6 Practice Tests for TOEIC® Listening and Reading

Special thanks to the team who made this book possible:

Sumi Aktar, Kim Bowers, Louise Cook, Anthony Cooper, Scarlet Edmonds, Joanna Graham, Brian Holmes, Elise Johnson, Bharat Krishna, Shannon O'Brien, Priya Patel, Laura Pilkington, Jonathan Ridd, Emma Sagor, Traci Shackelford, Nimesh Shah

TOEIC® is a registered trademark of the Educational Testing Service, which neither sponsors nor endorses this product.

Published by Kaplan Publishing, a division of Kaplan, Inc.
750 Third Avenue
New York, NY 10017

10 9 8 7 6 5 4 3 2
ISBN: 978-1-5062-2441-1

TABLE OF CONTENTS

HOW TO USE THIS BOOK

WELCOME TO KAPLAN's 6 PRACTICE TESTS FOR TOEIC LISTENING AND READING

Congratulations on your decision to improve your English proficiency, and thank you for choosing Kaplan for your TOEIC preparation. You've made the right choice in acquiring this book—you're now armed with six full length TOEIC Reading and Listening practice tests, produced as a result of decades of researching the TOEIC and similar tests and teaching many thousands of students the skills they need to succeed.

Your Book

This book contains six TOEIC Reading and Listening practice tests, including audio tracks for the Listening Section, which can be accessed online.

Review the listening scripts, answers and explanations at the back of this book to better understand your performance. Look for patterns in the questions you answered correctly and incorrectly. Were you stronger in some areas than others? This analysis will help you to target specific areas when you practice and prepare for the TOEIC.

Go online to access your audio

The audio tracks for this book are all in digital format, and must be accessed online. You can also find additional resources and information about test updates in your online resources.

To listen to the audio for this book, access your audio tracks and other online resources through the Kaplan Study App at **www.kaptest.com/booksonline**. When registering, make sure you select the correct book title and ISBN (you can find this book's ISBN number at the front of the book).

Once you have registered, login at **kaptest.com/login**. Additionally, after registering, you can download the Kaplan Mobile Prep app on **Google Play** or the **App Store** from your Android or iOS device.

You should listen to your audio wherever you see this icon 🎧 in your book.

If you have any issues finding your audio online, please email us at **booksupport@kaplan.com**.

TOEIC Listening and Reading Practice Test 1

LISTENING TEST

In this section of the test, you will show your knowledge of spoken English. This section has four parts, and the entire section will last for around 45 minutes. Directions are given for each individual part of the test. Mark your answers on the answer sheet provided. To listen to the audio tracks for this section of the test, access the tracks in your Online Resources, by visiting **www.kaptest.com/booksonline** OR through the Kaplan Study App.

 Play Track 1 for Test 1, Part I

PART I: PHOTOGRAPHS

Directions: For each question in this part, you will hear four statements about a picture in your test book. When you hear the statements, you must select the one statement that best describes what you see in the picture. Then find the number of the question on your answer sheet and mark your answer. The statements will not be printed in your test book and will be spoken only one time.

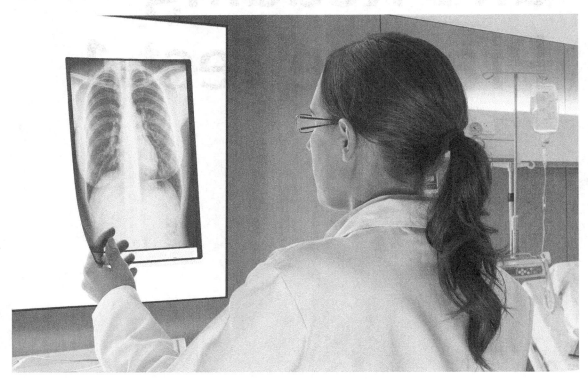

1

2

3

4

5

6

Play Track 2 for Test 1, Part II

PART II: QUESTION RESPONSE

Directions: You will hear a question or statement and three responses spoken in English. They will not be printed in your test book and will be spoken only one time. Select the best response to the question or statement and mark the letter A, B, or C on your answer sheet.

7	Mark your answer on your answer sheet.	20	Mark your answer on your answer sheet.
8	Mark your answer on your answer sheet.	21	Mark your answer on your answer sheet.
9	Mark your answer on your answer sheet.	22	Mark your answer on your answer sheet.
10	Mark your answer on your answer sheet.	23	Mark your answer on your answer sheet.
11	Mark your answer on your answer sheet.	24	Mark your answer on your answer sheet.
12	Mark your answer on your answer sheet.	25	Mark your answer on your answer sheet.
13	Mark your answer on your answer sheet.	26	Mark your answer on your answer sheet.
14	Mark your answer on your answer sheet.	27	Mark your answer on your answer sheet.
15	Mark your answer on your answer sheet.	28	Mark your answer on your answer sheet.
16	Mark your answer on your answer sheet.	29	Mark your answer on your answer sheet.
17	Mark your answer on your answer sheet.	30	Mark your answer on your answer sheet.
18	Mark your answer on your answer sheet.	31	Mark your answer on your answer sheet.
19	Mark your answer on your answer sheet.		

Play Track 3 for Test 1, Part III

PART III: SHORT CONVERSATIONS

Directions: You will hear some conversations between two people. You will be asked to answer three questions about what the speakers say in each conversation. Select the best response to each question and mark the letter (A), (B), (C), or (D) on your answer sheet. The conversation will not be printed in your test book and will be spoken only one time.

32 Who was supposed to go to the meeting in Brazil?

    A Andy

    B Michelle

    C Georgia

    D Tim

33 What does the man say about Georgina?

    A She might be able to go to Brazil.

    B She's leaving the company.

    C She's looking after her children.

    D She's put him in touch with someone who can go.

34 Why does the man not want to reschedule the meeting?

    A He doesn't want to make a bad impression.

    B He's confident they will find someone else to go.

    C He already tried but the client refused.

    D The client is usually difficult.

35 What are the speakers discussing?

    A where a conference is taking place

    B when a conference is taking place

    C who is attending a conference

    D where to stay when attending a conference

36 Why is the woman surprised?

    A because the man is upset

    B because the man booked non-refundable tickets

    C because the man booked tickets too early

    D because the man hasn't booked tickets yet

37 What is the woman's recommendation?

    A Cancel the flights.

    B Email the conference organizers.

    C Write to the airline.

    D Telephone the conference organizers.

38 What is this conversation about?

    A a customer survey

    B a customer complaint

    C a promotion

    D a technical issue

39 What does the woman say about reception?

    A It's still pretty bad.

    B It's been fixed.

    C She's booked an appointment with technical support.

    D It's been fine from the start.

40 Why dos the man say "I'm glad to hear it"?

    A Her old company's service was bad.

    B The subscription issues have been solved.

    C She is pleased with her current provider.

    D The engineer fixed the connection.

41 Why has the position not been filled yet?

    A It was only advertised recently.

    B The person who left gave no notice.

    C Most applicants haven't been that good.

    D The candidate they had chosen changed their mind.

42 What will the man do?

    A invite people to interviews

    B talk to applicants on the phone

    C look at resumes and applications

    D continue to observe the woman's work

43 What does the man say about the recruitment agency?

    A They've terminated their contract with them.

    B They're renewing their contract with them.

    C They're looking for a new recruitment agency.

    D He's looking forward to their new contract with them.

44 Who are the speakers likely to be?

    A a customer and a company representative

    B two colleagues

    C a boss and a subordinate

    D two family members

45 What does the woman imply about Thomas?

    A He caused the issues.

    B He's not a hard worker.

    C He's trying to resolve the issue.

    D He doesn't see what the problem is.

46 What is the man's suggestion?

    A to send someone to their offices

    B to charge a cancellation fee

    C to set a deadline on Tuesday

    D to refuse to send without receiving a purchase order

47 Why is the woman upset?

    A She accidentally ordered the wrong cake.

    B The cake was delivered late.

    C The cake tasted awful.

    D The cake was not made to her specifications.

48 How did the woman order the cake?

    A by telephone

    B she visited to the store

    C over the internet

    D someone else ordered for her

49 What does the man think is the reason for the mistake?

    A human error

    B technical issue

    C miscommunication

    D He doesn't give a reason.

50 What are the speakers discussing?

    A their cancelled flight

    B their plans tonight

    C what to do tomorrow evening

    D when to meet each other

51 How will their friends get to the hotel from the airport?

   A The man will take them.

   B They will use public transport.

   C They have booked a flight.

   D They are taking a cab.

52 Why does the man say "Oh, I don't mind"?

   A It doesn't matter that she's not free.

   B He is fine with waiting outside the office.

   C It's not a problem for him to pick her up.

   D It doesn't matter how they get there.

---

53 Who are the speakers likely to be?

   A two teachers

   B a teacher and a student

   C two students

   D a teacher and a parent

54 What has the teacher decided to do?

   A punish the student lightly

   B keep a lasting record of his actions

   C leave it up to the student's parents

   D not punish either of the students

55 What is the woman's reaction to the situation?

   A argumentative

   B humble

   C furious

   D overjoyed

---

56 What has prompted this discussion?

   A the review of a process

   B a new hire

   C a problem with a client

   D an argument between two colleagues

57 What does the woman say about their filing system?

   A The online platform is too slow.

   B The spreadsheets are confusing.

   C It's impossible to make small changes.

   D You need to make changes more than twice.

58 Why is the woman concerned about their filing system?

   A She thinks people don't want to share files.

   B She thinks things can go unnoticed.

   C She thinks people will riot against it.

   D She thinks it won't work.

---

59 Why has the woman called the man?

   A to warn him about a pile-up on the road

   B to check how long he's going to be

   C to see if he had issues with the car

   D to check if he was in an accident

60 What does the man tell the woman to do?

   A serve some appetizers until he's home

   B wait for him, as he won't be long

   C start eating before he arrives

   D call him to check where he is before they start eating

61 Why did the woman not get wine?

   A She forgot.

   B She couldn't go during her lunch break.

   C The supermarket was closed.

   D She thought the man would be getting it.

---

62 Why does the woman want to return the item?

   A She bought the wrong size.

   B It didn't look good on.

   C She didn't realize it was stained.

   D The pattern didn't look good at home.

63 Why must the item be exchanged?

   A   The price was reduced.

   B   They don't have any more in stock.

   C   The manager is not at work.

   D   The woman doesn't need the money.

64 Why does the woman say "that's not really a big deal"?

   A   She thinks she will find something else she likes.

   B   She received a refund.

   C   She decided to keep the item.

   D   She didn't mind that the store couldn't take the item back.

---

65 What are the speakers doing?

   A   reviewing the qualifications

   B   selling to a client

   C   conducting a job interview

   D   considering promoting an employee

66 What was David doing before he worked at E-Net?

   A   taking evening classes

   B   studying at university

   C   working as a copywriter

   D   managing a small team

67 What is David's current job title?

   A   Copywriter

   B   Head of Department

   C   Content Manager

   D   Editor

---

68 Why is the man unable to attend the talk?

   A   He's away on holiday.

   B   His boss won't give him the time off.

   C   He doesn't have any more holiday allowance left.

   D   He is able to attend, but he finds planes dull.

69 Look at the program. Which talk is the woman delivering?

   A   *The History of Aviation*

   B   *Safety and Security: can airlines do more?*

   C   *Amelia Earhart: 80 years of theories*

   D   *The Future of Aviation: Part 1*

PROGRAM–DAY 1

8.30 a.m.–10 a.m.

The History of Aviation

10.15 a.m.–11.45 a.m.

Safety and Security: can airlines do more?

1 p.m.–2.30 p.m.

Amelia Earhart: 80 years of theories

2.45 p.m.–4.15 p.m.

The Future of Aviation: Part 1

---

70 Why does the man say "that's ridiculous"?

   A   The flights are all fully booked.

   B   Flights with a stopover are more expensive.

   C   Flights with a stopover take four hours more.

   D   Flights with a stopover are half price.

Play Track 4 for Test 1, Part IV

PART IV: SHORT TALKS

Directions: You will hear some talks given by one speaker. You will be asked to answer three questions about what the speaker says in each talk. Select the best response to each question and mark the letter (A), (B), (C), or (D) on your answer sheet. The conversation will not be printed in your test book and will be spoken only one time.

71 Where is this speech likely to take place?

    A in a business meeting

    B in a TV or radio interview

    C during a sales pitch

    D during a family dinner

72 What does the woman say about entrepreneurs?

    A They enjoy bragging.

    B They're not as skilled as they think they are.

    C They like clichés.

    D They usually know what they're talking about.

73 What does the woman say about when she started her business?

    A She had to persevere a lot.

    B She received help from her parents.

    C She had no unique selling point yet.

    D She had worked hard to make contacts.

74 What is the topic of this speech?

    A how to improve communication within the company

    B what kind of changes might improve performance

    C why people within the company don't like change

    D how to let company employees know changes are coming

75 How does the man expect his colleagues to respond to pushback?

    A by using research to back themselves up

    B by ignoring what their employees say

    C by listening to their employees.

    D by expressing how upset they feel

76 What can be inferred from the man's speech?

    A The changes will not happen unless enough people complain about them.

    B People are unlikely to feel threatened by the changes.

    C The changes might cause problems they haven't predicted.

    D The changes should be implemented quickly.

77 Why has the company been in the news lately?

    A It had to close a lot of its shops.

    B It's announced it's going into administration.

    C The CEO, Mrs. Rossi, resigned.

    D It received a lot of investment.

78 What is implied about the company's former employees?

    A They are probably lying.

    B They are worried about fear of repercussions.

    C They come from various levels in the company hierarchy.

    D They came forward with their stories because of Mr. Edmonds.

79 What will happen at 8 o' clock?

   A   Mr Rossi will talk to the public.

   B   Two employees will complain about their treatment.

   C   All employees will be given anonymity.

   D   All former employees will be interviewed.

80 What does the speaker do?

   A   She works at an office.

   B   She works on the subway.

   C   She's an entrepreneur.

   D   She's a student.

81 What does the speaker NOT say about the fellow commuters on her journey?

   A   They were in a hurry.

   B   They shoved each other.

   C   They were reading newspapers.

   D   They didn't look at or speak to one another.

82 What would the woman's app do?

   A   tell people how to get to their destinations

   B   tell people how to avoid missing their connections

   C   show them a map of the Chicago "L" lines

   D   tell them which subway car opens nearest to the station exit

83 Where is this speech taking place?

   A   at a conference

   B   at a meeting

   C   at a party

   D   at a university

84 How many shares will the company own by September?

   A   10%

   B   23%

   C   97%

   D   100%

85 Why is it important for the company shares to be bought back?

   A   The speaker didn't like the investors.

   B   The speaker and the investors disagreed about future plans.

   C   The investors weren't very helpful.

   D   The investors wanted to expand to Europe and the speaker didn't.

86 Which button should the caller press to find out if their shipment has been delivered?

   A   1

   B   2

   C   3

   D   4

87 Which information can be found on the company's website?

   A   parcel size and weight limits

   B   the company's range of services

   C   information about next-day delivery

   D   how to arrange for re-delivery

88 What should the caller do if none of the options apply to them?

   A   listen to the menu again and choose the closest

   B   visit the company's website

   C   wait on the line

   D   ask to speak to a representative

89 How did the speaker receive feedback from the company's customers?

  A by completing surveys in the store

  B by contacting subscribers

  C by conducting interviews with customers

  D by testing the collection on customers

90 Look at the table below. Which product does the speaker describe as a fluke?

  A KY918

  B KG945

  C KY439

  D KM13T

First Quarter Sales			
Product	Jan	Feb	March
KY918	$5,543	$5,345	$2,789
KG945	$5,321	$7,689	$3,234
KY439	$2,345	$3,546	$2,324
KM13T	$3,452	$4,563	$4,546

91 What can be inferred about the product KG945?

  A It's a summery garment.

  B There was initial pushback against it within the company.

  C It was expected to outperform other products.

  D The design was viewed as too conservative.

92 Which reason is NOT given for why companies don't like remote working?

  A They are worried employee performance will drop.

  B It's not the status quo.

  C They've heard bad things about it.

  D They don't recognize the advantages of it.

93 What does the woman say about remote working in her company?

  A 50% of her employees work from home full-time.

  B All employees need to work from home once a week.

  C Some roles are exempt from it.

  D She expects it to increase certain costs.

94 What can be inferred from the woman's speech?

  A Travelling to work can cause anxiety.

  B Most parents will find it hard to work from home.

  C Some employees don't like remote working.

  D New parents in her company often quit their jobs.

95 Where is this speech likely to take place?

  A at a business meeting

  B at a radio interview

  C at a conference

  D at a high school lesson

96 Why was the woman upset with how her boss treated her after her husband's death?

  A She was careful with what she said around her.

  B She whispered about her in front of her.

  C She was deliberately insulting towards her.

  D She asked her to come back to work too soon.

97 What major life change did the woman make after her husband's death?

   A She became a professional speaker.

   B She left her company to join another.

   C She became a teacher.

   D She returned to college.

---

98 Look at the map. Which number marks the location of the Red Line?

   A 1

   B 2

   C 3

   D 4

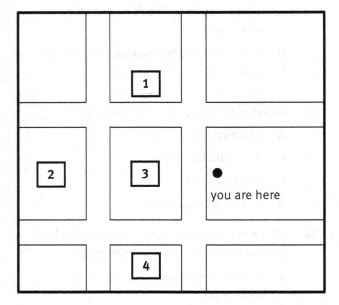

99 What can be inferred about the city gardens from the woman's speech?

   A They're within walking distance.

   B It can be reached by public transport.

   C It's not worth visiting.

   D They're better than the archeological museum.

100 Which sightseeing method of transport does the woman recommend?

   A the red hop-on hop-off bus

   B the green hop-on hop-off bus

   C the yellow hop-on hop-off bus

   D a private tour guide

READING TEST

In this section of the test, you will show your knowledge of written English. This section has three parts, and you have 75 minutes to complete all three sections. Directions are given for each individual part of the test. Mark your answers on the answer sheet provided.

PART V: INCOMPLETE SENTENCES

Directions: Complete the following sentences using one of the four answer choices provided. Mark the answer **A, B, C** or **D** on your answer sheet.

101 This isn't the first time the company has been in trouble with the law: just three years ago, the previous CEO _____ embezzling and sentenced to ten years in prison.

  A caught

  B was

  C was caught

  D had caught

102 The manuscript is a first edition in _____ condition, so it's going to be worth a lot of money.

  A precise

  B pristine

  C precious

  D profound

103 The bank said my credit score was too low, so they _____ to offer me a loan without a guarantor.

  A were unable

  B were incapable

  C couldn't

  D shouldn't

104 _____ light of these recent discoveries, the company director will be stepping down from his position.

  A On

  B At

  C In

  D With

105 What _____ all morning? You look so tired and sweaty!

  A did you do

  B have you been

  C have you been doing

  D had you done

106 He tends to take things at _____ value, so you can't be sarcastic or ironic with him.

  A face

  B hand

  C arm

  D head

107 I made it _____ clear to him that I was not going to accept any delays in the delivery of the final draft.

A perfect

B definitely

C scarcely

D abundantly

108 If we _____ time fighting over what to do, we would've finished by now.

A don't waste

B didn't waste

C hadn't wasted

D wouldn't have wasted

109 She _____ the alarm upon discovering a slew of confidential documents in an unlocked thumb drive abandoned on his desk.

A rose

B hit

C lifted

D raised

110 The area next to the bar will be cleared _____ all tables so the DJ can set up there.

A from

B of

C with

D to

111 The purpose of this _____ is to walk you through the main components and responsibilities of your new role.

A intention

B induction

C indentation

D inflection

112 It's probably a long _____ , but do you happen to know anyone who is fluent in Japanese and looking for a new role at the moment?

A possibility

B chance

C way

D shot

113 The company was contacted but _____ to comment on the proceedings.

A decline

B declined

C declining

D declination

114 The couple has confirmed that they have filed for divorce, _____ irreconcilable differences. The split is reported to be amicable, however.

A citing

B circulating

C chiding

D censuring

115 Following lengthy negotiations, the two conglomerates have finally reached an agreement and _____ by the end of the year.

A merge

B have merged

C will be merging

D will have been merging

116 The celebrations of the opening of the two new stations have been _____ by the union's decision to go on strike.

A poured

B marred

C charred

D scarred

117 I have repeatedly attempted to discuss the situation with him, but _____ with contempt and excuses.

- **A** met
- **B** have met
- **C** have been met
- **D** have been meeting

118 We are _____ to announce that we have now reached our target of 40 million customers in the US alone.

- **A** delight
- **B** delighted
- **C** delightful
- **D** delightfully

119 He might have studied at the most prestigious colleges and trained with some of the best in the field, but it is really his unique insight and _____ personality that allowed him to build such a successful business.

- **A** blithe
- **B** frivolous
- **C** temperamental
- **D** shrewd

120 _____the results you want, you will need to motivate your team better.

- **A** Achieve
- **B** Achieving
- **C** To achieve
- **D** To achieving

121 When we inquired about the status of the report, we were told it would be released in _____ course.

- **A** due
- **B** soon
- **C** rapid
- **D** quick

122 Can you help me out? I thought this was the right template, but when I try to open it, it says the file is _____.

- **A** corrupt
- **B** corrupting
- **C** corrupted
- **D** corruption

123 It would probably be_____ to apply directly through their website than to use an intermediary website.

- **A** easy
- **B** easier
- **C** easiest
- **D** the easiest

124 There are certain _____ that will need to be considered before we decide whether it would be smart to sign a contract with them.

- **A** material
- **B** facts
- **C** information
- **D** advice

125 The company has been _____ for its inappropriate response to a customer's complaint about the content on their website.

- **A** lauded
- **B** praised
- **C** lambasted
- **D** precipitated

126 It _____ ten years since a Canadian author was last nominated for this prestigious literary award.

- **A** was
- **B** has
- **C** has been
- **D** has gone

127 Until we receive _____ that the client has agreed to all the proposed changes to the program, we cannot proceed. Our hands are tied.

A sentence

B email

C word

D instruction

128 The union has agreed to _____ its planned action following successful negotiations with representatives at the top level of management.

A suspend

B sustain

C surrender

D surpass

129 It's up to us to lead _____ example and show our teams the kind of behavior we expect from them.

A through

B for

C by

D in

130 All of our memberships come with a 30 day _____ period, meaning that if you change your mind for any reason, you can request a full refund—no questions asked.

A cooling off

B cooling down

C coming off

D coming down

PART VI: TEXT COMPLETION

Directions: Read the following texts and select the best answer choice to complete the text. Mark the answer **A, B, C** or **D** on your answer sheet.

Questions 131–134 refer to the following email.

To: antonis.paterakis@email.com
From: amparo.lopez@cleanhouses.com
Date: 10/29/17
Subject: Customer Complaint Case #126543

Dear Mr. Paterakis,

Due to a technical issue, you _____ an email earlier this week informing you that your
                              131.
account with us will be deactivated unless you contact us via email or over the phone.

We are sincerely aware of the inconvenience our _____ email must have caused you.
                                                132.
We take pride in the service we provide to our customers, including our communications

to you, and we would like to take this opportunity to apologize that we failed to uphold our

standards on this occasion.

To compensate, we would like to offer you a special discount on your next booking with us:

simply use_____ code TECH10 and you will receive $10 off one of our services. The
            133.
code will be available for 12 months, _____. We will send you a reminder before that
                                      134.
happens, if you have not used your code in a years' time. Once again, please accept our

deepest apologies. Thank you for your continued patronage!

Kind Regards,
Amparo Lopez
Client Engagement Coordinator

---

131 **A** may receive

  B may have received

  C could receive

  D could have received

132 **A** erroneous

  B ravenous

  C ravishing

  D enormous

133 **A** prohibitive

  B promote

  C promotive

  D promotional

134 **A** at which point it will expire

  B and will last for 2 years.

  C so we'll see you next week

  D in order for your account to remain active

Questions 135–138 refer to the following email.

Hotel Booking Confirmation–Neptune Hotel

Dear Naveen Clayton,

Thank you for choosing Neptune Hotel for your next stay in Barcelona. We are _____ to
135.
host you from February 15th, 2018 to February 19th, 2018. The room you have selected is a
deluxe double room with breakfast included.

We would like to inform you that our hotel offers a pickup service from the Barcelona airport.
No pre-payment is required–all we will need are your credit card details, and the full amount
will be charged _____ arrival.
136.
Alternatively, you can use the Aerobus service, which is an express bus service from the
airport to the city center. The Aerobus can be taken both from Terminal 1 and Terminal 2 and
runs every five to ten minutes. If you decide to take the Aerobus, please _____ at Plaça
137.
de Catalunya and refer to the attached map for how to find us. We are a two minute walk
from the bus stop.

You can also take the RENFE train–please refer to our attached guide for more specific
instructions. Please note that reception is open 24 hours a day and check in is available
after 2 p.m. on the day of your arrival. You are welcome to leave your luggage with us if you
arrive earlier. We are also at your _____ if you have any questions or need any help with
138.
anything during your stay.

We look forward to welcoming you to Barcelona.

All the best,
Neptune Hotel

---

135 A delighted
B demulcent
C devoted
D desired

136 A at
B after
C upon
D from

137 A alight
B detrain
C dislodge
D eject

138 A availability
B disposal
C discretion
D request

Questions 139–142 refer to the following review.

Salt the Earth: A Selection of Poems

'Salt the earth and say goodbye. Let them burn, let them burn.'

Divided into five sections, each focusing on a year spent in a different city and _____
139.
a different stage of critically acclaimed poet Diego Sanchez's clinical depression, this new,
much anticipated collection of poems has arrived.

Diego Sanchez became famous for his unique style, one which combines lyrical, heart-
wrenching verse with stunning visuals that utilize every corner of every page—words
_____ across the paper, twisting and swirling and pulling the reader into a world of
140.
profound pain, but also profound talent.

A native of New Mexico, Diego Sanchez has lived in 25 states across the US and has used
all of these diverse locations as a source of inspiration for his poetry. _____ From the
141.
smoggy fire escapes of New York to the landlocked landscapes of Arkansas, you will be
_____ an exciting, though harrowing, journey through the US.
142.

---

139 A represent

　　B represents

　　C represented

　　D representing

140 A spoiled

　　B splintered

　　C strewn

　　D spurned

141 A You can find his poems on his website, www.diegosanchez.com.

　　B Diego's poetry has won several awards.

　　C Diego has never been to Europe, but plans to go for his next collection.

　　D This collection is, of course, no exception.

142 A taking on

　　B taken on

　　C taking to

　　D taken to

Questions 143–146 refer to the following email.

Hi all,

Apologies in advance for the group email. As most of you are likely already aware, we are going to be filming a documentary in Sicily this coming August. I know it's still a long way off, but we are currently looking into the logistics and trying to map out a route for the crew and everyone else who will be joining us. One of the things we still _____ to figure out
143.
is how we're going to get around when none of us can speak the language.

_____ that end, we have decided to recruit a native speaker for the duration of our stay
144.
at the island.

The guide should:

• Be a native speaker of Italian, or speak it at near-native level.

• Speak English at B1 level as a _____ minimum–preferably B2 or C1.
145.

• Be at least 21 years old and with a driving license.

• Be free for the two first weeks of August.

If you or any of your friends happen to know anyone who meets the above _____,
146.
please forward my email address to them. The role will be suitably paid, and there's a finder's fee in it for you.

Thanks,

Greg

---

143 A don't manage

B didn't manage

C haven't managed

D hadn't managed

144 A To

B For

C At

D When

145 A absolute

B varying

C bare

D very

146 A rules

B criteria

C measures

D caveats

PART VII: READING COMPREHENSION

Directions: In this part of the test, you will read different texts and then answer several questions about each text. Mark the answer A, B, C or D on your answer sheet.

Questions 147–149 refer to the following email.

To: ika.sumartini@email.com

From: pedro@petitions.com

Dear Ms. Sumartini,

Marble Hills High School has been a part of our community in Northampton for more than 100 years, since a generous donation from local resident and entrepreneur Roger Marble. In its 104 years of operation, the school and its excellent staff have educated the residents of Northampton, cared for us and motivated us to work hard and achieve our ambitions.

But, unless we can convince the local government to change its mind, Marble Hills High School will shut its doors forever on Friday, March 23rd. This decision was made against the wishes of parents and school officials, who argue that closing the school will force many kids to drop out of higher education, as their parents won't be able to afford the cost of the commute to neighboring towns. Additionally, it will damage the quality of the lessons given to our kids and the kids from every town in our district, as classes will become severely overcrowded.

So far, the local government has refused to entertain our misgivings, rejecting our requests for meetings. If we can get 50,000 people to sign our petition, however, they will have no choice but to listen to us and allow us to give voice to our children, who will be most adversely affected by this decision.

Will you sign our petition and share it on social media with your friends?

Kind regards,

Pedro Gomez

a concerned parent

147 What is the purpose of this email?

 A to explain why Marble Hills High School is closing

 B to describe the history of Marble Hills High School

 C to complain to the local government

 D to request action from the recipient

148 What does the email NOT say about the decision to close the school?

 A It will put undue strain on other schools in the area.

 B The decision might be reversible.

 C It will have a negative impact on graduation rates.

 D School officials weren't consulted about it.

149 What can be inferred about the author of the email?

    A He works for the closing school.

    B His child attends the closing school.

    C He's a resident of one of the neighboring towns.

    D He came up with the idea of the petition.

Questions 150–153 refer to the following table.

Plan Options		
SIM Only **Basic Plan–starting from $7 per month**	**SIM Only** **Tailored Plan - $20 per month**	**SIM and Phone** **Upgrade Plan–starting from $20 per month**
Our basic plan, perfect for those on a tight budget, comes with: • Unlimited texts and calls to our network • 100 texts to other networks • 200 minutes for calls to landlines and other networks • 2GB of mobile data Basic plans can last a year ($8 per month), two years ($7 per month), or can be on a month to month rolling basis ($10 per month)—it's all completely up to you!	Our tailored plan is our most popular plan on offer. It comes with a choice of: Either • Unlimited texts to other networks, 500 minutes for calls to landlines and other networks and 4GB of mobile data Or • 300 texts to other networks, 300 minutes for calls to landlines and other networks and 8GB of mobile data Both options include unlimited calls and texts to our network. Tailored plans are offered on a rolling basis only.	By far our most flexible plan, the upgrade plan comes with a brand new phone of your choice and either the basic or tailored plan. There is also the Gold option, for $10 extra per month, which combines the best of both worlds from the tailored plan, with unlimited texts, 500 minutes for calls outside our network and 8GB of mobile data.

150 What is TRUE about the basic plan?

    A It's the most popular plan.

    B It comes with 3GB of mobile data.

    C It can last for as little as a month.

    D It has a set price.

151 Which plan is best for someone who has just bought a new phone and sends 250 texts to other networks each month?

    A the basic plan

    B the tailored plan

    C the upgrade plan

    D All three plans are the same.

152 If someone on the tailored plan has 4GB of mobile data, what else do they have?

    A 500 minutes for calls to the same network

    B unlimited texts to all networks

    C 200 minutes for calls to landlines

    D 300 texts to other networks

153 What's the lowest price one can pay for the Gold option?

    A $10

    B $20

    C $30

    D $40

Questions 154–156 refer to the following instant messaging conversation.

Neil:	Are we still on for this week?
Elliot:	Yeah, definitely. When are you landing again?
Neil:	Flight was supposed to be on Tuesday at 9 a.m. but it's been cancelled because of the weather, so now I'm flying Wednesday morning–same time.
Elliot:	Weather's been horrible here for the past week. Bundle up before you come! Definitely bring boots for the snow. How many meetings do you have planned? How long are you staying again?
Neil:	I'm staying till Friday and then I'm flying directly to Florida to meet my wife and kids–I'm on leave for a month.
Elliot:	Wow, so we'd better get everything ready while you're here.
Neil:	I've got a pretty busy Wednesday (all my cancelled meetings got moved to Wednesday) but I've got some slots on Thursday or Friday if that works for you.
Elliot:	Friday's better. I've got a sales meeting all day Thursday.
Neil:	Great–lunch?
Elliot:	Cool, there's a nice new restaurant you're gonna love. Should I invite my boss?
Neil:	Nah, let's keep it casual for now. Don't worry, I'll be checking emails while I'm away and Denise will pick up the slack while I'm gone–we'll get your contract signed even if I'm across the country!
Elliot:	Cool. Ok. See you soon!

154 Why does Neil say "Are we still on"?

  A   He's confirming that Elliot and he will meet up.

  B   He's asking if the contract has been signed yet.

  C   He's asking if the heating is working in the office this week.

  D   He's asking if Elliot will come with him to meet the client.

155 Which day is good for Neil but not for Elliot to meet?

  A   Tuesday

  B   Wednesday

  C   Thursday

  D   Friday

156 What can be inferred from the conversation?

  A   Neil thinks Elliot is eager to do business.

  B   Elliot doesn't expect the meeting to be productive.

  C   Elliot's boss has expressed interest in joining the meeting.

  D   Denise will be present at the meeting.

Questions 157–159 refer to the following table.

Venues for Hire						
State	**Venue**	**Capacity**	**Weekday**	**Saturday**	**Sunday**	**Notes**
Maryland	*Mallowbrook Hall*	400	$6000	$8000	$7500	Not available on Mondays
Maryland	*Royal Oak Center*	50	$800	$1000	$1000	
New Jersey	*Belwyn Place*	100	$1500	$2400	$2600	Only available Wed-Sun
New Jersey	*Linburn Hall*	200	$2500	$3000	$3000	
New Jersey	*Brightbay Gardens*	300	$4000	$5000	$4500	Only available summer months
New York	*Vertigo Bay*	200	$3000	$3400	$3400	
New York	*Merricrest Hall*	150	$1700	$2000	$2400	
New York	*Belbridge Garden*	100	$2000	$2000	$2000	Only available May-October
New York	*Fogmill Home*	25	$500	$800	$650	Music restrictions apply
New York	*Beachwall Mansion*	300	$7000	$10000	$8000	
Pennsylvania	*Whitebush Hill House*	20	$300	$500	$400	Cannot be booked online - please call
Pennsylvania	*Oakhaven Center*	55	$1000	$1600	$1200	
Pennsylvania	*Hedgemont Place*	80	$500	$600	$500	
Pennsylvania	*Estermill Gardens*	410	$5500	$8000	$7000	Only available March-October

157 Which venue is cheapest for a group of 90 on a weekday?

   A Belwyn Place

   B Belbridge Garden

   C Hedgemont Place

   D Linburn Hall

158 In which state is the least expensive venue for more than 300 people located?

   A Pennsylvania

   B New York

   C New Jersey

   D Maryland

159 What CANNOT be inferred from the table?

A Whitebush Hill House can be booked online.

B Brightbay Gardens is probably an outdoor space.

C It's cheaper to book a venue on a Sunday than a Saturday.

D Mallowbrook Hall is available on Tuesdays.

Questions 160–162 refer to the following email.

To: francesca.astore@designer.com

From: anca.styles@bestsolutions.com

Dear Francesca,

Thank you for sending me the design so quickly! That was much faster than I anticipated, and it looks pretty good. I only have a few suggestions to make these fliers even better: (1) could we use a different font for the tagline below our company logo? I'm not entirely sure the current one works. (2) I've shown the design to my boss, and she's very happy with it, but she's asked to remove the purple background and replace it with something else. I know we agreed on the color, but perhaps we can go with our original choice of that slightly lighter hue?

I've been speaking with my boss about future events—as I mentioned on the phone, this particular conference is just the beginning, and we're hoping to secure a spot in at least two more conferences this year—so we might need a few more things from you, including additional flyers, depending on how everything goes in February. So far we've only discussed posters (we'd want consistency across the designs, so not much work), but I think it'd be a good idea to also offer some funky stuff like pens or even bookmarks, too—or anything else you can think of? Please do let me know.

At any rate—like I said, I'm very happy with it so far and look forward to receiving the updated version and hearing your thoughts for future designs.

Best wishes,

Anca

---

160 What is NOT TRUE about the purple background?

   A Anca's boss didn't like it.

   B Anca and Francesca picked it together.

   C It wasn't Anca and Francesca's first choice.

   D Anca thinks a darker shade might be better.

161 The work Anca has commissioned so far pertains to which type of product?

   A posters

   B flyers

   C lighters

   D bookmarks

162 What can be inferred from the email?

   A Anca is expecting Francesca to recommend something.

   B The designs of other products will be quite different.

   C Anca's boss likes the idea of bookmarks.

   D Anca's company is participating in three conferences this year.

Questions 163–164 refer to the following letter.

Dear all:

As you may have heard by now, we will be doing some essential work on the building over the Christmas holidays. This is to make space for new arrivals, as our little company is growing and we will need to fit 20 more people into our current space. Rest assured, however, that while we will be replacing all the desks, your new desks won't be smaller than your current ones. The new design is just more ergonomic, so we can take advantage of currently unoccupied space.

This work should be completed by the time we all return in January—though we might need to ask some of you to work from home for the first few days of the New Year; we'll keep you posted on that. What we would like you to do before you leave by the end of this week is take one of the boxes from the kitchen, write your name on it and fill it with all your belongings from your desk—as well as your keyboard, mouse and mousepad. The only things left on your desk by the end of the working day on Friday should be the cables and the monitors.

We appreciate your help with this. If you have any questions at all, just give me a shout.

Kind regards,

Noelle Tier

HR Administrator

163 In paragraph 1, what does the word "ergonomic" mean?

A efficient

B cramped

C laborious

D formidable

164 Which of the following should employees not remove from their desks?

A their keyboards

B their computer screens

C their personal items

D their boxes

Questions 165–168 refer to the following notice.

Ricotta restaurant chain coming to new york

Ricotta Restaurants has officially announced they will be opening their first US branch at the Rohampton Center this coming July.

Rumors were sparked about the successful Italian chain finally coming to the US after cryptic posters were put up in its—now confirmed—new location, advertising its iconic lunch menu with messages such as *"Can you smell the stone baked goods*?"—the famous motto of Ricotta's 2017 campaign in Canada. — [1] — The rumors were finally confirmed by the company's CEO, Francesca Besozzi, via her social media accounts on Friday morning, where she posted that "Ricotta and the Land of the Free" will be meeting in July. — [2] —

Ricotta Restaurants has been steadily building a reputation as a health-conscious yet tasty alternative to traditionally (and often calorie-laden) Italian dishes such as pizza and pasta, as well as for its environmentally-friendly and employee-focused approach to business with excellent development schemes, employee benefits and healthcare coverage—all of which has made it popular with Italian cuisine fans around the world. — [3] —

Established in Italy in 2001, Ricotta Restaurants now operates in 18 countries in Europe, America and Asia with more than 200 restaurants and has hinted that is may be expanding into the US market since last year, when it launched in Canada. — [4] — According to Ms. Besozzi, the plan is to open at least 15 stores in the coming 24 months in various key states such as New York, California, Florida and Texas. The opening of the New York restaurant will also be celebrated with the introduction of a new vegan pizza dish.

---

165 What prompted people to think a Ricotta restaurant might be opening in the US?

  A the pictures of the restaurant's lunch menu on a poster in Rohampton Center

  B the slogan on a poster in the Rohampton Center

  C the opening of a Ricotta restaurant in Canada

  D the CEO's social media activity

166 Which of the following is Ricotta Restaurants not known for?

  A the rights of its workers

  B its nutrition-focused recipes

  C its vegan dishes

  D the opportunities it offers for career progression

167 What can be inferred from the text?

  A The last country in which Ricotta opened a restaurant was Canada.

  B Ricotta currently has a two year expansion plan for the US market.

  C The next US store will open in California, Florida or Texas.

  D Ricotta will be opening only 15 restaurants in the US.

168 In which of the positions [1], [2], [3] or [4] does the following sentence best belong?
"The announcement was met with unabated enthusiasm."

  A [1]

  B [2]

  C [3]

  D [4]

Questions 169–171 refer to the following email.

From: darla.perez@mail.com

To: customerservice@brightlights.com

To Whom It May Concern:

I have now been waiting over an hour for one of your representatives to call me, though you promised you would be in touch at 11.00am in your email last week, and I would just like to inform you that you needn't bother: I have changed my mind and I will no longer be subscribing to your service.

I'd like to take this opportunity to reiterate how disastrous my experience has been in the hopes that perhaps you can learn something from it. Perhaps you can correct your service so that no other customer has to suffer through your horrible customer service: my payment last month did not go through due to insufficient funds. This was because of a bank error, not because I actually had insufficient funds in my account. However, instead of contacting me to inform me of the issue, you automatically cancelled my subscription and didn't even let me know. I had to find out for myself, after not receiving my monthly package and contacting you. I spent half an hour on hold, as you were taking too long to respond to my initial email. At no point did you offer an apology—only a promise to call me back at an agreed time and set up a new payment and subscription. You have now failed to fulfill that promise.

I'm not sure why you think it's acceptable to waste customers' time in this manner. I have been a loyal subscriber for three years. Please do not try to get in touch as I do not plan to spend any more of my time on this matter, other than to inform various relevant social media platforms.

Regards,

Darla

---

169 What was the purpose of the call Darla was expecting?

A   to subscribe to a new service

B   to complain about the service she received

C   to reinstate a service

D   to renew an existing subscription

170 Following Darla's issue, what was the first form of communication between the two parties?

A   The woman called the company.

B   The company called the woman.

C   The woman emailed the company.

D   The company emailed the woman.

171 How is the author of this email likely to feel?

A   incensed

B   crestfallen

C   content

D   bemused

Questions 172–173 refer to the following email.

From: damien.price@mail.com

To: arjun.patel@mail.com

Dear Arjun,

I hope this email finds you well. This is Damien—we sat next to each other on the flight from Chicago to San Francisco last week, and you gave me your email address to get in touch with you as I am currently looking for an internship in San Francisco and you mentioned that you might be able to help.

As I mentioned during our conversation on the plane, I am in my final year and will be graduating in June with a BA in Business Administration. — [1] — I have previously worked as a group leader for three consecutive summers at Blue Bay Summer Camp, and I also worked briefly as a barista at Yellow Oaks Café in Chicago. — [2] — I am also a great team player.

I have attached my resume for you, and I have asked my previous employers at Blue Bay Summer Camp and Yellow Oaks Café to get in touch with you to provide references. — [3] — I am really excited about the opportunity to work at your company, and I look forward to hearing from you.

— [4] — Thank you once again for offering me the chance to apply for the internship position.

Kind regards,

Damien

---

172 What is the main purpose of this email?

A to apply for a job

B to network

C to thank Arjun for an opportunity

D to remind the recipient of how they met

173 In which of the positions [1], [2], [3] or [4] does the following sentence best belong?
"I am diligent, determined, and extremely hard-working."

A [1]

B [2]

C [3]

D [4]

Questions 174–175 refer to the following letter

Dear Customers,

It is with great sadness we must announce that, after 56 years of service, *Andy's Diner* will be closing at the end of this month.

We would like you to know we have not taken this decision lightly: our father, Andy Brown, opened this diner when he was just 23 years old and never took a day off for 56 years. He and our mother loved this place, and treated it as one of their children. Every single customer meant the world to them, and we have no doubt each and every one of you were well accustomed to their kindness and hospitality.

Unfortunately, our father is no longer with us. While our mother, despite her own declining health, was keen to keep the diner open despite the loss, she has struggled to keep the diner in profit since the loss of our father eight months ago, it has simply not been possible– so we have decided the best option is to go out on a high note rather than provide our fantastic customers with a subpar experience.

We thank you for your loyalty and look forward to seeing you at our goodbye party on the February 27th.

All the best,

Andy's Diner

174 In the announcement, the word "lightly" in paragraph 2, line 1 is closest in meaning to?

  A carelessly

  B leniently

  C brightly

  D delicately

175 What is the main reason the diner is closing now?

  A the owner died

  B the owner's wife is ill

  C financial difficulties

  D foreclosure

Questions 176–180 refer to the following notice and email.

Casting call for "the great money maker"

Always dreamed of travelling the world, buying your own house, or opening your own business, but never had the money? Are you fascinated by trivia? If so, you might be the perfect candidate for America's favorite game show, *The Great Money Maker*, as we enter our second season.

Audition/Casting period: Ongoing

Restrictions: You need to be over 18 to participate in the program. You need to live in the US and be able to travel to one of our shooting locations in New York, San Francisco, Chicago, Charlotte or Seattle—the dates we will be shooting in each location will be announced in March. We welcome participants from all walks of life, and are particularly keen to cast people aged between 18-29 and 65+ for our *Generation Wars* charity specials.

How to apply: Please download and complete the application form, and send it together with a short cover letter about who you are and why you want to apply, as well as an interesting fact about yourself to moneymaker@channel8.com.

From: Christos88charlotte@email.com

To: moneymaker@channel8.com

To Whom It May Concern:

Please find attached my completed application for the new season of *The Great Money Maker*. My name is Christos Mavridis and I am 29 years old. I live in Charlotte, NC, where I work as a waiter in a restaurant. I also freelance as a comic artist, and my dream is to publish my own graphic novel.

I would like to participate in *The Great Money Maker* for two reasons: firstly, because I love the show and I'm always shouting at the TV when contestants answer a question incorrectly because I knew the right answer, so I think I'll do well if you accept me. Secondly, because I'm getting married to my partner, who I've been with since high school, next year and I would like us to have the wedding we both always dreamed of. Plus, we'd like to go to Europe for our honeymoon and we are even considering relocating to San Francisco after we marry, so some extra cash sure would be handy.

An interesting fact about me is that my dad is Greek and my mum is German, so I speak four languages fluently (including Spanish, which I studied at university).

I look forward to hearing from you.

Best,

Christos

---

176 What kind of game show is *The Great Money Maker* likely to be?

- **A** activity-oriented
- **B** puzzle-oriented
- **C** question and answer
- **D** essay based

177 What do the producers do for episodes aimed at raising money for a good cause?

- **A** They pit teams of young and old people against each other.
- **B** They look for contestants from all walks of life.
- **C** They buy a house for the winner.
- **D** They travel to a variety of locations, such as Charlotte and Seattle.

178 What does Christos NOT say he plans to use the winning money on?

- **A** expanding his wedding budget
- **B** travelling
- **C** a wedding present for his partner
- **D** moving to a new house

179 In the second paragraph of the email, why does Christos write, "handy"?

- **A** because is will be helpful to have some more money
- **B** because he is very dexterous
- **C** because he thinks he will win the competition
- **D** because he is confident in his ability to be entertaining

180 What can be inferred about Christos from the second text?

- **A** He will be asked to participate in a *Generation Wars* episode.
- **B** He has a knack for languages.
- **C** He will participate in a San Francisco episode if chosen.
- **D** He's not an American citizen.

Questions 181–185 refer to the following two emails.

From: maria.perez@homeandaway.com

To: yussef.batra@homeandaway.com

Date: April 3rd

Dear Mr. Batra,

We are delighted to invite you to this year's Global Sales Meeting, which will be taking place on November 15th–17th at our offices in Zurich, Switzerland. Please refer to the attached document for further details on location and timings, as well as the agenda for the meeting. Please note that the agenda is not finalized yet; we will be sending round a finalized version by August 31st.

If you or your assistant requires help with making travel and hotel arrangements, please let me know and I will have our travel team get in touch. Please always refer to our travel policy when booking flights and/or hotels, as expenses above the specified limits will not be honored.

We look forward to welcoming you in Zurich. Please confirm your attendance by July 20th.

Kind regards,

Maria

From: esther.port@homeandaway.com

To: yussef.batra@homeandaway.com

Date: November 19th

Dear Mr. Batra,

Thank you so much for forwarding me the above email, and my deepest apologies for the error in communication. Maria left the company back in June and, while she did leave a list of all of the people she had contacted with the previous dates for the sales meeting, she must have missed you. Not that this in any way excuses what happened here, and someone from either the Zurich or the Los Angeles office should have informed you of the changes before you had to come all the way here to discover for yourself.

I have taken the liberty of asking our travel team to book accommodation and travel for you for the meeting next week. A decision will be made soon regarding which office should swallow the costs of your unnecessary trip.

Once again, please accept my apologies.

Many thanks,

Esther

181 What does Maria say about the travel policy?

   A It's attached to her email.

   B It differs by country.

   C It needs to be observed for all trips.

   D It will be finalized in August.

182 What is the deadline for RSVPs?

   A April 3rd

   B July 20th

   C August 31st

   D November 15th

183 What can be inferred from the two emails?

   A Yussef travelled to Zurich on the wrong date.

   B Yussef travelled to the wrong location.

   C The meeting took place, but Yussef wasn't there.

   D Yussef was sent the wrong dates and noticed in time.

184 Whom does Esther blame for the mistake?

   A Maria

   B the Zurich office

   C the Los Angeles office

   D all of the above

185 In the 2nd paragraph of text 2, what does "swallow" mean?

   A bear

   B escalate

   C deliver

   D incur

Questions 186–190 refer to the following advertisement and two reviews.

Deluxe DVD Player

Was: ~~$49.99~~–NOW ONLY $24.99

- A stylish, affordable DVD player with multi-playback that includes multi-format DVDs and CDs

- Can be connected to a TV via HDMI or Scart cable

- USB outlet–recognizes most file formats, including MP4, MP3, MOV, AVI, MPEG-4 and VLC

- Multi-region DVD player–works with all DVDs from North America, South America, Europe and Australasia

- Comes with a 1-year warranty (can be extended to 3 years for a $14.99 additional fee)

★★★★☆ – **review by** Adiran Santxitz

I bought this DVD player when my trusty old DVD player died on me after seven years of faithful service. It arrived promptly and so far I have had no problems with it: it does exactly what it says on the box. I don't have any DVDs from a different region, so I haven't yet tried out that feature, but everything else works great. I've been using the USB slot a lot and I'm very satisfied with it: not only does it recognize every single format I've thrown at it (both for movies and for music), but it also accepts subtitles with all of them. The only thing you need to do is make sure the name of the file and the corresponding subtitles have an identical name and you're set to go. I even tried it out with subtitles that don't have Latin characters (Greek, Chinese, etc.) for fun and it works. I don't understand a word of it, but it works.

One thing I'd recommend to potential buyers is to also purchase a longer Scart cable if you plan to plug it into the TV using a Scart connection. The one it comes with is too short, especially if you want to keep the DVD player and the TV in separate shelves on your furniture. Also, it doesn't come with an HDMI cable, so you'll need one of those if that's what your TV port is.

★☆☆☆☆ – **review by** Clara Phoenix

Where do I start? First of all, the DVD player didn't arrive on time. When I called the company to ask where it was, no one even knew how to check up on orders. There doesn't seem to be a tracking system in place, and none of the employees seem to be competent enough to deal with customer issues.

Eventually, I managed to get them to send me a replacement–which arrived broken! Not only did it not recognize my DVDs, I got the "unsupported disc" error message for all of them (by the way, they are standard North American region 1 DVDs)–but it didn't even have an HDMI cable, so I had to go out and buy one. When I called to complain again, I was told it has been more than 14 days since I placed my order, so I am no longer entitled to a replacement! They can only fix it and send it back–and they had the nerve to say they would also be charging me for the postage. Stay away from this item–It's no wonder it was on sale. I guess you get what you pay for.

186 Which of the following is TRUE about the DVD player?

A It costs $49.99.

B A 3-year warranty is included in the price.

C It doesn't work with CDs.

D It works with mp3 files.

187 What has Adiran not tested out yet?

A whether DVDs from other countries work

B whether the DVD player works with an HDMI cable

C whether all USB file formats work

D whether the DVD player plays music

188 Why does Clara begin her review by writing, "Where do I start"?

A The reviewer is unfamiliar with the process.

B The reviewer has many criticisms.

C The reviewer did not understand how to use the item.

D The reviewer really liked the product.

189 Which issue do both reviewers mention?

A the short Scart cable

B the lack of an HDMI cable

C that the DVD player doesn't accept all DVD regions

D the delayed arrival of the product

190 Why did the company refuse to replace Clara's DVD player the second time?

A They had already replaced it once.

B She hadn't purchased a warranty.

C She complained too late.

D They claimed she was the one who had broken it.

Questions 191–195 refer to the following two emails and list of charges.

From: HR@wallets.com

To: charlotteoffice@wallets.com

Hi all,

Please have a look at the attached list of charges to the company credit card. Can those of you who recognize these charges please drop a line to Ruth with the invoice as well as the purpose of the charge, and whether it is billable to your client or not?

May I also remind you that you should always notify Ruth or Tom from HR whenever you use the company credit card and immediately send your invoices to us? This is extremely important and has been mentioned in numerous company-wide meetings. Please do not force us to resort to naming and shaming.

Thank you very much for your attention.

Kind regards,

HR Department

Highlight Airlines	$897.56
Airport Parking Lot	$60.00
TMR Airways	$430.91
Walker's Stationery	$29.99
Fly High Airways	$125.66
Opus Bus Company	$38.00
Joe's Coffee	$49.86
KDQ Airlines	$1,209.12
TMR Airways	$56.00
Joe's Coffee	$56.12
Furniture Ideas	$59.99

From: pablo@wallets.com

To: ruth@wallets.com

Hi Ruth,

Please find attached the invoice for the $897.56 charge, as well as the $60 associated parking lot charge. Both of these costs are associated with the meeting we had with one of our clients, Le Bateau, in Paris two weeks ago: they are John's flights, and the parking lot charge is for his car for the night.

I have to say, I'm a little bit confused with this. As you can see in the email I have attached, I already sent these a month ago when we booked the tickets and the parking lot spot—and you, in fact, acknowledged my email and assured me it had been filed properly. This isn't the first time I've sent my company credit card invoices only for my expenses to be added to your monthly email requesting "missing" invoices—same thing happened last month with John's flights to Peru.

Is there something that can be done to avoid this situation? I am happy to re-send invoices, but I do not appreciate being added to these emails and threatened with 'name and shame' when I have done everything I need to do.

Thanks,

Pablo

191 In the first email, in paragraph 1, line 2, the phrase "drop a line" is closest in meaning to

A send an email

B connect

C wire

D invite to lunch

192 What does the first email say about the need to send invoices to HR?

A It will be mentioned again in the next company-wide meeting.

B It helps to determine if charges are billable to the client or not.

C They will have to start publicly identifying wrongdoers if it continues.

D It should be done before the end of the month.

193 According to the list, how much money was spent on office supplies?

A $29.99

B $38.00

C $49.86

D $56.00

194 With which airline did John fly to Paris?

A Highlight Airlines

B TMR Airways

C Fly High Airways

D KDQ Airlines

195 How is the author of the second email likely to feel?

A ashamed

B frustrated

C smug

D petrified

Questions 196–200 refer to the following flight itinerary and two emails.

FLIGHT DETAILS	
*Outbound–**March 19***	*Inbound–**March 28***
San Diego ➜ Los Angeles (TMR9776)	London ➜ Los Angeles (TMR9731)
Departs: 10:31	Departs: 07:01
Arrives: 11:45	Arrives: 17:25
Check-in opens: 08:30	Check-in opens: 04:00
Check-in closes: 09:45	Check-in closes: 05:30
Los Angeles ➜ London (TMR9113)	Los Angeles ➜ San Diego (TMR9129)
Departs: 13:31	Departs: 19:04
Arrives: 08:15 +1	Arrives: 20:20
Check-in opens: 10:30	Check-in opens: 17:30
Check-in closes: 12:00	Check-in closes: 18:15

From: customerservice@TMR.com

To: rich.spencer@mail.com

Date: March 28th, 16:21

Dear Mr. Spencer,

We regret to inform you that your connecting flight has been cancelled. Please make your way to our information desk upon arrival to Los Angeles Airport to inquire about alternatives.

Our deepest apologies for the inconvenience caused.

Kind regards,

Customer service department—TMR Airways

From: rich.spencer@mail.com

To: customerservice@TMR.com

Date: March 30th, 09:45

Hi,

My name is Richard Spencer and I recently flew with you from San Diego to London and back. On my return, one of my flights was cancelled due to—as I was told at the airport—an issue with the aircraft.

As it was already quite late by the time I arrived at Los Angeles, there were no more seats available on any flights on the same day, and so I was forced to spend the night at a local hotel and fly out the next day.

Notwithstanding the issues caused by the delay, which included having to take an extra day off from work, the hotel I was booked into by your staff was unacceptable—and the voucher I was offered for my dinner there was a meager $15, which meant I had to fork out another $30 from my own pocket to have a decent meal. I have attached the receipt for you, and I expect to be compensated for my expenses, as they never would have occurred had you not messed up. I also expect some form of compensation for the trouble I was put through, and for having to sleep at that truly terrible hotel.

I look forward to hearing from you.

Regards,

Rich Spencer

196 What was the latest time the passenger could drop his bags at the counter on his first out-bound flight?

   A   08:30

   B   09:45

   C   10:31

   D   11:45

197 At what time was the passenger due to arrive to his final destination on his return trip?

   A   08:15

   B   11:45

   C   17:25

   D   20:20

198 According to the email from customer service, which flight was cancelled?

   A   TMR9776

   B   TMR9113

   C   TMR9731

   D   TMR9129

199 What was the problem with the flight that was cancelled?

   A   not enough staff

   B   engineering problem

   C   overbooking

   D   a delay

200 Which of the following is NOT a complaint made by Rich Spencer?

   A   The hotel he was booked in was not appropriate.

   B   He missed a day of work.

   C   He arrived late to Los Angeles.

   D   He had to pay extra for his meal.

TOEIC Listening and Reading Practice Test 2

LISTENING TEST

In this section of the test, you will show your knowledge of spoken English. This section has four parts, and the entire section will last for around 45 minutes. Directions are given for each individual part of the test. Mark your answers on the answer sheet provided. To listen to the audio tracks for this section of the test, access the tracks in your Online Resources, by visiting **www.kaptest.com/booksonline** OR through the Kaplan Study App.

 Play Track 5 for Test 2, Part I

PART I: PHOTOGRAPHS

Directions: For each question in this part, you will hear four statements about a picture in your test book. When you hear the statements, you must select the one statement that best describes what you see in the picture. Then find the number of the question on your answer sheet and mark your answer. The statements will not be printed in your test book and will be spoken only one time.

1

2

3

4

5

6

Play Track 6 for Test 2, Part II

PART II: QUESTION RESPONSE

Directions: You will hear a question or statement and three responses spoken in English. They will not be printed in your test book and will be spoken only one time. Select the best response to the question or statement and mark the letter A, B, or C on your answer sheet.

7	Mark your answer on your answer sheet.	20	Mark your answer on your answer sheet.
8	Mark your answer on your answer sheet.	21	Mark your answer on your answer sheet.
9	Mark your answer on your answer sheet.	22	Mark your answer on your answer sheet.
10	Mark your answer on your answer sheet.	23	Mark your answer on your answer sheet.
11	Mark your answer on your answer sheet.	24	Mark your answer on your answer sheet.
12	Mark your answer on your answer sheet.	25	Mark your answer on your answer sheet.
13	Mark your answer on your answer sheet.	26	Mark your answer on your answer sheet.
14	Mark your answer on your answer sheet.	27	Mark your answer on your answer sheet.
15	Mark your answer on your answer sheet.	28	Mark your answer on your answer sheet.
16	Mark your answer on your answer sheet.	29	Mark your answer on your answer sheet.
17	Mark your answer on your answer sheet.	30	Mark your answer on your answer sheet.
18	Mark your answer on your answer sheet.	31	Mark your answer on your answer sheet.
19	Mark your answer on your answer sheet.		

Play Track 7 for Test 2, Part III

PART III: SHORT CONVERSATIONS

Directions: You will hear some conversations between two people. You will be asked to answer three questions about what the speakers say in each conversation. Select the best response to each question and mark the letter (A), (B), (C), or (D) on your answer sheet. The conversation will not be printed in your test book and will be spoken only one time.

32 What are the speakers talking about?

    A   a conference

    B   a job interview

    C   a project meeting

    D   a presentation

33 Who asked questions?

    A   the personnel director

    B   a researcher

    C   the office manager

    D   a client

34 How does the man feel?

    A   pleased

    B   disappointed

    C   worried

    D   surprised

35 Who is the man?

    A   a job applicant

    B   an employee

    C   a government official

    D   a customer

36 Where will the speakers go?

    A   a factory

    B   a government office

    C   a conference

    D   a restaurant

37 What will the man need to wear?

    A   a suit and tie

    B   safety equipment

    C   an ID badge

    D   a microphone

38 When does the woman need the work finished?

    A   before April

    B   in four weeks

    C   before May

    D   in three weeks

39 Why does the man say "at the crack of dawn"?

    A   His workers will arrive early.

    B   He needs more time to finish.

    C   He thinks it's too late.

    D   He thinks she got there too soon.

40 Look at the plan. Which cubicle does the man think should be removed from the project?

    A   Cubicle 1

    B   Cubicle 2

    C   Cubicle 3

    D   Cubicle 4

Door	Cubicle 1	Cubicle 2	
			Cubicle 3
	Cubicle 4	Cubicle 5	
			Sink and Dryer

41 Where are the speakers?

A at a cafe

B an a supermarket

C in an office

D at home

42 Where is the man going?

A to a bank

B to the marketing department

C to the post office

D to a bookstore

43 What does the woman want?

A a copy of a report

B some food

C a book

D some stamps

44 Where does the man want to go?

A church

B a factory

C an Italian restaurant

D Chicago

45 What is Giuseppe's?

A an Italian restaurant in Chicago

B a local restaurant near the factory

C the restaurant where they took the clients

D the official restaurant of the Chicago Bears

46 Why were the clients disappointed?

A They couldn't spot a bear.

B It was too cold in Chicago.

C They didn't like the Italian restaurant.

D They thought they would see a different sport.

47 Why does the woman say "too good to be true"?

A She thinks products at TeckPak are too cheap.

B She thinks there might be something wrong with the online store.

C She thinks the eco printers are unreliable.

D She doesn't believe Wallace

48 Look at the graphic. Which product did they most likely buy?

A Smart TV Eco 42"

B Smart TV 4K 28"

C Ecojet Printer 4480

D Premi Printer 4680

Product	Store	
	Gadgets Online	TechPak
Smart TV Eco 42"	$400.00	$500.00
Smart TV 4K 28"	$349.99	$350.00
Ecojet Printer 4480	$200.00	$300.00
Premi Printer 4680	$405.00	$420.00

49 Who's Matteo?

A Wallace's friend

B Burcu's husband

C their boss

D a customer service advisor

50 How are the speakers probably feeling?

A excited

B tired

C frustrated

D hungry

51 Why does Nelson say "It's a bit of a nightmare"?

A He finds the new system difficult to use.

B He hasn't slept well for days.

C He doesn't like working with Colin.

D He doesn't like computers.

52 What does the woman say about IT?

A They work hard.

B They need a pay rise.

C They do unnecessary things.

D They should work harder.

53 What can't the woman find?

A her folder

B the invoices

C her box

D an internet link

54 What does the man say about the company?

A Staff don't follow the rules.

B The computers never work.

C The offices are too messy.

D The managers are too bossy.

55 Who is NOT one of the managers?

A Tatiana

B Sarah

C Marcelo

D Mikiko

56 Who is an architect?

A the first speaker

B the first speaker's wife

C Julie

D Rodrigo

57 What is the woman's suggestion?

A a trip abroad

B dinner out in an exotic restaurant

C an art course in London

D a long vacation in Brazil

58 Why does the man say "I'll text him later"?

A He'll ask Rodrigo for advice.

B He'll invite Rodrigo to the museum.

C He'll tell Rodrigo about Julie and Abu.

D He'll ask for Rodrigo's number.

59 What will Thomas do this weekend?

A He will go on a business trip.

B He will move to Germany.

C He will work with the new associates on the Mahamas case.

D He will visit his sister.

60 Who's the woman going to watch closely?

A Thomas

B Rawan

C the new associates

D Thomas's sister

61 How should the woman contact the man?

A in person

B by telephone

C by email

D by fax

62 How does the woman feel about the candidate?

A suspicious

B excited

C disappointed

D overjoyed

63 When did the candidate finish university?

A three years ago

B more than twenty years ago

C around 1999

D around 2002

64 What does the man say he'll do?

A He'll contact her former employers.

B He'll send her résumé to the woman.

C He'll see if he knows where to find her.

D He'll keep the woman better informed about the candidate's qualifications and work experience.

65 What did the man do the night before?

A He watched TV with some friends.

B He stayed home and listened to music.

C He entertained guests at home.

D He talked to some of his old school friends.

66 What was the documentary about?

A the amount of garbage in big cities

B where the garbage we produce ends up

C how to recycle trash

D how to stop beaches and mountains from being polluted

67 What does Rebecca say about San Francisco?

A She was there 10 years ago.

B The city does not produce a lot of waste.

C It's much more polluted than 10 years ago.

D It produces less garbage than her home-town.

68 What does the man say about his company?

A They import some of their parts from China.

B They import small components from China.

C They import half their parts from China.

D They import very few parts from China.

69 Which adjective does NOT describe the Chinese manufacturers?

A fast

B reliable

C less expensive

D creative

70 Look at the table. In which of the containers can you probably find the parts produced in the US?

A Container 1

B Container 2

C Container 3

D Container 4

Containers	Description	Quantity	Weight
01	ZTech Turbines	3	470 kg
02	W2 Chips	200	3.7 kg
03	Y71788 Cases	100	244 kg
04	TWK Boards	55	29.1 kg

Play Track 8 for Test 2, Part IV

PART IV: SHORT TALKS

Directions: You will hear some talks given by one speaker. You will be asked to answer three questions about what the speaker says in each talk. Select the best response to each question and mark the letter (A), (B), (C), or (D) on your answer sheet. The conversation will not be printed in your test book and will be spoken only one time.

71 What time does the coach service get to Heathrow Airport?

- **A** 7.45
- **B** 7.50
- **C** 8.35
- **D** 8.45

72 Why can't the bus get to terminals 4 and 5?

- **A** the traffic is too heavy
- **B** the roads are closed for repair
- **C** there are very few shuttles
- **D** there's a demonstration on the roads

73 How can passengers get to terminals 4 and 5?

- **A** by coach
- **B** by train
- **C** by shuttle bus
- **D** by car

74 What is the name of the premiere movie?

- **A** The Lone Fighter
- **B** The Young Orphan
- **C** The Heart of America
- **D** Women's Day

75 Which of the following has the premiere movie NOT been nominated for?

- **A** Best Special Effects
- **B** Best Soundtrack
- **C** Best Leading Actor
- **D** Best Picture

76 What promotion is mentioned in the announcement?

- **A** Women get free popcorn.
- **B** Women go free with another paying adult.
- **C** Women get a discount on International Women's Day.
- **D** Free ticket for women booking on their website.

77 What type of text is the recording?

- **A** an advertisement
- **B** a radio program
- **C** a mall announcement
- **D** an airport announcement

78 Which service is NOT mentioned in the recording?

- **A** mudding
- **B** hair treatment
- **C** oriental skin treatment
- **D** dietary advice

79 What does the speaker mean when he says '"the first day of the rest of your life"?

- **A** Their services can change a person's life.
- **B** Their services are cheap and reliable.
- **C** She's referring to a Hollywood movie.
- **D** The beauty center has opened just recently.

80 Where are you most likely to hear this talk

A in a meeting

B at a conference

C on the radio

D on an answering machine

81 Which area will be the wettest?

A West

B East

C Central

D South

82 Which of the following is NOT mentioned in the report?

A fog

B heavy rain

C frost

D snow storms

83 Who is the speech most likely addressed to?

A undergraduates

B high school students

C teachers

D psychologists

84 Look at the itinerary below. Which of the scheduled items hasn't been updated with the correct information?

A Opening Speech

B Why study here?

C Lunch Break

D Lectures

Eastern University Open Day			
09.00	Opening Speech	Reception Hall	Sally Cruz
09.30	Campus Tour		Jason Beele
10.25	Why study here?	Main Auditorium	Federico Albuquerque
11.05	Personal Development	Rooms 3–26	Vocational Psychology Group
12.20	Lunch Break	Kiosk Café	
13.20	Lectures	Auditoriums A–F	

85 Which of the following is NOT mentioned in the woman's speech?

A changes to the original schedule

B grants and scholarships

C lunch

D the weather

86 What's the new restaurant called?

A La Bella Vita

B La Bella Express

C Panini's

D La Ciabatta

87 What kind of food will the new restaurant serve?

A traditional food

B American food

C fast food

D frozen meals

88 How does the speaker describe *La Bella Vita?*

A expensive

B cheap

C traditional

D successful

89 Which benefits are offered by the company?

A free fuel, insurance, and road assistance

B free fuel, satnav, and student discount

C insurance, satnav, and student discount

D discount fuel, insurance, and satnav

90 How many of their stores also sell cars?

A 30

B 24

C 12

D 7

91 What does the woman NOT say about their cars for sale?

A They all have low mileage.

B A 12-month warranty is included.

C All cars are in good condition.

D You can see car prices on their website.

92 Where will the flight land?

A Atlanta

B Munich

C Frankfurt

D Berlin

93 What does the woman say about the flight?

A Passengers can now get on the plane.

B The boarding gate has changed to gate 27.

C The plane is ready to take off.

D It has been delayed.

94 Who has boarding priority?

A pregnant women

B the elderly

C small children

D passengers with a priority pass

95 What time does the clinic close on Tuesdays?

A 7:00 p.m.

B 5:00 p.m.

C 4:00 p.m.

D 3:00 p.m.

96 When is the clinic closed?

A on Sundays

B on weekends

C on Saturdays

D on Mondays

97 How can you book an appointment?

A only on their website

B by using their app or going to their website

C by phone or online

D only by calling them during office hours

98 What does Giovanna mean when she says "I just don't get it"?

A She didn't receive her order.

B She doesn't know where her order is.

C She wants to know why her order was damaged.

D She is surprised her order was left outside.

99 What does she say about the payment?

A She has asked for a refund.

B She has already paid for the order.

C She will not pay for it.

D She wants a discount after all the delivery problems.

100 Look at the invoice. Which IS INCORRECT?

A customer's email

B order number

C order items

D payment form

8th March 2018

Order #
DDW1299-62

DP 2298 Portable
Printer (1)

A5 Photo Quality
Paper (3)

Papadopoulos, Giovanna
109 Kinson Road BH9 3RR
gigi_papa68@email.com
(729) 927-2900

Paid with Paypoint on 8th March 2018 2:53 p.m.

READING TEST

In this section of the test, you will show your knowledge of written English. This section has three parts, and you have 75 minutes to complete all three sections. Directions are given for each individual part of the test. Mark your answers on the answer sheet provided.

PART V: INCOMPLETE SENTENCES

Directions: complete the following sentences using one of the four answer choices provided. Mark the answer **A, B, C** or **D** on your answer sheet.

101 _____ had seen any of the numbers before the presentation started.

   A Somebody

   B Anybody

   C Nobody

   D Everybody

102 The police had been _____ the rooms in the house for hours before they found the crime weapon.

   A looking

   B seeking

   C searching

   D finding

103 Once the meeting was over, we went _____ to the airport.

   A straight

   B direct

   C towards

   D along

104 Lucia didn't manage to convince Omar _____ his current job.

   A quits

   B quit

   C quitting

   D to quit

105 The government is _____ pass a new law on digital currencies.

   A going

   B due to

   C likely

   D about

106 The textile _____ has suffered a major blow this financial year.

   A industry

   B industrial

   C industrialization

   D industrious

107 My supervisor _____ on the day I left the company.

   A promoted

   B is promoted

   C got promoted

   D promotes

108 _____ , we managed to sign a new agreement.

   A Unfortunately

   B Usually

   C Fortunately

   D Rarely

109 What I most like about Masha is her ability _____ positively.

   A to always think

   B always thinking

   C to think always

   D always think

110 I am _____ to see that your proposal has been accepted.

   A pleased

   B please

   C pleasure

   D pleasing

111 Di Luca is seen as a _____ leader by his friends and colleagues.

   A visionary

   B vision

   C visual

   D visualize

112 Mrs. Patel's _____ of commitment has ultimately led to her dismissal.

   A miss

   B fault

   C foul

   D lack

113 Much to the shareholders' _____, Simpsons Ltd. shares plummeted to a new low last week.

   A declaration

   B deviant

   C dismay

   D delight

114 Farm workers were not _____ by the cuts.

   A effect

   B affect

   C affected

   D effective

115 Pierre is _____ have been accused of embezzlement.

   A believe

   B believe to

   C believed

   D believed to

116 They were well _____ of the fact that they were breaking the law.

   A known

   B aware

   C thought

   D seen

117 The group decided it was time to _____ their investments and leave.

   A cash in

   B pay in

   C take on

   D deposit

118 Stock prices _____ as a result of the corruption scandal.

   A improved

   B plummeted

   C rise

   D fall

119 Magali _____ with corporate law for years before she joined the firm.

   A has worked

   B was been working

   C used to have worked

   D had worked

120 The increase in the HR budget _____ us to organize a conference this year.

A will allow

B will have allowed

C will be allowing

D allow

121 The political _____ following the referendum is damaging the economy.

A tension

B tense

C tensely

D tenseness

122 _____ he had never worked in the area, Ali still managed to impress the interviewers and get the job.

A However

B Even though

C In spite of

D Despite

123 Nikita soon got used _____ late hours.

A to work

B to working

C of working

D at work

124 The jury's _____ will decide the company's fate.

A verification

B verdure

C veracity

D verdict

125 Isaac's _____ to detail is key to his success.

A attention

B obsession

C importance

D dedication

126 _____ getting a promotion, Ruth ended up being given a formal warning.

A Apart from

B As well

C Instead of

D On top of

127 We regret _____ that you have not been accepted on to the course at this time.

A saying

B say

C to say

D said

128 Millennials are usually very _____ on learning by using technology.

A interested

B important

C likely

D keen

129 The board has received _____ of his financial reports on the year to date.

A any

B none

C little

D every

130 All our employees get notifications about meetings _____ their smart phones.

A on

B in

C at

D into

PART VI: TEXT COMPLETION

Directions: Read the following texts and select the best answer choice to complete the text. Mark the answer **A**, **B**, **C** or **D** on your answer sheet.

Questions 131–134 refer to the following email.

With the enormous success of its new branches in Singapore and Indonesia, TDK Bank must now be _____ the world leader in innovative personal banking. We cannot deny
    131.
that HBWC has been providing strong competition for the past two decades, especially in Southern Europe, but TDK's new line of interest-only mortgages and easy-access loan products is more than enough to guarantee its global market leadership. _____ other
        132.
banks and building societies had the vision and courage of these two massive corporations, this new generation would have a better chance of setting up small businesses or climbing the property ladder. By adapting their financial products to the local markets they enter, TDK Bank and HBWC have achieved never before seen levels of success in a very short period of time. Hopefully, the refreshing and inventive attitude _____ these two giants will set
        133.
a new trend of personal banking that sees profit as the consequence of investing on the development of a more inclusive society. The main difference, however, is TDK's technical know-how, allowing it to open more branches _____ and explore markets with little if
        134.
any competition.

---

131 A seen

    B remembered

    C considered

    D recognized

132 A Perhaps if

    B Although

    C In spite of

    D Unless

133 A with

    B shown by

    C towards

    D to

134 A quicker

    B quick

    C quickest

    D more quickly

Questions 135–138 refer to the following email

To:	lizzie@teamcorp.com.it
From:	wu@smartbilling.co.uk
Date:	February 22, 2017
Subject:	3rd reminder on invoice #38266 (overdue by one month)

Hi Elisabeta Lavagna,

I have written to you several times, reminding you of the _____ amount of $12,700 for in-
                                                              135.
voice #38266, but it continues to remain unpaid even after a whole month.

If you have any queries regarding its payment or would like to renegotiate it, please let me know
by the end of this week, _____ .
                          136.

I'm afraid that if we don't hear back from you by Friday we will have to assign this matter to our
legal team and you will have to cover the _____ as agreed in the contract you signed when you
                                           137.
placed your order with us.

_____ you reply to this message to let me know you have received it?
    138.

Regards,

Jane Doe

---

135 A pending
B missing
C check
D profits

136 A look forward to meeting you
B otherwise, please organize for settlement of this invoice immediately.
C I hope you will accept this position.
D we consider you an important asset to our team.

137 A income
B expenses
C balance
D left

138 A Could
B Should
C When
D If

Questions 139–142 refer to the following advertisement.

IT Manager

EWY Remanufacturing - Cincinnati

$70,000 – $95,000 a year

EWY is rapidly becoming the international market leader in the manufacture of electronics. We are now looking for a creative professional who is able to _____ when managing product design and development administration.
139.

Responsibilities

- Build and upgrade systems on Azure Cloud Platform

- Recommend and/or develop innovative approaches for system administration tasks

- _____ user requests are addressed promptly
  140.

Requirements

- Familiar with Azure Cloud Administration

- Good _____ and eager to learn
  141.

- Proactive with great interpersonal skills

- Impeccable verbal and written communication skills

Perks

- Freedom to develop own products

- Company reimbursed _____ for a wide range of training programs
  142.

Salary

Salary range is between $70K – $95K per year, depending on skills and experience.

Required experience:

Systems administration: 3 years

139
  A dread to think
  B think out loud
  C think the world of
  D think outside the box

140
  A Ensure
  B Allow
  C Reinforce
  D Reassure

141
  A solving-problem skills
  B solve-the-problem skill
  C problem-solving skills
  D problem-solved skills

142
  A tuition
  B fares
  C expenditure
  D scholarship

Questions 143–146 refer to the following notice.

To all residents

Electrical safety is critical

Under section 11, from the Landlord and Tenant Act of 1985, the landlord is responsible _____ the maintenance of all electrical wiring and electricity supply. _____ ,
143.   144.
landlords and letting agents are also required by law to check the safety of the electrical appliances that come with the property.

In the UK, approximately 4000 people are seriously injured in electrical incidents each year. Half of these accidents result from poor maintenance and DIY jobs.

IT'S IMPORTANT THAT TENANTS DO NOT ATTEMPT TO REPAIR ELECTRICAL EQUIPMENT THEMSELVES, _____ THEY ARE CERTIFIED ELECTRICIANS.
145.
Please contact us at **healthandsafety@managekings.co.uk** if you have any queries or need the help of a certified electrician.

_____
146.
Management

---

143 A to

B for

C in

D on

144 A And

B Without this

C With reference to

D In addition

145 A IF

B UNLESS

C AS LONG AS

D IN CASE

146 A We look forward to hearing back from you.

B Should you need any further information, please contact your line manager.

C Your cooperation in this matter is highly appreciated.

D To whom it may concern.

PART VII: READING COMPREHENSION

Directions: In this part of the test, you will read a number of different texts and then answer several questions about each text. Mark the answer **A**, **B**, **C** or **D** on your answer sheet.

Questions 147–149 refer to the following tables.

City Metro Fare — [1] —				
	Adult	**Over 60**	**Under 18**	**Under 6**
One way	$2.50	$1.50	$1.50	Free
Return	$4.00	$2.50	$2.50	Free
Day Pass — [2] —	$7.50	$4.00	$4.00	Free

— [3] — For travels outside Zone A, the following surcharges will be added for each zone crossed.

	Adult	**Over 60**	**Under 18**
One way	$1.00	$0.75	$0.75
Return	$1.50	$1.00	$1.00
Day Pass	$2.00	$1.50	$1.50

— [4] —

147 How much should a senior citizen pay for a return ticket within the same zone?

A $4.00

B $2.50

C $1.50

D $1.00

148 How much would a 12-year-old pay for unlimited travel between zones A and B on the same day?

A $4.00

B $1.50

C $5.50

D $4.75

149 In which of the positons [1], [2], [3] and [4] does the following sentence best belong? "The fares above are valid for travel within Zone A (downtown)."

A [1]

B [2]

C [3]

D [4]

Questions 150–153 refer to the following warranty.

Warranty

— [1] — All of our smart televisions are guaranteed for a decade. We take great pride in the high quality of all the components used to build our entertainment systems, and this why our warranty is limited to the repair or replacement of such components. — [2] — The warranty does not cover equipment misuse, intentional damage, product modification, 'jailbreaking', abuse, or negligence. We are confident our range of smart TVs, when used according to the recommendations on your users' manual (www.sambahd.com/smarttv/usersmanual), will provide you with family entertainment for a lifetime. — [3] — Any and all claims made with this warranty must be accompanied by your unique registration number. We cannot repair products which have not been registered within 90 days of purchase (www.sambahd/warranty/termsandconditions). — [4] — For further information, contact us on info@sambahd.com or direct message on our Friendbook page.

---

150 How long does the warranty last?

A   6 months

B   5 years

C   10 years

D   90 days

151 Which of the following is covered?

A   intentional damage

B   product modification

C   negligence

D   components replacement

152 What is required when making a claim?

A   a user's manual

B   a copy of the receipt

C   a distinctive customer number

D   a product registration number

153 Which of the positons [1], [2], [3] and [4] does the following sentence best belong?
"Thank you for choosing a Samba model for your new television."

A   [1]

B   [2]

C   [3]

D   [4]

Questions 154–155 refer to the following table.

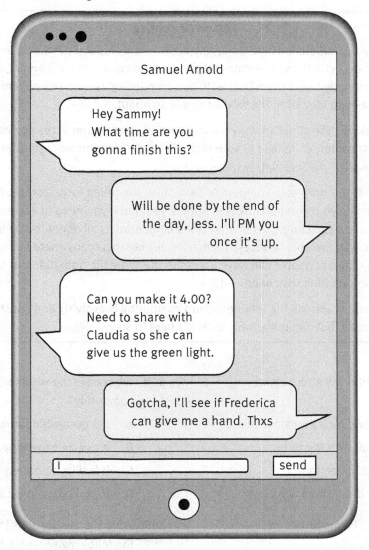

154 What does Jess mean by "green light"?

    A   Samuel needs to provide permission.

    B   Claudia needs to open the gates.

    C   Samuel needs to work faster.

    D   Claudia needs to authorize the work.

155 What will Samuel do?

    A   share the workload with a colleague

    B   work through lunch to finish on time

    C   submit the work tomorrow

    D   finish the work at 5pm

Questions 156–159 refer to the following text.

Cloud Computing

The cloud. We hear about it all the time; 'the file is in the cloud'. But what is the 'cloud'? Is it a cabinet? Where is it? These questions might seem ridiculous to a millennial, but I'm pretty sure you've probably heard them before. 'Cloud computing' is now everywhere and a lot of people still have no idea what the whole thing is all about. — [1] —

Roughly speaking, 'cloud' technology means remotely storing and accessing data and programs on the internet instead of your laptop's hard disk or memory stick. In the simplest terms, the 'cloud' is the internet. — [2] —

When you save files onto your computer's hard drive, it's called local storage. All the data you need is inside your computer right in front of you, but if you need to access it from another computer, you can't. This is what cloud computing is all about: by saving your files on the internet you are able to access them from any computer anywhere in the world. And not only that, different people can have access to the same file from different locations and share all the information they need. — [3] —

Just like everything else on the internet, cloud computing is evolving and constantly changing its rules, but one thing is for sure: it's here to stay. — [4] —

---

156 What does the writer say about cloud computing?

A It's been around for a thousand years.

B He's unfamiliar with the term.

C It's difficult to understand.

D Many people don't know what it is.

157 What is "the cloud" a metaphor for?

A the weather in Britain

B the internet

C a computer lab

D an old computer

158 What does the writer NOT say about cloud computing?

A It's everywhere nowadays.

B It can be expensive.

C It facilitates access to files and data.

D It won't disappear any time soon.

159 Which of the positons [1], [2], [3] and [4] does the following sentence best belong?
"Cloud computing also prevents people from losing their work because data is no longer stored on their computers."

A [1]

B [2]

C [3]

D [4]

Questions 160–162 refer to the following message.

February 16, 2018

To all employees:

Purposes

1. To provide employees with the opportunity to choose their own professional development path

2. To provide HR with the tools to design a professional development program that intrinsically motivates staff

3. To specify professional development goals according to areas of interest

Guidelines

Management is responsible for conducting impartial needs analysis during performance appraisals of all staff. Needs analysis procedures and forms will be distributed by HR by the end of the month. If any staff members strongly disagree with their line manager in terms of which professional development path would best suit their careers, the employee and manager should come to an agreement, since HR will only authorize programs which are signed by both the employee and their direct supervisor.

---

160 What does the text say about the professional development program?

- **A** It will be personalized.
- **B** It's a great opportunity to obtain a promotion.
- **C** It's a tool to increase the company's profit.
- **D** It will allow employees to spend more time at home.

161 Who needs to agree on the best program for each employee?

- **A** The employees will choose.
- **B** employees and management
- **C** employees and HR
- **D** management and HR

162 Which of the following is NOT mentioned in the memo?

- **A** who is responsible for employees' needs analysis
- **B** HR will provide the documentation for the needs analysis.
- **C** the different professional development programs
- **D** who authorizes professional development choices

Questions 163–165 refer to the following invoice.

White North Office Goods

339 Lakeside Drive

Orlando, FL 32803

Bill to	Ship to	**Invoice Date:** 10/23/19
Bharat Yasin	Mary Gordon	
91 Amsterdam Avenue #3A	5 Modern Red Square #16C	
New York, NY 10023	Long Island City, NY 10022	

Qty.	Description	Unit Price	Amount
13	A4 Plastic Wallets (Package 100 each) × 13	$1.20	$15.60
7	PrintJet HB4500 BW cartirdges × 7	$5.50	$38.50
5	Cash Box 8" Silver × 5	$16.00	$80.00

Subtotal	**$134.10**
Sales Tax 5.0%	**$6.70**
TOTAL	**$140.81**

Terms and Conditions
Payment is due within 7 days

Santander Bank
Account Number: 65100933
Routing: 011075150

163 Where is the supplier located?

  A Orlando

  B Amsterdam

  C New York

  D Long Island City

164 How much was spent on printer ink?

  A $15.60

  B $5.50

  C $38.50

  D $80.00

165 When is the invoice due?

  A October 23

  B October 30

  C 2020

  D there is not enough information

Questions 166–168 refer to the following document.

Car Rental Terms

Please be advised that if you do not adhere to the Terms & Conditions, our cancellation policy will be enforced.

Cancellations

If you cancel your pre-paid reservation within 24 hours of placing the booking, a full refund will be issued. If you cancel your reservation more than 24 hours from the time of making the booking, no refund will be given.

If you do not collect your vehicle (no show):

Unless you have cancelled your reservation, if you do not collect your vehicle at the time specified during the booking, no refund will be given.

Driver Age

All drivers must be age 21 or over. Drivers age 21–24 may only rent cars up to Standard category. Drivers of vehicle categories Prestige, Luxury and Elite must be age 28 or over.

Fuel Policy

All vehicles are supplied with a full tank of fuel. Customers may choose to purchase this tank of fuel at a preferential rate and return the vehicle empty or return the vehicle with a full tank at the end of the rental.

Payment

Payment is required by credit card or debit card. Cash and cheques are not accepted.

---

166 In which situation would a customer be entitled to a refund?

   A   The booking was cancelled on the same day it was made.

   B   The booking was cancelled before the collection date.

   C   The customer does not have a license.

   D   The customer is under 21.

167 How old do customers to be to rent a luxurious car?

   A   21 or older

   B   24 or older

   C   over 27

   D   younger than 45

168 Which of the following is NOT mentioned in the text?

   A   the refund policy

   B   the amount of gas or diesel in each car

   C   forms of payment

   D   which credit cards are accepted

Questions 169–171 refer to the following table.

These figures show how the cost of a 3-mile ride in a standard taxi cab compares with VroomX and Vroom Black Car.

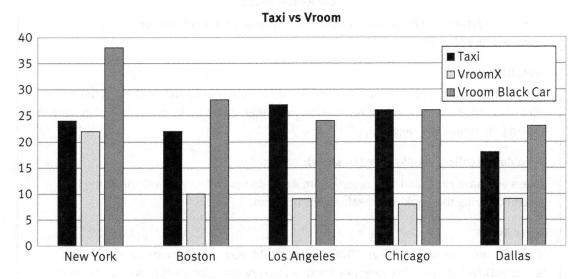

Fare estimates are in US Dollars and were calculated using mobile apps from Vroom and local taxi cab companies in October 2017.

169 Where are taxis more expensive than Vroom Black Cars?

  A New York

  B Boston

  C Los Angeles

  D Chicago

170 How much does a 3-mile taxi ride cost in Chicago?

  A more than $25

  B between $15–$20

  C between $10–$15

  D less than $10

171 Where can you travel 3 miles by taxi for less than $20?

  A Dallas

  B Chicago

  C Los Angeles

  D New York

Questions 172–173 refer to the following table.

Leroy 122K Smart TV Troubleshooting		
Problem	**Possible Cause**	**What to do**
No Image	Input and Output settings do not match	Menu > Settings > Image > Reset Settings
No Sound	1. Volume muted or too low. 2. Bluetooth headphones connected	1. Check volume with SmartRemote® 2. Menu > Settings > Bluetooth > Disconnect
No Internet	1. Cable unplugged 2. Wi-Fi disconnected	1. Remove and insert ethernet cable on TV and router 2. Menu > Settings > Internet > Wireless > Settings

172 What is the purpose of the table?

  A   to show various models of TVs

  B   to report problems with a television

  C   to help customers upgrade their televisions

  D   to explain how to fix issues for a TV

173 Which of the following problems is NOT caused by wireless technology?

  A   no image

  B   no sound

  C   no internet

  D   none of the above

Questions 174–175 refer to the following specifications.

Parkston T77 Single Sim Cell Phone–Black

- Modern, ergonomic design to better fit your hands and pockets

- Up to 22 hours talk time and 6 weeks on standby

- 3.5" QQVGA display for better texting and internet browsing

- Curved key mat for easier texting and dialing

- 64GB storage

- FM Radio built-in (no need for apps)

Important Information: This product has an IMEI that uniquely identifies it. When your order is dispatched, we will scan the IMEI and add it to the order history to help prevent fraudulent use.

---

174 Which of the following is NOT mentioned in the text?

A screen size

B storage capacity

C battery life

D operating system

175 Which of the following is a feature of the cell phone?

A a classic design

B an ultra-definition display

C can play music from the radio

D unlimited text messages

Questions 176–180 refer to the following text message chain and email.

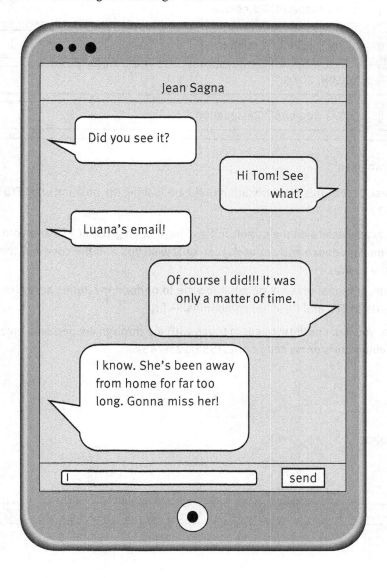

To:	cambiasso@etbltd.com.ar
From:	negreiros@etbltd.com.ar
Date:	July 08, 2016
Subject:	Luana Negreiros' Resignation

Dear Mr. Cambiasso

— [1] — Please accept this as notification that I am leaving my position with ETB effective August 22.

— [2] — I truly appreciate all the opportunities I have been given at ETB and your valuable professional guidance and support. I can only wish you and the company the best success in the future.

Unfortunately, personal reasons do not allow me to perform my duties according to the high standards of ETB and its sister companies. — [3] —

In the future, you can continue to get in touch with me through my personal email, lulu1979br@email.com, or my cell phone, (555)123-7454.

Sincerely,

— [4] —

Luana Negreiros

176 What does Jean mean when he says "It was only a matter of time"?

   A it was inevitable

   B it could have been avoided

   C it was a surprise

   D it was too late

177 What does Tom think the problem with Luana is?

   A she doesn't like her job

   B she misses her old job

   C she's homesick

   D she needs a professional challenge

178 Why does Luana email Mr Cambiasso?

   A to ask for advice

   B to notify him of her law suit against the company

   C to resign from her post

   D to request a promotion

179 In which of the positons [1], [2], [3] and [4] does the following sentence best belong?
"If I can be of assistance during this transition, please let me know."

   A [1]

   B [2]

   C [3]

   D [4]

180 Which of the following is NOT mentioned in either of the two texts above?

   A why Luana has written the email

   B what Jean thinks about Luana's decision

   C the name of the company Luana works for

   D Luana's current position at the company

Questions 181–185 refer to the following two texts.

International Inventors Association (IIA)
Awards Ceremony 2018
Friday, February 23, 2018 6.30 p.m.
Ball Room, Corcovado Hall
AGENDA

1.	Welcome Cocktails	Lucas Pietr
2.	Past Winners	Alexa Ilker
3.	Grants & Budget	Robin Giroud
4.	Presentation of Awards	João Bezerra
5.	Gala Ball	

To:	Ilker67@unitedforever.com
From:	bezerrajj@email.com.br
Date:	September 12, 2017
Subject:	IIA Rio 2018

Dear Ms. Ilker,

My name is João Bezerra and I am the new head of IIA. We would like to invite you to present our Past Winners retrospective during our awards ceremony this year. It would be an honor to have a successful entrepreneur two-time winner of the awards as our speaker during the most traditional part of our ceremony.

For this year we would like to focus on our first under 18 winner, Natasha Akinfeev, who stunned the world with her robot vacuum cleaner working model when she was only 17 years old. Should you accept our offer, we would like to offer you an all-expenses paid trip to visit her company's headquarters in Moscow.

I would like to say that I am speaking for all us at IIA when I say what an honor it would be to have you present our Past Winners retrospective.

Look forward to hearing back from you.

Warm regards,

João Bezerra

181 Who will talk about the finances at IIA2018?

A Lucas Pietr

B Mustafa Ilker

C Robin Giroud

D João Bezerra

182 Why does Mr Bezerra email Ms Ilker?

A to ask her to talk for item 2 of the agenda

B to invite her to present the awards

C to invite her to attend IIA 2018 in Rio

D to invite her to present her old inventions

183 How does Mr Bezerra describe the Past Winners retrospective?

A established

B resists change

C honorable

D popular

184 Who has designed a cleaning prototype?

A Lucas Pietr

B Robin Giroud

C João Bezerra

D Natasha Akinfeev

185 What's in Moscow?

A IIA 2018

B Natasha's company

C Mr. Bezerra's headquarters

D the Past Winners retrospective

Questions 186–190 refer to the following text chain, email and article.

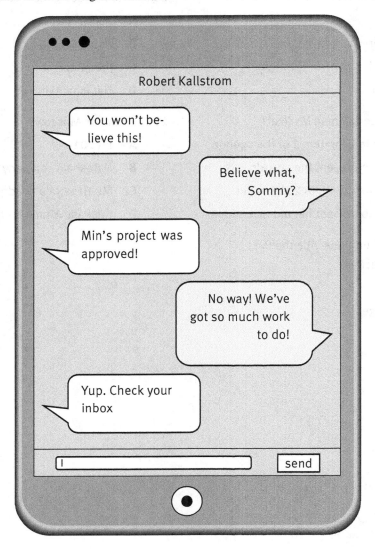

To:	robkit@mailme.se
From:	‹Samputchara› sommy@email.com.th
Date:	April 2, 2018
Subject:	FW: Lemur Park Redevelopment Proposal

Take a look at the forwarded message below. I can't wait for us to work on this!

_____

From: info@citycouncil.com

Sent: April 1, 2018

To: zhaomin@mailme.com

Subject: Lemur Park Redevelopment Proposal

Dear Ms. Zhao,

We are very happy to inform you that your redevelopment proposal has been accepted. We would like to invite you for a first meeting next Friday March 16 at 2 p.m. Would that suit you? If not, please let us know by tomorrow so we can find a more convenient time and date.

We are truly excited about this project and hope to discuss the details with you soon.

Yours sincerely,

Shaun Jeffers

City Council Chair

— [1] —

Work will begin early in 2019 and includes a soccer pitch, water park and restaurants. — [2] — The council has appointed developer Min Zhao of ModCit Designs to lead the regeneration, after a tendering process which saw several other international developers competing for the work.

Zhao, who graduated in architecture from New Minds University, has designed a project which celebrates the history of the coastal town while bringing it into the 21st century. — [3] — The new Lemur Park will be the home of a brand new soccer pitch, indoor waterpark, new shops, and a bespoke gourmet area with various cafés, restaurants, and gastro pubs.

— [4] — The first phase of the redevelopment, which will see the construction of the waterpark and part of the gourmet area, is expected to begin in January 2019.

186 What does Sommy mean when she says "Check your inbox"?

A Read your emails.

B Open the box I sent you.

C Refresh your browser.

D Go to the post office.

187 What does Sommy email Robert?

A a copy of the proposal

B an email addressed to Min Zhao

C an email from Min Zhao

D a link to an online article

188 Where does Robert work?

A City Council

B ModCit Designs

C Lemur Park

D New Minds University

189 Which of the following is NOT part of the redevelopment project?

A a soccer pitch

B a waterpark

C bowling alley

D restaurants and cafés

190 In which of the positons [1], [2], [3] and [4] does the following sentence best belong? "Lemur Park to undergo imaginative $200 million regeneration starting in 2019."

A [1]

B [2]

C [3]

D [4]

Questions 191–195 refer to the following three texts.

Luiz Pereyra

We're thinking of getting some tablets for the meeting room. Any recommendations?

What's the budget?

We've got $25,000 in the budget for the total renovations, so maybe $10,000?

Great! We should get some great ones with that, if we don't need too many. I'll send you some options.

send

Welcome to the future.
Welcome to the world of Npad.

No matter what, no matter where, the new Npad is always up to the task. With its 4K crystal display, it offers far more power than a typical office computer, in a compact, portable design. Npad Standard and Npad Pro, everything you want an office computer to be, anywhere you want it to be. Prices start at $450.

PRICES ($)		
	Npad	**Npad Pro**
150GB	$450	$650
200GB	$550	$750
250GB	$950	$1,250

TekPak Store
303 Bellevue Square
Bellevue, WA 98005
(425) 555-0029

Bill to	**Ship to**	**Invoice Date:** 08/12/17
Rawan Al-Halil	Luiz Pereyra	**Due Date:** 08/26/17
Winton Island Bank	Winton Island Bank	
4561 Erskine Way SW	4563 Erskine Way SW	
Seattle, WA 98112	Seattle, WA 98112	

12	NPAD: PRODUCT CODE 2356SFH-SD3-45	$750.00	$9000.00
	Sales Tax 5%	$37.50	$450.00
			$9450.00

191 What is being discussed in the text message chain?

    A   Luiz's promotion

    B   buying new equipment

    C   a home renovation

    D   where to buy new cell phones

192 Which type of tablet did the Luiz Perez purchase for the company?

    A   Npad, 150GB

    B   Npad Pro, 150GB

    C   Npad Pro, 200GB

    D   Npad, 250GB

193 What do the texts NOT say about the tablets?

    A   They can be more powerful than a computer.

    B   Only four thousand copies have been manufactured.

    C   They're easy to carry around.

    D   They have been designed for a work environment.

194 Who does Mr Pereyra work for?

    A   Npad Pro

    B   TekPak Store

    C   Bellevue Square

    D   Winton Island Bank

195 What was the total cost of tax for the purchase of the tablets?

    A $37.50

    B $450

    C $750

    D $9000

Questions 196–200 refer to the following three texts.

To:	frankhr@sweetlife.com
From:	kluivert@sweetlife.com
Date:	October 29, 2017
Subject:	New sugar mill in Hawaii

Hi Frank,

— [1] —

Linda and I have just attended the board meeting and the proposal for a new mill in Hawaii has been approved. The next step is to start the recruitment process and we have all agreed that you are the best person to head this next phase of the project. — [2] —

We will be holding another meeting before the end of the week, so I will get back to you as soon as I know the details. — [3] —

Regards,

— [4] —

Clarence Kluivert

Proposals for new sugar mill in Maui

Early planning documents have been submitted for the construction of a new sugar mill in Maui, Hawaii.

Environmental impact assessment documents outline plans to build the new mill on a 65-hectare site on what is predominantly former agricultural land. In the proposal submitted by sugar giants *SweetLife*, the applicant states that the development will regenerate the site and generate approximately 2500 jobs in the area.

New opportunities in Hawaii.

SweetLife is opening a new sugar mill in Maui, Hawaii. The positions available can be found in the link below.

Maui, Hawaii—Positions Available: 200—Click here for more information

Positions will be available internally for the first four weeks. Then the remaining positions will be posted on our careers webpage and sent to our partner recruitment agencies.

Do not hesitate to contact me in case you need more information about the positions available.

Regards,

Frank Palmer—HR Manager

196 In which of the positons [1], [2], [3] and [4] does the following sentence best belong? "Hope this finds you well."

A [1]

B [2]

C [3]

D [4]

197 Who will be responsible for staff recruitment for the new mill?

A Mr. Kluivert

B Frank

C recruitment agencies

D the government

198 Where will the new sugar mill be built?

A land in Maui previously used for farming

B in a 65-hectare area by the sea

C in the industrial district in Maui

D in unprofitable agricultural lands in Ohio

199 How many jobs are being offered by SweetLife?

A 4

B 65

C 200

D 2500

200 Who will be able to apply for the new positions first?

A local residents

B current employees

C recruitment agency candidates

D HR professionals

TOEIC Listening and Reading Practice Test 3

LISTENING TEST

In this section of the test, you will show your knowledge of spoken English. This section has four parts, and the entire section will last for around 45 minutes. Directions are given for each individual part of the test. Mark your answers on the answer sheet provided. To listen to the audio tracks for this section of the test, access the tracks in your Online Resources, by visiting **www.kaptest.com/booksonline** OR through the Kaplan Study App.

 Play Track 9 for Test 3, Part I

PART I: PHOTOGRAPHS

Directions: For each question in this part, you will hear four statements about a picture in your test book. When you hear the statements, you must select the one statement that best describes what you see in the picture. Then find the number of the question on your answer sheet and mark your answer. The statements will not be printed in your test book and will be spoken only one time.

1

2

3

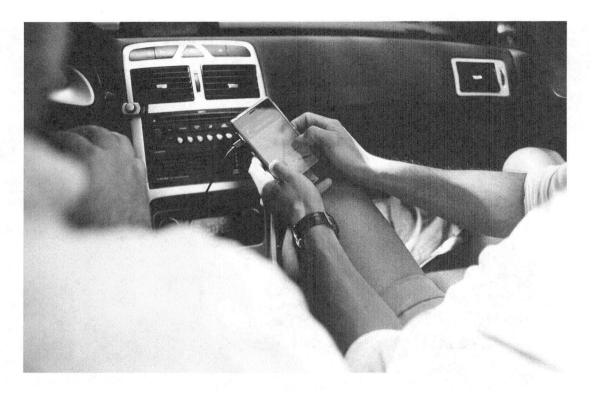

4

5

6

Play Track 10 for Test 3, Part II

PART II: QUESTION RESPONSE

Directions: You will hear a question or statement and three responses spoken in English. They will not be printed in your test book and will be spoken only one time. Select the best response to the question or statement and mark the letter A, B, or C on your answer sheet.

7	Mark your answer on your answer sheet.	20	Mark your answer on your answer sheet.
8	Mark your answer on your answer sheet.	21	Mark your answer on your answer sheet.
9	Mark your answer on your answer sheet.	22	Mark your answer on your answer sheet.
10	Mark your answer on your answer sheet.	23	Mark your answer on your answer sheet.
11	Mark your answer on your answer sheet.	24	Mark your answer on your answer sheet.
12	Mark your answer on your answer sheet.	25	Mark your answer on your answer sheet.
13	Mark your answer on your answer sheet.	26	Mark your answer on your answer sheet.
14	Mark your answer on your answer sheet.	27	Mark your answer on your answer sheet.
15	Mark your answer on your answer sheet.	28	Mark your answer on your answer sheet.
16	Mark your answer on your answer sheet.	29	Mark your answer on your answer sheet.
17	Mark your answer on your answer sheet.	30	Mark your answer on your answer sheet.
18	Mark your answer on your answer sheet.	31	Mark your answer on your answer sheet.
19	Mark your answer on your answer sheet.		

Play Track 11 for Test 3, Part III

PART III: SHORT CONVERSATIONS

Directions: You will hear some conversations between two people. You will be asked to answer three questions about what the speakers say in each conversation. Select the best response to each question and mark the letter (A), (B), (C), or (D) on your answer sheet. The conversation will not be printed in your test book and will be spoken only one time.

32 Why does the woman want to buy a tablet?

   A It's her son's birthday.

   B Her son will need it for his studies.

   C Her laptop is too slow.

   D She needs it for her job.

33 What will the tablet be used for?

   A scientific research

   B research and career management

   C writing articles and using the internet

   D internet research and audiovisual projects

34 Look at the graphic below. Which tablet does the man recommend?

   A Tab Jr

   B Tab X

   C Tab Pro 2.5

   D Tab Pro 3.0

Tab Jr	Tab V	Tab Pro 2.5	Tab Pro 3.0
8.5" screen	8.5" screen	9.7" screen	10.5" screen
B5 chip 32-bit	B8 chip 64-bit	B9 chip 64-bit	B10 chip 64-bit
Impact-absorbing hard case	State-of-the-art Real Leather Case	Impact-absorbing hard case	State-of-the-art Real Leather Case

35 What does the woman want from the man?

   A She's having problems with the new software.

   B Her computer's not working.

   C She doesn't know where the conference is.

   D She needs help with her correspondence.

36 What does Roy mean when he says "Mr. Wells is going to kill me"?

   A Mr. Wells is a violent man.

   B Mr. Wells is going to get very angry.

   C He will lose his job.

   D He might go to prison.

37 Where will Mrs. Sanchez be waiting for Pablo?

   A in the computer room

   B in the conference room

   C in her office

   D in the correspondence room

38 Why is the man calling?

   A He needs Mrs. Lee's email address.

   B He wants some information about management software.

   C He wants to speak to Mrs. Lee.

   D He wants the woman to give his contact details to Mrs. Lee.

39 Why does the woman say "she was feeling a bit under the weather"?

   A Mrs. Lee didn't go to work because she's feeling sick.

   B The weather is bad this time of the year.

   C Mrs. Lee doesn't like the weather there.

   D Mrs. Lee is sick because of the weather.

40 What does the woman suggest?

   A She can book another meeting with Mrs. Lee.

   B The man should call her back on Friday.

   C sending an email to Mrs. Lee

   D trying to contact Mrs. Lee by video call

---

41 What does the man want to avoid?

   A taking the clients out for lunch

   B taking Mr. Jung to the airport

   C keeping Mr. Jung waiting

   D staying at the hotel

42 What time will the clients have their lunch?

   A 12:00 p.m.

   B 3:00 p.m.

   C 9:55 p.m.

   D 10:05 p.m.

43 How are the clients going to the hotel?

   A by taxi

   B in an executive car

   C in a limo

   D Rita will pick them up.

---

44 What does Andrew do?

   A He works for HR.

   B He works with finances.

   C He's an event planner.

   D He's responsible for the career development program.

45 Why does the woman say "I'm a bit disappointed"?

   A because she didn't get the job

   B because she has to attend a lecture

   C because nobody from Andrew's department is going to the lecture

   D because Andrew told her that she might have to work during Christmas

46 What does Andrew not want to happen?

   A He doesn't want his team to work overtime this time of year.

   B He doesn't want to attend any of the lectures.

   C He wants to avoid going to the Christmas party.

   D He doesn't want to pay a Christmas bonus to some of his staff.

---

47 Why is the man at the store?

   A He's looking for new laptops for his office reception.

   B He's looking for new desks for reception.

   C He wants to buy some tablets for reception.

   D He's waiting to meet his architect there.

48 What does HR think looks better?

   A desks

   B computers

   C tablets

   D floorboards

49 Where's the architect?

   A on the second floor

   B on her way to the store

   C in the office

   D He doesn't know.

---

50 Why does Claire call the restaurant?

A to cancel her reservation

B to change her reservation

C to ask for a copy of the menu

D to ask for some information about the menu

51 What's the name of the restaurant?

A Little Italy

B Pepe's

C Manning's

D Alfredo's

52 Look at the graphic. Which set menu is Claire's client most likely to order?

A Set Menu 1

B Set Menu 2

C Set Menu 3

D Set Menu 4

	Set Menu 1	**Set Menu 2**
Starter	Meatballs al sugo	Green Salad
Main	Spaghetti Carbonara	Chicken Risotto
Dessert	Chocolate Ice-Cream	Tiramisu
	Set Menu 3	**Set Menu 4**
Starter	Tomato Salad	Ham Bruschetta
Main	Penne with fresh olives and tomatoes	Eggplant Lasagna
Dessert	Fruit Salad	Strawberries and Cream

53 Why didn't the man call?

A He was sick.

B He was out of the office.

C He was in a restaurant.

D He had a busy day at work.

54 Where does the woman invite the man to?

A a club on Saturday

B an office party

C an Italian restaurant

D Sally's new job

55 What does the man offer to do?

A He offers her a job promotion.

B He offers to give her a lift to the restaurant.

C He offers to call the restaurant.

D He offers to take her to Italy.

56 What kind of problem does the woman's company have?

A They have a legal problem.

B One of the photocopiers is not working.

C One of the elevators is not working.

D The printer is not making double-sided copies.

57 What does the woman tell the man?

A to take the elevator on his right

B to go to the second floor

C that she works for the legal department

D that her elevator is jammed

58 Where can the man find Kurt?

A on the fifth floor

B at the reception downstairs

C by the elevator on the right

D on the second floor

59 When is the meeting supposed to start?

A at 3 o'clock

B at 4:15

C in 30 minutes

D in an hour

60 What does the man say about the candidate?

    A she's an hour late

    B her name's Anita

    C she has experience in Marketing

    D her qualifications are excellent

61 Why will the woman send a text message?

    A to cancel the meeting

    B to change the time of the meeting

    C to interview Anita

    D to top up her cell phone

62 What does the woman say about Mrs. Chan?

    A She was offered a job.

    B She was impressed with the man's qualifications.

    C She has impressive skills.

    D She needs better qualifications

63 Why does the man say "I'm flattered"?

    A The candidate he is interviewing praised his skills.

    B His background check was successful.

    C He hasn't had much sleep lately.

    D He has been offered a job.

64 What does Ms. O'Keefe say she's going to post?

    A an offer letter

    B information about a company called *Watchdog Security*

    C the contract

    D background checks

65 What's the woman's problem?

    A She's going to miss her flight.

    B She won't get to the station in time.

    C the traffic in Barcelona

    D She needs to be in Barcelona in an hour.

66 What does the man say about the woman's ticket?

    A It's non-refundable.

    B It can't be changed.

    C It's a first-class ticket.

    D It can be upgraded to first-class.

67 Look at the graphic below. Which service is the woman going to take?

    A BC 2201

    B BC2202

    C BC2203

    D BC2204

Services to Barcelona Saturday March 24			
BC2201	BC2202	BC2203	BC2204
10:30 to 19:45	10:45 to 20:15	13:30 to 23:45	15:30 to 01:45
$22.50	$27.00	$22.50	$17.80

68 Who was very angry after a meeting?

    A Giovanna

    B Mr. Yun

    C Matthew

    D Pietra

69 What do they say about the budget?

   A It was reduced by nearly 30%.

   B It will not cover the multimedia campaign.

   C It's increased 27.8% since last year.

   D It can't be implemented.

70 Why does Giovanna say Matt is stressed?

   A He doesn't want to talk about Mr. Yun's personal affairs.

   B He won't be able to set up his cloud system project.

   C He can't implement the multimedia campaign.

   D He doesn't want to work with Mr. Yun.

Play Track 12 for Test 3, Part IV

PART IV: SHORT TALKS

Directions: You will hear some talks given by one speaker. You will be asked to answer three questions about what the speaker says in each talk. Select the best response to each question and mark the letter (A), (B), (C), or (D) on your answer sheet. The conversation will not be printed in your test book and will be spoken only one time.

71 Why is the college closed?

    A because of a snow storm

    B It's a national holiday.

    C The teachers went on strike.

    D There's been an accident in the library.

72 What information can you NOT find on their website?

    A the weather

    B online courses

    C course fees and dates

    D course work deadlines

73 What does the message say about student essays?

    A The teachers will not extend their deadlines.

    B They may be submitted electronically.

    C Sample copies can be found in the library.

    D The teachers will not be able to mark them.

74 Who complained about the patio door?

    A Mr. Amorim

    B Wayne

    C Mr. Romsey

    D Mr. Yen

75 How did the janitor feel when he heard about the complaints?

    A worried

    B angry

    C upset

    D surprised

76 What do we learn about Mr. Yen?

    A He's a janitor.

    B He's a wood specialist.

    C He works for a property management group.

    D He works in a different building.

77 When is the announcement being broadcast?

    A on a Friday

    B on a spring afternoon

    C in the morning

    D on a Saturday

78 Who helps students stay away from drugs?

    A Jackie Adams

    B a local charity

    C the community center

    D the radio station

79 Why does the woman say "Go Leopards"?

    A She doesn't think the Gainsville team can win.

    B She supports the Gainsville team.

    C She's excited about raising money for charity.

    D She's going to the football field.

80 What's the flight number?

    A 420

    B 955

    C 1776

    D 35,000

81 What does the man say about the flight?

  A   They'll arrive in 15 minutes.

  B   It might be late due to the weather.

  C   It's on schedule.

  D   They'll get to Paris 25 minutes early.

82 Look at the graphic below. When is the flight arriving in Paris?

  A   Monday

  B   Tuesday

  C   Wednesday

  D   Thursday

Monday	Tuesday	Wednesday	Thursday
64–71 °F	53–59 °F	50–60 °F	61–66 °F
Sunny and clear	Cloudy with short rainy spells	Cloudy with light wind.	Strong rain and possibility of thunderstorms

83 Why's the man calling?

  A   He has some information about a smart watch.

  B   He wants to buy a watch.

  C   He's selling a watch.

  D   His friend is selling a watch.

84 What does he say about the watch battery?

  A   He needs a new one.

  B   He wants to make sure it's good.

  C   His friend told him to buy one.

  D   His friend needs an extra one.

85 When's the best time to return his call?

  A   Before 8:30 p.m.

  B   Before 8:30 a.m.

  C   After 8:30 p.m.

  D   After 8:30 a.m.

86 What is Grandma Lucy?

  A   a restaurant

  B   a frozen food company

  C   a food market

  D   a company that sells recipe boxes.

87 How does the ad describe the food?

  A   organic

  B   low in calories

  C   decent

  D   fat free

88 What does the woman mean when she says "No, they don't cost an arm and a leg"?

  A   The product is really cheap.

  B   Some products are cheaper than others.

  C   People expect products like this to be expensive, but theirs aren't.

  D   People don't buy their products because they think they're too expensive.

89 Where is the store?

  A   Miami

  B   Colombia

  C   Italy

  D   New York

90 Which of the following is NOT mentioned in the announcement?

  A   clothes

  B   the name of the store

  C   the view from the restaurant

  D   opening hours

91 Look at the graphic below. Which of the sales does the announcement refer to?

    A 01

    B 02

    C 03

    D 04

01	02	03	04
Summer Mega Sale	**Summer Mega Sale**	**Winter Mega Sale**	**Winter Mega Sale**
Up to 40% Womenswear and Toys.	Up to 50% Menswear	Up to 50% Menswear	Up to 50% Menswear
Ends on Saturday June 12	Ends on Sunday June 13	Ends on Sunday February 20	Ends on Tuesday February 22

92 What number should you press if you're having problems with your phone?

    A 1

    B 2

    C 3

    D 6

93 Who should contact the company by a different number?

    A people who want to buy any of their products

    B people interested in one of their phones

    C people having problems with their bills

    D people who want to upgrade their phones

94 What is the new product called?

    A WPhones

    B NPhone 10

    C Npad Jr

    D easy upgrades

95 How does the man describe his experience as a guest?

    A unsuccessful

    B appalling

    C too short

    D boring

96 Which of the following does the man NOT complain about?

    A the restaurant

    B the management

    C the pool area

    D the rooms

97 What does the man threaten to do?

    A talk to the press

    B talk to the owner

    C write a negative review

    D contact his lawyers

98 Where does Dr. Antonescu work?

    A Manhattan

    B Budapest

    C Asia

    D South America

99 What will Dr. Antonescu talk about?

    A university courses

    B becoming a dentist in a competitive market

    C the dental implants market

    D opening a dental clinic

100 What does the text say about "large and small companies"?

    A Both can benefit from the talk.

    B They should help each other.

    C They have different market positions.

    D They can achieve similar results.

READING TEST

In this section of the test, you will show your knowledge of written English. This section has three parts, and you have 75 minutes to complete all three sections. Directions are given for each individual part of the test. Mark your answers on the answer sheet provided.

PART V: INCOMPLETE SENTENCES

Directions: complete the following sentences using one of the four answer choices provided. Mark the answer **A, B, C** or **D** on your answer sheet.

101 The company is run _____ two Chinese brothers.

  A at

  B by

  C in

  D through

102 Mrs. Suleyman is the managing director of DDW _____ the chairman of the faculty of science at Toronto University.

  A as well as

  B moreover

  C in addition

  D also

103 _____ the elections are over we'll have a better understanding of the economic situation.

  A Until

  B In case

  C Once

  D Twice

104 The board is _____ about the constant delays.

  A worried

  B will worry

  C worry

  D worryingly

105 Mr. Sagamoto has designed a plan that _____ into consideration the needs of local wildlife.

  A makes

  B has

  C takes

  D does

106 Both Jacques and Desiree applied _____ the same position with JC Electronics.

  A to

  B with

  C for

  D by

107 All members of staff _____ to take part in our charity dinner party.

  A are encouraged

  B are encouraging

  C encouraged

  D will encourage

108 Mrs. Hyun _____ to CFO of Lynix Industries.

  A has been just promoted

  B has just been promoted

  C just has been promoted

  D has been promoted just

109 We must do something. We cannot _____ to lose another client.

A afford

B risk

C depend

D take

110 Intrapersonal employees work better _____ .

A lonely

B on their own

C themselves

D solitaire

111 Our main _____ is to offer our customers safe and reliable solutions.

A objective

B object

C objection

D objectiveness

112 Mr. Ming is _____ the most intelligent man I've ever worked with.

A probably

B true

C possible

D sure

113 The _____ villain was arrested during one of many police raids in the area.

A fame

B infamous

C famously

D famousness

114 They used to be one of the biggest textile _____ in Turkey.

A manufacture

B manufactured

C manufacturing

D manufacturers

115 The _____ of the new factory will only be revealed during the gala ball.

A placement

B location

C local

D post

116 Mr. Gumbel's business is expanding _____ .

A rapid

B rapids

C rapidly

D rapidness

117 Helmets _____ at all times.

A must wear

B must be wearing

C must have worn

D must be worn

118 The company has faced _____ a few problems in the past five years.

A pretty

B very

C quite

D various

119 The critic was full of _____ for the new ballet.

- **A** praise
- **B** appraisal
- **C** praised
- **D** praising

120 Cineville is not responsible for personal _____ left in the vehicle.

- **A** belong
- **B** belongs
- **C** belongings
- **D** belonged

121 The store _____ offered to replace the faulty television.

- **A** prompt
- **B** promptly
- **C** prompted
- **D** prompts

122 Mr. Barbosa trusts them _____ his life.

- **A** with
- **B** for
- **C** in
- **D** by

123 This is the town in _____ he opened his first store.

- **A** where
- **B** what
- **C** when
- **D** which

124 The contract contains all the terms and conditions _____ to by the landlord and the tenant.

- **A** agree
- **B** agreed
- **C** agrees
- **D** agreeing

125 All board members are obliged to _____ party functions.

- **A** seeing
- **B** go
- **C** attend
- **D** be

126 This movie is not _____ for young children.

- **A** suitable
- **B** suitably
- **C** suit
- **D** suitability

127 The new director of operations should be highly _____ to change.

- **A** agile
- **B** versatile
- **C** adaptable
- **D** volatile

128 Most of their services and solutions are _____ designed for small companies.

- **A** excluded
- **B** exclusively
- **C** absolutely
- **D** very

129 By the time the article gets published, the culprits _____ all the evidence.

- **A** will destroy
- **B** will be destroying
- **C** will have destroyed
- **D** will have been destroyed

130 All imports of steel are in _____ with regulations.

- **A** compliant
- **B** compliance
- **C** complying
- **D** complied

PART VI: TEXT COMPLETION

Directions: Read the following texts and select the best answer choice to complete the text. Mark the answer **A**, **B**, **C** or **D** on your answer sheet.

Questions 131–134 refer to the email that follows.

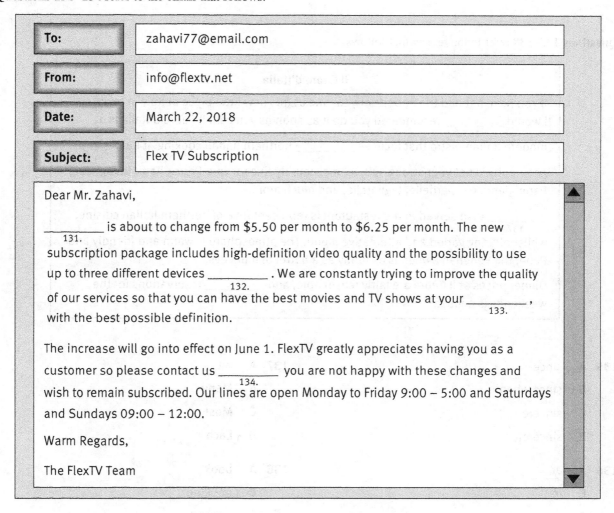

To:	zahavi77@email.com
From:	info@flextv.net
Date:	March 22, 2018
Subject:	Flex TV Subscription

Dear Mr. Zahavi,

_____ is about to change from $5.50 per month to $6.25 per month. The new
   131.
subscription package includes high-definition video quality and the possibility to use
up to three different devices _____ . We are constantly trying to improve the quality
                                    132.
of our services so that you can have the best movies and TV shows at your _____ ,
                                                                            133.
with the best possible definition.

The increase will go into effect on June 1. FlexTV greatly appreciates having you as a
customer so please contact us _____ you are not happy with these changes and
                                134.
wish to remain subscribed. Our lines are open Monday to Friday 9:00 – 5:00 and Saturdays
and Sundays 09:00 – 12:00.

Warm Regards,

The FlexTV Team

131 **A** We are writing to inform you that your FlexTV subscription fee

   B Thank you for your email

   C Please let us know if we can do anything else, as this

   D Unfortunately, your preferred payment method is no longer valid

132 **A** simultaneous

   B simultaneously

   C simultaneousness

   D simulate

133 **A** dispose
    B disposal
    C disposable
    D disposer

134 **A** in case
    B as long as
    C provided
    D suppose

Questions 135–138 refer to the review that follows.

Il Cuore d'Italia

If you have not had the opportunity to dine at this new little piece of Italy in town,
I would _____ recommend you do it as soon as you can. Il Cuore d'Italia is a
        135.
modern Italian bistro that focuses _____ northern Italian cooking. If Italian
                                    136.
geography is not your strong suit, let me simplify this for you: Parma ham, Bolognese,
Parmigiano, pappardelle, tagliatelle, and much more.

_____ dish served in the restaurant is representative of northern Italian cuisine,
    137.
whilst offering varied and alternative menu. The atmosphere is warm and friendly and
Pepe, the Venetian owner, is as funny as a barrel of monkeys.

Dinner prices at Il Cuore are fairly reasonable, and _____ reservations for the
                                                      138.
weekends is a must.

---

135 **A** since
    B since when
    C sincere
    D sincerely

137 **A** All
    B Many
    C Most
    D Each

136 **A** at
    B in
    C on
    D for

138 **A** book
    B booking
    C booked
    D books

Questions 139–142 refer to the advertisement that follows.

Jamie's Bakery

All our baked goods are handmade here at Jamie's with fresh organic _____ from
139.
local farms. Why not come in and try some of our delicious cakes, fruit pies, pastries,
cookies, and cupcakes?

Feeling just a little hungry? Try some of our miniature quiche, brownie bites, or
chocolate balls.

So hungry you could eat a horse? Here at Jamie's we serve a _____ variety of
140.
sandwiches, baguettes, and wraps.

We also provide catering _____ anniversaries, weddings, and corporate events.
141.
To learn more about our special occasion packages, visit our website on
www.jamiesbreadandbutter.com, or _____ call us at (602) 555–8620.
142.

---

139 A produce
B productivity
C product
D production

140 A We can help you learn how to master the art of horse-riding.
B We'd love to hear your recommendations for improvement!
C Please contact your doctor to book at appointment at your earliest convenience.
D Here at Jamie's we serve a wide variety of sandwiches, baguettes, and wraps.

141 A through
B for
C into
D on

142 A simple
B simpler
C simply
D simplicity

Questions 143–146 refer to the notice that follows.

Clothing donations required

The *Love Thy Brother* community center is asking for donations of warm clothing. The center will be _____ for any donations provided that they are in decent condition
143.
and that they demonstrate compassion and respect for those _____ need of help.
144.

Comforters and blankets are also welcome, as winter is a particularly difficult season for fighting _____ . Please drop off any donations at the front desk of the community
145.
center or at any of our partner stores. All donations _____ to create a warm and
146.
comfortable environment for those who are not lucky enough to have a place to stay in the cold season.

Please visit our website www.lovethybrother.org or call us at 1 800 555 1017 for further details.

---

143 A dreadful

　　B thankful

　　C pitiful

　　D wonderful

144 A in

　　B with

　　C on

　　D from

145 A homeless

　　B homelessly

　　C homelessness

　　D homeland

146 A will use

　　B will be used

　　C will be using

　　D will have used

PART VII: READING COMPREHENSION

Directions: In this part of the test, you will read a number of different texts and then answer several questions about each text. Mark the answer **A**, **B**, **C** or **D** on your answer sheet.

Questions 147–150 refer to the following schedule.

Rosie McGill Consultants Staff Day Out May 10 Penn Hill Farm–Perth 10:00 a.m.–5:00 p.m.		
Time	**Activity**	**Goal**
10 a.m.	Country Breakfast	Getting to know staff from different departments and branches
11 a.m.	Welcome to new staff	Sharing the company's belief, vision and mission for the future
12 p.m.	Murder Mystery Lunch	Promoting and developing teamwork through cooperation and collaboration
1:30 p.m.	Guest Talks	Giving staff the opportunity to consider the next steps in their career development
3:30 p.m.	Coffee Break Tales	Motivating staff through footage of success stories
4:00 p.m.	Chairperson's Update	Updating staff on company's new deals, prospective clients and future businesses

147 Which activity encourages staff to meet new people?

- **A** Country Breakfast
- **B** Murder Mystery Lunch
- **C** Coffee Break Tales
- **D** Chairperson's Update

148 When will staff think about their future professional goals?

- **A** 12 p.m.
- **B** 1:30 p.m.
- **C** 3:30 p.m.
- **D** 4:00 p.m.

149 What will happen at 11am?

- **A** breakfast
- **B** an outline of the company's goals
- **C** a guide for hiring new staff
- **D** staff will be awarder promotions

150 How long is the chairperson's speech?

- **A** 1 hour
- **B** 2 hours
- **C** 3 hours
- **D** 4 hours

Questions 151–154 refer to the following email.

To:	camiteacher@email.com
From:	hr@wandw.com
Date:	January 12, 2017
Subject:	Science Teacher Year 3 – Camilla Anderson

Dear Camilla,

— [1] — Welcome to Wellie & Waldorf Academies.

I am pleased to attach an offer letter and contract for you, along with the new starter forms. Can I please ask you to sign, complete and return everything to me at your earliest convenience? Feel free to either scan in and email everything back to me, or send it back by mail. — [2] —

I will then need to see three forms of ID, including one proof of address (must be dated within three months) to validate your application. Please can we arrange a convenient time for you to come into the school with your ID and qualification documentation?

— [3] —

We will also need to have medical clearance for you. You will shortly receive an email with log in details from a company called DMAIS, our health insurance provider, with details for completing an online health questionnaire. I have also attached our staff handbook, and I will forward some safeguarding information separately in due course.

— [4] —

Please let me know if you have any questions. I look forward to hearing from you soon.

Kind regards,

Denis Sukur

151 What is the main purpose of the email?

A   to offer a job

B   to invite to an interview

C   to request documentation from new staff

D   to invite to a university open day

152 What is NOT enclosed in the email?

A   an offer letter

B   a contract

C   log in details

D   staff handbook

153 What will Denis send Camilla in a future email?

   A   starter forms

   B   qualification documentation

   C   an online health questionnaire

   D   safeguarding information

154 In which of the positions market [1], [2], [3] and [4] does the following sentence best belong? "We look forward to you joining the team."

   A   [1]

   B   [2]

   C   [3]

   D   [4]

Questions 155–157 refer to the following product description.

Sommy SS75MM6600 75-Inch Ultra HD Smart TV

4K Ultra High Definition - 4X More Pixels Than Full HD

The Sommy MM6600 Ultra HDTV redefines the television concept by producing a mind-blowing colorful High Dynamic Range (HDR) viewing experience. Sommy's Smart TV hands-on user interface with voice navigation capability provides faster access to your favorite streaming content choices such as *Cine@Home, FlexTV, Sports24/7*, and much more.

Main Features:

- Full Wi-Fi connectivity, allowing you to connect a wireless network and stream music, videos and much more.

- HDMI ports, 3 USB ports, 1 Ethernet port, 1 component input, 1 composite input, 1 RF input, and 1 digital audio output.

- 4K Color Drive, which allows your TV to accurately reproduce a revolutionary spectrum of colors.

---

155 How can TV owners access some of their televisions functions more quickly?

A by using voice control

B by streaming content

C they can use the TV's full Wi-Fi connectivity

D by connecting to a wireless network

156 What does the text mean when it says "redefines the television concept"?

A It greatly improves the experience of watching TV.

B It allows you to watch TV anywhere.

C It gives a new definition to home entertainment.

D It enables users to stream high-definition content.

157 Which of the following is NOT a feature of the television?

A a hands-on user interface

B full Wi-Fi connectivity

C 1 digital video output

D a revolutionary spectrum of colors

Questions 158–160 refer to the following review.

Far Away from Home

Far Away from Home is a much different offering than we're used to from the critically acclaimed Russian author Andrey Djorkaeff, yet somehow, we were gripped from start to finish all the same. — [1] — Set in Chile. Eleanor and Alan are tourists from the UK. They find a baby on a trip to the Andes and decide to adopt her as their daughter. — [2] — As always, Djorkaeff inspires awe with his ability to find balance between drama and mystery, romance and fear. The story is simply yet eloquently told, and Djorkaeff's years in a Chilean vineyard allow him to transport you from your sofa to the breathtaking sceneries of the Aconcagua. — [3] — *Far Away From Home* is an astonishing tale that poignantly teaches us the lesson that nothing is quite as it seems. — [4] —

---

158 Where does the narrative take place?

A Russia

B Chile

C UK

D US

159 What is the critic most likely to mean by the phrase: "nothing is quite as it seems"?

A The book isn't as good as the critic expected it to be.

B People are too quick to judge.

C The book contains surprising or unexpected elements.

D The story seems to be a drama, but in fact it's a thriller.

160 In which of the positions marked [1], [2], [3] and [4] does the following sentence best belong?

"Djorkaeff's writing allows you to connect to Eleanor and Alan before a terrible secret is revealed."

A [1]

B [2]

C [3]

D [4]

Questions 161–163 refer to the following notice.

Professional Workshops with Linda Patel

Get motivated and keep going!

— [1] — Some find it really easy to get motivated and can easily find themselves immersed in a sea of excitement. Others find it almost impossible to find a way to motivate themselves and end up plagued by procrastination. — [2] — This workshop will provide you with some useful ideas based on recent research on how to get and, most importantly, stay motivated. — [3] —

During this practical workshop, Dr. Linda breaks down the science behind short-term motivation and how to feed it for the long-run. — [4] — Whether you're trying to figure out how to find your motivation or how to help others find theirs, Dr. Linda is sure to cover everything you need to know in order to foster motivation in the workplace.

---

161 Who is more likely to benefit from this workshop?

A someone who wants to enjoy working

B someone looking for a job promotion

C someone looking for a new job

D someone who wants to learn more about themselves

162 Where did Dr. Linda get some of her ideas for the workshop from?

A a study

B a practical workshop

C some of her colleagues' ideas

D a book

163 In which of the positions marked [1], [2], [3] and [4] does the following sentence best belong?
"Struggling to rediscover your passion for work?"

A [1]

B [2]

C [3]

D [4]

Questions 164–165 refer to the following email.

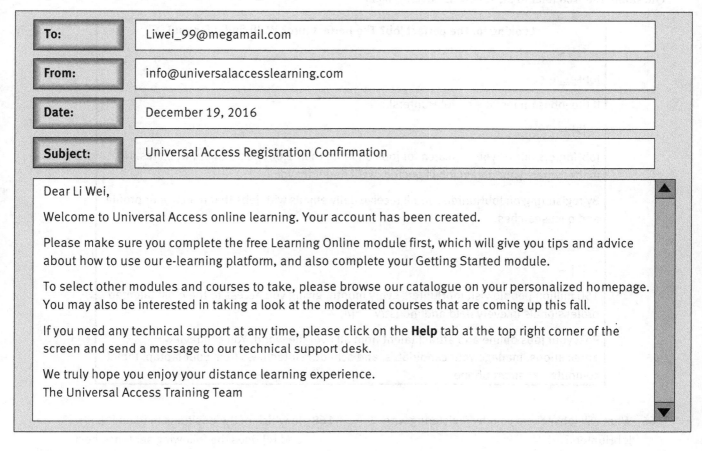

To:	Liwei_99@megamail.com
From:	info@universalaccesslearning.com
Date:	December 19, 2016
Subject:	Universal Access Registration Confirmation

Dear Li Wei,

Welcome to Universal Access online learning. Your account has been created.

Please make sure you complete the free Learning Online module first, which will give you tips and advice about how to use our e-learning platform, and also complete your Getting Started module.

To select other modules and courses to take, please browse our catalogue on your personalized homepage. You may also be interested in taking a look at the moderated courses that are coming up this fall.

If you need any technical support at any time, please click on the **Help** tab at the top right corner of the screen and send a message to our technical support desk.

We truly hope you enjoy your distance learning experience.
The Universal Access Training Team

164 What is Universal Access?

  A   a company providing services such as web design and web hosting

  B   an online learning provider

  C   a college which offers various IT courses

  D   a government service

165 Where can you learn more about the learning platform?

  A   the Learning Online module

  B   the Getting Started module

  C   the personalized homepage

  D   the technical support desk

Questions 166–168 refer to the following advertisement.

Looking for the perfect job? The perfect hire? We'll find it for you!

— [1] —

<u>Jobseekers</u>

If the job is online, it's on JobHunters!

— [2] —

JobHunters allows you to search for jobs on more than 1,000 recruitment websites. No matter where your dream job is posted, we'll find it for you.

By registering on JobHunters, you'll receive daily emails with jobs that match your profile and past searches.

<u>Employers</u>

— [3] —

150 million people visit JobHunters every month, giving you access to the most talented professionals in every field and industry. — [4] —

Post your jobs online and attract talent from all over the world. You can review applications, manage your candidates, and schedule interviews from your laptop, tablet computer, or smart phone.

---

166 What will jobseekers gain by registering with JobHunters?

A access to approximately 1000 jobs

B access to company profiles and their recruitment policies

C personalized emails with suitable roles

D daily emails containing their job search history

167 Which is NOT a benefit for employers who want to post an ad on JobHunters?

A access to talented professionals

B reviewing applications from portable devices

C booking interviews online

D managing candidates through instant messaging

168 In which of the positions marked [1], [2], [3] and [4] does the following sentence best belong?
"JobHunters helps millions of jobseekers and employers worldwide find what they need—a perfect fit!"

A [1]

B [2]

C [3]

D [4]

Questions 169–170 refer to the following letter.

Guildford Court Management

5510 N. Lakewood Avenue

Chicago, IL 60640

Mrs. Joan Chambers

Dean Park Resort

5600 W. Tremont Street

Block C–Apartment 105

Chicago, IL 60621

Dear Mr Chambers,

— [1] —

Multiple warnings have been issued regarding the number of people residing in your apartment. Your rental agreement clearly states that tenants are not allowed to sublet their apartments or offer temporary accommodation on websites and magazines.
Due to the failure on your part to uphold the agreement of your rental, Guildford Court Management has no choice but to submit this letter. — [2] —

You have been given a total of seven days to remedy the situation and make sure that the only tenants in the property are those stated in the current rental agreement. — [3] — — Failure to comply will result in legal action, including physical removal of all tenants from the apartment and the property.

— [4] —

Sincerely,

Garcia Gaston

Property Manager

---

169 What type of letter is it?

A a final request before eviction

B a letter of complaint

C a legal inquiry

D a proposal

170 In which of the positions marked [1], [2], [3] and [4] does the following sentence best belong?
"If you have any questions regarding this issue, please contact our legal team at 1 800 555 3299."

A [1]

B [2]

C [3]

D [4]

Questions 171–173 refer to the following information.

Vancouver Medical College
Facilities

- There is a student lounge with a cafe, internet, Wi-Fi and TV. You can relax, chat with friends over a coffee and a snack and use the internet. The Wi-Fi password can be found in the student lounge, in reception and on the notice boards. — [1] —

- We also have a modern library with digital and hard copies of newspapers, journals, magazines, and books. Your library card can be obtained from reception. A $30 deposit is required for registration. When you finish your studies with us, we will refund your deposit. The materials must be returned in the same condition as they were given to you. Some materials cannot be removed from the library. — [2] —

- Please make sure you keep your personal belongings with you at all times. — [3] —

- You may also leave your personal belongings in a locker. Please speak with reception should you require one.

- Please check the notice board every week as we have regular student activities. In summer there are also football matches, barbeques and volleyball at the park. — [4] —

---

171 Where will you NOT find information about the wireless connection?

- **A** student lounge
- **B** café
- **C** reception
- **D** notice boards

172 What should students do with their personal belongings?

- **A** leave them in reception
- **B** leave them in a locker
- **C** never take them to class
- **D** sign them in with reception

173 In which of the positions marked [1], [2], [3] and [4] does the following sentence best belong?
"The college does not take responsibility for lost or stolen property."

- **A** [1]
- **B** [2]
- **C** [3]
- **D** [4]

Questions 174–175 refer to the following article.

Guedes Optimistic about 2018 Tour

Ayrton Guedes is very optimistic about the performance of his new F4 car, which finally managed to achieve its full potential on the final week of the World Motor Racing Series opening test in Colorado.

The six-time world champion, who will begin the defense of his title in Auckland on April 12, managed to set the fastest time of the year after 33 laps in the oval circuit.

Because of the freezing weather conditions over the past week, Guedes had completed only 19 laps on a low track temperature that prevented his car being pushed to its limit.

On sunny Friday everything changed. With the track reaching over 73° F, the Brazilian driver was able to get the best out of his car and show us a glimpse what it can do during the 2018 WMR Series.

174 How does Ayrton Guedes feel about his new car?

   A hopeful

   B worried

   C happy

   D excited

175 Why did Guedes only manage to improve his car's performance after Friday?

   A The weather was difficult to drive in.

   B It's a new car.

   C He's not particularly fond of oval circuits.

   D They had to change the car.

Questions 176–180 refer to the following email and text message chain.

To:	gracefefa@megamail.com
From:	sanders@lifeofsummers.com
Date:	February 21, 2018
Subject:	Activity Leader Post – Grace Fernandes Farias

Dear Ms. Farias,

— [1] — As a result of your application for the position of Activity Leader with Life of Summers, I would like to invite you to attend an interview on Friday March 2 at 2:30 p.m. — [2] —

Please bring a copy of your passport/photo ID and proof of address to the interview.
If the date or time of the interview is inconvenient, please contact me by email (sander-sa@lifeofsummers.com) to arrange another appointment. — [3] —

I look forward to seeing you.

— [4] —

Best regards,

Adam Sanders

Activity Manager

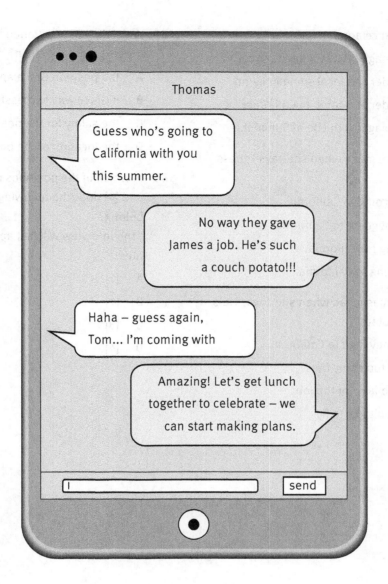

176 What job has Grace applied for?

A activity manager at a language school

B activity leader at a local summer camp

C activity leader at a camp in California

D activity manager with Life of Summers

177 What does Grace mean when she says "guess again"?

A Tom is not going to California.

B James is not going to California.

C Tom is going to California.

D Adam is going to California.

178 What does Thomas mean when she says "He's such a couch potato"?

A James will never go to California.

B James eats too many fries.

C James is too lazy for the job.

D James doesn't like to fly.

179 Which is NOT mentioned in either the email or the text message chain?

A the position Grace applied for

B if Grace was successful in the interview

C the salary for the position

D the location of the position

180 In which of the positions marked [1], [2], [3] and [4] does the following sentence best belong?
"The interview will last approximately 30 minutes."

A [1]

B [2]

C [3]

D [4]

Questions 181–185 refer to the following email and appointment calendar.

To:	park@fawcettsolutions.com
From:	beale@fawcettsolutions.com
Date:	January 11, 2018 2:45 p.m.
Subject:	Meeting Tomorrow

Dear Mrs. Park,

Please find the files attached. I am so sorry it has taken me this long to send you the reports you asked Mr. Smith for on Monday. Due to unforeseen circumstances, I had to be away from the office on Tuesday and Wednesday, so please accept my sincere apologies.

I do hope it is not too late for you to go through all the paperwork before our meeting tomorrow. I understand the importance of this project and would like to say that I am free on Monday all day should you prefer to reschedule the meeting.

Please accept my apologies once again. I look forward to speaking with you soon.

Sincerely,

Sarah Beale

Project Manager – PWF Media

Appointment Calendar Week 2–2018 Mrs. Jang-Mi Park	
Monday **January 8**	9:00 a.m.–Video Meeting (Wilson Smith–PWF Media) 10:00 a.m.–Board Meeting (new overseas branches) 1:00–2:30 p.m.–Lunch with Japanese investors (BBQ Lounge)
Tuesday **January 9**	8:30 a.m.–Avalon Group Presentation (Auditorium 1) 10:30 a.m.–Video Meeting (Paulo Barbosa–Aragorn Inc.) 12:00–1:00 p.m.–Interview PA (Janet Andrews–Room 3)
Wednesday **January 10**	9:45 a.m.–Team Meeting (presentation slides) 1:30 p.m.–5:00 p.m.–American Media Conference (Plaza Hotel)
Thursday **January 11**	9:30 a.m.–Interview Personal Assistant (Chiara Blanco–Room 3) 11:00 a.m.–Interview Personal Assistant (John Bose–Room 4) 2:30–6:00 p.m.–Safeguarding Training (Auditorium 1)
Friday **January 12**	8:30 a.m.–Video Meeting (Sarah Beale–PWF Media) 12:00–2:30 p.m.–Lunch with Mr. Castillo (El Toro - Colombia VP)

181 On which day does Mrs. Park have no meetings?

A Monday

B Tuesday

C Wednesday

D Thursday

182 What is suggested about Mrs. Park?

A She is recruiting for a personal assistant.

B She does not like talking about business during lunch.

C She is a partner at Avalon Group.

D She's a safeguarding specialist.

183 Why does Sarah apologize?

A She couldn't finish the reports.

B She might be late for the meeting.

C She took longer than expected to send the files.

D She had other priorities.

184 Why does Sarah suggest rescheduling the meeting?

A Mrs Park might not have time to check the paperwork.

B The meeting is too early.

C Mr feels disrespected.

D She doesn't have the reports.

185 What do we learn about Sarah?

A She is Mrs. Park's employee.

B She works with Mr. Smith.

C She is an audiovisual specialist.

D She always submits work on time.

Questions 186–190 refer to the following article, email and text message chain.

Coming soon!!!

Araki Dining

Araki is proud to be the first restaurant in San Antonio to serve the original Kobe beef, or as it's called outside Japan, the "caviar of meat". Why not ask for a full omakase menu and experience the chef's choices for a mind-blowing 12-course banquet? From well-marbled wagyu sirloin to a series of vegan dishes, there's something for everyone. Lunchtime sushi and sashimi boxes are also a work of art, designed by Tokyo graphic artists. Araki Dining opens on March 24.

www.arakidiningexperience.com

To:	bale_88@email.com
From:	contact@arakidiningexperience.com
Date:	March 7, 2018
Subject:	Grand Opening – Araki Dining Experience

Dear Mr. Edward Bale,

My name is Akemi Ito and I am the chef patron of Araki Dining Experience in San Antonio.

We are hosting a opening night and would love to have you as one of our guests. I have followed your work very closely both as a critic and connoisseur and it would be an honor to hear what you have to say about our restaurant.

Araki Dining Experience is a new concept I have had in my mind for nearly 10 years. Our menus are interactive, and customers use their phones or one of our tablets to do a multiple-choice food questionnaire on which our sous-chefs base their dish selections. I have enclosed an invitation for you plus one. Our opening night will be held on March 17, a week before we open to the public. Please RSVP before March 10 by replying to this email or by calling us at (210) 555 3391.

Sincerely,

Akemi Ito

Araki Dining Experience

186 Which of the following best describes Araki Dining Experience?

A a modern restaurant for vegans and vegetarians

B a new venture with unusual aspects

C traditional Japanese cuisine

D Japanese food for young people

187 Which of the following is NOT true about the restaurant?

A It serves vegan dishes.

B It offers a delivery service.

C It's good value for money.

D Customers use devices to order food.

188 When does the restaurant open to the public?

A March 24

B March17

C March 10

D next Saturday

189 What is most likely Edward's job?

A restaurant inspector

B food hygiene tester

C professional chef

D restaurant critic

190 When and where will the opening night take place?

A March 17, San Antonio

B March 17, Tokyo

C March 24, San Antonio

D March 24, Tokyo

Questions 191–195 refer to the following advertisement, receipt and email.

Enjoy a coffee on us!

Today until Sunday, buy one drink, get one free! Crispa Coffee Rewards Account members can enjoy a free hot beverage when buying any other hot beverage.

To claim your free coffee, simply present your rewards card, or show the access code on your mobile app to the barista. It's as easy as that!

Please note that the cheapest beverage will be free. Free beverages must be of the same size or smaller than the purchased beverage. Offer not valid without rewards card or access code. For the full list of terms and conditions, visit www.crispacoffeerewards.com/bogofbev12.

Crispa Coffee		
530 Lavaca St, Austin, TX 78701.		
Served by Mandy		
01/21/18 10:34:12		
2344679	Drawer: 1	Reg:2
TO GO		
1 x large latte		$2.70
with soy milk		$0.90
1 x small cappuccino		$1.90
with soy milk		$0.50
BOGOF promo		− $1.90
Subtotal		$4.10
Tax 8.75%		$0.34
Amount paid		$4.44
XXXXXXXXXXX9187		
284788		

To: Customer Complaints <complaints@crispacoffee.com>

From: Vikesh Chakladar <vikesh.chak.1992@onmail.com>

Subject: Buy One Get One Free Offer Query

Hello,

I wanted to get in contact to discuss a recent purchase made in your store on Lavaca Street, Austin. I'm a member or your rewards club, and I went in to take advantage of the buy one get one free offer released on Monday. I ordered a large latte with soy milk and a small cappuccino with soy milk. The barista did give me a discount at the till, but she only refunded me for the price of the smaller drink, excluding the soy milk. I don't think this can be correct, as the advert didn't mention anything about soy milk not being discounted. It was part of the cheapest drink, so I feel like it should also have been free.

I've been a loyal customer with you for many years, and I'd hate for this to impact my opinion of your stores. Let me know if there's anything you can do about this, or if I'm mistaking the offer in some way.

Thanks,

Vikesh Chakladar

---

191 What is being offered in the advertisement?

- **A** A free coffee when you open a new Rewards Account.
- **B** A free drink when you purchase a drink.
- **C** Buy one get one free on smaller meals.
- **D** A free upgrade to a Rewards Account.

192 How much was deducted from the bill?

- **A** $0.34
- **B** $0.50
- **C** $1.90
- **D** $4.10

193 On which days does the advertised offer run?

- **A** Monday - Wednesday
- **B** Monday - Sunday
- **C** Friday - Wednesday
- **D** Friday - Sunday

194 In the email, the phrase "take advantage of" in paragraph 1, line 2, is closest in meaning to

- **A** use.
- **B** extract.
- **C** gain.
- **D** exploit.

195 What problem does Mr. Chakladar mention in his email?

- **A** He received a different drink to the one he ordered.
- **B** He only received the discount on one drink.
- **C** The barista refused to discount his order.
- **D** He only received the discount on part of the drink.

Questions 196–200 refer to the article, chart and job advertisement that follow.

Technology is creating jobs, not taking them away.

The rise of robotics has raised many eyebrows in terms of what the future holds for human workers. New research conducted by the World Economic Forum disagrees and suggests that millennials aren't really worried about technology's negative impact on the job market — actually, they strongly believe that recent advances in technology will generate more jobs than it will destroy. — [1] —

— [2] — Approximately 25,000 participants shared their views on topics ranging from the current global economic outlook to the role of technology in the workplace. 78.6 percent believed that technology was leading to more jobs, not less.

— [3] — There are obviously still plenty of people that are not so sure about what automation brings to the table. — [4] —

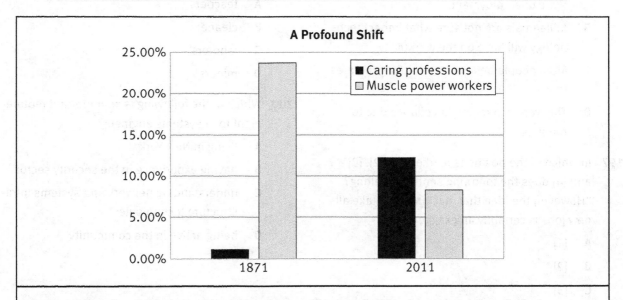

Caring professions include health and teaching professionals. Muscle power workers include cleaners, laborers and miners.

Systems Engineer (three positions)

Syscorp is looking to recruit Systems Engineers based out of its sites in New York, London and Sidney. The successful candidates will be working in the Enterprise Security team, whose main aim is to develop secure information systems to be delivered to customers within defense, government or public sector organizations.

The successful candidate will lead their own specialized engineering team and be responsible for supervising multiple active projects. The successful candidate must also have excellent working knowledge of network and systems infrastructure technologies.

---

196 What is the main finding of the research?

   A People are afraid that technology will generate unemployment.

   B Millennials are not sure what impact technology will have on the workplace.

   C Most people believe technology generates jobs.

   D The work market might collapse due to robotics.

197 In which of the positions marked [1], [2], [3] and [4] does the following sentence belong? "However, the idea that machines will take all new jobs is certainly an exaggeration."

   A [1]

   B [2]

   C [3]

   D [4]

198 What does the bar chart show?

   A labor has shifted from physically strenuous jobs to specialized, caring roles

   B technology is generating more jobs than expected

   C job requirements are more demanding than they were in the 19th century

   D robotics will have a negative impact on the world of work

199 Which of the following are NOT considered muscle power workers?

   A teachers

   B cleaners

   C laborers

   D miners

200 Which of the following is an important requirement for a systems engineer?

   A living in New York

   B having experience in the security sector

   C understanding network and systems infrastructure technologies

   D being active in the community

TOEIC Listening and Reading Practice Test 4

LISTENING TEST

In this section of the test, you will show your knowledge of spoken English. This section has four parts, and the entire section will last for around 45 minutes. Directions are given for each individual part of the test. Mark your answers on the answer sheet provided. To listen to the audio tracks for this section of the test, access the tracks in your Online Resources, by visiting **www.kaptest.com/booksonline** OR through the Kaplan Study App.

 Play Track 13 for Test 4, Part I

PART I: PHOTOGRAPHS

Directions: For each question in this part, you will hear four statements about a picture in your test book. When you hear the statements, you must select the one statement that best describes what you see in the picture. Then find the number of the question on your answer sheet and mark your answer. The statements will not be printed in your test book and will be spoken only one time.

1

2

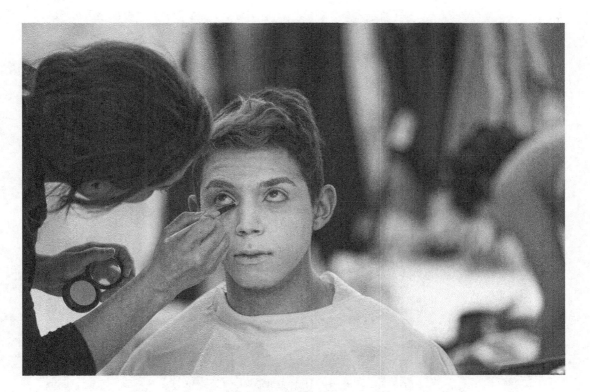

3

4

5

6

Play Track 14 for Test 4, Part II

PART II: QUESTION RESPONSE

Directions: You will hear a question or statement and three responses spoken in English. They will not be printed in your test book and will be spoken only one time. Select the best response to the question or statement and mark the letter A, B, or C on your answer sheet.

7	Mark your answer on your answer sheet.	20	Mark your answer on your answer sheet.
8	Mark your answer on your answer sheet.	21	Mark your answer on your answer sheet.
9	Mark your answer on your answer sheet.	22	Mark your answer on your answer sheet.
10	Mark your answer on your answer sheet.	23	Mark your answer on your answer sheet.
11	Mark your answer on your answer sheet.	24	Mark your answer on your answer sheet.
12	Mark your answer on your answer sheet.	25	Mark your answer on your answer sheet.
13	Mark your answer on your answer sheet.	26	Mark your answer on your answer sheet.
14	Mark your answer on your answer sheet.	27	Mark your answer on your answer sheet.
15	Mark your answer on your answer sheet.	28	Mark your answer on your answer sheet.
16	Mark your answer on your answer sheet.	29	Mark your answer on your answer sheet.
17	Mark your answer on your answer sheet.	30	Mark your answer on your answer sheet.
18	Mark your answer on your answer sheet.	31	Mark your answer on your answer sheet.
19	Mark your answer on your answer sheet.		

Play Track 15 for Test 4, Part III

PART III: SHORT CONVERSATIONS

Directions: You will hear some conversations between two people. You will be asked to answer three questions about what the speakers say in each conversation. Select the best response to each question and mark the letter (A), (B), (C), or (D) on your answer sheet. The conversation will not be printed in your test book and will be spoken only one time.

32 What are the speakers using?

   A a computer

   B a printer

   C a filing cabinet

   D a window

33 What advice does the woman give the man?

   A Close the window.

   B Always save your files.

   C Use the wireless printer.

   D Eject the memory stick before removing it.

34 What does the man want the woman to do?

   A Save the file.

   B Eject the memory stick.

   C Press enter.

   D Show him how to use the printer.

35 Why does the man have a new laptop?

   A He has been promoted.

   B His old one crashed.

   C IT have updated all the computers.

   D His old one is out of date.

36 What is causing the laptop issues?

   A The battery has died.

   B It needs to be unlocked.

   C The man is using it incorrectly.

   D The software is out of date.

37 What does the woman ask for at the end?

   A an extension on her deadline

   B more information about his promotion

   C the man's number

   D his email address

38 Whom is the conversation likely to be between?

   A a nurse and a doctor

   B two doctors

   C a doctor and a receptionist

   D a patient and a receptionist

39 On which day is this conversation taking place?

   A Monday

   B Wednesday

   C Friday

   D Saturday

40 Why does the woman prefer Friday?

   A because it's sooner

   B because she works on Monday

   C because Monday is too early in the morning

   D because Monday is with a different doctor

41 Why didn't the woman send the email?

   A She was sick.

   B She was away on vacation.

   C She couldn't find his email address.

   D She forgot.

42 What does the man suggest doing?

A making a phone call

B sending another email

C sending a fax

D offering the woman a new contract

43 What does the woman offer to do?

A clean his office

B solve the problem she created

C call the cleaners

D fix his computer

44 At what time will Ricardo have his IT induction?

A 9 a.m.

B 9:30 a.m.

C 10 a.m.

D 10:30 a.m.

45 Why does the woman prefer to do a tour?

A One of her colleagues is better equipped for the other option.

B She's new in her department.

C She's not good at explaining processes.

D She's not available at 11 a.m.

46 What does the man say at the end?

A He's going to do one of the two tours.

B The woman's idea about the tours is better.

C The tours have to happen one by one.

D The woman doesn't need to do both tours.

47 Between whom is the conversation likely to take place?

A two students

B a student and a tutor

C two tutors

D a student and an administrator

48 Why was the man concerned about the dissertation?

A There wasn't enough research on social movements.

B Marginalized groups are a sensitive topic.

C There weren't enough interviews included.

D He thought finding more interviewees would be difficult.

49 When is the latest the man can submit his dissertation?

A Thursday 12 p.m.

B Thursday 4 p.m.

C Friday 12 p.m.

D Friday 4 p.m.

50 Look at the graphic below. Which shows the budget that the man has created?

A Budget A

B Budget B

C Budget C

D Budget D

BUDGET A		BUDGET B	
Kitchen	– $10k	Kitchen	– $10k
Bedrooms	– $10k	Bathroom	– $20k
Misc.	– $10k	Bedrooms	– $15k
Total:	– $30k	Total:	– $45k
BUDGET C		BUDGET D	
Kitchen	– $10k	Kitchen	– $10k
Bedrooms	– $20k	Bathroom	– N/A
Misc.	– $15k	Bedrooms	– $20k
Total:	– $45k	Total:	– $30k

51 Which of the following does the woman NOT suggest to cut costs?

   A skipping the bathroom expansion

   B not refurbishing one of the rooms

   C not refurbishing the kitchen

   D selecting less expensive materials for the kitchen

52 What does the man say about the woman's parents?

   A He doesn't want to be indebted to them.

   B They recently refurbished their own home.

   C He thinks their offer is very kind.

   D They can help with looking at the numbers again.

---

53 Why does the man want to reschedule the meeting?

   A He's not in the office tomorrow morning.

   B They do not know when the proposals will arrive.

   C He thinks there isn't enough time to prepare for it.

   D He thinks it will last all day, so it should start sooner.

54 What is the timeline of the project?

   A four months

   B five months

   C six months

   D eight months

55 What does the woman say about the proposals so far?

   A She can't decide which one she likes more.

   B They're below average.

   C They're above average.

   D She hasn't read them yet.

56 Why has the man asked for an engineer?

   A His TV does not switch on.

   B His PC has been giving him an error message.

   C Some of the channels on his TV have vanished.

   D Her TV is not picking up a signal.

57 What has been causing the problem?

   A The man had picked the wrong source.

   B Something wasn't connected properly.

   C A device was unplugged.

   D The satellite dish is broken.

58 How is the man likely to feel at the end of the conversation?

   A foolish

   B foolhardy

   C reckless

   D crotchety

---

59 Why does the woman want to go to the cinema?

   A There's a specific movie she wants to see.

   B She doesn't want to miss an offer.

   C Someone recommended a movie to her.

   D She was given the movie schedule and it made her think of it.

60 What is the woman referring to when she says "Can you imagine?"

   A fighting with your siblings

   B having a lot of siblings

   C not having any sisters

   D having a big family inheritance

61 Look at the schedule below. Which screening do the man and woman pick?

- **A** *We Were Infinite*–6:10
- **B** *What Was Forgotten*–16:10.
- **C** *We Were Infinite*–20:00.
- **D** *What Was Forgotten*–18:00.

```
┌─────────────────────────────────────┐
│           MOVIE SCHEDULE             │
│                                      │
│  Screen 1                            │
│  We Were Infinite–PG-13              │
│  4:20–6:10–8:00                      │
│                                      │
│  Screen 2–IMAX                       │
│  The Fifteen Brothers–R              │
│  4:40–7:10                           │
│                                      │
│  Screen 3                            │
│  What Was Forgotten–NC-17            │
│  (subtitled screening at 4:10)       │
│  4:10–6:00–7:50–9:40                 │
└─────────────────────────────────────┘
```

62 How many months ago did Alice change jobs?

- **A** 3
- **B** 4
- **C** 6
- **D** 7

63 What is Alice planning to do next?

- **A** request her old job back
- **B** seek a new position in a new company
- **C** return to school
- **D** apply for a different job at her old company

64 Why does the man say "Wow, that's odd"?

- **A** He's surprised Alice listened to her husband.
- **B** He's surprised Alice has agreed to move to Utah.
- **C** He's surprised Alice is interested in economics.
- **D** He's surprised Alice wants to leave town.

65 How many people haven't decided if they're coming yet?

- **A** 10
- **B** 20
- **C** 30
- **D** 50

66 Why is the man reluctant to book the room that fits 30 people?

- **A** Some of the people who said they would attend might decide not to go.
- **B** It might be a bit cramped.
- **C** The room that fits 50 people looks better.
- **D** He thinks some people who said they won't come might come after all.

67 Look at the price list below. Which room do the man and woman decide to book?

- **A** the Green Room
- **B** the Blue Room
- **C** the Yellow Room
- **D** the Black Room

CONFERENCE ROOMS	
Green Room	**Blue Room**
Capacity: 25	Capacity: 30
Price: $100	Price: $250
Yellow Room	**Black Room**
Capacity: 50	Capacity: 200
Price: $450	Price: $1,200

68 At what time are the people the group is talking about arriving?

  A 7:30

  B 8:30

  C 9:00

  D 10:00

69 How are the people the group is talking about getting to the office?

  A David will be picking them up.

  B They are taking a taxi.

  C They are taking the bus.

  D They are taking the train.

70 Why does the man say "fair enough"?

  A The woman has a better reason to be stressed than he does.

  B The woman has done more to prepare for the visit than he has.

  C The woman is the one who gave him his job.

  D The woman is the one who needs to sign the contract.

Play Track 16 for Test 4, Part IV

PART IV: SHORT TALKS

Directions: You will hear some talks given by one speaker. You will be asked to answer three questions about what the speaker says in each talk. Select the best response to each question and mark the letter (A), (B), (C), or (D) on your answer sheet. The conversation will not be printed in your test book and will be spoken only one time.

71 Who is giving this speech?

   A   a reporter

   B   a firefighter

   C   a police officer

   D   a local resident

72 What information does the woman NOT give about the fire?

   A   where it began

   B   when it began

   C   how it began

   D   how far it has spread

73 How many casualties are there so far?

   A   18

   B   32

   C   36

   D   46

74 What is the topic of this speech?

   A   Which new product to launch.

   B   Why the company's sales have dropped.

   C   How the company started out.

   D   Projections for the next two quarters.

75 What does the man say about the company's current products?

   A   They need to be replaced.

   B   They need to be supplemented by new products.

   C   They can't be re-branded.

   D   They won't be successful anymore in 10 years.

76 What can be inferred from the man's speech?

   A   The company used to take risks.

   B   Sales will go up soon.

   C   The world of cosmetics isn't lucrative anymore.

   D   The company's new products are not good enough.

77 Which of the following passwords would be acceptable for the website?

   A   jOH1

   B   jOHn@hughes1

   C   jOHnhughes1

   D   jOHnhugh$s1

78 What do you NOT need to do to achieve 'Confirmed' status?

   A   Upload a short video.

   B   Provide a document that proves your ID.

   C   Add photographs of your degrees.

   D   Select your preferences in terms of projects you want to win.

79 What does the man say at the end?

   A People offering projects usually take a while to pick someone.

   B You are allowed to bid on all projects.

   C Some projects will be hidden from you.

   D You can't communicate with the people offering projects.

80 What can be inferred about the woman from the speech?

   A She doesn't like Monday mornings.

   B She wants to change the length of the meetings.

   C She replaced Marina.

   D She has only recently joined the company.

81 Which of the following does the woman NOT suggest as topics for the catch-up?

   A finding solutions to problems

   B sharing successes

   C sharing lessons learned

   D asking for assistance

82 What does the woman say about the catch-up at the end?

   A It will happen once a month.

   B She thinks it will be beneficial.

   C She will stop them if people don't find them useful.

   D It will start in five minutes.

83 What is wrong with the cell phones being recalled?

   A They switch off out of the blue.

   B The software can't be updated.

   C The 'trace' feature does not work.

   D Applications shut down randomly.

84 What is the speaker referring to when he says, "This is commendable"?

   A waiting in long lines to fix a phone

   B inviting all customers to check if their phone is faulty

   C recalling all faulty phones

   D admitting that the fault originated in a software issue

85 Look at the graphic below. Which cell phone model cannot be fixed?

   A KY483462

   B KY484162

   C KZ112362

   D KZ115462

CELL PHONE MODELS	
Spring Mini 5	KY483462–10/2018 batch
Spring Mini 5	KY484163–11/2018 batch
Spring Mini 6	KZ112363–10/2018 batch
Spring Mini 6	KZ115462–11/2018 batch

86 Why is the project with the woman's company not going ahead?

   A The client is going with a competitor.

   B The client has no budget left.

   C The client has decided to attack a new market instead of launching in a new region.

   D The client has decided to focus on their existing market.

87 What did Desmond say about the project?

   A They will be coming back to them in a year or two.

   B They've already decided they won't hire the woman's company.

   C It's unlikely the woman's company will be considered for it.

   D It's unlikely the client will ever expand.

88 Look at the table below. Which month is the woman referring to in her speech?

   A January

   B February

   C March

   D April

	Mississippi	Las Vegas
January	$172,000	$60,000
February	$78,000	$22,000
March	$95,000	$44,000
April	$170,000	$23,000

89 What can the caller do online?

   A amend a booking

   B find out more about the company's services

   C find their booking reference

   D request a text message with their mover's cell phone number

90 Which number should the caller press to cancel a paid-for booking?

   A 2

   B 3

   C 4

   D 5

91 Which number should the caller press to make changes to an unpaid booking?

   A 2

   B 3

   C 4

   D 5

92 Which government promise does the speaker NOT mention?

   A addressing crime committed with the use of knives

   B fixing medical care

   C culling the cricket population

   D controlling how much universities can charge

93 Look at the table below. Which university does the speaker attend?

   A Marble University

   B University of Kew Hill

   C Oakwood University

   D Green Arch University

CURRENT UNIVERSITY FEES PER ANNUM	
Marble University	$5,400
University of Kew Hill	$10,800
Oakwood University	$12,900
Green Arch University	$10,000

94 How is the speaker likely to feel?

   A unmotivated

   B determined

   C glum

   D despondent

95 What does the woman say is strange about the weather?

  A how suddenly it changed

  B how long it has lasted

  C how untypical it is

  D how late in the day it changed

96 What is NOT forecast for Sunday?

  A strong winds

  B snow

  C rain

  D low temperatures

97 What CANNOT be inferred from the speech?

  A Hospitals will probably be busy.

  B The weather is often this bad in the state.

  C There might be a few car accidents.

  D Older people will need assistance.

---

98 What can be inferred about the woman from the speech?

  A She just found out about Mr. Smith's plans to close 30 libraries.

  B She thinks libraries are a luxury.

  C She's personally invested in saving libraries because of her child.

  D She can't afford to buy books.

99 Which of the following important library services is NOT mentioned?

  A They help people who are looking for a job.

  B They offer essay-writing help.

  C They make technology available to students.

  D They teach children to become fans of reading.

100 What does the woman recommend to save libraries?

  A relocating libraries

  B reducing the number of staff

  C closing the libraries with expensive rent

  D selling some of the books

READING TEST

In this section of the test, you will show your knowledge of written English. This section has three parts, and you have 75 minutes to complete all three sections. Directions are given for each individual part of the test. Mark your answers on the answer sheet provided.

PART V: INCOMPLETE SENTENCES

Directions: complete the following sentences using one of the four answer choices provided. Mark the answer **A**, **B**, **C** or **D** on your answer sheet.

101 We still _____ whether to move the offices to the new location in April or May.

   A decided

   B have decided

   C didn't decide

   D haven't decided

102 The stock market has been significantly up, by at least 30%, since the presidential election, but it is being _____ carefully.

   A monitor

   B monitored

   C monitoring

   D monitors

103 It has been reported that the CEO is preparing to _____ following corruption allegations.

   A stand out

   B stand down

   C stand away

   D stand off

104 The talks have been described as _____, and it is expected that an agreement will be reached very soon between the two parties.

   A frugal

   B frivolous

   C fruitful

   D fractious

105 A foundation has been created _____ the victim's name, with all proceeds to go towards improving literacy in impoverished neighborhoods.

   A at

   B in

   C for

   D by

106 According to the research published yesterday, the government's proposed solution is unlikely to produce the results they had previously _____ it would.

   A professed

   B propounded

   C proffered

   D protracted

107 Taking the car was a terrible decision. We _____ public transportation.

   A must use

   B must have used

   C should use

   D should have used

108 _____ our manager's reluctance to discuss what has prompted her decision to withdraw her support for the proposed changes in the contract, I'm not surprised there's so much dissent among the ranks.

- **A** Provided
- **B** Given
- **C** Supposed
- **D** Considered

109 It is definitely a critical moment for the company, as failure to _____ with the new regulations within the given timeframe could see it face hefty fines and even closure.

- **A** compel
- **B** compete
- **C** compose
- **D** comply

110 The movie has been _____ by both critics and audiences, who have described it as "disappointing" and "wildly offensive".

- **A** created
- **B** penned
- **C** praised
- **D** criticized

111 The highway has been _____ with traffic for hours following a multi-vehicle collision at 7 this morning. Miraculously, there have been no casualties so far and all those involved escaped with minor injuries.

- **A** constructed
- **B** contorted
- **C** congested
- **D** confounded

112 The president has hit back at critics, claiming that they have _____ attempted to mislead the public with unfounded allegations.

- **A** deliberate
- **B** deliberation
- **C** deliberately
- **D** deliberated

113 We stopped _____ Amy from her house and then we went straight to the party.

- **A** collect
- **B** to collect
- **C** collecting
- **D** to collecting

114 Trade unions have announced that, _____ their demands are met by noon tomorrow, they will have no option but to go ahead with their planned industrial action.

- **A** whether
- **B** unless
- **C** if
- **D** provided

115 Polls will remain open until 7 p.m. tonight, with the first exit polls _____ immediately thereafter.

- **A** arrive
- **B** arrival
- **C** arriving
- **D** arrived

116 The new version of the app is due to be released today, and we will fix the bug that has been causing the app to crash _____.

- **A** expect
- **B** expected
- **C** unexpected
- **D** unexpectedly

117 The company had to _____ 3.1 million cell phones after their 2018 Globe edition failed safety tests just a week after it was released.

A rehash

B recall

C retrain

D remit

118 The government has announced plans to crack down _____ companies that exploit gig economy workers, starting with changes to sick pay rights and zero-hour contracts.

A in

B on

C at

D with

119 The company's announcement that its flagship store would be shutting down has _____ rumors that the company is on the brink of collapse and will face liquidation unless new investors step in.

A fortified

B fueled

C fabricated

D fulminated

120 There will be a three-month _____ period during which jurisdiction will remain at the hands of local authorities, but it is expected that the power to pass new laws on the matter will be fully transferred to the federal government on March 1st.

A aberration

B implementation

C capitulation

D delimitation

121 Her refusal to _____ to pressure from top levels is not only consistent with her work ethic, but also one of the reasons she was offered the position in the first place.

A bow

B fall

C give

D obey

122 The backlash from the musician's inappropriate comments about a fellow artist almost _____ his career, with sales of his latest album plummeting immediately after his interview was broadcast.

A dedicated

B deprecated

C destroyed

D desecrated

123 Growing divisions amongst top-tier representatives of the political party mean the government will most likely have a hard time _____ the law this Friday.

A pass

B to pass

C passing

D to be passed

124 His inability to understand why there has been such high turnover in the team does not _____ much confidence in his leadership skills.

A import

B inspire

C increase

D intone

125 The company director has been accused of _____ following the appointment of his unqualified nephew to a senior leadership position.

A   favoritism

B   clienteles

C   bruxism

D   protectionism

126 It is perhaps unsurprising that the company's commitment to sell only cruelty-free products by 2020 has been met with skepticism, considering its terrible track record _____.

A   hence

B   henceforth

C   this far

D   thus far

127 Mayor Till's _____ activities came to light only a week after he was appointed, leading to his immediate resignation.

A   decorous

B   sordid

C   scrupulous

D   assiduous

128 The exchange left him visibly _____: he had to excuse himself immediately to get some fresh air.

A   perturbed

B   unruffled

C   biased

D   percipient

129 The organization has vowed to invest heavily _____ recruiting new talent as part of its five-year growth strategy.

A   on

B   at

C   in

D   to

130 _____ this with Claire, she has agreed that we need to address the issue immediately by releasing a press statement that explains our motivations behind the structural changes.

A   Discuss

B   Discussing

C   Have discussed

D   Having discussed

PART VI: TEXT COMPLETION

Directions: Read the following texts and select the best answer choice to complete the text. Mark the answer **A**, **B**, **C** or **D** on your answer sheet.

Questions 131–134 refer to the email that follows.

To:	will.savage@mail.com
From:	caitlyn.turner@NachoTV.com
Date:	July 9, 2018
Subject:	NachoTV Service

Dear Mr. Savage,

Thank you _____ Nacho TV.
        131.

I have had a look at your account and I can confirm that you are _____ to our monthly
                                                                   132.
HDTV service, which is $11.99 per month. Your previous plan, Basic Member, was upgraded in

December 2017 through a Smart TV.

We recommend to our members that they upgrade their plan when they _____ through a
                                                                     133.
device that supports HD, as it improves viewer experience. You should have received an email

from us confirming the change on the day your plan was upgraded.

Nevertheless, I have updated your account and given you a free trial of six months, during which

you will only be paying $8.99 – the Basic Member plan price. If, after six months, you no longer

wish to use our HDTV service, you can _____ this subscription it online by visiting your
                                         134.
account page.

Please let me know if you have any other questions.

Kind Regards,

Caitlyn Jennings

Customer Service Representative – Nacho TV

The *FlexTV* team

131
  A to contact
  B to contacting
  C for contact
  D for contacting

132
  A subscribe
  B subscriber
  C subscribed
  D subscription

133
  A sign up
  B sign in
  C sign off
  D sign over

134
  A discontinue
  B disallow
  C dismember
  D dislodge

Questions 135–138 refer to the review that follows.

Royal Woods Winner for Third Year in a Row!

Hi Everyone!

As you may have already been informed by your managers and colleagues, Royal Woods has been announced as the Winner of the Developing New Talent Award by the NAYTB (North American Youth Talent Board). This is the third year in a row that we have won this prestigious award, so I would like to extend my congratulations to you all. _____
135.

Without your commitment to recruiting and discovering new talent, I know we _____
this far.   136.

I would especially like to thank Laura, _____ New Talent graduate scheme was praised
137.
as "remarkably helpful to young people" and "designed to set new starters up for success", as well as Delfim, who took care of the program while Laura was away on maternity leave.

I am well aware, however, that this is an impressive achievement for the entire company, and I would like to _____ my personal thanks to each and every one of you. Well done, all!
138.
Rose Oliphant

Royal Woods CEO

---

135 **A** I hope this message finds you well.

   B I am extremely proud of you for your dedicated, hard work.

   C We will be applying for a new grant today.

   D Please let me know if you are unable to attend.

136 **A** will never come

   B would never come

   C never would have come

   D never come

137 **A** who

   B whose

   C who's

   D which

138 **A** extend

   B expand

   C expose

   D extoll

Questions 139–142 refer to the following letter.

Dear David Martinez,

We regret _____ you that your application has been unsuccessful on this occasion.
139.
The competition for the role of Educational Researcher was particularly _____ and,
140.
while we appreciated your experience in education and your passion for the media industry,
we ultimately felt that you were not suited for this role.

_____ While this role may not have been the one for you, we were very happy with your
141.
interview and we would be delighted to work with you in the future.

If you would like to receive more _____ feedback on your performance at the interview,
142.
please contact Francesco, who will be more than happy to assist you.

Thank you once again for applying to our Media Studies program.

Kind regards,

Kirsty Darrenogue

139 A inform

 B informing

 C to inform

 D to informing

140 A foul

 B fierce

 C facetious

 D forthcoming

141 A Please do not be discouraged from applying for other opportunities with us.

 B We hope you will consider accepting the role.

 C We wish you all the best in your job search.

 D Please remember that these things are very subjective.

142 A detail

 B detailing

 C details

 D detailed

Questions 143–146 refer to the notice that follows.

Voting Rights of Club Members

All members are entitled to vote in the club's board and committee elections, as well as all other matters which the club committee _____ appropriate to put up to a general vote.
143.

Elections are held on the first week of April every year, while decisions for an _____ vote
144.

are always announced at least 30 days before the vote is to be held.

In order to vote, members must be present at the club office, as _____ votes are not
145.

allowed. Members who are unable to attend may appoint a fellow member as a proxy voter.

Please note that you need to bring your club membership ID with you in order to be allowed to vote, and the relevant approved proxy form if applicable. _____ Voting is held during
146.

opening hours on the appointed date; opening hours are 9 a.m. to 6 p.m. on weekdays and 10 a.m. to midnight on weekends.

---

143 A deems

    B adjourns

    C submits

    D confers

144 A adjacent

    B anonymous

    C complementary

    D referendum

145 A post

    B posting

    C postal

    D postage

146 A You will not be permitted to vote without these items.

    B Non-members are only allowed to vote under exceptional circumstances.

    C The results are posted on our website the next day.

    D You should always book a room in advance.

PART VII: READING COMPREHENSION

Directions: In this part of the test, you will read a number of different texts and then answer several questions about each text. Mark the answer **A, B, C** or **D** on your answer sheet.

Questions 147–149 refer to the following email.

To: ana1989@mail.com

From: weiwei@babyfirst.com

Dear Mr. Swanson,

Thank you for getting in touch with Baby First. We are happy to hear that you are considering becoming an adoptive parent. — [1] —

I can imagine you have a lot of questions about the process of becoming approved and finding a suitable child. Our website has a comprehensive FAQ page, but we also have a variety of guides which go into further detail, depending on whether you are considering local, national or intercountry adoption, or you would like to adopt a step-child or relative. We can either email you these guides, or we can mail them to your home address if you prefer. You can also collect copies from our offices. — [2] —

The first step would be to book a meeting with us to discuss the specific processes entailed in the adoption process and any questions you might have. This is a very casual chat and it is not considered part of the application process. Anything you say or ask is completely confidential and no notes are taken by the social worker who will speak with you. — [3] —

If you would like to book an appointment, you can either use the online form or give us a call. We have appointments available throughout the week, though weekend appointments are harder to come by, as you can imagine. I would advise you to have a look on our website to check availability.

— [4] — I look forward to hearing from you.

Kind regards,

Weiwei

---

147 What is the purpose of this email?

A to explain how to book an appointment with the adoption agency

B to offer the results of an adoption application

C to respond to an initial query from a pro-spective adopter

D to send the adoption agency's guides to adoption

148 What does the email say about the first meeting with the agency?

A It will determine the applicant's suitability.

B It will not be a formal meeting.

C The applicant will receive notes at the end of the meeting.

D It will be with the social worker who takes on the applicant's case.

149 In which of the positions [1], [2], [3] or [4] does the following sentence best belong?

"If you have any further questions, please do not hesitate to get in touch."

A [1]

B [2]

C [3]

D [4]

Questions 150–152 refer to the following advertisement.

Travel to the Greek Islands with Orpheus Cruises

Looking for your perfect holiday? Look no further! Orpheus Cruises *is the most luxurious yet affordable option for those with limited time and an insatiable desire to see as many Greek islands as possible.*

From the idyllic beaches and Minoan palaces of Crete to the day-long parties of Mykonos and the blue-white architectural wonders of rocky Santorini, there's something to suit every taste with our 4-day, 7-day and 14-day cruises.

Just visit www.orpheuscruises.com and use our cruise tool to find the best cruise for you!

Use Promo Code SUMMER for a 15% discount–valid until January 31st!

- *4-day, 7-day and 14-day cruises available*
- *Spend a week touring the Greek islands from as little as $1,399**
- *Overnight stays at Mykonos, Santorini, Paros, and Crete***
- *Breakfast and dinner included, with excellent discounts at local bars and restaurants*
- *Open bar from noon till midnight on the ship every day*

*airfare not included

**depending on cruise (1 overnight stay for 4-day cruises, 2 overnight stays for all other cruises)

---

150 What can be inferred about Orpheus Cruises from the ad?

A It doesn't run cruises in the winter.

B It's based in Rome.

C It offers 2 week long cruises.

D It's an American company.

151 Which statement is NOT TRUE about Orpheus Cruises?

A Customers do not need to pay extra for their breakfast.

B The price of meals can be reduced at certain bars in Greece.

C The cheapest cruise costs $1,399.

D Customers can drink for free on the ship from 12 at midday to 12 at night.

152 How many overnight island stays are there on the 7-day cruise?

A 1

B 2

C 3

D 4

Questions 153–155 refer to the following product description.

Purchase Order			
Item	**Quantity**	**Price Per Unit**	**Price in Total**
Brown bread loaf	4	0.36	1.44
White bread loaf	6	0.36	2.16
Brown baguette	5	0.28	1.4
White baguette	15	0.28	4.2
Brown sandwich bread loaf	15	0.12	1.8
White sandwich bread loaf	20	0.1	2
Full-fat milk (1.5L)	2	0.79	1.58
Semi-skim milk (1.5L)	2	0.81	1.62
Skim milk (1.5L)	2	0.81	1.62
Almond milk (1L)	2	0.89	1.78
Soy milk (1L)	2	0.71	1.42
Chocolate muffin	3	0.56	1.68
Blueberry muffin	3	0.58	1.74
Lemon and poppy seed muffin	2	0.57	1.14
Palmier biscuit	6	0.79	4.74
Chocolate glazed donut	4	0.45	1.8
Raspberry jam donut	4	0.45	1.8
Croissant	10	0.12	1.2
Coffee beans (1kg)	3	8.45	25.35
Decaf coffee beans (1kg)	2	8.5	17
		Total:	77.47

153 Which item was the least money spent on in total?

A croissant

B lemon and poppy seed muffin

C brown baguette

D white sandwich bread loaf

154 Which type of milk is cheapest per unit?

A skim

B full-fat

C semi-skim

D soy

155 For which of the following products will the largest number of units be sent?

A   croissant

B   white sandwich bread loaf

C   coffee beans (1kg)

D   white baguette

Questions 156–159 refer to the following article.

Selling your stuff online does not only help to declutter your home and get rid of things you don't need, but it can also be a great source of income. Books you're not planning on reading again taking up space on your shelf? Sell them online. Upgrading your phone? Find a local buyer on social media. Selling online comes with certain pitfalls too, though, and it pays to be diligent when you're crossing the threshold from customer to seller.

One thing you need to consider carefully is the platform on which you are going to advertise. Most big players in the field are so popular with sellers, not just because they can give you access to a bigger pool of potential customers, but also because they offer insurance, both to the seller and the buyer, which gives both buyers and sellers more confidence. The downside, however, is that you will generally need to pay an upront fee for using the platform, and may also have to sacrifice a cut of your profit to the company. What's more, you need to build up a reputation before buyers can trust you—which means you might have to settle for lower prices until you have a high rating.

You can use some platforms that either charge a smaller fee for advertising or even no fee at all—but, in that case, what you will need to keep in mind is your safety, especially if the value of the product you're selling is high. Most prospective buyers will be genuine, but it's always best to meet during the day at a public place such as a coffee shop, a library, or a supermarket parking lot—anywhere monitored by security cameras is good. Always keep the product close to you, and check that the money has been released into your account or—if you're being paid by cash—that you have been given the full amount before relinquishing your items.

A few more things to keep in mind: always be accurate with your descriptions of the items you are selling, especially if advertising on a big platform. The last thing you want is to be accused of fraud and banned from the website. Moreover, be vigilant with your personal information: do not give out your home address or cell phone number unless you have to, and have a separate email address for selling online. Don't give out your full name, either—keep your last name private. Identity theft might be rare in such transactions, but it's always better to be careful.

You might think many of these sound like common sense rules, and they are, but many first-time sellers naively forget to take precautions when selling their stuff online. At the end of the day, it's up to you to decide the way in which you are comfortable with conducting business online—but remember that a smart, prepared seller is a happy seller.

156 Why are bigger platforms more popular according to the author?

A   They have a rating system.

B   They charge a small fee.

C   Their customer service is better.

D   They offer peace of mind.

157 What does the author NOT say about meeting with a buyer?

A   Avoid meeting at night.

B   Meet somewhere with other people around.

C   Avoid meeting if the product you are selling is very expensive.

D   Choose a place with cameras around.

158 Which of the following is likely safe to give out to buyers?

A   your first name

B   your personal email address

C   your home address

D   your cell phone number

159 What can be inferred from the text?

A   Using bigger platforms is better than using free platforms.

B   Selling online can be a great experience if you take precautions.

C   Knowing how to sell online requires expertise.

D   New online sellers experience many issues.

Questions 160–162 refer to the following instant messaging conversation.

Yussef: Hi Bill, are you at the office today?

Bill: Hi Yussef. Yeah, what's up?

Yussef: My computer's frozen, I can't access any of the files. Can you ping IT and ask them to take a look?

Yussef: I tried calling but no one picked up the phone

Bill: Sure, just give me a sec

Bill: How's the leg doing, btw?

Bill: Getting better?

Yussef: Yeah, had a doctor's appointment 2 days ago & he said the cast should be coming off soon

Bill: That's great, so will you be coming back to the office soon?

Bill: Tony from IT says he'll do a remote access thing

Yussef: Cool, thx. Yeah, should be back at the office in a couple of weeks

Bill: No prob. Listen, the guys and I are grabbing drinks this Friday if you wanna join? I mean, if you can hop over!

Yussef: Sure, just send me the details & I'll be there

Yussef: They're doing something, my screen's lit up again

Bill: Great! I'll see you on Friday then

Yussef: Yeah, cool–see ya Friday

160 Why has Yussef contacted Bill?

   A to ask him how he is

   B to request assistance

   C to make plans for Friday

   D to inform him about an IT issue

161 In line 3, what is the word "ping" closest in meaning to?

   A message

   B call

   C query

   D walk over to

162 Why is Yussef working from home?

   A He had a doctor's appointment.

   B He's ill.

   C He has broken his leg.

   D He's a remote worker.

Questions 163–164 refer to the following email.

From: Will.Eleftheriou@kingstores.com

To: NashvilleOffice@kingstores.com

Dear All:

It is with great sadness that I must announce my departure from the company at the end of this month.

It has been a great five years here at the Nashville office with you. We've had our highs and our lows (particularly during the move to the swanky new offices earlier this year!), but I've met many great people here and I am extremely grateful for the opportunities I was given to learn and develop, as well as for the friends I made.

As many of you already know, I will be moving to a new role at Stoked Ltd as a manager, for which I am extremely excited! Please do drop by if you'd like to say hi. You can also add me on social media (just search "Will Eleftheriou"–there aren't many of us!). My personal email address is will.eleftheriou@mail.com.

Once again, thank you for being so nice, everyone. You made my job that much more enjoyable.

I wish you all the best.

Will

---

163 What is the purpose of Will's email?

A to accept a resignation

B to bid his colleagues farewell

C to apply for a new job

D to inform everyone about his promotion

164 What can be inferred from the email?

A The company relocated recently.

B Will's new job is a higher-level position.

C Will met his best friend at his current job.

D The company has a high turnover rate.

Questions 165–168 refer to the following document.

Dating in the workplace is, if not a taboo, certainly a conundrum–not only for businesses, but also for the employees who find themselves falling for a co-worker. — [1] — Should it be allowed? Would it be authoritarian to ban it? Should employees inform their bosses of office relationships, or should they conceal them? Is requiring so-called "love contracts" to be signed by both parties before initiating a relationship even realistic?

— [2] — Most people spend 30 to 45 hours in the office each week–and with team-bonding activities, work celebrations and Friday drinks, it's normal for colleagues to build a bond with one another, especially if they find that they have more things in common than just their employer.

From the company's point of view, however, couples at work are a serious risk factor which must be mitigated. Without a proper dating policy in place, claims of sexual harassment and accusations of favoritism become a significant risk. It's not necessary to ban office romance (though you are certainly allowed to): but you do need to have clear rules in place, to ensure you're doing all you can to head off any potential issues. Ask, for example, that all employees who embark on a relationship have a sit-down, be it casual or formal, with HR. — [3] —

As for employees, there are two things to consider when you find yourself romantically interested in one of your colleagues: first of all, is it worth it? — [4] — Regardless of how your employer feels, office romance can be quite complicated–not only because you'll most likely be the target of gossip, but also because your work environment will be affected if the relationship does not work out. And secondly, what is your company's dating policy? If they have a zero-tolerance policy, do not risk your job or assume you will be able to keep your relationship on the down low. In the vast majority of cases, it's simply not possible.

Attitudes towards office romance are certainly changing, with more companies reassessing zero-tolerance policies and opting for a more casual approach to how their employees connect with one another. That said, however, office romance is still a complex issue, and it should be treated with gravitas.

165 Who is this article aimed at?

A companies

B employees considering a relationship with a colleague

C employees who are not in a relationship with a colleague

D all of the above

166 Which of the following do employees need to decide before starting an office romance?

A what their dating policy will be

B whether the advantages of it outweigh the disadvantages

C whether to inform the company

D whether to follow the company's dating rules

167 In paragraph 4, line 7, what does the author mean by the phrase "keep your relationship on the down low"?

    A   hiding your relationship

    B   making an example out of your relationship

    C   protecting your relationship

    D   creating rumors about relationships

168 In which of the positions [1], [2], [3] or [4] does the following sentence best belong?
"It is, of course, it is not surprising that relationships do form in the workplace."

    A   [1]

    B   [2]

    C   [3]

    D   [4]

Questions 169–171 refer to the following email.

To:	Massimo.Miolo@websolutions.com
From:	Laura.Southwood@websolutions.com
Date:	September 5, 2017
Subject:	New Spreadsheet Formats

Hi Laura,

As we discussed in our meeting earlier today, I have asked Lucas to send you an example of the reports we produce for our client at the end of every month. As you will see, this is a very manual process at the moment. We actually need to cut and paste data from about 15 different spreadsheets and then manipulate it to translate them into a presentable PDF which is easy to read for the client. This takes up a lot of time – and, worst of all, none of that time is billable so we're operating at a loss.

I just want your thoughts on how we can go about mainstreaming this process. At this point, the client has certain expectations, so we can't go back and ask him to pay or tell him we won't be providing this service anymore. At the same time, I don't think the current process is sustainable in the long-term and I think we need to find a better method of collating the data. This is where your expertise comes in.

I look forward to your thoughts. I'm sure you'll come up with something brilliant.

Thanks,

Massimo

Web Solutions – Senior Salesperson

169 Which of the following is NOT an issue with the current reporting system?

   A   It's not automatic.

   B   The company has to swallow the cost.

   C   The current PDF is not very presentable.

   D   It's time-consuming.

170 Why can't Massimo change the current process with his client?

   A   They have already set a precedent.

   B   The client has already refused to pay.

   C   It wouldn't be sustainable.

   D   The service has been discontinued.

171 How is the author of this email likely to feel?

   A   forlorn

   B   sanguine

   C   apprehensive

   D   overwrought

Questions 172–173 refer to the following information

Local Resident Discount Card–How to Apply

To apply for the Local Resident Discount Card, you will need to visit your local council's website and complete the form online. You will then need to email photographs of your supporting documents to the email address provided. Alternatively, you might be able to apply in person or via post–please check your local council's website for further information.

To support your Local Resident Discount Card, you will need:

- A photo ID (National ID card, passport, driver's license or student ID from a recognized local university);

- A proof of address (bank statement, utility bill–excluding cellular phone bills–or official letter from a bank, hospital, medical practice, government agency, etc.);

- two recent passport photographs;

- Your expired Local Resident Discount Card, if applicable.

To check your local council, enter your zip code here:

Zip Code

---

172 Which of the following is true about Local Resident Discount Card applications?

   A   You must apply online.

   B   You cannot apply via post.

   C   You can apply in person in some councils.

   D   You must always email your personal documents.

173 Which of the following is NOT a valid supporting document?

   A   an identity card

   B   a letter from your doctor

   C   a bill from a cell phone carrier

   D   a picture of you

Questions 174–175 refer to the following text message chain.

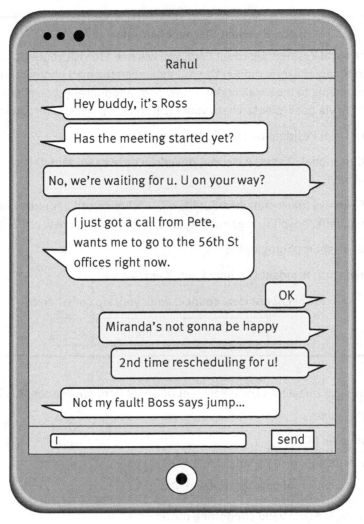

Rahul

Hey buddy, it's Ross

Has the meeting started yet?

No, we're waiting for u. U on your way?

I just got a call from Pete, wants me to go to the 56th St offices right now.

OK

Miranda's not gonna be happy

2nd time rescheduling for u!

Not my fault! Boss says jump…

I   send

174 What CANNOT be inferred from the conversation?

A Pete is Ross's boss.

B The meeting has been rescheduled because of Ross before.

C Ross should be in the same meeting as Rahul.

D Ross was expected to attend the meeting.

175 Why does Ross say "Boss says jump…"?

A He has to do what Pete says.

B He doesn't want to go to the meeting.

C He doesn't think Miranda will be annoyed.

D He doesn't believe that the meeting must be rescheduled.

Questions 176–180 refer to the following advertisement and review.

---

365 Holiday–Luxury Apartments by the Sea

If you're looking for a place that combines the comforts of a hotel with the convenience of a house by the sea, then look no further! Our apartments are suitable for 1, 2, 3 or 4 guests, available in numerous seaside locations across Europe and provide the perfect base for a relaxing break, with panoramic views, private beaches or boat moorings, and a range of free activities, suitable for adults and children alike.

All our apartments come equipped with:

- a private bathroom with a bathtub or shower, plus hair dryers

- a master bedroom with a king-sized bed

- a kitchen or kitchenette with a stove/oven, microwave, kettle, and fridge

- amenities such as TV, iron, ironing board, and safe

All apartments receive a regular cleaning service every two days, which is included in the price. We also offer services such as laundry and ironing for a small fee, and we even throw in a free massage at the local massage salon if you book before January 31st (where available). With prices starting from $119 per night, what are you waiting for? Your next holiday might be right around the corner!

Customer review by Jonathan Wells: ★☆☆☆☆

If you are considering booking with 365 HOLIDAY, I'd urge you to reconsider. In fact, I'd advise you to stay as far away from them as possible. I have just returned from a trip with them to the French Mediterranean, and it was a truly terrible experience.

Trouble started from the moment I arrived at the airport: while, according to the package my wife and I had purchased, we were entitled to a suitcase of 23kg each, the booking made by 365 HOLIDAY only included hand luggage, and we were forced to fork out $50 extra to take our bags with us.

Then, when we arrived at the airport in France, our driver was 20 minutes late—which, granted, gave us an opportunity to browse at the shops for tax-free bargains and visit the local bureau de change, but it was also another sign of just how disorganized this company is.

Nothing could've prepared us for the cherry on the cake, however. When we were taken to this supposedly "luxurious" apartment we found it not only looked nothing like the pictures—it was advertised as state-of-the-art with cutting-edge facilities—but in reality the paint was peeling off the walls and there was rust on the window frames and mold in the bathroom. It was also in the midst of renovations! This, of course, meant there was a crew around at 7 a.m. every morning, turning what was supposed to be a relaxing break into a daily nightmare.

I've already requested a refund from 365 HOLIDAY, but I'm not holding my breath.

---

176 Which of the following is NOT stated to be available at 365 HOLIDAY apartments?

- **A** facilities to cook meals
- **B** a place to protect personal belongings
- **C** things to do for families
- **D** boat tours

177 What can be inferred from the first text?

- **A** Apartments can be cleaned more often for a small fee.
- **B** One of the services included in the price is a massage.
- **C** Some of the apartment locations are at the seaside.
- **D** The company offers an early-bird discount.

178 What was the first issue Jonathan Wells encountered?

- **A** His flight was delayed.
- **B** He wasn't given a service he'd paid for.
- **C** The company booked the wrong tickets.
- **D** The company overcharged him by $50.

179 How were Jonathan and his wife likely to feel when they arrived at the apartment?

- **A** relieved
- **B** flabbergasted
- **C** euphoric
- **D** assertive

180 What does Jonathan Wells say about compensation?

- **A** He will be suing the company.
- **B** He doesn't expect to receive any.
- **C** He will not be asking for a refund.
- **D** He has been offered a refund.

Questions 181–185 refer to the following invoice and email.

Jameson Bank
January Bank Statement
Lachlan McDowell

	In	Out
January 1		
PANZERS RESTAURANT		$49.56
Peter Andrews	$750.00	
Ref: Rent & Bills		
January 2		
The Slender Box Concert	$89.00	
Ref: Refund		
Lilith Jones		$1,213.00
Ref: Rent		
January 5		
Pedro's Mexican Grill		$24.48
Great Seasons Bar		$10.99
Great Seasons Bar		$10.99
Great Seasons Bar		$10.99
Elements Club		$20.00
January 7		
Archeological Museum		$10.00
Oscar Thompson		$250.00
Ref: Personal Trainer		
January 15		
FOREVER TV		$38.40
Amparo Perez		$180.00
Ref: Spanish class		
January 18		
East Street Supermarket		$21.95
Spicy Ltd		$112.00
January 25		
Horton, Holmes & Baker	$3,415.46	
Energy Now		$45.00

Balance: $3,842

From: Riley.Wagner@jameson.com

To: Lachlan.McDowell@mail.com

Dear Mr. McDowell,

Thank you for your email regarding the suspicious activity on your account. Please note that, in urgent cases such as this, it is preferable to contact us through our web chat feature, which is available at all times to customers with hearing loss.

We have had a chance to investigate the charge from "Spicy Ltd" and can confirm that, while the charge appeared in your account on January 18th, the purchase was made on January 16th on 72nd Street, which is near your registered address. "Spicy Ltd" is the registered name of a shop called "Spices and Places".

I have authorized a refund of $112.00, which should reach your account by close of business today at the latest. If this purchase sounds familiar, please let us know and I will cancel the refund. I have also attached a short form for you to complete and return to us. Although your refund will be processed regardless of when you submit this form, it would be greatly appreciated if you completed it as soon as possible.

If there is anything else I can help you with, please do let me know.

Kind regards,

Riley Wagner

Accounts Manager

---

181 Based on the bank statement, with whom is Lachlan McDowell most likely to live?

A Peter Andrews

B Lilith Jones

C Oscar Thompson

D Amparo Perez

182 Which of the following is NOT one of Lachlan's expenses in January?

A exercising

B learning a foreign language

C home entertainment

D concerts

183 What can be inferred about Lachlan from the email?

A He used the web chat feature to contact the bank.

B He might have impaired hearing.

C He didn't think the suspicious charge was an urgent matter.

D He frequents "Spices and Places".

184 What does Lachlan NOT need to do, based on the email?

A Use the web chat if something similar happens in the future.

B Inform the bank if he recognizes the shop "Spices and Places".

C Let the bank know the money reached his account.

D Complete the form he has been sent.

185 What does Riley say about the refund?

    A   It is not contingent upon completion of the short form.

    B   It will arrive before tomorrow.

    C   It will arrive as soon as Lachlan confirms he doesn't recognize the charge.

    D   It will be confirmed once the short form has been received.

Questions 186–190 refer to the following advertisement, instant message and email.

BUBBLEGUM GYMS

***New Year, New Rules* Offer**

Are you looking to lose those extra pounds you gained from your Christmas turkey meal? Is getting fit your New Year's resolution? Then look no further! With our *New Year, New Rules* offer, you get **25% off**, plus you skip the registration fee!

~~**NORMAL MEMBERSHIP: $40 per month + $35 registration**~~

NEW YEAR NEW RULES: $30 per month + no registration!*

What are you waiting for? Get in touch on our social media pages!

*12-month minimum subscription required

Hi, I'm interested in your "New Year, New Rules" offer. Can you send me a bit more information, please? I live near your 31st St. branch, and I also work near the 77th St. branch, which I'd prefer as I'd like to also have access to a swimming pool. Can you email me at gabby.mendez@mail.com please? I don't use social media much so I don't check it often. Thanks! Gabby

To:	gabby.mendez@mail.com
From:	Jared.StJohn@bubblegumgyms.com
Date:	February 10, 2017
Subject:	New membership offer

Dear Gabby,

Thank you for getting in touch on our social media page.

Unfortunately, our *New Year, New Rules* offer expired on January 31st. However, we are currently running a new promotional offer which is quite similar and, unlike our previous offer, also includes access to our swimming pools. The offer is $40 per month (down from our normal $50 for gym + swim), plus 50% off all classes such as yoga and Pilates.

You do have to pay the registration fee, I'm afraid – but if you book by the end of this week I will be happy to throw in a free month for a 12-month membership, which works out better for you.

Please let me know if this sounds good to you and I will give you a call so we can arrange everything.

Kind regards,

Jared – Sales Representative

186 In which month was the ad most likely published?

    A   January

    B   February

    C   October

    D   November

187 What can be inferred from Gaby's message?

    A   She wants to have access to two different pools.

    B   She prefers to be contacted via social media.

    C   The 31st Street branch doesn't have a pool.

    D   She prefers to go to the gym after work.

188 What can be inferred from Jared's response?

    A   The new deal can last for less than 12 months.

    B   The *New Year, New Rules* deal didn't give access to swimming pools.

    C   The company has raised their prices.

    D   The new promotional offer expires on January 31st.

189 In Jared's email, in paragraph 3, the phrase "I will be happy to throw in a free month" is closest in meaning to

    A   I will be happy to replace the free registration with a free month.

    B   I will be happy to add a free month on top of the free registration.

    C   I will be happy to offer you a free month to compensate.

    D   I will be happy to give you a free month trial.

190 In Jared's email, in paragraph 4, what does "Please let me know if this sounds good to you" refer to?

    A   purchasing the *New Year, New Rules* membership plan

    B   not paying the registration fee

    C   receiving a month for free

    D   being contacted over the phone to arrange signing up

Questions 191–195 refer to the following job posting and two instant messages.

Sarah Walters Hi everyone! I've got an exciting new opening for a home-based graphic designer in a funky San Francisco-based start-up in the advertising and marketing industry! One year minimum experience in graphic design required, preferably in marketing and advertising, though not strictly necessary. Graduates with internship experience and notable academic performance will be considered. $22-25k per annum depending on experience, plus bonuses and numerous perks such as healthcare, a cycle to work scheme and discounted gym memberships. Must be local to SF—relocation help can be provided upon request. Immediate start preferred. If that sounds like you, DM me for details with a bit of info about yourself, education and experience. If you've got any friends who might be interested in this role, please tag them below and I promise to get in touch with them—there will be a referral reward in it for you if they pass probationary period! Thanks! Sarah

Hi Sarah! My name is Diego Sanchez and I'm interested in the graphic designer position you're advertising. I have two years of experience with an advertising company in Chicago and excellent references from my freelance work. Please have a look at my portfolio on my page. Could I get some more information, please? Also, two questions: a. I have to give one-months' notice at my current job. Will that be a problem? b. I've got holidays booked in July. Is that all right? Thanks! Diego

Hi, Diego! Thanks for getting in touch. I've looked at your portfolio and it looks good. Are you based in Chicago? If so, are you willing to move? The role is home-based but the company would prefer candidates based in SF so they could travel to their offices when needed. The offices are near Trocadero station. They'd also prefer an immediate start, but most candidates have a 1-month notice so I wouldn't worry about it. Not sure about the holidays but I can't imagine them posing an issue, either. Can you send me your resume at sarah@designrecruit.com please? Then I'll send you a task the company would like you to complete – it's nothing complicated, just designing a logo for a mock product based on their specifications. Thanks, Sarah

191 Which of the following is NOT TRUE about the advertised role?

   A   The company is in San Francisco.

   B   The employee will work from home.

   C   It's a freelance position.

   D   The salary is negotiable.

192 In Sarah's post, line 4, the phrase "notable academic performance" is closest in meaning to

   A   an excellent track record at work

   B   remarkable achievements in education

   C   many years in education

   D   a university degree

193 Which of the following is Diego worried about?

   A   whether his experience is relevant

   B   whether his current job will ask for a one-month notice

   C   whether he can work from Chicago

   D   whether his booked vacation will be a problem

194 In Sarah's instant message, line 7, what does "I wouldn't worry about it" refer to?

   A   Diego's location

   B   Diego's one-month notice

   C   Diego's holidays

   D   Diego's references

195 What does Diego NOT need to do for his application to be considered?

   A   share his portfolio

   B   design something

   C   forward his resume

   D   confirm he lives in or can move to San Francisco

Questions 196–200 refer to the following entrance pass, receipt and email.

CONCEPTS

BUSINESS FAIR—2018

March 12th–15th

This entrance pass allows access to the holder + one (1) more person to all events throughout the duration of the fair.

Please keep this ticket with you at all times. You and your guest must remain together throughout your visit to the fair, as random ticket inspections are carried out.

Access Code:

U V 3 8 9 K Z 1 X

Absolutely Vegan Ltd

03/13/18 11:26:34

Number:	XXXXXXXXXXXX9876
Type:	CREDIT
Entry mode:	Swiped
Response:	APPROVED
Approval Code:	813421
1 x Access Pass	$29.99
Subtotal	$29.99
Tax 9%	$2.69
Total	$32.68

Thank you

To:	contact@concepts.com
From:	Silvia.Hinton@email.com
Date:	March 16, 2018
Subject:	Complaint & Refund Request

To Whom it May Concern,

My name is Silvia Hinton and my business partner and I attended the business fair you held this week in Miami using your Every Day + Guest pass, which I purchased on your website for $179.99 last month. I have attached a picture of my ticket - the access code is UV389KZ1X. — [1] —

According to your website and the confirmation email I received after I purchased this ticket, my partner and I would be allowed to access all parts and sections of the fair, including shows and talks and exhibitions. This is also clearly marked on the pass itself. However, while most of your vendors were happy to accept our shared ticket, one particular vendor, Absolutely Vegan, said our pass was not valid for two people for their show, and we were forced to pay an additional fee (see receipt attached) for both of us to be allowed in. — [2] — In fact, they were particularly rude about it, and made us look as if we were trying to trick them.

This vendor's behavior was completely unacceptable. The only reason we did not leave right there and then was because we are friends with one of the people in the show and did not want to miss it. — [3] — We do, however, expect a full refund for the fee we were forced to pay, as well as some form of compensation for the way we were treated — [4] —

I look forward to your response.

Regards,

Silvia Hinton

196 What can be inferred from the entrance pass?

A The pass holder and their guest cannot attend different shows

B The pass is only valid for one day

C The pass can be discarded once scanned

D The access code can only be used once

197 On which day did the ticket holder visit Absolutely Vegan?

A March 12th

B March 13th

C March 14th

D March 15th

198 Which of the following does Silvia NOT mention as proof that the entrance pass is valid for two?

A information provided online

B the email she was sent

C what she was told by ticket inspectors at the fair

D the entrance ticket

199 How is Silvia likely to feel based on her email?

A exhilarated

B exasperated

C exuberant

D exfoliated

200 In which of the positions [1], [2], [3] or [4] does the following sentence best belong?
"Despite our protestations, they did not relent."

A [1]

B [2]

C [3]

D [4]

TOEIC Listening and Reading Practice Test 5

LISTENING TEST

In this section of the test, you will show your knowledge of spoken English. This section has four parts, and the entire section will last for around 45 minutes. Directions are given for each individual part of the test. Mark your answers on the answer sheet provided. To listen to the audio tracks for this section of the test, access the tracks in your Online Resources, by visiting **www.kaptest.com/booksonline** OR through the Kaplan Study App.

 Play Track 17 for Test 5, Part I

PART I: PHOTOGRAPHS

Directions: For each question in this part, you will hear four statements about a picture in your test book. When you hear the statements, you must select the one statement that best describes what you see in the picture. Then find the number of the question on your answer sheet and mark your answer. The statements will not be printed in your test book and will be spoken only one time.

1

2

3

4

5

6

Play Track 18 for Test 5, Part II

PART II: QUESTION RESPONSE

Directions: You will hear a question or statement and three responses spoken in English. They will not be printed in your test book and will be spoken only one time. Select the best response to the question or statement and mark the letter A, B, or C on your answer sheet.

7	Mark your answer on your answer sheet.	20	Mark your answer on your answer sheet.
8	Mark your answer on your answer sheet.	21	Mark your answer on your answer sheet.
9	Mark your answer on your answer sheet.	22	Mark your answer on your answer sheet.
10	Mark your answer on your answer sheet.	23	Mark your answer on your answer sheet.
11	Mark your answer on your answer sheet.	24	Mark your answer on your answer sheet.
12	Mark your answer on your answer sheet.	25	Mark your answer on your answer sheet.
13	Mark your answer on your answer sheet.	26	Mark your answer on your answer sheet.
14	Mark your answer on your answer sheet.	27	Mark your answer on your answer sheet.
15	Mark your answer on your answer sheet.	28	Mark your answer on your answer sheet.
16	Mark your answer on your answer sheet.	29	Mark your answer on your answer sheet.
17	Mark your answer on your answer sheet.	30	Mark your answer on your answer sheet.
18	Mark your answer on your answer sheet.	31	Mark your answer on your answer sheet.
19	Mark your answer on your answer sheet.		

Play Track 19 for Test 5, Part III

PART III: SHORT CONVERSATIONS

Directions: You will hear some conversations between two people. You will be asked to answer three questions about what the speakers say in each conversation. Select the best response to each question and mark the letter (A), (B), (C), or (D) on your answer sheet. The conversation will not be printed in your test book and will be spoken only one time.

32 What is the man looking for?

- **A** car keys
- **B** a jacket
- **C** a cell phone
- **D** movie tickets

33 What does the woman say about the tickets?

- **A** They don't need them.
- **B** She can print another copy.
- **C** He might have left them in the taxi.
- **D** They were quite expensive.

34 Why is the woman in a hurry?

- **A** They have people waiting for them.
- **B** She doesn't like being late.
- **C** He's worried the taxi may leave without them.
- **D** Their friends are outside.

35 Why is the woman unhappy?

- **A** She thinks the problem is too big to be solved.
- **B** She doesn't want to get a quote for the job.
- **C** She thinks Mr. Wells is not reliable.
- **D** She needs to get the job done before Friday.

36 When did Mr. Wells have a problem with his vehicle?

- **A** Monday
- **B** Tuesday
- **C** Wednesday
- **D** Friday

37 What problem does the woman have?

- **A** One of the doors is not working.
- **B** She can't find her plumber.
- **C** The men are not available.
- **D** There's a leak in her office.

38 What does Gabriela say about her work?

- **A** She loves the atmosphere in Buenos Aires.
- **B** She has two new clients.
- **C** Her competitors are very powerful.
- **D** She misses Denver.

39 What does the man mean when he says "I miss the buzz of setting up a new office"?

- **A** He misses working in different places.
- **B** He misses the excitement of a new challenge.
- **C** He misses decorating new offices.
- **D** He misses traveling to new places.

40 What does the man say about the presentation?

A He left Gabriela alone because his first child was born.

B They were struggling to get through to the clients

C It was a successful presentation he'll never forget.

D He wishes he hadn't missed her presentation.

41 What do they say about Jackie?

A She opened her own restaurant.

B She wants to go out with them.

C She doesn't want to see Fiona because they had an argument.

D She really liked one of the dishes from the new restaurant.

42 When do they agree to meet?

A 12:30 pm.

B 1:00 p.m.

C 1:30 p.m.

D 2:00 p.m.

43 Where are they going together?

A to an Italian restaurant

B to see Fiona from IT

C to talk to Manuel

D to Helsinki

44 Why is Boris upset?

A Two of his clients have left him.

B His commission has been reduced to 20%.

C His new manager is taking his clients from him.

D Clara broke up with him.

45 What does the woman think Boris should do?

A talk to the board

B discuss the problem with Clara

C talk to his manager

D send an email to Mr. Fernandez

46 When did the problem start?

A after the merger

B in July

C after Clara's promotion

D last week

47 What does the woman say about her company?

A They're having financial difficulties.

B It's a very small company.

C It has a small budget.

D It's exploring a new market.

48 Where are her clients staying?

A in Maryland

B at the Royal Bath

C at the Shelton

D near the airport

49 Look at the fare prices below. Which type of vehicle does the woman choose?

A Economy

B Standard

C Luxury

D Premium

Class	Fare	Passengers Per Vehicle
Economy	$50	3
Standard	$75	4
Luxury	$100	4
Premium	$250	12

50 Who are they going to meet?

   A Murilo

   B Claire

   C Chuck

   D Mrs. Walcott

51 Where do the men work?

   A in finances

   B in reception

   C in the warehouse

   D in IT

52 Where will the speakers go?

   A to Claire's office

   B to a meeting

   C to the main reception

   D to the warehouse

53 What does the man think about Mr. Honda's email?

   A He disagrees with it.

   B He's not sure that what he proposes is a good idea.

   C It's frustrating.

   D He approves of the idea.

54 What does the man mean when he says "I'm just worried what our customers might think when the word gets out"?

   A He's worried about how customers will react once they learn their products are not manufactured in the US.

   B He's worried they will lose customers because of their advertising campaign.

   C He's worried customers will disapprove of the new designs.

   D He's worried customers will think their products are more expensive but not better quality.

55 What does the woman think about Mr. Honda's idea?

   A She thinks it's a great idea.

   B She thinks it's too risky.

   C She believes Mr. Honda has considered both the advantages and disadvantages.

   D She believes Mr. Honda is making a big mistake.

56 What do we learn from the conversation?

   A They're in the middle of a presentation.

   B The presentation is late because of a technical problem.

   C The woman has a lot of work to do before the end of the day.

   D The woman works in compliances.

57 What do they NOT say about their company?

   A They need to hire more staff.

   B They need to update their sales software.

   C The need more young people in management positions.

   D They still have fax machines.

58 What does the woman say about Mrs. Pollain?

   A She's old-fashioned.

   B She's frugal.

   C She's an excellent saleswoman.

   D She doesn't respect traditional values.

59 What does the woman say about Mrs. Kournikova?

   A She doesn't return calls.

   B She'll reply to his email later.

   C She's going away on Tuesday.

   D She's away from the office.

60 What does the man say about the event?

    A He's happy with the food and drink.

    B He needs a confirmation email from guests.

    C He thinks it should be moved to morning time.

    D He thinks there are too many people coming.

61 Look at the graphic below. Which movie festival is the man talking about?

    A The Manhatten Movie Awards

    B The Santa Fe Movie Festival

    C The Albuquerque Movie Festival

    D The Pennsylvania Movie Awards

Manhattan Movie Awards	Friday March 23 8 p.m.	100–200 guests
Santa Fe Movie Festival	Saturday March 24 10 a.m.	200–300 guests
Albuquerque Movie Festival	Saturday March 24 7:30 p.m.	200–300 guests
Pennsylvania Movie Awards	Sunday March 25 11 a.m.	50–80 guests

62 Where did the man put the boxes?

    A In the woman's office, behind her door

    B In the woman's office, opposite the side door

    C In another room next to the woman's office

    D In his office

63 What does the woman say about her own office?

    A It's too small for her.

    B It's too big for her.

    C She is cleaning it tomorrow.

    D It's cluttered and it needs to be sorted out.

64 What will happen at 7?

    A Cocktails will be served.

    B The boxes will be delivered.

    C The presentation will start.

    D The presentation will be over.

65 Who thinks the rooms should not be cleaned?

    A Mrs. Zhang

    B Mr. Cooper

    C Lucas

    D Mr. Beech

66 What does Mrs. Zhang say about the rooms?

    A The furniture is broken.

    B They haven't been cleaned.

    C She'll clean them herself.

    D She thinks they need renovating.

67 What does Mrs. Zhang say she's going to do?

    A She's going to talk to Mr. Beech.

    B She's going to call Lucas.

    C She's going to postpone one of the talks.

    D She's going to use one of the rooms during the conference.

68 What are the speakers discussing?

    A a meeting with a supervisor

    B the location of a meeting

    C the materials for a presentation

    D a new project design

69 What time is the visitor more likely to arrive?

    A 8:30–10:00 A.M.

    B 10:00–11:30 A.M.

    C 11:30–1:00 P.M.

    D 1:00–2:30 P.M.

70 Why is the woman worried?

    A She lives in Denver.

    B She has a busy schedule.

    C There aren't many plants in the office.

    D Some of the machines aren't working.

Play Track 20 for Test 5, Part IV

PART IV: SHORT TALKS

Directions: You will hear some talks given by one speaker. You will be asked to answer three questions about what the speaker says in each talk. Select the best response to each question and mark the letter (A), (B), (C), or (D) on your answer sheet. The conversation will not be printed in your test book and will be spoken only one time.

71 Why is Mrs. Hildenberg in Minnesota?

- **A** to lead a new marketing campaign
- **B** to learn more about local projects
- **C** to launch a new line of kitchen appliances
- **D** to lead a brainstorming session

72 What is Auntie Bella known for?

- **A** food
- **B** kitchen appliances
- **C** business strategies
- **D** business model

73 What does the woman say about their previous marketing campaign?

- **A** It didn't emphasize the quality of their products.
- **B** It should have paid more attention to looks and design.
- **C** It cost too much.
- **D** It was a huge success.

74 What is Luxville?

- **A** a movie
- **B** a shopping mall
- **C** a restaurant
- **D** a café

75 How does the woman describe Gigi Giglio?

- **A** a respected European brand
- **B** luxurious
- **C** the highlight of the opening party
- **D** overpriced

76 Which of the following is NOT mentioned in the news report?

- **A** who is responsible for the project
- **B** how Gigi feels about the US
- **C** how followers of fashion call Gigi's designs
- **D** the other shops Gigi is opening

77 Why was Susie arrested?

- **A** She had been stealing tablet computers from supermarkets.
- **B** She had been stealing information from personal accounts on different auction websites.
- **C** She attacked a man in a parking lot and stole his tablet computer.
- **D** She had been selling fake products.

78 Which of the following is true about Susie?

- **A** She met her victims in person.
- **B** She had been doing the same thing for 15 years before she got arrested.
- **C** She always lured her victims to a super-market parking lot.
- **D** She might spend up to 30 years in jail.

79 What is the best description of Susie according to the news report?

- **A** a violent person
- **B** a dangerous criminal
- **C** a person who cheats and deceives people
- **D** a person who smuggles goods

80 Who is a musician?

   A   Maurizio Biglia

   B   Amy Cartagena

   C   Ananda Prasit

   D   Bob Jones

81 What does the man say about the event?

   A   It's a photography exhibition.

   B   It's a small rock concert.

   C   People don't know exactly what they'll see there.

   D   It's a private party.

82 How do Ananda and Bob know each other?

   A   They were together in a band.

   B   They've know each other since they were children.

   C   They are cousins.

   D   They went to the same school.

83 Which number should someone looking to buy Euros press?

   A   1

   B   2

   C   3

   D   4

84 What does the message say about bank fraud?

   A   A number of Americans have been affected

   B   It has never happened to OneBank's customers.

   C   The number of cases has increased by 5%.

   D   It might ruin your vacations.

85 What's EasySave?

   A   a type of savings account

   B   a type of loan

   C   their most popular mortgage product

   D   OneBank's main competitor

86 What's the purpose of the message?

   A   to obtain information about a new insurance policy

   B   to verify personal information before processing a claim

   C   to make an insurance claim

   D   to check personal details to renew an insurance policy

87 Which of the following is NOT mentioned in the message?

   A   Mr. Lizaru's full name

   B   the speaker's full name

   C   the purpose of the call

   D   the speaker's contact details

88 Look at the graphic below. Which policy is more likely to be Mr. Lizaru's?

Policy # / Information	#99653	#99747	#99771	#99823
Current Address	√	√		
Contact Details		√	√	
Premium	√		√	√
Deadline	April 4	April 14	April 4	April 14

   A   #99653

   B   #99747

   C   #99771

   D   #99823

89 What does the man say about Mr. Hudson?

   A He retired two months ago.

   B He's the future chairman of DigiWorld.

   C He created the DigiWorld app.

   D He turned DigiWorld into a big company.

90 What does the man mean when he says "Who would be able to fill the shoes of the man"?

   A He's asking who could do the job as well as Mr Hudson.

   B He wants to know who the next director is going to be.

   C He's asking who would like to be a chairman in the future.

   D He wants to know which of the directors would make the best chairman.

91 What do we know about Ms. Flores?

   A She wants to be chairman in the future.

   B She helped DigiWorld reach small companies around the world.

   C She's responsible for updating the DigiWorld app.

   D She's Mr. Hudson's personal assistant.

92 What is the purpose of the announcement?

   A to inform passengers their flight has been delayed

   B to inform passengers their flight has been cancelled

   C to inform passengers their flight is now boarding

   D to inform passengers that the gate is now closed

93 Where's the announcement taking place?

   A in London

   B in Dublin

   C in Moscow

   D in Saudi Arabia

94 Which of the following is NOT mentioned in the announcement?

   A the flight destination

   B weather conditions in London Heathrow

   C how long the flight is

   D where the aircraft is

95 How does Alan describe Ibiza?

   A beautiful but expensive

   B beautiful and full of energy and life

   C quiet and isolated

   D noisy and not restful

96 What does the man mean when he says "where fun is as certain as death and taxes"?

   A He's saying that having fun in Ibiza is inevitable.

   B He's saying that most people who go to Ibiza have a wonderful time.

   C He's saying that it's cheaper to have fun in Ibiza because the island is tax free.

   D He's saying that there are different ways of having fun in Ibiza.

97 Which of the following is NOT mentioned in the talk?

   A who the passengers are

   B the name of the hotel where they're staying

   C different things people can do in Ibiza

   D what to do with their bags once they arrive at the hotel

98 Why are staff being asked to evacuate the building?

   A   There's a fire.

   B   Machinery in part of the warehouse is malfunctioning.

   C   There's an armed intruder in the building.

   D   It's an evacuation drill.

99 Where's the meeting point?

   A   a parking lot opposite the main building

   B   a parking lot behind the main building

   C   Warehouses A1, A2 and A3

   D   Warehouses B1 and B2

100 Look at the graphic below. Which department is being asked to evacuate the building?

   A   Logistics

   B   Assembly

   C   Sales

   D   Management

Department Areas	
Warehouses A1/A2/A3	**Logistics**
Warehouses B1/B2	**Assembly**
Main Building Floors 1-2	**Sales**
Main Building Floor 3	**Management**

READING TEST

In this section of the test, you will show your knowledge of written English. This section has three parts, and you have 75 minutes to complete all three sections. Directions are given for each individual part of the test. Mark your answers on the answer sheet provided.

PART V: INCOMPLETE SENTENCES

Directions: complete the following sentences using one of the four answer choices provided. Mark the answer **A, B, C** or **D** on your answer sheet.

101 It's about time employees _____ their terms of employment.

   A review

   B to review

   C reviewing

   D reviewed

102 Moving production to another plant is not an _____ at the moment.

   A option

   B optional

   C options

   D optionally

103 They _____ a huge profit last semester.

   A made

   B bought

   C had

   D did

104 Mrs. Lindgard works for one of the biggest _____ agencies in California.

   A recruit

   B recruiting

   C recruited

   D recruitment

105 The board _____ our future tomorrow.

   A have decided

   B will be deciding

   C will be decided

   D had decided

106 The CEO is on the verge _____ resigning from his position.

   A to

   B of

   C in

   D on

107 They _____ not expected to come to the meeting next week.

   A are

   B will

   C may

   D do

108 Donations have _____ in after the new celebrity campaign.

   A flooded

   B rained

   C snowed

   D stormed

109 All staff certificates and résumés are _____ in the system.

A store

B stored

C storing

D stores

110 The library is located _____ the second floor of the main building.

A in

B at

C on

D by

111 This is _____ year this office has ever seen.

A busy

B busier

C the busiest

D as busy as

112 _____ marketing works really hard, the sales team doesn't help much.

A Even though

B As soon as

C Unless

D However

113 There are still _____ issues we need to discuss.

A a few

B a little

C a lot

D very

114 Prof. Ranieri is seen _____ one of the most influential linguists in Europe.

A like

B as

C for

D how

115 Can you get me some stamps if you go to the post _____ ?

A box

B office

C service

D mail

116 The engineers have worked _____ hard to deliver this project in time.

A incredible

B incredibly

C more incredible

D credibility

117 The mayor _____ resigned after the tax scandal.

A should

B should be

C should have

D should get

118 Mrs. Takeda has worked for Eco International _____ she graduated in 1999.

A since

B for

C when

D from

119 Bankruptcy is only a _____ of time.

A problem

B issue

C concern

D matter

120 Cynthia _____ married for 12 years before she divorced last year.

A will be

B is

C has been

D had been

121 All their bad decisions will ultimately _____ to huge losses.

   A lead

   B result

   C end

   D make

122 The presentation has been cancelled _____ a power cut.

   A because

   B as

   C due to

   D as a result

123 _____ the firemen not arrived in time, many would have died.

   A If

   B Imagine

   C Should

   D Had

124 Employees _____ to be given a 30-minute break every four hours.

   A should

   B must

   C might

   D ought

125 The interns have been _____ selected by HR.

   A care

   B careful

   C careless

   D carefully

126 Her line manager, to _____ she had reported the problem, looked into the matter later that day.

   A who

   B whom

   C that

   D which

127 Staff _____ wear badges here at TGF Ltd.

   A do not need

   B does not need

   C need not

   D need

128 You need to log on _____ gain access to the database.

   A due to

   B in order to

   C so as it

   D for

129 Does anybody happen to know whose cell phone _____ ?

   A that is

   B that's

   C is that

   D that

130 Could you _____ me a hand with these boxes?

   A take

   B do

   C borrow

   D give

PART VI: TEXT COMPLETION

Directions: Read the following texts and select the best answer choice to complete the text.. Mark the answer **A, B, C** or **D** on your answer sheet.

Questions 131–134 refer to the report that follows.

Public Transport in the New Factory Area

The aim of this report is to look at the _____ in the area where our new factory is
                                          131.
located. The area benefits from both bus and tram services.

Traveling around the area is relatively easy due to the great number of bus and tram routes.
However, factory workers have suggested that even though tram services are reliable,
they are considered too expensive. Buses are the most economic option but, _____,
                                                                            132.
the majority of people have complained that they are never on time and are always
overcrowded.

We believe it is necessary to improve the transport system in the area _____ working
                                                                        133.
in partnership with the local government and bus and tram companies. An _____ in
                                                                         134.
the number of buses that serve the area or a monthly tram pass would make transport both
cheaper and more comfortable for the workers.

---

131 A transport ways

    B means of transport

    C method transport

    D transport roads

132 A fortunately

    B luckily

    C unfortunate

    D unfortunately

133 A by

    B for

    C at

    D on

134 A increase

    B increased

    C increasing

    D increasingly

Questions 135–138 refer to the following email

To:	lukbaba@mailnet.com
From:	recruitment@bankamerica.com
Date:	June 22, 2018
Subject:	Compliance Operations – Arban Luk

Dear Arban Luk

Thank you for expressing interest in the Compliance Operations – Disclosure Assistant position. We have received your profile and are _____ reviewing it.
135.

Please **click here** if you would like to review your profile.

Please note, your information will be stored in our database and, _____ specified
136.
during your application, will only be matched to jobs in Europe, North America and Japan. If your experience and qualifications _____ to our requirements, a member of
137.
human resources will contact you soon for a telephone interview.

_____
138.

Yours sincerely,

Janice Taylor

Human Resources Department

Bank of North America

135 **A** actually

B decisively

C currently

D proudly

136 **A** although

B despite

C in addition

D unless

137 **A** correspond

B akin

C resemble

D compare

138 **A** We look forward to hearing back from you.

B We thank you for your interest.

C We truly appreciate your collaboration.

D Let's keep in touch for the time being.

Questions 139–142 refer to the job ad that follows.

Personal Assistant

Paper World is seeking an individual to work as a PA to the managing director. We are looking for an individual who is _____ of dealing with various administrative
139.
situations in the director's absence and is _____ to take decisions on the director's
140.
behalf when required. Confidentiality is a fundamental _____ of this position, which
141.
requires building a strategic partnership with the managing director in order to achieve the organization's goals and the MD's short-term objectives.

We are looking for an individual with advanced skills in word processing and slideshows and at least an intermediate _____ of digital spreadsheets.
142.

---

139   **A**   able

      B   good

      C   capable

      D   interested

140   **A**   enough confidence

      B   too confident

      C   confident enough

      D   plenty of confidence

141   **A**   necessity

      B   requirement

      C   option

      D   obligation

142   **A**   ability

      B   skill

      C   fluency

      D   knowledge

Questions 143–146 refer to the following message.

Thank you, your grant application _____ . Now carefully follow these final steps so you
143.
know what you must do next.

1. Your unique reference number is provided below. _____ . You will need this number if
144.
you want to log in again to the university website and access your online application.

CU094851

2. A confirmation has been sent to your email address. Please note that if you do not receive
this email message it may be because you provided us with an incorrect email address or it
was incorrectly identified as junk mail. For this reason, we recommend that you take note of
the details shown here.

3. You should print your online forms for future reference. If you do not currently_____
145.
access to a printer, you can log in to your completed application again for the next seven
days, using the application security details you provided at the beginning. _____, you
146.
will also need to use your unique application reference number above.

---

143 **A** has been submitted successfully

B will not be able to proceed to the next stage

C has unfortunately been denied

D can now be applied for

144 **A** Please keep it safe for reference

B Please contact us should you require one

C Do not apply unless you are certain

D Please take two before breakfast

145 **A** gain

B obtain

C have

D buy

146 **A** For this reason

B However

C Having said that

D To do this

PART VII: READING COMPREHENSION

Directions: In this part of the test, you will read a number of different texts and then answer several questions about each text. Mark the answer **A, B, C** or **D** on your answer sheet.

Questions 147–149 refer to the following email.

To:	tadeshi78@mailnet.com
From:	contact@travelnetplus.com
Date:	January 22, 2018
Subject:	Inquiry – Mr. Tadeshi Nagamoto

Dear Mr. Tadeshi,

— [1] —

Warm greetings from TravelNetPlus.

Thank you for choosing us as your vacation provider.

— [2] —

Regarding your inquiries for the San Marco Resort (seven nights):

- All room types are available from March 26
- Premier Suite rate is $223.99 per night
- Family Room rate is $277.99 per night
- Family Premium Chalet is $597.99 per night
- Breakfast is included
- All rooms are wheelchair accessible
- Please find attached a file regarding the services and facilities at San Marco.

— [3] —

Book now!!!

— [4] —

Should you have any further inquiries, please do not hesitate to contact us.

Kind Regards,

Wilson Smith – Sales Consultant

147 What do we learn about the San Marco Resort?

A   It has three different room types.

B   Some of the rooms are not wheelchair accessible.

C   Families must stay in a chalet.

D   Room service is not available.

148 Which information has NOT been sent in the email?

A   room rates

B   hotel facilities

C   reservation fees

D   room availability

149 In which of the positions marked [1], [2], [3] and [4] does the following sentence best belong?

"If you would like to make a reservation, please click on the following link and choose your room type."

A   [1]

B   [2]

C   [3]

D   [4]

Questions 150–151 refer to the following memo.

To: All Staff

From: HR Department

The company annual meeting will be held on Friday April 13 at 4 p.m. in the main auditorium at The Benevue Hotel. Drinks and snacks will be offered at the bar after 6 p.m. All employees are asked to attend and bring a copy of their appraisal forms. Please contact your department heads should you require any further information.

150 What can be concluded from the memo?

A   The annual meeting happens every April at the Benevue Hotel.

B   Staff should confirm their presence with their department heads.

C   Dinner will be served after the meeting.

D   Attendance is compulsory.

151 What should staff take to the meeting?

A   drinks and snacks

B   friends and family

C   a copy of their résumés

D   their appraisal forms

Questions 152–154 refer to the letter that follows.

Mr. José Nogueira

99 Biscayne Blvd.

Miami, FL 33132

July 08, 2017

— [1] —

Dear Mr. Nogueira,

— [2] — Under the terms of your policy, outdoor water and gas pipes are not covered unless they run between different rooms within the property. — [3] —Your claim refers to the main water pipe so I suggest you contact your water supplier. — [4] — .

Claims Department

Master Insurance

152 What do we know about Mr. Nogueira?

A He has some problems with his car insurance.

B He had a problem with a water pipe.

C He sells insurance.

D He needs new gas pipes.

153 What does the letter recommend?

A contacting the insurance company

B revising his policy

C getting in touch with his water supplier

D making a new claim

154 In which of the positions marked [1], [2], [3] and [4] does the following sentence best belong?

"We regret to inform that your insurance claim reference number MI33865-4 has been denied."

A [1]

B [2]

C [3]

D [4]

Questions 155–158 refer to the article that follows.

Personal Trainer Jailed

A personal trainer who lived an extravagant lifestyle has been jailed for drug dealing, money laundering and fraud. — [1] — The 27-year-old, whose name will not be revealed due to ongoing investigations, was also found in possession of criminal property and weapons.

— [2] — Officers received information that a Rawrano Race Car had been obtained from a car dealer in Beverly Hills by deception in October 2016. After making further enquiries, federal agents located and seized the vehicle from the personal trainer's father in San Antonio, Texas.

— [3] —

The personal trainer was later arrested on suspicion of possession with intent to supply illegal drugs, which were found inside soup cans stored in the garage of his house.

— [4] —

---

155 What does the text mean by "who lived an extravagant lifestyle"?

A The man spent more money than he had.

B The man spent a lot of money on luxury items.

C The man borrowed money to buy things he didn't need.

D His lifestyle impressed his neighbors.

156 What does the article say about the Rawrano Race Car?

A It was found in Beverly Hills.

B It cost the man a fortune.

C The man's father had it.

D It hasn't been located yet.

157 Which of the following is the personal trainer NOT being accused of?

A murder

B fraud

C money laundering

D drug dealing

158 In which of the positions marked [1], [2], [3] and [4] does the following sentence best belong?
"The man pleaded guilty to all of the above offences at trial."

A [1]

B [2]

C [3]

D [4]

Questions 159–161 refer to the schedule that follows.

Tuesday April 10	
08:00–08:30	Registration Desk Open
08:45–09:30	Opening Announcements and Plenary Session
09:30–10:00	Coffee Break
10:00–10:45	Session 1–The Past, Present and Future of Graphic Design
10:45–11:30	Session 2–Breaking the Monotony of the Working Environment
11:30–12:15	Session 3–Developing Autonomous Designers through Project Work.
12:15–1:30	Lunch
1:30–2:15	Session 4–The Impact of Graphics Design in Advertising
2:15–3:00	Session 5–Real Challenges of the Profession
3:00–3:30	Drinks and Networking

159 Who is most likely to be attending the conference?

A university students

B graphic designers

C IT professionals

D advertising students

160 Which session can help people who might be bored at work?

A session 1

B session 2

C session 3

D session 4

161 Which of the following is NOT mentioned in the schedule?

A when people can register

B session speakers

C the topics of each session

D break times

Questions 162–165 refer to following email.

To:	maynard@creativemindco.com
From:	debbieadams@temail.com
Date:	April 08, 2018
Subject:	Junior Marketing Assistant Post

Dear Ms. Maynard,

— [1] — I recently applied for a job opening at Creative Minds for the position of junior marketing assistant on your online career site. — [2] —. You can learn more about me by viewing my BusinessLink Profile: www.businesslink/users/75735r688226.

I have been following you on BusinessLink for some time, and truly appreciated your recent article on digital marketing and the valuable resources you are providing for job seekers like me.

I'd love to set up a time to schedule a call and talk about the position and my experience. — [3] — I have some availability on Tuesdays and Thursdays after 3 p.m., but I am confident I can manage to talk to you at another time if these options are not convenient. — [4] — You can email me at debbieadams@email.com or call me at 555-6510. I look forward to scheduling some time with you.

Sincerely,
Deborah Maple-Adams

162 What is the purpose of this email?

A   to apply for the position of junior market-ing assistant

B   to learn more about a position she might apply for

C   to reinforce her interest in joining the company

D   to offer Ms. Maynard the junior marketing assistant position

163 Who is offering the junior marketing assistant position?

A   Creative Minds

B   BusinessLink

C   different online career sites

D   Deborah's company

164 What does Deborah say about Ms. Maynard?

A   Deborah liked one of her articles.

B   Ms. Maynard doesn't like being followed.

C   They've known each other for a long time.

D   Ms. Maynard has a busy schedule.

165 In which of the positions marked [1], [2], [3] and [4] does the following sentence best belong?

"I believe the position aligns perfectly with my experience and qualifications."

A   [1]

B   [2]

C   [3]

D   [4]

Questions 166–168 refer to the following article.

There has been an increase of nearly 10% in the number of vegetarians amongst teenagers over the last three years according to a new study published by the University of Rononda.

This has been attributed to the number of social media activists protesting against meat consumption and animal cruelty. There also has been a large number of teen celebrities, YouTubers and bloggers defending vegetarianism and veganism as a more environmentally friendly lifestyle.

The Animal Farming Association is planning to develop materials that explain how organic meat from local farms can also be considered eco-friendly in an attempt to reestablish the image of a sector which has been the victim of many protests in recent months.

166 Which of the following is stated about teenagers in the article?

A   Less than 10% are vegetarian.

B   The number of vegetarians has increased.

C   Many support animal cruelty.

D   They're organizing a protest.

167 Why does the article say teenagers are changing their eating habits?

A   influence from peers

B   a healthier lifestyle

C   the economy

D   their parents

168 Who is trying to change what others think of them?

A   teenagers

B   social media activists

C   YouTubers and bloggers

D   The Animal Farming Association

Questions 169–171 refer to the following pamphlet.

Money Saving Tips from Cell 121

— [1] — Welcome to our second top tips email, we hope you found the first one useful. Here you'll find some more useful tips on how to save money on your calls and get the most out of your cell phone. Save up to $32 a year by setting up online billing, where you can view your bills and see any payments you've made. Simply update your preferences in My Account and start saving today. — [2] —

Another great idea is to **set up a calling circle**. Enjoy a 15% savings on up to 20 phone numbers including international and cell phone numbers. It won't cost you a dime and you can start saving immediately! — [3] —

And why not get the **calling features**? The Calling Features package includes a bundle of useful features so you'll never miss a call again. — [4] —.

Cell 121–Your last cell phone provider

---

169 How much can one save by not receiving paper bills?

A $32 a year

B   15%

C   15–20%

D   More than $300 in a year

170 What does the text mean when it says "It won't cost you a dime"?

A   It's free to set up a calling circle.

B   It's cheap to join a calling circle.

C   There's a fee to join a calling circle.

D   Some calls are free when you join a calling circle.

171 In which of the positions marked [1], [2], [3] and [4] does the following sentence best belong?

"Features include call divert, call waiting and our special reminder call."

A   [1]

B   [2]

C   [3]

D   [4]

Questions 172–173 refer to the email that follows.

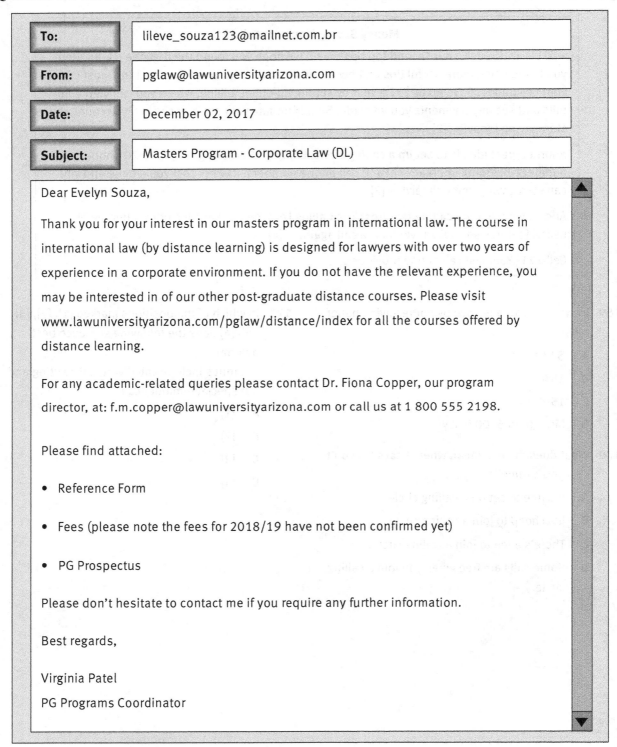

To: lileve_souza123@mailnet.com.br

From: pglaw@lawuniversityarizona.com

Date: December 02, 2017

Subject: Masters Program - Corporate Law (DL)

Dear Evelyn Souza,

Thank you for your interest in our masters program in international law. The course in international law (by distance learning) is designed for lawyers with over two years of experience in a corporate environment. If you do not have the relevant experience, you may be interested in of our other post-graduate distance courses. Please visit www.lawuniversityarizona.com/pglaw/distance/index for all the courses offered by distance learning.

For any academic-related queries please contact Dr. Fiona Copper, our program director, at: f.m.copper@lawuniversityarizona.com or call us at 1 800 555 2198.

Please find attached:

• Reference Form

• Fees (please note the fees for 2018/19 have not been confirmed yet)

• PG Prospectus

Please don't hesitate to contact me if you require any further information.

Best regards,

Virginia Patel
PG Programs Coordinator

172 Which of the following is a requirement to attend the course Evelyn is interested in?

   A having a master's degree

   B being a lawyer

   C experience working in the field

   D having a degree in international law

173 Which of the following is NOT included in the email?

   A a reference form

   B details of the program director

   C course fees for 2018/19

   D PG prospectus

Questions 174–175 refer to the following job advertisement.

Assistant Architect

— [1] —

We are looking for an architect with minimum two years' experience with the ability to work in a team environment. The applicant should have excellent design skills and a vast working knowledge of building and planning regulations. They must also have a proven flair for creativity and innovation.

— [2] —

The ability to work on a range of modern building projects.

Proficiency in Autocad is required.

— [3] —

The successful candidate will have the opportunity to expand their skills and experiences by working with a renowned senior architect.

— [4] —

---

174 Which of the following is least likely to get the position?

   A a young creative architect that enjoys working in teams

   B an experienced architect who solely works with vintage and traditional projects.

   C an architect with a particular interest in town planning

   D an innovative architect who is very good with computers

175 In which of the positions marked [1], [2], [3] and [4] does the following phrase best belong? "Job Requirements"

   A [1]

   B [2]

   C [3]

   D [4]

Questions 176–180 refer to the following text message chain and email.

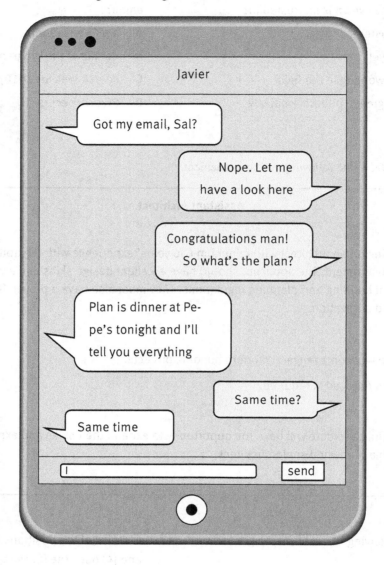

To:	salomong88@email.com, marijoviedo@mailnet.com
From:	fernandez_us@email.com
Date:	May 31, 2017
Subject:	FW: Application Status: J. Fernandez, Bid Writer

Hi Sal, Hi Mari:

— [1] — Take a look at this! Thanks so much for your help with the application, I owe you big time.

Original Message

To: fernandez_us@email.com

From: youth@lagalaxy.com

Subject: Trial with LA Galaxy – Dae-Jung Son

Dear Mr. Fernandez,

— [2] — After careful consideration we believe that your skills and professionalism would be a great addition to our team

Our director, Mr. Schmidt, was very impressed with your personal experience, as well as your knowledge of our company. We're really looking forward to see what you can do here

We will be contacting you later this week to set up a meeting with Mr. Schmidt, so you and he can talk through your new role personally. — [3] —

I am attaching information about our training schedule, new hiring documents, and probationary period terms, so that you understand a bit more about your role at the company over the first few months.

Please contact me if you have any questions. — [4] —

Pete Sanders

Recruitment

AOR Enterprise

176 Why does Javier text Sal?

   A to check if Sal read his email

   B to ask for help

   C He can't check his email.

   D to invite Sal for lunch

177 Which of the following gives the most likely reason for Javier writing "I owe you big time."

   A He is grateful for the opportunity Pete has given him.

   B He is thankful to Sal for lending him some money.

   C He is thankful to his friends for helping with his application.

   D He is thankful for the appreciation Mr. Schmidt has shown.

178 Who was impressed with Dae-Jung's experience?

   A Sal

   B Mr. Schmidt

   C Mari

   D Pete Sanders

179 Which of the following is NOT mentioned in either text?

   A Javier's plans for tonight

   B the salary for his new role

   C The title of the position Javier applied for

   D the reason he has been offered a job

180 In which of the positions marked [1], [2], [3] and [4] does the following phrase best belong? "Thank you for attending an interview for our advertised position."

   A [1]

   B [2]

   C [3]

   D [4]

Questions **181–185** refer to the following product review and text message chain.

★★★★★

This is the perfect kit for a first time printer builder. — [1] — All parts supplied are excellent quality and really well packaged. — [2] — The install time depends on the builder's knowledge, and the learning curve is not actually hard if you have the patience.

The frame is cut to the right length, making it perfectly square and easier for manual levelling.

TriD Prints's support staff are very helpful. — [3] — They helped me understand the system and sent me loads of information about how to make the best of my 3D printer.

Also, I considered many other printers and this one seemed to be the best option available within this price-range. — [4] — Five stars because I can't give six!

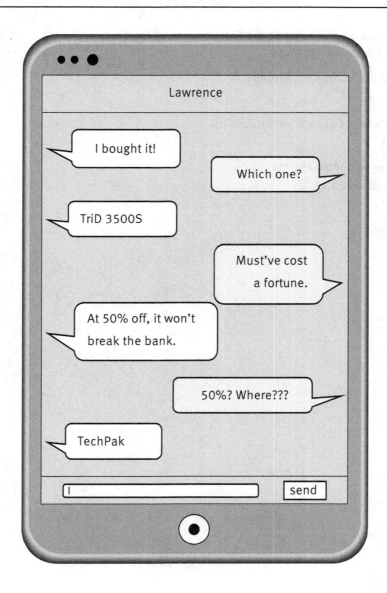

181 What does the review say about the product?

   A   It's not appropriate for beginners.

   B   The frame needs improving.

   C   Manual levelling is very helpful.

   D   It is the most cost-efficient on the market.

182 What can vary from one product buyer to another?

   A   the install time

   B   manual levelling

   C   the packaging

   D   performance

183 What does Lawrence mean when he says "At 50% off, it won't break the bank"?

   A   The discount is a unique opportunity.

   B   He can't afford it.

   C   He doesn't think it's expensive because of the discount.

   D   He won't have to borrow any money because of the discount.

184 Which of the following is NOT mentioned in either text?

   A   the price of the product

   B   some of the product's features

   C   the shop where he bought the printer

   D   the printer model

185 In which of the positions marked [1], [2], [3] and [4] does the following phrase best belong? "Before I go into detail, let me just say that I am so thrilled with my choice."

   A   [1]

   B   [2]

   C   [3]

   D   [4]

Questions 186–190 refer to the following notice, advertisement and article.

To all staff:

Our new line of products arrives in stores next week. Please check the staff catalog for full collection and product information. Customer catalogs will not be available for this collection, as these are no longer being produced. However, customers should be reassured that they can find all the information they need on our website and mobile app.

Management

Tired of the same, humdrum choices?

So are we! That's why Tiara's new summer collection was designed for the modern woman who likes to take risks. Our team of designers endured a long journey into the depths of the Brazilian rainforest in their search for inspiration. The results? New colors, new trends and new cuts waiting to be worn. Curious? Well, tomorrow's the day. Go to www.tiarabeachwear.com tomorrow after 12:00 a.m. and be the first to experience Tiara's new collection.

From the Jungle to Your Wardrobe
by Marisa Stones

It may not come as a surprise that the jungle offers fabulous fashion inspiration. — [1] — It is capable of giving old styles a reenergized look that conveys both nature and the wild. Designers from all over the world have explored this trend at one time or another. — [2] — However, such designs very rarely had the opportunity to leave the catwalk and be embraced by the public. Thank goodness that this is about to end.

— [3] —

From head-to-toe animal prints to crocodile camouflage gear with crocodile accessories, the new beachwear collection by Tiara is perfect for those who enjoy fun, exoticism and vibrancy. Fashion of this nature is not always available for everyday wardrobes, but Tiara has made this accessible as well as extravagant with this audacious new collection designed by Kevin Alonso and Osvaldo da Silva. The adaptable "Mother Nature" qualities and exoticism give the line a particular edge that make it perfect for both sunny days by the pool and nights in a cabana by the sea.

— [4] —

186 What does the notice say about customer catalogs?

   A They'll arrive later this year.

   B They have been discontinued.

   C They contain the full collection.

   D They have all the product information.

187 The word "humdrum" in the advertisement is closest in meaning to

   A different things.

   B old.

   C boring.

   D sleepy people.

188 What do we learn about the new collection?

   A It's made in Brazil.

   B It's inspired by modern women.

   C It's been created by a modern fashion designer.

   D It's considered wild and exotic.

189 Who's happy people will get to wear something that was exclusively for fashion models?

   A management

   B Marisa Stones

   C Kevin Alonso

   D Osvaldo da Silva

190 In which of the positions marked [1], [2], [3] and [4] does the following phrase best belong?

"The new Tiara collection will be available from May 1 in Tiara's stores across the country and also on their website, www.tiarabeachwear.com"

   A [1]

   B [2]

   C [3]

   D [4]

Questions 191–195 refer to the job ad, text message chain and email that follows.

Accounts Assistant

We are looking to recruit an accounts assistant to be based in our Manhattan North American headquarters. The accounts assistant will take responsibility for a number of key financial account processes for our growing business in the US.

This role involves working as one member of a two-person aggregation team within the central finance function of McQueen US. The successful candidate will be responsible for the production of financial documents, including statements and invoices, for the US mobile payments business.

This challenging and interesting position is available for an ambitious candidate who not only meets but exceeds the requirements. McQueen offers the opportunity to develop and progress while gaining formal qualifications within a fast growing company.

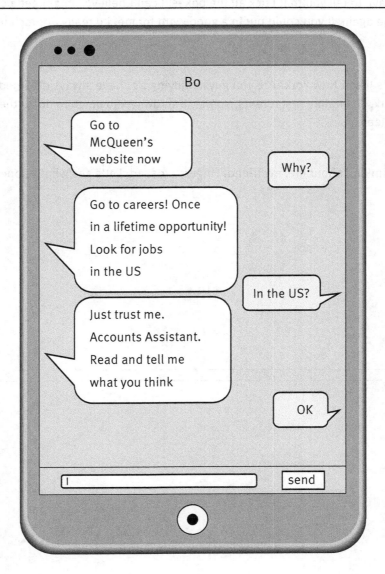

To:	bo_xing@mcqueenus.com
From:	samuelarnold_78@mailnet.com
Date:	May 31, 2017
Subject:	Accounts Assistant Position

Hi Bo,

— [1] —

I can't tell you how excited I am. Thank you so much for the referral. I have just applied for the position and I have to tell you that I tick all the boxes. I can't believe I might get a chance to work with you and Sue again. If you could put in a good word for me, I'd really appreciate it.

— [2] —

So tell me. How's life in New York? Are you guys enjoying it? I have always dreamed about living in New York. The Italian restaurants, sports, Broadway—so much to do all the time. The city that never sleeps.

Thank you for thinking about me, my friend. Fingers crossed. Let's see what happens.

— [3] —

A million thanks,

— [4] —

Samuel

191 Which of the following is true about the position offered by McQueen US?

    A Candidates must have at least two years' experience.

    B There are two positions available.

    C It involves traveling around North America.

    D It offers professional development opportunities.

192 Why does Bo text Samuel?

    A He thinks Samuel should apply for the job.

    B He wants Samuel to revise the text for him.

    C Bo wants to apply for the job.

    D Bo thinks Samuel could help him with the job.

193 What does Samuel mean when he says "I tick all the boxes"?

    A He completed the application form.

    B He meets all the job requirements.

    C There's nothing he would like more than this job.

    D He thinks he is better suited for the job than Bo.

194 What does Samuel say about New York?

    A He'd like to live there.

    B It's very big.

    C It's not easy to sleep in such a busy city.

    D There are too many Italian restaurants.

195 In which of the positions marked [1], [2], [3] and [4] does the following phrase best belong? "Miss you guys loads. Send my regards to Sue."

    A [1]

    B [2]

    C [3]

    D [4]

Questions 196–200 refer to the following advertisement, invoice and email.

Fun on the Go with the NX-SP2 Wireless Speaker

The NX-SP2 is compact, wireless and easy to move. With a long battery life lasting up to 16 hours and a water-resistant surface, you're free to take it with you anywhere. You can choose from a range of 6 different colors and connect up to six wireless speakers for stereo sound in different parts of the house or, if you prefer, party! And no Bluetooth hassle—connect your smartphone with One-touch technology and get the party going in an instant.

Tech Pak

125 Lakeside Drive

Orlando, FL 32805

Bill to	**Ship to**	**Invoice Date:** 12/12/17
Theo Collins	Noah Collins	
91 Amsterdam Avenue	5 Modern Red Square	
New York, NY 10023	Long Island City, NY 10022	

Qty.	Description	Unit Price	Amount
2	NX-SP2 Red	$44.00	$88.00
1	NX-SP2 Green	$44.00	$44.00
1	NX-SP2 Black	$44.00	$44.00
2	NX-SP2 Yellow	$39.60	$79.20

Subtotal		$255.20
Sales Tax 5.0%		$11.26
TOTAL		$236.46

To:	noahgunner@email.net
From:	theocollins10@email.net
Date:	December 13, 2017
Subject:	Speakers Christmas Party

Hi Noah

Bought those speakers we talked about last week. Got six of them so we could have a couple downstairs, two upstairs, and the other two on the terrace. Dad's gonna love it. Since Christmas's at yours this years, I asked them to deliver them to you. Should be with you in a couple of days. Just let me know when you get them.

As for the food, mom said she's going to make the turkey. I asked Bella to make the veggies so was wondering if you guys would make, or buy, desserts and stuff.

By the way, how's Livy doing? Did she like the ring? Bella was over the moon when I told her about the engagement.

Gotta go now - your nephew's up to no good. See you in a couple of weeks.

Love you

Theo

196 Which of the following is NOT a feature of the wireless speaker?

  A It's portable.

  B It can be connected to five other speakers.

  C It's water-resistant.

  D You can choose from twelve different colors.

197 Who bought the speakers and why?

  A Theo for the Christmas party

  B Noah to surprise his father

  C Theo for Noah's birthday

  D Noah as Christmas gift to his father

198 Which speakers were most likely on sale?

  A the red ones

  B the green ones

  C the black ones

  D the yellow ones

199 What does Theo mean when he says "desserts and stuff"?

  A different types of desserts

  B desserts or something else

  C desserts and other similar foods

  D desserts and drinks

200 Why was Bella happy?

  A because Noah and Livy are going to get married

  B She loves spending Christmas at Noah's.

  C She really wanted the wireless speakers.

  D She loves turkey.

TOEIC Listening and Reading Practice Test 6

LISTENING TEST

In this section of the test, you will show your knowledge of spoken English. This section has four parts, and the entire section will last for around 45 minutes. Directions are given for each individual part of the test. Mark your answers on the answer sheet provided. To listen to the audio tracks for this section of the test, access the tracks in your Online Resources, by visiting **www.kaptest.com/booksonline** OR through the Kaplan Study App.

 Play Track 21 for Test 6, Part I

PART I: PHOTOGRAPHS

Directions: For each question in this part, you will hear four statements about a picture in your test book. When you hear the statements, you must select the one statement that best describes what you see in the picture. Then find the number of the question on your answer sheet and mark your answer. The statements will not be printed in your test book and will be spoken only one time.

1

2

3

4

5

6

Play Track 22 for Test 6, Part II

PART II: QUESTION RESPONSE

Directions: You will hear a question or statement and three responses spoken in English. They will not be printed in your test book and will be spoken only one time. Select the best response to the question or statement and mark the letter A, B, or C on your answer sheet.

7	Mark your answer on your answer sheet.	20	Mark your answer on your answer sheet.
8	Mark your answer on your answer sheet.	21	Mark your answer on your answer sheet.
9	Mark your answer on your answer sheet.	22	Mark your answer on your answer sheet.
10	Mark your answer on your answer sheet.	23	Mark your answer on your answer sheet.
11	Mark your answer on your answer sheet.	24	Mark your answer on your answer sheet.
12	Mark your answer on your answer sheet.	25	Mark your answer on your answer sheet.
13	Mark your answer on your answer sheet.	26	Mark your answer on your answer sheet.
14	Mark your answer on your answer sheet.	27	Mark your answer on your answer sheet.
15	Mark your answer on your answer sheet.	28	Mark your answer on your answer sheet.
16	Mark your answer on your answer sheet.	29	Mark your answer on your answer sheet.
17	Mark your answer on your answer sheet.	30	Mark your answer on your answer sheet.
18	Mark your answer on your answer sheet.	31	Mark your answer on your answer sheet.
19	Mark your answer on your answer sheet.		

Play Track 23 for Test 6, Part III

PART III: SHORT CONVERSATIONS

Directions: You will hear some conversations between two people. You will be asked to answer three questions about what the speakers say in each conversation. Select the best response to each question and mark the letter (A), (B), (C), or (D) on your answer sheet. The conversation will not be printed in your test book and will be spoken only one time.

32 What is NOT true about the sweater?

    A It was picked by the man's wife.

    B The man was wearing it before his 10 a.m. meeting.

    C It was a birthday present.

    D It's blue and patterned.

33 Why does the woman say "Oh, I don't know about that"?

    A She doesn't know the answer.

    B She doesn't know where the sweater is.

    C She thinks someone might've stolen the sweater.

    D She doesn't know why things are going missing in the office.

34 How is the man likely to feel?

    A moody

    B grateful

    C tenacious

    D distressed

35 On which day are the man and woman going to the theater?

    A April 7th

    B April 13th

    C April 15th

    D April 22nd

36 Why does the man say "that sucks"?

    A The woman can't pay more than $100.

    B The woman can't come to the theater this month.

    C The woman is working a lot.

    D The show finishes on the 23rd.

37 Look at the graphic. Which seats do the man and woman select?

    A A13–A14

    B G19–G20

    C L4–L5

    D H11–H12

Fiddler on the Roof – Seats available	
A13–A14 (Orchestra Center)	$192.50
G19–G20 (Orchestra Center)	$67.50
L4–L5 (Orchestra Right)	$49.50
H11–H12 (Balcony)	$25.00

38 Where is this conversation likely to take place?

    A a college

    B a museum

    C an art gallery

    D a photography class

39 What is NOT TRUE about the woman?

    A She thinks her photographs are better.

    B She sells photographs.

    C She's a student.

    D She thinks the photographs are overrated.

40 What does the woman say "Yeah, I get that" about?

  A The men agree with each other.

  B The men disagree with her.

  C She understands why the photographs are so popular.

  D She understands the theme behind the photographs.

41 Why does the man need the woman's help?

  A He spilled tea on his laptop.

  B He can't locate a program he needs.

  C He needs a replacement laptop.

  D He doesn't know how to install Yellow Studio.

42 Why does the man say "oh, right"?

  A He understands now.

  B He remembered something.

  C He agrees with something.

  D He's being sarcastic.

43 What does the woman say about Andrew?

  A He gave her remote worker privileges.

  B He needs bribery to do anything.

  C He really likes chocolate.

  D He's a tricky person to deal with.

44 What is the conversation mainly about?

  A Mr. Renton's latest changes

  B where the staff will go for lunch

  C the team dinner last night

  D a new member of staff

45 What is the COO going to do?

  A Organize a dinner for the team.

  B Introduce new arrivals to the rest of the team.

  C Create longer working hours.

  D Remove lunch breaks.

46 What does the man disagree with the women about?

  A that the COO's changes will be a good thing

  B that the new COO is ruthless

  C that the COO is new

  D the date for the dinner

47 What kind of company is the woman likely to own?

  A website hosting services

  B a travel agency

  C security services

  D cobbling

48 Which of the following is NOT a perk of the Gold Plan?

  A tech support every day of the year

  B tech support during business hours only

  C more RAM

  D assistance with customizing the control panel

49 Look at the graph below. Which membership does the woman choose?

  A Basic

  B Bronze

  C Silver

  D Gold

MEMBERSHIP OPTIONS	
Basic Plan	Free
Bronze Plan	$6.99 per month
Silver Plan	$12.99 per month
Gold Plan	$29.99 per month

50 Why does the woman say "What's up"?

A She's asking how the man is.

B She's asking what's going on.

C She's asking why the man is sad.

D She's asking what the man's plans are.

51 What is the name of the man's contact in New York?

A Carol

B Alex

C Chris

D Agustin

52 Why does the man not want the woman to write an email for him?

A He's waiting for a phone call.

B He wants to write his own email.

C He doesn't know what to write in the email.

D He doesn't want the client to expect emails in Spanish.

53 Who are the speakers talking about?

A a national celebrity

B a mutual friend

C a co-worker

D a newspaper publisher

54 What does Bobby Edmonds plan to do?

A cover city politics

B stop writing a column

C pay his dues

D accept a new job

55 Where do the speakers work?

A at an online publication

B at city hall

C at an institution

D at a news stand

56 Where did the woman spend time during the summer?

A the Suzuki Building

B Los Angeles

C Colorado

D Arizona

57 What department does the woman work in?

A Finance and Accounting

B General operations

C Database management

D Food services

58 What do the speakers make plans to do?

A Study databases

B Eat lunch together

C Go on a trip

D Go to the eighteenth floor

59 Who currently teaches Crime and Media Representation?

A Professor Whitworth

B Professor Stone

C Professor Dominguez

D Professor Fuller

60 Look at the graphic below. Which elective module do the man and woman choose?

   A History of Crime and Punishment

   B Penology

   C Youth and Crime

   D Sociology of Violence

ELECTIVE MODULES

History of Crime and Punishment

Mondays, 9 a.m.–11 a.m.

Penology

Tuesdays, 9 a.m.–11 a.m.

Youth and Crime

Wednesdays, 11 a.m.–1 p.m.

Sociology of Violence

Thursdays, 5 p.m.–7 p.m.

---

61 What can be inferred from the conversation?

   A The man can't wait to graduate.

   B The woman doesn't like early morning classes.

   C The man and the woman are seniors.

   D The man has a job.

---

62 How long did it used to take the man to go to work?

   A 25 minutes

   B 40 minutes

   C 45 minutes

   D 50 minutes

63 What can be inferred from the conversation?

   A The man takes a car to work.

   B The man and the woman used to work together.

   C The man really likes his new colleagues.

   D The man finds his new colleagues too chatty.

64 Why does the man say "Tell me about it"?

   A He wants the woman to share something with him.

   B He agrees with the woman.

   C He disagrees with the woman.

   D He doesn't understand what the woman is talking about.

---

65 What problem does the man have?

   A He lost his credit card.

   B He is a victim of theft.

   C He misplaced his ATM card.

   D He has run out of money.

66 What does the man want to do?

   A purchase a new wallet

   B cancel his bank accounts

   C replace his cards

   D phone the police department

67 What does the man need to do next?

   A give his account numbers to the customer service person

   B thank the person and hang up the phone

   C hang up and look for his wallet on the subway

   D send a bank statement to the woman in the post

---

68 What can be inferred from the conversation?

A The woman recommended the book to the man.

B The woman didn't expect the man to like the book.

C The man thought the book was a slog.

D The man couldn't wait to finish the book.

69 Why is the man not into romance novels?

A He doesn't think they're good enough.

B He prefers literary fiction.

C He doesn't like the style of writing.

D They're not commercial enough.

70 What do the man and woman agree on?

A science fiction is better than romance novels.

B The prose in literary fiction is pompous.

C Science fiction is commercial fiction.

D The language in romance novels isn't simple.

Play Track 24 for Test 6, Part IV

PART IV: SHORT TALKS

Directions: You will hear some talks given by one speaker. You will be asked to answer three questions about what the speaker says in each talk. Select the best response to each question and mark the letter (A), (B), (C), or (D) on your answer sheet. The conversation will not be printed in your test book and will be spoken only one time.

71 Where are you most likely to hear this talk?

  A at a company

  B at a private function

  C at a table over dinner

  D at a graduation ceremony

72 What will happen next?

  A Janet Richardson will speak to the audience

  B the speaker will explain the plans for next year

  C students will speak to the audience

  D the speaker will explain why the school is life changing

73 What is the speaker doing?

  A thanking the audience

  B introducing Janet Richardson

  C bidding everyone goodnight

  D giving the first speech of the evening

74 What is the topic of this speech?

  A why most people are not in the right career

  B why we shouldn't listen to our parents when it comes to career paths

  C what makes people happy

  D how to identify the best career option

75 Which of the following is NOT a reason parents sometimes give the wrong advice?

  A They don't take a pragmatic approach.

  B They think lucrative careers are better.

  C Their own past aspirations affect them.

  D They often want you to carry on the family legacy in a field.

76 What does the man say about jealousy at the end?

  A It can be the source of happiness.

  B It can reveal your true desire.

  C We are constantly bombarded with ideas about what it means.

  D It's often a result of other people having a better career than you.

77 Which country first introduced alcohol-free January?

  A the US

  B Great Britain

  C the Soviet Union

  D Finland

78 Why do Dry January critics dislike the choice of January?

  A It's the beginning of the year.

  B People spend a lot of money over the holiday period.

  C The weather is terrible.

  D It's a depressing month.

79 What does the speaker say about doctors and psychologists?

A   They agree on the effects of Dry January.

B   They disagree on how Dry January can affect mood.

C   They both think Dry January can improve sleeping patterns.

D   They have different priorities.

80 How many surveys received a response from every person surveyed?

A   10

B   18

C   55

D   60

81 What did most visitors dislike about the vineyard visit?

A   the tour

B   the video

C   the tasting

D   the timings offered

82 What solution does the man offer at the end?

A   having the tour earlier in the day

B   shortening the tour

C   offering snacks with the wine tasting

D   removing the second tour

83 On which floor is the room in which the guests will be having their breaks?

A   basement floor

B   first floor

C   second floor

D   third floor

84 Whose duty is it to prepare the identification for the guests?

A   Tanya

B   Mario

C   Joao

D   the speaker

85 Look at the graph below. Given the mistake mentioned by the speaker, at what time will the Paris group presentation start?

A   9:30 a.m.

B   12 p.m.

C   1 p.m.

D   3:45 p.m.

Event Schedule

9:00–9:30 a.m.
Introductions
9:30–12:00 p.m.
London Group Presentation
12:00–1:00 p.m.
Lunch break
1:00–3:30 p.m.
Paris Group Presentation
3:45 p.m.–4:15 p.m.
Wrap-up

86 Which number should the caller press if they can't attend their appointment?

A   1

B   2

C   3

D   4

87 What does the caller need to do to activate their online account?

A press 3

B send a picture of their passport

C visit the medical practice

D visit the medical practice's website

88 How many people will speak to advisors before the caller?

A 3

B 4

C 8

D 10

89 What can be inferred from the speech?

A The company needed to recruit three new people.

B The speaker has resigned.

C The speaker is moving to the head office.

D One of the new recruits visited the store recently.

90 Look at the table below. Where does the man work?

A Store 235

B Store 541

C Store 199

D Store 675

SHOE SALES BY SHOP (PERCENTAGE OF OVERALL SALES)	
Store 235	21%
Store 541	12%
Store 199	10%
Store 675	19%

91 What is going to change at the store where the man works?

A They will be selling more men's and women's clothing.

B They will not be stocking any shoes anymore.

C There won't be a dedicated shoe section anymore.

D The children's corner will be replaced by a shoe corner.

92 What can be inferred about the speaker?

A She's a concerned member of the public.

B She holds a public office position.

C She's the transport minister.

D She carried out the research mentioned in the speech.

93 When the speaker says "Isn't that appalling", what is she referring to?

A the government's inaction

B the fact that some motorcyclists don't wear helmets

C how many lives are lost in car accidents every year

D the results of the research in general

94 How many deadly accidents happen per week?

A 3

B 4

C 8

D 9

95 What can be inferred from the speech?

    A Teachers are in favor of removing uniforms.

    B Many people disagree with the decision.

    C The woman is a teacher.

    D The woman's children are happy not to wear uniforms.

96 Why does the woman say "please"?

    A to ask for something politely

    B to confirm something

    C to beg

    D to express incredulity

97 Which of the following arguments does the woman NOT mention?

    A Uniforms don't allow students to express themselves.

    B Uniforms don't make rich and poor students indistinguishable.

    C Uniforms are not a logical dress code.

    D Students are aware of what constitutes proper school clothing.

---

98 What will the finalist in 2nd place get?

    A $1,000

    B $5,000

    C the opportunity to exhibit their art in a gallery

    D nothing

99 Look at the table below. Which finalist has removed themselves from the competition?

    A John Krakow

    B Maria Sanchez

    C Donald Wreck

    D Rose O'Brien

FINALISTS
Deep Blue Sky, by John Krakow – Judge Score: 8.7
Irreverent, by Maria Sanchez – Judge Score: 9.1
My Sister Emily, by Donald Wreck – Judge Score: 7.9
The Weight of Light, by Rose O'Brien – Judge Score: 9

100 How is the woman likely to feel as she announces the results?

    A furious

    B annoyed

    C surprised

    D concerned

READING TEST

In this section of the test, you will show your knowledge of written English. This section has three parts, and you have 75 minutes to complete all three sections. Directions are given for each individual part of the test. Mark your answers on the answer sheet provided.

PART V: INCOMPLETE SENTENCES

Directions: complete the following sentences using one of the four answer choices provided. Mark the answer A, B, C or D on your answer sheet.

101 While the president has signaled that he is open _____ the options, he has been clear that there will be no kowtowing to pressure from violent protestors.

  A discuss

  B to discussion

  C discussing

  D to discussing

102 Politicians from both sides of the political spectrum have warned that, _____ a solution is found soon, the consequences for the country's economy will be dire.

  A if

  B when

  C unless

  D as soon as

103 According to a survey published today, public opinion has _____ considerably: while only six months ago 65% were in favor of new elections, only 38% still support the idea today.

  A swaggered

  B shifted

  C shunted

  D swirled

104 In a move that is likely to surprise many, Mr. Smith has announced his decision to _____ from his role as CEO of Hedging Inc.

  A step off

  B step out

  C step down

  D step over

105 Even her most outspoken critics will agree that Ms. Claremont's promise to donate 5% of the company's yearly profits to charity is _____.

  A commendable

  B ceremonial

  C cantankerous

  D convalescent

106 It's been seven years in the _____, but fans of the popular trilogy will finally be able to enjoy the final installment this coming weekend.

  A make

  B making

  C makes

  D makings

107 The committee is disappointed with the government's response, which they say has failed to address their safety concerns _____ the introduction of road toll booths.

A at

B for

C over

D in

108 The court has agreed that the cost of installing ramps at the school should be _____ by the council and that the parents of disabled student Kumiko Jones should not be charged a cent.

A conflated

B subsidized

C allocated

D destabilized

109 The media mogul fought off critics of his most popular newspaper, claiming their accusations of "fake news" were _____ and motivated by jealousy.

A unctuous

B unfounded

C unruly

D unabashed

110 A damning report has found that 20% of single parents struggle to provide _____ their children.

A for

B to

C with

D over

111 We have yet _____ confirmation that this is going ahead, so we cannot book travel or accommodation until we hear back from them.

A received

B not received

C to receive

D not to receive

112 His _____ need to micromanage everyone has left him with few friends in the company.

A inexorable

B inalienable

C infallible

D inadmissible

113 It was only after the company's _____ attracted social media attention that it decided to apologize to its customer for their employee's response to her complaint.

A blister

B blather

C blinker

D blunder

114 The new TV series has taken audiences _____ storm, with more than 20 million viewers in the 18-49 demographic after just three episodes.

A on

B by

C at

D with

115 My father, who died in 2001, _____ Europe, so it has been my lifelong dream to visit it for him.

A never visits

B never visited

C has never visited

D did never visited

116 Speculation about the king's health began to run _____ the moment it was announced he would not be joining the prime minister on her trip to Canada next week.

A rampant

B raucous

C restless

D ruthless

117 Our flight was delayed by three hours, and not once _____ any food or water. It was a dreadful experience.

A we offered

B offered we

C we were offered

D were we offered

118 Motivation is certainly an issue around the office. We need to _____ what has worked in the past and why our current methods of motivating workers are not producing results.

A zero in on

B zero out on

C zero off of

D zero on in

119 The client has requested the agenda for next Friday's meeting, and has also asked whether we could move it back by half an hour _____ she can make it on time.

A as long as

B so that

C in order to

D in hopes of

120 The communications piece went out on Friday at 5 p.m., which is _____ why most people haven't taken a look at it yet.

A presumed

B presumption

C presumptive

D presumably

121 Despite the accusations _____ against him, Mr. Smith has ruled out resigning from office.

A levied

B levitated

C levered

D leveraged

122 With the weather as it is, people _____ to avoid traveling when possible until tomorrow morning.

A warn

B are warning

C are being warned

D warning

123 This stunning revelation comes at a very troubling time for the company, which has struggled _____ paying off its growing debts.

A to

B at

C on

D with

124 Her _____ performance definitely played a role in the decision not to renew her contract.

A unilateral

B unremarkable

C unrelenting

D unrequited

125 If the government wants to convince the public that they have their best interests _____, they'll have to take meaningful measures to tackle the housing crisis.

A at hand

B at heart

C at mind

D at arms

126 I don't even want to think of the potentially catastrophic series of events which would have occurred if you _____ the alarm when you noticed what was going on.

A didn't raise

B haven't raised

C hadn't raised

D wouldn't have raised

127 The president has been urged to put the country ahead of political interests and not to _____ to irrational demands from the more radical members of his party.

A retort

B resort

C reinstate

D repose

128 I have nothing but _____ for him: it's because of his rash decision to go ahead even though we were unprepared that our proposal was unsuccessful.

A contempt

B respect

C hostility

D avidity

129 Mr. Ireland, who has more than 20 years of experience in mediation, waded _____ the dispute to help the two companies find an appropriate solution.

A on

B in

C to

D in to

130 I know Marc has already gone through the procedure with you. _____ that as it may, I would like to go through it with you as well.

A Is

B Be

C Being

D Was

PART VI: TEXT COMPLETION

Directions: Read the following texts and select the best answer choice to complete the text. Mark the answer A, B, C or D on your answer sheet.

Questions 131–134 refer to the following notice.

NOTICE TO ALL RESIDENTS

Dear resident:

We would like to inform you that essential maintenance work will be taking place in the building's water supply pipework over the next two weeks, _____ on Monday February 12th.
131.

_____ the cold water supply will not be affected by this, the hot water supply will
132.

occasionally need to be switched off in certain apartments for a minimum of four hours during the course of the project to allow the maintenance crew to complete their work.

_____, and will be during working hours (9-5) Monday to Friday.
133.

If you are subletting your property, please advise your tenants of the upcoming works and the potential disruption associated. _____
134.

Kind regards,

The Management

---

131 A commences

    B commenced

    C commencing

    D commence

132 A When

    B While

    C As

    D However

133 A You will be informed of this beforehand

    B This will always be advertised to each apartment concerned beforehand

    C We will let each of you know in advance

    D You will not need to do anything yourself

134 A We are outraged by the inconvenience.

    B We thank you for your cooperation.

    C We would appreciate your thoughts.

    D We look forward to welcoming you.

Questions 135–138 refer to the following email.

From: Blandine.Guilhot@frenchcourses.com

To: Elsken.Bakker@mail.com

Subject: **French Course Confirmation**

Dear Elsken,

We are pleased to confirm that your 10-week Beginners (A1) January-March course has now _____.
135.

Please note that we have a number of partnerships with schools in the area and the location of our classes depends on availability. _____ We will be emailing you directions the
136.
week before your course is due to begin.

All of our evening courses begin at 6:30 p.m. Textbooks are provided, as well as bags (_____ this is the first time you are booking with us), but you will need to bring your
137.
own notebook and pen – as well as your enthusiasm! Please arrive 15 minutes early for your first lesson to _____ your student ID card.
138.
If you have any questions about the course, please get in touch.

Kind regards,

Blandine

135 **A** booked

    B was booked

    C book

    D been booked

136 **A** Please confirm receipt of our directions to the correct location.

    B All of our locations, however, are within walking distance from Western Station.

    C We will let you know once we have enough bookings for the course.

    D Our partner schools offer German, Spanish and Italian courses.

137 **A** only

    B whether

    C if

    D while

138 **A** obtain

    B contrive

    C ordain

    D undertake

Questions 139–142 refer to the following advertisement.

Do you have a great idea for a comic or a graphic novel but you can't put pen to paper? Do you find it hard to _____ the image in your mind to the page in front of you?
139.

Then come to our

DRAWING THE PERFECT COMIC

OR GRAPHIC NOVEL COURSE

February 13 – April 24, 2018

_____ by Michaela Roy, the award-winning author of *Races and Hiccups* and *We've Got*
140.

it Covered, our popular course will teach you basic techniques in drawing and narrative in a fun, interactive way.

While this course is aimed _____ beginners, intermediate-level artists are also
141.

welcome. All you need to bring is a pen, a pencil and lots of enthusiasm!

At the end of the course, you will be given the opportunity to present your work to a group of experienced graphic novelists, including our successful alumni Indira Jones and Pedro Cervantes, and to pitch to representatives of three major publishing houses.

_____ Book now at www.graphicnovelcourses.com!
142.

---

139 **A** transfer

B transcribe

C transpire

D transport

140 **A** Teach

B Teaching

C Taught

D Were taught

141 **A** to

B at

C on

D for

142 **A** We'll be in touch soon!

B for a chance to get a 15% discount

C We have been teaching for 10 years.

D So, what are you waiting for?

Questions 143–146 refer to the following email.

TO: bookings@thegeorge.com

FROM: Emily.Stinson@savage.com

SUBJECT: Booking for November 10th

Hi,

_____ I would like to make a booking for 15 people for the November 10th at 6 p.m.
143.

We would like it to be in your private executive room – could you please confirm what the minimum charge is? I tried to find it on your website but I couldn't see it anywhere.

No one has any allergies or special _____ requirements that I'm aware of, though three
144.

of the guests are vegetarians. Having checked your menu, I can see you have plenty of
_____ vegetarian options so I imagine that won't be a problem.
145.

We _____ at around 5:30 p.m., so we would like to have some drinks at the bar first.
146.

Please let me know if you would prefer us to order in advance or if you are happy for us to order when we arrive.

Yours sincerely,

Emily Stinson

---

143   **A**   I trust this email finds you well.

     B   Thank you for choosing us.

     C   We look forward to your reply.

     D   You can contact me via email.

144   **A**   diet

     B   dietary

     C   dieting

     D   dietician

145   **A**   edible

     B   delectable

     C   edifying

     D   duplicitous

146   **A**   arrived

     B   have arrived

     C   will be arriving

     D   will have arrived

PART VII: READING COMPREHENSION

Directions: In this part of the test, you will read a number of different texts and then answer several questions about each text. Mark the answer A, B, C or D on your answer sheet.

Questions 147–149 refer to the following email.

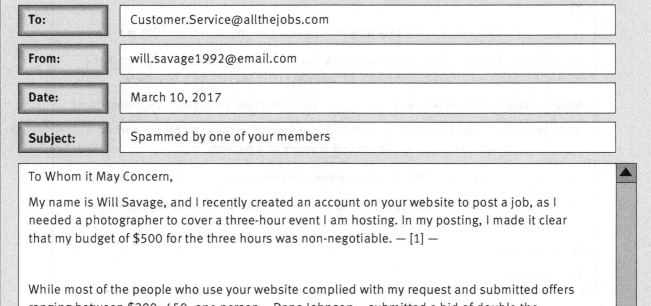

To:	Customer.Service@allthejobs.com
From:	will.savage1992@email.com
Date:	March 10, 2017
Subject:	Spammed by one of your members

To Whom it May Concern,

My name is Will Savage, and I recently created an account on your website to post a job, as I needed a photographer to cover a three-hour event I am hosting. In my posting, I made it clear that my budget of $500 for the three hours was non-negotiable. — [1] —

While most of the people who use your website complied with my request and submitted offers ranging between $300–450, one person – Dana Johnson – submitted a bid of double the maximum amount of $500. — [2] — When I politely declined her bid, explaining that it was above my (clearly stated) budget, I was subjected to a barrage of abusive remarks about how I'm a part of the problem by underpaying photographers and I should be ashamed of myself. — [3] — I reported the message and blocked Dana from contacting me on your website immediately.

However, since then, Dana has tracked me down on my social media, as well as my place of work. I have been on the receiving end of a steady stream of abuse for a week now, and she has even emailed my employer with allegations that I was abusive towards her. — [4] — I'm also very close to pressing charges against her. Can you please intervene and ensure that this woman stops stalking me?

Many thanks,

Will Savage

147 How much money did Dana offer for the job Will posted?

A $300

B $450

C $500

D $1,000

148 How is Will likely to feel, based on the email?

A overjoyed

B nonchalant

C vexed

D lackadaisical

149 In which of the positions marked [1], [2], [3] or [4] does the following sentence best belong? "I'm at the end of my rope here."

A [1]

B [2]

C [3]

D [4]

Questions 150–152 refer to the following text chain.

150 What's the purpose of Ian's text?

  A to complain about the hotel

  B to ask for assistance from Kris

  C to inform Kris about a mistake he made

  D to ask Kris if she's off today

151 Why does Kris say "What's up"?

  A She is asking where Ian is.

  B She is asking how Ian feels.

  C She is asking why Ian needs her.

  D She is asking if Ian is at work.

152 Based on the conversation, how does Kris think Ian feels?

  A stressed

  B grief-stricken

  C frustrated

  D nonplussed

Questions 153–155 refer to the following notice.

EYE SPY

2-for-1 Deal on all Glasses

Why not treat yourself to a brand new pair of glasses this summer? With our 2-for-1 deal, you can get any combination of named brand glasses or choose from our own, incredibly stylish range of frames for all ages!

NO NEED TO BOOK AN APPOINTMENT!

Just pop into any of our stores before July 31st 2018 and quote **2-for-1**!

Don't forget to bring a prescription with you if you are buying prescription glasses.

To book a free** appointment with our optometrist, go to our website: www.eyespy.com/optometrist and use code 2FOR1.

With our 2-for-1 deal you can:

- *Buy two pairs of prescription glasses, two pairs of sunglasses, or one of each – all combinations allowed!**
- *Buy two pairs from our own range, two brand pairs, or one of each!**

All orders must be placed on or before July 31st 2018.

Deal can be used online or in store.

Deal only includes frames – lenses for prescription glasses not included.

*Only 2 pairs per person. Cheapest pair free.

Cannot be combined with any other voucher or deal.

**Optician appointment normal price of $20 will be discounted from 2-for-1 purchase.

---

153 Which of the following can customers NOT do based on the ad?

- **A** buy one pair of prescription glasses and one pair of sunglasses
- **B** buy two pairs of sunglasses
- **C** buy two pairs from Eye Spy's own range
- **D** buy two named brand pairs and two pairs from Eye Spy's own range

154 Which of the following is NOT free in the 2-for-1 deal?

- **A** the least expensive prescription frames
- **B** the least expensive pair of sunglasses
- **C** the least expensive lenses
- **D** the optometrist appointment

155 Which of the following is NOT TRUE based on the ad?

- **A** Eye Spy caters to both young and old customers.
- **B** Eye Spy offers free optometrist appointments to everyone.
- **C** The 2-for-1 deal can still be used on July 31st 2018.
- **D** The 2-for-1 deal cannot be used in conjunction with another deal.

Questions 156–159 refer to the following article.

SHOULD EMPLOYEES WEAR NAME TAGS?

It's a question that divides opinions: should companies – particularly those in customer service, such as clothing retailers and coffee shops or restaurant chains – force their employees to wear name tags? Most companies seem to think so: walk into any shopping mall in America and you're bound to be greeted by shop assistants with cheery MY NAME IS **** AND I'M HERE TO HELP name tags. But what are the benefits of this practice, and do they outweigh the drawbacks?

There are a few ways that introducing name tags can be beneficial for your business, the most obvious being that they allow customers to start a conversation with your employees more easily – something that can break ice and build rapport, which is exactly the kind of thing you want if you're looking for loyal customers. It can also make it easier for customers to give credit where credit's due by naming the employee who made them happy with their visit in feedback forms. Conversely, if a customer has a problem with one of your employees, being able to name the person who served them will make it easier for them to complain, and easier for you to deal with their complaint. What's more, employees will be more motivated to do their best when helping a customer, knowing that their name is out there for everyone to see.

Critics of the practice, however, claim that name tags can have the opposite effect: they can make interactions impersonal and stilted, perhaps even awkward. Is it, after all, enjoyable for a stranger, even if that stranger is a customer, to be able to address you by your first name when you don't know theirs? In an age when privacy is so valued, this can feel like an intrusion, which might explain why employees, particularly millennials, dislike name tags – and, as any seasoned entrepreneur will tell you, unhappy employees mean unhappy customers.

So, what should you do? The answer depends on the nature of your business, and what you expect name tags to achieve. If you want your coffee shop or restaurant to feel more casual, like a friend's house, skip the tags. If you want it to look professional, and to highlight the difference between the customer and the staff, then go for it.

---

156 Who is this article aimed at?

- **A** customers
- **B** employees
- **C** business owners
- **D** millennials

157 Which of the following benefits of name tags is NOT mentioned in the article?

- **A** Customers can chat with employees.
- **B** Customer feedback is more positive.
- **C** It's easier for customers to complain about bad service.
- **D** Employees are likely to provide better service.

158 In paragraph 3, what does "seasoned" mean?

   A   rudimentary

   B   callow

   C   accomplished

   D   cumbersome

159 What can be inferred about millennials from the article?

   A   they value privacy

   B   they hate working in customer service

   C   they make customers unhappy

   D   their opinions about name tags differ from those of other employees

Questions 160–162 refer to the following email.

To:	Wolfgang.Springstein@doetrips.com
From:	Elliott.McFarlane@recruit4best.com
Date:	October 19, 2017
Subject:	Reschedule call

Hi Wolfgang,

I'm so sorry I missed your call yesterday. — [1] — I was dragged into a meeting out of the blue and it lasted until late in the evening.

As I mentioned in my email earlier this week, we have identified three candidates we think might be suitable for the B2C role. — [2] — I have spoken with two of them on the phone, and have a phone call interview with the last one later today. — [3] — The two people I have interviewed so far seem good, so I will be forwarding you their resumes so you can take a peek.

With regards to the B2B role, we are still actively looking for potential candidates. The ad has only been live for five days so I'm not concerned – we have received quite a few resumes, just nothing we think would be suitable just yet. I will let you know once I have more news. — [4] —

Many thanks,

Elliott McFarlane

Recruitment Consultant

---

160 Why did Elliott miss Wolfgang's call?

- **A** He had a scheduled meeting.
- **B** He was asked to join a meeting.
- **C** He wasn't available in the evening.
- **D** He was feeling blue.

161 In paragraph 2, line 5, what is the phrase "take a peek" closest in meaning to?

- **A** have a look
- **B** examine closely
- **C** make a decision
- **D** share your thoughts

162 In which of the positions marked [1], [2], [3] or [4] does the following sentence best belong?
"Shall we have a call tomorrow?"

A   [1]

B   [2]

C   [3]

D   [4]

Questions 163–164 refer to the following online post.

| Kelly_Was_Waiting
Newbie

Joined: Mon Feb 1, 2011 7:03 am

Posts: 27

Location: London, UK

Age: 41 | ▶LAST **Trip to London – tips?**
Posted at 10.28.2018 3.41 p.m.

I've lived in London for 10 years, but I originally come from Indiana so this would be my advice as a fellow American:
• Book your tickets in advance for attractions that need admission. You'll skip massive queues & save a lot of money.
• For heaven's sake, don't buy single tickets for the tube (this is what Brits call the subway). Either buy an Oyster card (a rechargeable card that works with most methods of public transport in London) or use your wireless bank card if you have one. Buses don't take cash – you'll need a card.
• Plan your meals. Many pubs stop serving food after a certain time, so be aware of that.
• London is a safe city overall, but like any other big city it requires a certain level of vigilance. Don't keep your wallet in your back-pocket, and don't be absentminded when you use your cell phone, especially at traffic lights. Thieves on motorbikes could snatch it from you in a second.
• Layers are your friend. You may have been warned about the fickle English weather. You can have four seasons in a single day, so carry an umbrella with you and opt for lots of layers you can shed if the sun decides to grace you with its presence. |

163 What CANNOT be inferred about the author from the post?

A   He is American.

B   He moved to London at age 31.

C   He joined the website over 7 years ago.

D   He originally visited London as a tourist.

164 The author says "layers are your friend" in the last bullet point. What does he mean by that?

A   You should wear a winter coat.

B   You should wear waterproof clothing.

C   You should wear many garments on top of one another.

D   You should wear a t-shirt in case the sun comes out.

Questions 165–168 refer to the following article.

It's the fourth day of strikes for WiseWay's 50,000 store employees across the country, including not just sales assistants, but also assistant store managers and store managers, and WiseWay is finally starting to feel the heat.

WiseWay, a chain of electronic stores that has grown rapidly since its establishment in 2011, now has more than 400 locations. Out of these, only 11 are still open. — [1] — The rest are barricaded by disgruntled employees who, with picket signs and slogans, are protesting what they call "fat-cat" bonuses handed out to those at management level while they struggle to make ends meet with their minimum-wage salaries.

— [2] — Back in 2015, WiseWay was taken to court over its refusal to allow its employees to form a union. When it lost the case, amidst a storm of negative media attention, WiseWay capitulated: they would not be taking the case to the Supreme Court, they said, and unions would be allowed to form. It's a decision they're probably regretting now.

— [3] — However, WiseWay's employees have every right to be upset. For the last three years, salaries have remained pretty much stagnant, growing at a much slower rate than inflation. Top-level salaries and bonuses, in the meantime, have skyrocketed. — [4] — WiseWay announced just 10 days ago that its profits for the last fiscal year had grown by 5.4% compared with the previous year. Two days later, following failed talks between the union and the management, the union announced the strike.

If history is any indication, WiseWay will reach an agreement with its employees soon. Customers are already starting to complain – and they're overwhelmingly on the employees' side. Some members of the public have even joined the protesters on the front line, and #UnwiseWay is trending on social media. At this stage, giving in to the – quite frankly, reasonable – demands of their employees might be the only way out of this PR disaster for WiseWay.

165 In paragraph 1, line 2, the phrase "WiseWay is finally starting to feel the heat" is closest in meaning to

A WiseWay's stores are getting too warm.

B WiseWay is beginning to get angry.

C The consequences of the strike are becoming apparent to WiseWay.

D WiseWay is starting to come up with solutions to stop the strike.

166 Which of the following CANNOT be inferred from the text?

A The disparity in salaries between top and low level employees led to the strike.

B The union attempted to make a deal with management before deciding to strike.

C WiseWay has announced that they want to reach an agreement soon.

D Most customers are supporting the cause of the employees.

167 Based on the article, what does the author think about the employees' behavior?

    A   He thinks they are being petulant.

    B   He thinks their requests are sensible.

    C   He thinks they are exaggerating.

    D   He expresses no view.

168 In which of the positions marked [1], [2], [3] or [4] does the following sentence best belong?
"This isn't the first time WiseWay has been in trouble."

    A   [1]

    B   [2]

    C   [3]

    D   [4]

Questions 169–171 refer to the following email.

To:	Andrea@properton.com
From:	Jon@properton.com; Ella@properton.com; Yashmeen@properton.com
Date:	October 15, 2017
Subject:	Revised manual

Hi everyone,

I know I promised I'd get this to you three weeks ago but with all the last-minute meetings and stuff, I've only just now managed to get around to it. — [1] — Here's the updated version of the manual for the marketing team.

As you will see in the attached, I've made all the changes you requested and added the two new chapters we discussed in our meeting last month. — [2] — I also added an appendix with links to the folders in the open drive where you can find all the documents relevant to the marketing department. — [3] —

Before I send it off to HR, could you sense-check it and let me know if there's anything I've missed by EOD Friday? I've also highlighted three or four sections where I'm not sure about the wording, and a couple of parts where I wasn't sure if we still do things that way or if the procedures described are different now. — [4] —

Thanks,

Andrea

Senior Marketing Director

---

169 Why did it take Andrea so long to complete the manual?

  A She didn't have the time.

  B She forgot.

  C She didn't have everything she needed.

  D She needed to have a meeting with the marketing team first.

170 Which of the following does Andrea not ask the team to check the manual for?

  A grammatical mistakes or typos

  B incomplete sections

  C unnatural or incorrect sentence structure

  D outdated information

171 In which of the positions marked [1], [2], [3] or [4] does the following sentence best belong?
"I look forward to your thoughts."

A [1]

B [2]

C [3]

D [4]

Questions 172–173 refer to the following notice.

GIFT CARD @ THE REDHILL CAFÉ

If you or one of your friends is a regular customer at the Redhill Café, why not get one of our gift cards?

Doubling as a loyalty card, the Redhill Café gift card can be charged with as little as $5 to start and with any amount after it's been activated.

With the Redhill Café gift card, you can:

•   Get your 10th cup of coffee for free after nine beverage purchases* in any size;

•   Benefit from our 10% discount on special occasion cakes and desserts;

•   Collect points** which can be used on anything in store, from lunch to coffee beans and merchandise such as travel mugs or even coffee machines;

•   Get 2 coffees + 2 desserts for free on your birthday***.

What are you waiting for? Come and collect your gift card in store now!

*Excludes bottled and canned beverages

**5 points per dollar spent on drinks, 10 points per dollar spent on food and merchandise. 100 points are equivalent to 50 cents

***Valid ID required

---

172 On which of the following occasions do you NOT get a free coffee?

A when you have previously purchased nine coffees

B when it's your birthday

C when you buy a special occasion cake

D when you have enough points on your card to use on the coffee

173 How many points per dollar do you get if you buy a travel mug?

A 5

B 10

C 50

D 100

Questions 174–175 refer to the following text chain.

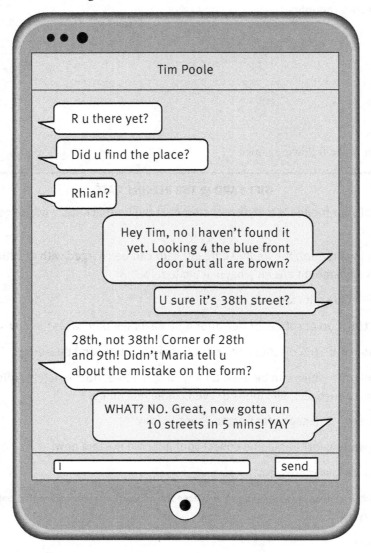

174 Where does Rhian need to go?

   A   a building with a brown door on the corner of 9th and 28th

   B   a building with a brown door on the corner of 9th and 38th

   C   a building with a blue door on the corner of 9th and 28th

   D   a building with a blue door on the corner of 9th and 38th

175 How is Rhian likely to feel at the end of this conversation?

   A   stressed

   B   terrified

   C   fortunate

   D   skeptical

Questions 176–180 refer to the following sign-in sheet and email.

Full name	Company	Here to Visit	Vehicle	Time in	Time out	Signed out by
Polly Thwaites	WDS	Amy Jones	NWH 634	9:15 a.m.	10:30 a.m.	Amy Jones
Aaron Gorski	-	Rian Dodeigne	-	9:45 a.m.	11:40 a.m.	Wren Tyler
Anna Vandi	Ela Ela	Mrs. Baker	-	9:45 a.m.	-	-
Angela Monto	Fork & Sons	Lola Geller	-	10:20 a.m.	11:30 a.m.	Lola Geller
Prisha Laghari	-	Rian Dodeigne	NVU 920	10:45 a.m.	12:10 p.m.	Wren Tyler
Sami Abboud	St Claire	Amy Jones	-	11:30 a.m.	-	-
Jessica Thorne	S&S	Theo Holmes	JBO 110	11:30 a.m.	11:45 a.m.	Niamh Baker
Lachlan Summers	WWBD	Cordelia Fuller	GDV 885	11:45 a.m.	12:30 p.m.	Cordelia Fuller
Becky St James	-	Rian Dodeigne	-	2:45 p.m.	4:10 p.m.	Wren Tyler
Kana Sato	-	Amy James	-	3:30 p.m.	4:00 p.m.	-

To:	HR@taffy.com
From:	**+ALLSTAFF**
Date:	May 15th, 2017
Subject:	Signing guests in and out

Hi everyone,

I would like to draw your attention to a safety and security rule that some of you have been neglecting to follow. As you know, our company deals with sensitive government data and, as a result, we take security extremely seriously – as I'm sure you all remember from the vetting process you went through when you first joined the company.

Due to this, we must always make sure that we know who is in the building at all times. As you can see from the sign-out sheet attached, however, just two days ago we had two people who never signed out and one person who signed themselves out but was not escorted by anyone.

Please remember that you should under **no circumstances** allow your guests to leave the premises without personally escorting them out of the building. You should always allow extra time between meetings to escort guests out, and if for any reason you are unable to do so you should either ask one of your colleagues to do so for you or, if push comes to shove, contact someone from reception or HR.

Please be aware that repeated failure to comply with this very important rule may lead beyond verbal warnings to disciplinary action or even dismissal. Thank you for your understanding.

Kind regards,

HR Management

176 From the people who signed out, who stayed on the premises for the shortest time?

   A   Lachlan Summers

   B   Jessica Thorne

   C   Kana Sato

   D   Anna Vandi

177 Which person had the most visitors?

   A   Rian Dodeigne

   B   Amy Jones

   C   Wren Tyler

   D   Cordelia Fuller

178 What is the problem, according to the email?

   A   Visitors are staying for too long.

   B   The information is being entered incorrectly.

   C   Visitors are not being escorted out of the building.

   D   Employees are not using the sign-up sheet.

179 In paragraph 3, line 4, the phrase "if push comes to shove, contact someone from reception or HR" is closest in meaning to?

   A   You should always inform reception or HR.

   B   You should never inform reception or HR.

   C   Reception or HR should be your first choice.

   D   Reception or HR should be your last choice.

180 What is NOT mentioned as a consequence of not following the rules?

   A   being fired

   B   being given a spoken warning

   C   performance reviews

   D   disciplinary measures

Questions 181–185 refer to the following schedule and email.

GIUILIO MALAVASI – CALENDAR VIEW

	June 4	June 5	June 6	June 7
9:00			Meeting with Allie *Blue room*	
10:00	Planning meeting with Melanie *Boardroom*		Logistics for Athens, GA meeting *Yellow room*	Meeting with Jo *Yellow room*
11:00	Interview with Angie *Meeting room*	Interview with Sami *Meeting room*	Interview with Reggie *Boardroom*	Interview with Lorena *Meeting room*
12:00	Interview with George *Blue room*		Interview with Ariel *Meeting room*	Interview with Willa *Boardroom*
1:00		TEAM LUNCH *the pizza place down the road*		
2:00	Interview with Roanna *Meeting room*			Meeting with Yashmeen & Pip *Boardroom*
3:00		Interview with Eleanor *Meeting room*	Interview with Andreas *Meeting room*	
4:00	Operations meeting *Boardroom*	Interview with Tahani *Meeting room*	Interview with Polly *Meeting room*	

To:	Bozena.Hanusz@firefly.com
From:	Giulio.Malavasi@firefly.com
Date:	May 28, 2017
Subject:	Interviews for business analyst position

Hi Bozena,

How are you? I hope you had a good time in Arizona last week!

As you may have seen, I have added a few interviews to your diary for next week. I needed a second person to conduct the interviews with me and since Phoebe from HR is on holiday, I thought you might want to join me for a few of them. Please let me know if you can't make any of them and I will find someone else – but I think it would a be great experience for you, and since you will be working closely with the new recruit, it will be better for you to play a role in the decision-making process to ensure you get along with them. Plus, you were right when you said we should hire Raymond, so I trust your insights.

On a similar note: I've booked one of the interviews in the wrong room. We're supposed to be having all interviews in either the boardroom or the meeting room, but they were both busy. I asked Phil if I could borrow the boardroom but he has a client meeting – but you are holding the meeting room for an internal meeting, so do you mind if we swap? Phoebe will bite my head off if she finds out I held an interview in one of the torture chambers!

One final thing: I've attached the new template for interview notes. There are 20 questions in it and we need to ask at least 15 of them. I've selected eight I'd like to ask, can you select another eight and we can discuss during our meeting tomorrow?

Thanks!

Giulio

181 On which day does Giulio have the most interviews?

   A June 4th

   B June 5th

   C June 6th

   D June 7th

182 Which time period is always free of meetings and interviews on Giulio's calendar?

   A 9:00–10:00

   B 10:00–11:00

   C 12:00–1:00

   D 1:00–2:00

183 Which of the following is NOT a reason Giulio wants Bozena to help with the interviews?

   A He wants to make sure she will like the new recruit.

   B It will increase her familiarity with the process of hiring.

   C Phoebe from HR recommended her.

   D He believes she will be good at selecting the right candidate.

184 In his email, Giulio says "I've booked one of the interviews in the wrong room". Which interview is he referring to?

   A George's

   B Allie's

   C Sami's

   D Willa's

185 In paragraph 3, line 4, the phrase "Phoebe will bite my head off" is closest in meaning to

   A Phoebe will be disappointed in me.

   B Phoebe will be furious with me.

   C Phoebe will not want to speak to me.

   D Phoebe will be indifferent towards me.

Questions 186–190 refer to the following advertisement and messages.

RAINBOW PARTY LIMOS

Celebrate in style with one of our luxurious party limousines! With space for up to 20 people and prices starting as low as $500 for six hours, you can now party the way you deserve!

What you get with Rainbow Party Limos:

- Professional, fully licensed drivers

- Spacious back with A/C, mirrored ceiling, fiber optic lighting & one-way privacy glass

- TV monitors, DVD/CD players, USB

- Mini fridge and coolers available

- Numerous decoration styles for you to choose from, including: 21st birthday party, prom party, wedding, bachelor / bachelorette, anniversary

BOOK ONLINE NOW AT: www.rainbowpartylimos.com

info@rainbowpartylimos.com

Book by October 31st for a 10% discount!

Jess.Pink1999	▶LAST **Rainbow Party Limos – any good?**
Guru	**Posted at 10.24.2018 11:11 a.m.**
Joined: Apr 1 2016 8:15 am	Hi guys! Hoping to use your wisdom here… Has anyone ever used Rainbow Party Limos? I'm looking for a limo to hire for my cousin's 21st birthday party and they're running a promotion with a 10% discount. Their prices are already pretty low compared to everything else I've found, plus on their website they say they only need a $100 deposit – every other company I've contacted either wants the full amount up front or they ask for a $300-$400 deposit, and I don't have that kind of money right now. But I don't wanna use them if anyone else has had any bad experiences with them, so…what's the verdict?
Posts: 564	
Location: Philadelphia	
Age: 19	

PortiaWinchester

Guru

Joined: Nov 19 2014 6:21 pm
Posts: 821
Location: Philadelphia
Age: 25

Rainbow Party Limos – any good?

Posted at 10.24.2018 3:51 p.m.

STAY AS FAR AWAY AS POSSIBLE FROM RAINBOW PARTY LIMOS!

Got your attention? Good. You should not give any of your hard-earned cash to these guys. My friend was lured in by the same promotion that caught your eye (I swear, they just re-print the ad with a different deadline every month to capture innocent victims) and booked a limo for her sister's bachelorette party, and it was. The worst. Experience. Ever.

Where do I even start? First of all, the limo was two hours late. We tried calling and calling but no one picked up the phone. When the limo finally showed up, the driver was rude and he responded with snide remarks when we complained about his tardiness. The "privacy glass" was out of order, so the guy could look through and we didn't feel like we could relax, and when we asked for a different car with a functioning glass, he called us "princesses" and said all the other limos were out. Not to mention that the car had clearly not been cleaned, and the speakers had this sort of echo that ruined the music we tried to play. Of course, there was no mini fridge and no coolers. And the best part? After we complained, they had the audacity to charge $300 to my friend's credit card for "damages to the vehicle". She contested the charge and got her money back from the bank, but it took ages.

If you want a good limo company, go with either Lime Limo or Treasure Bus. They're both a bit pricier but they're still affordable, and your experience will be much better.

186 Which of the following is NOT mentioned as a perk in the advertisement?

A a place to store cold drinks

B abundance of room in the vehicles

C air conditioning

D exterior lighting

187 How much is the deposit for Rainbow Party Limos?

A $100

B $300

C $400

D the full amount

188 In the first post, in line 8, the phrase "what's the verdict?" is closest in meaning to

A Has anyone used Rainbow Party Limos?

B Why is Rainbow Party Limos so cheap?

C Is Rainbow Party Limos a good or a bad choice?

D Does anyone have any limo recommendations?

189 Which of the following is TRUE about the friend of the second post's author?

A She never retrieved the money she was charged for damages

B She was celebrating her sister's 21st birthday.

C She booked with Rainbow Party Limos because of the 10% discount.

D She recommends Lime Limo or Treasure Bus.

190 Based on the second post, what is the author's opinion on Rainbow Party Limos?

A It's a horrendous company.

B It's a mediocre company.

C It's an average company.

D It's a magnificent company.

Questions 191–195 refer to the following price list, receipt and email.

BOAT TOURS AT SWEETWATER RIVER	
Prices	
60-minute tour	
Adult	$15
Child	$7
Student*	$10
Senior* (over 65)	$12
90-minute tour	
Adult	$18
Child	$10
Student*	$13
Senior* (over 65)	$15
*Senior's Card or Student ID required	

Sweetwater River Boat Tours	

08/24/18 10:36:40	
Number:	XXXXXXXXXXX5632
Type:	CREDIT
Entry mode:	Swiped
Response:	APPROVED
Approval Code:	443987
Ticket x 2	$18.00
Ticket	$15.00
Subtotal	$51.00
Tax 12%	$6.12
Total	$57.12
Thank you for your order	

To:	info@sweetwatertours.com
From:	Adeyayo.Eze@email.com
Date:	September 4th, 2017
Subject:	Complaint about charges

To Whom it May Concern,

Last week my daughter and I took one of your 90 minute boat tours at Sweetwater River and, while our experience was mostly positive, there was a bitter note to it: I was overcharged for the tickets.

As you can see in the receipt attached, my credit card was charged for three tickets: two at $18 and one at $15. The $15 ticket was mine, for which I used my driving license to apply the discount. One of the other two tickets was for my daughter. There was, however, no one else with us – so we paid an extra $18 for a non-existent person.

What makes this even more frustrating is that the mistake was not only not identified at the register, but it was also not identified by the tour guide who examined our tickets. At no point were we questioned about who the third person in our group was, and no one pointed out the mistake. If my daughter had not insisted on examining the ticket closely before discarding it, we never would've discovered the problem.

To make matters worse, when we attempted to request a refund at the register, we were told that it's company policy not to offer refunds once a ticket has been stamped as "used" – regardless of the problem. I take issue with this policy and I would like my $18 to be refunded to me immediately, otherwise I will seek a refund through the bank.

Thank you,

Adeyayo

191 How much does a 70-year-old man need to pay for a 1-hour tour?

   A $7

   B $10

   C $12

   D $15

192 What combination of tickets has been charged in the receipt?

   A two adult tickets and one senior ticket

   B two adult tickets and one student ticket

   C two student tickets and one child ticket

   D two student tickets and one senior ticket

193 How is the author of the email NOT likely to feel?

   A cheated

   B galled

   C exasperated

   D ebullient

194 Why was the man refused a refund at the ticket office?

   A He didn't notice the mistake when he paid.

   B The company has a no-refund policy.

   C The ticket had been used already.

   D The tour guide didn't examine the ticket.

195 In the email, in paragraph 4, line 3, the phrase "I take issue with this policy" is closest in meaning to

   A I am not happy about this policy.

   B I don't understand how this policy works.

   C I was not aware of this policy.

   D I think this policy does not apply to my situation.

Questions 196–200 refer to the following notice and emails.

SORRY WE MISSED YOU!

Dear Silvia Till

Date: 12/08/2018

Today we called to deliver a

☑ **Parcel**

❑ **Box**

❑ **Letter**

❑ **Other:** _____

We have left your shipment

❑ **With your neighbor at:** _____

❑ **In your garage / shed**

❑ **In your agreed safe place**

❑ **Other:** _____

We were unable to deliver because

❑ **The shipment was too big.**

☑ **A signature was required.**

❑ **It was not safe to do so.**

❑ **Other:** _____

Please go to www.FLP.com/redelivery to pick a new date for your shipment to be delivered.

To:	info@FLP.com
From:	Silas.Till@email.com
Date:	December 9th, 2018
Subject:	My package was not delivered

To Whom it May Concern,

My name is Silas Till, and today I was supposed to receive a package from you. I specifically took a day off work to make sure I would be at home, as it was extremely important that I receive the package, which contained my son's birthday present, today. I was told it would be delivered between 9 a.m. and 1 p.m., so I did not leave the house at all during that time or do anything noisy (such as laundry) that might prevent me from hearing the doorbell ring.

At 1 p.m., since the package still had not arrived, I decided to call the driver using the phone number you had sent me in a text. However, the driver never picked up. I then tried to call your offices but, after 30 minutes on hold, I hung up. It was at that point I decided to go outside and check... and that was when I discovered the SORRY WE MISSED YOU card on the doormat of my front door.

As it turns out, the driver never even bothered to ring the bell, or even shove their card through the mail slot: they just threw it on my front step and drove off. Now I am short a birthday present and I have wasted a day off work. What's more, I will be forced to waste another in order to reschedule delivery, as you only offer daytime slots, and I am not even sure I will receive the package this time.

Words cannot express how furious I am. If this is how you treat loyal, long-term customers, I hate to imagine how you treat newcomers. I expect a satisfactory solution immediately.

Thank you,

Silas Till

To:	Silas.Till@email.com
From:	Info@FLP.com
Date:	December 10th, 2018
Subject:	RE: My package was not delivered

Dear Mr. Till,

We are sorry to hear that our driver did not ring the bell when they came to deliver your package or insert our SORRY WE MISSED YOU card through the mail slot. We pride ourselves on focusing on quality rather than quantity, which is why we do not have delivery quota for our drivers and use our customers' feedback as a performance indicator instead. In this case we have clearly failed to meet our very strict standards and we apologize for this. You can rest assured that we have launched an internal investigation to identify why our driver did not deliver the package when you were clearly at home. Please let me know if you would like to be informed of the outcome of our investigation.

In the meantime, I would like to confirm that we have arranged for special evening delivery for you today at no cost to you. Can you please let us know which time works best for you between 5 p.m. and 10 p.m.? We will then ensure that our driver arrives at the exact time you request. We would also like to offer you a $20 voucher for any future services you purchase with us, which you can find attached to this email.

I look forward to your response.

Kind regards,

Sergio Torres

Customer Service Assistant

196 According to the card, why did the driver not deliver the package?

   A It was too large.

   B The recipient needed to sign for it.

   C It was unsafe to deliver it.

   D There were no neighbors available to take it.

197 What can be inferred from Silas's email?

   A The package contained a birthday present for his wife.

   B He has never used FLP before.

   C He has been an FLP customer for a while.

   D He was on hold for half an hour when he called the driver.

198 Based on his email, how is Silas likely to feel?

   A cross

   B content

   C complacent

   D callous

199 In the second email, in paragraph 1, line 3, the phrase "we do not have delivery quota for our drivers" is closest in meaning to

   A We do not ask our drivers to deliver at a specific time.

   B We do not ask our drivers to make a minimum amount of deliveries.

   C We expect our drivers to try their hardest to deliver products.

   D We do not ask our drivers how many deliveries they made at the end of the day.

200 Which of the following does FLP NOT offer to Silas Till?

   A an update on what comes out of their internal investigation

   B a free special delivery

   C free delivery on a future purchase

   D $20 off his next purchase

Listening Scripts

PRACTICE TEST 1

Part I

Track 1

(Narrator)		For each question, you will hear four statements about a picture in your test book. When you hear the statements, you must select the one statement that best describes what you see in the picture. Then find the number of the question on your answer sheet and mark your answer. The statements will not be written in your test book, and will be spoken just once.
(Narrator)		Look at the example item below.
(Narrator)		Now listen to the four statements.
(Woman A)	**A**	She's reading the paper.
	B	She's applying the body.
	C	She's studying the test.
	D	She's looking at the X-ray.
(Narrator)		Statement **A**, 'She's looking at the X-ray' best describes the photograph. Therefore, you should mark answer **A** in your test book.
(Narrator)		Now Part 1 will begin.
(Narrator)		Look at the picture marked number 1 in your test book.
(Man A)	**A**	The vehicles are parked side by side.
	B	A car is being towed away.
	C	The truck is travelling the wrong way.
	D	A vehicle is making a turn at the corner.
(Narrator)		Look at the picture marked number 2 in your test book.
(Woman B)	**A**	The people are standing behind the railing.
	B	The people are climbing over the railing.
	C	The people are seated on the railing.
	D	The people are all holding on to the railing.
(Narrator)		Look at the picture marked number 3 in your test book.
(Man B)	**A**	The hostess is entertaining her guests.
	B	The woman is slicing the meat.
	C	The waitress is serving her customers.
	D	The chef is placing the meat onto the platter.
(Narrator)		Look at the picture marked number 4 in your test book.
(Woman A)	**A**	The woman is taking a selfie.
	B	She's hanging up the telephone.
	C	The woman is painting the scenery.
	D	She's holding a photograph.
(Narrator)		Look at the picture marked number 5 in your test book.

(Man A)	A	The building is very upmarket.
	B	The people are looking for shelter.
	C	The market has many different stalls.
	D	The building is newly painted.
(Narrator)		Look at the picture marked number 6 in your test book.
(Woman B)	A	She is looking for her cup of tea.
	B	She is reading on a device.
	C	She is taking her tablets.
	D	She is working through equations.

Part II

Track 2

(Narrator)	You will hear a question or statement and three responses spoken in English. They will not be written in your test book, and will be spoken just once. Select the best response to the question or statement and mark the letter A, B, or C on your answer sheet.
(Narrator)	For example, you will hear:
(Man B)	Where are the marketing interns?

(Narrator)		You will also hear:
(Woman A)	A	The market closes at three.
	B	It's just round the corner, past the butcher's.
	C	Rohan took them to lunch.
(Narrator)		The best response to the question "Where are the marketing interns?" is choice **C**, "Rohan took them to lunch," so **C** is the correct answer. You should mark answer **C** in your test book.
(Narrator)		Now let us begin with question number 7.
(Woman A)	7	Have you booked a car for the trip?
(Man A)	A	We're taking a taxi.
	B	The parking lot's around the corner.
	C	I don't care who's coming.
(Man B)	8	Is it OK if I bring a friend with me?
(Woman A)	A	You can use the front entrance.
	B	Sure, I can take it with me.
	C	The more the merrier.
(Woman A)	9	You weren't supposed to tell him.
(Man B)	A	Well, nobody warned me they would be here.
	B	I know, I'm really sorry I'm late.
	C	Well, the cat's out of the bag now.
(Woman B)	10	Why was she complaining to the waitress?

(Man A)	**A**	I think I need a refill.
	B	There was a hair in her coffee.
	C	I'm on a carb-free diet.
(Woman A)	**11**	When was the last time we had lunch together?
(Man A)	**A**	Oh, it's been ages.
	B	They don't serve lunch here.
	C	Actually, I wasn't even born then.
(Man B)	**12**	I'm really surprised by the turnout at the event.
(Woman A)	**A**	I know, I didn't think there would be half the people.
	B	I've never tried one of these before.
	C	You should really talk to your lawyer about this.
(Woman A)	**13**	Does he always ask so many questions?
(Man B)	**A**	It was a questionable decision.
	B	Interrogating people is his hobby.
	C	I forgot he was planning on bringing someone.
(Woman B)	**14**	Are you having a summer or winter wedding?
(Man A)	**A**	We're not married yet.
	B	May 15th, so spring actually.
	C	It really *has* been cold winter, hasn't it?
(Man A)	**15**	Who does this blue notebook belong to?
(Woman B)	**A**	I'm not sure, I just found it here.
	B	We've run out of blue notebooks.
	C	Let me make a note of that.
(Man B)	**16**	It's such a shame about his father passing.
(Woman B)	**A**	I'll be sure to pass on the message.
	B	He was so young, too.
	C	My father was happy to hear about you.
(Woman B)	**17**	Are you available to come into the office this Saturday?
(Man B)	**A**	I'm away for the weekend.
	B	Yeah, nobody knew about it.
	C	It's going to be on Sunday morning.
(Woman A)	**18**	Whose idea was it to postpone the meeting by a week?
(Man A)	**A**	Meetings are on Monday mornings at 11.
	B	It was the client's request, actually.
	C	I was in another meeting, so I couldn't join you.
(Woman B)	**19**	How many bags are we allowed to bring on the plane?
(Man B)	**A**	The flight is going to be delayed by 30 minutes.
	B	That's just wrong–plain and simple.
	C	According to the website, only two.

(Man B)	20	Has she been informed of this yet?
(Woman A)	A	No, I don't think it's a good idea to lie to him.
	B	Yes, we haven't mentioned it to her yet.
	C	No, she's still in the dark.
(Woman A)	21	When will the new policy be implemented?
(Man B)	A	It's not been decided yet.
	B	It's starting to look a bit bad.
	C	I guess we'll never know.
(Man A)	22	Do you prefer sweet or savory?
(Woman B)	A	I would prefer it if we waited a bit first.
	B	That's very sweet of you to say.
	C	I'm not very picky with food, I like everything.
(Woman B)	23	Who is the guy who just said hello to you?
(Man A)	A	He's the company's new Chief Operating Officer.
	B	I only said hello to be friendly.
	C	He wasn't supposed to talk to you.
(Man A)	24	Where are you taking her for her birthday?
(Man B)	A	I'm not taking anything for granted.
	B	I'm throwing her a surprise party at home.
	C	She's turning thirty this year.
(Man B)	25	Don't we have a meeting in five minutes?
(Woman B)	A	It takes me more than 10 minutes, normally.
	B	That's been pushed back. It's in two hours.
	C	OK, I'll call him back in five minutes.
(Woman A)	26	The item I ordered from you has still not arrived.
(Man A)	A	I'm sorry to hear that.
	B	I didn't order any items.
	C	I was told that wasn't the correct form.
(Woman B)	27	What's your favorite book?
(Man B)	A	I've got a lot of things to do.
	B	I took literature in college.
	C	I'm not a big fan of reading.
(Man A)	28	Have you decided what to do yet?
(Woman A)	A	I'm not going to be on time.
	B	I didn't know she was going to do it.
	C	I'm still on the fence about it.
(Man B)	29	I bought these new posters for my office.
(Man A)	A	I'm on my way to the post office, too.
	B	Oh, they look very nice!
	C	And whose fault is it?

(Woman A)	30	How long before the game begins?
(Woman B)	A	It's been a long day.
	B	My favorite game is chess.
	C	It's already started.
(Woman B)	31	Were you upset that they didn't invite you?
(Woman A)	A	They did. I just didn't want to go.
	B	I told you already, I'm not upset with you.
	C	You'll feel better in the morning.

Part III

Track 3

(Narrator)	You will hear some conversations between two or more people. You will be asked to answer three questions about what the speakers say in each conversation. Select the best response to each question and mark the letter (A), (B), (C), or (D) on your answer sheet. The conversation will not be written in your test book, and will be spoken just once.
(Narrator)	Now let us begin with question number 32.
(Narrator)	Questions 32–34 refer to the following conversation.
(Woman A)	Morning, Andy. Any idea who we're sending to Brazil for that meeting?
(Man A)	I was actually discussing this with Michelle this morning. It's becoming a bit of a nightmare, to be honest... Tim was originally scheduled to go, but you know he gave his notice last week, so he won't be around. I thought Georgia might be able to go, but she's got her kids to take care of that week.
(Woman A)	It's such a shame I've booked my holidays to Spain that week already. I would've loved to go! Excellent opportunity to see the sales pitch first hand.
(Man A)	Yeah, and I've got a meeting in Florida that week with a different client, so I can't make it either.
(Woman A)	Have we tried to reschedule with the client?
(Man A)	Well, the thing is they're a new client, so it would look unprofessional.
(Narrator)	Who was supposed to go to the meeting in Brazil?
(Narrator)	What does the man say about Georgina?
(Narrator)	Why does the man not want to reschedule the meeting?
(Narrator)	Questions 35–37 refer to the following conversation.
(Man A)	Hey, can you have a look at this email for me? I just want to know your take on it. I don't think I'm reading it right. Does it really say they've moved the conference back two months?
(Woman B)	Let's see... umm... Yeah, see here: the new date is November 10th to November 15th.
(Man A)	I thought so! This is unbelievable... I've already booked flights and accommodation, and none of it is refundable. I'm going to be out of pocket by thousands of dollars.

(Woman B)	You booked already? The conference isn't happening for another ten months! Twelve now.
(Man A)	You know I like to plan things in advance. I don't like to be stressed. This is just typical, I can't catch a break at the moment.
(Woman B)	Just give them a call. I'm sure they'll have no choice but to reimburse you. It's their fault, after all.

(Narrator)	What are the speakers discussing?
(Narrator)	Why is the woman surprised?
(Narrator)	What is the woman's recommendation?

(Narrator)	Questions 38–40 refer to the following conversation.
(Man B)	Hi, I'm calling on behalf of Max TV. Do you have a couple of minutes to spare? I'd just like to ask you a few questions.
(Woman A)	Um, sure.
(Man B)	Great. Okay, so I can see you've been signed up with us for a month... how have you been getting on with your subscription to our service so far?
(Woman A)	It's been all right, I guess... Well, I did have a problem with reception at first–some of the channels were acting up and the feed was interrupted, but I called your helpline and they sent an engineer the next day so it's all good now.
(Man B)	Excellent. And is there anything you feel is missing from your subscription, any service you'd like us to add?
(Woman A)	Nothing comes to mind... my previous provider was horrendous and they charged extortionate fees–the technical service wasn't free, either. You've been great.
(Man B)	I'm glad to hear it!. Now, if you could just...

(Narrator)	What is this conversation about?
(Narrator)	What does the woman say about reception?
(Narrator)	Why dos the man say "I'm glad to hear it"?

(Narrator)	Questions 41–43 refer to the following conversation.
(Woman A)	God, I'm so tired. I've been looking at resumes all morning.
(Man A)	Are you still trying to fill that assistant position? I thought you'd offered it to someone.
(Woman A)	I had, but then he called and said he'd been offered a better position elsewhere so I'm back to square one now. Urgh, well, I've narrowed it down to five people. I've got phone interviews with most of them in the next few days. I just hope one of them works out.
(Man A)	I can do a couple of the interviews if you like? I've got some spare time this week.
(Woman A)	Can you? That would actually be great help. Honestly, ever since we terminated our contract with that recruitment agency, finding new people has been a nightmare.
(Man A)	Well, good news. I heard through the grapevine that we're looking into signing a contract with a different agency.

(Narrator)	Why has the position not been filled yet?
(Narrator)	What will the man do?
(Narrator)	What does the man say about the recruitment agency?
(Narrator)	Questions 44–46 refer to the following conversation.
(Man A)	What they need to understand is that we don't run a charity here. Unless we have a signed purchase order, we can't provide them with services that we're not going to be able to charge them for.
(Woman B)	I totally agree. I've raised this numerous times with Thomas, and he feels exactly the same way. To be honest with you, I think he's a bit embarrassed about the whole situation. He's been asking his boss to sign the purchase order for ages, but he's just been ignored every time.
(Man A)	Well, I think it's about time we did something about it. When is the next time we're supposed to send someone to their offices?
(Woman B)	Monday morning, I think. No, wait, they cancelled that. It's Tuesday now.
(Man A)	Well, let's tell them we'll have to cancel that order if we haven't received a signed purchase order for it by noon on Monday. Maybe that'll get a response.
(Narrator)	Who are the speakers likely to be?
(Narrator)	What does the woman imply about Thomas?
(Narrator)	What is the man's suggestion?
(Narrator)	Questions 47–49 refer to the following conversation.
(Woman A)	I can't believe this has happened. Have you even looked at this? It's awful! First of all, my husband's name is misspelled–it's Stephen with a P H, not Steven with a V– and secondly, we explicitly said no nuts in the cake and there are nuts sprinkled all over the top! It's just unacceptable. I have a party in five hours and about a hundred other things to do–I can't be going around looking for a new cake. I just can't.
(Man B)	Of course, I understand, madam. When you came over to order the cake, we did ask you how to spell the name and you signed the order with the name spelled with a V, but –
(Woman A)	You must be mistaking me with a different customer. I placed my order online and, trust me, I know how to spell my husband's name. I also wrote, very clearly, that my husband is deathly allergic to nuts. Even the smell of this cake could throw him into anaphylactic shock. Are you trying to get him killed?
(Man B)	I'm really sorry, madam. There must've been a glitch in the system. Would you like to have a look at our other cakes? You can pick two different ones, and we'll decorate them quickly for you right now with the correct name.
(Narrator)	Why is the woman upset?
(Narrator)	How did the woman order the cake?
(Narrator)	What does the man think is the reason for the mistake?
(Narrator)	Questions 50–52 refer to the following conversation.
(Woman B)	I thought we had dinner plans with your friends tomorrow? Aren't they supposed to be arriving tomorrow morning?

(Man B)	Didn't I tell you? Their flight got cancelled because of the weather. They've been booked on the evening flight, so they won't be here until midnight.
(Woman B)	That's awful. Are you still picking them up?
(Man B)	I offered, but the airline's booked a taxi to the hotel for them so I don't have to.
(Woman B)	Well, it's been a long week. If we have the evening off I wouldn't mind going out to eat, I guess.
(Man B)	Great. Do you want me to pick you up from work or should we meet somewhere?
(Woman B)	Let's meet somewhere. I've got a meeting right at the end of the day and it might run over, so I don't want to keep you waiting outside the office.
(Man B)	Oh, I don't mind. I'll pick you up with the car, so I won't be outside.
(Narrator)	What are the speakers discussing?
(Narrator)	How will their friends get to the hotel from the airport?
(Narrator)	Why does the man say "Oh, I don't mind"?
(Narrator)	Questions 53–55 refer to the following conversation.
(Man A)	Welcome, Mrs. Denton. Take a seat. The reason we called you in is because your son was involved in... an altercation with another student.
(Woman A)	An altercation? What kind of altercation?
(Man A)	Verbal, and physical. Both boys maintain the other started it, of course, but we have several witnesses who have reported the fight began because your son called his classmate a... well, a swear word I'm not inclined to repeat.
(Woman A)	I'm so sorry. This is... This is very unlike him. I don't know what to say.
(Man A)	I agree, and I think it would be best to be lenient on this occasion because his record, up until now, has been excellent. We wouldn't want something like this on his permanent record to affect his chances when he applies to colleges. There will need to be repercussions, of course. Your son will need to write a letter of apology and he will be in detention for the rest of the week. It would perhaps be a good idea to have a chat with him, see what prompted this behavior.
(Woman A)	Thank you. Absolutely, I will. Thank you so much.
(Narrator)	Who are the speakers likely to be?
(Narrator)	What has the teacher decided to do?
(Narrator)	What is the woman's reaction to the situation?
(Narrator)	Questions 56–58 refer to the following conversation.
(Man A)	Well, what's the problem now? I thought we'd all agreed the way we do things was fine.
(Woman B)	We did. But now that Paul has left and Kayla has taken his place, she's decided we should be reviewing our procedures... She wants to see where we can improve performance and remove any convoluted processes that waste time.
(Man A)	Well, I don't see what's wrong with the current filing system.
(Woman B)	She thinks it's a bit repetitive—and you have to agree, it is. When you make a small change, you need to update not just our online platform, but two different spreadsheets, too. It's such a waste of time.

(Man A)	We tried to improve it last year. We said we would all store the information in the same place and update the same spreadsheet and there was uproar. People don't want to share files. They want to do things their own way.
(Woman B)	Well, they'll have to learn. The way we do things now, small details can slip through the net too easily. It's a big risk.
(Narrator)	What has prompted this discussion?
(Narrator)	What does the woman say about their filing system?
(Narrator)	Why is the woman concerned about their filing system?
(Narrator)	Questions 59–61 refer to the following conversation.
(Man B)	Oh, my God, you're OK. Thank goodness! I was watching the news and there was a big pile-up accident on your route. I thought I saw one of the cars that looked like yours.
(Woman A)	Wow. No, I'm fine. That would explain the traffic—it's horrendous! I don't think I'll be home for at least another hour.
(Woman A)	Never mind that, at least you're OK.
(Man B)	True. What time are your parents arriving tonight?
(Woman A)	My mom's already here. Dad's off work and he's on his way over right now.
(Man B)	Well, don't wait for me to start eating. It's a slog out here, I don't want to keep you guys waiting.
(Woman A)	Nonsense. I'll just put out some appetizers, we should all be fine until you get home. Just don't forget to grab a bottle of wine on your way. It completely slipped my mind when I went to the supermarket.
(Man B)	Oh, I did that already. I got it during my lunch break.
(Woman A)	Awesome. See you soon, then. Drive safe.
(Narrator)	Why has the woman called the man?
(Narrator)	What does the man tell the woman to do?
(Narrator)	Why did the woman not get wine?
(Narrator)	Questions 62–64 refer to the following conversation between three speakers.
(Woman B)	Excuse me, I'd like to return this item, please.
(Man A)	Of course—let me scan that for you. Do you have the receipts? ... Thanks... so, it looks like you bought this in the sale?
(Woman B)	Yeah, that's correct. I just bought it without trying it on, because it was such a good deal, but when I got home and tried it on... well, it just didn't work... I don't really suit A-lines...
(Man A)	Ah, I see. One moment, let me just grab my manager. Marge?
(Woman A)	Hey Stuart. What's up?
(Man A)	This lady would like to return an item, but it was bought in the sale.
(Woman A)	Oh right, okay. Unfortunately, we can't refund you for an item you got in the sale, as they're exchange only. You'll have to pick out something else from the store so we can swap it for you—if it's more expensive you'll need to just pay the difference.

(Woman B)	Gotcha. Well, I love your store, so that's not really a big deal, I'm sure I can find something... does it have to be in the sale?
(Woman A)	Nope, you can pick out anything you like.
(Narrator)	Why does the woman want to return the item?
(Narrator)	Why must the item be exchanged?
(Narrator)	Why does the woman say "that's not really a big deal"?
(Narrator)	Questions 65–67 refer to the following conversation between three speakers.
(Man A)	Hi David, thanks for coming back in to see us.
(Man B)	It's my pleasure! It's great to be back for the next round.
(Man A)	Great! We love a positive attitude here. I've asked our Head of Department, Sabrina, to join us today.
(Woman A)	Hi David, nice to meet you. I wondered if you might be able to tell me a bit about the sort of work you're doing in your current role... your CV says you've been at E-Net for 6 years?
(Man B)	Yep, so I'll just talk you through it from the beginning... so, I started working there fresh out of college, as a copywriter. I wrote articles and marketing content for their website... After a couple of years I was promoted to editor, so I was looking over the content of the other writers, making sure the quality was good, the tone was right, you know? The company didn't actually have a style guide so I created one... then the following year I was promoted again, now I'm the Content Manager for online presence.
(Woman A)	Thanks for taking us through that... so, you've been at E-Net for quite a while, why is it that you want to leave now?
(Man B)	Well, to be honest, I've been working there for a while, and I've really enjoyed it, but I just feel like I've learned as much as I can there, and I want to keep developing my skills...
(Narrator)	What are the speakers doing?
(Narrator)	What was David doing before he worked at E-Net?
(Narrator)	What is David's current job title?
(Narrator)	Questions 68–70 refer to the following conversation and program.
(Woman B)	Morning Mark! Sorry about all this paper, I'm still practicing for this talk.
(Man A)	Of course! Do you know what time your speech is? I wish I hadn't used all my holiday days at work, I'd have loved to come and see you.
(Woman B)	I haven't actually checked the program—let me see. Oh, *The History of Aviation*—I'm really looking forward to that. I'm glad I'm not right after it or I would not be able to focus... My talk is the one just before the first part of *The Future of Aviation*.
(Man A)	So, are you flying home right after?
(Woman B)	No, I actually checked for flights but they were all fully booked—unless I wanted to fly via another airport, which would take four more hours. And cost double, too!
(Man A)	That's ridiculous. They should be half price, if anything.
(Woman B)	Right? That's why I'm flying back the next morning.

(Narrator)	Why is the man unable to attend the talk?
(Narrator)	Look at the program. Which talk is the woman delivering?
(Narrator)	Why does the man say "that's ridiculous"?

Part IV

Track 4

(Narrator)	Questions 71–73 refer to the following talk.
(Woman A)	Well, to be totally honest with you, off the top of my head I think I could answer that question with a couple dozen clichés about what it takes to become successful—and it's all stuff you've heard before in different variations, I mean, this is what a cliché is after all, but it's also that sort of thing that gives people the impression I know exactly what I'm talking about, that I possess this sort of…unique insight which is what allowed me to build an innovative, highly capitalized business. But it's all smoke and mirrors. We entrepreneurs like to boast, we like to claim that it was our perseverance and our talent and our intelligence that got our businesses off the ground and turned us into millionaires—and it's true, to a certain degree. Building a successful business requires skill, it requires gusto and it requires perseverance. But, first and foremost, it takes luck. I was incredibly lucky that I came up with my idea at the right time, when the market was ready for it. And I was lucky because I had funds, I had a support network in my parents, who also own their own business, and I was able to take out a loan thanks to them. So, I guess, my advice to first time entrepreneurs would be… [fade]

(Narrator)	Where is this speech likely to take place?
(Narrator)	What does the woman say about entrepreneurs?
(Narrator)	What does the woman say about when she started her business?

(Narrator)	Questions 74–76 refer to the following talk.
(Man A)	I think you've hit the nail on the head there, Jong-Ki. The key here is communication, more specifically finding the right way to communicate this to everyone. We know we should expect pushback because we're implementing major changes, and nobody likes change—but, while our instinctive reaction could be to dismiss people's concerns because we've got our research to back us up, I think we should do exactly the opposite: we should listen to them, listen to what they have to say. These are key changes to the structure of the company, and people are bound to feel upset, or even threatened, and we should acknowledge that. To be clear, I'm not saying we should entertain all their ideas or suggestions, as that will give the wrong impression that our decision is up for debate, when it absolutely isn't. But we should allow people to feel however they feel, and we should give them time to adjust to the new reality in the company. We should answer their questions, let them talk about how they feel, identify genuine issues they raise that we might've not thought of, and just try our best to make this exciting new path for the company a success. What does everyone think? Are we all on board?

(Narrator)	What is the topic of this speech?
(Narrator)	How does the man expect his colleagues to respond to pushback?
(Narrator)	What can be inferred from the man's speech?

| (Narrator) | Questions 77–79 refer to the following talk. |
| (Man B) | What's worse, these allegations come at a particularly turbulent period for the company, which only recently announced it would be shutting more than fifty of its stores across the country, including its flagship store in New York, leading to a loss of at least three hundred jobs. The company's CEO, Mrs. Rossi, has been fervently trying to allay concerns that liquidation or administration might be on the horizon, but investors don't seem convinced, as is evident from the company's incredibly poor performance in the stock market ever since the announcement was made last month—and things look like they are only going to get worse from now on. In the last 24 hours, two more former employees of the company have come forward with stories similar to Mr. Edmonds', describing a toxic work environment and a bullying culture that, based on their varied roles, seems to be present from the top level all the way down to the bottom ranks. These two employees have chosen to remain anonymous, but they have spoken of cases where proper working standards were not maintained. We'll speak to one of these former employees at 8, so stay tuned. |

(Narrator)	Why has the company been in the spotlight lately?
(Narrator)	What is implied about the company's former employees?
(Narrator)	What will happen at 8 o' clock?

| (Narrator) | Questions 80–82 refer to the following talk. |
| (Woman B) | OK, so, I got this idea while I was taking the subway to the office. It was early morning and it was hot outside and even hotter inside and I was sweating and I was starting to get a little claustrophobic and I looked around me and I saw, you know, so many different people—young, old—and they were all…rushing. Pushing each other and ignoring each other, messing with their phones and listening to music, and as soon as the doors opened they jumped, fighting to be the first out onto the platform. And I'm exactly the same: I always have to be the first out. I actually have this habit, I…sort of know what the best spot is when I take the subway. I mean, I know where to stand so the doors open in front of the exit— which, you know, it can shave off at least a couple of minutes from your commute. It can make the difference between catching and missing your connection. So, I thought—that would make a great app. People on the platform putting in their journey, and their phone telling them where to stand so they can find themselves right at the exit when they get to their destination. So, then I started looking into the sort of specifications such an app would require. For example, I mean, the Chicago "L" only has eight lines, but that's 145 stations and I'd need to know every single variation of a journey between all of them, which amounts to… |

(Narrator)	What does the speaker do?
(Narrator)	What does the speaker NOT say about the fellow commuters on her journey?
(Narrator)	What would the woman's app do?

(Narrator) Questions 83–85 refer to the following talk.

(Man A) As most of you know, our company will be celebrating 30 years of operation this coming September. I know, I know, it's party time—but I'll leave that conversation to the party committee. What I would like to talk to you about is where we stand at this moment, and the exciting times ahead. As you might remember from our last company-wide meeting, I told you we were negotiating with our external investors to buy back the shares we had to sell ten years ago, when the economic crisis started. I'm happy to announce that negotiations are over and before our thirtieth anniversary in September, we will have bought back 23% of our shares, bringing our ownership back up to 97%, with an aim to reach 100% in the next ten months. This is extremely important for us because, while our investors were of great help during a very difficult period for the company, they also didn't share our vision for the future of the company. We have long discussed the possibility of expanding to European markets, more specifically Germany and France to start with, and later on Spain, Italy and the United Kingdom—but we have not been able to do so because of pushback. Now our plan to open a small office in Germany can go ahead, and we anticipate…

(Narrator) Where is this speech taking place?

(Narrator) How many shares will the company own by September?

(Narrator) Why is it important for the company shares to be bought back?

(Narrator) Questions 86–88 refer to the following talk.

(Man B) Thank you for contacting Athena Couriers. If you are calling to inquire about an existing shipment, please have your tracking number to hand. If you would like to know the status of your shipment, please press 1. If you would like to arrange for re-delivery, please press 2. If you are a new customer and would like to know more about the services we offer, please press 3 or visit our website at www.athenacouriers.com. If you would like to know about parcel size and weight limits, please press 4. If you would like to know more about our guaranteed next-day delivery service, please press 5. If your parcel is experiencing delays at customs and you would like advice, please press 6. For all other enquiries, please hold and you will be connected to a representative soon. If you would like to hear the menu again, please press 0.

(Narrator) Which button should the caller press to find out if their shipment has been delivered?

(Narrator) Which information can be found on the company's website?

(Narrator) What should the caller do if none of the options apply to them?

(Narrator) Questions 89–91 refer to the following talk and table.

(Man A) I think it's pretty clear that most of our winter collection has been quite successful, and even the products that didn't quite manage to capture our customers' attention, judging by what's left in stock in our stores, there's very little compared with last year. The main thing we got out of the feedback surveys from our mailing list last year was that people wanted us to be more innovative, to take more risks, and having taken that feedback to heart and tested it with this collection, we can see the results are quite remarkable. If we ignore the strange flukes, like this pair of jeans, whose sales were consistently lower than the rest of our products even during our sales in February, the rest of the line has performed really well. I want to draw your attention to this particular pair of trousers, KG945. Now, if you remember, some of you were very reluctant to go ahead with it when the design was revealed because you thought it was too daring—but as you can see, it's outperformed all our other products even in March, when we began to experience a slump as people started looking for more summery clothes. What I think we need to do is...

(Narrator)	How did the speaker receive feedback from the company's customers?
(Narrator)	Look at the table below. Which product does the speaker describe as a fluke?
(Narrator)	What can be inferred about the product KG945?

| (Narrator) | Questions 92–94 refer to the following talk. |
| (Woman A) | The truth is that remote working is the future. Companies are reluctant to accept this for a variety of reasons—because it's not what they're used to, because they're afraid their employees will slack off if they're not in the office, because they just don't see the benefits in allowing their employees to work from home—but those companies that have embraced remote working, and I mean fully embraced, have seen it for what it is: an excellent opportunity to evolve. About 50% of our full-time, permanent employees now work from home at least three days a week, and the other 50% work from home one day a week, with the exception of departments such as finance, HR and reception. And you know what that means? It means we can rent a smaller space and lower our monthly overhead costs. It means our employees who have children no longer need to give up their job to take care of them, nor do we need to provide them with day care facilities: they can stay at home with their kids, look after them and at the same time respond to phone calls and emails. It means that our employees are happy, because they save money and time and avoid the stress of commuting, and we are happy because they are doing their job better as a result of their flexibility. |

(Narrator)	Which reason is NOT given for why companies don't like remote working?
(Narrator)	What does the woman say about remote working in her company?
(Narrator)	What can be inferred from the woman's speech?

| (Narrator) | Questions 95–97 refer to the following talk. |
| (Woman B) | Thank you for coming to listen to me. My name is Emma Thorne. I worked as a Chief Operating Officer for 20 years in three different Fortune 500 companies. I was happily married, and I had two kids. Then, one morning, my husband had a heart attack on his way to work and passed away—and the whole world collapsed under my feet. My company offered me a couple of days off to mourn, and then they politely asked me to return. Which I felt was a bit too soon, but it was OK, because the world continues to turn and I still had bills to pay and kids to feed. Plus, I welcomed the distraction. As soon as I returned to the office, though, my company, which had been great up until then, did everything wrong. My boss walked on eggshells around me. She fed me clichés... I don't know how many times I was told that 'time heals all wounds'... These statements were unhelpful and, frankly, insulting. People whispered in front of me. It just made me think that companies can do better. There must be a way to teach them to do better, to treat |

grieving employees better. And that's why I left my job as a Chief Operating Officer and went back to school at age 45 to study psychology. To use my experience, my very common experience, to change the way companies operate when it comes to death in an employee's family. Let's look at some figures...

(Narrator)	Where is this speech likely to take place?
(Narrator)	Why was the woman upset with how her boss treated her after her husband's death?
(Narrator)	What major life change did the woman make after her husband's death?
(Narrator)	Questions 98–100 refer to the following talk.
(Woman A)	So, the hotel is here—see the red dot? That's where we are. When you exit through those doors behind you, you can either turn left or right. We've got two subway stations nearby, one on the blue line, one on the red, both equidistant from the hotel. For the blue line, turn left. For the red, turn right. Now, since you guys are only staying for a couple of days, what I'd recommend you definitely visit is the archaeological museum, which is just two blocks from here. When you exit, just turn left, follow the road down and turn right when you see a mini market with a yellow door. It's very distinctive, you can't miss it. You should also visit the city gardens—you'll need to take the red line for that. It's just five stations from here—see? It's here on the map. There are three different hop-on hop-off bus companies: the red, the yellow and the green. I prefer the green: it's cheaper, and the ticket lasts for 48 hours. The other two are only 24. Or, if you prefer, we can set you up with a private tour guide tomorrow, though it's a Sunday so it might be pricier than usual. If you have time on Monday, that might be cheaper—though the hop-on is just as good.
(Narrator)	Look at the map. Which number marks the location of the Red Line?
(Narrator)	What can be inferred about the city gardens from the woman's speech?
(Narrator)	Which sightseeing method of transport does the woman recommend?

PRACTICE TEST 2

Part I

Track 5

(Narrator)	For each question in this part, you will hear four statements about a picture in your test book. When you hear the statements, you must select the one statement that best describes what you see in the picture. Then find the number of the question on your answer sheet and mark your answer. The statements will not be written in your test book, and will be spoken just once
(Narrator)	Look at the example item below.
(Narrator)	Now listen to the four statements.
(Woman A)	**A** They're talking about their food.
	B The men are making chopsticks.
	C They're making the dinner.
	D They're having a meal together.

(Narrator)	Statement **D**, 'They're having a meal together' best describes the photograph. Therefore, you should mark answer **D** in your test book.
(Narrator)	Now Part 1 will begin.
(Narrator)	Look at the picture marked number 1 in your test book.

(Man A)	**A**	Everyone has finished.
	B	They will eat outside.
	C	The cutlery is missing.
	D	The dishes need to be discarded.

(Narrator)	Look at the picture marked number 2 in your test book.

(Woman B)	**A**	They are attending a screening.
	B	They are monitoring their staff.
	C	The files are grouped on the table.
	D	The colleagues are looking at their work.

(Narrator)	Look at the picture marked number 3 in your test book.

(Man B)	**A**	He's looking at a document.
	B	He's driving his car.
	C	He's working from home.
	D	He's playing a game.

(Narrator)	Look at the picture marked number 4 in your test book.

(Woman A)	**A**	The baskets are next to each other.
	B	The wires are on the floor.
	C	The technician is wearing a glove.
	D	They are reading a novel.

(Narrator)	Look at the picture marked number 5 in your test book.

(Man A)	**A**	The plants are in the basket.
	B	The woman is talking to the child.
	C	The woman is laying the table.
	D	The man is falling asleep.

(Narrator)	Look at the picture marked number 6 in your test book.

(Woman B)	**A**	There is a fire in the hallway.
	B	The cans of food are on the floor.
	C	The bedroom is cluttered.
	D	The trash can is on the left-hand side.

Part II

Track 6

(Narrator)	You will hear a question or statement and three responses spoken in English. They will not be printed in your test book and will be spoken only one time. Select the best response to the question or statement and mark the letter A, B, or C on your answer sheet.

(Narrator)		For example, you will hear:
(Man B)		When will you send me your notes?
(Narrator)		You will also hear:
(Woman A)	**A**	I can get them to you this afternoon.
	B	Noted, thanks.
	C	He notes everything down.
(Narrator)		The best response to the question "Where are the marketing interns?" is choice **C**, "Rohan took them to lunch," so **C** is the correct answer. You should mark answer **C** in your test book.
(Narrator)		Now let us begin with question number 7.
(Woman A)	**7**	What time do you think the bank closes?
(Man A)	**A**	On Saturdays.
	B	I don't think so.
	C	Usually at 5.
(Man B)	**8**	Why are you leaving?
(Woman A)	**A**	I'm going back to college.
	B	The leaves on the trees look wonderful.
	C	Yes, I'm leaving at the end of this week.
(Woman A)	**9**	When do you expect to visit the new clients?
(Man B)	**A**	In San Francisco
	B	With Mary, I think.
	C	The day after tomorrow.
(Woman B)	**10**	How expensive are the new computers?
(Man A)	**A**	I like the new computers.
	B	Not very, and we really need them.
	C	Life is expensive in New York.
(Woman A)	**11**	Do I have any meetings today?
(Man A)	**A**	Yes, your sister called.
	B	Sometimes.
	C	Yes. Mr. Smith from ITC at 2.
(Man B)	**12**	Where is the fax we received this morning?
(Woman A)	**A**	On your desk.
	B	Yes, please.
	C	I faxed it last night.
(Woman A)	**13**	It's supposed to snow tonight.
(Man B)	**A**	No, I'm pretty warm right now.
	B	It'll be difficult to get to work tomorrow then.
	C	It'll be quite warm tonight.

(Woman B)	**14**	Can I get you some tea?
(Man A)	**A**	Yes, please.
	B	Yes, occasionally.
	C	No, I don't.
(Man A)	**15**	Whose phone is this?
(Woman B)	**A**	I think it's Gisele's.
	B	I don't know where.
	C	It's an old one.
(Man B)	**16**	Mrs. Aubameyang's train arrives at seven this morning.
(Woman B)	**A**	Matt will pick her up at the station.
	B	She'll be here tonight.
	C	Trains are expensive in Europe.
(Woman B)	**17**	Where should I take the candidates?
(Man B)	**A**	Tomorrow, please.
	B	By car, I hope.
	C	To the meeting room.
(Woman A)	**18**	Which do you prefer, computers or tablets?
(Man A)	**A**	Not sure. I guess I like both.
	B	Computers are getting cheaper and cheaper.
	C	I'll take an aspirin tablet, thanks.
(Woman B)	**19**	How many emails do you usually get every day?
(Man B)	**A**	I didn't get her email.
	B	Nearly a hundred, I'd say.
	C	6 o' clock.
(Man B)	**20**	When will they announce the new CEO?
(Woman A)	**A**	Beginning of April I've been told.
	B	In Moscow.
	C	That's in room 301
(Woman A)	**21**	Is your office warm in winter?
(Man B)	**A**	It's a corner office.
	B	It's a warm country.
	C	Very.
(Man A)	**22**	I come to this restaurant a lot.
(Woman B)	**A**	Me too. I love the noodles.
	B	Me too. It's a great movie.
	C	No, I don't.
(Woman B)	**23**	Ms. Aranha called when you were away.
(Man A)	**A**	What did she want?
	B	I'll call him later.
	C	It was amazing.

(Man A)	**24**	What are these people doing here?
(Man B)	**A**	They're six and eight.
	B	They're here for the interview.
	C	She wants to see you.
(Man B)	**25**	Why don't you take the rest of the day off?
(Woman B)	**A**	It's a beautiful day.
	B	I'll turn it off for you.
	C	Thank you, sir.
(Woman A)	**26**	What color is the replacement car?
(Man A)	**A**	It's the blue one by the exit.
	B	Yellow taxis.
	C	It's already been replaced.
(Woman B)	**27**	How much time will it take them to finish the new kitchen?
(Man B)	**A**	I heard it was yesterday.
	B	Two to three weeks.
	C	Six months ago.
(Man A)	**28**	Did the papers come yet?
(Woman A)	**A**	Yes, they're on your desk.
	B	No, they won't.
	C	Yes, they are.
(Man B)	**29**	Why are you still here?
(Man A)	**A**	It's green.
	B	Because I will.
	C	I need to finish this report today.
(Woman A)	**30**	Can you recommend a good French teacher?
(Woman B)	**A**	No, thanks.
	B	Not really. I'm sorry.
	C	Yes, tomorrow is the day.
(Woman B)	**31**	This printer is always breaking down.
(Woman A)	**A**	I'm on my lunch break.
	B	Can you print it for me, please?
	C	It's time to get a new one, I suppose.

Part III

Track 7

(Narrator) You will hear some conversations between two or more people. You will be asked to answer three questions about what the speakers say in each conversation. Select the best response to each question and mark the letter (A), (B), (C), or (D) on your answer sheet. The conversation will not be printed in your test book and will be spoken only one time.

(Narrator)	Now let us begin with question number 32.
(Narrator)	Questions 32–34 refer to the following conversation.
(Woman B)	Jane told me that your interview went quite well. Who interviewed you?
(Man B)	The office manager, but the personnel director dropped by to explain some procedures. He didn't ask me any questions though. It was the office manager who did all the interviewing, but she was very nice. I think it all went very well, actually, so I'm happy about that.
(Woman B)	That's encouraging. I bet the office manager doesn't interview every applicant. Did you get a chance to talk about the research you've been doing recently?
(Man B)	Yes, I did. She asked me a lot of questions about it and she seemed pretty impressed.
(Narrator)	What are the speakers talking about?
(Narrator)	Who asked questions?
(Narrator)	How does the man feel?
(Narrator)	Questions 35–37 refer to the following conversation.
(Woman B)	I always think it's a good idea for customers to see how we run our production process, so if you have time, Mr. Bidwell, I thought I'd show you around the plant.
(Man B)	That's a great idea. I don't have much time, though. How long will it take? If it's not more than half an hour, that should be fine.
(Woman B)	Not long-about twenty minutes or so. I'm afraid I'll have to ask you to put on this hard hat, thought. It's government regulations... we can't risk you getting injured.
(Man B)	No, I understand, no problem.
(Narrator)	Who is the man?
(Narrator)	Where will the speakers go?
(Narrator)	What will the man need to wear?
(Narrator)	Questions 38–40 refer to the following conversation and plan.
(Woman A)	Here's your check, Mr. Kanu. How long do you think until it's all up and running?
(Man B)	Three or four weeks I'd say.
(Woman A)	I don't need to remind you that we need the work completed by the end of April?
(Man B)	I know that, Ms. Webster. The boys will be here right at the crack of dawn.
(Woman A)	That's good to know. And as agreed, I'll give you the other half of the payment once work's completed.
(Man B)	That's fine. Can I just ask you a question about the new toilets?
(Woman A)	Sure. What do you want to know?
(Man B)	I'm just a bit worried about the number of cubicles. It's one thing to fit five cubicles in that area on paper, but another to make something in which people can feel comfortable. Perhaps four cubicles, two on each side would be better? Then we can add another sink and dryer.

(Narrator)	When does the woman need the work finished?
(Narrator)	Why does the man say "at the crack of dawn"?
(Narrator)	Look at the plan. Which cubicle does the man think should be removed from the project?
(Narrator)	Questions 41–43 refer to the following conversation.
(Man B)	I'm just popping out to the bank to deposit a check in my account. Do you want me to pick anything up for you while I'm out?
(Woman A)	Well, actually, if you pass by the mini-market could you get me a sandwich for lunch? Cheese if you can find one, chicken if not. Hang on a moment and I'll get some money.
(Man B)	No, no. My treat! I'll pick up sandwiches for us both on my way back. Oh, and by the way, |I'm expecting a call from the marketing department. If they call, could you tell them i'll be back at my desk in half an hour or so?
(Woman A)	Okay. I'll do that.
(Narrator)	Where are the speakers?
(Narrator)	Where is the man going?
(Narrator)	What does the woman want?
(Narrator)	Questions 44–46 refer to the following conversation.
(Man A)	So, after the church you'll have get in the right lane because you'll have to turn right at the first roundabout. That's the main road and I think you can remember how to get to the factory from there.
(Woman B)	Yes, I do. But are you sure I have to turn right at the roundabout? I remember going straight and then past that Italian restaurant... What's it called? We had lunch there once...
(Man A)	Giuseppe's.
(Woman B)	Yes, that's it.
(Man A)	That was in Chicago, Mesut. Remember? We took the Japanese clients to see the Bears... it was freezing...
(Woman B)	You're right... I remember that. When we said football they thought they were going to see a soccer match.
(Man A)	Exactly. They were so disappointed.
(Narrator)	Where does the man want to go?
(Narrator)	What is Giuseppe's?
(Narrator)	Why were the clients disappointed?
(Narrator)	Questions 47–49 refer to the following conversation.
(Man B)	We ordered those new eco printers over two weeks ago and still nothing. I must say I'm thinking about cancelling the order and going back to TechPak.
(Woman A)	You get what you pay for. Told you it was too good to be true. How on earth can they be $100 cheaper than TechPak? It's just impossible.

(Man B)	Come on, Burcu. It's easy to say that now. I can't remember you saying that when I found this online store. On the contrary... you were quite excited. You even texted the link to your husband and asked him to look at the smart TV on sale.
(Woman A)	That's not entirely true, Wallace. I told you I would never buy anything from an online store... and this is why I sent the link to Matteo. And guess what? He was a bit suspicious about the whole thing... He even called you!!!
(Man B)	He called me to ask if I'd ever heard about one of the TV makes. He thought they were too cheap. He didn't say anything about the store.
(Narrator)	Why does the woman say "too good to be true"?
(Narrator)	Look at the graphic. Which product did they most likely buy?
(Narrator)	Who's Matteo?
(Narrator)	Questions 50–52 refer to the following conversation with three speakers.
(Man A)	Do you want me to help you with those? I've already uploaded all the data and have nothing else to do for the day.
(Woman B)	That's okay, I've got it covered, thanks. But I think Nelson here is struggling a little with the new system.
(Man B)	It's a bit of a nightmare, actually. It's taking me twice the time to export the spreadsheets. I can't find anything!!! It's not practical at all.
(Man A)	Why did they change it? I never had any issues.
(Woman B)	Right? We only had the other system for two years and it was working just fine. Sometimes I think IT is only trying to justify their salaries, you know. Look how busy we are, we have a new system, new software, all these files to process. It's madness!
(Narrator)	How are the speakers probably feeling?
(Narrator)	Why does Nelson say "It's a bit of a nightmare"?
(Narrator)	What does the woman say about IT?
(Narrator)	Questions 53–55 refer to the following conversation.
(Woman A)	Could you tell me where you keep the invoices?
(Man A)	There's a folder on Dropdrive. Invoices 2018.
(Woman A)	Let me see. I can't find anything. Are you sure it's there?... oh hang on, got it. Ugh, it's so difficult to find what we need here. Some save their files on Dropdrive, others use the intranet... It's such a mess.
(Man A)	I know. The problem is that everybody thinks they can do whatever they want in this place. People arrive whenever they want, they go home whenever they want, they use the computers to do whatever they want... It's chaos.
(Woman A)	But what do you expect to happen with such laid-back management? Tatiana is never here, Sarah is always on the phone, and what about Marcelo...
(Man A)	Oh, don't get me started! He's the worst, Mikiko. I have never seen anyone this lazy in my entire life.

(Narrator)	What can't the woman find?
(Narrator)	What does the man say about the company?
(Narrator)	Who is NOT one of the managers?

(Narrator)	Questions 56–58 refer to the following conversation with three speakers.
(Man A)	Hi Julie. Hi Abu. I was wondering if you could do me a favor. It's my wife's birthday this Thursday and I have no idea what to get her. Every year I get her something I think she's going to like but she always takes it back to the store. It's so frustrating.
(Man B)	Oh! We can try to help, but I'm not promising anything! What's she like?
(Man A)	She's an architect. She loves her job more than anything. She's also a big art fan… She loves modern art and all those things I don't understand.
(Woman B)	Does she have any hobbies? Anything she likes doing on the weekend?
(Man A)	She loves cooking, Julie. Not every day cooking. She likes cooking for friends and family… we always have people over on the weekend.
(Man B)	Why don't you get her one of those experience day gifts? She could spend a whole day with a chef and learn some new recipes… Different cuisines, different flavors… I think she'd like that.
(Woman B)	That's a good idea. And also, if she likes modern art, you could give her a holiday as a present… You could go to London and visit the modern art museum.
(Man B)	Or Sao Paulo, in Brazil. I've heard they've got a great modern art museum there. Actually, Brazilian food is really good. She could visit the museum and take a cookery course there. I'm sure Rodrigo from IT can help you with that - he used to live there.
(Man A)	That's a great idea, thanks! I'll text him later.

(Narrator)	Who is an architect?
(Narrator)	What is the woman's suggestion?
(Narrator)	Why does the man say "I'll text him later"?

(Narrator)	Questions 59–61 refer to the following conversation.
(Man B)	Rawan, do you have a minute?
(Woman A)	Of course Thomas. What do you need?
(Man B)	I'm going to Germany for the weekend and I was wondering if you could keep an eye on the new associates. I just want to make sure they know what they're doing. We can't afford any surprises in the Mahamas's case.
(Woman A)	No problem. I'll monitor the whole thing and if I need your input I'll send you an email.
(Man B)	Just call me. It's easier and I might not be able to check my email all the time while I'm there. My sister lives in the countryside and she told me they still don't have 4G there.
(Woman A)	Don't worry. I'll call you if anything happens. You're going on Wednesday, is that right?
(Man B)	Tomorrow. I'm spending the night at Newark tonight, though. My flight leaves really early in the morning.
(Woman A)	Well, enjoy your vacation. You've earned it.

(Narrator)	What will Thomas do this weekend?
(Narrator)	Who's the woman going to watch closely?
(Narrator)	How should the woman contact the man?
(Narrator)	Questions 62–64 refer to the following conversation.
(Man A)	You didn't send me her résumé as you promised. What happened?
(Woman B)	I'm not sure she's what we're looking for. She certainly has the experience and the qualifications. But don't you think it's a bit strange that she's had all these different jobs? The longest she's managed to stay with the same company was three years, from 1999 to 2002. And that was nearly twenty years ago when she had just finished university.
(Man A)	That doesn't look very good. Did you talk you talk to her about that? What did she have to say?
(Woman B)	She said it was because she wanted to learn all the facets of corporate law. She also told me I could contact every single former employer from her résumé to ask for references.
(Man A)	So why don't you do that? At least you'll be better informed before you make a decision. And I might know someone who's worked with her before. Just send me her résumé today and I'll get touch with some of her former employers. Then we'll see what we want to do.
(Narrator)	How does the woman feel about the candidate?
(Narrator)	When did the candidate finish university?
(Narrator)	What does the man say he'll do?
(Narrator)	Questions 65–67 refer to the following conversation with three speakers.
(Woman A)	Were you home last night guys? Did you see the documentary on IBC2?
(Man B)	No, we had some friends over for dinner so we didn't get a chance.
(Woman B)	What was it about, Rebecca?
(Woman A)	It was about what happens with all the trash we produce and how some of the most beautiful beaches and mountains all around the world have been turned into these filthy landfills.
(Man B)	Is this the one with Jeremy Irons?
(Woman A)	Yeah.
(Woman B)	We saw it at the movies a couple of years ago. It was so depressing. I remember the part where some marine biologists found all sorts of plastic residue inside a whale's stomach.
(Man B)	Okay, I agree it was a bit sad. But it also said that it's not too late to change things around.
(Woman A)	You're right. Look at San Francisco, where nearly all garbage is recycled. You know, they managed to sort the city out in less than 10 years.

(Narrator)	What did the man do the night before?
(Narrator)	What was the documentary about?
(Narrator)	What does Rebecca say about San Francisco?
(Narrator)	Questions 68–70 refer to the following conversation.
(Man A)	We only make the small components here. All the other parts are imported from China for obvious reasons.
(Woman B)	What do you mean by obvious reasons?
(Man A)	Well, the Chinese are able to manufacture high quality parts with a much lower cost. They're also capable of manufacturing at a speed we'd never be able to match here in the US. They're fast, they're reliable, and much less expensive.
(Woman B)	Okay. So why do you still manufacture those parts here? Why not import the whole lot?
(Man A)	We believe it's important to have control over the product. We're only a small company, so we hire a couple of Chinese manufacturers to make the big parts for us. By producing some of the small parts here, and ordering the other parts from different manufacturers, we are able to not only protect our products and ideas, but also upgrade them as we like.
(Woman B)	I see.
(Narrator)	What does the man say about his company?
(Narrator)	Which adjective does NOT describe the Chinese manufacturers?
(Narrator)	Look at the table. In which of the containers can you probably find the parts produced in the US?

Part IV

Track 8

(Narrator)	Questions 71–73 refer to the following talk.
(Man A)	Attention passengers. Attention passengers. The 7:45 direct coach from London Victoria to Heathrow Airport is about to depart. Attention all passengers. The 7:45 direct coach to Heathrow Airport is about to depart. This is a 50-minute journey and the coach is due to arrive at Heathrow Terminals 1, 2 and 3 at 8:35 a.m. Passengers going to terminals 4 and 5 must use the airport bus shuttle service due to road works in the area. Attention passengers. This 7:45 to Heathrow airport will terminate at terminals 1, 2 and 3. Passengers traveling to terminals 4 and 5 can make use of the Heathrow shuttle service at no extra cost.
(Narrator)	What time does the coach service get to Heathrow Airport?
(Narrator)	Why can't the bus get to terminals 4 and 5?
(Narrator)	How can passengers get to terminals 4 and 5?

(Narrator)	Questions 74–76 refer to the following talk.
(Woman A)	Hello. You have reached Capital Movies, the home of entertainment. Tonight in Studio A we are showing our premiere movie *The Lone Fighter*. A young orphan conquers the hearts of America in a journey of self-discovery and struggles. *The Lone Fighter* has been nominated for 7 Academy Awards including Best Picture, Best Soundtrack, and Best Leading Actor. For more information about *The Lone Fighter* and all the other movies being shown at the Capital, access our website at www.capitalmoviesentertainment.com or visit our social media pages. To celebrate International Women's Day, women get a free ticket when accompanied by another paying adult. For more information about our events and promotions, visit our website at www.capitalmoviesentertainment.com or visit our social media pages.

(Narrator)	What is the name of the premiere movie?
(Narrator)	Which of the following has the premiere movie NOT been nominated for?
(Narrator)	What promotion is mentioned in the announcement?

(Narrator)	Questions 77–79 refer to the following talk.
(Man B)	Are you tired of your old style? Does your hair look like a broom and does your skin feel like sand paper? Alicia's Beauty Center can turn your old dull look into a fresh new style. We specialize in alternative hair treatments, mudding, and oriental massages. We also provide dietary advice through our nutritionists and fitness experts. We help you not only choose the best beauty treatment but also make the correct decisions to ensure that your day at Alicia's becomes the first day of the rest of your life. Wanna know the secret behind Hollywood actress Angie Jules's looks? Wanna know how NBA heroes look after their bodies? Come see us. Go to our website www.aliciasbeautycenter.com or call us at 1 800 555 1274.

(Narrator)	What type of text is the recording?
(Narrator)	Which service is NOT mentioned in the recording?
(Narrator)	What does the speaker mean when he says "'the first day of the rest of your life"?

(Narrator)	Questions 80–82 refer to the following talk.
(Woman B)	This is the weather report for this evening, Thursday June 10th. Showers will fade this evening, allowing many areas to become clear and cold with light winds. Patchy fog and frost will form for some, especially through west and central swathes of the countryside. Across the east coast further wintry showers will push in. Friday will see fog in central areas clear by lunch time, leaving many dry and bright. Showers will continue across the east coast, while drizzle will quickly spread across the south and west, particularly in the southwest. As for Saturday and Sunday it will stay unsettled, with further rain and strong winds in the south in particular. Additional hail storms are also possible in the east coast.

(Narrator)	Where are you most likely to hear this talk
(Narrator)	Which area will be the wettest?
(Narrator)	Which of the following is NOT mentioned in the report?

(Narrator)	Questions 83–85 refer to the following talk.
(Man A)	Welcome to Eastern University Open Campus Day. We are truly excited to have you all here with us and we hope that by the end of the day you will have realized that Eastern University is the right place for those who want to evolve as professionals and develop themselves. Before we get started with our tour of the campus, I'd like to go over some changes to the schedule. Professor Albuquerque will begin his speech fifteen minutes earlier than the original time. He will now speak at 10:25 instead of 10:40 in our main auditorium. This means that you will get an extra fifteen minutes during the question and answer session with our vocational psychologists. The rest of the schedule remains unchanged with the exception of lunch, which will now be served in the main restaurant due to the weather forecast for this afternoon.
(Narrator)	Who is the speech most likely addressed to?
(Narrator)	Look at the itinerary below. Which of the schedule items hasn't been updated with the correct information?
(Narrator)	Which of the following is NOT mentioned in the woman's speech?
(Narrator)	Questions 86–88 refer to the following talk.
(Man B)	The Italian chain of restaurants *La Bella Vita* has announced its intentions to expand business and enter the fast food market. *La Bella Express* will be the fast food version of the successful chain which attracts millions of Americans to their restaurants every week. *La Bella Express* will serve *paninis,* a type of Italian sandwich made from different combinations of cold meats and cheese served in a ciabatta or sourdough bread. It will also serve pizza slices, beef and veggie lasagna, and fresh salads. Everything over the counter with the usual quality that has made *La Bella Vita* the most successful restaurant chain in America. The first fast food restaurant is set to open its doors this Saturday at Miami International Airport with 12 new locations following in the next three weeks.
(Narrator)	What's the new restaurant called?
(Narrator)	What kind of food will the new restaurant serve?
(Narrator)	How does the speaker describe La Bella Vita?
(Narrator)	Questions 89–91 refer to the following talk.
(Man A)	Rent-your-way lets you rent a car by the day, week, month, or even year if that's what you need. Our rent-your-way service allows you to drive the car you want, whenever and wherever you want. With more than 100 stores nationwide, we offer all types of cars ranging from the modern economic Smart to the timeless classic limo. All our contracts include a full tank of gas can be refilled at no further expense, comprehensive insurance, 24/7 road assistance, and a satnav. Not interested in renting? Would you like to buy your own car? No problem. You can buy the car of your dreams at one of our 12 mega stores. All our used cars have low mileage, a 12-month warranty, and are in impeccable condition. Visit us at www.rentyourwaycars.com and get behind the wheel today.

(Narrator)   Which benefits are offered by the company?

(Narrator)   How many of their stores also sell cars?

(Narrator)   What does the woman NOT say about their cars for sale?

(Narrator)   Questions 92–94 refer to the following talk.

(Woman A)   Your attention please. This is the boarding announcement for passengers for Municho Airways flight 5665 departing from Jackson Atlanta International Airport to Frankfurt. Your flight is now ready for boarding from gate 27. Please have your passport and boarding pass ready to show the gate attendant. Remember, you are allowed one small carry-on bag only. Passengers with extra hand luggage will be asked to check it before boarding the plane. Passengers with small children or requiring special assistance may go to the head of the line. All passengers who have not already done so should proceed through passport control immediately.

(Narrator)   Where will the flight land?

(Narrator)   What does the woman say about the flight?

(Narrator)   Who has boarding priority?

(Narrator)   Questions 95–97 refer to the following talk.

(Woman B)   You have reached Happy Pets Veterinary Clinic. If this is an emergency, please hang up and contact our afterhours clinic at 1 800 555 8722, and one of our night specialists will assist you. For other inquiries, our clinic is open from 08:00 a.m. to 7:00 p.m. on Mondays and Wednesdays, 08:00 a.m. to 5:00 p.m. on Tuesdays and Thursdays, and 08:30 a.m. to 3:00 p.m. on Fridays and Saturdays. If you wish to make an appointment, please call again during our regular opening hours. You can also book an appointment online by visiting our website at www.happypets.com, or by downloading our app. If you wish to leave a message, please wait for the tone, and then begin recording your message. Please press the hash key to stop recording your message.

(Narrator)   What time does the clinic close on Tuesdays?

(Narrator)   When is the clinic closed?

(Narrator)   How can you book an appointment?

(Narrator)   Questions 98–100 refer to the following talk.

(Woman A)   Hello. My name is Giovanna Papadopoulos and I'm calling regarding a problem with my order. The box was left outside the house by your courier service and I'm afraid the product has been damaged. I just don't get it. Why would someone leave a box containing an expensive electronic device behind the garbage can in my front yard? Anyway, my order number is DDW1299-62. I made an order of a portable printer with three boxes of photo paper. Also, I was promised one-day delivery and that was three days ago. I paid for the item with Paypoint and the amount has already been charged to my account. I would still be interested in having the product if you could get it delivered by the end of the day tomorrow. I tried to talk to you through social media and webchat service with no success. If I don't hear back from you within a couple of hours, I will ask Paypoint for a refund. My email address is gigi_papa78@email.com and my cell phone number is (729) 927–2900.

(Narrator)	What does Giovanna mean when she says "I just don't get it"?
(Narrator)	What does she say about the payment?
(Narrator)	Look at the graphic. Which is INCORRECT?

PRACTICE TEST 3

Part I

Track 9

(Narrator)	For each question in this part, you will hear four statements about a picture in your test book. When you hear the statements, you must select the one statement that best describes what you see in the picture. Then find the number of the question on your answer sheet and mark your answer. The statements will not be written in your test book, and will be spoken just once.
(Narrator)	Look at the example item below.
(Narrator)	Now listen to the four statements

(Woman A)	A	The class is trying to understand.
	B	The speaker is laughing a lot.
	C	The men are playing a game.
	D	The audience are having a good time.

(Narrator)	Statement **D**, 'The audience are having a good time,' best describes the photograph, Therefore, you should mark answer **D** on your answer sheet.
(Narrator)	Now Part 1 will begin.
(Narrator)	Look at the picture marked number 1 in your test book.

(Man B)	A	The cargo is being loaded.
	B	The plane is ready to take off.
	C	The passenger's bags are full.
	D	The suitcases will be dropped.

| (Narrator) | Look at the picture marked number 2 in your test book. |

(Woman B)	A	The floor is very dirty.
	B	The man is on the right of the trolley.
	C	The sign is in the trolley.
	D	The man is not alone.

| (Narrator) | Go on to the next page. |
| (Narrator) | Look at the picture marked number 3 in your test book. |

(Man A)	A	He is learning to drive.
	B	He is tuning the radio.
	C	He is finding directions.
	D	He is looking for his keys.

(Narrator)	Look at the picture marked number 4 in your test book.
(Woman A)	**A**	They are winding the thread.
	B	They are preparing the dinner.
	C	They are wrapping the gifts.
	D	They are packing the items.
(Narrator)	Look at the picture marked number 5 in your test book.
(Man B)	**A**	She's leaving the building.
	B	She's currently engaged.
	C	She's going up.
	D	She's waiting for his secretary.
(Narrator)	Look at the picture marked number 6 in your test book.
(Woman A)	**A**	The snacks have all been eaten.
	B	The canapés are all prepared.
	C	The sandwiches are being used.
	D	The burgers have been stacked.

Part II

Track 10

(Narrator)	You will hear a question or statement and three responses spoken in English. They will not be printed in your test book and will be spoken only one time. Select the best response to the question or statement and mark the letter A, B, or C on your answer sheet.
(Narrator)	For example, you will hear:
(Man B)	What did Ms. Ono want us to do?
(Narrator)	You will also hear:
(Woman A)	**A**	She's really bossy.
	B	She asked us to send out the samples.
	C	Ms. Ono wants to get a promotion.
(Narrator)	The best response to the question "What did Ms. Ono want us to do?" is choice **B**, "She asked us to send out the samples," so **B** is the correct answer. You should mark answer **B** on your answer sheet.
(Narrator)	Now let us begin with question number 7.
(Woman A)	**7**	When did you move to the US?
(Man A)	**A**	Six months ago.
	B	Yes, I did.
	C	Tomorrow or the day after.
(Man B)	**8**	Who's meeting with Professor Klaus on Monday?
(Woman A)	**A**	The meeting will be really interesting.
	B	I believe it's Dr. Lucchese.
	C	At 3:30.

(Woman A)	9	What are these things on your desk?
(Man B)	A	Oh, just some toys for my kids.
	B	It's an oak desk.
	C	My cousins.
(Woman B)	10	Would you like me to take you to the airport?
(Man A)	A	Yes, I did.
	B	I've already taken it.
	C	Don't worry. I'll take a cab.
(Woman A)	11	Should we stay late tonight and finish the slides?
(Man A)	A	I suppose we have to now.
	B	It's really cold out there.
	C	The slides were on your memory stick.
(Man B)	12	Who will be responsible for the new project?
(Woman A)	A	I think it's an interesting project.
	B	I have never been there.
	C	Mrs. Silva.
(Woman A)	13	When will we start selling the new software?
(Man B)	A	In a couple of weeks.
	B	Last week.
	C	Two weeks ago.
(Woman B)	14	Why don't we give Mr. Wu a chance?
(Man A)	A	I don't really like it there.
	B	Actually, that's not a bad idea.
	C	They seem like a good option.
(Man A)	15	That workshop was really interesting, wasn't it?
(Woman B)	A	It's good to work here.
	B	He's not interested in arts.
	C	I loved it.
(Man B)	16	You've worked in Italy before, haven't you?
(Woman B)	A	Yes, five years ago.
	B	No, I won't.
	C	I don't speak Italian.
(Woman B)	17	Do I have to fill this in now?
(Man B)	A	Yes, you are.
	B	Yeah, but it won't take a minute.
	C	I'm full, too.
(Woman A)	18	Your new manager seems quite bossy.
(Man A)	A	She *can* be difficult sometimes.
	B	I'm his boss.
	C	The main boss is on leave at the moment.

(Woman B)	19	Have the computers been updated?
(Man B)	A	Yes, they're all working now.
	B	Yes, they do.
	C	No, the computers are over there.

(Man B)	20	Has Mrs. Russet finished her report?
(Woman A)	A	Yes, she will.
	B	No, she doesn't.
	C	I'm not sure. I'll ask her.

(Woman A)	21	Why don't we take a break for a few minutes?
(Man B)	A	That's a good idea.
	B	Because it's broken.
	C	I don't know the main reason.

(Man A)	22	How was your stay in Beijing?
(Woman B)	A	I really enjoyed it.
	B	It was 12:30.
	C	Really tall.

(Woman B)	23	When should I send out the emails?
(Man A)	A	Last night.
	B	First thing tomorrow morning.
	C	Maybe.

(Man A)	24	Lenny, is this your tablet?
(Man B)	A	Yes, I am.
	B	No, I can't.
	C	Doesn't look like it; mine's a bit smaller.

(Man B)	25	You're responsible for the associates, aren't you?
(Woman B)	A	No, thanks.
	B	Yes, for the past seven years.
	C	She's not here.

(Woman A)	26	Does Leandro work in IT or HR?
(Man A)	A	He's one of the IT consultants.
	B	HR is on the third floor.
	C	Leandro is really talented.

(Woman B)	27	Which car should I take?
(Man B)	A	The old one, please.
	B	This is my car.
	C	Yes, of course.

(Man A)	28	Why's everyone waiting outside Mrs. Fraser's office?
(Woman A)	A	I have no idea.
	B	Mrs. Fraser's in the restroom.
	C	This is her office.

(Man B)	29	Shouldn't we do something about her situation?
(Man A)	A	I shouldn't have eaten that much.
	B	The situation is very clear to me.
	C	Perhaps. She does seem to be struggling.
(Woman A)	30	The printer's out of paper.
(Woman B)	A	It's a new printer.
	B	There's some more in the drawer on the right.
	C	Where are you?
(Woman B)	31	Where will the meeting be held?
(Woman A)	A	5:00 p.m.
	B	Next Thursday.
	C	Room 303.

Part III

Track 11

(Narrator)	You will hear some conversations between two or more people. You will be asked to answer three questions about what the speakers say in each conversation. Select the best response to each question and mark the letter (A), (B), (C), or (D) on your answer sheet. The conversation will not be printed in your test book and will be spoken only one time.
(Narrator)	Now let us begin with question number 32.
(Narrator)	Questions 32–34 refer to the following conversation with three speakers.
(Woman A)	Hello. I'm looking for a tablet for my son who's going to high school next month. Can I have a look at this one here, please?
(Man A)	Of course, ma'am. Is this the sort of thing you're looking for?
(Woman A)	I'm not sure... it does look nice, but would it be suitable for you, Norman?
(Man B)	Err, well... I'll be taking it to school with me every day in my backpack. Do you think this is strong enough? It needs to be something I can read pdfs on, do research with, and also use with a word processor to write essays.
(Man A)	I understand. Well, in that case I think you should take a look at the Tab Pro. It comes in a hard shell which can absorb impact and it's faster than most laptops we sell here. Let me show you what it can do...
(Narrator)	Why does the woman want to buy a tablet?
(Narrator)	What will the tablet be used for?
(Narrator)	Look at the graphic below. Which tablet does the man recommend?
(Narrator)	Questions 35–37 refer to the following conversation.
(Woman B)	Roy, can you help me? IT has sent the link for the software update but I have no idea what to do here. I'm useless with computers.

(Man A)	I'm sorry Mrs. Sanchez but if I don't take these boxes to the conference room right now, Mr. Wells is going to kill me. If you give me a few minutes, I'll be more than happy to help you.
(Woman B)	Don't worry. I'll be in my office so just come in when you're free. You don't have to knock.
(Man A)	No problem. Just give me 10 minutes.
(Woman B)	OK. In the meantime, I'll catch up on my correspondence.
(Narrator)	What does the woman want from the man?
(Narrator)	What does Roy mean when he says "Mr. Wells is going to kill me"?
(Narrator)	Where will Mrs. Sanchez be waiting for Pablo?
(Narrator)	Questions 38–40 refer to the following conversation.
(Man B)	Hi, this is Roman Uzmanov. I'm calling for Mrs. Lee. I sent her an email with some information about our management software, Kazoom, and she asked me to video call her this morning but I couldn't reach her.
(Woman A)	I'm sorry but Mrs. Lee didn't come to the office today. She was feeling a bit under the weather so she decided to stay at home and get better before the conference.
(Man B)	I see. I hope she gets better soon. There's no hurry. So what I'll do is, I'll send her an email so we can reschedule the meeting for next week.
(Woman A)	She won't be back until Friday next week. If you want, I can book a video meeting for you for Friday afternoon... Just let me have a look at her calendar here. Shall we say 3:30 p.m.? How does that sound to you?
(Man B)	It sounds perfect. Thank you so much.
(Woman A)	You're welcome. It should be fine. But if anything happens and she can't take the meeting, I'll contact you myself.
(Man B)	That's fine. Thanks again.
(Narrator)	Why is the man calling?
(Narrator)	Why does the woman say "she was feeling a bit under the weather"?
(Narrator)	What does the woman suggest?
(Narrator)	Questions 41–43 refer to the following conversation with three speakers.
(Man B)	Peter, the clients are visiting us on Tuesday, so I'd like you to take them out for lunch.
(Man A)	Absolutely. I'll take them to that new place on Broadway.
(Man B)	That's fine. Take them wherever you want as long as they're back here by 3:00. Mr. Jung is flying down here just to meet them and I don't want to be alone in a room with him waiting for you guys to come back.
(Man A)	Don't worry. I'll book a table for 12:00.
(Man B)	Perfect. Rita, can you sort the airport transfer for me? They arrive on Monday 9:55 p.m. at Newark. They're staying at the hotel just around the corner.
(Woman A)	Consider it done. Should I get a regular executive car or something a bit more special?
(Man B)	The usual is fine. Thank you, guys. I don't know what I'd do without you.

(Narrator)	What does the man want to avoid?
(Narrator)	What time will the clients have their lunch?
(Narrator)	How are the clients going to the hotel?
(Narrator)	Questions 44–46 refer to the following conversation.
(Woman B)	Hi, Andrew. This is Sofia from HR. I'm calling about the lecture at the Plaza tomorrow. I haven't heard anything back from you guys. Is anyone from the finance department coming at all?
(Man A)	Hi, Sofia. I'm so sorry. James was supposed to email yesterday. We're on a tight schedule here with the winter holidays coming up. Would it be OK if we skipped this one? I do understand how important these things are, but I don't want to ask people around here to do any extra hours just before Christmas.
(Woman B)	I have to say I'm a bit disappointed, Andrew. This is the third time in a row we'll have no one from finances in one of our CPD sessions. Everyone was complaining that the company had no career development program and now that we have one, you all have excuses not to come.
(Man A)	I'm sorry you feel that way, Sofia. And yes, I do believe that what you're doing is very important for this company. But Christmas is three days from tomorrow and everyone here has small kids, so I can't make them work long hours. Not this week. I'm really sorry but we can't come this time.
(Narrator)	What does Andrew do?
(Narrator)	Why does the woman say "I'm a bit disappointed"?
(Narrator)	What does Andrew not want to happen?
(Narrator)	Questions 47–49 refer to the following conversation.
(Man B)	Excuse me. I'm planning to acquire some office desks from your store, but I can't seem to find anyone to help me.
(Woman A)	Hello, sir. Sorry about that. Are you looking for any desks in particular?
(Man B)	Not exactly. You see, we have just replaced our reception laptops for tablets. HR says they look better. IT says they're easier to maintain. Anyway, I don't want to bore you with any of that. So I'd like someone to talk to one of our architects, so I can be on my way and go back to the office.
(Woman A)	I can certainly help you with that. Is your architect here with you this morning?
(Man B)	Yes, but she went to have a look at the flooring options on the second floor. I'll call her now and she'll be here in a second. I mean, if you don't mind waiting.
(Woman A)	Not at all, sir. We're here to help.
(Narrator)	Why is the man at the store?
(Narrator)	What does HR think looks better?
(Narrator)	Where's the architect?
(Narrator)	Questions 50–52 refer to the following conversation.
(Woman B)	Hello. I have a reservation for five people at 1:00 p.m. tomorrow. My name's Claire Manning.

(Man B)	Hello, Mrs. Manning. This is Pepe. I can see your reservation here. How can I help you?
(Woman B)	I have just realized that one of my guests is a vegan. That means he doesn't eat any meat or anything that comes from animals. I was wondering if you had anything in your menu that would cater to his needs. He's a very important client and I think he'd love the view from your terrace, so I need to know if the chef can prepare anything special for him.
(Man B)	Don't worry, Mrs. Manning. We have a selection of vegan dishes that I am sure will make your special client more than happy. Here at Alfredo's we always try to cater to our customers' individual needs so you can rest assured your client will love both the view and the food.
(Woman B)	That's great. Thank you very much.
(Man B)	You're welcome, Mrs. Manning. See you tomorrow.
(Narrator)	Why does Claire call the restaurant?
(Narrator)	What's the name of the restaurant?
(Narrator)	Look at the graphic. Which set menu is Claire's client most likely to order?
(Narrator)	Questions 53–55 refer to the following conversation.
(Woman A)	You said you would call yesterday, but I didn't hear from you. Was everything okay?
(Man A)	I'm so sorry. I had a really busy day in the office so it must have slipped my mind.
(Woman A)	Anyway, Sally just got promoted and we're going out to celebrate on Saturday. She said that you're more than welcome to come.
(Man A)	Sure, I'd love to. Do you know where you're going?
(Woman A)	We're going to that new Italian restaurant downtown.
(Man A)	Great! What time should I pick you up then?
(Narrator)	Why didn't the man call?
(Narrator)	Where does the woman invite the man to?
(Narrator)	What does the man offer to do?
(Narrator)	Questions 56–58 refer to the following conversation.
(Man A)	Hi. I'm from Colatte Printing Solutions. We got a call saying you have a problem with one of the photocopiers.
(Woman B)	Yeah, that's right. It's one of the machines in our legal department. Apparently, they can't get it to do double-sided copies anymore. I think it's jammed.
(Man A)	No problem. I'll go and have a look. Where is it?
(Woman B)	Our legal department is on the fifth floor. So if you take that elevator on your right, it'll take you straight to reception. There you can ask for Kurt, who will explain what the problem is in more detail.
(Man A)	Thank you. So elevator on the left, fifth floor, ask for Kurt.
(Woman B)	Elevator on the right, please. The one on the left only goes to the second floor.

(Narrator)	What kind of problem does the woman's company have?
(Narrator)	What does the woman tell the man?
(Narrator)	Where can the man find Kurt?
(Narrator)	Questions 59–61 refer to the following conversation.
(Man A)	I have a question before we interview the next candidate. Do you think we will have the time to hold the afternoon meeting? I told Marketing we'd be starting at 4.15 and it's nearly 3.00 now.
(Woman B)	This is the last interview and I don't think it'll take more than an hour.
(Man A)	What if we like her? Her qualifications are outstanding, and she has the experience we're looking for. We might just have to put the meeting off.
(Woman B)	Ok. This is what I'll do. While you get the next candidate, I'll text Anita from Marketing and let her know we'll be starting the meeting 30 minutes later than scheduled.
(Narrator)	When is the meeting supposed to start?
(Narrator)	What does the man say about the candidate?
(Narrator)	Why will the woman send a text message?
(Narrator)	Questions 62–64 refer to the following conversation.
(Woman A)	Hello. This is Margaret O'Keefe from Atlantis International. Is this a good time to speak?
(Man B)	Yes, of course. How can I help you, Mrs. O'Keefe?
(Woman A)	I'd like to say that both Mr. McAdams and Mrs. Chan were impressed with your skills and qualifications. We think you're exactly what we're looking for and would like to offer you the position of Director of Operations.
(Man B)	That's very good news. I'm flattered. I have been following Atlantis International for a couple of years now, waiting for the right position to become available. So I must say, this is a dream come true.
(Woman A)	That's very good to hear, Mr. Hillenweck. What I'm going to do now is send you an offer letter along with a request for some documentation we need from you. You'll also be contacted by a company called Watchdog Security. They run all our background checks. So as soon as we get everything back we can sort your contract and everything else. How much notice do you need to give?
(Man B)	As I told Mr. McAdams last week, I have to give three weeks' notice. That means I'll be ready to start by the end of the month.
(Woman A)	That's fine. So I guess that's it. I'm going to post your job offer letter now, and welcome to Atlantis International.
(Man B)	Thank you, Mrs. O'Keefe.
(Narrator)	What does the woman say about Mrs. Chan?
(Narrator)	Why does the man say "I'm flattered"?
(Narrator)	What does Ms. O'Keefe say she's going to post?

(Narrator)	Questions 65–67 refer to the following conversation.
(Woman B)	Excuse me. I have a ticket for the 4 o'clock coach to Barcelona. But I'm still stuck in traffic and there's no way I can get to the station in the next hour. I was wondering if I could change the ticket for tomorrow. Would that be possible?... my name's Maria Vidal Garcia.
(Man B)	Thanks. Let me check your booking details. It won't be a minute... I can see that you have purchased a first-class ticket so we can change that for you with no incurring fees. However, tomorrow's coach is fully booked so you'll have to travel on Saturday or Sunday.
(Woman B)	Oh no. My sister's wedding is on Sunday. What time does the Saturday coach leave?
(Man B)	It's a morning service and it's scheduled to arrive in Barcelona at 7:45 p.m.
(Woman B)	That should be fine. Would you do that for me, then?
(Man B)	Of course, ma'am. You'll receive an email in the next two hours with a new booking number and all the information about your journey. Please remember that you should get to the station at least 45 minutes in advance.
(Woman B)	No problem. Thanks for your help.
(Narrator)	What's the woman's problem?
(Narrator)	What does the man say about the woman's ticket?
(Narrator)	Look at the graphic below. Which service is the woman going to take?
(Narrator)	Questions 68–70 refer to the following conversation.
(Woman A)	Hi Giovanna. Can you tell me what happened during the meeting this morning? I heard Mr. Yun was furious when he left the building.
(Woman B)	I honestly don't know. They had an emergency downstairs so I had to leave before the meeting was finished. Do you know what happened, Matthew?
(Man A)	Mr. Yun was told his budget for next year and he didn't like it one bit. He was hoping to launch a new multimedia campaign, but apparently he can't now.
(Woman A)	But I have the figures with me. What was he expecting? We increased his budget by nearly 30% the past three years. 27.8% to be more precise. That's more than any other department.
(Man A)	Yeah, he should be thrilled to have that much.
(Woman B)	Matthew's stressed because they told him he'll have to wait until next year to implement the new cloud system.
(Woman A)	I'm sorry to hear that, Matt. It's not fair...
(Narrator)	Who was very angry after a meeting?
(Narrator)	What do they say about the budget?
(Narrator)	Why does Giovanna say Matt is stressed?

Part IV

Track 12

(Narrator)	Questions 71–73 refer to the following talk.
(Woman A)	Hello and thank you for calling United World International College, the leading marketing school in Cleveland. Due to last night's blizzard, we will not be opening today. Please check our website for more weather information. We will also be unable to deliver any of our distance and online courses today since most of our teachers work from our computer lab in the main building. Please check our website and social media for more information about tomorrow. We would also like to remind students that essays and research projects will not have their deadlines extended. Most books from our library can now be accessed through our online library service. For more information on work deadlines and how to use our online library service, please visit our student portal at www.unitedworld.students.org.
(Narrator)	Why is the college closed?
(Narrator)	What information can you NOT find on their website?
(Narrator)	What does the message say about student essays?
(Narrator)	Questions 74–76 refer to the following talk.
(Man A)	Hi, Mr. Amorim. This is Wayne from Glenville Property Management. I got your call about the patio door. I've contacted the janitor, Mr. Romsey, who told me he wasn't aware of the problem so I don't really know what's going on here. He told me no one had said anything about it and he was quite surprised when I told him about your complaints. Anyway, we're sending someone to get the door fixed tomorrow morning and we're also trying to find someone to have a look at the floor. We have used a wood specialist before for the same type of problem in another building and he did a really good job. As soon as we get hold of him, I'll let you know. Well, I guess that's it. Have a good day and I'll call you once I hear back from Mr. Yen.
(Narrator)	Who complained about the patio door?
(Narrator)	How did the janitor feel when he heard about the complaints?
(Narrator)	What do we learn about Mr. Yen?
(Narrator)	Questions 77–79 refer to the following talk.
(Man B)	Hello, Radio 7 listeners. This is Jackie Adams with the news on this beautiful spring morning in Gainesville. This Friday, the Gainesville Community Center will be hosting a charity barbecue with all the funds going to Say No! For those of you who don't know, Say No! is a local charity that works in partnership with schools and colleges to make students aware of the risks and consequences of the use of what are considered soft drugs. So it's this Friday at 5:30 p.m. on the football field at Gainesville Community Center. And this Saturday the Gainesville Leopards will be playing against their local rivals the Jacksonville Jaguars. We're counting on your presence to support the boys. Go Leopards!

(Narrator)	When is the announcement being broadcast?
(Narrator)	Who helps students stay away from drugs?
(Narrator)	Why does the woman say "Go Leopards"?

| (Narrator) | Questions 80 –82 refer to the following talk. |
| (Woman B) | Good afternoon, passengers. This is your captain speaking. First I'd like to welcome everyone on Sunnywest Airlines Flight 1776. We are currently cruising at an altitude of 35,000 feet at an airspeed of 420 miles per hour. The time is now 9:55 p.m. local time. The weather doesn't look too good, but with the tailwind on our side we are expecting to land in Paris approximately 25 minutes ahead of schedule. The weather in Paris is cloudy and damp, with a high of 60 degrees for tomorrow. The cabin crew will be coming around in about 15 minutes' time to offer you a light snack and beverage, and the inflight entertainment system will become available shortly after that. I'll talk to you again in the morning before we reach our destination. Until then, sit back, relax and enjoy the rest of the flight. |

(Narrator)	What's the flight number?
(Narrator)	What does the man say about the flight?
(Narrator)	Look at the graphic below. When is the flight arriving in Paris?

| (Narrator) | Questions 83–85 refer to the following talk. |
| (Man A) | Hello. My name's Arturo Camacho and I'm calling about the smart watch ad you placed on youbuywesell.com. I've just started training for a half marathon and thought a smart watch would be helpful. I really like the one you've got so I was wondering if you still have it. Also, if you don't mind, I'd like to have a look at it. A friend told me to be careful with the battery if I'm gonna buy a used watch, because it's pretty expensive to replace them. Anyway, I'd really appreciate it if you could call or text me when you get this. My phone number is 555-7611. I'm going to a play tonight so I might not be able to pick up your call after 8:30. You can text me and I'll call you back or something. Thanks! |

(Narrator)	Why's the man calling?
(Narrator)	What does he say about the watch battery?
(Narrator)	When's the best time to return his call?

| (Narrator) | Questions 86–88 refer to the following talk. |
| (Man B) | Tired of cooking every day? Can't stand the idea of peeling and chopping? Your problems are now over! Grandma Lucy offers a variety of quality meals that you can easily prepare in less than 10 minutes. No, they don't cost an arm and a leg. No, we're not talking about ready meals that you heat up in the microwave and then pray they're decent enough to eat. I'm talking about recipe boxes with organic ingredients for restaurant quality food that you can prepare for the whole family in less than 10 minutes. No washing, no peeling, no chopping, no cleaning! How does it work? Grandma Lucy sends you a package with seven boxes, one for each day of the week. Inside each box you will find one of our exciting easy-to-follow recipes, and all the ingredients you need to prepare them. All our vegetables and meats come pre-washed and ready to cook. Too good to be |

true? Get in touch today for a free box of a dish of your choice. All you have to do is check out www.grandmalucy.com/freebox and change your life today!

(Narrator) What is Grandma Lucy?

(Narrator) How does the ad describe the food?

(Narrator) What does the woman mean when she says "No, they don't cost an arm and a leg"?

(Narrator) Questions 89–91 refer to the following talk.

(Man A) Attention all customers. Attention all customers. The winter mega sale has now started in menswear. Thousands of items can now be purchased with reductions of up to 50%. That's right. 50% off jeans, shirts, jackets, coats, sweaters and much, much more. Our mega menswear sale ends on Sunday so don't waste any time. Why go elsewhere when you can save with Maggie's? And why not visit our restaurant on the top floor? With magnificent views of Miami Bay, you and your family can enjoy a freshly roasted cup of Colombian coffee, or a slice of one of our heavenly cheesecakes. Feeling hungry? We offer a variety of hot dishes and sandwiches. Il Viaggio restaurant is on the top floor by the toy department.

(Narrator) Where is the store?

(Narrator) Which of the following is NOT mentioned in the announcement?

(Narrator) Look at the graphic below. Which of the sales does the announcement refer to?

(Narrator) Questions 92–94 refer to the following talk.

(Woman A) Thank you for calling WPhones. All our operators are busy helping other customers. If you'd like a call back press one now, for other options please hold. Thank you for calling WPhones. If you have any queries regarding the new NPhone 10, call our sales team at 1 800 555 2097. They will be able to help you with any information you might need about the newest phone on the market and all of its incredible features. And our customers get a free NPad Jr when buying their NPhone 10 with WPhones. Talk to our sales team to find out more. Please hold. If you'd like to talk about a bill or contract, press 2 now. For information regarding upgrades press 3. For anything else, please press 6 and we'll redirect your call to one of our advisors.

(Narrator) Who should contact the company by a different number?

(Narrator) What is the new product called?

(Narrator) What number should you press if you're having problems with your phone?

(Narrator) Questions 95–97 refer to the following talk.

(Woman B) Hello. My name is Miss Sokolov. I have been trying to speak to the hotel owner for a couple of days now with no success. I have to say, this is truly disappointing for a five-star hotel, especially with the amount of money we spent during our stay with you. My family and I stayed at the Hotel Chandelier for three nights last week and the whole experience was, just utterly appalling... none of your waiters could speak Russian, even though I have an email from you assuring us that there would be a minimum of two Russian speaking staff on every shift... you had noisy kids' activities and water polo competitions by the pool non-stop, it made it really difficult to relax. When expressing our concerns to the manager, Mr. Lewis, not only was he unable to provide us with a space where we could relax and read our books, but he also told us that smoking was not allowed in the hotel, although, again, we checked this before our stay and you told us that smoking outdoors was permitted. Please get back to me as soon as you get this message or I will have to take these matters to my legal team.

(Narrator)	How does the man describe his experience as a guest?
(Narrator)	Which of the following does the man NOT complain about?
(Narrator)	What does the man threaten to do?
(Narrator)	Questions 98–100 refer to the following talk.
(Woman A)	Good afternoon and welcome to the second day of our annual American Dental Conference and Dentistry Show. I'm honored to introduce Dr. Antonescu, whose grandfather organized our first dentistry show here in Manhattan more than 100 years ago. Dr. Antonescu is a professor at Budapest University and has more than 58 years experience with dental prostheses. Today, he will talk about the Dental Prosthesis market segment and analyze manufacturers by region, type, and application. Dr. Antonescu will provide us with a global understanding of the market so that we can determine how the market will evolve and decide how to plan our next move. He will present results of his latest research in East Asia and South America, research that will help large and small companies to achieve their preferred market position. And now, please join me in welcoming Dr. Antonescu.
(Narrator)	Where does Dr. Antonescu work?
(Narrator)	What will Dr. Antonescu talk about?
(Narrator)	What does the text say about "large and small companies"?

PRACTICE TEST 4

Part I

Track 13

(Narrator)	For each question, you will hear four statements about a picture in your test book. When you hear the statements, you must select the one statement that best describes what you see in the picture. Then find the number of the question on your answer sheet and mark your answer. The statements will not be written in your test book, and will be spoken just once.
(Narrator)	Look at the example item below.
(Narrator)	Now listen to the four statements.
(Woman A)	**A** They're buying groceries.
	B She's pointing at the pepper.
	C They're working in the lotion.
	D She's counting all the cauliflowers.
(Narrator)	Statement **B**, "She's pointing at the pepper," best describes the photograph. Therefore, you should mark answer **B** on your answer sheet.

(Narrator)	Now Part 1 will begin.
(Narrator)	Look at the picture marked number 1 in your test book.
(Man A)	**A** She's reaching for a copy.
	B She's calling them out.
	C She's hailing a cab.
	D She's trying to get out.
(Narrator)	Look at the picture marked number 2 in your test book.
(Woman B)	**A** He's made up with his progress.
	B He's making it up to her.
	C She's doing his makeup.
	D She's watching him work.
(Narrator)	Look at the picture marked number 3 in your test book.
(Man B)	**A** He's screwing the bolts.
	B He's twisting the wheel.
	C He's changing the locks
	D He's moving the lever.
(Narrator)	Look at the picture marked number 4 in your test book.
(Woman A)	**A** The ruin is crumbling.
	B The flat is being made.
	C The tiles are being laid.
	D The house is up for sale.
(Narrator)	Look at the picture marked number 5 in your test book.
(Man B)	**A** They are eating their meals.
	B They are cooking vegetables.
	C They are leaving their plates.
	D They are serving out the food.
(Narrator)	Look at the picture marked number 6 in your test book.
(Woman B)	**A** He's donating his clothes.
	B He's giving a speech.
	C He's labelling the information.
	D He's presenting an award.

Part II

Track 14

(Narrator)	You will hear a question or statement and three responses spoken in English. They will not be written in your test book, and will be spoken just once. Select the best response to the question or statement and mark the letter A, B, or C on your answer sheet.
(Narrator)	For example, you will hear:
(Man B)	When will they fix the lifts?
(Narrator)	You will also hear:

(Woman A)	A	No one has told me where it is either.
	B	I can lift it up for you.
	C	The maintenance team should be here in an hour.
(Narrator)		The best response to the question "When will they fix the lifts?" is choice **C**, "The maintenance team should be here in an hour," so **C** is the correct answer. You should mark answer **C** on your answer sheet.
(Narrator)		Now let us begin with question number 7.
(Woman A)	7	What have you been up to all morning?
(Man A)	A	We're meeting in an hour.
	B	Just taking a nap.
	C	Mornings are better than evenings.
(Man B)	8	Did you find your phone in the end?
(Woman A)	A	Yeah, it was in the bathroom.
	B	No, my number's still the same.
	C	I'm not sure I can help.
(Woman A)	9	I didn't notice you arrive.
(Man B)	A	I was right behind you.
	B	I put the note up on the board.
	C	I'm on my way right now.
(Woman B)	10	What's wrong with him?
(Man A)	A	She's just really tired.
	B	His bad knee is acting up.
	C	I've got some painkillers here.
(Woman A)	11	Did you remember to print the report?
(Man A)	A	I tried, but the printer wasn't working.
	B	I'm sending him the report just now.
	C	I've reported the issue.
(Man B)	12	Can we move the meeting to tomorrow same time?
(Woman A)	A	I'm actually on holiday starting this evening.
	B	The meeting hasn't happened yet.
	C	I know it's supposed to be tomorrow same time.
(Woman A)	13	I don't like how the new office looks.
(Man B)	A	It wasn't official until now.
	B	Oh, it looks appalling, doesn't it?
	C	It looks like I'm going to be late.
(Woman B)	14	When did they say they were arriving?
(Man A)	A	I'm not saying that's the case.
	B	The arrivals hall is on the left.
	C	Their plane is landing in an hour.

(Man A)	15	Do you prefer to sit at the front or at the back?
(Woman B)	A	My back has been hurting all morning.
	B	I'm short, so the front is better.
	C	I'm waiting by the front door.
(Man B)	16	I'm so sorry I didn't tell you sooner.
(Woman B)	A	I apologized already.
	B	You can't tell me what to do.
	C	It's all right—I found out from Anna.
(Woman B)	17	Are you sure this is the correct spreadsheet?
(Man B)	A	That's the one she sent me.
	B	The sheets are in the dryer.
	C	You didn't answer correctly.
(Woman A)	18	How many times a week do you have classes?
(Man A)	A	I go to the gym twice a week.
	B	every Monday and Tuesday
	C	I think it's next week.
(Woman B)	19	Where should I put this?
(Man B)	A	Just leave it by the door.
	B	I'm put off by this.
	C	We need to put a stop to it.
(Man B)	20	Have you found a new assistant yet?
(Woman A)	A	I don't need any assistance, thank you.
	B	I'm still recruiting.
	C	My assistant isn't new.
(Woman A)	21	Don't be discouraged by what he said.
(Man B)	A	I'll try, but my confidence took a hit.
	B	Yeah, his words were very encouraging.
	C	It took a lot of courage to do this.
(Man A)	22	Are you a morning or an evening person?
(Woman B)	A	I have meetings all morning.
	B	I'm totally a night owl.
	C	I'd prefer to meet in the evening, if possible.
(Woman B)	23	Why didn't you bring your partner with you?
(Man A)	A	I'm not going to bring it up, don't worry.
	B	It's a very successful partnership.
	C	He's out of state, visiting his parents.
(Man A)	24	Have you read her latest book?
(Man B)	A	I didn't like her last one, so I didn't bother.
	B	I haven't published any books.
	C	I'm an avid reader of fiction.

(Man B)	25	Did anything happen after I left?
(Woman B)	A	Take a left turn, then a right.
	B	No, you didn't miss anything.
	C	No, it's not happening yet.
(Woman A)	26	I can't believe how rude he was!
(Man A)	A	He doesn't believe us, either.
	B	He tends to be quite blunt, to be honest.
	C	It's happening everywhere.
(Woman B)	27	Have we met before? You look familiar.
(Man B)	A	The meeting is tomorrow at noon.
	B	I'm familiar with him too.
	C	I just have one of those faces.
(Man A)	28	Do you eat fish?
(Woman A)	A	Something smells fishy here.
	B	Of course—I'm an omnivore.
	C	I've fed the fish already.
(Man B)	29	Who delivered this package?
(Man A)	A	It was a courier—he just left.
	B	The package is for Sandra.
	C	I asked for home delivery.
(Woman A)	30	I can't remember where I left my keys!
(Woman B)	A	The key to success is persistence.
	B	You should retrace your steps.
	C	We're leaving in a minute.
(Woman B)	31	Would you like me to do that right now?
(Woman A)	A	It's fine—it can wait.
	B	I wasn't done with it.
	C	I like to do a lot of stuff.

Part III

Track 15

| (Narrator) | You will hear some conversations between two or more people. You will be asked to answer three questions about what the speakers say in each conversation. Select the best response to each question and mark the letter (A), (B), (C), or (D) on your answer sheet. The conversation will not be written in your test book, and will be spoken just once. |
| (Narrator) | Now let us begin with question number 32. |

(Narrator)	Questions 32–34 refer to the following conversation.
(Woman A)	Ok. So what you have to do now is press enter and we're done.
(Man A)	I know, I know. And make sure the file is saved before I close the window. I remember everything you've told me.
(Woman A)	Good. And don't remove the memory stick without ejecting it first. You might damage the file and lose all your work.
(Man A)	All right, all right. I get it. Will you please now show me how to use the wireless printer?
(Narrator)	What are the speakers using?
(Narrator)	What advice does the woman give the man?
(Narrator)	What does the man want the woman to do?
(Narrator)	Questions 35–37 refer to the following conversation.
(Man A)	Excuse me, is this the IT department?
(Woman A)	Yeah, that's us. Did you need help with that laptop?
(Man A)	Yeah, I got a promotion recently, and they gave me this company laptop to go with it, but it keeps crashing. I kind of wish I could just have my old one back, you know?
(Woman A)	Oh! But this is actually a really good model, *and* it's got huge amounts of storage. Let me take a quick look at it, I have an idea of what might be wrong with it... Yup, here it is... it hasn't been used for a while, so the software needs updating. I bet you've been trying to open documents in the new format, and that's been causing the laptop to crash... also, it looks like it hasn't been cleared after the last user. I'll clear it, too, then it should be a lot faster. Do you have much stored on here yet? I might need to wipe all the files.
(Man A)	No, I haven't managed to save anything on there yet, so feel free to wipe it clean. That's brilliant, thanks so much! Should I just leave it here with you then?
(Woman A)	Yep, I'll give you a call when it's ready. What's your office extension?
(Narrator)	Why does the man have a new laptop?
(Narrator)	What is causing the laptop issues?
(Narrator)	What does the woman ask for at the end?
(Narrator)	Questions 38–40 refer to the following conversation.
(Man B)	47th Street Medical Practice, this is Phoenix speaking, how may I help you?
(Woman A)	Hi, I would like to book an appointment, please.
(Man B)	May I have your date of birth, please?
(Woman A)	Sure, it's December 13th 1989.
(Man B)	And your first name?
(Woman A)	Maria.
(Man B)	Great. Hi Mrs. Gonzalez. May I ask what the appointment is about?

(Woman A)	I'm just worried because one of my toenails is cracked and I think I've got an infection. I'd like a doctor to have a look at it.
(Man B)	Do you feel any serious pain, or is there any discoloration?
(Woman A)	No, nothing like that. Just some discomfort when I wear shoes.
(Man B)	I'm afraid our earliest appointment is in two days, this Friday the 14th at 11 a.m. Would that work for you?
(Woman A)	I work at that time, is there any other appointment available? I don't mind waiting a bit longer.
(Man B)	Next appointment is Monday the 17th at 8:30 a.m. but it's not with your usual doctor.
(Woman A)	Oh. I'll take the appointment on Friday then, thanks. I'll just have to tell my boss first.
(Man B)	Would you like me to hold Monday while you call?
(Woman A)	No, that's fine, thanks.
(Narrator)	Whom is the conversation likely to be between?
(Narrator)	On which day is this conversation taking place?
(Narrator)	Why does the woman prefer Friday?
(Narrator)	Questions 41–43 refer to the following conversation.
(Man B)	You didn't send that email yesterday like you promised. Is everything alright?
(Woman B)	I'm so sorry. I can't believe I forgot about it.
(Man B)	Well, if you had sent it, we could have gotten the contract. It's all very disappointing. We're going to have to give them a call and see if they'll open an exception.
(Woman B)	I'll do that Mr. Lopez. This is my mess and I'll get it fixed.
(Narrator)	Why didn't the woman send the email?
(Narrator)	What does the man suggest doing?
(Narrator)	What does the woman offer to do?
(Narrator)	Questions 44–46 refer to the following conversation.
(Man A)	Are you in the office on Monday?
(Woman B)	Yeah, why?
(Man A)	We have a couple of new starters and I'm planning their induction. Do you have any spare time at all to help out?
(Woman B)	Yeah, sure. What would you like me to do?
(Man A)	There's two of them—Hui Yin and Ricardo. I've asked Hui Yin to be here at 9:30 a.m. and Ricardo at 10 a.m. so I can go through the HR stuff with them one by one—you know, emergency contact details, copies of degrees, that stuff. Then, at 10 and 10:30 a.m. respectively, they have their inductions with IT to set them up at their desks. I've also got a few meetings set up for them with a representative of each department so they can go through how their job relates to the different departments in the company and what the processes and

	expectations are. I'm just missing someone who can do the tour of the office, preferably after the IT inductions, and someone to represent your department.
(Woman B)	I can do the tour. I think Priya would be better for the meeting about our department—she did it last time.
(Man A)	Great, can you do 11 a.m.?
(Woman B)	Sure. Will it be both of them together or just one?
(Man A)	Well, it was going to be one by one, but now that you ask, maybe both might be more efficient. Let's do that.
(Narrator)	At what time will Ricardo have his IT induction?
(Narrator)	Why does the woman prefer to do a tour?
(Narrator)	What does the man say at the end?
(Narrator)	Questions 47–49 refer to the following conversation.
(Woman A)	I've now had a look at your dissertation, and I have to say I'm quite impressed with what you've done.
(Man B)	Really?
(Woman A)	Definitely. I think you've addressed all my points about connecting your argument to the existing research on social movements and adjusting your research methodology to include people who are less marginalized but decide to participate in such events.
(Man B)	That's great. I was really worried about the second part—adjusting my research methodology—because I'd already interviewed everyone but it wasn't as hard as I thought it'd be to find more people, especially since the pool of candidates was bigger. It's easier to find non-marginalized people who are willing to talk.
(Woman A)	Well, yes—and the chapter you wrote up using those interviews is brilliant. It provides a good contrast to your chapter on the interviews with marginalized groups. Now, I've marked down a few spots where you haven't cited your sources properly, but other than that you're ready to submit.
(Man B)	Perfect, thanks! I'll have a look today and submit by Thursday, after my 4 p.m. class.
(Woman A)	Don't forget the deadline is Friday at noon! Don't be late.
(Man B)	I won't, thanks.
(Narrator)	Between whom is the conversation likely to take place?
(Narrator)	Why was the man concerned about the dissertation?
(Narrator)	When is the latest the man can submit his dissertation?
(Narrator)	Questions 50–52 refer to the following conversation.
(Man B)	I've been crunching the numbers for the refurbishment and we're going to need more than $45,000 if we want to do it right.
(Woman B)	I thought we'd agreed on $30,000.
(Man B)	That was before we decided to expand the bathroom. We need at least $10,000 for the kitchen and another $20,000 for the bedrooms, plus all the small stuff like painting once the work is done... There's nothing left for the bathroom.

(Woman B)	So we don't expand the bathroom, then. Or we wait another year or two before we do it.
(Man B)	It's going to cost more if we wait—it's better to get it all done at the same time. And we can't skip the bathroom! We need a bigger bathroom.
(Woman B)	Isn't there a way to save money from everything else? Maybe we can pick cheaper tiles for the kitchen, or we can stick to just painting one of the bedrooms rather than redoing the whole thing.
(Man B)	I guess… We need to sit down and look at the numbers together.
(Woman B)	If that doesn't work, we can always ask my parents to pitch in. They already offered.
(Man B)	Yeah, but I'd rather not take them up on it. I don't want to owe anyone anything, especially family, and your parents need the money for their own refurbishment plans anyway.
(Narrator)	Look at the graphic below. Which shows the budget that the man has created?
(Narrator)	Which of the following does the woman NOT suggest to cut costs?
(Narrator)	What does the man say about the woman's parents?
(Narrator)	Questions 53–55 refer to the following conversation with three speakers.
(Man A)	What's the plan?
(Woman B)	The plan is to sit down tomorrow and have a look at all the proposals. We're waiting for one more company to come back to us by the end of the day and then we'll have all of them.
(Man A)	It's a bit soon, isn't it? If we're still waiting for proposals, shouldn't we get at least a day to read through all of them properly?
(Woman A)	The meeting's at 12 tomorrow, so you'll have all morning.
(Man A)	Still, it's a bit tight.
(Woman B)	The whole timeline is tight. These sorts of projects normally take six to eight months from conception to completion, and we've only got four months to do everything. We really need to make a decision on who to go with as soon as possible and get started.
(Man A)	That's fair. I didn't know we only had four months. I thought we had six.
(Woman A)	We did, originally. Then it got shortened to five, and then to four. It's not ideal, but it is what it is.
(Man A)	Do either of you have any of the other proposals? Can you send them to me so I can have a look at them this evening?
(Woman B)	I'll email them to you. Between us, I'm hoping the last proposal is really good, because what we've received so far is subpar.
(Narrator)	Why does the man want to reschedule the meeting?
(Narrator)	What is the timeline of the project?
(Narrator)	What does the woman say about the proposals so far?

(Narrator)	Questions 56–58 refer to the following conversation.
(Woman A)	Hi. Are you Mr. Tombs?
(Man B)	Yes. Come in.
(Woman A)	You asked for an engineer?
(Man B)	I did, yes. I don't know what's going on, but I haven't been getting any signal on my TV since last Thursday. It just…vanished, out of the blue. I've been getting this error message since.
(Woman A)	I assume you've tried all the troubleshooting instructions online?
(Man B)	Yeah. I spent three hours just going through every step twice and three times, but nothing.
(Woman A)	Let me have a look. OK, you've picked the right source and everything is plugged… Oh, wait. I see what the problem is. You're going to feel very silly.
(Man B)	What is it?
(Woman A)	The cable that connects to your satellite dish is loose, so it must've come off. See? It works now.
(Man B)	Wow. It was that simple? I can't believe I wasted a day off for this!
(Woman A)	Yeah. Might be a good idea to store the ironing board somewhere else. It must've pulled the cable out at some point when you used it.
(Man B)	Ugh. Thank you so much! You were right, this was so stupid.
(Woman A)	Don't—you can't imagine how many people make the same mistake.
(Man B)	Oh, well. Makes your job easier, I guess, right?
(Narrator)	Why has the man asked for an engineer?
(Narrator)	What has been causing the problem?
(Narrator)	How is the man likely to feel at the end?
(Narrator)	Questions 59–61 refer to the following conversation.
(Woman A)	We need to use the movie vouchers this weekend. They're expiring next week!
(Man B)	I'd forgotten about those! Well, there's quite a few movies I wanna watch. One of my colleagues recommended this new movie—what was the name? I can't remember.
(Woman A)	I have the movie schedule here.
(Man B)	It's none of these.
(Woman A)	Well, we need to pick one of them. Have you seen any of the trailers?
(Man B)	Yeah, they're all good. This one's about 15 brothers fighting over the family inheritance.
(Woman A)	Well, with so many of them… Can you imagine? I have a hard time with one brother, let alone fourteen. OK, how about this? I've heard it's good.
(Man B)	Sure, which screening? I'm off work at 3 p.m. so I can make any of them.
(Woman A)	Not the 4-something one, I hate subtitles. They're so distracting. Let's go to the one after.
(Man B)	Alright.

(Narrator)	Why does the woman want to go to the cinema?
(Narrator)	What is the woman referring to when she says "Can you imagine?"
(Narrator)	Look at the schedule below. Which screening do the man and woman pick?
(Narrator)	Questions 62–64 refer to the following conversation between three speakers.
(Woman B)	Did you hear about Alice?
(Man A)	No, what happened?
(Woman B)	Her new company's closing down.
(Woman A)	For real?
(Woman B)	Yeah, I spoke to her yesterday and she said they broke the news to them last Friday. Apparently, it's been doing badly for the past few months and they'd been relying on some big investment that fell through, so they've got no choice but to close down.
(Man A)	That's awful! She's only been working there for what, three, four months?
(Woman A)	Six, isn't it?
(Woman B)	No, seven.
(Woman A)	So, what's she going to do? Is she going to ask for her old job back, or is she looking for a new one?
(Man A)	She could apply for that new opening we've got in marketing. It's not her old job, but she's got the skills and it pays well.
(Woman B)	She's actually decided to leave town and go to university. She's going to Utah with her husband, and she's going to study economics there.
(Man A)	Wow, that's odd.
(Woman A)	What d' you mean?
(Man A)	I never pegged Alice for the kind of person who could live in a place like Utah.
(Narrator)	How many months ago did Alice change jobs?
(Narrator)	What is Alice planning to do next?
(Narrator)	Why does the man say "Wow, that's odd"?
(Narrator)	Questions 65–67 refer to the following conversation.
(Woman A)	What do you think?
(Man B)	Well, on one hand, this room is bigger and can fit more people. On the other hand, we don't know how many people are going to turn up and we might end up paying more for a service we don't need.
(Woman A)	How many have confirmed attendance so far?
(Man B)	We've invited 50, and 20 of those have said they're not coming. Another 10 are tentative, and 20 have confirmed—so the numbers could fluctuate between 20 and 30.
(Woman A)	Well, in that case, the room that only fits 25 is no good.
(Man B)	No, definitely not. And we don't need this one either—it's way bigger than we need.
(Woman A)	Yeah, definitely. Why don't we just book the one that fits 30 people and be done with it?

(Man B)	Well, I worry some of the people who said no might change their minds. You know how fickle they are. Maybe the room with 50 people is better.
(Woman A)	Well, tough luck if they change their minds. We can't waste $200 just in case they decide to show up.
(Man B)	I guess you're right. Let's go for this one, then.
(Narrator)	How many people haven't decided if they're coming yet?
(Narrator)	Why is the man reluctant to book the room that fits 30 people?
(Narrator)	Look at the price list below. Which room do the man and woman decide to book?
(Narrator)	Questions 68–70 refer to the following conversation with three speakers.
(Woman B)	Do we know what time their plane lands?
(Man A)	They were supposed to take the 7:30 one in the morning, weren't they?
(Man B)	I think it was the 8:30 one.
(Woman B)	No, no, I remember now–it was the 7:30 one, so they should be here at 9.
(Man B)	Well, if it's the 7:30 one it was delayed, so they'll be here at 10. I was checking earlier.
(Woman B)	Oh, all right. And David's picking them up to bring them to the office, right?
(Man A)	Well, he's booked a cab for them, so the driver should be waiting for them at arrivals. They wanted to take the public transport at first, but...
(Man B)	Well, they'd take ages if they took the bus, and the train's not working today, is it?
(Man A)	No, it's closed.
(Woman B)	I really hope all goes well. We can't afford any issues at this stage.
(Man B)	Don't worry, it will be fine. We just need to give them a good time and show them some hospitality and that's it.
(Woman B)	Easy for you to say. You're not the one whose job relies on them signing the contract.
(Man B)	Fair enough–but it'll be fine, I promise.
(Man A)	Yeah, Abigail, relax. We've planned everything down to the minutest detail. We've got this.
(Narrator)	At what time are the people the group is talking about arriving?
(Narrator)	How are the people the group is talking about getting to the office?
(Narrator)	Why does the man say "Fair enough"?

Part IV

Track 16

(Narrator)	Questions 71–73 refer to the following talk.
(Woman A)	I'm at the scene now, Dolores, and as you can see behind me, there's a big crowd gathering and a dozen ambulances waiting to pick up casualties from the building. We don't have a lot of information yet, the police have been very busy speaking to residents, but what we do know is that the blaze started somewhere on the third

story and spread through the building very rapidly around 9 p.m. tonight. Now, there are six stories in this building and most of the residents from the first three stories have been accounted for, but we still don't know what's going on in stories four to six. As you can see, the fire is mostly under control, though there are billows of smoke behind me, and the firefighters we've spoken to are confident that the fire has been contained and it won't be jumping to any of the surrounding buildings. It certainly helps that it's not a very windy night tonight, though I predict the heat is making the firefighters' job pretty uncomfortable. Now, I've been told that there's a list of the residents and there are 120 people living here, out of whom 46 are downstairs. About 18 have confirmed they weren't in the building when the fire started, and about 32 are receiving treatment either here or at the hospital. 36 people are still unaccounted for, and...

(Narrator)	Who is giving this speech?
(Narrator)	What information does the woman NOT give about the fire?
(Narrator)	How many casualties are there so far?

(Narrator)	Questions 74–76 refer to the following talk.
(Man A)	I know I've only been here for a few weeks so I haven't really had the chance to go through everything or speak to everyone but, from my perspective, I believe the approach we've been taking with our products and our customers has been overly cautious—the company as a whole has been loath to take risks lately and I think that's partly what's causing the slump in sales we've experienced for the last two quarters. I mean, we clearly started out with a unique product that became successful very quickly, and this is how this company became one of the world leaders in the cosmetics market, but—but what worked 20, 15, even 10 years ago won't necessarily work today, which you guys have identified but, you know, you've been focused on re-branding what we have, but what I think is we don't just need a major overhaul of how we present the products we have: we need to create new products, too. New lines, new... We need to attack new markets in the cosmetics world, we need to be seen once again as the sort of risk-takers that launched this company from the ground up and—and we, I believe we will see a marked improvement in sales very soon if we focus on that.

(Narrator)	What is the topic of this speech?
(Narrator)	What does the man say about the company's current products?
(Narrator)	What can be inferred from the man's speech?

(Narrator)	Questions 77–79 refer to the following talk.
(Man B)	OK, so the first thing you'll want to do, obviously, is log in. Careful when you type in the URL—use .net, not .com as that's a different website. You should have received an email with a temporary password—use that with your email address as the username and you will be prompted to select a new password. Your password should be a combination of letters and numbers, more than five characters, and it can use capitals. You can also use symbols, but you can't use the @ sign or any underscore. You should have at least one symbol for the password to be accepted. Now—once you've changed your password, you can start on building your

profile—you'll need to add details on what kind of work you are looking for, what your qualifications are, and you'll also need to upload a short bio and copies of your degrees and certificates, as well as your passport. Oh, and your bank details, obviously. One of the administrators will check your documents to confirm they're genuine and then you will reach 'Confirmed' status. That means you are allowed to bid on projects. You can't bid on projects that you're not qualified to work on—they'll be filtered out so you won't even be able to see them. Once you bid, you just sit back and wait for the person offering the project to pick someone and that's it, really!

(Narrator)	Which of the following passwords would be acceptable for the website?
(Narrator)	What do you NOT need to do to achieve 'Confirmed' status?
(Narrator)	What does the man say at the end?
(Narrator)	Questions 80 –82 refer to the following talk.
(Woman B)	Thank you, everyone, for coming in earlier today. I know all of you have extremely busy schedules and you're eager to get on with today's tasks, but I was told by Marina that you used to do these Monday morning…well, I don't really want to call them meetings because a meeting, to me, is a sit-down where everyone discusses a topic and tries to come up with a solution to something and they can often be dull and repetitive and I don't want you to think of this like that. This is just a quick catch-up for the whole team, an opportunity to raise a point— something you're focusing on this week, something you might need help with, or even a recent success you'd like to share or feedback on something you found troublesome and you think your colleagues might benefit from what you learned through trial and error. So, I will start by saying what I will probably need your help with is navigating the offices here, as I've gotten lost twice already! But, seriously, this is just a five-minute catch-up and we're going to try it out for a few weeks, how does a month sound? A month, we'll try it out for a month and if you find it beneficial, then excellent, if not, we can always discuss different ways of catching up—and I want you to feel comfortable, so…
(Narrator)	What can be inferred about the woman from the speech?
(Narrator)	Which of the following does the woman NOT suggest as topics for the catch-up?
(Narrator)	What does the woman say about the catch-up at the end?
(Narrator)	Questions 83–85 refer to the following talk.
(Man A)	Finally, the company has broken its silence and announced that it will be recalling all of the cell phones affected by the fault which was discovered two weeks ago in its latest model of the Spring Mobile Mini series, Spring Mini 6. Now, not every Spring Mini 6 will be affected by the fault. As the company representative explained, they have traced the origin of the fault that is making Spring Mini 6 phones shut down unexpectedly and they believe that only approximately 3,000 phones are affected. Some of the phones can be fixed by simply updating the software, they say, and they encourage customers who have purchased a Spring Mini 6 to bring it in to a Spring Mobile store even if it hasn't exhibited the behavior reported. I think this is commendable, by the way, but I would urge you to wait unless you want to face long lines. Other cell phones, however, are not fixable—mostly the ones that failed within the first week—and those will be replaced, free of charge. The ones

which are not fixable have a model number that ends with -62 from the November 2018 batch. You can check the back of the box to see if yours is one of them.

(Narrator)	What is wrong with the cell phones being recalled?
(Narrator)	What is the speaker referring to when he says, "This is commendable"?
(Narrator)	Look at the graphic below. Which cell phone model cannot be fixed?

| (Narrator) | Questions 86–88 refer to the following talk. |
| (Man B) | OK, so I've just got off the phone with Desmond and I'm afraid it's not good news. It's just as we suspected: excitement for the project has fizzled at the top level and his boss has lost all interest in enlisting our help to launch in Ohio. At first I thought it was because they were going with a competitor or because they'd just run out of budget, but according to what Desmond told me, the main reason is that they've decided to focus on what they already have rather than attack new markets or launch in new regions and countries. It's just a short-term thing, they anticipate looking into it in a year or two, but even when they do, Desmond's not so sure we'll be in the running after our poor performance in Las Vegas—and I can't say I blame him, to be honest. Look at this: this month is one of the busiest in their Mississippi stores, and it was one of the worst-performing months in Las Vegas. I think we really need to go back to the drawing board with this and come up with a plan that will wow them if we want to stay in the running for any future projects with them. |

(Narrator)	Why is the project with the woman's company not going ahead?
(Narrator)	What did Desmond say about the project?
(Narrator)	Look at the table below. Which month is the woman referring to in her speech?

| (Narrator) | Questions 89–91 refer to the following talk. |
| (Man A) | Thank you for calling Joe's Moving Services. All of our lines are busy at the moment—please hold and one of us will get to you as soon as possible. If you are enquiring about a specific booking you have made, please have your booking reference ready. If your booking is today and you have received a text message with the cell phone number of your mover, please call that number instead. To better redirect your call, please follow the instructions on the home menu: for any questions about a booking not taking place today, please press one. To inquire about our services or make a new booking, please press two or visit our website at www.joesmoving.com. If your booking is today and you have not yet received a text message from us or your driver is not picking up their phone, please press three. To modify or cancel a booking for which you have been charged, please press four. To modify or cancel a booking for which you have not been charged yet, please press five. For all other enquiries, please hold. |

(Narrator)	What can the caller do online?
(Narrator)	Which number should the caller press to cancel a paid-for booking?
(Narrator)	Which number should the caller press to make changes to an unpaid booking?

(Narrator)   Questions 92–94 refer to the following talk.

(Woman A)   This is the third promise the government has gone back on since they were sworn into office. Why are we even surprised anymore? I'm honestly curious. They promised they would fix healthcare, and they made it less accessible. They promised they'd introduce new measures to tackle knife crime in the capital and, so far, all I've heard is crickets. And now they've gone back on their promise to limit university fees by allowing universities to raise prices by 20%. Think about it. My university, they currently charge more than $5,000 per semester—that's more than $10,000 a year. With the new prices, they'll be able to charge $12,000 a year, which will leave new students with a debt of $48,000 by the time they graduate—and that's not even taking into account the cost of living, with landlords in university towns and cities taking advantage of the bubble in the housing market to extort students. I think it's about time we showed the government that they can't just walk all over us and expect us to taking it lying down. We will fight this. We will protest and take the fight to Washington. We will kick them out of office if they don't pledge to fulfill the promise they made to cut fees by half. We might be young, but we are the future of this country, and we will decide its destiny—not them.

(Narrator)   Which government promise does the speaker NOT mention?

(Narrator)   Look at the table below. Which university does the speaker attend?

(Narrator)   How is the speaker likely to feel?

(Narrator)   Questions 95–97 refer to the following talk.

(Woman B)   What's most surprising is not the ferocity with which these adverse weather phenomena have hit us—it is the way it happened, so abruptly, late this Wednesday. Just a week ago we were enjoying temperatures in the range of 60 to 70 degrees Fahrenheit and now they've plummeted to 30 with severe wind and rain in most areas. This drop is expected to continue well into the weekend and next week—falling as low as 10 in some areas, with strong gusts until next Monday. Snowfall, as you can imagine, is expected in the northernmost regions of the state throughout this time, while the heavy downpour is not expected to ease until Saturday evening, which I imagine will be little consolation to those who had plans to go out this weekend. The state government has advised residents to stay at home where they can and to avoid unnecessary trips until Sunday, but they have also recommended that people keep an eye on older family members or neighbors and children to ensure their safety. Hospitals are braced for a busy weekend, too, not just because of the potential road accidents with the rain but also due to vulnerable people such as the elderly and children, who are more likely to be affected by the drop in temperatures. Keep in mind that the last time we experienced such weather was 10 years ago, when...

(Narrator)   What does the woman say is strange about the weather?

(Narrator)   What is NOT forecast for Sunday?

(Narrator)   What CANNOT be inferred from the speech?

(Narrator)	Questions 98–100 refer to the following talk.
(Woman A)	Thank you for taking my call. What I wanted to ask Mr. Smith is whether he has given any consideration to the real-life effects of his plans to close 30 public libraries across the state because, from what I'm hearing, I don't think he has. I have a five-year-old daughter and every Sunday morning we go to a reading group for kids and their parents at our local library, and it's the most exciting part of her day—it makes her eager to learn how to read because she wants to start reading books on her own. I have neighbors who love reading but can't afford to buy books and the local library allows them to read literature without having to skip a meal or heating. You might think libraries are a luxury, Mr. Smith, but they're not. They are essential, the services they offer are essential. Teenagers whose parents can't afford to buy them a laptop can use the computers to do research and write essays for school. Unemployed adults can receive help with their resumes and learn pivotal employability skills. Children learn to love books, which turns them into educated adults. I urge Mr. Smith to reconsider—I understand the need to make cuts, but not by sacrificing an essential, life-changing service that people rely on. Why not hire more volunteers? Why not move some of the libraries to buildings with lower maintenance costs or rent? There must be a better way.
(Narrator)	What can be inferred about the woman from the speech?
(Narrator)	Which of the following important library services is NOT mentioned?
(Narrator)	What does the woman recommend to save libraries?

PRACTICE TEST 5

Part I

Track 17

(Narrator)	For each question, you will hear four statements about a picture in your test book. When you hear the statements, you must select the one statement that best describes what you see in the picture. Then find the number of the question on your answer sheet and mark your answer. The statements will not be written in your test book, and will be spoken just once.
(Narrator)	Look at the example item below.
(Narrator)	Now listen to the four statements.
(Woman A)	A He's typing up a presentation.
	B The computer is broken.
	C He's showing him the data.
	D He's listening to the podcast.
(Narrator)	Statement **C**, "He's showing him the data," best describes the photograph. Therefore, you should mark answer **C** on your answer sheet.
(Narrator)	Now Part 1 will begin.
(Narrator)	Look at the picture marked number 1 in your test book.

(Man B)	A	They are having a long walk.
	B	They're meeting in the conference room.
	C	She's taking notes while they talk.
	D	She's noticed the time.
(Narrator)		Look at the picture marked number 2 in your test book.
(Woman A)	A	The plates have fallen down.
	B	The sauce is on the middle shelf
	C	The teapot is on the lowest shelf.
	D	The dishes are being cleared.
(Narrator)		Look at the picture marked number 3 in your test book.
(Man A)	A	The pedals are being pulled up.
	B	They're cycling on the road.
	C	The gears are on the move.
	D	The cycles are being renewed.
(Narrator)		Look at the picture marked number 4 in your test book.
(Man B)	A	They're all watching the cell.
	B	They're leaning over the table.
	C	They're looking for the laptop.
	D	He's showing them the tablet.
(Narrator)		Look at the picture marked number 5 in your test book.
(Man B)	A	They're discussing the weather forecast.
	B	There is not enough seating.
	C	They're taking part in the meeting.
	D	They're looking at the photograph.
(Narrator)		Look at the picture marked number 6 in your test book.
(Woman B)	A	The dancer has fallen down.
	B	The woman is putting on pumps.
	C	The singer is taking a break.
	D	The ballerina is learning to dance.

Part II

Track 18

(Narrator)	You will hear a question or statement and three responses spoken in English. They will not be written in your test book, and will be spoken just once. Select the best response to the question or statement and mark the letter A, B, or C on your answer sheet.
(Narrator)	For example, you will hear:
(Man B)	How do you know Jemima?

(Narrator)			You will also hear:
(Woman A)		**A**	We met last year at Chang's birthday party.
		B	I don't know what that means either.
		C	You know, the one with the short blonde hair.

(Narrator) The best response to the question "How do you know Jemima?" is choice **A**, "We met last year at Chang's birthday party," so **A** is the correct answer. You should mark answer **A** on your answer sheet.

(Narrator) Now let us begin with question number 7.

(Woman A)	**7**		When was the plane supposed to land?
(Man A)		**A**	No, not today.
		B	I don't know where it is.
		C	About an hour ago.
(Man B)	**8**		Have you seen Mrs. Yun lately?
(Woman A)		**A**	Yes, she was at the conference last week.
		B	No, I won't.
		C	Yes, I am going to call him later.
(Woman A)	**9**		Where can I find the Wi-Fi password?
(Man B)		**A**	Yesterday or the day before, I'm not sure.
		B	I have it here. It's FR33WIFI.
		C	In Orlando.
(Woman B)	**10**		Does Mr. Nazario work in IT or Marketing?
(Man A)		**A**	He used to work in Marketing, but then joined IT last April.
		B	No, he doesn't really like it.
		C	Tea, please.
(Woman A)	**11**		Where did you leave the forms?
(Man A)		**A**	On your desk.
		B	This morning.
		C	By car.
(Man B)	**12**		What time is the meeting starting?
(Woman A)		**A**	In room 22.
		B	Two or three times.
		C	In half an hour.
(Woman A)	**13**		Haven't you heard about BWC Bank?
(Man B)		**A**	Yes, he loved it.
		B	No, what happened to her?
		C	Yes, what a mess.
(Woman B)	**14**		Can you send this fax for me, please?
(Man A)		**A**	Of course. Whom to?
		B	Yes, it arrived this morning.
		C	No, I don't.

(Man A)	15	When did they say the components would arrive?
(Woman B)	A	On Friday.
	B	I wouldn't if I were you.
	C	Through the mail.
(Man B)	16	How soon can you repair the computers?
(Woman B)	A	It'll be a couple of days, at least.
	B	I'll turn them on.
	C	Three weeks ago.
(Woman B)	17	Is the restroom door locked?
(Man B)	A	Yes, you need a rest.
	B	It shouldn't be. Have you checked?
	C	It's mine.
(Woman A)	18	Who's in charge of the new development project?
(Man A)	A	I don't think they will.
	B	There's a socket behind your desk.
	C	I believe it's Sally.
(Woman B)	19	How long will the presentation last?
(Man B)	A	An hour or so.
	B	It's about ten feet long.
	C	I don't think it'll last.
(Man B)	20	Whose cell phone is that?
(Woman A)	A	It's 555 6100.
	B	It must be Nora's. This is her desk.
	C	I'll text you if you don't mind.
(Woman A)	21	Where do I sign up for the basketball team?
(Man B)	A	Every Friday at 6:30.
	B	There's a pen in my drawer.
	C	Go to HR and speak to Cassio.
(Woman B)	22	May I borrow your ruler?
(Man A)	A	Sure. There you go.
	B	No, you won't.
	C	Yes, every other week.
(Man A)	23	How old are your children?
(Woman B)	A	About 15 years ago.
	B	She's 8 and he's 10.
	C	We have two boys and a girl.
(Man A)	24	How much is this contract worth?
(Man B)	A	I'd say 2 or 3 million dollars.
	B	It's been a while.
	C	A couple of years.

(Man B)	25	Where are you going for Easter?
(Woman B)	A	Saturday morning.
	B	We'll take the train. It's just easier.
	C	To Luke's sister's. She lives in Miami.
(Woman A)	26	When will I receive your invoice, then?
(Man A)	A	It should be with you by the end of the day.
	B	By email.
	C	Sales will contact you to book an appointment.
(Woman B)	27	What's the factory's ZIP code?
(Man B)	A	We're quite proud of it.
	B	It's 44561.
	C	The one on the left. Under the mattress.
(Man A)	28	How many people are going to the party?
(Woman A)	A	I hired a DJ and a Japanese buffet.
	B	Almost everyone from the office. 50, 60 perhaps?
	C	I love the swimming pool there.
(Man B)	29	Give me one reason why I shouldn't fire you.
(Man A)	A	I don't know what to say. It won't happen again.
	B	It's really hot in LA this year.
	C	We're lucky the firemen arrived quickly.
(Woman A)	30	Is the photocopier broken?
(Woman B)	A	Yes, but you can use the printer.
	B	No, it doesn't.
	C	No, but there's coffee in the staff room.
(Woman B)	31	Do you recommend this brand?
(Woman A)	A	No, I'm really tired. Can we do it tomorrow?
	B	No, my cousin bought one of those and said they're awful.
	C	No, I think they're excellent.

Part III

Track 19

(Narrator)	You will hear some conversations between two or more people. You will be asked to answer three questions about what the speakers say in each conversation. Select the best response to each question and mark the letter (A), (B), (C), or (D) on your answer sheet. The conversation will not be written in your test book, and will be spoken just once.
(Narrator)	Now let us begin with question number 32.
(Narrator)	Questions 32–34 refer to the following conversation.
(Woman B)	The taxi will be here any minute. Are you ready?
(Man B)	I can't find my jacket. I'm pretty sure I left it in the kitchen. Did you take it?

(Woman B)	I did see it in the kitchen but that was this morning. I haven't seen it since you got back from work. Maybe you left it in the car. What do you need it for, anyway? We're going to be late.
(Man B)	I printed the tickets at work and put them in my pocket.
(Woman B)	Don't worry. I have them in my email. We don't need to print those things anymore. They can scan it straight from the phone screen. By the way, just got a text saying the taxi is downstairs. Let's go.
(Man B)	OK. You go ahead. I'll have a look in the car, just in case. At least I won't spend the whole play wondering where my jacket is.
(Woman B)	Sure. But don't take too long. Mark and Vera are waiting for us.
(Narrator)	What is the man looking for?
(Narrator)	What does the woman say about the tickets?
(Narrator)	Why is the woman in a hurry?
(Narrator)	Questions 35–37 refer to the following conversation with three speakers.
(Man A)	How soon can we have the quotes? We really need to sort this out before the clients arrive from China.
(Man B)	It'll take us a couple of days. I don't want to give you a number now and then later have to say it was wrong. You'll just have to be patient.
(Woman A)	Patient? You said you were coming on Monday and then you had a problem with your van. Then on Tuesday it was the snow. And now you're telling us you can't give us a quote until Friday?
(Man B)	I understand your frustration, ma'am. But there's nothing I can do. This is not a simple job.
(Man A)	But there's got to be something you can do. Let's say you give us the quote on Friday and we're happy to proceed. How soon can you start?
(Man B)	It depends. I'd have to check with my men what their availability is and, er, we need to order the parts. It's not that easy…
(Woman A)	Well, it seems pretty easy to me. We have a leak in the office, we need a plumber to fix it and it seems to me that you're not the man for the job, Mr. Wells. Thank you for your time. The door is on your left. Take care and good luck.
(Narrator)	Why is the woman unhappy?
(Narrator)	When did Mr. Wells have a problem with his vehicle?
(Narrator)	What problem does the woman have?
(Narrator)	Questions 38–40 refer to the following conversation.
(Man A)	How are things going at the Buenos Aires office, Gabriela?
(Woman A)	Everything's fine. We've recently managed to take two major clients from one of our main competitors. We're really making a name for ourselves down there. How are things in Ohio?
(Man A)	I'm not sure. We've been doing the same thing for far too long, I guess. I don't know. Sometimes I think I'd be better off in Orlando or Oregon. There's so much going on at the new branches. I miss the buzz of setting up a new office, the

	targets, the mission. But it's impossible to move all the time now. It was fine when the kids were younger, but now…
(Woman A)	I know. How old are they, anyway?
(Man A)	Chloe's 12 and Jake's 9.
(Woman A)	Wow. I can't believe it. It feels like yesterday when you got the call in the middle of our presentation, remember?
(Man A)	How could I forget? It was your first week and I left you alone with a roomful of new clients and rushed to the hospital. By the time I got there, Monica already had Chloe in her arms.
(Woman A)	Time flies. It's just ridiculous.
(Narrator)	What does Gabriela say about her work?
(Narrator)	What does the man mean when he says "I miss the buzz of setting up a new office"?
(Narrator)	What does the man say about a presentation?
(Narrator)	Questions 41–43 refer to the following conversation.
(Woman A)	What do you want for lunch? I feel like Italian today.
(Man A)	Italian is fine. Shall we go that new place on 52nd? Jackie said their risotto is to die for.
(Woman A)	Great idea. I still have to go through these files, though. Can you give me another half hour?
(Man A)	No problem. I'm going to see Fiona from IT now so we could meet downstairs in half an hour.
(Woman A)	One o' clock it is, then. Can I ask Manuel if he would like to join us?
(Man A)	I'd rather you didn't. We had a bit of an argument yesterday because of the Helsinki project. He was pretty rude and I just don't want to pretend nothing happened. He owes me an apology.
(Woman A)	I understand. Just the two of us, then. Anyway, I'd better get going or no lunch at all.
(Man A)	Okay. See you in a bit.
(Narrator)	What do they say about Jackie?
(Narrator)	When do they agree to meet?
(Narrator)	Where are they going together?
(Narrator)	Questions 44–46 refer to the following conversation with three speakers.
(Man A)	What's wrong, Boris? You look upset.
(Woman B)	Is everything OK? Does it have anything to do with the new manager?
(Man B)	Everything. He's giving two of my best clients to Clara. No explanation, nothing. He didn't talk to me in person, not even a phone call. He just sends me an email saying that even though he appreciates my effort in bringing them to the company, he thinks that Clara should handle them from now on.
(Man A)	That's ridiculous. What about your commission?

(Man B)	He said, well, his email said I'll be getting the usual 20% for the first two months but since they'll be Clara's clients, she'll get the commission after July.
(Woman B)	He can't do that! You have to take it to the board. This has to stop. Since the merger, he's been giving all the good clients to his people. This is unprofessional. If Mr. Fernandez finds out, he'll put an end to this.
(Man B)	I don't know. I have always taken care of my own problems.
(Man A)	This is not about taking care of your own problems. He's doing this to everyone. Listen to me, Boris. If you don't talk to Mr. Fernandez, I will.
(Narrator)	Why is Boris upset?
(Narrator)	What does the woman think Boris should do?
(Narrator)	When did the problem start?
(Narrator)	Questions 47–49 refer to the following conversation.
(Woman A)	Hi. Is this Maryland Taxis? I need three taxis for 8 o' clock tonight. I'm taking some clients out for dinner.
(Man B)	Why not hire one of our premium vehicles?
(Woman A)	Not so sure. We're a new company and our budget is quite low.
(Man B)	That shouldn't be a problem. If you allow me, I can look into it for you. You might even save a little bit if you use one of our premium vehicles... It won't take a minute, I promise. I can see your address in the system already... just tell me where you want to go.
(Woman A)	We'll finish our meeting at 8 and then I was going to take them to the restaurant at The Royal Bath.
(Man B)	Ok. And after dinner?
(Woman A)	They're staying at the Shelton.
(Man B)	And when you say they, how many people are we talking about?
(Woman A)	12. Including me.
(Man B)	So, three taxis would cost you $225.00... they're 75 bucks each. You could have a limo for $250.00. What do you think?
(Woman A)	It's not a bad idea but I think I'll pass this time. Maybe another time.
(Man B)	No problem, ma'am. Three taxis at 8 then.
(Woman A)	Thank you.
(Man B)	No problem. And thanks for choosing Maryland Taxis.
(Narrator)	What does the woman say about her company?
(Narrator)	Where are her clients staying?
(Narrator)	Look at the fare prices below. Which type of vehicle does the woman choose?
(Narrator)	Questions 50–52 refer to the following conversation with three speakers.
(Woman A)	Excuse me, can you tell me how to get to the main reception? I'm new here and someone is waiting for me there.
(Man B)	No problem. All you have to do is...

(Man A)	Murilo! Claire! I see you two have already met. Well, let's go. Mrs. Walcott is waiting for us.
(Man B)	Hi, Chuck. What do you mean "waiting for us"? I was only telling her how to get to the main reception.
(Man A)	Didn't you get the email? This is Claire Dawson, the new HR director. Mrs. Walcott called a meeting to introduce her to everyone in finances. And that includes you, my friend.
(Man B)	Really? I didn't get anything. Anyway, my name's Murilo Pinto. Nice to meet you, Ms. Dawson.
(Woman A)	Nice to meet you too. And please call me Claire.
(Man B)	Well, since we're all going to the same place, why don't you follow us, Claire? We'll take a shortcut through the warehouse.
(Narrator)	Who are they going to meet?
(Narrator)	Where does the woman want to go?
(Narrator)	Where do the men work?
(Narrator)	Questions 53–55 refer to the following conversation.
(Woman B)	Did you read the email Mr. Honda sent his morning, Pete?
(Man A)	Yes, I did. Do you think it's a good idea? I'm not so sure.
(Woman B)	Well, you have to understand how frustrating it must be for him. His designs are excellent and if we don't have the resources for manufacturing the goods here in the US, why not send them elsewhere?
(Man A)	I know. I'm just worried what our customers might think when the word gets out. It wasn't even two years ago when we had a massive advertising campaign focusing on how our products are 100% American and all that stuff. It's a dangerous move.
(Woman B)	I think it's a calculated risk. And most of them will still be assembled here in the US, so I think he's got a point there.
(Man A)	I hope you're right.
(Narrator)	What does the man think about Mr. Honda's email?
(Narrator)	What does the man mean when he says "I'm just worried what our customers might think when the word gets out"?
(Narrator)	What does the woman think about Mr. Honda's idea?
(Narrator)	Questions 56–58 refer to the following conversation.
(Man B)	When's the presentation going to start? We've been here for nearly half an hour. I've got a pile of contracts to go through on my desk.
(Woman A)	I don't know. They're trying to get the projector to work now since the screen is not working. Anyway, how're things in compliances?
(Man B)	Don't ask. We're really short-staffed. I can't remember the last time I got home before 9. And Maria is really upset with me. As if there was anything I could do about it.

(Woman A)	Sorry to hear that, Waleed. But it's the same thing at sales. Our software is outdated, we have no digital marketing whatsoever. It seems as if this company stopped in the 90's. We still have fax machines and filing cabinets up there.
(Man B)	You're kidding me, right?
(Woman A)	No. Mrs. Pollain asks us to print every single quote and file them in alphabetical order. We tried to explain that it would be cheaper to update the system and have everything stored in a cloud.
(Man B)	And...
(Woman A)	She tells us that she has been in this business for 50 years and all that traditional nonsense.
(Man B)	I know. Look. It's finally starting.
(Narrator)	What do we learn from the conversation?
(Narrator)	What do they NOT say about their company?
(Narrator)	What does the woman say about Mrs. Pollain?
(Narrator)	Questions 59–61 refer to the following conversation.
(Man B)	Hello. May I speak to Mrs. Kournikova? This is Mr. Andreolli. I need to talk to her about the movie festival next month.
(Woman A)	I'm afraid Mrs. Kournikova is not in the office today. She's attending a conference in Santiago and won't be back until Tuesday next week.
(Man B)	Would it be possible for you to give her a message? I have already emailed it to her but I thought I should call since she never returns any of my emails.
(Woman A)	She never returns anyone's emails. What's the message?
(Man B)	We are happy with the dinner menu and wine selection. However, we have increased the number of guests from 280 to 300. I just want to make sure this is not a problem.
(Woman A)	She did get your email, then. She told me about it when I spoke to her this morning. It's all taken care of, Mr. Andreolli, we'll see you the evening of the 24th.
(Man B)	That's good to know. Thanks for everything, Mrs. Challen
(Narrator)	What does the woman say about Mrs. Kournikova?
(Narrator)	What does the man say about the event?
(Narrator)	Look at the graphics below. Which movie festival is the man talking about?
(Narrator)	Questions 62–64 refer to the following conversation.
(Man A)	There wasn't room here in your office so I put the boxes next door. Just make sure you don't leave them there overnight.
(Woman A)	There's really not much space in here. I really need to get this sorted. It's such a mess. I can't seem to find anything.
(Man A)	Anyhow, what time does the presentation start?
(Women A)	Cocktails will be served at 6. The presentation itself should start an hour later.

(Narrator)	Where did the man put the boxes?
(Narrator)	What does the woman say about her own office?
(Narrator)	What will happen at 7?

(Narrator)	Questions 65–67 refer to the following conversation.
(Woman B)	Hi, Mr. Cooper. You're in charge of maintenance here, right? I was just wondering why these rooms aren't being cleaned. What if we had a problem with the auditorium downstairs and had to move one of the talks up here?
(Man B)	I'm so sorry, Mrs. Zhang, but my manager asked me not to do any of the rooms upstairs because it's a waste of cleaning products. He even told me off when I said we might need to use these rooms.
(Woman B)	I see. In this case, I'm going to have a word with Mr. Beech this afternoon. And don't worry. I won't mention our little chat here.
(Man B)	Thank you, Mrs. Zhang. I really appreciate that.
(Woman B)	You're welcome. And in the meantime, just leave it as it is. I'll make sure he sorts this mess out himself.

(Narrator)	Who thinks the rooms should not be cleaned?
(Narrator)	What does Mrs. Zhang say about the rooms?
(Narrator)	What does Mrs. Zhang say she's going to do?

(Narrator)	Questions 68–70 refer to the following conversation.
(Man A)	The supervisor just sent me an email to see if he can visit the plant tomorrow at lunchtime.
(Woman B)	Does it have to be tomorrow? I can be there to let him in, but I have a meeting in Denver at 3. It'll take me at least an hour to get there.
(Man A)	I think all he wants is to make sure the new machines are up and running. You probably won't need to stay. And even if he stays a bit longer, I can fill him in on the latest developments here at the plant.
(Woman B)	No problem then. But please make sure he knows that I have another meeting.

(Narrator)	What are the speakers discussing?
(Narrator)	What time is the visitor more likely to arrive?
(Narrator)	Why is the woman worried?

Part IV

Track 20

| (Narrator) | Questions 71–73 refer to the following talk. |
| (Woman A) | Hello everyone and thanks for coming. First, I'd like to introduce Mrs. Hildenberg from our German branch in Munich. She'll be joining us to learn more about our projects here in Minnesota and she'll also be sharing some of her ideas and visions for the future of this company tomorrow during the conference. So now that the introductions have been made, let's get down to business. Our meeting |

today is about the new marketing campaign for Auntie Bella. Customers have a lot of confidence in the quality of our baked goods, but the same cannot be said about our range of kitchen appliances. We believe that our previous marketing campaign gave too much importance to the looks and design of our range of appliances but did not emphasize their quality. So what I propose we do is find a way to link our baked goods to our kitchen appliances. The idea is to create a campaign that makes our cakes and breads look even better when made with one of our appliances. Today is our first brainstorming session, so all ideas are welcome.

(Narrator)	Why is Mrs. Hildenberg in Minnesota?
(Narrator)	What is Auntie Bella known for?
(Narrator)	What does the woman say about their previous marketing campaign?
(Narrator)	Questions 74–76 refer to the following talk.
(Man A)	Last night was the grand opening of Luxville, the newest development by Erin Brothers. The luxurious shopping mall is located in a prime location only three minutes away from Miami Beach. Luxville is home to more than 150 stores, including the first Gigi Giglio store in the US. The Italian designer was present at the opening party last night and told us why he waited so long before opening a store for what is now one of the most revered brands in Europe. Gigi spoke of his love for the country, and how he was waiting for the correct opportunity to take his posh rags, as they're called by fashionistas, to American shores. Gigi Giglio is not the only surprise revealed during the opening, with three other stores making their first appearances in an American mall.
(Narrator)	What is Luxville?
(Narrator)	How does the woman describe Gigi Giglio?
(Narrator)	Which of the following is NOT mentioned in the news report?
(Narrator)	Questions 77–79 refer to the following talk.
(Man B)	And now, a breaking news story. A local woman has been charged with forgery. Susie Crab, 44, has been charged with selling counterfeit Npad tablet computers. She placed ads on different auction websites and then agreed to meet prospective buyers to deliver the Npad computers, which were nothing more than painted wood filled with sand. Since her "computers" were delivered in unopened boxes that looked like the original versions, victims did not suspect they were buying a piece of wood and not a computer. The scam was only uncovered when one of the victims saw Mrs. Crab in a supermarket parking lot carrying two Npad boxes. The man instantly recognized the trickster and called the police, who arrested her with more than 30 counterfeit tablet computers in her car. If convicted, Mrs. Crab could serve 10–15 years in a federal prison.
(Narrator)	Why was Susie arrested?
(Narrator)	Which of the following is true about Susie?
(Narrator)	What is the best description of Susie according to the news report?

(Narrator)	Questions 80 –82 refer to the following talk.
(Man B)	Hello and welcome to "Brooklyn, Now", the one and only daily show covering only local news for Brooklyn, New York. I'm Maurizio Biglia and today's special correspondent is Amy Cartagena, who has been covering the opening of the new art gallery by the photographer and collector, Ananda Prasit. Tonight's opening exhibition is a bit of a mystery. This is the first time Mr. Prasit will show his private collection and critics and art lovers are not sure what to expect. Even more hype was generated early this morning, when British pop star Bob Jones not only confirmed his presence at the opening, but also revealed he'll be playing an acoustic show. Childhood friends Ananda and Bob are said to be partners in the new art gallery.
(Narrator)	Who is a musician?
(Narrator)	What does the man say about the event?
(Narrator)	How do Ananda and Bob know each other?
(Narrator)	Questions 83–85 refer to the following talk.
(Man A)	You have reached OneBank's automated current account information line. Press 1 for your current balance. Press 2 for PIN services and online banking ID. Press 3 for credit cards. Press 4 for traveler's checks and foreign currency. Press 5 for savings account and investments. To hear these options again, please press 6. You have reached OneBank's automated current account information line. Did you know that one in five Americans has been a victim of bank fraud? Speak to one of our advisors today to learn how to protect your savings and the future of your family. One of our advisors will be with you shortly. OneBank's Easysave is the perfect solution for those who need a friendly hand to help them save for the future. A new car? The vacation of a lifetime? With payments starting at $3 a month, Easysave is the ideal savings account for those who find it hard to put some money aside at the end of the month.
(Narrator)	Which number should someone press who is looking to buy Euros?
(Narrator)	What does the message say about bank fraud?
(Narrator)	What's Easysave?
(Narrator)	Questions 86–88 refer to the following talk.
(Man B)	Hello, Mr. Lizaru. My name is Antonina Skirtel and I'm calling on behalf of Mars Insurance. We have received your claim but would like to ask you a few questions before processing it. It seems to me that you were not living at the same address provided when you took out our policy and we just want to make sure we have all the information we need before looking into your claim. If you could get back to us at 1 800 555 2881, we can then confirm all your details and process your claim. Alternatively, you can email us at claims@marsinsurance.com and provide us with the following: your current address, your driver's license number and the names of any other residents currently living at your property. If we you don't hear back from you by April 4th, we will not be able to process your claim.
(Narrator)	What's the purpose of the message?
(Narrator)	Which of the following is NOT mentioned in the message?
(Narrator)	Look at the graphic below. Which policy is more likely to be Mr. Lizaru's?

(Narrator)	Questions 89–91 refer to the following talk.
(Man A)	Before we start our 27th Annual Marketing Conference, I have a very important announcement to make. As most of you know, our chairman, Mr. Hudson, is due to retire at the end of the year. What will we do without the man who transformed this small family company into a global force in digital marketing? Therefore, for the past two months, we've been discussing who his ideal replacement could be. Well, ladies and gentlemen, our search is over and I would like to announce that Ms. Flores will become the new chairman of DigiWorld. We couldn't think of anyone with better qualifications or experience to keep us on the same path of success set by Mr. Hudson. For those of you who don't know Ms. Flores, she is the mastermind behind our DigiWorld app, which has allowed us to offer our products and services to small entrepreneurs all over the world. I know she'd like to say a few words, so please join me in welcoming our new chairman, Ms. Elizaveta Flores.
(Narrator)	What does the man say about Mr. Hudson?
(Narrator)	What does the man mean when he says "Who would be able to fill the shoes of the man"?
(Narrator)	What do we know about Mr. Flores?
(Narrator)	Questions 92–94 refer to the following talk.
(Woman A)	Attention passengers waiting to board Saudi Airlines flight 9911 to London. Attention all passengers waiting to board Saudi Airlines flight 9911 to London Heathrow. Your plane has been delayed due to thick fog in London. We do not expect the plane to arrive here in Dublin for the next two hours, so we will inform you as soon as we have an approximate boarding time. We apologize for the inconvenience and we'll update you as soon as we have an approximate boarding time. Again, passengers waiting to board Saudi Airlines flight 9911 to London Heathrow. Due to thick fog, the aircraft has not taken off from London Heathrow and boarding will not take place for at least two more hours. We'll continue to update you as soon as we receive additional information.
(Narrator)	What is the purpose of the announcement?
(Narrator)	Where's the announcement taking place?
(Narrator)	Which of the following is NOT mentioned in the announcement?
(Narrator)	Questions 95–97 refer to the following talk.
(Man A)	Hello everyone. My name is Alan. On behalf of Medi Travel I'd like to welcome you all to Ibiza, where fun is as certain as death and taxes. The bus ride to your hotel will take about 20 minutes. I am pretty sure you are going to enjoy your stay here in Ibiza. This is a beautiful, vibrant city where you can relax and sit by the beach or enjoy some of the best clubs in Europe. You can walk into town and enjoy the local shops and restaurants or take a moonlit walk along the water if you prefer some peace and quiet. We're going to be pulling up to the Marina Hotel in just a few minutes. Please sit back and enjoy the view of the ocean on the right hand side of the bus as we go over the bridge. I kindly ask that you remain in your seats and do not eat or drink on the bus. Manuel will be meeting us at the entrance to give you a warm welcome and help you with your bags. Please make sure your

bag has a tag and has been taken off the bus. On behalf of Medi Travel, I wish you all a wonderful vacation in Ibiza and I hope to see you around the resort.

(Narrator)	How does Alan describe Ibiza?
(Narrator)	What does the man mean when he says "where fun is as certain as death and taxes"?
(Narrator)	Which of the following is NOT mentioned in the talk?
(Narrator)	Questions 98–100 refer to the following talk.
(Woman A)	Attention all staff! Attention all staff! An immediate evacuation of warehouses A1, A2 and A3 is required due to fire. Please remain calm and follow the fire procedures and instructions of emergency. After leaving the area, go to the parking lot opposite the main building. Please do not attempt to collect any personal belongings or try to contact other staff on their cell phones. Office staff, please limit phone use so phone lines are available for emergency messaging. Personnel in warehouses B1 and B2, or areas of the company not listed for evacuation should remain in place, and be alert to changing conditions. Do not leave the building unless you are in warehouses A1, A2 or A3.
(Narrator)	Why are staff being asked to evacuate the building?
(Narrator)	Where's the meeting point?
(Narrator)	Look at the graphic below. Which department is being asked to evacuate the building?

PRACTICE TEST 6

Part I

Track 21

(Narrator)	For each question, you will hear four statements about a picture in your test book. When you hear the statements, you must select the one statement that best describes what you see in the picture. Then find the number of the question on your answer sheet and mark your answer. The statements will not be written in your test book, and will be spoken just once.
(Narrator)	Look at the example item below.
(Narrator)	Now listen to the four statements.
(Woman A)	**A** He's telling him how to farm.
	B They're having a conversation.
	C The farmer is ploughing the field.
	D The tractor is broken down.
(Narrator)	Statement **B**, "They're having a conversation," best describes the photograph. Therefore, you should mark answer **B** on your answer sheet.
(Narrator)	Now Part 1 will begin.

(Narrator)		Look at the picture marked number 1 in your test book.
(Man A)	**A**	The tallest skyscraper is on the far right.
	B	The buildings are being constructed.
	C	The gherkins have all been eaten.
	D	The city has lots of fillings.
(Narrator)		Look at the picture marked number 2 in your test book.
(Man B)	**A**	The pupils are enjoying their vacation.
	B	They're taking notes on the lecture.
	C	He's offended by her comments.
	D	The students have gone outside to work.
(Narrator)		Look at the picture marked number 3 in your test book.
(Man B)	**A**	The men are all on the phone.
	B	The group are presenting the information.
	C	The women are sharing a joke.
	D	The family is clearing the table for dinner.
(Narrator)		Look at the picture marked number 4 in your test book.
(Woman A)	**A**	He's reading her the headlines.
	B	The wine has spilled onto her hands.
	C	The bottle is old and dusty.
	D	She's showing him the wine label.
(Narrator)		Look at the picture marked number 5 in your test book.
(Man A)	**A**	They're comparing the different pictures.
	B	The students are having their work graded.
	C	They're critiquing the portraits at the gallery.
	D	They're choosing their favourite story.
(Narrator)		Look at the picture marked number 6 in your test book.
(Woman B)	**A**	The florist is closing his shop.
	B	He's taking an order over the phone.
	C	The garden is full of flowers.
	D	He's ordering more flowers for his house.

Part II

Track 22

(Narrator)	You will hear a question or statement and three responses spoken in English. They will not be written in your test book, and will be spoken just once. Select the best response to the question or statement and mark the letter A, B, or C on your answer sheet.
(Narrator)	For example, you will hear:
(Man B)	How do I access the web-based accounting report?

(Narrator)		You will also hear:
(Woman A)	A	The accountants are reporting to the CEO now.
	B	It's encrypted, you need the login and password.
	C	You need a keycard to get up there, Bill has one you can borrow.

(Narrator) The best response to the question "How do I access the web-based accounting report?" is choice (B), "It's encrypted, you need the login and password," so (B) is the correct answer. You should mark answer (B) on your answer sheet.

(Narrator) Now let us begin with question number 7.

(Woman A)	7	Have you decided on a name yet?
(Man A)	A	I was named after my grandfather.
	B	We don't even know the gender yet.
	C	She was named salesperson of the year.

(Man B)	8	I hate speaking on the phone.
(Woman A)	A	I'm about to call them right now.
	B	There's a payphone across the street.
	C	Me too—I prefer texting, for sure.

(Woman A)	9	Did you apply for the job?
(Man B)	A	I missed the deadline.
	B	No, I didn't get it.
	C	I wish I had your job, too!

(Woman B)	10	What did you want to be when you were a kid?
(Man A)	A	I didn't like cheese or vegetables.
	B	I don't have any kids.
	C	An astronaut, or a football player.

(Woman A)	11	Did you renew your membership after all?
(Man A)	A	I negotiated a discount first.
	B	I don't know what the best option is.
	C	No way I'm helping out with that.

(Man B)	12	I'm feeling a bit under the weather this morning.
(Woman A)	A	The forecast says tomorrow will be nice.
	B	It's been a beautiful morning indeed.
	C	There's a lot of sick people in the office—you must've caught something.

(Woman A)	13	What's gotten into him?
(Man B)	A	Something must've upset him.
	B	I'm not that into him.
	C	He's gotten a new car.

(Woman B)	14	Did she tell you what she's bringing to the party?
(Man A)	A	The party is on Saturday.
	B	I'm bringing nothing, to be honest.
	C	I think she's bringing a casserole.

(Man A)	15	Whose song is this?
(Woman B)	A	It's an indie band–I found them online.
	B	I don't like listening to music.
	C	I love singing in the shower.
(Man B)	16	Did you go for the first or the second candidate?
(Woman B)	A	This won't take a second.
	B	I tanked my interview.
	C	I'm still deciding.
(Woman B)	17	What were you guys talking about?
(Man B)	A	He just wanted to know what time we're meeting tomorrow.
	B	I'm sorry if I offended you.
	C	I'll go and talk to her right now if you want.
(Woman A)	18	Did I do something to upset you?
(Man A)	A	Yes, he's really upset with you.
	B	I just wish you'd listen to me sometimes.
	C	I haven't done it yet.
(Woman B)	19	Are you going to the coffee shop?
(Man B)	A	The coffee shop is just down the road.
	B	She doesn't drink coffee.
	C	Yeah, do you want me to get you anything?
(Man B)	20	Why didn't you just bring him with you?
(Woman A)	A	This is not his kind of thing.
	B	I'm still looking for a new assistant.
	C	I forgot to bring my glasses with me.
(Woman A)	21	I wouldn't take it personally if I were you.
(Man B)	A	I know, everyone says this is just how he is.
	B	He's the right kind of person for the job.
	C	I'm not sure I'm allowed to take that with me.
(Woman B)	22	Do you prefer pancakes or scones for breakfast?
(Man A)	A	Breakfast is served at 7:30.
	B	Can we have croissants instead?
	C	I haven't eaten yet.
(Man A)	23	Do you want to give it a try?
(Woman B)	A	I've already given it to her.
	B	We've got a long way to go.
	C	I'm good, thanks.
(Man A)	24	What is wrong with the printer?
(Man B)	A	I've printed everything we need.
	B	I think it's jammed again.
	C	It's in the printer room.

(Man B)	25	Did you understand what he said?
(Woman B)	A	I don't know who he is.
	B	Yeah, he said to meet him there.
	C	He hasn't told me yet.

(Woman A)	26	This is all I could find.
(Man A)	A	I'm finding it really hard.
	B	It'll have to do, then.
	C	I will find out for you.

(Woman B)	27	You didn't need to pay much, did you?
(Man B)	A	We accept credit or cash.
	B	I'm not paid enough for this.
	C	No, it was half price.

(Man A)	28	Can you tell me where the bathroom is?
(Woman A)	A	It's down the hall, on your left.
	B	I'm all right, thank you.
	C	The house has three rooms.

(Man B)	29	What happened between them?
(Man A)	A	It's happening this weekend.
	B	They had a massive fight.
	C	It's between 3 and 5 p.m.

(Woman A)	30	Do you like the blue or the red tie more?
(Woman B)	A	I'm wearing the blue suit.
	B	I'd like to be there.
	C	Why don't you just wear a bow tie?

(Woman B)	31	I brought you some sweets from Europe.
(Woman A)	A	He's a very sweet guy.
	B	Oh, you shouldn't have!
	C	I've been to Europe a few times.

Part III

Track 23

(Narrator)	You will hear some conversations between two or more people. You will be asked to answer three questions about what the speakers say in each conversation. Select the best response to each question and mark the letter (A), (B), (C), or (D) on your answer sheet. The conversation will not be written in your test book, and will be spoken just once.
(Narrator)	Now let us begin with question number 32.
(Narrator)	Questions 32–34 refer to the following conversation between three speakers.
(Man B)	Has either of you seen my striped blue sweater?
(Woman B)	Where did you last leave it, do you remember?

(Man B)	It was on the back of my chair before I went to my 10 a.m. meeting, but now it's disappeared. Did anyone come into my office?
(Woman A)	Are you sure you left it there? When I came in to remind you about the meeting I didn't see it.
(Man B)	Really? Oh, man. I was sure I'd left it there.
(Woman B)	Let's just look for it together. It couldn't have disappeared. Maybe you just left it somewhere and forgot.
(Man B)	It's my favorite sweater, too. My wife bought it for my 40th. I hope no one took it!
(Woman B)	They wouldn't...would they?
(Woman A)	Oh, I don't know about that. A lot of stuff's gone missing in the office lately. Marco left his cell phone in the bathroom the other day and by the time he went back, it was gone.
(Woman B)	Yeah, but that's different. Everyone's got access to the bathroom—we share it with three other companies. Who would come into Brian's office to steal a sweater?
(Man B)	Unless I forgot it somewhere... Damn it...
(Narrator)	What is NOT true about the sweater?
(Narrator)	Why does the woman say "Oh, I don't know about that"?
(Narrator)	How is the man likely to feel?
(Narrator)	Questions 35–37 refer to the following conversation.
(Man A)	I've been looking at tickets for *Fiddler on the Roof* and I think I've got a few options for us.
(Woman A)	Which date?
(Man A)	Well, I was looking for the April 7th but it's all extremely expensive, and then I'm on holiday between the 15th and the 22nd and the show finishes on the 23rd so I went for the 13th. Is that all right?
(Woman A)	Yeah, should be fine. It's not a Friday, is it?
(Man A)	No, it's a Tuesday.
(Woman A)	Cool. I'm working late every Friday this month.
(Man A)	That sucks!
(Woman A)	I know! OK, let's see... Definitely not these ones, I'm not paying more than $100 for theater tickets.
(Man A)	How about these ones?
(Woman A)	They're cheap...but I might get vertigo if we're high up. I'd rather pick orchestra seats.
(Man A)	Well, in that case I think it's worth paying a bit extra so we're in the middle, don't you think?
(Woman A)	Oh, yes—definitely. These ones, then. Let's go for them.
(Narrator)	On which day are the man and woman going to the theater?
(Narrator)	Why does the man say "that sucks"?
(Narrator)	Look at the graphic. Which seats do the man and woman select?

(Narrator)	Questions 38–40 refer to the following conversation with three speakers.
(Man B)	I really like this photograph. It reminds me of my mother's house in Denver. It's a shame it's been sold already or I would buy it for her.
(Man A)	Yeah, it's a really good one. The whole exhibition is really good.
(Woman A)	I heard this is his third exhibition in the US, and he sold out in both his previous ones.
(Man B)	Really? That's impressive!
(Woman A)	Yeah. I'm kind of surprised, to be honest.
(Man A)	Why? Do you not like his work?
(Woman A)	It's not that, it's just... I mean, it's good–but is it really *that* good, you know?
(Man B)	I think somebody's jealous...!
(Woman A)	I'm not jealous! My photographs are doing pretty well and I haven't even finished school yet. I just don't see what's so special about them. They're so...bland to me. There's nothing unique about them.
(Man A)	But that's the whole point, isn't it? They're all about everyday life and how common it can be.
(Man B)	Yeah, I agree with Tom.
(Woman A)	Yeah, I get that. I can see what he's trying to do. And I get why people like it; I just don't get why they like it so much. In my opinion, it's average at best.
(Narrator)	Where is this conversation likely to take place?
(Narrator)	What is NOT TRUE about the woman?
(Narrator)	What does the woman say "Yeah, I get that" about?
(Narrator)	Questions 41–43 refer to the following conversation.
(Man B)	Hey, Sierra. When you have a minute, can you come over to my desk and help me install Yellow Studio? I tried looking for it on the shared drive, but I couldn't find it.
(Woman B)	Didn't I install Yellow Studio on your computer, like, a month ago?
(Man B)	Yeah, funny thing about that... I spilled hot tea on my laptop the other day and it went caput. Well–it didn't explode or anything, though there were some sparks–but, yeah, it's dead. I got a replacement yesterday.
(Woman B)	Wow. How in the world did you manage that?
(Man B)	Well, it was early in the morning and I just plopped down on my chair and the mug kind of flew out of my hand and –
(Woman B)	No, I mean, how did you manage to get a replacement? Jo dropped milk on her laptop the other week and she had to sit at reception and use that archaic computer that's been gathering dust for years now.
(Man B)	Oh, right! Well, Jo doesn't need a new laptop to do her job as much as I do, I guess. I might've also buttered Andrew up with some chocolates.
(Woman B)	That'll do the trick. Andrew's notoriously susceptible to bribery in the form of any kind of chocolate.
(Man B)	I know. That's how I got him to promise he'll give me remote worker privileges when we launch the trial next month.

(Narrator)	Why does the man need the woman's help?
(Narrator)	Why does the man say "oh, right"?
(Narrator)	What does the woman say about Andrew?

(Narrator)	Questions 44–46 refer to the following conversation with three speakers.
(Woman B)	Have you two met the new COO yet?
(Man B)	No, but Mr. Renton's gonna organise a dinner for our department tomorrow, so we can all meet her then.
(Woman A)	I heard she's pretty ruthless.
(Man B)	Me too. Isn't she planning to shorten lunch breaks and crack-down on late arrivals?
(Woman B)	Yeah, but don't you think that's exactly what we need?
(Man B)	No! I like the way things are now. Working in a relaxed environment is more enjoyable.
(Woman A)	I think we'd get more done if people actually turned up on time.
(Woman B)	Exactly. Her changes could make us so much more efficient.

(Narrator)	What is the conversation mainly about?
(Narrator)	What is the COO going to do?
(Narrator)	What does the man disagree with the women about?

(Narrator)	Questions 47–49 refer to the following conversation.
(Man B)	Websites 4U, Fernando speaking, how may I help you?
(Woman A)	Hi, Fernando. My name's Beatrice and I'm using your service for my website. I was interested in upgrading my account and I would like to talk about my options.
(Man B)	Of course. May I ask what your website is?
(Woman A)	Yeah, it's www.beatricetraveldeals.com.
(Man B)	Great, thanks. And your full name, membership ID and security word?
(Woman A)	Beatrice Cobbler, and my ID is 19875642. No security word.
(Man B)	Great, thanks. So I see your current membership is Bronze, which means you have some access to our premium services but it's restricted. Do you know what you'd like to upgrade to?
(Woman A)	Well, I'm not sure I understand the difference between the other two plans.
(Man B)	Well, obviously, with the Gold Plan you get more GBs of RAM and you have access to our tech support 24/7 365 days a year, whereas with the Silver Plan you only get tech support during business hours. With the Gold Plan you also get help in setting up your control panel in a way that works for you.
(Woman A)	OK. I'm not exactly an expert, but...
(Man B)	It all depends on the size of your business and where you want to take it. The bigger the business, the more you'll need out of your website.
(Woman A)	Well, my business is medium-sized but I think 30 bucks is a reasonable price so let's go for that.

(Narrator)	What kind of company is the woman likely to own?
(Narrator)	Which of the following is NOT a perk of the Gold Plan?
(Narrator)	Look at the graphic. Which membership does the woman choose?

(Narrator)	Questions 50–52 refer to the following conversation.
(Man A)	Hey, Carol. Do you have a minute? You speak Spanish, right?
(Woman A)	Hey, Alex. Yeah, I do. Why? What's up?
(Man A)	I just received this email from one of my clients but it's in Spanish and I'm not sure what they're asking for.
(Woman A)	Why's your client emailing you in Spanish?
(Man A)	Well, it's not my client exactly. It's a person that works for my client—I work with the headquarters in New York, but they operate in South America as well and one of their associates in Chile was supposed to get in touch with me, but I don't think he realizes we're an American company.
(Woman A)	Let me have a look. OK, yeah—he's introducing himself. Your contact in New York must've misinformed him or they must've misunderstood each other, because he's saying it's nice to be working with someone who speaks Spanish.
(Man A)	Ugh, this is so typical of Chris—he never listens to me when I speak. I told him we have people who speak Spanish and they'd be on my team to help out, but I never said I speak Spanish myself!
(Woman A)	Do you want me to write a reply to him?
(Man A)	No, I don't want to set a precedent. I'll just call Chris and tell him what happened. Maybe I can even call this guy, Agustin, and introduce myself and explain.

(Narrator)	Why does the woman say "What's up"?
(Narrator)	What is the name of the man's contact in New York?
(Narrator)	Why does the man not want the woman to write an email for him?

(Narrator)	Questions 53–55 refer to the following conversation.
(Woman B)	Have you heard the news about Bobby Edmonds? He's moving over to the Herald. They're giving him his own blog.
(Man B)	Really? He's a great writer and copyeditor, and I'll miss his terrible jokes around the office. How long has he been with us, about 30 years?
(Woman B)	Not that long! Only around a decade but it certainly does seem longer, now that you mention it. The rumor is that he asked the publisher, Mr. Smith, for his own column and online blog last year, but he was turned down.
(Man B)	What a shame. If anyone deserves his own blog, it's Bobby Edmonds. I wonder who going to take over his current job here, now that he is moving on. Have you heard anything, Rachel?

(Narrator)	Who are the speakers talking about?
(Narrator)	What does Bobby Edmonds plan to do?
(Narrator)	Where do the speakers work?

(Narrator)	Questions 56–58 refer to the following conversation.
(Man B)	Mariko, is that you? I haven't seen you since the company barbecue last summer. Are you still working in the finance and accounting department in the Suzuki Building?
(Woman A)	Tony, it's so nice to see you again! I still work in that department, but I've been out of the office this summer doing database programming and training at the regional training center in Colorado. The company wants me to transform our current accounting procedures and upgrade our internal software systems.
(Man B)	Really? That sounds great. I'm hoping to take a training course there, too. It's in online marketing and social media. Would you mind if I asked you some questions about your experience this summer?
(Woman A)	Sounds great. Let's do lunch, and you can fill me in on everything that I missed while I was away. It looks like the entire eighteenth floor has been renovated.

(Narrator)	Where did the woman spend time during the summer?
(Narrator)	What department does the woman work in?
(Narrator)	What do the speakers make plans to do?

(Narrator)	Questions 59–61 refer to the following conversation.
(Woman B)	Have you got this semester's schedule yet?
(Man A)	Yeah, there's quite a few new classes, aren't there? I didn't know Professor Whitworth was even teaching anymore, but he's got Crime and Media Representation.
(Woman B)	Oh, yeah, I'm really excited about that one. But it's not Professor Whitworth anymore. He retired.
(Man A)	I thought he had—both he and Professor Stone. Who's teaching it, then?
(Woman B)	Well, I thought it was Professor Dominguez but if you look at the schedule, it's actually Professor Fuller. She's a good one, from what I've heard.
(Man A)	Oh, yeah. What about electives, have you picked your elective yet?
(Woman B)	No, I thought we'd pick together. I know you're not going to be able to wake up in time for a class at 9, so these two are out, but do you prefer a late morning or evening class?
(Man A)	Evening, normally, but the late morning one sounds much more interesting.
(Woman B)	Oh, yeah. Let's go for that one, then. Oh, I'm so excited. I can't believe it will all be over in six months.
(Man A)	I know, right? I'm trying not to think about it.

(Narrator)	Who teaches Crime and Media Representation?
(Narrator)	Look at the graphic. Which elective module do the man and woman choose?
(Narrator)	What can be inferred from the conversation?

(Narrator)	Questions 62–64 refer to the following conversation.
(Woman A)	So, how's the new job?
(Man B)	It's all right, you know? It's not too bad. I'm still learning the ropes but I'm really enjoying it. My new manager's great: she's been tracking my training to make sure that everyone takes time to help me out and to show me how all the tools work, but she's not overbearing or anything—and she's very friendly, too. Friendliest manager I've ever had.
(Woman A)	That's good. I'm glad you're enjoying it.
(Man B)	I'm not sure I like the job yet—it's very different from what I'm used to—but the company, for sure. I miss my old commute, though.
(Woman A)	Well, you were lucky before. A 25-minute commute is the dream. It takes me 40 minutes on a good day, 50 if there's traffic.
(Man B)	Yeah, it takes me about 45 now, but it's because I'm taking the bus.
(Woman A)	And what about your new colleagues? Are they nice?
(Man B)	Not like you guys. They're all right, but I think they're a bit uptight. I miss what we had.
(Woman A)	I know what you mean. It's one of the reasons I don't want to change jobs. Finding nice colleagues is so hard.
(Man B)	Tell me about it. I think my new colleagues are robots, to be honest.
(Narrator)	How long did it used to take the man to go to work?
(Narrator)	What can be inferred from the conversation?
(Narrator)	Why does the man say "Tell me about it"?
(Narrator)	Questions 65–67 refer to the following conversation.
(Woman A)	Alliance Bank customer service. How may I help you today?
(Man B)	Yes, my wallet has just been stolen on the subway. I need to cancel my ATM card and credit card and would like to request new ones.
(Woman A)	I'm sorry to hear that sir. Just a moment, please... OK, now, what is the name on the ATM and credit card? And what is the account number?
(Man B)	Oh. I know the name, obviously, but I'll need to go and find a bank statement for my account number. The name on the ATM is my name. David Stephenson, spelled D-A-V-I-D, for the first name, and S-T-E-P-H-E-N-S-O-N for the surname. I'll go grab a statement now.
(Narrator)	What problem does the man have?
(Narrator)	What does the man want to do?
(Narrator)	What does the man need to do next?
(Narrator)	Questions 68–70 refer to the following conversation.
(Woman A)	So? Did you finish it?
(Man A)	I did.
(Woman A)	And? What did you think?

(Man A)	I don't even have words. It's been... An emotional rollercoaster, that's what it's been.
(Woman A)	See, I told you it was good.
(Man A)	I've got to say, I'm surprised. I'm not normally into romance novels—not because I don't think they have their merits, more because I just find the prose too elaborate. It's the same reason I don't like literary fiction. I'm a very impatient reader and I hate it when writers take their time getting to the point. But this... This was beautiful.
(Woman A)	I don't think I agree with you about romance novels. Literary fiction, yes, for sure, it tends to be flowery and bombastic and I have no patience for it either. But romance novels are a type of commercial fiction—they appeal to a broader audience and, as such, they need to use simpler language.
(Man A)	Oh, no, I don't mean the language isn't simple. What I mean is that there's too much description, too much scene-setting, too much exposition. That's why I prefer science fiction: it's snappy. It's bold and it takes risks, but it's snappy.
(Woman A)	Depends on the book, though, doesn't it? I've read sci-fi books that could speak to anyone, but then there are also dozens of science fiction books which are full of clichés.
(Man A)	Yeah, that's true. So, do you have any other recommendations?
(Narrator)	What can be inferred from the conversation?
(Narrator)	Why is the man not into romance novels?
(Narrator)	What do the man and woman agree on?

Part IV

Track 24

(Narrator)	Questions 71–73 refer to the following talk.
(Woman A)	Hello everyone, thanks for giving me such a warm welcome. Well, I think we all know why we're here tonight, but let me just take a few moments to remind you all. We're here to support Janet Richardson and her school for disadvantaged young children. Earlier tonight, we heard from the woman herself, who described the plans for the school next year, plans such as creating a new practical learning room, to teach students new skills that will help them to begin their careers after graduation. Next, we'll hear from the students themselves, who will tell us a bit about their lives before they found the school, and how things have changed for them since joining. Before we do that, I'd like to thank you all for coming tonight, for helping us to fund this incredibly worthy cause, and for spreading the word about this fantastic school. Thank you, we really do appreciate your presence.
(Narrator)	Where are you most likely to hear this talk?
(Narrator)	What will happen next?
(Narrator)	What is the speaker doing?

(Narrator)	Questions 74–76 refer to the following talk.
(Man A)	You know, a lot of people ask this question: how do I know what the right career is for me? And there's a very simple answer to it. Of course, a lot of people throughout the course of your life will try to tell you what's right for you—parents, teachers, friends—and in most cases they'll have your best interests in mind, but what they'll think is right for you might not be the career you want. Parents tend to think more pragmatically—they'll take talent into account, of course, but at the end of the day they want to see you in a field that makes money, or a field that they themselves built a career in or always wanted to go into but never had the chance. But, for me, there's a very simple way to find out what the right path is for you, and that's to answer this question truthfully: who are you most jealous of? Forget about what you think might make you happy. We are always told where happiness comes from—money, success, family. We're constantly bombarded with ideas about the source of happiness, but it's really jealousy, a primal and frowned-upon feeling, that reveals your true self. Are you jealous of your colleague's promotion, or are you more jealous of your neighbor's successful career in another field? Who do you envy the most? The person you envy the most probably has the thing you want the most, and that's what you need to get for yourself to find happiness.

(Narrator)	What is the topic of this speech?
(Narrator)	Which of the following is NOT a reason parents sometimes give the wrong advice?
(Narrator)	What does the man say about jealousy at the end?

(Narrator)	Questions 77–79 refer to the following talk.
(Man B)	It's an initiative sneered at by many as ill-conceived and ill-timed, but also praised by some as life-changing and the reason behind improved health and better sleeping patterns. But what is Dry January, and could it become a custom in the US as it has for our friends across the pond? Dry January is a campaign attributed to Alcohol Concern, a British charity whose stated aim is to discourage and protect people from excessive drinking and its associated risks. Though it became popular only in recent years, Dry January has been around for a long time—since 1942, in fact, when the Finnish government attempted to persuade its citizens to observe what they called "Sober January" for a month in the midst of war with the Soviet Union. Dry January, as the name suggests, is a month where participants forgo alcohol. January is a popular choice because it's the start of a new year and comes after Christmas, when most of us have spent the holidays overindulging on food and drink, but it's also why most of its critics refuse to observe it, claiming that January, with its post-Christmas blues, is the worst month to stop drinking. And what about the effects of Dry January? They are just as controversial. While some participants and doctors claim abstaining from alcohol can have a positive effect on mood, sleep and energy, psychologists warn that it can actually induce feelings of sadness, and suggest...

(Narrator)	Which country first introduced alcohol-free January?
(Narrator)	Why do Dry January critics dislike the choice of January?

(Narrator)   What does the speaker say about doctors and psychologists?

(Narrator)   Questions 80–82 refer to the following talk.

(Man B)   As you can see here, the average response rate tended to fall somewhere between 55–60%, with only about 10% of the surveys receiving a response from more than 70% of the participants–and only 18 surveys had a 100% response rate. In the question "What did you most enjoy about your visit?" the most popular response was "the tasting session", followed by "the tour". The least popular part of everyone's visit was overwhelmingly the film about the vineyard's history, only preferred by 0.8% of visitors overall. This is even more evident in the "What would you change?" question, where more than 40% of the participants responded with "Other" and added as a comment to remove the "boring" and "unnecessary" film. As you all know, we have two tour visits per day, one at 11 a.m. and one at 1:30 p.m. Monday to Friday. We have looked at the differences between the two and what we've discovered is that morning visitors tend to find that the tour "lasted just long enough", whereas 30% of afternoon visitors claim that it "could be shorter". In both groups, only about 3-5% of visitors think it "could be longer". Now, this discrepancy could be because afternoon visitors are more likely to be hungry by the time the tour takes place, so they're more eager to have some snacks and taste our wines, so perhaps we should consider changing the time of the second tour. I think we should have a vote on the matter, and if a majority is in favour of changing the time, we should set about changing this as soon as possible, to prevent any further issues. Okay, so now let's…

(Narrator)   How many surveys received a response from every person surveyed?

(Narrator)   What did most visitors dislike about the vineyard visit?

(Narrator)   What solution does the man offer at the end?

(Narrator)   Questions 83–85 refer to the following talk.

(Man A)   So, just to walk you all quickly through the logistics of the event on March 10th, we'll be using the large conference room downstairs, on the basement floor. I know some of you raised concerns about the fact that there's no natural light in the room and we did consider the conference room on the second floor or the one on the third floor, but they're just not spacious enough. We did decide to use the small conference room on the first floor as the break room, so hopefully that'll compensate. Now, our guests will be arriving after 8:30 in the morning, so tea and coffee should be ready, plus breakfast. Tanya has contacted all our guests to find out any dietary requirements for lunch, and we've got the final list of guests so Mario will have lanyards ready for everyone. Obviously, the room is not properly set up for the event yet and we can't set it up until the day before because it's being used for another event on the 9th, but Joao and I have agreed to come in earlier on the 10th to take care of it. We'll store the flipcharts and the supplies we'll need in the storage room overnight. Oh, before I forget: there's a mistake in the program. The Paris group will be presenting first, not the London group. What else? I…

(Narrator)	On which floor is the room in which the guests will be having their breaks?
(Narrator)	Whose duty is it to prepare the identification for the guests?
(Narrator)	Look at the graph below. Given the mistake mentioned by the speaker, at what time will the Paris group presentation start?

(Narrator)	Questions 86–88 refer to the following talk.
(Man B)	Thank you for calling Haywood Medical Practice. Please note that phone calls may be recorded for training purposes. If you would like to book an appointment, please press 1. If you would like to reschedule or cancel your appointment, please press 2 and leave your first name and date of birth after the beep. If you would like to set up an online account to be able to book appointments on our website, please press 3. Please note that we will be switching to online appointments only on April 1st, and you will need to come in with your passport to activate your online account. If you would like to receive your test results, please press 4. If you would like to speak to an advisor or a nurse, please hold. We are experiencing high call volumes at the moment and will be with you shortly. You are currently the...fifth person in line. Approximate waiting time: 10 minutes.

(Narrator)	Which number should the caller press if they can't attend their appointment?
(Narrator)	What does the caller need to do to activate their online account?
(Narrator)	How many people will speak to advisors before the caller?

(Narrator)	Questions 89–91 refer to the following talk.
(Man A)	Hi everyone. I promise I won't keep you long, I know you've all got busy schedules and you'd rather be getting on with your jobs than listening to me rattle on about stuff, but... I've got some news to share with you. As you know, there were some changes to the top-level management recently. Nothing that directly affects you and your job, but two people resigned and one person was laid off. Now the company is restructuring and we've merged two roles into one, which is what the guy you met on Friday, Mateusz, will be doing at the head office. But the thing that concerns you is the change that was announced recently, which is about what we're going to be selling in store. As you know, the shoe department has been underperforming for months—our score is particularly bad, we have the second lowest percentage of shoe sales in the region—so the company has decided that we won't be stocking as many shoes anymore—we'll have only the ones we expect to sell the most, and our shoe corner will be turning into a children's corner. Menswear and womenswear won't be affected...

(Narrator)	What can be inferred from the speech?
(Narrator)	Look at the table. Where does the man work?
(Narrator)	What will be changing at the store where the man works?

(Narrator)	Questions 92–94 refer to the following talk.
(Woman A)	Thank you, Dan. What I think we need at this point is real change, and I mean real, radical change in the way we police our streets and the way we enforce the rules we currently have. This research illustrates the point I've made since the

moment I took office: rules and regulations are all good, but unless we force people to follow them, they're not worth the paper they're written on. It defies belief that out of all the fines that were handed out in the last year, more than 35% were for speeding in populated areas, and more than 20% were for drinking and driving. Not to mention the fact that 17% of drivers apparently admit to not wearing a seatbelt for short trips, and a whopping 8% of motorcycle riders don't wear helmets. And the government is doing nothing to address this. Isn't that appalling? We have tried to draw attention to this time and time again, but nobody's listening, and it's costing lives and money and putting a strain on our healthcare system. This government's negligence is costing lives. What's it going to take for the transport minister to take notice? For the past four years, we've had three deadly vehicle accidents per week, and nine non-deadly accidents. I propose that what we need to focus on ...

(Narrator)	What can be inferred about the speaker?
(Narrator)	When the speaker says "Isn't that appalling", what is she referring to?
(Narrator)	How many deadly accidents happen per week?

(Narrator)	Questions 95–97 refer to the following talk.
(Woman B)	Hi, my name is Winnie and I'm a mother of two girls and one boy. My oldest is 16 and my youngest is 12. I have to say, I'm a bit surprised at the backlash that this is receiving, especially from teachers. I would've thought people would be happy that we're finally abolishing this archaic system of school-mandated uniforms and allowing our children to express themselves in a way they see fit. I don't agree with the two main arguments, either: I don't think that uniforms make all kids look the same, rich or poor. Do you think kids can't tell if a uniform is brand new or if it's a hand-me-down from an older sibling or second-hand bought from a thrift shop? Please. Trust me, it's quite easy to spot the difference. And to the second point: yes, kids will be dressing the way they want to. What's wrong with that? As long as there's a comprehensive–and logical–dress code in place, there's nothing to worry about. Believe it or not, kids know how to dress appropriately and rules can be implemented and enforced even if uniforms are removed. Not to mention–what kind of message are we sending to our kids by dictating that they all look the same? That they should be–pardon the pun–uniform, no uniqueness whatsoever. Ridiculous. We should be encouraging them to thrive in their individuality, not suppressing it.

(Narrator)	What can be inferred from the speech?
(Narrator)	Why does the woman say "please"?
(Narrator)	Which of the following arguments does the woman NOT mention?

(Narrator)	Questions 98–100 refer to the following talk.
(Man A)	And now, finally, the time has come to announce the winner of our art competition. I know you're all excited to be here and looking forward to finding out which artist will be getting the opportunity to display their art in exhibitions at our art galleries across the country, as well as the $5,000 cash prize. We'll also announce the lucky runner-up, who will be going home with a $1,000 cash prize.

Before I start, I have to tell you that one of the contestants has decided to remove herself from the competition as she was offered an opportunity elsewhere—which is not surprising, considering she had the second highest score given by the judges. But let's focus on our remaining three contestants, all of whom deserve recognition and congratulations for making it this far. It has been a very tough competition with more than a thousand entries, so you should all be very proud of yourselves. So, after tallying up the votes from our gallery's members and combining them with the judges' scores, we are happy to announce that the winner of the competition is... Oh, wow... Incredibly, the winner is our youngest contestant, with no formal art training... Congratulations to Donald Wreck, with My Sister Emily!

(Narrator)   What will the finalist in 2nd place get?

(Narrator)   Look at the table below. Which finalist has removed themselves from the competition?

(Narrator)   How is the woman likely to feel as she announces the results?

Answers and Explanations

PRACTICE TEST 1 ANSWER KEY

Part I	Part II	Part III	Part IV	Part V	Part VI	Part VII
1. D	7. A	32. D	71. B	101. C	131. B	147. D
2. A	8. C	33. C	72. A	102. B	132. A	148. D
3. B	9. C	34. A	73. B	103. A	133. D	149. B
4. A	10. B	35. B	74. D	104. A	134. A	150. C
5. C	11. A	36. C	75. B	105. C	135. A	151. B
6. B	12. A	37. D	76. C	106. A	136. C	152. B
	13. B	38. A	77. A	107. D	137. A	153. C
	14. B	39. B	78. C	108. C	138. B	154. A
	15. A	40. C	79. A	109. D	139. D	155. C
	16. B	41. D	80. A	110. B	140. C	156. A
	17. A	42. B	81. C	111. B	141. C	157. A
	18. B	43. C	82. D	112. D	142. B	158. A
	19. C	44. B	83. B	113. B	143. C	159. C
	20. C	45. C	84. C	114. A	144. A	160. D
	21. A	46. D	85. B	115. C	145. C	161. B
	22. C	47. D	86. A	116. B	146. B	162. A
	23. A	48. C	87. B	117. C		163. A
	24. B	49. B	88. C	118. B		164. B
	25. B	50. C	89. B	119. D		165. B
	26. A	51. D	90. C	120. C		166. C
	27. C	52. C	91. B	121. A		167. B
	28. C	53. D	92. C	122. C		168. B
	29. B	54. A	93. C	123. B		169. C
	30. C	55. B	94. A	124. B		170. C
	31. A	56. A	95. C	125. C		171. A
		57. D	96. A	126. C		172. A
		58. B	97. D	127. C		173. B
		59. D	98. A	128. A		174. A
		60. C	99. B	129. C		175. C
		61. A	100. C	130. A		176. C
		62. B				177. A
		63. A				178. C
		64. A				179. A
		65. C				180. B
		66. B				181. C
		67. C				182. B
		68. C				183. A
		69. C				184. D
		70. B				185. A
						186. D
						187. A
						188. B
						189. B
						190. C
						191. A
						192. C
						193. A
						194. A
						195. B
						196. B
						197. D
						198. D
						199. B
						200. C

PRACTICE TEST 1

Part I—Photographs

1. (D)

The photograph shows a white van turning a corner. (**D**) correctly describes the photograph. There are parked cars, but they are not side by side. No cars are being towed. The vehicles are all travelling in the same direction.

2. (A)

The photograph shows a group of people standing near railings and looking down. (**A**) correctly describes the photograph; the people are behind the railing. They are standing, not climbing or seated. Only some of the people are holding onto the railing.

3. (B)

The photograph shows a woman cutting or carving meat. (**B**) correctly describes the photograph. There are no guests or customers in the photograph, it is unclear that the woman is a hostess or a waitress. The woman is cutting meat, not putting it onto a plate.

4. (A)

The photograph shows a woman taking a picture of herself on a mobile phone. (**A**) correctly describes the photograph. (**B**) is incorrect; she's taking a picture, not ending a phone conversation. (**C**) is incorrect; She's taking a picture of herself, not painting a view. (**D**) is incorrect; she's holding her phone, not a photograph.

5. (C)

The photograph shows a large warehouse filled with market stalls and shoppers. (**C**) correctly describes the different stalls. (**A**) confuses the word market with the word upmarket. The people are shopping not looking for shelter (**B**). One of the stalls is selling paintings but it is not clear whether the building is newly painted (**D**).

6. (B)

The photograph shows a woman holding a mug and reading something on an electronic tablet. (**B**) correctly describes the image. (**A**) she is holding her drink, not looking for it. She is using a tablet not taking tablets (medication) (**C**). there is no indication that she is solving equations (**D**).

Part II—Question-Response

7. (A)

The question asks *Have you booked a car for the trip?* (**A**) correctly answers: they are taking a taxi instead of a car. (**B**) talks about a parking lot, not a trip, and (**C**) talks about the people coming, not the vehicle used.

8. (C)

The question asks *Is it OK if I bring a friend with me?* (**A**) talks about an *entrance*, not a *friend*. (**B**) talks about a thing (*it*), not a *friend*. (**C**) says *the more the merrier*, which is an expression that means *more* people are better than fewer, so it's *OK* to *bring a friend*.

9. (C)

The sentence says *You weren't supposed to tell him.* (**A**) is incorrect because the person says they weren't *warned* about who *would be here*, not what to *tell*. (**B**) apologises for being *late*, but does not discuss what they *weren't supposed to do*. (**C**) is correct because *the cat's out of the bag* means a secret has been revealed, i.e. something you're not *supposed to tell*.

10. (B)

The question asks *Why was she complaining to the waitress?* (**B**) gives a reason someone might be upset and *complain*: finding a *hair* in their *coffee*. (**A**) says the speaker *needs a refill*, but that's no reason to *yell*. (**C**) talks about a *diet*, not a reason to *yell*.

11. (A)

The question is *When was the last time we had lunch together?* (**A**) is the only answer that gives a time that makes sense (*ages*). (**B**) talks about whether they *serve lunch* in a place, not the *last time* they *had lunch*, whereas (**C**) says the speaker *wasn't even born yet*, but you have to be born in order to have lunch.

12. (A)

The sentence is *I'm really surprised with the turnout at the event.* (**A**) agrees with the speaker about the *turnout*, i.e. how many *people* showed up, saying they expected *half*. (**B**) talks about *trying* something, which has nothing to do with a *turnout*. (**C**) talks about speaking to *your lawyer*, but having a lot of people at an *event* is no reason to contact a *lawyer*.

13. (B)

The question asks *Does he always ask so many questions?* (**A**) talks about a *questionable* decision, i.e. dubious – nothing to do with *questions*. (**C**) talks about *bringing someone*, not about *questions*. (**B**) says *interrogating people*, i.e. *asking many questions*, is his *hobby* – so he does *always ask so many questions*.

14. (B)

The question is *Are you having a summer or winter wedding after all?* (**A**) says *we're not married yet*, which is redundant as it's already clear the *wedding* is in the future. (**C**) talks about the weather being *cold* in the *winter*, not the *wedding*. (**B**) gives a date (*May 15th*) and the correct season (*spring*) for the *wedding*.

15. (A)

The question is *Who does this blue notebook belong to?* (**A**) responds to the question with *I'm not sure*, and that they *just found it*. (**B**) talks about *running out of blue notebooks*, but the question was about a specific *blue notebook*, not *blue notebooks* in general. (**C**) talks about *making a note*, i.e. writing something down, not a *blue notebook*.

16. (B)

The sentence is *It's such a shame about his father passing*, which means the *father* has died. (**B**) is the only answer that addresses this by saying how *young* he was. (**A**) talks about *passing on the message*, not someone *passing*. (**C**) talks about the speaker's *father* being *happy to hear about you*, not about a *father* being dead.

17. (A)

The question asks *Are you available to come into the office this Saturday?* (**A**) explains the speaker is *away for the weekend*, so not *available*. (**B**) talks

about people *knowing* something, not being *available*. (**C**) talks about something not happening *on Sunday morning*, not about being *available* on *Saturday*.

18. (B)

The question is *Whose idea was it to postpone the meeting by a week?* (**B**) explains it was *the client's request*, or *idea*. (**A**) talks about when *meetings* happen regularly (*Monday mornings*), not this particular *meeting*. (**C**) talks about why the speaker *couldn't join* the *meeting*, not why it was *postponed*.

19. (C)

The question is *How many bags are we allowed to bring on the plane?* (**A**) talks about a *flight*, but about how it's *going to be delayed*, not about *bags*. (**B**) talks about something being *wrong – plain and simple*, i.e. clearly *wrong*, not about a *plane*. (**C**) is the correct answer because it gives the number of *bags* (*two*).

20. (C)

The question asks *Has she been informed of this yet?* (**C**) explains that *she's still in the dark*, which means she has not been informed. (**B**) agrees with the statement, but says *we haven't mentioned it to her* which opposes the statement, so it cannot be the correct response. (**A**) Talks about telling *him* a lie, but they're talking about informing *her* of something.

21. (A)

The question asks *When will the new policy be implemented?* (**A**) explains they haven't *decided yet* when it will be *implemented*. (**B**) talks about something *starting to look bad*, but this is not related to the *policy* referenced. (**C**) gives a resigned answer (*I guess we'll never know*) which is inappropriate here because the *policy* is going to be *implemented*, so it's possible to *know* when.

22. (C)

The question is *Do you prefer sweet or savory?* This is a question about food preferences. (**A**) says they *would prefer* to *wait*, but this is not related to the options given. (**B**) says something is *sweet*, i.e. kind *to say*, which has nothing to do with food. (**C**) is the only answer that talks about *food* and says the speaker is not *picky*, so they *like* both.

23. (A)

The question asks *Who is the guy who just said hello to you?* (A) is the only answer that explains who the person is (*Chief Operating Officer*). (B) talks about why they *said hello*, not who the person is, whereas (C) talks about whether they were *supposed to talk* to each other, not who the person is.

24. (B)

The question is *Where are you taking her for her birthday?* (B) explains they are not *taking her* anywhere but are *throwing her a surprise party at home*. (A) talks about *taking* something *for granted*, i.e. assuming it will always be there, not *taking* someone somewhere. (C) talks about how old *she* is *turning this year*, not what the *birthday* plans are.

25. (B)

The question asks *Don't we have a meeting in five minutes?* (A) is incorrect because are talking about how long something usually takes, not when the meeting is. (C) talks about *calling* someone, not a *meeting*. (B) is correct because the *meeting* was *pushed back*, i.e. postponed, by *two hours*.

26. (A)

The sentence is *the item I ordered from you has still not arrived*. This is a complaint, and (A) offers an apology (*sorry to hear that*). (B) says they *didn't order any items*, but that has nothing to do with the complaint. (C) talks about a *form* not being *correct*, but the question is about a delayed order.

27. (C)

The question is *what's your favorite book?* (A) talks about *things to do*, i.e. commitments, not *books*. (B) talks about *literature* as a class, not a hobby – and doesn't address the question of the favorite book. (C) responds to the question by saying they are *not a big fan of readings*, i.e. they don't like *books*.

28. (C)

The question is *have you decided what to do yet?* (C) says they're *on the fence*, which means they're undecided. (A) talks about being *on time*, not about a decision. (B) talks about something someone already did, not something they are *deciding* still.

29. (B)

The sentence is *I bought these new posters for my office*. (B) responds with a comment about how *nice* they are. (A) talks about the *post office*, not *posters*. (C) talks about somebody's *fault*, but there's nothing wrong with buying *posters*.

30. (C)

The question is *how long before the game begins?* (A) talks about the *day* being *long* but doesn't say when *the game* will start. (B) talks about the speaker's *favorite game*, but likewise not about when *the game* will start. (C) is the only one that answers the question: *the game* has *already started*.

31. (A)

The question is *were you upset that they didn't invite you?* (A) explains that *they did invite* them, but they *just didn't want to go*. (B) talks about being *upset* with the other speaker, not a third party, and (C) talks about *feeling better in the morning*, not about whether they are *upset* now or not.

Part III—Short Conversations

32. (D)

The man says *Tim was originally scheduled to go,* so (D) is correct. (A) is incorrect because Andy (the male speaker) says he has *got a meeting in Florida*. (B) is incorrect because he was talking to Michelle about it, but she wasn't supposed to be going. (C) is incorrect because the man says he *thought Georgia might be able to go, but she's got her kids to take care of that week*.

33. (C)

The man says he *thought Georgia might be able to go, but she's got her kids to take care of that week,* so (C) is the correct answer. (A) is incorrect because he thought she might be able to go until she told him she was busy. (B) is incorrect because the man says *Tim gave his notice*, not Georgia, and (D) is incorrect because she only told him she couldn't go, she didn't give him someone who could.

34. (A)

The man says *they're a new client, so it would look unprofessional*, which means he's worried about making a *bad impression*, so (A) is correct. (B) is incorrect because the man never says he's *confident they will find someone*, and (C) is incorrect because he never says they *already asked*. (D) is incorrect because the client is new, so the man is not sure how they usually act.

35. (B)

The man says *does it really say they've moved the conference back two months?* This means that (B) is correct, as it talks about the *when*, i.e. the date. (A) is incorrect because it mentions *where*, i.e. the place, not the date. (C) is incorrect because *who is attending* is never mentioned, and (D) is incorrect because the man never talks about *where to stay* when he goes to the conference, only that he's booked *accommodation*.

36. (C)

The woman says *you booked already? The conference isn't happening for another ten months!* This means she's surprised the man booked tickets so soon, so (C) is correct. (A) is incorrect because the woman is not surprised *the man is upset*. (B) is incorrect because the woman never comments on the fact that *none* of the tickets are *refundable*. Finally, (D) is incorrect because the man did book *tickets*.

37. (D)

The woman says *just give them a call. I'm sure they'll have no choice but to reimburse you* and claims it is *their fault*, so she clearly means the organizers. This means (A) and (C) are incorrect. Since she says to *call*, not to *email*, (B) is also incorrect, making (D) the correct answer.

38. (A)

The man says *would like to ask you a few questions*. He then proceeds to say *I just wanted to know how you've been getting on with your subscription to our service*, which means he's completing a *survey*, so (A) is correct. (B) is incorrect because the woman has no *complaints* about the provider. (C) is incorrect because no *promotion* is mentioned, and (D) is incorrect because a *technical issue* is mentioned, but it's not the main topic of the conversation.

39. (B)

The woman says she *did have a problem with reception at first*, but it's *all good now*, so it's been *fixed*, making (B) correct. (A) is incorrect because it's been *fixed* so it can't be still *bad*, and (C) is incorrect because the woman says they already *sent an engineer*. Finally, (D) is incorrect because the woman says there *was a problem with reception at first*.

40. (C)

The woman says *I'm quite happy so far... you've been great* and the man replies *I'm glad to hear it* meaning he's glad that her current service has been good. (D) is mentioned earlier in the passage, but is not the reason he is glad. The woman does mention that her previous service was bad, but the man would not say he was happy about that to the woman, so (A) cannot be correct. (B) is incorrect as this was an issue with her previous provider.

41. (D)

The woman says she *offered* the position to *someone*, but *he called and said he'd been offered a better position elsewhere*, which means they *changed their mind*, so (D) is correct. The woman says nothing about when the *position* was *advertised*, so (A) is incorrect. She also says nothing about what *notice* the departing employee *gave*, so (B) is incorrect. Finally, the woman never comments on how *good* the *applicants* were, so (C) is incorrect.

42. (B)

The man says *I can do a couple of the interviews if you like*, and the woman says *that would actually be a great help*. The woman also says they're *phone interviews*, so (B) is correct. (A) is incorrect because, while the man offers to *help*, the woman says she has *already narrowed it down to five people now*. (C) is incorrect for the same reason, whereas (D) is incorrect because the man will be helping the woman with *interviews*.

43. (C)

The man says *I heard through the grapevine that we're looking into signing a contract with a different agency*, which means they're *looking for a new one*, so (C) is correct. (A) is incorrect because it's the woman who says they've *terminated their contract*, not the man. **(B)** is incorrect because the *contract* is *terminated* so they won't be *renewing* it and **(D)** is incorrect because, once more, it's the woman who is *looking forward* to the *new contract*, not the man.

44. (B)

The man says *what they need to understand is that we don't run a charity here*, and the woman says *I totally agree*, which suggests the man is talking about a company and the two of them work for the same company. This means that **(B)** is correct. **(A)** is incorrect because the man and the woman are both talking about a client signing a *purchase order*. **(C)** is incorrect because neither the man nor the woman say anything to suggest one of them is the *boss*, e.g. no instructions, and **(D)** is incorrect because neither the man nor the woman say anything to suggest they are *family*.

45. (C)

The woman says *Thomas* is *a bit embarrassed about the whole situation* because *he's been asking his boss to sign the purchase order for ages, but he's just been ignored every time*. Since *Thomas* has been trying so hard but is reliant upon his *boss*, it can't be his *fault they're having issues*, so **(A)** is incorrect. **(D)** is incorrect because *Thomas* clearly recognizes the *issues* and he's *embarrassed* about them, and **(B)** is incorrect as neither speaker says that Thomas is not a hard worker. **(C)** is therefore correct, as *Thomas* has been *asking for ages* for *his boss to sign* and is feeling *embarrassed about the whole situation*.

46. (D)

The man says *Well, let's tell them we'll have to cancel that order if we haven't received a signed purchase order for it by noon on Monday.*. This means he's not going to send the order unless he receives a purchase order, so **(D)** is correct. **(A)** is incorrect because the man says *we're supposed to send someone to their offices*, which suggests this is the service they offer, not an action to resolve the problem. **(B)** is incorrect because the man talks about *cancellation*, but never mentions *fees*, and **(C)** is incorrect because the woman mentions *Tuesday* as the day they're *supposed to send someone*, but the man mentions *Monday noon* as a *deadline*, not *Tuesday*.

47. (D)

The woman says her *husband's name is misspelled*. She also says *we explicitly said no nuts in the cake and there are nuts sprinkled all over the top*. Both of these are *specifications* that were not followed, so **(D)** incorrect. The woman never says it was her fault, so **(A)** is incorrect. She also never says the *cake was delivered late*, so **(B)** is incorrect. While she calls the cake *awful*, she never says it *tasted awful*, so **(C)** is incorrect.

48. (C)

The woman says *I placed my order online*, which means she used the *internet*, so **(C)** is correct. **(A)** is incorrect because neither the man nor the woman mention a *telephone*, and **(D)** is incorrect because the woman says *I placed my order* – not *someone else*. Finally, **(B)** is incorrect because, while the man says *you came over to order the cake*, the woman corrects him and says *you must be mistaking me with a different customer* before saying she did it *online*.

49. (B)

The man says *there must've been a glitch in the system*, which means he thinks it was a *technical issue*, so **(B)** is the correct answer. **(A)** is incorrect because the man never blames himself or any of his colleagues, and **(C)** is incorrect because the man never mentions *miscommunication*. Finally, **(D)** is incorrect because the man does *give a reason*: the *glitch in the system*.

50. (C)

The man says *their flight got cancelled* so they're talking about someone else's flights. The man and woman are discussing plans *tomorrow*, not *tonight*, so **(B)** is incorrect and **(C)** is correct. They don't discuss a time to meet, so **(D)** is incorrect.

51. (D)

The man says he *offered* to *pick up* his *friends, but the airline's booked a taxi to the hotel for them so I don't have to*. As *taxi* is a synonym for *cab*, **(D)** is correct, **(A)** is incorrect because the man is not taking them. **(B)** is incorrect they are taking a taxi, not public transport. **(C)** is incorrect because they have taken a flight to the airport, but they cannot take one to the hotel.

52. (C)

The man says *I don't mind* after the woman says *I don't want to keep you waiting outside the office*. The man also says *I'll pick you up with the car, so I won't be outside*, so the man doesn't mind because he doesn't mind picking her up. **(C)** is correct. **(A)** is incorrect because she is free, **(B)** is incorrect because he won't be waiting outside, and **(D)** is incorrect because they have already decided how they will get there.

53. (D)

The man says *the reason we called you in is because your son was involved in an... altercation with another student*. From the way the man speaks about the *altercation* and the way he uses *we* to represent the school, it is clear he is a *teacher*, so **(C)** is incorrect. Since the man refers to the woman's *son*, it is clear she is a *parent*, so **(D)** is the correct answer. This means that **(A)** and **(B)** are incorrect, because the woman is neither a *teacher* nor a *student*.

54. (A)

The man says *I think it would be best to be lenient*. To be *lenient* means to dole out *punishment* which is *light*, so **(A)** is correct. **(B)** is incorrect as the man says they do not want to keep a permanent record of his behavior. While the man does suggest the woman should *have a chat* with the student, he is also giving him a *punishment* (*detention*, *letter of apology*), so **(C)** and **(D)** are incorrect.

55. (B)

The woman says *I'm so sorry* to the man, and then says *thank you* twice. She also says *absolutely* when the man describes her *son*'s *punishment*. This is the opposite of *argumentative* and *furious*, so **(A)** and **(C)** are incorrect. **(D)** is also incorrect because although the woman is grateful that her son is not being harshly punished, she cannot be described as overjoyed, as she is disappointed in her son's behaviour. **(B)** is correct because the woman is *humble* in the way she agrees the man's decision and *thanks* him.

56. (A)

The woman says *now that Paul has left and Kala has taken his place, she's decided we should be reviewing our procedures*. While a *colleague* (Paul) has *departed*, that's not why she is speaking with the man, so **(B)** is incorrect.

While the man asks what the *problem* is, he never mentions a *client*, so **(C)** is incorrect. **(D)** is also incorrect because neither the man nor the woman ever mention an *argument between two colleagues*. **(A)** is correct because the woman mentions *reviewing* their *procedures* and this is what has upset the man and started the *discussion*.

57. (D)

The woman says that the *system* is *a bit repetitive*, meaning they need to *file changes more than twice*, so **(D)** is the correct answer. While the woman mentions the *online platform*, she never calls it *slow*, so **(A)** is incorrect. She mentions the *spreadsheets*, but never calls them *confusing*, so **(B)** is incorrect. Finally, **(C)** is incorrect because the woman says *when you make a small change*, which means that it's not *impossible to make small changes*.

58. (B)

The woman says *the way we do things now, small details can slip through the net too easily*. To *slip through the net* means to *go unnoticed*, so **(B)** is correct. **(A)** is incorrect because it's the man who says *people don't want to share files*, not the woman. Similarly, **(C)** is incorrect because it's the man who talks about an *uproar*, not the woman. Finally, **(D)** is incorrect because the woman never says anything to suggest she *thinks it won't work*.

59. (D)

The woman sounds relieved to hear the man: *you're OK. Thank goodness*. This suggests she worried he *was in an accident* and called to *check*, so **(D)** is correct. While the woman mentions the *pile up*, it's not in the context of *warning* the man, so **(A)** is incorrect. She also never asks the man *how long he's going to be*, so **(B)** is incorrect. Finally, while the woman mentions the *car*, she never mentions *issues* with it, so **(C)** is incorrect.

60. (C)

The man says *don't wait for me to start eating*, which means they can *start eating before he arrives*, so **(C)** is correct. **(A)** is incorrect because it's the woman who says she will *serve some appetizers*. **(B)** is incorrect because the man says the exact opposite: *don't wait*. Finally, **(D)** is incorrect because the man never tells the woman to *call him*.

61. (A)

The woman says *it completely slipped my mind* about the wine, which means she *forgot* – so (A) is correct. (B) is incorrect because it's the man who mentions his *lunch break*, and that he *got* the wine then. (C) is incorrect because the woman mentions going to the *supermarket* but never says it was *closed*, and (D) is incorrect because the woman asks the man to *get the wine*, but never says she *thought* he was supposed to.

62. (B)

The woman says *when I got home and tried it on... it just didn't work...I don't really suit A lines...* The woman didn't think the dress looked good on her. The answer is (B).

63. (A)

The manager says *Unfortunately, we can't refund you for an item you got in the sale, as they're exchange only*. The item cannot be refunded and must be exchanged because it was *in the sale*, meaning the price had been reduced. (A) is correct.

64. (A)

The woman says *I love your store, so that's not really a big deal*, after the other woman says that she must exchange the item, rather than receive a refund. The woman doesn't think it's a big deal as she thinks she will find something else she likes. The answer is (A).

65. (C)

The woman asks about the man's current role at a different company, and then asks why he wants to leave. The man and woman are interviewing David for a job at their company. The answer is (C).

66. (B)

David says *I started working there fresh out of college* so David was studying at university before he started working at E-Net. (B) is correct.

67. (C)

David says *now I'm the Content Manager for online presence*, so David is a Content Manager now. The answer is (C).

68. (C)

The man says *I've used up all my holiday days for this year.* This means he has no more *holiday allowance*, so (C) is correct. The man never says he is *away on holiday* and never mentions *his boss*, so (A) and (B) are incorrect. (D) is incorrect because the woman says the *talk* will be *dull*, not the man.

69. (C)

The woman says *oh, The History of Aviation – I'm really looking forward to that.* This means she is not *delivering* (A), as she is excited to see it, or (B), as it's *straight after*. Then, when the man points out *part 1*, she explains that *one of my colleagues is doing a two-parter*, which means she's not *delivering* (D). She must therefore be *delivering* (C), *Amelia Earhart: 80 years of theories*.

70. (B)

When the woman says that *flights via another airport* (i.e. with a *stopover*) *cost double*, the man says that they *should be half price*. This means his comment is about the fact that they are *more expensive*, so (B) is correct. It also means they are not *half price*, so (D) is incorrect. The man doesn't comment on (A) and (C), so they are incorrect.

Part IV—Short Talks

71. (B)

The woman talks about *what it takes to become successful* in order to give *advice to new-starters*. This isn't something that would be discussed in a *business meeting*, as she's not talking to colleagues (A) is incorrect. The tone suggests this is a speech, not a casual conversation during *dinner*, so (D) is incorrect. A sales pitch for clients would be unlikely to give *advice to new-starters*, so (C) is incorrect. The most likely answer is (B), as giving *advice* to people is something an *entrepreneur* would usually be asked to do in a *TV or radio interview*.

72. (A)

The woman says *we entrepreneurs like to boast. Boast* is a synonym of *brag*, so (A) is correct. (B) is incorrect because the woman says *building a successful business requires skill.* (C) is incorrect because the woman says she could *spew* some *clichés* but never says other *business people* like them, and (D) is incorrect because the woman says she can *give you the impression I know exactly what I'm talking about.*

73. (B)

The woman says *I had a support network in my parents*, and since *support* is a synonym for *help*, (B) is correct. While she does mention *perseverance*, she never links it to *when she started her business*, so (A) is incorrect. (C) is incorrect because the woman clearly says she did have a *unique selling point*, and (D) is incorrect because she mentions *new-starters* but never says she was one.

74. (D)

The man never says that communication needs to be *improved*, so (A) is incorrect. The man mentions *changes* but never says they will *improve performance*, so (B) is incorrect. The man says *nobody likes change*, not just *people within the company*, and never explains *why*, so (C) is incorrect. (D) is correct because the man talks about *finding the right way to communicate this to everyone.*

75. (B)

The speaker says *our instinctive reaction will be to dismiss people's concerns*, so (B) is correct. (A) is incorrect because *research* is mentioned as the reason the man and his *colleagues* might *dismiss people's concerns*. (C) is incorrect because the man says *listening to their employees* is what they *should do*, but also the *exact opposite* of their *instinctive reaction*. (D) is incorrect because the man says the *people* receiving the news (i.e. the employees) will *feel upset.*

76. (C)

The man says he doesn't want to *give the wrong impression that our decision is up for debate, when it absolutely isn't*, meaning that *changes* cannot be prevented, so (A) is incorrect. He also says *people are bound to feel upset, or even threatened*, which means they are likely to *feel threatened*, so (B) is incorrect. He also says *we should give them time to adjust to the new reality in the company*, which means he doesn't

want the *changes* to happen *quickly*, so (D) is incorrect. What the man says is some employees might *identify genuine issues they raise that we might've not thought of*, so (C) is the correct answer.

77. (A)

The man says the company *recently announced it would be shutting more than fifty of its stores*, so (A) is correct. Mr Rossi is denying claims that the company is going into *administration*, (B) is incorrect. The CEO has not resigned, (C) is incorrect. *Investors* are mentioned, but it is not stated that the company has received a lot of investment, (D) is incorrect.

78. (C)

Nothing is said to suggest the *former employees* are *probably lying*, so (A) is incorrect. While the man says they *chose to remain anonymous*, he never speculates why, so (B) is incorrect. The man never says *Mr. Edmonds* is the reason they *came forward*, so (D) is incorrect. The man says that *bullying* is present at *various levels in the hierarchy*, from the *top level* to the *bottom ranks*, so (C) is the correct answer.

79. (A)

The man says *We'll speak to one of these former employees at 8, so stay tuned*, so one of these employees will be interviewed at 8 o' clock. (D) is correct.

80. (A)

The woman says *I got this idea while I was taking the subway to the office*, so (A) is correct. While the woman mentions the *subway*, she doesn't say she *works* there, so (B) is incorrect. She also never mentions being an *entrepreneur*, even though she talks about an idea for an *app*, so (C) is incorrect. Finally, the woman clearly says she was on her way to *class*, so (D) is incorrect.

81. (C)

The woman says they were all *rushing*, i.e. *in a hurry*, so (A) is incorrect. She also says they were *pushing*, i.e. *shoving each other*, so (B) is incorrect. They were *ignoring each other*, so (D) is incorrect. The speaker does not say that they were *reading newspapers*, so (C) is correct.

82. (D)

The woman says that commuters would *put in their journey* but never says the *app* would *tell them how to get to their destination*, so (**A**) is incorrect. The woman says the app's service *can make the difference between catching and missing your connection*, so (**B**) is incorrect. The woman also mentions *the Chicago "L"* and its *eight lines*, but never mentions its *map*, so (**C**) is incorrect. (**D**) is correct because the woman says the *app* would tell commuters *where to stand so they can find themselves right at the exit*.

83. (B)

The man says *as you might remember from our last company-wide meeting*, which suggests this is another *company-wide meeting*, so (**B**) is correct. The man never mentions a *conference* or a *university* or students, so (**A**) and (**D**) are incorrect. Finally, while the man mentions a *party*, it's in the context of *celebrating 30 years of operation* and something the *party committee* will need to organize, so (**C**) is incorrect.

84. (C)

The man mentions *ten months*, not *10%*, so (**A**) is incorrect. The man also says they will have *bought back 23%* by *September*, so (**B**) is incorrect. This, he says, will *bring* their *ownership* back to *97%*, making (**C**) the correct answer. (**D**) is incorrect because the man says they will need *ten months* after *September* to get to *100%*.

85. (B)

The speaker never says whether he *liked* the *investors* or not, so (**A**) is incorrect. The man explicitly says that they were *of great help*, so (**C**) is also incorrect. The man also says that the *investors* presented *pushback*, i.e. didn't *want to expand to Europe* – the exact opposite of (**D**). (**B**) is the correct answer because the man says the *investors* didn't *share our vision for the future*.

86. (A)

The voice message says *if you would like to know the status of your shipment, please press 1*. The *status* would be either *delivered* or not *delivered*, so (**A**) is correct. (**B**) is incorrect because *2* is about *re-delivery*. (**C**) is incorrect because *3* is for *new customers*, who

wouldn't have a *shipment* already, and (**D**) is incorrect because *4* is about *parcel size and weight limits*.

87. (B)

The voice message says *if you are a new customer and would like to know more about the services we offer, please press 3 or visit our website at www.athenacouriers.com*, so (**B**) is correct. While the voice message mentions *parcel size and weight limits*, *next-day delivery* and *re-delivery*, it never says information about these is on the website, so (**A**) (**C**) and (**D**) are all incorrect.

88. (C)

The voice message says *for all other enquiries, please hold*, so the correct answer is (**C**). While the voice messages mentions how to *hear the menu again*, it never recommends this, so (**A**) is incorrect. Also, while the voice message mentions the *company's website*, it never says to go there if *none of the options apply*, so (**B**) is incorrect. Finally, if the *caller* decides to *hold*, they will *be connected to a representative* automatically, so (**D**) is incorrect.

89. (B)

The speaker mentions *feedback surveys from our mailing list*–not done *in store*, and not *interviews*, which means that (**A**) and (**C**) are incorrect. (**B**) is correct, however, as a *mailing list* is a *list of subscribers*.

90. (C)

The speaker mentions *flukes like this pair of jeans, whose sales were consistently lower than the rest of our products even during our sales in February*. The item in the table with the lowest sales is KY439. The answer is (**C**).

91. (B)

The speaker says about this *product* that *some of you were very reluctant to go ahead with it when the design was revealed because you thought it was too daring*. This means *some* people *within the company* expressed their dislike for the product, so (**B**) is correct. (**A**) is incorrect because the speaker says that in *March we began to experience a slump as people started looking* *for more summery clothes*. (**C**) is incorrect because the *pushback* suggests the opposite and the speaker mentions it *outperformed other products* to further his point. (**D**) is incorrect because the *product* is described as *too daring* – the exact opposite of *conservative*.

92. (C)

The woman mentions *they're afraid their employees will be lazy*, which means *employee performance will drop*, so (**A**) is incorrect. She says *it's not what they're used to*, i.e. the *status quo*, so (**B**) is incorrect. She also says *they just don't see the benefits*, which means they don't *recognize the advantages*, so (**D**) is incorrect. The woman never says whether they have *heard bad things about it* or not, so (**C**) is correct.

93. (C)

The woman says *50% of our full-time, permanent employees now work from home at least three days a week*. This means the *employees* have *full-time* contracts, but don't *work from home full-time*, so (**A**) is incorrect. Other employees *work from home once, with the exception of departments such as finance, HR and reception*, so (**B**) is incorrect. (**C**) is correct because to be *exempt* is to be an *exception*. Finally, (**D**) is incorrect because the woman says they *have been able to diminish our monthly overhead costs*, which includes *rent*.

94. (A)

The woman says remote workers can *avoid the stress of commuting*, so (**A**) is correct. While the woman says *parents can stay at home with their kids*, but never comments on how *hard* it is, so (**B**) is incorrect. She also says about remote workers that *our employees are happy*, so (**C**) is incorrect. Finally, (**D**) is incorrect because the woman says *our employees who have children no longer need to give up their job to take care of them*.

95. (C)

The woman says *thank you for coming to listen to me*. This means there are people in the same room *listening to her*, and they decided to *come*. This means that (**B**) and (**D**) are incorrect. (**A**) is also incorrect because the woman is talking about her personal history and how she decided to change careers, which is not a *business meeting* topic. This is more likely to be a *conference* speech topic, so (**C**) is the correct answer.

96. (A)

The woman says *my boss walked on eggshells around me*, which is an expression that means the *boss was careful with what she said around her*, so (**A**) is the correct answer. (**B**) is incorrect because the woman says *people whispered about her*, not her *boss*. (**C**) is incorrect because the woman says the *clichés* her *boss fed* her were *insulting*, but never that she did it *deliberately*. (**D**) is incorrect because, while the woman says she f*elt it was a bit too soon* when the *boss asked her to come back*, she said it was *OK*, so she wasn't *upset* about it.

97. (D)

The woman never says she *became a professional speaker*, so (**A**) is incorrect. The woman says that after everything that happened she *left* her *job as a Chief Operating Officer and went back to school at age 45 to study psychology*, so (**B**) is incorrect. She also didn't *become a teacher*, so (**C**) is incorrect. What she did was *go back to school*, i.e. *return to college*, so (**D**) is correct.

98. (A)

The woman says *see the red dot? That's where we are*, then she says *for the red line, turn right*. Only position 1 is to the right of the hotel, so the answer must be (**A**)

99. (B)

The woman says *you should also visit the city gardens – you'll need to take the red line for that*. If she suggests taking the *subway*, the *city gardens* can't be *within walking distance*, so (**A**) is incorrect, and (**C**) is incorrect because she recommends they visit it. The woman also says the *gardens* are *just five stations from here*, which means can take public transport, so (**B**) is the correct answer. (**D**) is incorrect because, while the woman mentions the *archeological museum*, she never says whether it's *better* or worse.

100. (C)

The woman says *there are three different hop-on hop-off bus companies: the red, the yellow and the green. I prefer the green*, so (**A**) and (**C**) are incorrect. The woman says *we can set you up with a private tour* *guide tomorrow*, but then she says *the hop-on is just as good, and cheaper*. This means that (**D**) is incorrect, and (**C**) is the correct answer.

Reading

Part V—Incomplete Sentences

101. (C)

The missing word is a verb. Since it's impossible for the *CEO* to *catch* themselves *embezzling* (i.e. stealing money from the company or the company's clients), someone else has to *catch* them, so the verb needs to be in the passive voice. The only verb in the passive voice is (**C**) *was caught*. Therefore, (**A**) (**B**) and (**D**) are all incorrect.

102. (B)

The missing word collocates with *condition* to mean 'excellent' *condition*. (**B**) *pristine* means 'excellent' and collocates with *condition*, so it's correct. (**A**) is incorrect because *precise* means 'accurate', not excellent. (**C**) is incorrect because a *manuscript* can be *precious* (i.e. valuable) but not in a *precious condition*, and (**D**) is wrong because *profound* means either intense or exhibiting great insight, but can only apply to humans, feelings or statements – not a *manuscript*.

103. (A)

The missing word needs to convey inability. This automatically excludes (**D**) *shouldn't*, which conveys rules. What also excludes *shouldn't* is that it's followed by an infinitive without 'to'. (**C**) *couldn't* is incorrect for the same reason, even though it conveys inability. (**B**) *were incapable* is incorrect because it's followed by of + gerund. (**A**) *were unable* is the only option followed by infinitive with 'to', so it's the correct answer.

104. (A)

The missing word is a preposition that collocates with *light of* to mean 'as a direct result of'. (**C**) *in* is the preposition that collocates with *light of*, so it's the correct answer. This means that (**A**) *on*, (**B**) *at* and (**D**) *with* are all incorrect.

105. (C)

The missing word is a verb. All four options are verbs in different tenses. As the person says *you look tired and sweaty*, talking about the present, (**A**) and (**D**) are incorrect. Since the person says *all morning*, the action must have been continuous, so (**C**) is correct and (**B**) is incorrect.

106. (A)

The missing word collocates with *value* to mean that somebody does not seek hidden meanings in what they are told. The correct collocation is *at face value*, so (**A**) is correct. This means that (**B**) *hand*, (**C**) *arm* and (**D**) *head* are all incorrect.

107. (D)

The missing word collocates with *clear* to mean it's very *clear*. While perfectly collocates with *clear*, the adjective *perfect* doesn't, so (**A**) is incorrect. (**B**) is incorrect because *definitely* cannot collocate with *clear* or go in that position in the sentence. (**C**) is incorrect because *scarcely* means 'barely', the opposite of very. (**D**) *abundantly* means very, so it's the correct answer.

108. (C)

The missing word is a verb. Since the sentence starts with *if*, it's a conditional sentence. Also, both parts of the sentence are about the past, so the sentence should be in the third conditional – a wish about the past. The structure for the third conditional is 'if + past perfect, would/could/might + have + past participle'. This means that (**A**) *don't waste* (present tense) and (**B**) *didn't waste* (past simple) are both incorrect. Since we already have *would've finished*, we are missing the past perfect, i.e. (**C**) *hadn't wasted*. Therefore, (**C**) is correct and (**D**) *wouldn't have wasted* is incorrect.

109. (D)

The missing word is a verb that collocates with *alarm* to mean 'express concerns'. The verb that collocates with *alarm* is *raise*, so (**D**) *raised*, the past tense of the verb, is correct. This means that (**A**) *rose* (past tense of rise), (**B**) *hit* (past tense of hit) and (**C**) *lifted* (past tense of lift, a synonym of *raise*) are all incorrect.

110. (B)

The missing word is the preposition that follows the verb *clear* to mean that something is moved away, in this case the *tables* from *the area next to the bar*, to make space. The correct preposition for this is *of*, so (B) is the correct answer. This means that (A) *from*, (C) *with* and (D) *to* are all incorrect.

111. (B)

The missing word is a noun that describes the process of introducing someone to their new job. (B) *induction* means exactly that, so it's the correct answer. (A) *intention* is incorrect because it means planning to do something, and (C) *instruction* is incorrect because it means telling someone what to do, not explaining their role to them. (D) *inflection* is incorrect because it has nothing to do with jobs: it describes speech.

112. (D)

The missing word here collocates with *a long* to create an expression that means something is unlikely. (D) *shot* is the word missing from the collocation. (A) and (B) are incorrect because they cannot collocate with *long*. (C) *way* collocates with *long*, but it's used to describe distance or time, not probability.

113. (B)

The missing word is a verb connected to the subject of the sentence, *the company*. This automatically excludes (D) *declination*, as it's a noun, and (C) *declining*, as it's a gerund. The sentence is talking about the past (*was contacted*); therefore, (B) *declined* is the correct answer. (A) *decline* is not only incorrect because it's in the present tense: it's also in the first or second person. In the present, the verb must be *declines*, as we are talking about something *the company* does.

114. (A)

The missing word is a verb that means to refer to something as evidence. (A) *citing* means exactly that, so it's correct. (B) *circulating* means to flow or distribute. (C) *chiding* and (D) *censuring* are synonyms that mean to scold or express disapproval.

115. (C)

The missing word is a verb. Since it's followed by the expression *by the end of the year*, we are talking about a deadline in the future. This means that (A) *merge* (present simple) and (B) *have merged* (present perfect) are both incorrect. (D) *will have been merging* is incorrect because it focuses on the duration of the action, not the result. (C) *will be merging* is the only verb form that talks about the future and focuses on the result, not the duration of the action of *merging*.

116. (B)

The missing word is a verb that means to spoil. (B) *marred* is a synonym of spoil. (A) *tarred* means to cover with *tar*, a material normally used in making roads. (C) *charred* means to burn something, and (D) *scarred* means to leave a mark on something.

117. (C)

The missing word is the verb *meet*. To *meet with* means to have a physical meeting, which you can only do with a human or animal – not with *contempt and excuses*. To *be met with* something, however, means to receive it as a reaction, and *contempt and excuses* can be reactions. This means that the verb needs to be in the passive voice, and (C) *have been met* is the only passive voice option. This means that (A) *met*, (B) *have met* and (D) *have been meeting* are all incorrect.

118. (B)

The missing word follows the verb 'to be' (*are*), so it needs to be an adjective. (A) *delight* is a noun, and (D) *delightfully* is an adverb, so they're both incorrect. To be *delighted* means to be very happy, whereas to be *delightful* means to cause happiness. The news can be *delightful*, but the person announcing it can't: they can be *happy* about it, so (B) is the correct answer.

119. (D)

The missing word is an adjective that describes a personality. Since it's the reason for somebody's *success*, it must be a positive adjective. (D) *shrewd* is the only positive adjective, as it means to have excellent judgment.

Therefore **(D)** is correct. **(A)** *blithe* and **(B)** *frivolous* both mean to be carefree, and **(C)** *temperamental* means to be moody – neither of which are qualities that tend to make someone *successful*.

120. (C)

The missing word is a verb. The verb needs to convey the purpose of an action: the action is *to motivate the team better*, and the purpose is *the results you want*. The grammatical structure for this is known as the 'infinitive of purpose', and it's the infinitive + to, i.e. **(C)** *to achieve*. This means that **(B)** and **(D)** are incorrect because they are gerunds (*achieving*), not infinitives, and **(A)** is incorrect because it's the infinitive without 'to' (*achieve*).

121. (A)

The missing word is an adjective that collocates with *course* to create an expression that means something will happen relatively soon, or within the appropriate timeframe. The correct collocation is *in due course*, so **(A)** is the correct answer. **(B)** is incorrect because *soon* is an adverb, not an adjective, so it can't go before a noun like *course*. **(C)** *rapid* and **(D)** *quick* are both incorrect because, while both adjectives, they don't collocate with *course* in that way.

122. (C)

The missing word is an adjective used to describe *files* that have errors. **(B)** *corrupting* is either the gerund or an adjective describing someone who corrupts someone else, which is not what the sentence wants to convey here, so it's incorrect. **(D)** *corruption* is a noun, so it's incorrect. **(A)** *corrupt* is an adjective, but normally used to describe a person without morals, not a damaged *file*. **(C)** *corrupted* is the correct way to describe a damaged *file*.

123. (B)

The missing word is an adjective. Since it's later followed by the word *than*, the adjective needs to be in the comparative form, and **(B)** *easier* is the only option in the comparative, so it is the correct answer. **(A)** is incorrect because *easy* is in the positive degree, and **(C)** *easiest* and **(D)** *the easiest* are both incorrect because they are in the superlative.

124. (B)

The missing word is a noun. Since it's preceded by *there are*, it must be in the plural. The only option in the plural is *facts*, so **(B)** is correct. **(A)** *material* is incorrect because it's in the singular, whereas **(C)** *information* and **(D)** *advice* are incorrect because they're both uncountable nouns, so they cannot be in the plural form.

125. (C)

The missing word is a verb which means the *company has been* criticized, since it gave an *inappropriate response* to a *complaint*. **(A)** *lauded* and **(B)** *praised* both mean the opposite of criticize – they are used to express approval. **(D)** *precipitated* has nothing to do with approval: it means to cause something. **(C)** *lambasted* is the only available synonym for criticizing, so it is the correct answer.

126. (C)

The missing word is a verb that describes passage of time between the past (*the last time a Canadian author was nominated*) and the present (where, presumably, another *Canadian author* has been *nominated*). The present perfect is normally used to link events in the past and present, so **(A)** *was* (past tense) and **(B)** *has* (present simple) are both incorrect. The correct verb for expressing time passing is the verb 'to be', not 'to go', so **(C)** *has been* is correct, and **(D)** *has gone* is incorrect.

127. (C)

The missing word is a noun that collocates with the verb *receive* to mean that someone is informed about something. The correct collocation is to *receive word*, so **(C)** is correct. **(A)** is incorrect because *sentence* doesn't collocate with *receive*. **(B)** and **(D)** are incorrect because an *email* is countable, so it would need an article (*an*) after *receive*.

128. (A)

The missing word is a verb that means to either delay or stop something, and *suspend* means exactly that, so the correct answer is **(A)**. To **(B)** *sustain* means to strengthen, so it's incorrect. To **(C)** *surrender* means to give up, and you can only *surrender* yourself or something physical, not *planned action*. To **(D)** *surpass* means to exceed.

129. (C)

The missing word is the preposition that completes an expression that means to be the kind of leader that teaches their team how to work by working the same way. The correct expression is to *lead by example*, so (C) is the correct answer. (A) *through* and (D) *in* are the incorrect prepositions. (B) *for* is used with the word *example* when you want to give examples of something (*for example*), but not with the verb *lead*.

130. (A)

The missing word is a phrasal verb that collocates with the word *period* to describe the right consumers often have to cancel a purchase. The correct expression is a *cooling off period*, so (A) is correct. (B) *cooling down* means to make something *cooler*, i.e. colder. (C) *coming off* means to become detached, and (D) *coming down* means to collapse.

Part VI—Text Completion

131. (B)

In this sentence, the verb is missing. Since the sentence is about something that happened *earlier this week*, the verb should be in the past, so (A) *may receive* is incorrect. The verb needs to express that something probably happened as a result of a *technical issue*. (C) *could receive* and (D) *could have received* talk about ability, not probability, so they are both incorrect. (B) is correct because *may have received* is about possibility/probability in the past.

132. (A)

This sentence is missing an adjective that describes the email. Since the email was a mistake caused by a *technical issue*, *erroneous* is the best option. (B) *ravenous* means extremely hungry, which can't apply to an *email*. (C) *ravishing* means delightful or beautiful, which also can't apply to the particular *email*. (D) *enormous* means extremely large, so it cannot be the answer.

133. (D)

This sentence is missing a word that collocates with *code* to describe a *code* used to apply a *promotion*. The correct collocation is *promotional code*, so (D) is correct. This mean that (A) *prohibitive*, (B) *promote* and (C) *promotive* are all incorrect.

134. (A)

The first half of the sentence explains that the code will be valid for 12 months, and the following sentence talks about reminding the customer about the code expiring, so (A) is the most appropriate answer, as it related to both of these points. (B) is not correct, as it talks about the code lasting for 2 years, but we know if only lasts for one year. (C) cannot be the answer, as it talks about next week, but the code lasts for a year. (D) is not the answer, because it talks about the account remaining active, but this is the problem the customer originally complained about, and is not related to the 12 month code.

135. (A)

This sentence is missing the adjective that means happy. (A) *delighted* is a synonym of happy, so it's correct. (B) *demulcent* means soothing, and (D) *desired* means wanted. While (D) *devoted*, which means dedicated, might've worked, it can't because it's followed by to + gerund, and here we have to + infinitive (*to host*).

136. (C)

This sentence is missing the preposition that collocates with *arrival* to mean after someone has arrived. The correct collocation is *upon* or *on arrival*, but only *upon* is available, so (C) is the correct answer. This means that (A) *at*, (B) *after* and (D) *from* are incorrect. *After* is the only option that could be used to convey the same message, but only with the verb version of *arrival*: *after* you arrive.

137. (A)

This sentence is missing the correct verb that means disembarking from a *bus*. (A) *alight* means to disembark from a vehicle or train, so it's correct. (B) is incorrect because to *detrain* means to disembark from a train, not a bus. (C) is incorrect because to *dislodge* means to remove something that's been stuck, and (D) is incorrect because to *eject* means to remove someone or something forcefully, i.e. to kick them out, not to disembark willingly.

138. (B)

This sentence is missing the noun that completes a collocation meaning the writer of this email is available at all times *if* the receiver has *any questions*. The correct collocation is *at your disposal*, so (B) is correct. (A) is incorrect because there's no *at your availability* collocation. (C) is incorrect because the collocation *at your discretion* means a decision rests upon you, not that someone is available for you, and (D) is incorrect because *at your request* means after you have *requested* something – so a correct sentence would be: we are available *at your request*.

139. (D)

This sentence is missing a word that completes a secondary clause (beginning from *divided* and ending at *depression*). Since this is not the main clause, it can only have a verb accompanied by a wh- word, e.g. *this collection of poems,* which *represents…, has arrived.* Since there is no wh- word here, we can't use a verb. This means that (A) *represent* and (B) *represents* are both incorrect, as they are verbs. (C) *represented* can be a verb, but it can also be a passive adjective if it describes something happening to the noun attached to it. However, here the *collection* is the one *representing* the *stages* of *clinical depression*, not *represented* by them. Therefore, (D) is the correct answer.

140. (C)

This sentence is missing a verb that describes how *words* are written *across the paper. Words* in this case are *twisting* and *swirling,* which means they are thrown onto the *page* randomly, or (C) *strewn* on it. (A) is incorrect because *spoiled* means ruined. (B) is incorrect because *splinted* means to be supported with a *splint,* which is used for broken bones. (D) is incorrect because *spurned* means to be rejected with contempt.

141. (C)

The text in this paragraph describes how *location* has always served as an *inspiration* for the *poet,* and carries on to say the reader will experience an *exciting* trip as they read. Since this *collection* follows the pattern of previous *collections,* it is *no exception,* so (D) makes sense in the gap. (A) does not fit in the middle of the paragraph: the link would normally go at the end of the text. (B) and (C) are irrelevant, as the paragraph does not talk about *awards* or future *collections.*

142. (B)

This sentence is missing the verb that describes what will happen to the reader of the *poem collection.* The

gap is followed by the noun *journey.* The correct collocation is to *take* someone *on a journey,* not *take to,* so (C) and (D) are incorrect. The sentence has a subject (*you*), but it doesn't have an object, so we need to use the passive voice. This means the reader is the one going on a *journey* and the book is the one *taking* them there. So (B) *taken on* is the correct answer and (A) *taking on* is incorrect, as it's in the active voice.

143. (C)

This sentence is missing a verb. It talks about actions in the present – the company is looking for a *native speaker,* but they don't have one yet. (B) *didn't manage* and (D) *hadn't managed* are incorrect because they talk about the past. However, if the company is looking and has had no results, they must've started looking in the past – and the past is affecting the present. The correct tense to convey this is the present perfect, so (C) *haven't managed* is correct. (A) is incorrect, as it's the present simple.

144. (A)

This sentence is missing the preposition that, when preceding *that end,* creates a collocation synonymous to 'for that reason'. The correct expression for this is *to that end,* so (A) is correct. This means that (B) *for,* (C) *at* and (D) *with* are incorrect.

145. (C)

This sentence is missing the adjective that collocates with *minimum.* The only two adjectives that collocate with *minimum* are (A) *absolute* and (C) *bare.* However, the article before the gap is *a,* not 'an', so we need an adjective that begins with a consonant, so (C) is correct.

146. (B)

This sentence is missing the noun that describes specifications for a job, so (B) *criteria* is the correct answer. (A) *rules* are something you must follow, not something you need to be able to do. Similarly, (C) *measures* are actions taken to ensure something happens or doesn't happen, while (D) *caveats* are a type of warning that there are certain stipulations attached to an agreement, so they are all incorrect.

Part VII—Reading Comprehension

147. (D)

The email starts with a bit of information around the (**B**) *history* of *Marble Hills High School*. It then goes on to (**A**) *explain why* it's *closing* and explain (**C**) what the *local government* has to do with the *decision*. However, it's not until the end that the sender asks: *Will you sign our petition and share it on social media with your friends?* This is, essentially, the *action* he would like the *recipient* to take, so (**D**) is the correct answer.

148. (D)

The email says *classes will become severely overcrowded*, which is *undue strain*, so (**A**) is incorrect. It also says that *unless we can convince the local government to change its mind, Marble Hills High School will shut its doors*, which means that the author thinks they might be able to *reverse* the *decision*, so (**B**) is incorrect. It also says that it will *force many kids to drop out*, which will have *a negative impact on graduation rates*, so (**C**) is incorrect. Finally, the email says *this decision was taken against the wishes of parents and school officials*. This, however, means that *school officials* disagree – not that they *weren't consulted*. Therefore, (**D**) is correct.

149. (B)

The author signs the email as *a concerned parent*, which seems to suggest he has a *child* who *attends the closing school*, so (**B**) is correct. He never says anything about his *work*, so (**A**) is incorrect. He also says the *school's excellent staff have educated us residents of Northampton*, which means he lives in the town where the *school* is located, so (**C**) is incorrect. Finally, he continually uses the phrase *our petition*, not 'my', so it's impossible to know if he *came up with the idea*, so (**D**) is incorrect.

150. (C)

The text says *our tailored plan is our most popular plan on offer*, so (**A**) is incorrect. It also says the *basic plan comes with 2GB of mobile data*, so (**B**) is incorrect. *Basic plans can last a year ($7 per month), two years ($8 per month), or can be on a month to month rolling basis ($10 per month)* – so the *price*

is not *set* but changes based on duration, so (**D**) is incorrect. (**C**) is correct because the *basic plan* can be *on a month to month rolling basis* – i.e. no minimum contract, so it can *last for as little as a month*.

151. (B)

The basic plan only offers 100 texts, so (**A**) is incorrect. (**C**) and (**D**) are incorrect because the upgrade plan offers a new phone, but the customer already has a new phone. (**B**) the tailored plan is the best option.

152. (B)

(**A**) is incorrect because it talks about *500 minutes to the same network*, not *landlines* and *other networks*. (**C**) is incorrect because the *plan* clearly comes with *500*, not *200 minutes to landlines*. (**D**) is also incorrect because the *plan* comes with *unlimited texts to other networks*, not *300*. (**B**) is the correct answer because the text says *unlimited texts to other networks*, and later on also *unlimited calls and texts to our network*, so *unlimited texts to all networks*.

153. (C)

The *Gold option* sits within the *upgrade option* and is available for *$10 extra per month*. This means *$10* on top of the regular fee of the *upgrade option*, not just *$10* – so (**A**) is incorrect. Since the text says the *upgrade plan* is *starting from $20 per month*, the *lowest price* for the *Gold option* must be *$20* plus the *$10 extra* required for the *Gold option*, i.e. (**C**) *$30*, not (**B**) *$20* or (**D**) *$40*, both of which are incorrect.

154. (A)

Neil asks 'Are we still on for this week' to confirm that he and Eliot will meet up, (**A**) is correct. (**B**) is incorrect as the contract is mentioned later, but this is not why Neil asks 'are we still on', as he is already aware that the contract has not been signed yet. (**C**) is not correct as although Eliot mentions that the weather is bad, this is not the reason Neil asks if they're still on. (**D**) must be incorrect as Neil is most likely to be Elliot's client.

155. (C)

Neil's *Tuesday flight* has been *canceled* and he won't be arriving until *Wednesday*, so (**A**) is incorrect. (**B**) is also incorrect because *Neil* says he's got *a pretty busy*

Wednesday. (**D**) is incorrect because *Neil* and *Elliot* agree to meet on *Friday* and *Elliot* specifically says *Friday* is *better*. (**C**) is the correct answer because Neil offers *some slots on Thursday* but *Elliot* says he has *got a sales meeting all day Thursday.*

156. (A)

(**B**) is incorrect because *Elliot* offers to *invite* his *boss* – he wouldn't do that if he didn't *expect the meeting to be fruitful*, i.e. to produce results. (**C**) is incorrect because, while *Elliot* offers to *invite* his *boss*, he never says his *boss has expressed interest in joining the meeting.* Likewise, (**D**) is incorrect because, while *Neil* mentions *Denise* will be covering for him while he's away (*picking up the slack*), he never says she *will be present at the meeting.* (**A**) is correct because *Neil* tells *Elliot*: *Don't worry, I'll be checking emails while I'm away and Denise will pick up the slack while I'm gone – you'll get your contract signed even if I'm across the country!* This sounds like *Neil* is trying to appease *Elliot* that things will get going, which he would only do if he thought *Elliot* is *keen* for them to do business.

157. (A)

Hedgement Place only has a *capacity* of *80*, so (**C**) is incorrect. The other three options have a *capacity* of *100* or more, so they are eligible. *Belwyn Place* costs *$1500, Belbridge Garden* costs *$2000* and *Linburn Hall* costs *$2500*, so (**A**) *Belwyn Place* is the cheapest, making (**B**) and (**D**) incorrect.

158. (A)

Since the *venue* needs to be for *more than 300*, all *venues* for *300* or fewer *people* can be excluded. That leaves us with just two *venues: Mallowbrook Hall* and *Estermill Gardens.* This means that (**B**) *New York* and (**C**) *New Jersey* are incorrect, as *Mallowbrook Hall* is in *Maryland* and *Estermill Gardens* are in *Pennsylvania. Mallowbrook Hall* costs more than *Estermill Gardens.* Since the latter is in *Pennsylvania*, (**A**) is correct and (**D**) is incorrect.

159. (C)

In the *Comment* column, next to *Whitebush Hill House*, it says *cannot be booked online - please call*, so (**A**) is

incorrect. In the *Comment* column for *Brightbay Gardens* it says *only available summer months*, so (**B**) can't be correct. *Mallowbrook Hill* is *not available on Mondays* – but since nothing is said about *Tuesdays*, we can assume it's *available* then, so (**D**) is incorrect. While some *venues* are *cheaper on a Sunday*, other places are the same price. Some places, such as *Merricrest Hall*, are even more expensive *on a Sunday*, so (**C**) is correct.

160. (D)

The email says *Anca's boss* has *asked to remove the purple background*, which must mean she *didn't like it*, so (**A**) is true. Anca also says *I know we agreed on the color*, which must mean they *picked it together*, so (**B**) is true. She then says they should return to their *original choice*, meaning the current *color wasn't* their *first choice*, so (**C**) is true. (**D**) is NOT TRUE because Anca says the *hue*, i.e. *shade* of the *original choice* is *lighter*, not *darker.*

161. (B)

Anca says that if things go well she will need *additional flyers*, which means she has ordered some already – so (**B**) is correct. (**A**) is incorrect because Anca mentions she has *discussed posters* with her *boss*, meaning they haven't ordered *posters* yet. (**C**) and (**D**) are both incorrect because Anca says *it'd be a good idea to also offer some funky stuff like pens or even bookmarks*, and since she is using the second conditional (*it'd* = it would), she's talking about something unreal that hasn't happened yet.

162. (A)

Anca says: *I think it'd be a good idea to also offer some funky stuff like pens or even bookmarks, too – or anything else you can think of?* The question shows she wants *Francesca to recommend something*, so (**A**) is the correct answer. (**B**) is incorrect because Anca says they'd *want consistency across the designs*, meaning they'd want them to be similar. (**C**) is incorrect because Anca says she's only *discussed* the *posters* with her *boss*, so it's impossible to know what the *boss* thinks of *bookmarks.* (**D**) is incorrect because Anca says *we're hoping to secure a spot in at least two more conferences this year*, which means that nothing is confirmed yet.

163. (A)

According to the email, the *new design* will be *more ergonomic* so they can *take advantage* of unused *space*. This means they'll be able to do more with what they already have, so the correct answer is (A) *efficient*. (B) is incorrect because *cramped* means people will have less *space*, but the email says the size of the *desks* won't change. (C) is incorrect because *laborious* means strenuous, requiring effort, and (D) is incorrect because *formidable* means inspiring fear.

164. (B)

The email says *take one of the boxes in the kitchen, write your name on it and fill it with all your belongings from your desk – as well as your keyboard.* This means that (A) is incorrect, as *keyboards* must go in the *boxes*. (C) is incorrect because *personal stuff* is a synonym for *belongings*, which also go in the *boxes*, and (D) is incorrect because the email doesn't say where the *boxes* should be left once filled. (B) is the correct answer because the email says *the only things left on your desk should be the cables and the monitors*, and *monitors* is a synonym for *computer screens*.

165. (B)

Since the *motto*, or *slogan*, was the same as the one used in another country (*Canada*), it's logical to suspect the company might be *opening in the US*, so (B) is correct. No reference is made to *pictures* on the *poster* (A), and the *Canada* stores *opened* in *2017*. Finally, (D) is wrong because *the CEO's social media confirmed* the suspicions – they didn't start the *rumors*.

166. (C)

The text mentions *employee benefits* (A), *health-conscious* food (B), and *excellent development schemes* (D), which usually lead to *career progression*. While the text mentions a *new, vegan pizza dish* at the end, it never says the company's *vegan dishes* are what it's *known for*, so (C) is correct.

167. (B)

While the text mentions the company *launched in Canada last year*, we don't know if it also *launched* elsewhere afterwards, so (A) is incorrect. Likewise, while the text mentions *California*, *Florida* and *Texas*,

these are just examples of *key states* the company *plans to focus on* – the *next US store* might *open* in any other *key state*, so (C) is incorrect. (D) is incorrect the text clearly mentions *at least fifteen stores*, not *only*. (B) is the correct answer because the text mentions the *plan* for the *coming 24 months* – suggesting that *Ricotta has a 2-year expansion plan*.

168. (B)

Since the sentence mentions an *announcement*, the position needs to follow one. [1] appears beforethe announcement, so cannot be correct. [2] appears after the announcement, so must be the correct answer. [3] and [4] do not appear after an announcement.

169. (C)

At the beginning of the text, *Darla* says *I have changed my mind and I will no longer be subscribed to your service*. This means the purpose of the call was to discuss her *subscription* – meaning (B) is incorrect. Further down, however, we find out her original *subscription* was *cancelled* and the company *promised to call* in order to *set up a new payment and subscription*. This means they just going to *reinstate* what was *cancelled*, so (C) is correct.

170. (C)

The woman says *instead of contacting me to inform me of the issue, you automatically cancelled my subscription and didn't even let me know* – so the *company* never contacted the *woman*, making (B) and (D) incorrect. Since the *email* was *initial*, it came first – so (C) is correct.

171. (A)

Based on the language the woman uses, it's safe to assume she's angry – and since (A) *incensed* means extremely angry, it's correct. It's possible the woman could've felt (B) *crestfallen*, which means sad and disappointed, but the language in her email is more aggressive than suggestive of disappointment. On the other hand, it's not likely the woman feels (C) *content*, which means satisfied, and there is nothing in the text suggesting she is (D) *bemused*, which means confused, so both answers are incorrect.

172. (A)

The author of the email lists his skills and experience. This suggests he is *applying for a job*, so (A) is correct. While the author does *remind the recipient of how they met* and thanks him *for the opportunity*, these are both in the context of *applying for a job*, not the purpose of the email. As far as *networking* is concerned, this already happened on the *plane* where the author and *recipient* met.

173. (B)

This sentence describes the author's skills. Being a *great team player* is a skill, so [2] is correct – especially as this sentence includes the word *also*, which means other skills preceded it. Position [1] is surrounded by the author's experience, not his skills, and positions [3] and [4] have moved on to the final part of the email, where the author lists the actions he's taken (e.g. sending his *resume*).

174. (A)

The sentence says the *decision* was not *taken lightly*. This is an expression that means a lot of thought was put into the *decision*. In other words, it was not done (A) *carelessly*, which is correct. While *lightly* might also means (B) *leniently* (e.g. when someone is punished *lightly*) and the adjective *light* is a synonym of (C) *bright*, this is not the case here. (D) *delicately* is also incorrect as it would mean the *decision* was made in a harsh manner.

175. (C)

The text mentions that the *mother* has *tried hard to keep the diner in profit* but it *has not been possible*, and that has prompted the decision. To keep a business *in profit* means to have enough *finance* for it, so (C) is correct. While the text does mention *the loss of our father eight months ago* and the *mother's declining health*, these are not the *main reasons* for the decision – and, according to the text, they are *closing before the bank forces* them to, so *foreclosure* hasn't happened yet.

176. (C)

The first text asks *are you fascinated by trivia?* As *trivia* means unimportant information, this suggests the game show asks random knowledge questions – which is then confirmed in the second text where Christos references *knowing* the *right answer* to the *questions*. This means

that the *game show* is a *question –answer* show, so (C) is correct. This means that (A) *activity-oriented*, (B) *puzzle-oriented* and (D) *essay based* are all incorrect.

177. (A)

The casting call asks for *people aged between 18-30 and 65+* and calls the episodes *Generation Wars*, suggesting that these two *age* groups will be asked to compete *against each other*, so (A) is correct. (B) and (D) are incorrect because the casting call says they *look for people from all walks of life* in general, not just for *charity specials*. (C) is wrong because, while the ad mentions *buying a house*, it's meant to entice contestants – they never say the game show will *buy a house for the winner*.

178. (C)

(A) is incorrect because Christos says *I'm getting married to my partner […] next year and I would like us to have the wedding we both always dreamt of.* (B) is incorrect because Christos says *we'd like to go to Europe*, and (D) is incorrect because he says *we are even considering relocating to San Francisco*. (C) is correct because, while Christos mentions the *wedding*, he never mentions a *wedding present*.

179. (A)

Christos writes *some extra cash sure would be handy*, because he and his wife are planning ot move after getting married *handy* means helpful, so (A) must be the correct answer.

180. (B)

(A) is incorrect because, while Christos is *29 years old*, and the first text mentions *people aged 18-30* for the *Generation Wars* episode, we can't know definitively that he *will be asked to participate* in that episode. (C) is incorrect because Christos says he wants the winning money for his *wedding*, and he might *move to San Francisco after* his *wedding* – so he'd probably *participate* in *Charlotte*, where he lives now. (D) is incorrect because, while Christos says his *dad* is *Greek* and his *mum* is *German*, he never mentions whether he has *American* citizenship or not. (B) is correct because to have a *knack* for something means to have a talent for it, and Christos clearly has a talent for *languages* since he *speaks four* of them.

181. (C)

(A) is incorrect because *Maria* says the *attached document* includes *further details on locations and timings* and the *agenda*, not the *travel policy*. (B) is incorrect because the email never says the *travel policy* is different in each *country*. (D) is incorrect because *Maria* says the *agenda* is *not finalized*. (C) is correct because *Maria* says *please always refer to our travel policy*, so it *needs to be observed*.

182. (B)

RSVP is a synonym for *confirming attendance* and the email says *please confirm your attendance by July 20th*, so (B) is correct. (A) is incorrect because *April 3rd* is when the email was sent. (C) is incorrect because *August 31st* is the deadline for the *finalized agenda*, not the *attendance*. (D) is incorrect because *November 15th* is the day of the *Sales meeting*.

183. (A)

The second email mentions *previous dates*, so (A) is correct. (B) is incorrect because the mistake was with the *dates*, not the *location*. (C) is incorrect because *Esther* says she has *booked accommodation and travel* for the *meeting next week*, so the *meeting* clearly hasn't taken place yet. (D) is incorrect because *Yussef* didn't *notice in time*.

184. (D)

The email says *Maria left the company back in June... and someone from either the Zurich or the Los Angeles office should have informed you.* This means Esther doesn't *blame* someone specifically, but *all of the above*, so (D) is the correct answer and (A), (B) and (C) are incorrect.

185. (A)

The email says *a decision will be made soon regarding which office should swallow the costs of your unnecessary trip*, which means someone will have to pay, or *bear* the *cost*, so (A) is correct. (B) is incorrect because to *escalate* something means to raise it higher. (C) is incorrect because to *deliver* something means to take it to someone, and (D) is incorrect because to *incur* a *cost* means to create a *cost*, not to pay it.

186. (D)

The text says the *DVD player was $49.99* but is now *$24.99*, so (A) is incorrect. It also says a *3-year warranty* requires a *$14.99 additional fee*, so (B) is incorrect. (C) is incorrect because the text mentions both *DVDs and CDs*. (D) is the correct answer because the *player* comes with a *USB outlet*, which means it accepts *USB*, or *flash drives*.

187. (A)

Adiran says *I don't have any DVDs from a different region, so I haven't yet tried out that feature*, so (A) is correct. Adiran mentions an *HDMI cable*, but doesn't say if he has used one. He does say he has *been using the USB slot a lot and* is *very satisfied with it* because *it recognizes every single format I've thrown at it (both for movies and for music*, so (C) and (D) are incorrect.

188. (B)

The second reviewer says *Where do I start? First of all, the DVD player didn't arrive on time. When I called the company to ask where it was, no one even knew how to check up on orders. There doesn't seem to be a tracking system in place, and none of the employees seem to be competent enough to deal with customer issues.* The reviewer has lots of negative points to raise, and isn't sure which one to discuss first. The correct answer is (B).

189. (B)

While Adiran mentions the *short Scart cable (the one it comes with is too short)*, Clara doesn't, so (A) is incorrect. Adiran says *I don't have any DVDs from a different region, so I haven't yet tried out that feature*, which means he can't know whether (C) is true, so it's incorrect. (D) is incorrect because Adiran says the *DVD player arrived promptly*, which means fast. (B) is the correct answer because Adiran says *it doesn't come with an HDMI cable* and Clara says *it didn't even have an HDMI cable*.

190. (C)

Clara says *when I called to complain again, I was told it has been more than 14 days since I placed my order, so I am no longer entitled to a replacement*. This means she was *too late*, so (C) is correct. While Clara does mention they *already replaced it once*, she doesn't give this as a reason for the *refusal* when she *called* again, so (**A**) is incorrect. She also never says anything about them *claiming* she *had broken it* (**D**) – and the *DVD player* comes with a *1-year warranty* (**B**), so she didn't need to *purchase one*.

191. (A)

To *drop a line* means to correspond, either via *email* or by *letter*, which means (**A**) must be correct.

192. (C)

The email says this *has been mentioned in numerous company-wide meetings*, not that it *will be mentioned*, so (**A**) is incorrect. While *HR* does request the *invoices* and to know whether *charges are billable*, it never says the *invoices* can *help to determine* that, so (**B**) is incorrect. The email also says the *invoices* need to be sent *immediately*, not *before the end of the month*, so (**D**) is incorrect. What the email does say is they might eventually have to *resort to naming and shaming*, which means *publicly identifying wrongdoers*, so (**C**) is correct.

193. (A)

Office supplies is a synonym for *stationery*, and the list includes a *$29.99* charge from *Walker's Stationery*, so (**A**) is correct. It's unlikely that companies named *Opus Bus Company*, *Joe's Coffee* and *TMR Airways* would sell *office supplies*, so all other options are incorrect.

194. (A)

The second email mentions *costs associated with* a trip to *Paris* for *John*, and also mentions the *charge* was *$897.56*. That charge is from *Highlight Airlines*, so (**A**) is correct. None of the other three options are mentioned in the second email and none of them have an *$897.56 charge*, so they're all incorrect.

195. (B)

The author suggest he's not happy with being targeted, and probably also quite *frustrated*, so (**B**) is the correct answer. It's unlikely he feels (**A**) *ashamed* or (**D**) *petrified* (i.e. scared), as he has *done everything* correctly, and he gives no indication that he might be feeling (**C**) *smug* just because he *did everything* right.

196. (B)

The *bag drop* usually happens at *check-in*, and the *first outbound flight* is *TMR9776* where, according to the *flight details*, *check-in closes* at *09:45*, so (**B**) is correct. (**A**) *08:30* is the earliest, not the *latest time*, whereas (**C**) and (**D**) are the arrival and departure times – nothing to do with *check-in* or *dropping bags*.

197. (D)

The *return trip* is the *inbound trip*, and the *final destination* is the last leg of the *trip*. This means the question is asking about flight *TMR9129*, and the *arrival* time for this is *20:20*, so (**D**) is correct. All the other options are the *arrival* times of the other three flights, so they're incorrect.

198. (D)

The *email from customer service* arrived on *March 28th*, so it can't be either of the *outbound* flight – meaning (**A**) and (**B**) are incorrect. Since the email mentions *arriving to Los Angeles*, the first flight on March 28th can't have been *cancelled*, so (**D**) is the correct answer.

199. (B)

The second email says *on my return, one of my flights was cancelled due to – as I was told at the airport – an issue with the aircraft*. An *issue with the aircraft* is an *engineering problem*, so (**B**) is correct. While the text mentions *staff*, it never says there weren't enough (**A**), and while the text mentions there were *no more seats*, this was in other *flights*, not the original one (**C**). Similarly, the *delay* mentioned in the text was due to the original flight having been *cancelled* – not the cause of the *cancellation* (**D**).

200. (C)

(**A**) is incorrect because *Rich* calls the *hotel filthy* at the end of his email. (**B**) is also incorrect because *Rich* mentions *having to take an extra day off from work*. (**D**) is incorrect because *Rich* complains about the fact he *had to fork out* (i.e. pay) *another $30 from my own pocket to have a decent dinner*. (**C**) is the correct answer: while *Rich* does say *it was already quite late by the time I arrived at Los Angeles*, this is to explain why he had to stay over in a *hotel*, not a *complaint* per se.

PRACTICE TEST 2 ANSWER KEY

Part I	Part II	Part III	Part IV	Part V	Part VI	Part VII
1. A	7. C	32. B	71. C	101. C	131. C	147. B
2. D	8. A	33. C	72. B	102. C	132. A	148. C
3. A	9. C	34. A	73. C	103. A	133. B	149. C
4. C	10. B	35. D	74. A	104. D	134. D	150. C
5. B	11. C	36. A	75. A	105. B	135. A	151. D
6. D	12. A	37. B	76. B	106. A	136. B	152. D
	13. B	38. C	77. A	107. C	137. B	153. A
	14. A	39. A	78. C	108. C	138. A	154. D
	15. A	40. C	79. A	109. A	139. D	155. B
	16. A	41. C	80. C	110. A	140. A	156. D
	17. C	42. A	81. B	111. A	141. C	157. B
	18. A	43. B	82. D	112. D	142. A	158. B
	19. B	44. B	83. B	113. C	143. B	159. C
	20. A	45. A	84. C	114. C	144. D	160. A
	21. C	46. D	85. B	115. D	145. B	161. B
	22. A	47. B	86. B	116. B	146. C	162. C
	23. A	48. C	87. C	117. A		163. A
	24. B	49. B	88. D	118. B		164. C
	25. C	50. C	89. A	119. D		165. B
	26. A	51. A	90. C	120. A		166. A
	27. B	52. C	91. D	121. A		167. C
	28. A	53. B	92. C	122. B		168. D
	29. C	54. A	93. A	123. B		169. C
	30. B	55. D	94. C	124. D		170. A
	31. C	56. B	95. B	125. A		171. A
		57. A	96. A	126. C		172. D
		58. A	97. C	127. C		173. A
		59. D	98. D	128. D		174. D
		60. C	99. B	129. B		175. C
		61. B	100. A	130. A		176. A
		62. A				177. C
		63. C				178. C
		64. A				179. C
		65. C				180. D
		66. B				181. C
		67. B				182. A
		68. A				183. A
		69. D				184. D
		70. B				185. B
						186. A
						187. B
						188. B
						189. C
						190. A
						191. B
						192. C
						193. B
						194. D
						195. B
						196. A
						197. B
						198. A
						199. C
						200. B

PRACTICE TEST 2

Part I—Photographs

1. (A)

The photograph shows a table with used plates and cutlery, the people who were sitting here have recently finished their meal. (A) describes this, no one is still eating. (B) confuses the tense, the diners have finished eating, they are not about to eat. (C) is incorrect, the cutlery is on the table. The dishes should be cleaned, not *discarded* (D).

2. (D)

The photograph shows four colleagues looking at a computer monitor. (D) describes the situation; they are looking at their work. (B) confuses the word *monitor* with the word *monitoring*. The *people* are grouped around the table, not the *files* (C). (D) confuses the computer *screen*, with the word *screening*.

3. (A)

The photograph shows a businessman in the back of a car, using his phone and looking over documents. (A) correctly describes the photograph. The man is in a car, but he is not *driving* a car (B). The man is working in the *car*, not a *home* (C). The man is *working*, not *playing a game* (D).

4. (C)

The photograph shows a gloved technician examining wired equipment. (C) correctly describes the photograph, the technician is wearing a glove. There are no baskets in the photograph (A). The wires are in a box on the *wall*, not on the *floor* (B). No one in the photograph is *reading* (D).

5. (B)

The photograph shows two adults and a child sitting in a field. The woman is talking to the child, (B) is correct. The basket does not have any plants in it (B). There is no *table* in the photograph (C). The man is taking his medication, not falling asleep (D).

6. (D)

The photograph shows a hallway with a trashcan to the left-hand side of the hall. (D) correctly describes the photograph. The is a *fire extinguisher* in the hallway, but no *fire* (A). There is a *trashcan*, but no *cans* in the hallway

Part II—Question-Response

7. (C)

The question asks *what time*, so (C) is the correct answer. (A) is wrong because it's a day, not time. (B) is impossible because it doesn't answer a *Wh- question.*

8. (A)

The speakers asks *Why are you leaving?* The correct response will give a reason. (A) gives an appropriate reason, the other speaker is *going back to college.* (B) confuses *leaving* with *leaves* on trees. (C) answers a yes/no question.

9. (C)

The question asks *when*, so (C) is the correct answer. (A) is wrong because it answers *where*. (B) is also incorrect because it answers a who question.

10. (B)

(B) is the correct answer because when it says *not very* it means *not very expensive.* (A) is wrong because it says *I like* but doesn't say if the computers are expensive or not. (C) is incorrect because it talks about a place, *New York,* not computers.

11. (C)

(A) is wrong because it talks about a *phone call,* not a meeting. (B) says *how often* but doesn't confirm the information the speakers wants to know (whether they have a meeting). This means (C) is the only possible answer.

12. (A)

The questions asks *where,* so (A) is the right answer. (B) is wrong because it accepts an offer. (C) is wrong because it talks about sending a fax the night before.

13. (B)

(B) is the correct answer because it talks about the consequences of snow falling. **(A)** is wrong because it's not a yes/no question. **(C)** does not make sense because if it's going to snow it will be cold, not warm.

14. (A)

(A) is the correct answer because it replies to the offer by accepting some *tea*. **(B)** is incorrect because *occasionally* refers to frequency, not an offer. **(C)** is also incorrect because it answers a Yes/No question.

15. (A)

The question asks *whose*, so **(A)** is the correct answer. **(B)** is wrong because it talks about *tonight*, but she'll arrive this morning. **(C)** is not possible because it says the phone is old but does not say *whose* phone it is.

16. (A)

(A) is the best answer because it says *pick her up at the station (train station)*. **(B)** is wrong because it says *he* as opposed to *she*. **(C)** is also incorrect because it talks about train fares in Europe.

17. (C)

The question asks *where*, so **(C)** is the correct answer. **(A)** is wrong because it answers *when*. **(B)** is also incorrect because it answers *how*.

18. (A)

(B) is incorrect because it talks about prices, not *preference*. **(C)** uses the word *tablet* with a different meaning (*aspiring tablets*), so it isn't possible either. This means **(A)** is the only possible answer.

19. (B)

The question asks *how many*, so **(B)** is the correct alternative. **(A)** is incorrect because it doesn't say a *number*. **(C)** is also wrong because it answers *what time*.

20. (A)

The question asks *when* and **(B)** answers *where*, so it is incorrect. **(C)** answers a where question.

21. (C)

The question asks *if the office is warm*, so *very* is an appropriate answer and **(C)** is correct. **(A)** is not possible because it describes the office, not its temperature. **(B)** is incorrect because it says *country*, not *office*.

22. (A)

(A) is correct because it agrees with the statement. **(B)** also agrees but it talks about *movies*, not a restaurant. **(C)** is wrong because it is an answer to a question, not a reply to a statement.

23. (A)

(A) is the correct answer because it replies to the statement by asking *what Ms Aranha wanted*. **(B)** is wrong because it says *him*, and Ms Aranha is a woman. **(C)** is impossible because it talks about a situation, not a person's missed call.

24. (B)

The question asks for a reason and **(A)** talks about *age*, so it's incorrect. **(C)** is wrong because it says *she* but the question says *people*. This means **(B)** is the correct answer.

25. (C)

The question is an offer (*take the day off*), so **(C)** is an appropriate reply. **(A)** is wrong because it talks about the *weather*. **(B)** is incorrect because it talks about turning something off, not a *day off*.

26. (A)

The question asks for the color of a replacement car, so **(A)** is the correct answer. **(B)** is wrong because it talks about *taxis*, not a replacement car. **(C)** does not answer the question *what color*, so it isn't possible either.

27. (B)

The question asks *how much time*, so **(B)** is the correct answer. **(A)** and **(B)** are wrong because they are in the past, and the question is about the future.

28. (A)

The question is checking for information (*if newspapers arrived*), so **(A)** is the correct answer. The question is in the past and (**B**) is in the future, so it is incorrect. (**C**) is also wrong because it is in the present.

29. (C)

(**A**) answers *what color* but the question asks *why*, so it is incorrect. (**B**) is wrong because it talks about the future and the question asks about the present. This means (**C**) is the only possible answer.

30. (B)

The question asks for a recommendation, so (**B**) is the best possible answer. (**A**) is wrong because it refuses an offer. (**C**) is also incorrect because it talks about *when* something is going to happen but fails to make a recommendation.

31. (C)

The statement talks about a problem with the printer, so (**C**) is the correct answer. (**A**) is wrong because it talks about a *lunch break*, not a printer that always *breaks down*. (**B**) is incorrect because it asks for a favor instead of replying to a problem with a recommendation.

Part III—Short Conversations

32. (B)

The man says *it was the office manager who did all the interviewing*, (**B**) is correct. (**A**), (**C**) and (**D**) are not mentioned in the conversation.

33. (C)

The man says *it was the office manager who did all the interviewing*, (**C**) is correct. (**B**) and (**D**) are not mentioned in the conversation. The *personnel manager* (**A**) spoke, but didn't ask any questions.

34. (A)

The man says *I think it all went very well, actually so I'm happy about that*, (**A**) is correct. The man does not express any different emotions in the conversation, so (**B**) (**C**) and (**D**) are incorrect.

35. (D)

The woman says *it's a good idea for customers to see how we run our production process, so if you have*

time, Mr Bidwell, I thought I'd show you around the plant, the man is a customer (**D**). (**A**), (**B**) and (**C**) are not mentioned in the conversation.

36. (A)

The woman says *I thought I'd show you around the plant*, the speakers will go to a *factory* (**A**). (**B**), (**C**) and (**D**) are not mentioned in the conversation.

37. (B)

The woman says *I'll have to ask you to put on this hard hat*, the man needs to wear *safety equipment* (**B**). (**A**), (**C**) and (**D**) are not mentioned in the text.

38. (C)

(**C**) is the correct alternative because the woman says *I don't have to say we need the work completed by the end of April*, and May is the month that follows April. The man says *Three or four weeks* when asked how long it would take him to finish the job. This doesn't mean this is when the woman needs the job done, so (**A**) and (**B**) are wrong. They don't say anything about *the end of the year*, so (**D**) is impossible.

39. (A)

When the man says *The boys will be here right at the crack of dawn*, *the boys* means *his workers*, and *the crack of dawn* means *very early*, so (**A**) is the correct answer. He doesn't say he needs more time, so (**B**) is wrong. The man doesn't say anything about whether it's late or not, so (**C**) is not possible either. (**D**) is incorrect because he doesn't say anything about what time she gets to work.

40. (C)

The man says *The boys will be here right at the crack of dawn*. In order to remove one cubicle and still have two cubicles on each side, cubicle 3 is the one which needs to be removed. This means alternatives (**A**), (**B**), and (**D**) are incorrect and (**C**) is the only possible answer.

41. (C)

The man says *I'm expecting a call from the marketing department. If they call, could you tell them I'll be back at my desk in half an hour or so?* The speakers must be at the office (**C**). (**A**), (**B**) and (**D**) are not mentioned in the conversation.

42. (A)

The man says *I'm just popping out to the **bank** to deposit a check in my account*, the man is going to the bank (**A**). (**B**), (**C**) and (**D**) are not mentioned in the conversation.

43. (B)

The woman says *if you pass by the mini-market could you get me a sandwich for lunch?* The woman wants some food (**B**). (**A**), (**C**) and (**D**) are not mentioned in the text.

44. (B)

(**B**) is the best possible answer because the woman says *I think you can remember how to get to the factory from there.* (**A**) is wrong because the woman says *after the church you'll have get in the right lane.* The woman also says the Italian restaurant was in Chicago (*That was in Chicago, Mesut. Remember?*), so (**C**) is not possible either. Chicago is where the Italian restaurant is located but not where Mesut wants to go, so (**D**) is also incorrect.

45. (A)

The man says *I remember going straight and then past that Italian restaurant... What's it called* and the woman replies *Giuseppe's.* She later says *That was in Chicago,* so (**A**) is the only possible answer. (**B**) is wrong because if the restaurant is in Chicago, it isn't near the factory. The woman says *We took the Japanese to see the Bears* but doesn't say they went to the restaurant as well, so (**C**) and (**D**) are impossible.

46. (D)

The man says *When we said football they thought they were going to see a soccer match* and the woman replies *Exactly. They were so disappointed.* This means (**D**) is the right option. Chicago Bears is an American football team, so (**A**) is impossible. (**B**) is wrong because even though the woman says *it was freezing,* this is not the reason why the Japanese were disappointed. We don't know if the Japanese went to an Italian restaurant, so (**C**) is incorrect.

47. (B)

The woman says *Told you it was too good to be true. How on earth can they be 20% cheaper that TechPak? It's just impossible,* so (**A**) is incorrect. She doesn't say anything about the quality of the printers, she's only worried that they haven't been delivered yet. This means (**C**) is also wrong. She doesn't trust the store, not Wallace, so (**D**) is not the answer. This means (**B**) is the only possible answer.

48. (C)

(**C**) is the best answer because the man says *We ordered those new eco printers* and the woman later says *$100 cheaper than TechPak.* (**A**) and (**B**) are wrong because they're not printers. (**D**) is wrong because it's not an Eco printer, or $100 cheaper than the same model at TechPak.

49. (B)

Wallace says *You even texted the link to your husband* and then Burcu replies *this is why I sent the link to Matteo,* which means Matteo is her husband and (**B**) is the correct answer. We know Matteo knows Wallace (*he even called you*), but that doesn't necessarily mean they're friends so (**A**) is unlikely. (**C**) and (**D**) are wrong because they don't mention a boss or customer service advisor.

50. (C)

They all complain about the fact that there is a new system. They don't say anything about being tired, and they do not seem to be happy, so (**A**) and (**B**) are wrong. They don't say anything about food, either. This means (**D**) is also incorrect and (**C**) is the only possible answer.

51. (A)

The woman says *I think Nelson here is struggling a little bit with the new system* and then Nelson says *It's a bit of a nightmare, actually.* This means (**A**) is the best answer. They don't talk about sleeping, so (**B**) is wrong. We don't know if Colin and Nelson work well together or not, so (**C**) is impossible. Nelson doesn't like the new system but that doesn't means he doesn't like computers, so (**D**) is also incorrect.

52. (C)

The woman says *We only had the other system for two years and it was working just fine. Sometimes I think IT is only trying to justify their salaries,* so (**C**) is the right answer. If she says *only trying to justify their salaries,* she means they have nothing important to do so (**A**) is incorrect. She says *justify their salaries,* which doesn't mean they need better salaries and (**B**) is wrong. (**D**) is not possible because she doesn't say what she thinks they should do.

53. (B)

The woman says *could you tell me where you keep the invoices?* so (**B**) is the correct alternative. The man says *there's a folder,* but he doesn't say it's her folder. This means (**A**) is wrong. There's no mention of a link or a box, so (**C**) and (**D**) are impossible.

54. (A)

The man says *People arrive whenever they want, they go home whenever they want, they use the computers to do whatever they want,* so (**A**) is the best possible answer. He doesn't complain about the computers, so (**B**) is not possible. He says *it's chaos* when talking about people's attitudes, not the office. This means (**C**) is not possible either. The woman says *laid-back management* and the man agrees (*Oh, don't get me started!*), so (**D**) is also wrong.

55. (D)

The woman says *But what do you expect to happen with such laid-back management? Tatiana is never here, Sarah is always on the phone, and what about Marcelo,* so (**A**), (**B**), and (**C**) are all incorrect. This means (**D**) is the only possible answer.

56. (B)

The first speaker says *Hi Julie. Hi Fatima. I was wondering if you could do me a favor. It's my wife's birthday this Thursday and I have no idea what to get her* and *She's an architect.* This means (**B**) is the correct answer. Julie and the first speaker are talking when the first speaker says in the third person *She's an architect,* so (**A**) and (**C**) are impossible. (**D**) is also wrong because Fatima says *Rodrigo from IT.*

57. (A)

The woman says *you could give her a holiday as a present... You could go to London and visit the modern art museum.* So the woman suggests a trip abroad. The answer is (**A**). They talk about cooking, but the woman doesn't recommend dinner, the man recommends a trip to Brazil, and the woman recommends visiting an art museum in London. not taking an art course.

58. (A)

Abu says *I'm sure Rodrigo from IT can help you with that* and the man replies *That's a great idea, thanks! I'll text him later.* so (**A**) is the correct alternative. The man doesn't talk about inviting Rodrigo to go anywhere with him, so (**B**) is wrong. There's nothing to say to Rodrigo about either Julie or Fatima, so (**C**) is impossible. (**D**) is also incorrect because the man says *I'll text him later,* which means he already has Rodrigo's number.

59. (D)

Thomas says *I'm going to Germany for the weekend* and *and I might not be able to check my email all the time while I'm there. My sister lives in the countryside,* so (**D**) is the correct option. He doesn't say it's a business trip, so (**A**) is wrong. He says *I'm going to Germany for the weekend,* so (**B**) and (**C**) are incorrect.

60. (C)

Thomas says *I was wondering if you could keep an eye on the new associates* and Rawan replies *No problem.* This means (**C**) is the correct answer. If Thomas is the man in the conversation and Rawan the woman, options (**A**) and (**B**) are impossible. Thomas's sister lives in Germany, so (**D**) is also wrong.

61. (B)

The man says *just call me,* so (**B**) is correct. The man discusses why *email* would not be a good idea, and meeting in person or contacting by fax are not mentioned.

62. (A)

The woman says *She certainly has the experience and the qualifications. But don't you think it's a bit strange she's had all these different jobs,* which probably means she thinks there's something wrong with the candidate. This means (**A**) is the best answer. She seems worried (*I'm not sure if she's what we're looking for*), so (**B**) and

(D) are impossible. (C) is wrong because she thinks there's something wrong but it's just a feeling. She can't be disappointed about something she doesn't know.

63. (C)

The woman says *The longest she managed to stay with the same company was three years from 1999 to 2002. And that was nearly twenty years ago when she had just finished university,* so (C) is the correct answer. The woman says *three years from 1999 to 2002,* so (A) is wrong. She says *nearly twenty years ago* which means it's been less than twenty years and (B) is incorrect. (D) is wrong because 2002 is when the candidate left one of her jobs.

64. (A)

(A) is the correct answer because the man says *Just send me her résumé today and I'll get touch with some of her former employers.* The man says *Just send me her résumé,* so (B) is not possible. He doesn't say anything about *finding her,* so (C) is wrong. The woman already has information about the candidate's experience and qualifications, so (D) is also incorrect.

65. (C)

The man says *we had some friends over for dinner,* so (C) is the correct answer. The man says *we had some friends over for dinner so we just listened to music and talked,* so (A) and (B) are incorrect. He doesn't say anything about his guests being old friends from school, so (D) is also wrong.

66. (B)

Rebecca says *It was about what happens with all the trash we produce and how some of the most beautiful beaches and mountains all around the world have been turned into these filthy landfills,* so (B) is the correct answer. (A) is wrong because Rebecca says *some of the most beautiful beaches and mountains all around the world have been turned into these filthy landfills.* (C) is not possible because even though Rebecca says *They give the example of San Francisco where nearly all garbage is recycled,* that doesn't mean this is the main focus of the documentary. Rebecca says *It was about what happens with all the trash we produce,* so (D) is not possible either.

67. (B)

She says *they managed to get this done in less than 10 years,* so (A) is not possible. (C) is impossible because she says *Take the example of San Francisco where nearly all garbage is recycled and how they managed to get this done in less than 10 years.* She doesn't mention her hometown, so (D) is also wrong. This means (B) is the only possible answer.

68. (A)

(A) is the correct answer because the man says *We only make the small components here. All the other parts are imported from China for obvious reasons.* (B) is incorrect because he says *We only make the small components here.* He doesn't say the number or percentage of parts imported from China, so (C) and (D) are both wrong.

69. (D)

The man says *They're fast, they're reliable, and much less expensive,* so alternatives (A), (B), and (C) are all incorrect. This means (D) is the only possible answer.

70. (B)

The man says *We only make the small components here.* (A) is wrong because *small components* can't weigh 470 kg. The same applies to (C) and (D) which are heavier and have a small number of items than (B), which is lightest, so most be the correct answer.

Part IV—Short Talks

71. (C)

The man says *the coach is due to arrive at Heathrow Terminals 1, 2 and 3 at 8.35 a.m.,* so (C) is the correct answer. The bus leaves at 7.45, so (A) is incorrect. The man says *50-minute journey,* so (B) is also impossible. (D) is wrong because *8.45* is not mentioned in the text.

72. (B)

The man says *Passengers going to terminals 4 and 5 have to use the airport shuttle service due to road works in the area,* so (B) is the correct alternative. The man doesn't say anything about traffic or demonstrations, so (A) and (D) are incorrect. (C) is not possible because he says *Passengers going to terminals 4 and 5 have to use the airport shuttle.*

73. (C)

(C) is the only possible answer because the man says *Passengers going to terminals 4 and 5 have to use the airport shuttle service.* The coach will stop at terminals 1, 2, and 3, but not at terminals 4 or 5. This means (A) is incorrect. The man doesn't mention a *train* or *car*, so alternatives (B) and (D) are both incorrect.

74. (A)

(A) is the only possible answer because the woman says *our premiere movie The Lone Fighter.* The woman says *A young orphan conquers the hearts of America in a journey of self-discovery and struggles,* when talking about the movie plot, so (B) and (C) are incorrect. (D) is not possible because she says *To celebrate International Women's Day, women get a free ticket when accompanied by a paying adult.*

75. (A)

The woman says *7 Academy Awards including Best Picture, Best Soundtrack, and Best Leading Actor,* so alternatives (B), (C) and (D) are incorrect. This means (A) is the only possible answer.

76. (B)

(B) is the right option because the woman says *To celebrate International Women's Day, women get a free ticket when accompanied by a paying adult.* She doesn't say anything about *popcorn* or *discount,* so options (A) and (C) are both incorrect. (D) is also wrong because she says *women get a free ticket when accompanied by another paying adult. For more information about our events and promotions visit our website.*

77. (A)

The speaker is making the services offered by a company more attractive when he says *Alicia's Beauty Center can turn your old dull look into a fresh young style.* He also uses the first person plural *We help you not only choose the best beauty treatment but also.* This means the recording is an ad and (A) is the best possible answer. Even though it might be an ad made for the radio, it isn't a *radio program,* so (B) is

incorrect. The same applies to (C). (D) is impossible because airport announcements don't usually talk about stores, products, and services.

78. (C)

The speaker says *We specialize in alternative hair treatments, mudding...* so (A) and (B) are incorrect. (D) is also wrong because he says *We also provide dietary advice.* This means (C) is the correct answer.

79. (A)

The phrase *the first day of the rest of your life* means that your life will be different after using their services, so (A) is the correct answer. The speaker doesn't talk about prices, so (B) is not possible. He says *Hollywood actress,* not *movie.* This means (C) is not possible either. (D) is wrong because he doesn't say when the center was opened.

80. (C)

The man says *This is the weather report for this evening Thursday 10th June,* so the talk is a weather report, which you are most likely to hear on the television or the radio. The answer must be (C).

81. (B)

The man says *Across the east coast further wintry showers will push in.* He also says *Showers will continue across the east coast* and *Additional hail storms are also possible in the east coast.* This means the forecast predicts wet weather in the east for the next four days, so (B) is the best answer. He talks about fog and frost and drizzle in the west, which is not as wet as the showers mentioned for the east. This means (A) is incorrect. He talks about *fog* in central areas, so (C) is also wrong. (D) is not possible because he only mentions rain in the south once.

82. (D)

The man says *Patchy fog and frost will form for some,* so (A) and (C) are wrong. (B) is incorrect because *showers* means *heavy rain.* This means (D) is the only possible answer.

83. (B)

The woman says *we hope that by the end of the day you will have realized that Eastern University is the right place,* which means she's addressing a group of people who are interested in going to university. *Undergraduates* are already studying in a university, so (**A**) is incorrect. The same applies to (**C**) and (**D**). *High school students* is the only group who will not have gone to university yet, so (**B**) is the correct answer.

84. (C)

The woman says *The rest of the schedule remains unchanged with the exception of lunch, which will now be served in the main restaurant,* so (**C**) is the only possible answer. The place and the name of the speaker for the opening speech are not mentioned, so (**A**) is incorrect. The same applies to (**B**). (**D**) is also wrong because she says *This means that you will get an extra fifteen minutes during the question and answer sessions with our vocational psychologists.*

85. (B)

The woman says *I'd like to go over some changes to the schedule,* so (**A**) is wrong. (**C**) is also incorrect because she says *with the exception of lunch, which will now be served.* She also says *due to the weather forecast,* so (**D**) is not possible either. This means (**B**) is the only possible answer.

86. (B)

(**B**) is the only possible answer because the man says *La Bella Express will be the fast food version of the successful chain.* (**A**) is wrong because it's the name of an established chain of restaurants. (**C**) and (**D**) are types of food to be served in the new restaurant.

87. (C)

The man says *La Bella Express will be the fast food version of the successful chain,* so (**C**) is the correct answer. He doesn't say anything about *Traditional food,* so (**A**) is not possible. (**B**) is also incorrect because there's no mention of an *American food.* The man doesn't say anything about *frozen food,* so (**D**) is wrong.

88. (D)

The man says *the usual quality that has made La Bella Vita the most successful restaurant chain in America,* so (**D**) is the correct alternative. He doesn't talk about

prices, so (**A**) and (**B**) are both incorrect. He doesn't use the adjective *traditional* to describe the chain, so (**D**) is also wrong.

89. (A)

The woman says *All our contracts include a full tank which can be refilled at no further expense, comprehensive insurance, road assistance 24/7 service, and a satnav,* so (**A**) is the correct answer. She doesn't say anything about *student discounts,* so (**B**) and (**C**) are wrong. She says *a full tank which you don't have to refill,* do (**D**) is also incorrect.

90. (C)

The woman says *You can buy the car of your dreams at one of our 12 mega stores,* so (**C**) is the right answer. They have 100 stores but not all of them sell cars, so (**A**) is wrong. (**B**) and (**D**) are incorrect because she says *road assistance 24/7 service.*

91. (D)

The woman says *All our used cars have low mileage, impeccable conditions, and a 12-month warranty,* so options (**A**), (**B**) and (**C**) are all incorrect. This means (**D**) is the only possible answer.

92. (C)

The woman says *from Jacson Atlanta International Airport to Frankfurt,* so *Frankfurt* is the final destination. This means (**C**) is the correct alternative.

93. (A)

The woman says *Your flight is now ready for boarding from gate 27,* so (**A**) is the correct answer. She doesn't mention a *change,* so (**B**) is wrong. (**C**) is also incorrect because she says *Passengers with small children or requiring special assistance may go to the head of the line.* There's no mention of a *delay,* so (**D**) is not possible either.

94. (C)

The woman says *Passengers with small children or requiring special assistance may go to the head of the line,* so (**C**) is the best answer. She doesn't say anything about *pregnant women, the elderly* or a *priority pass,* so alternatives (**A**), (**B**) and (**D**) are all incorrect.

95. (B)

The recording says *08.00 a.m. to 5.00 p.m. on Tuesdays and Thursdays,* so (B) is the correct answer. The clinic closes at 7 on Mondays and Wednesdays, so (A) is wrong. It closes at 3 on Fridays and Saturdays, so (C) is also incorrect. (D) is not possible because the recording doesn't mention *4.00 p.m.*

96. (A)

The only day not mentioned when the man talks about the opening times is *Sunday,* so (A) is the best possible answer. The recording talks about *Saturday,* so (B) and (C) are incorrect. (D) is not possible because he says *our clinic is open from 08.00 a.m. to 7.00 p.m. on Mondays and Wednesdays.*

97. (C)

(C) is the right option because the man says *If you wish to make an appointment, please call again during our regular opening hours. You can also book an appointment online by visiting our website at www.happypets.com, or by downloading our app.* (A) and (B) are wrong because you can book an appointment over the phone. (D) is not possible because they take online bookings.

98. (D)

She says *I just don't get it. Why would someone leave a box containing an expensive electronic device behind the garbage can in my front garden?* In disbelief, so (D) is the best answer. She has received her order, so (A) and (B) are not possible. (C) is wrong because she says *The box was left outside the house by your courier service and I'm afraid the product has been damaged.*

99. (B)

She says *I paid for the item with Paypoint and the amount has already been to charged to my account,* so (B) is the correct alternative. (A) is wrong because she says *If I don't hear back from you within a couple of hours, I will ask Paypoint for a refund,* which means she hasn't asked for a refund yet. (C) is incorrect because she says *I paid for the item with Paypoint.* She doesn't say anything about a *discount,* so (D) is not possible either.

100. (A)

(A) is the right answer because her email in the system information is different to then one she says in the recording. The rest of the information matches what is said in the recording, so alternatives (B), (C) and (D) are incorrect.

Reading

Part V—Incomplete Sentences

101. (C)

The sentence says *any of the numbers* so a negative context is required. This means (C) is the only possible answer. (A), (B), and (D) do not infer a negative meaning, so they're not possible.

102. (C)

The sentence requires a verb which means *trying to find something within,* so (C) is the only possible answer. (A) has a similar meaning, but we would need *looking in* to complete the sentence. To *seek* the rooms would mean to look for the rooms, but the sentence means they were looking *in* the rooms. (D) is also wrong because it means *discovering.*

103. (A)

The sentence requires an *adverb* which means *directly,* so (A) is the correct alternative. (B) is not possible because it is an *adjective.* (C) is incorrect because it is a *preposition.* When (D) is used as an adverb it means *in company with others,* so it is also wrong.

104. (D)

(D) is the only possible answer because the sentence needs an *infinitive with to* form. (A) is wrong because it is in the *3rd person singular present form.* (B) is not possible because even though it is in the *infinitive,* it does not carry the preposition *to.* (C) is also wrong because it is in the *gerund.*

105. (B)

The sentence needs an adjective which means *expected at a certain time,* so (B) is the correct answer. (A) and

(D) aren't *adjectives,* so they're both incorrect. (C) is wrong because it means *probable.*

106. (A)

The sentence needs a *noun* which means *a particular branch of commercial activity,* so (A) is the correct answer. (B) and (D) are both *adjectives,* so they're not possible. (C) is wrong because it means *the development of industries.*

107. (C)

The sentence requires a verb in the *past passive form,* so (C) is the only possible option. (A) and (D) are wrong because they're *active* sentences. (B) is incorrect because it's in the *present.*

108. (C)

The sentence requires an adverb which means *it is fortunate that,* so (C) is the correct option. (A) is wrong because it has the opposite meaning. (B) and (D) are *adverbs of frequency,* so they're both incorrect.

109. (A)

Adverbs of frequency usually come before the *main verb,* so (A) is the correct answer. (B) is wrong because the *adverb* is before a *preposition,* not the *main verb.* (C) is also incorrect because the *adverb* is *after the main verb.* (D) is not possible because when the noun *ability* is followed by a verb, the verb is in the *infinitive with to* form.

110. (A)

The gap needs an *adjective* which means *showing or feeling pleasure and satisfaction,* so (A) is the only possible answer. (B) and (C) are wrong because they aren't adjectives. (D) is also incorrect because even though it is an adjective, it means *satisfying.*

111. (A)

The gap requires an *adjective* which means *planning the future with imagination or wisdom,* so (A) is the correct answer. (B) and (D) are incorrect because they aren't *adjectives.* (C) is an adjective but it means *relating to sight.*

112. (D)

The sentence needs a noun which means *not having enough of something,* so (D) is the correct alternative. (A) and (C) are incorrect because they aren't *nouns.* (B) is wrong because it means *an unattractive or unsatisfactory feature.*

113. (C)

The shareholders would not be happy about share prices falling, so the answer must be a word that describes a negative emotion. (C) must be the correct answer. (D) is a positive word, (A) means saying something, and (B) means to be a bad person, but we need a word that means *unhappiness.*

114. (C)

The sentence needs an *adjective* which means *influenced by an external factor,* so (C) is the correct option. (A) and (B) are wrong because they're not *adjectives.* (D) is an adjective, but it is incorrect because it means *successful in producing a desired result.*

115. (D)

The gap needs a verb in the *past participle form* to form a *passive* structure. This means (D) is the correct answer. (A) and (B) are wrong because they are *not in the past passive form.* (C) is incorrect because it doesn't have the preposition *to.*

116. (B)

The sentence needs an *adjective* which means *having knowledge or perception of a situation,* so (B) is the correct option. (A) does not collocate with *of,* so it is incorrect. (C) and (D) are wrong because they are verbs in the *past participle* form.

117. (A)

The sentence needs a *phrasal verb* which means *convert investments into money,* so (A) is the correct answer. (B) means *pay money into a bank account,* so it's wrong. (C) means *get upset,* so it is also incorrect. (D) is not possible because it means *set down in a specific place.*

118. (B)

The gap needs a verb in the *past simple form* which means *drop down at high speed*, so **(B)** is the only possible answer. **(A)** is wrong because it means *become better.* **(C)** and **(D)** are not possible because they are in the *infinitive form.*

119. (D)

(D) is the only possible answer because the sentence requires a verb in the *past perfect simple.* The other alternatives are wrong because **(A)** is in the *present perfect simple,* **(B)** in *present perfect continuous,* and **(C)** is *used to + infinitive* to talk about routines.

120. (A)

The sentence needs a verb in the *future simple form,* so **(A)** is the correct answer. **(B)** is wrong because it is *future perfect.* **(C)** is *future continuous,* so it is also incorrect. **(D)** is not possible because it is in the *infinitive form.*

121. (A)

The gap needs a noun which means *emotional strain,* so **(A)** is the correct answer. **(B)** and **(C)** are incorrect because they are *not nouns.* **(D)** is wrong because it means *stretched tight or rigid.*

122. (B)

The sentence needs a conjunction which means *despite the fact that,* so **(B)** is the correct answer. **(A)** is wrong because it is usually *followed by a comma.* **(C)** and **(D)** should be *followed by a noun,* and not a clause. This means they are both incorrect.

123. (B)

The structure *get used to + gerund* is required in this sentence, so **(B)** is the correct answer. **(A)** is wrong because it is the *infinitive.* **(C)** and **(D)** are incorrect because *get used* is usually followed by *to.*

124. (D)

The gap needs a noun which means *a decision on an issue of fact in a civil or criminal case,* so **(D)** is the

correct answer. **(A)** means *the process of establishing the truth,* so it's wrong. **(B)** is incorrect because it means *lush green vegetation.* **(C)** means *accuracy,* so it isn't possible either.

125. (A)

(B) is wrong because *obsession* can't be followed by *to.* The same applies to **(C)**. **(D)** is wrong because *dedication* does not collocate with *detail.* This means **(A)** is the only possible answer.

126. (C)

The gap needs a conjunction which means *in place of,* so **(C)** is the correct option. **(A)** is incorrect because it means *except for.* **(B)** and **(D)** are wrong because they mean *in addition.*

127. (C)

The verb *regret* is usually followed by *infinitive with to* when used to express *apology for* or *sadness over something.* This means **(C)** is the only possible option. **(A)** is wrong because it is in the *gerund.* **(B)** is incorrect because it is in the *infinitive,* but *without to.* **(D)** is not possible because it is in the *past simple form.*

128. (D)

The only option that can be followed by the preposition *on* is **(D)**. **(A)** is usually followed by *in.* **(B)** can be followed by *to* or *for.* **(C)** is usually followed by *to.*

129. (B)

The gap needs a pronoun which means *not any,* so **(B)** is the correct answer. **(A)** is wrong because it does not contain *not.* **(C)** should be followed by an uncountable noun, so it is also incorrect. **(D)** is not possible because it is not commonly followed by *to.*

130. (A)

The noun *notifications* is commonly followed by the preposition *on,* so **(A)** is the correct answer. **(B)**, **(C)**, and **(D)** do not collocate with *notifications,* so these options are all incorrect.

Part VI—Text Completion

131. (C)

The gap needs a *past participle* which means *thought to be*, so **(C)** is the best answer. **(A), (B),** and **(D)** are usually followed by the conjunction *as,* so these options are incorrect.

132. (A)

The sentence needs an adverb which expresses *uncertainty,* so **(A)** is the only possible answer. **(B)** and **(C)** are wrong because they express *contrast.* **(D)** is incorrect because it means *except if.*

133. (B)

The sentence needs a preposition which *identifies the agent performing the action,* so **(B)** is the correct answer. **(A)** is wrong because it means *accompanied by.* **(C)** and **(D)** collocate with the noun attitude, but they mean *directed at.*

134. (D)

The sentence requires a *comparative adverb,* so **(D)** is the only possible answer.

135. (A)

The gap needs an adjective which means *awaiting settlement,* so **(A)** is the only possible answer. **(B)** is wrong because it means *not able to be found.* **(C)** is incorrect because it is *not an adjective.* **(D)** is wrong because it is the *past participle* of the verb *leave.*

136. (B)

The text does not mention a meeting, so **(A)** is incorrect. **(C)** is wrong because the text does not talk about any positions. The text does not say whether the reader is a member of the company's staff, so **(D)** is not possible either. This means **(B)** is the only possible answer.

137. (B)

The gap needs a *noun* which means *the cost required for something,* so **(B)** is the correct alternative. **(A)** is incorrect because it means *money received.* **(C)** is also wrong because it means *an order to a bank to pay a stated amount.* **(D)** is not possible as it means *a financial gain.*

138. (A)

The gap needs to be completed with *could,* as the sentence is asking Elisabeta to complete a task. **(A)** is correct.

139. (D)

The sentence needs an *idiom* which means *think differently and creatively,* so **(D)** is the correct alternative. **(A)** is incorrect because it is *not an idiom.* **(B)** means *think aloud,* so it is also wrong. **(C)** is not possible because it means *to have a very high regard for.*

140. (A)

The sentence requires a verb which means *make certain that,* so **(A)** is the correct option. **(B)** is wrong because it means *let someone do something.* **(C)** means *strengthen,* so it is also incorrect. **(D)** is not possible as it means *say something to remove doubts.*

141. (C)

The gap needs a phrase which means *the ability to solve problems.* Options **(A), (B),** and **(D)** do not collocate. This means **(C)** is the only possible answer.

142. (A)

The gap needs a noun which means *a sum of money charged by a college or university,* so **(A)** is the correct alternative. **(B)** is *the money paid for a journey on public transport,* so it's wrong. **(C)** is also incorrect because it means *the act of spending funds.* **(D)** is not possible as it means *a grant to support a student's education.*

143. (B)

The adjective *responsible* does not collocate with **(C)** or **(D)**, so these alternative are wrong. *Responsible to* means *having to report to* and should be followed by a person or institution, so **(A)** is also incorrect. This means **(B)** is the only possible answer.

144. (D)

The missing word must connect the sentence with the previous one. This sentence explains that landlords must *also* complete further tasks, so the best option is *in addition*, as this shows that there is a further step required. (D) is correct.

145. (B)

The gap needs a conjunction which means *except if*, so (B) is the correct answer. (A) is wrong because *if* is the opposite of *unless*. (C) is not possible because it means *on condition that*. (D) is incorrect because it means *as a provision against something happening*.

146. (C)

(A) is commonly used in formal letters or emails, so it is incorrect. (B) mentions a *line manager* which is not related to a notice addressing the residents of a building, so it is also wrong. (D) is not possible because it should be used at the beginning of a formal letter or email. This means (C) is the only possible answer.

Part VII—Reading Comprehension

147. (B)

Pensioner means *a person who receives the retirement pension,* so this means the person is over 60 and (B) is the correct answer. (A) is the amount to be paid by *adults,* so it is incorrect. (C) is wrong because it is the surcharge for an extra zone for passengers over 60, but *not the fare.* (D) is the surcharge paid by adults.

148. (C)

Unlimited travel for under 18s is $4.00. Because the question says *zones A and B,* a surcharge of $1.50 is added to the fare. This means (C) is the correct answer. (A) is the fare for a day ticket for *one zone only,* so it is wrong. (B) is incorrect because it is only the surcharge and does not include the fare. The surcharge of $0.75 is for a *one way ticket,* so (D) is not possible either.

149. (C)

The sentence says *the fares above* so it should be placed under the fares. This means (C) is the only possible answer. The other alternatives are wrong because the sentence cannot be placed above the fares (A), next to one of the ticket types (B), or under the surcharges (D).

150. (C)

The text says *guaranteed for a decade,* so (C) is the correct answer. The text does not mention *six months* or *five years,* so (A) and (B) are impossible. (D) is incorrect because *90 days* is the period customers have to register their products.

151. (D)

The text says *The warranty does not cover equipment misuse, intentional damage, product modification, 'jailbreaking', abuse or negligence,* so alternatives (A), (B), and (C) are incorrect. This means (D) is the only possible answer.

152. (D)

The text says *Any and all claims made this warranty must be accompanied by your unique registration number,* so (D) is the right answer. The text only mentions the user's manual to help customers make better use of their smart TVs, so (A) is incorrect. (B) and (C) are not possible because they are not mentioned in the text.

153. (A)

The sentence is better placed at the beginning of the text to be used as an *introduction* before more serious matters like the warranty are addressed. This means (A) is the best answer. (B) and (C) are in the middle of the terms and conditions for the warranty so they are not possible. (D) is also incorrect because it comes near the end, before the concluding sentence.

154. (D)

Jess says *Need to share with Claudia so she can give us the green light,* this means that Claudia needs to say that the work is okay, or authorize it, before it can move on to the next stage. (D) is correct.

155. (B)

Samuel says *I'll get Frederica to give me a hand,* so he's going to ask a colleague to help him. (A) is the correct answer.

156. (D)

The text says *"Cloud computing" is now everywhere and a lot of people have no idea what the whole thing is all about*, so (D) is the correct answer. *Millennials* are the generation born around the year 2000, so it is not related to 1000 years and (A) is incorrect. The text says *"Cloud computing" is now everywhere*, so (B) is also wrong. (C) is not possible because the text does not say how difficult it is to understand this technology.

157. (B)

The text says *In the simplest terms, the "cloud" is the internet*, so (B) is the correct option. There's no mention of *weather* or *Britain*, so (A) is incorrect. The text mentions computers but no *labs*, so (C) is not possible. (D) is also wrong because the text does not say anything about *old computers*.

158. (B)

The text says *Cloud computing" is now everywhere*, so (A) is wrong. It also says *by saving your files on the internet you are able to access them from any computer anywhere in the world*, so (C) is not possible either. (D) is incorrect because the text says *one thing is for sure: it's here to stay*. This means (B) is the only possible answer.

159. (C)

The sentence says *Cloud computing also prevents people from losing their work* so the reader is expected to already knows some information about *cloud computing*. This means the sentence cannot be placed at the beginning of the text and (A) is incorrect. (B) is wrong because the sentence talks about the benefits of *cloud computing* which are only mentioned in the 3rd paragraph. (D) is not possible because it would require a closing sentence. This means (C) is the only possible answer.

160. (A)

The text says *To provide employees with the opportunity to choose their own professional development path*, so (A) is the correct answer. The text does not mention a *promotion*, so (B) is incorrect. (C) is also wrong because the text doesn't talk about *profits*. Also, the text doesn't say anything about *working from home*, so (D) is not possible.

161. (B)

The text says *the employee and manager should come to an agreement since HR will only authorize programs which are signed by both the employee and their direct supervisor*, so (B) is the correct answer. Because the text says *the employee and manager*, alternatives (A), (C), and (D) are all incorrect.

162. (C)

The text says *Management is responsible for conducting impartial needs analysis during performance appraisals of all staff*, so (A) is incorrect. (B) is wrong because the text says *Needs analysis procedures and forms will be distributed by HR*. (D) is not possible because the text says *HR will only authorize programs*. This means (C) is the only possible answer.

163. (A)

The text says White North Office Goods *339 Lakeside Drive Orlando, FL 32803*, so (A) is the correct alternative. *Amsterdam Avenue, New York* is the billing address so (B) and (C) are incorrect. *Long Island City* is the goods will be shipped to, so (D) is not possible either.

164. (C)

The total amount for *PrintJet HB4500 BW* is *$38.50*, so (C) is the correct option. (A) is the total amount for *A4 Plastic Wallets*, so this option is incorrect. (B) is the *unit price* for *PrintJet HB4500 BW*, so this alternative is also wrong. (D) is not possible because it's the total amount for *Cash box 8" Silver.*

165. (B)

The text says Invoice Date: *23/10/19* and *Payment is due within 7 days*, so (B) is the correct answer. (A) is wrong because it's the invoice date. The year is *2019*, so (C) is incorrect. (D) is not possible because the date can be found in the invoice as explained above.

166. (A)

The text says *If you cancel your pre-paid reservation within 24 hours of placing the booking, a full refund will be issued*, so (A) is the correct answer. (B) is wrong because the text says *If you cancel your reservation more than 24 hours from time of making the booking, no refund will be made.* There is no mention of a *license*, so (**C**) is not possible. (**D**) is also incorrect because the text says *All drivers must be aged 21 or over.*

167. (C)

(**C**) is the right answer because the text says *Drivers of vehicle categories Prestige, Luxury and Elite must be aged 28 or over.* (**A**) and (**B**) are wrong because the text says *Drivers aged 21-24 may only rent cars up to Standard category.* The text says *28 or over*, so (**D**) is also incorrect.

168. (D)

The text says *If you cancel your pre-paid reservation within 24 hours of placing the booking, a full refund will be issued,* so (**A**) is not possible. (**B**) is wrong because the text says *All vehicles are supplied with a full tank of fuel.* (**C**) is also incorrect because the text says *Payment is required by credit card or debit card.* This means (**D**) is the only possible answer.

169. (C)

Taxis are represented by the *black bars* and Vroom black cars are *dark gray.* The only city in which the black bar is higher than the dark gray bar is Los Angeles, so (**C**) is the correct answer. (**A**) and (**B**) are wrong because the dark gray bar is higher in those cities. Both bars are at the same height in Chicago, so (**D**) is also incorrect.

170. (A)

Taxi fares are represented by the black bars. A 3-mile taxi ride in Chicago costs just over $25, so (**A**) is the correct answer.

171. (A)

Taxis are represented by the black bars. The only city where the black bar is under the $20 line is Dallas, so (**A**) is the correct answer. The black bar is above the $20 line in every other city, so alternatives (**B**), (**C**) and (**D**) are incorrect.

172. (D)

The table shows how to fix various problems in a particular TV. The answer must be (**D**). (**A**) is incorrect, as

only one model of television is discussed. (**B**) is incorrect, as the table shows people how to fix general issues, it is not reporting issues on a specific TV. (**C**) is incorrect, as there is no mention of 'upgrading' in the table.

173. (A)

Bluetooth is a type of wireless technology, so (**B**) is incorrect. (**C**) is also wrong because the text says *Wi-Fi disconnected.* (**D**) is not possible because there is no mention of wireless technology in *no image.* This also means (**A**) is the right answer.

174. (D)

The text says *3.5" QQVGA display,* so (**A**) is wrong. (**B**) is not possible because the text says *3.5" QQVGA display.* (**C**) is also incorrect because the text says *Up to 22 hours talk time and 6 weeks on standby.* This means (**D**) is the only possible answer.

175. (C)

The text says *FM Radio built-in (no need for apps),* so (**C**) is the correct answer. (**A**) is wrong because the ad says *Modern, ergonomic design.* (**B**) is not possible because the text says *3.5" QQVGA display.* (**D**) is also incorrect because the text doesn't mention that text messages are free with the phone.

176. (A)

The expression *only a matter of time* means *inevitable,* so (**A**) is the correct answer. Options (**B**), (**C**), and (**D**) are incorrect because they are not related to the expression.

177. (C)

(**C**) is the correct answer because Tom says *She's been away from home for far too long.* There's nothing saying whether Luana likes or dislikes her job, so (**A**) is incorrect. Neither text mentions her old job, so (**B**) is not possible. (**D**) is also wrong because the texts don't say anything about a professional challenge.

178. (C)

The email says *Please accept this as notification that I am leaving my position,* so (**C**) is the correct answer. Luana does not ask for any device, so (**A**) is not possible. (**B**) is wrong because the email says *notification that I am leaving my position.* **(D)** is also incorrect because there's no mention of a *promotion.*

179. (C)

This is not an opening sentence, so **(A)** is incorrect. **(B)** is wrong because the second paragraph talks about her experience with ETB, and the sentence should come after that. It is not common to place a sentence after *Sincerely,* so **(D)** is not possible either. This means **(C)** is the only possible answer.

180. (D)

The text says *Please accept this as notification that I am leaving my position,* so **(A)** is incorrect. **(B)** is wrong because Jean says *it was only a matter of time.* **(C)** is not possible because the email says *all the opportunities I have been given at ETB.* This means **(D)** is the only possible answer.

181. (C)

The text says *Grants & Budget Robin Giroud,* so **(C)** is the correct answer. **(A)** is wrong because the first text says *Welcome Cocktail Lucas Pietr.* **(B)** is not possible because the agenda says *Past Winners Mustafa Ilker.* **(D)** is also incorrect because the first text says *Presentation of Awards João Bezerra.*

182. (A)

(A) is the right answer because the email says *We would like to invite you to present our Past Winners retrospective.* The awards will be presented by *Mr Bezerra,* so **(B)** is wrong. **(C)** is not possible because the email says *invite you to present.* **(D)** is also incorrect because the text says *present our Past Winners retrospective.*

183. (A)

The email says *the most traditional,* so **(A)** is the correct answer. **(B)** is not possible because neither text talks about *changes.* **(C)** is also wrong because the email says *It would be an honor to have a successful entrepreneur two-time winner of the awards as our speaker.* **(D)** is incorrect because the email says *to have a successful entrepreneur.*

184. (D)

The email says *Natasha Akinfeev, who stunned the world with her robot vacuum cleaner working model*

when she was only 17 years old, so **(D)** is the correct answer. The text does not say anything about the past of *Lucas Pietr, Robin Giroud,* or *João Bezerra.* This means alternatives **(A), (B),** and **(C)** are wrong.

185. (B)

The email says *we would like to offer you an all paid trip to visit her company's headquarters in Moscow,* so **(B)** is the correct option. IIA 2018 is in Rio, so **(A)** and **(D)** are incorrect. **(C)** is wrong because there's no mention of *Mr Bezerra's headquarters* in either text.

186. (A)

Inbox is the folder in which people receive their emails, so **(A)** is the correct answer. *Inbox* is not a physical box, so **(B)** is wrong. Sommy means *look at your emails,* not *refresh your browser* or go to the post office.

187. (B)

The text on the email says *To: zhaomin@mailme.com,* so **(B)** is the correct answer. There isn't a copy of the proposal in any of the texts, so **(A)** is not possible. The original email was primarily sent by *info@citycouncil.com,* so **(C)** is also wrong. **(D)** is incorrect because even though one of the texts is an article, there isn't a link to it in the email.

188. (B)

In the text chain, Robert says *we've got so much work to do,* meaning Sommy and Robert work together. The email shows that they also work with Min Zhao, and the article explains that Min Zhao works at ModCit designs. The answer is **(B)**.

189. (C)

The text says *includes a soccer pitch, water park, and restaurants,* so alternatives **(A), (B),** and **(D)** are not possible. This means **(C)** is the correct answer.

190. (A)

The sentence follows the structure of a headline, so **(A)** is the best answer. The use of the infinitive *to undergo* indicates the sentence is a headline and headlines are the *first lines of an article.* This means alternatives **(B), (C),** and **(D)** are all incorrect.

191. (B)

Luiz texts *we're thinking of getting some tablets for the meeting room. Any ideas?* So the speakers are discussing buying new equipment. (**B**) is correct.

192. (C)

The invoice tells us that Luiz spent $750 on each tablet, looking at the advertisement, the price of an Npad Pro with 200GB is $750, so the answer must be (**C**).

193. (B)

The ad says *offers far more power than any office computers,* so (**A**) is incorrect. (**C**) is not possible because the ad says *anywhere you want it to be.* (**D**) is also wrong because the ad says *office computers* twice. This means (**B**) is the only possible answer.

194. (D)

The invoice says *Luiz Pereyra Winton Island Bank,* so (**D**) is the right option. (**A**) is wrong because *Npad Pro* is the brand of the tablets purchased by Mr Pereyra's company. *TekPak Store* is the store where Mr Pereyra's company bought the tablets, so (**B**) is not possible. (**C**) is also wrong because *Bellevue Square* is the address for the store.

195. (B)

(**C**) is the unit price of each tablet, so it's incorrect. (**A**) is the tax amount paid for each unit, so it's also wrong. (**D**) is the total amount for 12 tablets without tax, so this alternative isn't possible either. This means (**B**) is the only possible answer.

196. (A)

This sentence is commonly used at the beginning of an email, so (**A**) is the correct answer. This sentence should not be used in the middle of the text, so (**B**) is incorrect. (**C**) would require a closing sentence, so this option is also wrong. (**D**) is not possible because *Regards* is not commonly followed by anything but the name of the sender.

197. (B)

The email addressed to Frank says *we have all agreed that you are the best person to head this next phase of the project,* so (**B**) is the correct answer. Mr Kluivert sent the email, so (**A**) is not possible. (**C**) is incorrect because the notice says *Positions will be available internally for the first four weeks. Then the remaining positions will be posted on our careers webpage and sent to our partner recruitment agencies.* (**D**) is also wrong because *the government* is not mentioned in any of the texts.

198. (A)

The article says *plans to build the new plant on a 65-hectare site on what is predominantly former agricultural land,* so (**A**) is the correct answer. The article does say *65-hectare site* but it doesn't say it's *near the sea,* so (**B**) is incorrect. (**C**) is wrong because none of the texts say anything about the *industrial district in Maui.* There's no mention of *profits,* so alternative (**D**) isn't possible either.

199. (C)

The notice says Positions Available: 200, so (**C**) is the correct alternative. The article says *65-hectare,* so (**A**) is not possible. (**B**) is incorrect because *2500* is the estimate number of jobs to be generated in the area according to the article. *Four* is the number of weeks jobs will be available internally, so (**D**) is also wrong.

200. (B)

The notice says *Positions will be available internally for the first four weeks,* so (**B**) is the correct option. None of the texts talk about *locals* being offered positions first, so (**A**) is not possible. (**C**) is wrong because the third text says *Then the remaining positions will be posted on our careers webpage and sent to our partner recruitment agencies. HR professionals* are not mentioned in any of the texts, so (**D**) is also incorrect.

PRACTICE TEST 3 ANSWER KEY

Part I	Part II	Part III	Part IV	Part V	Part VI	Part VII
1. A	7. A	32. B	71. A	101. B	131. A	147. A
2. B	8. B	33. C	72. C	102. A	132. B	148. B
3. C	9. A	34. C	73. A	103. C	133. B	149. B
4. D	10. C	35. A	74. A	104. A	134. A	150. A
5. A	11. A	36. B	75. D	105. C	135. D	151. A
6. B	12. C	37. C	76. B	106. C	136. C	152. C
	13. A	38. C	77. C	107. A	137. D	153. D
	14. B	39. A	78. B	108. B	138. B	154. D
	15. C	40. A	79. B	109. A	139. A	155. A
	16. A	41. C	80. C	110. B	140. D	156. A
	17. B	42. A	81. D	111. A	141. B	157. C
	18. A	43. B	82. C	112. A	142. C	158. B
	19. A	44. B	83. B	113. B	143. B	159. C
	20. C	45. C	84. B	114. D	144. A	160. B
	21. A	46. A	85. A	115. B	145. C	161. A
	22. A	47. B	86. D	116. C	146. B	162. A
	23. B	48. C	87. A	117. D		163. A
	24. C	49. A	88. C	118. C		164. B
	25. B	50. D	89. A	119. A		165. A
	26. A	51. D	90. D	120. C		166. C
	27. A	52. C	91. C	121. B		167. D
	28. A	53. D	92. B	122. A		168. A
	29. C	54. C	93. B	123. D		169. A
	30. B	55. B	94. D	124. B		170. D
	31. C	56. B	95. B	125. C		171. B
		57. A	96. D	126. A		172. B
		58. A	97. D	127. C		173. C
		59. B	98. B	128. B		174. A
		60. D	99. C	129. C		175. A
		61. B	100. A	130. B		176. C
		62. B				177. B
		63. D				178. C
		64. A				179. C
		65. B				180. B
		66. C				181. D
		67. A				182. A
		68. B				183. C
		69. B				184. A
		70. B				185. B
						186. B
						187. C
						188. A
						189. D
						190. A
						191. B
						192. C
						193. B
						194. A
						195. D
						196. C
						197. D
						198. A
						199. A
						200. C

PRACTICE TEST 3
Part I—Photographs

1. (A)

The photograph shows a plane being loaded with sacks of cargo. **(A)** correctly describes the photograph. The plane is not ready to take off **(B)**, as cargo is still being loaded. The *sacs of cargo* are full, there are no *passenger's bags* **(C)** or *suitcases* **(D)** in the photograph.

2. (B)

The photograph shows a cleaner moping the floor clean. **(B)** correctly describes the photograph, the man is standing on the right-hand side of the trolley. The room is being *cleaned* but it is not *dirty* **(A)**. The sign is *next to* the trolley, not *in* it **(C)**. The man is alone **(D)**.

3. (C)

The photograph shows a man using gps maps on his cell phone. **(C)** correctly describes the photograph; he is *finding directions*. He is in a car, but he is not *driving* or *learning to drive* **(A)**. He is using gps on his cell phone, not *tuning the radio* **(B)**. He is looking *at* his cell phone, not looking *for* his keys.

4. (D)

The photograph shows employees wrapping spools of thread with plastic. **(D)** correctly describes the photograph; they are *packing* the items. They are not *winding* the thread **(A)**. They are preparing the *items*, not *dinner* **(B)**. They are wrapping the *items*; they are not wrapping *gifts* **(C)**.

5. (A)

The photograph shows a woman waiting for a lift, pressing the button to indicate she wants to travel upwards. *She's going up* best describes the photograph. She's *currently waiting*, not *currently engaged*. She's *waiting for a lift*, not *leaving the building*. She's waiting for the *lift*, not a *secretary*.

6. (B)

The photograph shows a tray filled with entrées, or canapés. **(B)** best describes the photograph. The snacks are all on the tray, they have not *all been eaten*. The food is ready, but it is not *being used*. The food is placed on the tray, it is not *stacked*.

Part II—Question-Response

7. (A)

The question asks *when did* so the answer needs a *past time expression*. This means **(A)** is the correct answer. **(B)** is wrong because *wh- questions* should not be answered with a *yes* or *no*. **(C)** is incorrect because it's a *future time expression*.

8. (B)

The question asks *who* and the only answer to provide a *person* is **(B)**. **(A)** is wrong because it describes the meeting but doesn't say *who*. **(C)** is also incorrect because it answers *what time*.

9. (A)

The question asks *what are* and the only answer that talks about things in the plural is **(A)**. **(B)** is incorrect because it's in the *singular*. **(C)** is not possible because it answers *who*, not *what*.

10. (C)

(A) is incorrect because it says something has been done, it does not respond to an offer. **(B)** talks about taking *it*, but the question asks about taking *you*. This means **(C)** is the only possible answer.

11. (A)

The question asks for an opinion, and **(A)** is the only answer that addresses that (*I suppose we have to now*). **(B)** is wrong because the question does not talk about the *weather*. **(C)** is also incorrect the question doesn't ask *where*.

12. (C)

The question asks *who,* so **(C)** is the only possible answer. **(A)** is not possible because it talks about the project but doesn't say *who*. **(B)** is also wrong because the question is in the future and the answer is in the *present perfect*.

13. (A)

The question asks *when will*, so the answer needs a *future time expression*. This means (A) is the only possible answer. (B) and (C) are wrong because they are *past time expressions*.

14. (B)

The question asks about Mr. Wu. (A) is wrong because it talks about a place, not a person. (C) is not possible because it says *they*. This means (B) is the right answer.

15. (C)

The question tag is checking an opinion, so (C) is the only possible answer. (A) is wrong because it doesn't refer to the *workshop*. (B) is also incorrect because it talks about *arts*.

16. (A)

The question tag is checking a person's *past experience,* so (A) is the right answer. (B) is wrong because it's in the *future*. (C) is not possible because it's in the *present*.

17. (B)

(A) is wrong because the question asks *Do I* and can't be answered with *you are*. (C) is not possible because it talks about a state and the question is asking about an action. The question is verifying whether something needs to be done, so (B) is the only possible answer.

18. (A)

The uses a negative adjective (*bossy*) to describe a person's new manager. (A) is correct because it's the only answer to address that (*she can be difficult*). (B) is wrong because you can't be your manager's boss. (C) is incorrect because it answers a *where* question.

19. (A)

(B) is incorrect because you cannot answer a question with *have* using a short answer with *do*. (C) is not possible because it talks about *where* the computers are, not if they have been updated. This means (A) is the only possible answer.

20. (C)

(A) and (B) are wrong because you should not use a short answer with *will* or *doesn't* to answer a question using *has* as an auxiliary. This means (C) is the right answer.

21. (A)

(A) is the correct answer because it's the only alternative that replies to a *suggestion*. (B) confuses the meaning of break (to stop working) with broken (a damaged item). (C) responds to a *reason*, but the question is asking about a break.

22. (A)

The question asks information about a trip, so (A) is the correct answer. (B) is wrong because it answers *what time*. (C) is incorrect because it describes a person.

23. (B)

The question needs an answer with a *future time expression,* so (A) is wrong. (C) is wrong because *when* cannot be answered with *maybe*. This means (B) is the correct alternative.

24. (C)

The question asks *is this,* so (A) is incorrect. The same applies to (B) because you cannot use a short answer with *can't* to answer a question with *is*. Therefore, (C) is the only possible answer.

25. (B)

The question tag is verifying information and the only answer to give a confirmation is (B). (A) is not possible because it replies to *an offer* or *suggestion*. (C) is also wrong because it uses *she* (third person) to reply to a sentence in the second person.

26. (A)

The question asks about Leandro's job, so (A) is the correct answer. (B) is wrong because it doesn't talk about Leandro. (C) is wrong because it doesn't talk about his job.

27. (A)

The question asks *which* and (A) is the only alternative that chooses something (*the old one*). (B) is wrong because it answers *whose*. (**C**) is wrong because it answers a Yes/No question.

28. (A)

The question asks *why*. (**B**) I wrong because it answers *where*. (**C**) is also incorrect because it answers *whose*. This means (**A**) is the right answer.

29. (C)

The question *shouldn't we* is asking whether she needs help or not. The only option to address that is (**C**) (*Perhaps*). (**A**) is not possible because it talks about food. (**B**) is wrong because even though it uses the word *situation*, it doesn't say anything about *her*.

30. (B)

(**A**) is wrong because the fact that the printer is new has nothing to do with the printer not having paper. (**C**) does not talk about the printer, so it's not possible. This means (**B**) is the only possible answer, it correctly gives the place where more paper can be found.

31. (C)

The question asks *where* and (**A**) answers *what time*, so it's wrong. (**B**) is not possible because it answers *when*. This means (**C**) is the right answer

Part III—Short Conversations

32. (B)

The woman says *I'm looking for a tablet for my son who's going to high school*, so (**B**) is the correct answer. She doesn't say anything about her son's birthday, so (**A**) is incorrect. (**C**) is also wrong because the man says the tablet is *faster than most laptop computers*, but we don't even know if the woman has a laptop. (**D**) is not possible because she doesn't mention her job.

33. (C)

(**C**) is the correct answer because the woman's son says *It needs to be something that I can read pdfs on, do research with, and also use with a word processor to write essays.* (**A**) is wrong because the boy says *internet for research*, not *scientific research*. Nobody

says anything about career management, so (**C**) is not possible. (**D**) is also incorrect because they don't mention *audiovisual projects*.

34. (C)

The man says *you should take a look at the Tab Pro. It comes in a hard shell which can absorb impact,* so (**C**) is the right answer. (**A**) and (**B**) are wrong because the man says *Tab Pro*. (**D**) is not possible because the man says *It comes in a hard shell which can absorb impact*.

35. (A)

The woman says *IT has sent the link for the software update but I have no idea what to do here*, so (**A**) is the correct answer. She doesn't say anything about her computer *not working*, so (**B**) is not possible. (**C**) is wrong because the man says *he needs to take these boxes to the conference room right now*. (**D**) is also incorrect because she says *I'll catch up on my correspondence*.

36. (B)

Pablo says *if I don't take these boxes to the conference room right now, Mr. Wells is going to kill me.* This means he has a job to do and doesn't want to upset Mr. Wells. This doesn't mean Mr. Wells is a violent man, so (**A**) is not possible. He doesn't mention any punishment, so (**C**) and (**D**) are also incorrect. This means (**B**) is the only possible answer.

37. (C)

The woman says *I'll be in my office so just come in when you're free*, so (**C**) is the right answer. The woman has a problem with her computer but doesn't say anything about a *computer room*, so (**A**) is wrong. (**B**) is also incorrect because the man says *if I don't take these boxes to the conference room*. (**D**) is not possible because they don't mention a *conference room*.

38. (C)

(**C**) is the right answer because the man says *I'm calling for Mrs. Lee.* (**A**) is not possible because the man says *I sent her an email*, which means he has her email address. (**B**) is also incorrect because he says *an* email with some information about our management software. (**D**) is wrong because he says *she asked me to video call her this morning,* which means Mrs. Lee knows how to contact him.

39. (A)

To feel under the weather is an idiom which means *to feel sick.* The woman says *She was feeling a bit under the weather so she decided to stay at home and get better,* so (**A**) is the only possible answer. (**B**) and (**C**) are wrong because *to feel under the weather* is an idiom. Mrs. Lee might be sick but we don't know the reason, so (**D**) is also incorrect.

40. (A)

The woman says *If you want, I can book a video meeting for you,* so (**A**) is the correct alternative. The woman doesn't ask the man to call again, so (**B**) is not possible. The woman doesn't mention an email, so (**C**) is not possible either. (**D**) is wrong because she says *I can book a video meeting for you,* but doesn't say the man should try to contact Mrs. Lee for a video call by himself.

41. (C)

The man says *I don't want to be alone in a room with him waiting for you guys to come back.* so (**C**) is the correct answer. (**A**) is wrong because even though the man says *the Chinese clients are visiting us on Tuesday, so I'd like you to take them out for lunch,* that doesn't necessarily mean he's trying to avoid them. (**B**) is wrong because the man says *Mr. Jung is flying down here,* but doesn't say anything about picking him up at the airport. (**D**) is not possible because the man says *They're staying at the hotel just around the corner.*

42. (A)

Peter says *I'll book a table for 12.00,* so (**A**) is the right answer. (**B**) is wrong because the man says *as long as they're back here by 3.00.* The man also says *They arrive on Monday at 9.55 p.m. at Newark,* so (**C**) is incorrect. (**D**) is not possible because *10.05 p.m.* is not mentioned in the conversation.

43. (B)

The woman asks *Should I get a regular executive car or something a bit more special?* and the man replies *The*

usual is fine. This means (**B**) is the correct alternative. Taxis and limos are not mentioned, so (**A**) and (**C**) are incorrect. (**D**) is wrong because the man says *Rita, can you sort the airport transfer for me?,* which means she's not gong to pick them up herself.

44. (B)

The woman says *I haven't heard anything back from you guys. Is anyone from the finance department coming at all,* which implies that Andrew works in finances. This means (**B**) is the best possible answer. (**A**) is wrong because the woman introduces herself by saying *This is Sofia from HR.* (**C**) and (**D**) are also incorrect because she says *in one of our CPD sessions,* which means her team is organizing the CPD events.

45. (C)

(**C**) is the correct alternative because when Andrew says he and his team are not going to the lecture, Rita replies *I have to say I'm a bit disappointed, Andrew.* Rita doesn't talk about a new job, so (**A**) is not possible. Rita is organizing the event, so (**B**) is incorrect. (**D**) is wrong because when Andrew says *But Christmas is three days from tomorrow and everyone here has small kids, so I can't make them work long hours,* he's not including her.

46. (A)

Andrew says *But Christmas is three days from tomorrow and everyone here has small kids, so I can't make them work long hours,* so (**A**) is the correct answer. Andrew can't attend the lecture but he doesn't say he's not going because he doesn't want to. This means (**B**) is incorrect. He doesn't say anything about a party or a bonus, so (**C**) and (**D**) are impossible.

47. (B)

The man says *I'm planning to acquire some office desks from your store,* which means (**B**) is the most likely answer. (**A**) is wrong because he says *we have just replaced our reception laptops for tablets.* (**C**) is wrong because the laptops have already been replaced by tablets, so he probably doesn't need to buy any more tablets. (**D**) is wrong because he says *I'd like someone to talk to one of our architects who's here with me.*

48. (C)

The man says *we have just replaced our reception laptops for tablets. HR says they look better,* so (C) is the right answer. The man is still looking for new desks, so (A) is not possible. (B) is wrong because the computers have been replaced. The man doesn't say anything about floor boards, so (D) is not possible.

49. (A)

The man says *she went to have a look at the flooring options on the second floor,* so (A) is the correct alternative. (B), (C) and (D) are wrong because the man says *one of our architects who's here with me.*

50. (D)

Claire says *I was wondering if you had anything in your menu that would cater for his needs,* so (D) is the correct answer. She says *I have a reservation for five people at 1.00 p.m. tomorrow,* but doesn't mention a cancellation or a change. This means (A) and (B) are incorrect. (C) is also wrong because she says *I was wondering if you had anything in your menu,* but doesn't ask for a copy.

51. (D)

The name *Little Italy* is not mentioned, so (A) is incorrect. The man's name is *Pepe,* so (B) is not possible. The woman's name is *Claire Manning,* so (C) is also wrong. The man says *Here at Alfredo's we always try to cater for our customers' individual needs,* so (D) is the correct alternative.

52. (C)

Claire says *I have just realized that one of my guests is a vegan. That means he doesn't eat any meat or anything that comes from animals.* The only set menu that doesn't contain any meat is *Set Menu 3,* so (C) is the correct answer. (A) is wrong because of the *meatballs.* (B) is incorrect because of the *chicken risotto.* (D) is not possible because of the *ham bruschetta.*

53. (D)

The man says *I had a really busy day in the office* so (D) is correct. (A) is incorrect because the man does not say anything about his health. (B) is also incorrect because the man says *I had a really busy day in the office* so

he wasn't *out of the office.* (C) is incorrect because the woman is the one to mention the restaurant (*we're going to that new Italian restaurant downtown*), not the man.

54. (C)

The woman says *…you're more than welcome to come* and later she says *…to that new Italian restaurant downtown* so (C) is the correct answer. (B) is wrong because even though the man mentions the office *I had a really busy day in the office,* the woman doesn't say anything about it. (A) is also incorrect because although the woman uses the word *Saturday,* she talks about a restaurant, not a club. The woman says *Sally just got promoted and we're going out to celebrate on Saturday* but she doesn't say they'll be going to Sally's *new job.* (D) is not correct.

55. (B)

The man says *What time should I pick you up then?* so (B) is the correct answer. (A) is not possible since there is no indication that the man and woman work together and the woman is the person to mention a job *promotion: Sally just got promoted.* (C) is also incorrect because it is the woman who mentions the restaurant *we're going to that new Italian restaurant downtown.* (D) is wrong because the man offers to pick her up to go the restaurant, not to *take her to Italy.*

56. (B)

The man says *We got a call saying you have a problem with one of the photocopiers,* and the woman replies *Yes.* This means (B) is the correct answer. The woman says *It's one of the machines in our legal department,* so (A) is not possible. The woman says *take that elevator on your right,* so the elevator is working and (C) is the correct answer. The woman says *they can't get it to do double-sided copies anymore* when talking about one of the photocopiers, so (D) is wrong.

57. (A)

The woman says *take that elevator on your right,* so (A) is the right answer. (B) is wrong because she says *Our legal department is on the fifth floor.* The woman doesn't say anything about her position in the company, so (C) is not possible. (D) is incorrect because she says *I think it jammed* when talking about the photocopier, not the elevator.

58. (A)

The woman says *Our legal department is on the fifth floor. So if you take that elevator on your right, it'll take you straight to reception. There you can ask for Kurt,* so (A) is the correct alternative. She tells him to use the elevator, so (B) is not possible. (C) is also wrong because she tells the man to take the elevator in the right to get to the fifth floor. (D) is incorrect because she says *Elevator on the right, please. The one on the left only goes until the second floor.*

59. (B)

The man says *I told Marketing we'd be starting at 4.15.* (B) is correct. (A) refers to the current time, not the time of the meeting. (C) and (D) are incorrect, as the meeting is more than an hour away.

60. (D)

The man says *her qualifications are outstanding.* (D) is correct. (A) repeats *hour,* but this refers to the length of the interview will take, not how late the candidate is. (B) repeats *Anita,* but she already works for the company, in *marketing,* so she cannot be the candidate. The man says *she has the experience we're looking for* but he doesn't say that this experience is in marketing so (C) is also incorrect.

61. (B)

The woman says *I'll text Anita from Marketing and let her know we'll be starting the meeting 30 minutes later than scheduled.* She's delaying the meeting. (C) is correct. (A) and (D) are not mentioned in the conversation. (B) repeats *Anita,* who is not the candidate.

62. (B)

The woman says *both Mr. McAdams and Mrs. Chan were impressed with your skills and qualifications,* so (B) is the correct answer. Mrs. Chan interviewed the man, so (A) is not possible. (C) and (D) are wrong because the woman says *both Mr. McAdams and Mrs. Chan were impressed with your skills and qualifications.*

63. (D)

The man says *That's very good news. I'm flattered* after the woman says *Mr. McAdams and Mrs. Chan were*

impressed with your skills and qualifications. We think you're exactly what we're looking for and would like to offer you the position of Director of Operations so the man is flattered to be offered a job, (D) is correct. (A) is incorrect as he is being offered a job, not interviewing a candidate. (B) is incorrect as the background check is mentioned later, and (C) is incorrect as there is no mention that he is tired, and flattered is a positive emotion.

64. (A)

Margaret says *What I'm going to do now is send you an offer letter,* so (A) is the right answer. (B) is wrong because she says *You'll also be contacted by a company called Watchdog Security.* (C) is also incorrect because she says *as soon as we get everything back we can sort your contract,* which means she's not going to send it now. Margaret also says *You'll also be contacted by a company called Watchdog Security. They run all our background checks,* so (D) is not possible either.

65. (B)

The woman says *I'm still stuck in traffic and there's no way I can get to the station in the next hour,* so (B) is the right answer. (A) is wrong because she wants to take a coach, not a plane. If she wants to go to Barcelona, she can't be in Barcelona. This means (C) is not possible either. (D) is incorrect because she says *there's no way I can get to the station in the next hour.*

66. (C)

The man says *I can see that you have purchased a first-class ticket,* so (C) is the correct alternative. He doesn't say anything about the ticket being *non-refundable,* so (A) is incorrect. (B) is wrong because the man says *so we can change that for you with no incurring fees.* The woman ticket *is* a first-class ticket, so (D) is not possible either.

67. (A)

The man says *it's scheduled to arrive in Barcelona at 7.45 p.m.* and (A) is the correct answer. The only service that gets to Barcelona at 7.45 p.m. is the *BC2201.* This means alternatives, (B), (C) and (D) are all incorrect.

68. (B)

(B) is the correct answer because Pietra says *I heard Mr. Yun was furious when he left the building.* Pietra asks *Giovanna* why Mr. Yun was angry, so (**A**) is not possible. Giovanna doesn't know the answer so she asks Matthew. This means (**C**) is also incorrect. (**D**) is wrong because is the one who wats to know why Mr. Yun was furious.

69. (B)

Matthew says *Mr. Yun was told his budget for next year and he didn't like it a bit. He was hoping to launch a new multimedia campaign.* This means (**B**) is the right answer. Pietra says *We increased his budget by nearly 30% in the past three years,* so (**A**) and (**C**) are wrong. The campaign can't be implemented, not the budget. This means (**D**) is not possible either.

70. (B)

Giovanna says *Matthew's stressed because they told him he'll have to wait until next year to implement the new cloud system,* so (**B**) is the correct answer.

Part IV—Short Talks

71. (A)

The message says *Due to last night's blizzard, we will not be opening today. A blizzard* is a heavy snow storm, so (**A**) is the correct alternative. (**B**) is wrong because the message doesn't mention a holiday. The message says teachers can't make it to the building, but doesn't say anything about a strike. This means (**C**) is also incorrect. (**D**) is not possible because there's no mention of an accident.

72. (C)

The message says *Please check our website for more weather information.,* so (**A**) is not possible. (**B**) is also wrong because the message says *We will also not be able to deliver any of our distant and online courses today.* (**D**) is incorrect because the message says *We would just like to remind students that essays and research projects will not have their deadlines extended.* This means (**C**) is the only possible answer.

73. (A)

The message says *We would just like to remind students that essays and research projects will not*

have their deadlines extended, so (**A**) is the right answer. The message doesn't mention how course work should be submitted, so (**B**) is wrong. The message says most books can be found in the online library, but it doesn't say anything about sample copies. This means (**C**) is not possible either. (**D**) is also incorrect because the message doesn't say anything about marking.

74. (A)

The man says *Hi Mr. Amorim* and then *I got your call about the patio door.* This means (**A**) is the right answer. (**B**) is wrong because Wayne is the man speaking. (**C**) is wrong because Mr. Romsey is the janitor. Mr. Yen is the wood specialist, so (**D**) is also incorrect.

75. (D)

Wayne says *he was quite surprised when I told him,* so (**D**) is the right option. The voice message doesn't say anyone is feeling worried, so (**A**) is not possible. The same applies to (**B**), which is not mentioned inn the recording. (**C**) is not possible for the same reason, the only adjective used to describe a feeling in the message is *worried.*

76. (B)

Wayne says *We have used a wood specialist before for the same type of problem in another building and he did a really good job. As soon as we get hold of him, I'll let you know* and then he says *I'll call you once I hear back from Mr. Yen.* Therefore, we can safely assume that Mr. Yen is the wood specialist and (**B**) is the correct answer. The janitor is Mr. Romsey, so (**A**) is not possible. Wayne works for a property management group, so (**C**) is wrong. (**D**) is also incorrect because Wayne says *We have used a wood specialist before for the same type of problem in another building,* but that doesn't mean he's there right now.

77. (C)

The woman says *This is Jackie Adams with news in this beautiful spring morning in Gainesville,* so (**C**) is the correct alternative. She says there's barbecue on Friday so the broadcast can't be on the same day or she would have said tonight or this evening. This means (**A**) is wrong. (**B**) is wrong because she says *beautiful spring morning.* (**D**) is not possible because Saturday is the day of the match between the *Leopards* and the *Jaguars.*

78. (B)

The woman says *Say No! is a local charity that works in partnerships with schools and colleges to make students aware of the risks and consequences of the use of what are considered soft drugs*, so **(B)** is the correct answer. Jackie Adams is the speaker, so **(A)** is wrong. **(C)** is incorrect because even though the community center is holding the charity barbecue, it's the charity that is responsible for the project. The radio station talks about the charity barbecue and the sports match, but doesn't say anything about sponsoring *Say No!* This means **(D)** is not possible either.

79. (B)

(A) is wrong because she says 'Go Leopards' to show support for the team, not because she doesn't think they can win. **(C)** is also incorrect because it is the barbecue that raises money for charity, not the match. The woman says *we're counting on your presence*, but doesn't say anything about being there herself. This means **(D)** is also wrong and **(B)** is the only possible answer.

80. (C)

The man says *I'd like to welcome everyone on Sunnywest Airlines Flight 1776*, so **(C)** is the right answer. **(A)** is wrong because the man says *an airspeed of 420 miles per hour.* **(D)** is also incorrect because he says *an altitude of 35,000 feet.* He says *The time is now 9:55 pm local time*, so **(B)** is not possible either.

81. (D)

The man says *we are expecting to land in Paris approximately twenty-five minutes ahead of schedule*, so **(D)** is the correct answer.

82. (C)

The man says *The weather in Paris is cloudy and damp, with a high of 60 degrees for tomorrow*, so **(B)** is the correct answer. **(A)** and **(D)** are wrong because it's warmer than 60 degrees. **(B)** is also incorrect because Monday doesn't mention rain and the captain says cloudy and *damp.*

83. (B)

The man says *I've just started training for a half marathon and thought a smart watch would be helpful*

when calling someone who placed an ad for a smart watch. This means he wants to buy a watch and **(B)** is the correct answer. He asks for information, so **(A)** is wrong. **(C)** is wrong because he says *I'm calling about the smart watch ad you placed.* **(D)** is not possible because we don't know if the person selling the watch is his friend.

84. (B)

The man says *if you don't mind, I'd like to have a look at it. A friend told me to be careful with the battery*, so **(B)** is the correct answer. **(A)** is wrong because he says *A friend told me to be careful with the battery if I were to a buy a used watch.* **(C)** and **(D)** are both incorrect because he only mentions his friend when he says *A friend told me to be careful with the battery if I were to a buy a used watch.*

85. (A)

The man says *I'm going to a play tonight so I might not be able to pick up your call after 8.30*, so **(A)** is the correct answer. **(B)** and **(D)** are wrong because he says *I'm going to a play tonight* so we know he means 8.30 p.m. **(C)** is also incorrect because after 8.30 he'll be at the play and won't be able to take any calls.

86. (D)

The woman says *I'm talking about recipe boxes with organic ingredients*, so **(D)** is the correct answer. She says *restaurant quality food* but the business is not a restaurant, so **(A)** is wrong. She also says, *we're not talking about ready meals that you heat up in the microwave* and doesn't mention anything about *frozen food*, so **(B)** is not possible either. **(C)** is wrong because she doesn't say anything about a market, only that the recipe boxes ingredients are organic.

87. (A)

The woman says *recipe boxes with organic ingredients*, so **(A)** is the correct alternative. She doesn't mention *calories* **(B)**, or *fat* **(D)** so these alternatives are incorrect. **(C)** is wrong because she says *we're not talking about ready meals that you heat up in the microwave and then pray they're decent enough to eat.*

88. (C)

When the woman says *No, they don't cost an arm and a leg. No, we're not talking about ready meals that you heat up in the microwave and then pray they're decent enough to eat,* she's telling us that these are assumptions which are not true. The idiom *cost an arm and a leg* means *extremely expensive.* For both these reasons, (C) is the correct answer. (A) is wrong because we know the product is not *extremely expensive,* but that doesn't mean it's really cheap. She doesn't talk about different prices, so (B) is not possible. She doesn't say anything about people not buying their products for a reason, so (D) is also incorrect.

89. (A)

The man says *why not visit our restaurant on the top floor? With magnificent views of Miami bay,* which means the store is in Miami and (A) is the correct answer. He says *Colombian coffee,* so (B) is wrong. (C) is also incorrect because the restaurant has an Italian name (*Il Viaggio*), but that doesn't mean the store is in Italy.

90. (D)

The man says *The winter mega sale has now started in Menswear,* which is department in the store that sells clothes for men. This means (A) is not possible. (B) is wrong because the man says *Why go elsewhere when you can save with Maggies?* (C) is also incorrect because he says *why not visit our restaurant on the top floor? With magnificent views of the Orlando bay.*

91. (C)

The man says *The winter mega sale,* so options (A) and (B) are wrong. (D) is also incorrect because he says the restaurant is near where the toys are but doesn't say anything about a toy's sale. This means (C) is the only possible answer.

92. (B)

The message says *If you have any queries regarding the new NPhone 10, call our sales team on 0800 555 209 751,* so (B) is the right answer. (A) is wrong because they say *queries regarding the NPhone,* and not any of their products. (C) is incorrect because the woman says

If you'd like to talk about a bill or contract, press 2 now. She also says *For information regarding upgrades press 3,* so (D) is not possible either.

93. (B)

The message says *If you have any queries regarding the new NPhone 10, call our sales team on 0800 555 209 751,* so (B) is the correct answer. (A) is wrong because *WPhones* is the name of the store. (C) is also incorrect because the message says And our customers get a free *NPad Jr* when buying their *NPhone 10* when advertising the new *NPhone 10.* There's no mention of *easy upgrades,* so (D) is not possible.

94. (D)

The recording says *If you'd like a call back press 1 now,* so (A) is not possible. (B) is wrong because the woman says *to talk about a bill or contract, press 2.* (C) is also incorrect because the message says *For information regarding upgrades press 3.* This means (D) is the only possible answer.

95. (B)

The man says *the whole experience was appalling,* so (B) is the correct alternative. (A) is wrong because he says *I have been trying to speak to the hotel owner for a couple of days now with no success.* He doesn't say anything about his stay being *too short* (C) or *boring* (D), so these options are both incorrect.

96. (D)

The man says *none of your waiters,* so (A) is incorrect. (B) is wrong because the man says *When expressing our concerns to the manager, Mr. Lewis, not only was he unable to provide us with a space.* (C) is not possible because he says *when we decided to sunbathe by the pool, we found, to our horror, that you had kids' activities.* This means (D) is the only possible answer.

97. (D)

The man says *Please get back to me as soon as you get this message or I will have to take these matters to my legal team.* so (D) is the correct alternative. (A) is wrong because the man doesn't mention *the press.* (B) is also incorrect because he says *I have been trying to speak to the hotel owner for a couple of days now with no success,* which means he's already trying to contact the owner. He doesn't say anything about a review, so (C) is not possible either.

98. (B)

The woman says *Dr. Antonescu is a professor at Budapest University,* so (B) is the right answer. (A) is wrong because the conference is in Manhattan, but he works in Budapest. (C) and (D) are incorrect because even though she says *He will present results of his latest research in East Asia and South America,* that doesn't mean he works there.

99. (C)

The woman says *Today, he will talk about the Dental Prosthesis market segment,* so (C) is the correct alternative. (A) is wrong because even though she says *Dr. Antonescu is a professor at Budapest University,* that's not the topic of his talk. (B) is incorrect because she doesn't say anything about *becoming a dentist.* The same applies to (D), because she doesn't mention any *dental clinics.*

100. (A)

The woman says *research that will help large and small companies to achieve their preferred market position,* so (A) is the correct answer. (B) is wrong because she doesn't talk about companies helping one another. (C) is also incorrect because she says *help large and small companies to achieve their preferred market position,* which doesn't necessarily mean they already have different positions. (D) is not possible because she says *He will present results of his latest research.*

Reading

Part V—Incomplete Sentences

101. (B)

(B) is the correct answer because the preposition *by* is used to indicate what or who is responsible for an action in a passive sentence. *At, in* and *through* cannot be used to introduce the agent of a passive sentence, so alternatives (A), (C) and (D) are incorrect.

102. (A)

The gap requires a phrase which means *and also,* so (A) is the correct option. (B) is wrong because it is usually followed by a clause. (C) and (D) would be correct if they followed the conjunction *and,* which they don't. This means these alternatives are not possible either.

103. (C)

The gap requires a conjunction which means *as soon as,* so (C) is the correct answer. (A) is wrong because it means *up to.* (B) is also incorrect because it is used *as a provision against something happening.* (D) means *two times,* so it's not possible either.

104. (A)

The sentence needs an adjective which means *anxious or troubled,* so (A) is the correct answer. (B) is wrong because it means *causing anxiety about potential problems.* (C) and (D) are not possible because they're not adjectives.

105. (C)

Take something into consideration is a fixed phrase which means *take something into account,* so (C) is the only possible answer. The other verbs do not collocate with the rest of the phrase, so alternatives (A), (B) and (D) are all incorrect.

106. (C)

When the verb *apply* is used with the meaning of *put oneself forward as a candidate for a job,* it requires the preposition *for.* This means (C) is the correct answer. (B) and (D) do not collocate with the verb *apply,* so they're not possible. (A) is wrong because the verb *apply* takes the preposition *to* when it's used with the meaning of *make a formal request.*

107. (A)

The sentences asks for a passive structure, so (A) is the only possible answer. (B), (C) and (D) are incorrect because they are active.

108. (B)

The adverb *just* when placed in a passive sentence should go before the verb *be,* so (B) is the correct alternative. The position of the adverb *just* in the other sentences does not follow that rule, so options **(A)**, **(C)** and **(D)** are incorrect.

109. (A)

(B) is incorrect because it is usually followed by *gerund*. **(C)** is also wrong because it is usually followed by *on*. The verbs *take* and *lose* do not go well together, so **(D)** is not possible. This means **(A)** is the only possible answer.

110. (B)

The gap requires a phrase which means *unaccompanied by others*, so **(B)** is the correct answer. **(A)** is wrong because it's a *feeling*. **(C)** would only be correct if preceded by the preposition *by*. **(D)** is wrong because it's a noun.

111. (A)

The sentence needs a noun which means *a goal*, so **(A)** is the correct answer. **(B)** is wrong because it means *a material thing which can be touched*. **(C)** is also incorrect because it means *an expression of disapproval*. **(D)** is not possible because it's the noun which derives from the adjectives *objective* which means *not influenced by personal feelings in considering facts*.

112. (A)

The sentence needs an adverb which means *almost certainly*, so **(A)** is the correct answer. **(B)**, **(C)** and **(D)** are incorrect because they are *adjectives*.

113. (B)

The gap requires an adjective which means *well known for some bad quality*, so **(B)** is the correct answer. Alternatives **(A)**, **(C)** and **(D)** are not adjectives, so they're all incorrect.

114. (D)

The sentence needs a noun which means *a company that makes goods for sale*, so **(D)** is the only possible answer. The other alternatives are incorrect because they are verbs. **(A)** is a verb in the *infinitive*, **(B)** is *past participle*, and **(C)** *is gerund*.

115. (B)

(B) is the correct answer because the sentence needs a noun which means *a particular place*. **(A)** means *the action of placing someone*, so it's incorrect. **(C)** is not possible because it's an adjective. **(D)** is wrong because it means *an item of content published online*.

116. (C)

The sentence needs an adverb, so **(C)** is the only possible answer. **(A)** is wrong because it's an adjective. **(B)** and **(D)** are wrong because they're nouns.

117. (D)

The sentence needs a *passive structure,* so **(D)** is the only possible alternative. Options **(A)**, **(B)** and **(C)** are wrong because they're active.

118. (C)

The gap needs a phrase which means *a fairly large number,* so **(C)** is the correct answer. **(A)** does not collocate with *few,* so it's wrong. **(B)** is not usually followed by *a,* so it's also incorrect. **(D)** has the opposite meaning of *few,* so it's not possible either.

119. (A)

The gap needs a noun which means *the expression of approval or admiration for someone,* so **(A)** is the correct answer. **(B)** is wrong because it means *an act of assessing something.* **(C)** and **(D)** are not possible because they're verbs.

120. (C)

The sentence needs a plural noun which means *possessions.* Alternatives **(A)**, **(B)** and **(D)** are wrong because they're verbs.

121. (B)

The sentence needs an *adverb,* so **(B)** is the only possible answer. The other alternatives are wrong because **(A)** is an adjective, and **(C)** and **(D)** are verbs.

122. (A)

Trust someone with something, means *to allow someone to look after something valuable with confidence.* This means **(A)** is the correct answer. **(B)** is wrong because it does not collocate with the verb *trust.* **(C)** is incorrect because *trust* is not commonly followed by *in.* The same applies to **(D)**, which is not frequently used with *trust.*

123. (D)

In which means *where,* so **(D)** is the correct answer. *In* is not usually followed by *where,* so **(A)** is incorrect. A *town* is a place, so it should not be followed by the relative pronouns *what* or *when.* This means options **(B)** and **(C)** are incorrect.

124. (B)

The gap needs a verb in the *past participle,* so **(B)** is the only possible answer. **(A)** is wrong because it's *infinitive.* **(C)** is also incorrect because it's conjugates in the *3rd person singular of the present simple.* **(D)** is *gerund,* so it's not possible either.

125. (C)

Board members must *attend* functions, so **(C)** is correct. For *be* to fit, it would need to be followed by *at,* and for *go* to fit in the sentence it would need to be followed by *to.*

126. (A)

(A) is the only possible alternative because the sentence requires an adjective. The other options are wrong because **(B)** is an adverb, **(C)** can be a noun or a verb, and **(D)** is a *noun.*

127. (C)

The gap needs an adjective which can be followed by the preposition *to,* so **(C)** is the only possible answer. **(A), (B)** and **(D)** aren't usually followed by *to change,* so they're incorrect.

128. (B)

The gap requires an *adverb* which means *to the exclusion of others,* so **(B)** is the correct answer. **(A)** is wrong because it's not an adverb. **(C)** is not possible because it means *totally.* **(D)** is incorrect because it means *in a high degree.*

129. (C)

The gap requires a verb in the *future perfect active* to indicate that an action will be finished in the future. This means **(C)** is the correct answer. **(A)** and **(B)** are wrong because they're *not future perfect.* **(D)** is also incorrect because it's in the *passive voice.*

130. (B)

The gap requires a *noun* which means *the state of meeting rules,* so **(B)** is the correct answer. **(A)** is wrong because it's an adjective. **(C)** and **(D)** are wrong because they're verbs.

Part VI—Text Completion

131. (A)

Only **(A)** correctly completes the setnence, which is disucssing a change in fees. **(B)** is a general opening for an email response, but it cannot be followed by *is about to expire* as it is not clear what *it* is. **(C)** is incorrect and the increase in fee is not discussed, and **(D)** is incorrect as it discusses a payment method not working, not an increase in a fee.

132. (B)

The gap needs an adverb, so **(B)** is the only possible answer. **(A)** is wrong because it's an adjective. **(C)** is also incorrect as it's a noun. **(D)** is a verb so it's not possible either.

133. (B)

The phrase *at one's disposal* means *available for one to use whenever and however one wishes,* so **(B)** is the only possible answer. Since this is a fixed phrase, alternatives **(A), (C)** and **(D)** are incorrect.

134. (A)

The gap needs a phrase which means *if it is true that,* so **(A)** is the correct answer. **(B)** and **(C)** means *on condition that,* so they are both incorrect. **(D)** is also wrong because it means *imagine.*

135. (D)

The gap requires an adverb, so **(D)** is the only possible answer. *Since* refers to a time in the past and *sincere* is an adjective.

136. (C)

The only preposition that collocates with the verb *focus* is *on*. This means (C) is the only possible answer. (A), (B) and (D) are wrong because these prepositions do not collocate with the verb *focus*.

137. (D)

The only alternative that can be followed by a singular noun is *each*, so (D) is the correct answer. (A), (B) and (C) should be followed by a plural noun, so they are incorrect.

138. (B)

When a verb is used as the subject of a sentence, it usually needs to be in the *gerund*. This means (B) is the correct answer. (A) is wrong because it's *infinitive*. (C) is also incorrect because it's *past*. (D) is not possible because it's a *noun*.

139. (A)

The gap needs a noun which means *agricultural and other natural products collectively*. This means (A) is the correct answer. (B) is wrong because it means *the state or quality of being productive*. (C) is also incorrect because it means *an article or substance that is manufactured*. (D) is not possible because it means *the act of manufacturing from components or raw materials*.

140. (D)

The previous sentence discusses being *hungry* and the advertisement is about a new restaurant, so (D) must be the correct answer. (A) talks about horse-riding, but horse is mentioned in the idiom *so hungry you could eat a horse*, which means to be very hungry. (B) asks for recommendations for improvement, but this assumes that the reader has already been to the restaurant, but the advertisement is aimed at new customers. (C) talks about contacting a doctor, but the advertisement is about food, not medical help.

141. (B)

Provide catering needs the dependent preposition *for*, so (B) is the right answer. The other prepositions do not collocate with *cater*, so options (A), (C) and (D) are not possible.

142. (C)

The gap requires an adverb, so (C) is the only possible answer. (A) is wrong because it's an adjective. The same applies to (B), which is a comparative adjective. (D) is wrong because it's a noun.

143. (B)

The sentence needs an adjective which means *pleased*, so (B) is the correct answer. (A) and (C) are wrong because they have negative meanings. (D) is not possible because it means *inspiring delight, pleasure, or admiration*.

144. (A)

In need of is a fixed phrase which means *needing something*, so (A) is the only possible answer. Since it's a fixed phrase, other prepositions cannot be used and alternatives (B), (C) and (D) are incorrect.

145. (C)

The sentence needs a noun which means *the state of having no home*, so (C) is the correct option. (A) is not possible because it's an adjective. (B) is also wrong because it's an adverb. (D) is also a noun, but it's incorrect because it means *a person's native land*.

146. (B)

(B) is the only possible answer because the gap needs a verb in the *future simple passive*. All the other verb forms are active, so alternatives (A), (C) and (D) are incorrect.

Part VII—Reading Comprehension

147. (A)

The text says *Getting to know staff from different departments and branches* when describing the goals for *Country Breakfast,* so (A) is the correct answer. (B) is wrong because it's about team work, but not necessarily with people one hasn't met before. (C) is incorrect because it involves watching videos. (D) is not possible because it's a speech.

148. (B)

The text says *Giving staff the opportunity to consider the next steps on their career development* when describing the *Guest Talks* that start at 1.30 p.m. This means (**B**) is the correct answer. (**A**) is not possible because *Murder Mystery Lunch* is about promoting collaboration. (**C**) is also incorrect because during *Coffee Break Tales* staff will be watching videos. (**D**) is wrong because it's the chairperson's speech.

149. (B)

At 11am, new staff will be welcomed. The table states that they will go over the company goals and aims, so (**B**) is correct.

150. (A)

The text says *10.00 a.m. – 05.00 p.m.* Since the chairperson's speech starts at 4.00 p.m., (**A**) is the most likely answer. The other options would mean that the speech would finish after 05.00 p.m., so (**B**), (**C**) and (**D**) are all incorrect.

151. (A)

The email says *I am pleased to attach an offer letter,* so (**A**) is the correct answer. (**B**) is wrong because an invitation would not come with an offer letter attached. Even though the email asks for some documents, (**C**) is incorrect because Camilla hasn't accepted the job offer yet. There's no mention of an *open school day,* so (**D**) is not possible.

152. (C)

The email says *I am pleased to attach an offer letter and contract for you,* so (**A**) and (**B**) are incorrect. (**D**) is also wrong because it says *I have also attached out staff handbook.* This means (**C**) is the only possible answer.

153. (D)

The email says *I will forward some safeguarding information separately in due course,* so (**D**) is the correct answer. The text says The email says *I am pleased to attach an offer letter and contract for you, along with the new starter forms.* This means (**A**) is incorrect. The email *asks* for qualification documentation, so (**B**) is not possible either. (**C**) is also wrong because another company will send the health questionnaire.

154. (D)

The sentence is a fixed email convention which has to go towards the end of the email, so (**D**) is the only possible answer. Because email writing conventions usually have to go in pre-determined places of the text, alternatives (**A**), (**B**) and (**C**) are not possible.

155. (A)

The text says *voice navigation capability provides faster access to your favorite streaming content,* so (**A**) is the correct answer. *Streaming content* is one of the television's functions, but not a way of gaining faster access to other functions. This means (**B**) is incorrect. (**C**) and (**D**) are also wrong because Wi-Fi connections allows access to the internet, but that doesn't necessarily mean faster access to other TV functions.

156. (A)

To *redefine a concept* in this text means to *make something old seem new and better,* so (**A**) is the correct answer. There's no mention of portability, so (**B**) is incorrect. (**C**) is wrong because it talks about *home entertainment* in general and not TV sets only. (**D**) is only one of many TV features, so this option is not possible either.

157. (C)

The text says *Sommy's Smart TV hands-on user-interface,* so (**A**) is incorrect. The text mentions *Full Wi-Fi connectivity* as one of the features, so (**B**) is not possible either. (**D**) is also wrong because the text says *your TV to accurately reproduce a revolutionary spectrum of colors.* This means (**C**) is the only possible answer.

158. (B)

The text says *set in Chile,* so (**B**) is the correct option. The author is Russian but the story takes place in Chile, so (**A**) is incorrect. The review says *Eleonor and Alan have travelled there from the UK,* so they're not in the UK and (**C**) is wrong. The text doesn't mention the US, so (**D**) is not possible.

159. (C)

The expression *nothing is quite as it seems* means that things might turn out different from what we expected them to be. This means **(C)** is the best answer. It is likely that the critic is hinting that there may be some unexpected twists in the book, so **(C)** is correct. The critic does not state that he though he would enjoy the book but did not, so **(A)** is incorrect. **(B)** is not correct in the context of the text and **(D)** cannot be correct as we are not told about the genre of the book.

160. (B)

(A) is incorrect because the text hasn't started talking about the narrative yet. **(C)** is not possible because the review is not addressing the protagonists in this part of the text anymore. **(D)** is also wrong because the critic has already wrapped up his review by saying his general description and opinion about the book. This means **(B)** is the only possible answer.

161. (A)

(A) is the best answer because someone who is unhappy at work is likely to benefit from a workshop on motivation. The other alternatives talk about people in situations which do not necessarily involve a lack of motivation, so **(B)**, **(C)** and **(D)** are incorrect.

162. (A)

The text says *This workshop will provide you with some useful ideas based on recent research,* so **(A)** is the correct option. It is a practical workshop but this is not where Dr. Linda got her ideas from, so **(B)** is wrong. **(C)** and **(D)** are not possible because the text doesn't mention any colleagues or books.

163. (A)

This is an introductory sentence presenting the topic of the workshop, so **(A)** is the correct answer.

164. (B)

The text says *Welcome to Universal Access online learning,* so **(B)** is the best answer. **(A)** is wrong because the text doesn't talk about *web design* or *web hosting.* We know different courses but there's no mention of *Universal Access* being a college, so **(C)** is incorrect. **(D)** is not possible because the text doesn't say anything about the government.

165. (A)

The text says *Please make sure you complete the free Learning Online module first, which will give you tips and advice about how use our e-learning platform,* so **(A)** is the correct answer. We don't know the content of the *Getting Started* module, so **(B)** is not possible. **(C)** is incorrect because the email says *browse our catalogue on your personalized homepage.* **(D)** is also wrong because the text says *click on the* Help tab at the top right of the screen and send a message to our technical support desk.

166. (C)

The text says *emails with jobs that match your profile,* so **(C)** is the correct answer. **(A)** is incorrect because the text says *1000 recruitment websites,* not *jobs.* **(B)** is also wrong because the text doesn't say anything about *recruitment policies.* The ad says *daily emails with jobs that match your profile and past searches.* This doesn't mean *job search history* is the main content of the emails, so **(D)** is not possible either.

167. (D)

The text says *giving you access to the most talented professionals,* so **(A)** is incorrect. **(B)** is also wrong because the text says you can *review applications* from a *tablet computer or smart phone.* The ad also says you can *schedule interviews from your laptop,* so **(C)** is not possible either. This means **(D)** is the correct alternative.

168. (A)

(A) is the best answer because the sentence talks about both employers and jobseekers. **(B)** is wrong because any sentence in that place should only address jobseekers. The same applies to **(C)** and **(D)** where sentences should only address employers.

169. (A)

The letter talks about consequences of a rental agreement not being respected. The text says *Failure to comply will result in legal action, including physical removal of all tenants from the apartment and the property,* so **(A)** is the only possible answer. **(B)** is wrong because even though the writer is unlikely to be happy with the situation, this is not a letter of complaint because it does not complain about a product or a service. **(C)** is not possible because the letter doesn't ask for information. **(D)** is incorrect because the letter doesn't put anything forward for consideration.

170. (D)

Sentences containing contact details usually go at the end of a letter, so **(D)** is the correct answer. Since this is a writing convention, alternatives **(A)**, **(B)** and **(C)** are not possible.

171. (B)

The text says *The Wi-Fi password can be found in the student lounge, in reception and on the notice boards,* so alternatives **(A)**, **(C)** and **(D)** are all incorrect. This means **(B)** is the only possible answer.

172. (B)

The text says *You may also leave your personal belongings in a locker,* so **(B)** is the correct answer. **(A)** and **(D)** are wrong because it says *You may also leave your personal belongings in a locker. Please speak with reception should you require one.* **(C)** is also incorrect because the text says *Please make sure you keep your personal belongings with you at all times.*

173. (C)

The paragraph where **(A)** is talks about the internet, so it's incorrect. **(B)** is not possible because that paragraph talks about the library. **(D)** is wrong because any sentences in this paragraph should be related to extra-curricular activities. This means **(C)** is the only possible answer.

174. (A)

The text says *Ayrton Guedes is very optimistic over the performance of his new F4 car. Optimistic* means *hopeful and confident,* so **(A)** is the right answer. **(B)** is wrong because there's no mention of negative feelings towards the new car. The text says Guedes feels *optimistic,* which doesn't necessarily mean he's either *happy* or *excited.* Therefore, alternatives **(C)** and **(D)** are also incorrect.

175. (A)

The text says *Because of the freezing weather conditions over the past week, Guedes had completed only 19 laps on a low track temperature that prevented his car being pushed to its limit.* This means the weather prevented his car from achieving its full potential and **(A)** is the correct answer. The text says it's a new car but doesn't say this is related to poor performance before Friday, so alternatives **(B)** and **(D)** are incorrect. **(C)** is wrong because the text doesn't say anything about Guedes's racing preferences.

176. (C)

The email says *As a result of your application for the position of Activity Leader* and a text message says *Guess who's going to California with you this summer,* so **(C)** is the correct answer. The mail says *the position of Activity Leader* but doesn't talk about a language school, so **(A)** is incorrect. If Grace is going to California, it can't be a local summer camp. This means **(B)** is also wrong. **(D)** is not possible because the email says *Adam Sanders Activity Manager.*

177. (B)

Grace says *guess again* after Thomas asks is James got the job, which means that Thomas's first guess was incorrect, so James did not get the job. **(B)** is correct.

178. (C)

Couch potato is an idiom which means a person is lazy or not very active, so **(C)** is the best possible answer. Even though Grace says *No way they gave James a job,* this is not the meaning of *couch potato* so **(A)** is incorrect. **(B)** is wrong because although we she refers to James as a *couch potato,* it doesn't necessarily mean he spends all day sitting on a couch. **(D)** is not possible because the texts don't say anything about James's eating or sleeping habits.

179. (C)

(A) is not possible because the email says *your application for the position of Activity Leader.* When

Grace says *I'm coming with you*, we can assume she was offered the position so (**B**) is also wrong. (**D**) is incorrect because Grace says *Guess who's going to California with you this summer.* This means (**C**) is the only possible answer.

180. (B)

(**B**) is the correct answer because it's positioned in the paragraph that talks about the interview details. (**A**) is wrong because the interview hasn't been mentioned yet. (**C**) is also incorrect because this part of the email talks about whether Grace would like to reschedule the interview. (**D**) is impossible because it's not common to add anything between the closing sentence (*I look forward to hearing from you*) and the signature.

181. (D)

(**A**) is wrong because the appointment calendar says *9.00 a.m. – Video Meeting (Wilson Smith – PWF Media)* and *10.00 a.m. – Board Meeting (new oversea branches)* on Monday. (**B**) is incorrect because it says *10.30 a.m. – Video Meeting (Paulo Barbosa – Aragorn Inc.)* on Tuesday. (**C**) is not possible because it says *09.45 a.m. – Team meeting (presentation slides)* on Wednesday. This means (**D**) is the only possible answer.

182. (A)

The agenda says *12.00 – 1.00 p.m. – Interview PA (Janet Andrews – Room 3), 09.30 a.m. – Interview PA (Chiara Blanco – Room 3)* and *11.00 a.m. – Interview PA (John Bose – Room 4).* Therefore, we can assume Mrs. Park is looking for a PA and (**A**) is the best possible answer. (**B**) is wrong because Mrs. Park has two lunch meetings. We don't know her current position, so (**C**) and (**D**) are not possible either.

183. (C)

Sarah says *I am so sorry it has taken me this long to send you the reports you asked Mr. Smith,* so (**C**) is the correct alternative. (**A**) is wrong because she says *the reports you asked Mr. Smith.* (**B**) is also incorrect because the email says *before our meeting tomorrow,* so she can't be late for the meeting. Sarah doesn't say anything about her priorities, so (**D**) is not possible.

184. (A)

The appointment calendar says the *Safeguarding Training* starts at 2.00 p.m. and does not end until 6.00 p.m. on Thursday and the meeting is planned for 08.30 on Friday morning. If the email was sent at 2.45 p.m., the most likely problem is that she might have no time to check all the reposts. This means (**A**) is the best answer. (**B**) is wrong because the problem is not the time of the meeting, but the fact that the reprts were sent too late. There's no mention of *disrespect,* so (**C**) is impossible. (**D**) is also incorrect because the emails says *Please find the files attached.*

185. (B)

The email says *I am so sorry it has taken me this long to send you the reports you asked Mr. Smith,* so Sarah is very likely to work with Mr. Smith and (**B**) is the best answer. (**A**) is wrong because we don't know Mrs. Park's position at the company. There's no mention of Sarah's positon either, so (**C**) is incorrect. (**D**) is not possible because Sarah was delayed with her submission.

186. (B)

The email says *Araki Dining Experience is a concept I have had in my mind for nearly ten years. Our menus are interactive,* so (**B**) is the correct answer. The ad says *From well-marbled wagyu sirloin to a series of vegan dishes,* which means the restaurant serves *beef* and (**A**) is incorrect. The word traditional is not used to describe the restaurant in any of the texts, so (**C**) is also wrong. (**D**) is not possible because none of the texts talk about age groups.

187. (C)

(**A**) is wrong because the ad says *a series of vegan dishes.* (**B**) is also incorrect because the ad says *delivered to your office in beautifully handmade Japanese boxes.* (**D**) is not possible because the email says *Our menus are interactive.*

188. (A)

The ad says *Araki Dining opens on March 24,* so (**A**) is the correct option. (**B**) is wrong because the email says *Our pre-opening night will be held on March*

17. (**C**) is not possible because the email says *Please RSVP before March 10.* (**D**) is also incorrect because Edward's text message says *Got any plans for next Saturday* when Edward is inviting Sally for the pre-opening night.

189. (D)

The email invites Edward to an opening night, and mentions that he is a respected *critic*. (**D**) is most likely correct.

190. (A)

The flyer mentions that the restaurant is in San Antonio, and the email mentions that the opening night is on the 17th March. (**A**) is correct.

191. (B)

This question asks what is being offered in the advertisement. The first sentence of the advertisement says 'Today until Sunday, buy one drink, get one free!' The advertisement is offering a free drink with the purchase of anotehr drink, (**B**) is correct. The offer is only available to people who have a Rewards Account, but it is not a free coffee for people who open a new account. The offer is for drinks, not meals, so (**C**) is incorrect. *Upgrades* are not mentioned, so (**D**) cannot be correct.

192. (C)

The question asks for the amount taken off the bill. Looking at the receipt, $1.90 is removed from the cost; (**C**) is correct. $0.34 gives the tax, but this is added to the bill, not deducted from it. $0.50 is the cost of adding soy milk, but again, this is added to the bill, not removed from it. $4.10 gives the subtotal for the bill, rather than a deduction.

193. (B)

The advertisement says the offer runs from *today until Sunday*, so the offer must end Sunday; which removes answer choices (**A**) and (**C**). The email says that the buy on get one free offer was *released on Monday*; so the offer must have run from Monday to Sunday. (**B**) is correct.

194. (A)

This question asks you to choose the answer with the closest meaning to 'take advntage of' in the email. Locating the phrase in the email, Vikesh writes that he went into the store to *take advantage of* the buy one get one free offer. As we know he used the buy one get one free offer in the store, we can infer that *to take advantage of* means *to use*, (**A**) is correct. (**B**) means to take, but Vikesh used the offer. (**C**) *to gain* means to add, or to increase. (**D**) to exploit offers another meaning for *to take advantage of* but carries negative connotations, and implies acting unfairly, which Vikesh did not do.

195. (D)

In his email, Mr. Chakladar says that he was not refunded for the soy milk in his cheaper drink, but he believes he should have been 'as the advert didn't mention anything about soy milk not being discounted'. Mr. Chakladar believes that as 'it was part of the cheaper drink... it should also have been free.' Mr. Chakladar complains because he only received part of his drink for free, when he believes he should have received the whole drink for free. (**D**) is correct. (**A**) is incorrect, as he received the drinks he ordered. (**C**) is incorrect, as the offer was only for one drink to be free. (**C**) is incorrect, as the barista does apply a discount, Mr. Chakladar's issue is that he feels the barista should have applied a greater discount.

196. (C)

The article says *78.6 percent believed that technology was leading to more jobs, not less*, so (**C**) is the correct answer. Even though people might be afraid of technology, this is not what the research found out. This means (**A**) is incorrect. (**B**) is wrong because the article says *millennials aren't really worried about technology's negative impact on the job market.* (**D**) is not possible because none of the texts talk about a collapse.

197. (D)

(**A**) is not possible because *However* should offer information that contrasts the sentence it follows, which is not the case in this part of the text. (**B**) and (**C**) are incorrect because *however* does not usually go at the beginning of a paragraph. This means (**D**) is the only possible answer.

198. (A)

The chart shows a drastic shift from manual to specialized work, so (**A**) is the correct answer. (**B**) is wrong because the information in the chart is in percentage, so we don't know the number of jobs. (**C**) is also incorrect because the chart does not say anything about requirements, it contains information about how specialized work has surpassed manual work in terms of number of workers. (**D**) is not possible because the chart doesn't say whether this shift is positive or negative.

199. (A)

The chart caption says *Caring professions include health and teaching professionals. Muscle power* *workers include cleaners, laborers, and miners*, so (**A**) is the correct answer. Since the caption says *Muscle power workers include cleaners, laborers, and miners*, alternatives (**B**), (**C**) and (**D**) are incorrect.

200. (C)

The ad says *The successful candidate must also have excellent working knowledge of network and systems infrastructure technologies*, so (**C**) is the correct answer. The positions offered are in New York, London and Sidney. However, this does not mean living in those cities is a requirement so (**A**) is not possible. (**B**) is incorrect because the ad says *The successful candidates will be working in the Enterprise Security team*, which does mean that experience in the security sector is a requirement. (**D**) is impossible because the ad doesn't say anything about *communities*.

PRACTICE TEST 4 ANSWER KEY

Part I	Part II	Part III	Part IV	Part V	Part VI	Part VII
1. C	7. B	32. A	71. A	101. D	131. D	147. C
2. C	8. A	33. D	72. C	102. B	132. C	148. B
3. D	9. A	34. D	73. B	103. B	133. B	149. D
4. C	10. B	35. A	74. B	104. C	134. A	150. C
5. D	11. A	36. D	75. B	105. B	135. B	151. C
6. B	12. A	37. C	76. A	106. A	136. C	152. B
	13. B	38. D	77. D	107. D	137. B	153. B
	14. C	39. B	78. A	108. B	138. A	154. D
	15. B	40. D	79. C	109. D	139. C	155. B
	16. C	41. D	80. D	110. A	140. B	156. D
	17. A	42. A	81. A	111. C	141. A	157. C
	18. B	43. B	82. C	112. C	142. D	158. B
	19. A	44. D	83. A	113. B	143. A	159. B
	20. B	45. A	84. B	114. B	144. B	160. B
	21. A	46. B	85. D	115. C	145. C	161. A
	22. B	47. B	86. D	116. D	146. A	162. C
	23. C	48. D	87. C	117. B		163. B
	24. A	49. C	88. D	118. B		164. A
	25. B	50. C	89. B	119. B		165. D
	26. B	51. C	90. C	120. B		166. B
	27. C	52. A	91. D	121. A		167. A
	28. B	53. C	92. C	122. C		168. B
	29. A	54. A	93. B	123. C		169. C
	30. C	55. B	94. B	124. B		170. A
	31. A	56. D	95. A	125. A		171. B
		57. B	96. C	126. D		172. C
		58. A	97. B	127. B		173. C
		59. B	98. C	128. A		174. A
		60. B	99. B	129. C		175. A
		61. C	100. A	130. D		176. D
		62. D				177. C
		63. C				178. B
		64. B				179. B
		65. A				180. B
		66. D				181. A
		67. B				182. D
		68. D				183. B
		69. B				184. C
		70. A				185. A
						186. A
						187. C
						188. B
						189. C
						190. C
						191. C
						192. B
						193. D
						194. B
						195. A
						196. A
						197. B
						198. C
						199. B
						200. B

PRACTICE TEST 4
Part I—Photographs

1. (C)

The photograph shows a woman on the street lifting her arm to hail a cab. (C) best describes the photograph. She's *lifting her arm for a cab*, not *reaching for a copy*, or *calling them out*. She's trying to get *a cab*, she's not *trying to get out*.

2. (C)

The photograph shows a woman applying stage makeup to a man. (C) best describes the photograph. She's putting on his makeup, he's not *made up with his progress*, or *making it up to her*. She's doing his makeup, not *watching him work*.

3. (D)

The photograph shows a man operating a machine by moving a lever. (D) best describes the photograph. He's not using *bolts*, a *wheel* or *locks*.

4. (C)

The photograph shows a house being built. On the roof, tiles are being laid by builders. (C) best describes the photograph. The house is new, not a *ruin*. The photograph shows a *house*, not a *flat*. The house is being made, it is not *up for sale*.

5. (D)

The photograph shows a man and a woman serving food to people. (D) best describes the photograph. They're serving food, not *eating their meals*. The food is already prepared, they're not *cooking the vegetables*. They're distributing the plates, not *leaving* them.

6. (B)

The photograph shows a man giving a speech to a crowd. (B) best describes the photograph. He's talking to people, not *donating his clothes*, or *labelling information*. He's giving a speech, not *presenting an award*.

Part II—Question-Response

7. (B)

The question asks *what have you been up to all morning?* (B) correctly answers the speaker has been *taking a nap*. (A) talks about the future (*in an hour*), not the past, while (C) talks about *mornings* in general, not this specific *morning*.

8. (A)

The question asks *did you find your phone after all?* (A) replies positively, giving a location (*the bathroom*). (B) talks about the *number*, not the *phone* itself, and (C) talks about the possibility of offering *help*, but if someone lost their *phone* they would need *help*, not offer it.

9. (A)

The sentence says *I didn't notice you arrive.* (A) is the correct answer because it explains why this happened (*I was right behind you*). (B) talks about a *note*, not *noticing* something (C) talks about being *on* their *way* which can't be right if they've already *arrived*.

10. (B)

The question asks *what's wrong with him?* (B) explains *what's wrong*: *his bad knee is acting up*, i.e. hurting. (A) talks about *she*, but the question asks about *he*. (C) offers *painkillers*, but doesn't explain *what's wrong* – and it's not even the person asking the question that might need *painkillers*, but a third person (*him*).

11. (A)

The question is *did you remember to print the report?* (A) says they *tried*, but it wasn't possible because *the printer wasn't working*. (B) talks about *sending* the report, not *printing* it. (C) talks about *reporting* an issue, not *printing* a *report*.

12. (A)

The question is *can we move the meeting to tomorrow same time?* (A) explains that's not possible because the speaker is *on holiday*. (B) talks about how the *meeting hasn't happened yet*, which is obvious. (C) talks about when the *meeting* is *supposed to be*, not whether it can be *moved* – and also says the *meeting* is *tomorrow same time*, which is impossible if they are discussing *moving* it there.

13. (B)

The sentence says *I don't like how the new office looks.* (**B**) agrees, describing it as *appalling*, i.e. horrible. (**A**) talks about something *official*, not an *office*. (**C**) says *it looks like I'm going to be late*, which has nothing to do with appearance – *it looks like* here means 'it seems as if'.

14. (C)

The question is *when did they say they were arriving?* (**C**) says *their plane is landing in an hour*, which means they *are arriving* in an hour. (**A**) talks something being *the case*, i.e. what's happening, not when someone is *arriving*. (**B**) talks about the location of *the arrivals hall*, not when someone is *arriving*.

15. (B)

The question is *do you prefer to sit at the front or at the back?* (**A**) talks about someone's *back*, i.e. the body part, not the *back* of a place when you can *sit*. (**C**) talks about *waiting by the front door*, not about where to *sit*. (**B**) is correct because the person picks the *front* because they're *tall*.

16. (C)

The sentence is *I'm so sorry I didn't tell you.* (**A**) talks about having *apologized already*, but the person responding is the one receiving an *apology*, not giving one. (**B**) talks about *telling* someone *what to do*, not something they should be told. (**C**) is correct because the person accepts the apology (*it's all right*) and explains they *found out* already *from Anna*.

17. (A)

The question asks *are you sure this is the correct spreadsheet?* (**A**) explains that this was *the one* the speaker was *sent*, implying it must be *correct*. (**B**) talks about *sheets* in the *dryer*, i.e. bedsheets, not *spreadsheets*. (**C**) talks about *answering* something, not a *spreadsheet*.

18. (B)

The question is *how many times a week do you have classes?* (**B**) explains it's *every Monday and Tuesday*, i.e. twice. (**A**) talks about going *to the gym*, not *classes*. (**C**) talks about something happening *next week*, not a regular *weekly* thing like *classes*.

19. (A)

The question is *where should I put this?* (**A**) gives a location to *put* it (*by the door*). (**B**) talks about being *put off*, i.e. disliking something, not *putting* it somewhere, and (**C**) talks about *putting a stop to* something, i.e. ending it.

20. (B)

The question asks *have you found a new assistant yet?* (**A**) refuses an offer of *assistance* but doesn't talk about an *assistant*. (**C**) talks about whether their *assistant* is *new* or not, not about *finding* one. (**B**) is correct because if you are looking for an assistant, it means you are *recruiting* for one, and they say they are *still recruiting*.

21. (A)

The sentence says *don't be discouraged by what he said.* (**A**) says they *will try* not to be *discouraged*, but that *what he said* affected their *confidence*. (**B**) talks about receiving *encouraging words*, not *discouraging*. (**C**) talks about *courage* to *do* something, not about being *discouraged* by someone.

22. (B)

The question is *are you a morning or an evening person?* (**B**) says they are a *night owl*, which means they prefer *nights*. (**A**) talks about when they *work*, not whether they prefer *mornings* or *evenings*. (**C**) talks about when they would *prefer to meet*, not what they *prefer* in general.

23. (C)

The question asks *why didn't you bring your partner with you?* (**C**) explains it wasn't possible because the *partner* is *out of the country*. (**A**) talks about *bringing* something *up*, i.e. mentioning it, not *bringing* someone somewhere. (**B**) talks about a *successful partnership*, not why the *partner* is not present.

24. (A)

The question is *have you read her latest book?*
(A) explains they *didn't bother* with it because they *didn't like her last* book. (B) talks about *publishing books*, not *reading* them. (C) talks about *reading fiction* in general, not a specific *book*.

25. (B)

The question asks *did anything happen after I left?*
(B) says they didn't miss anything. (A) talks about directions (*left* and *right*), not to be confused with the past tense of 'leave', which is also *left*. (C) talks about something *not happening yet*, but the question is about the past, not the future.

26. (B)

The sentence is *I can't believe how rude he was!*
(B) explains *he* can be *quite blunt*, i.e. direct, which can sometimes appear *rude*. (A) talks about not *believing* someone, but the first speaker doesn't *believe* something (the *rudeness* of the person in question), not someone. (C) talks about something *happening everywhere*, not about this specific *rude* person.

27. (C)

The question is *have we met before? You look familiar.*
(A) talks about a *meeting* in the future (*tomorrow*), not in the past. (B) talks about being *familiar* with another person (*him*), not the person in front of them. (C) responds to the question by explaining they *have one of those faces*, which means a lot of people think they *look familiar.*

28. (B)

The question is *do you eat fish?* (B) says they're *an omnivore*, which means they *eat* everything. (A) talks about something being *fishy*, i.e. dodgy, and (C) talks about *feeding* the *fish*, not *eating.*

29. (A)

The question is *who delivered this package?*
(A) explains it *was a courier* who *just left*. (B) talks about who the *package* belongs to (*Sandra*), not who *delivered* it. (C) talks about *asking for home delivery*, not the person who *delivered*.

30. (C)

The sentence is *I can't remember where I left my keys!*
(A) talks about the *key to success*, which is a figurative *key*, not a literal one. (C) talks about when they are *leaving*, not where the *key* is. (B) suggests the speaker *retrace* their *steps*, i.e. go backwards to *remember where* they *left* their *key.*

31. (A)

The question is *would you like me to do that right now?*
(A) explains that *it can wait*, so *it's fine* not to *do that right now*. (B) talks about being *done*, i.e. finished, not *doing* something. (C) talks about *what* someone *likes*, not when *to do* something.

Part III—Short Conversations

32. (A)

Some of the expressions used by both the woman (*press enter, don't remove the memory stick*) and the man (*make sure the file is saved*) can only be used to describe things we do on a computer so (A) is the correct answer. The man uses a future tense to talk about the printer (*will you please now show me how to use the wireless printer?*) so they can't be using it at the moment, which means (B) is incorrect. (C) confuses *file* with *filing cabinet*. (D) confuses the meaning of *window* in the conversation-it refers to a browser window, not a physical window.

33. (D)

The woman says *and don't remove the memory stick without ejecting it first.* (D) is correct. (A) is incorrect because it is the man who talks about closing the *browser window*, not the woman. (B) is also not possible for the same reason, the man talks about saving the file, even though the woman might have given similar advice before the conversation took place. (C) is wrong because the man asks *Will you please now show me how to use the wireless printer?*, but the woman does not say anything about a printer.

34. (D)

The man asks *will you please now show me how to use the wireless printer?*, so (D) is the correct alternative.

The man mentions previous advice given by the woman when he says *and make sure the file is saved before I close the window*, but this is not what he wants from the woman, so (**A**) is incorrect. (**B**) and (**C**) are not mentioned in the conversation.

35. (A)

The man says *I got a promotion recently, and they gave me this company laptop*. The answer is (**A**).

36. (D)

The woman says *it hasn't been used for a while, so the software needs updating*. The answer is (**D**).

37. (C)

At the end of the conversation, the woman asks *what's your office extension?* She's asking for the number to call to get hold of him at work, so the answer is (**C**).

38. (D)

The man says *47th Street Medical Practice, this is Phoenix speaking, how may I help?* This seems to suggest he is answering the phone, so he must be a *receptionist*. This is further evidenced by the woman's response, as she asks to *book an appointment*, which means she must be a *patient*, as this is a *medical practice* she has called. So, (**D**) is correct. This means that (**A**), (**B**) and (**D**) are incorrect – as, even though the *doctor* is mentioned, it is as a third person so there is no suggestion one of the two speakers is a *doctor*.

39. (B)

The man says *our earliest appointment is in two days, this Friday*. This means that the *conversation is taking place two days* before *Friday*, i.e. (**B**) *Wednesday*. That means that, even though *Monday* and *Friday* are mentioned, (**A**), (**C**) and (**D**) are incorrect.

40. (D)

The woman says *I don't mind waiting*, so she doesn't care which *appointment* is *sooner*, so (**A**) is incorrect. She also says *I work at that time* when the man mentions the *appointment* on *Friday*, not *Monday*, so (**B**) is incorrect. While the *appointment* on *Monday* is indeed *early* at *8.30 a.m.*, the woman never comments

on this, so (**C**) is incorrect. (**D**) is correct because, when the man says that the *appointment on Monday* is *not with your usual doctor*, the woman picks *Friday*.

41. (D)

The woman says *I can't believe I have forgotten about it*, when the man asks her why she didn't send the email. (**D**), the woman tells the man that she had *forgotten*, which matches the answer choice (*forgot*). (**A**) is incorrect, as although the man asks 'are you alright?', the woman does not mention being unwell. (**B**) is incorrect as the woman says she had *forgotten* about the email, not that she was away on vacation. (**C**) is incorrect as although the conversation is about emails, the woman does not say she couldn't *find* his emails address, she says she had *forgotten* to send an email.

42. (A)

The man says *We're going to have to give them a call*. (**A**) matches this (the man suggests making a *phone call*). For the record, (**B**), the man suggests a *call*, not an *email*. (**C**) describes a *fax*, not a *call*. (**D**) is a trap answer, based on the man's comment that if the woman had sent the email, they 'could have gotten the *contract*'. As this is not a suggestion, and as the contract does not specifically relate to the woman, (**D**) must be incorrect.

43. (B)

The woman says *I'll do that Mr. Lopez. This is my mess and I'll get it fixed*. (**B**) is correct. Even though the woman uses the word *mess*, she doesn't talk about *cleaners* or *cleaning*, so (**A**) and (**C**) are not possible. (**D**) is also wrong because when the woman says *This is my mess and I'll get it fixed*, she's talking about not sending the email, not a *computer* that needs fixing.

44. (D)

The man says *I've asked Hui Yin to be here at 9.30 a.m. and Ricardo at 10 a.m. so I can go through the HR stuff with them one by one* and *at 10 and 10.30 a.m. respectively, they have their inductions with IT. Respectively* means in the order previously mentioned, so *Hui Yin* has hers first at *10* and *Ricardo* has his at *10.30 a.m.* This means that (**D**) is correct and (**A**), (**B**) and (**C**) are incorrect.

45. (A)

The woman says *I can do the tour* and *I think Priya would be better for the meeting about our department – she did it last time.* It's safe to assume *Priya* is a *colleague* and, since she *did it last time*, she is *better equipped* to do it again, so (A) is correct. (B) is incorrect because the woman never says how long she has worked *in her department*, and (C) is incorrect because, while the man says the purpose of the *meeting* would be to *explain processes*, the woman never comments on it. (D) is wrong, finally, because the *tour* is at *11 a.m.* and the woman agrees to do it, so she is clearly *available* at that time.

46. (B)

The woman asks *will it be both of them together or just one?* The man says *it was going to be one by one, but now that you ask, maybe both might be more efficient. Let's do that.* This means he had one *idea*, but the *woman's idea* is *better*, so (B) is right. (A) is wrong because the man says he is doing the *HR induction*, not the *tour*. (C) is wrong because the man says the *tours* were *going to be one by one*, not that they *have to happen* like that – and in fact changes his mind about them being *one by one*. Finally, (D) is incorrect because the woman asks if the *tours* will be *together* and the man says *let's do that*, so she will *need to do both*.

47. (B)

The woman says *I've now had a look at your dissertation, and I have to say I'm quite impressed with what you've done.* She then says *I think you've addressed all my points.* This suggests the woman is not a student but a university official, so (A) is wrong. Since she is reading the *dissertation* and giving feedback, she must be a *tutor*, so (D) is incorrect. The person she is talking to wrote the *dissertation*, so he must be a *student*, so (C) is incorrect and (B) is the right answer.

48. (D)

The man says *I was really worried about the second part – adjusting my research methodology – because I'd already interviewed everyone but it wasn't as hard as I thought it'd be to find more people.* This means (D) is correct. (A) is wrong because the woman mentions the *existing research* but the man never comments on it. (B) is wrong because the man mentions *marginalized groups* being the focus, but never calls them *sensitive*. (C) is incorrect because the woman says the *dissertation* should *include people who are less marginalized* and this is why the man needs *more interviewees*; they never mention the number of *interviews*.

49. (C)

The woman says *the deadline is Friday noon. Noon* means *12 p.m.*, so (C) is the correct answer. The man says he will *submit by Thursday, after my 4 p.m. class*, but that's not related to the *deadline*, so (B) is wrong. (A) and (D) are incorrect because these combinations of time and day are never mentioned.

50. (C)

The man says *I've been crunching the numbers for the refurbishment and we're going to need more than $45,000*, which means the *budget* he is referring to is *$45k*. Therefore, *budget A* and *D* are wrong. (*Budget D* is actually what the woman mentions.) The man then says *we need at least $10,000 for the kitchen and another $20,000 for the bedrooms, plus all the small stuff like painting once the work is done… There's nothing left for the bathroom.* If there's *nothing for the bathroom*, *budget B* is wrong. (The numbers are also wrong in *budget B*, as the *bedrooms* are *20k*, not *15k*.) *Budget C* accounts for everything the man mentions: *10k* for the *kitchen*, *20k* for the *bedrooms*, and the remaining money for *misc.*, i.e. miscellaneous, which refers to *all the small stuff*. (C) is, therefore, the correct answer.

51. (C)

The woman says *so we don't expand the bathroom, then* as a first *suggestion*, so (A) is incorrect. She then says *maybe we can pick cheaper tiles* (i.e. *less expensive material*) for the kitchen, or we can stick to just painting one of the bedrooms rather than redoing (i.e. *refurbishing*) *the whole thing*, so (B) and (D) are wrong. The woman never suggests *not refurbishing the kitchen*, though, so (C) is correct.

52. (A)

The man says *I don't want to owe anyone anything, especially family*, which means he *doesn't want to be indebted* to them, so (A) is correct. (B) is wrong because the man mentions *refurbishment plans*, which means *refurbishment* hasn't happened yet. (**C**) is wrong because the man never comments on how *kind* the *offer* is, and (**D**) is wrong because the man says *we need to sit down and look at the numbers together* to the woman – he never mentions the *parents* for this.

53. (C)

The man says about the meeting *it's a bit soon, isn't it? If we're still waiting for proposals, shouldn't we get at least a day to read through all of them properly?* This means he wants to *prepare properly* but *there isn't enough time*, so (**C**) is correct. The man never says *he's not in the office tomorrow*, so (**A**) is incorrect. (**B**) is incorrect as they know when the last proposal will reach them. (**D**) is wrong because the man says he wants *a day* in order to *prepare*, not that the *meeting* will *last all day* – and in fact says the *meeting* is *a bit soon*, so he can't want it to *start sooner*.

54. (A)

One of the women says *these sorts of projects normally take six to eight months from conception to completion, and we've only got four months to do everything.* This means that (**A**) is correct and (**C**) and (**D**) are wrong. As for (**B**), it's wrong because the woman says the project *got shortened to five* at first, but *then to four.*

55. (B)

The woman says *what we've received so far is subpar.* *Subpar* is a synonym for *below average*, which means that (**B**) is correct. This also means that (**A**) is wrong because she can't *like* something and call it *subpar*, (**C**) is wrong because *above average* is the opposite of *subpar*, and (**D**) is wrong because the woman can't know the *proposals* are *subpar* if *she hasn't read them yet.*

56. (D)

The man says *I haven't been getting any signal on my TV*, which means the *TV is not picking* it *up*, so (**D**) is correct. (**A**) is wrong because the man mentions an *error message*, which he wouldn't be able to see if the *TV* didn't *switch on.* (**B**) is wrong because the man never mentions his *PC* – the *error message* is on the *TV.* (**C**) is wrong because the man says he has no *signal*, which means all of the *channels* must have vanished, not *some.*

57. (B)

The woman says *you've picked the right source and everything is plugged*, so (**A**) and (**C**) are wrong. She then says *the cable that connects to your satellite dish is loose, so it must've come off*, which means that the *satellite dish* is not *broken*, but the *cable* is not *connected properly*, so (**B**) is correct and (**D**) is wrong.

58. (A)

The man says *you were right, this was so stupid.* If *this was so stupid*, he must be feeling a bit *stupid*, or *foolish*, himself – so (**A**) is correct. (**B**) *foolhardy* and (**C**) *reckless* mean the same thing: being bold and not thinking of the risks, which is unlikely to be how the man *feels*, so they're both wrong. Finally, *crotchety* means irritable, and the man does not express anger or irritation at any point, so (**D**) is incorrect.

59. (B)

The woman says *we need to use the movie vouchers this weekend. They're expiring next week!* The *vouchers* are a form of *offer* and she doesn't want to *miss* it, so (**B**) is correct. The woman mentions the *movie schedule*, but she never says she *was given* it or that it inspired her, so (**D**) is wrong. The woman never mentions *wanting to see* a *specific movie* or receiving a *recommendation* – both of these are mentioned by the man.

60. (B)

The man says *this one's about fifteen brothers fighting over the family inheritance*, to which the woman responds *well, with so many of them... Can you imagine? I have a hard time with one brother, let alone fourteen.* With *can you imagine* she is clearly referring to how *many* the *brothers* are, and since *brothers* are siblings, (**B**) is correct. While *fighting* amongst the *brothers* is mentioned, this is not what the woman focuses on – and the woman never mentions *not having a sister* or the *inheritance* being *big.*

61. (C)

The woman says they should *not* go to *the 4-something one* because *I hate subtitles.* The only movie with *subtitles* is *What Was Forgotten*, so (**A**) and (**C**) are wrong. However, according to the *schedule* the *16:10 screening* of *What Was Forgotten* is *subtitled* and the woman says *no* to that, so the only option is (**D**) at *6:00*, i.e. *the one after*.

62. (D)

The man says *she's only been working there for what, three, four months?* Then, the woman says *six, isn't it?* However, the woman corrects both of them by saying *no, seven*. This means that (**D**) is correct and all other options are incorrect.

63. (C)

The woman says that *Alice* has *decided to leave town and go to university*, which means she is *returning to school*, so (**C**) is correct. While the woman does suggest she could *ask for her old job back* or *look for a new one*, and the man suggests she *could apply for that new opening we've got in Marketing*, none of these are what *Alice* herself is *planning*: they are merely ideas from the speakers.

64. (B)

After the man says *wow, that's odd*, the woman asks him to explain and he says *I never pegged Alice for the kind of person who could live in a place like Utah*. This means he didn't expect her to *agree to move to Utah*, so (**B**) is correct. (**A**) is wrong because the man never says anything about the *husband*, even though he is also *moving* there. While *Alice* is planning to *study economics*, the man never comments on this either – and he never says it's *odd* she *wants to leave town*: he's just amazed at her choice of destination, which he finds unlike her.

65. (A)

The man says *10 are tentative*, which means they might or might not *come*, so (**A**) is correct. *20* is the number of people who *have confirmed*, and *30* is the number up to which the *attendance* might *fluctuate*, whereas *50* is the number of people the man and woman have *invited*.

66. (D)

The man says *I worry some of the people who said no might change their mind*. This means *he thinks some people who said they won't come might come after all*, so (**D**) is correct. (**A**) is wrong because even if *more people confirm their attendance*, the total number

won't be higher than *30* – unless people *change their mind*. The man never says the *room* with *30* is *cramped* – and what he says is *maybe* the *room with 50 people is better*, meaning a *better* option, not that it *looks better*.

67. (B)

Early on, the woman says *the room that only fits 25 is no good* – and the man replies *we don't need this one either – it's way bigger than we need*. This means that (**A**) and (**D**) are wrong. The man and woman go on to discuss the merits of booking the *room for 30* and the *room* for *50*, i.e. the *Blue* or *Yellow room*. In the end, though, the woman says *we can't waste $200 just in case they*, meaning people who declined the invite, *decide to show up*. The *Yellow room* is *$200* more expensive and bigger than the *Blue room*, so they've clearly *decided to book* the *Blue room*, meaning (**B**) is correct.

68. (D)

The man says *they'll be here at 10*, so (**D**) is correct. *7.30* and *8.30* are times the three speakers mention that *they* will be departing, not *arriving*, so (**A**) and (**B**) are wrong – while (**C**) is wrong because, while the woman says *they should be here at 9*, the man then says their flight has been *delayed*, so they won't *arrive* until *10*.

69. (B)

The man says that *David* has *booked a cab* (i.e. *taxi*) *for them, so the driver should be waiting for them at arrivals* – so (**B**) is correct. The man says *they'd take ages if they took the bus, and the train's not working today*, so (**C**) and (**D**) are incorrect – while (**A**) is incorrect because, while the woman asks if *David's picking them up to bring them to the office*, the man replies that he *booked a cab*, so he clearly won't be *picking them up*.

70. (A)

The woman says *you're not the one whose job relies on them signing the contract*, to which the man responds *touché*. If her *job relies on* a successful outcome, this means she *has a better reason to be stressed*, so (**A**) is correct. The man says *we've planned everything down to the minutest detail* but nobody says who did *more*, so (**B**) is wrong. Nobody mentions how they got their *job* either. The woman says it's *them* who *need* to be *signing the contract*, not her, so (**D**) is incorrect.

Part IV—Short Talks

71. (A)

The question asks who is giving this speech. The woman says *I'm at the scene now, Dolores, and as you can see behind me, there's a big crowd gathering.* She then talks about *the police* not giving her *a lot of information* and the *firefighters* working in tough conditions. All of this suggests she is neither (**B**) *a firefighter* nor (**C**) *a police officer* herself, and from the way she reports the facts, it's unlikely she's (**D**) *a local resident*. The most logical explanation is that she is (**A**) *a reporter* at the *scene* of an event (a *fire*).

72. (C)

The question asks what information the woman does NOT give about the fire. The woman says *the blaze started somewhere on the third story and spread through the building very rapidly around 9 p.m. tonight*, which means she tells us (**A**) *where* and (**B**) *when* the *fire began*. The woman says *the blaze started around the third floor and spread through the building*, the woman then says *the fire has been contained and won't be spreading to any of the surrounding buildings*, so (**D**) is not the answer. The only thing she does not tell us is (**C**) *how it began*, so that's the correct answer.

73. (B)

The question asks how many casualties there are so far. *Casualty* means injured and/or dead people, and the woman says *about 32 are receiving treatment either here or at the hospital*, so (**B**) is correct. (**A**) is wrong because *18* is the number of *people* who *have confirmed they weren't in the building when the fire started*. (**C**) is wrong because *36* is the number of *people still unaccounted for*, and (**D**) is wrong because *46* is the number of *people downstairs*.

74. (B)

The question asks what the topic of this speech is. The man talks about a *slump in sales* and *what's causing* it, as well as how to cause *a marked improvement in sales*. This means the topic is the *company's sales*, so (**B**) is correct. While the man speaks about *launching new products*, he never says *which* is best to *launch*, so (**A**) is wrong. Also, while the man talks about *how the*

company started out (*with a unique product*), this is in the context of why that business model from *twenty years ago* doesn't *work* now, so (**C**) is wrong. Finally, (**D**) is wrong because the man talks about the *last two quarters*, i.e. the past, not about *projections* for the future.

75. (B)

The question asks what the man says about the company's current products. The man says *what I think is we don't just need a major overhaul of how we present the products we have: we need to create new products, too*. This means that the man doesn't think they *need to be replaced* or that they *can't be re-branded*, but they *need to be supplemented by new products*, so (**B**) is correct and (**A**) and (**C**) are wrong. Finally, (**D**) is wrong because the man never talks about *ten years* in the future; only about *ten years ago*.

76. (A)

The question asks what can be inferred from the man's speech. The man *we need to be seen once again as the sort of risk-takers that launched this company from the ground*. This suggests that the *company* was once a *risk-taker* or *used to take risks*, so (**A**) is correct. While the man talks about *a marked improvement in sales soon*, this is dependent on *focusing* on the creation of *new products*, so (**B**) is wrong. (**C**) is wrong because the man talks about *attacking new markets in the cosmetics world*, which he wouldn't suggest if he thought *the world of cosmetics isn't lucrative*, i.e. making money anymore. (**D**) is wrong, finally, because the man talks about the *need* for *new products* – which means they don't exist yet, so they can't be *not good enough*.

77. (D)

The question asks which of the following passwords would be acceptable for the website. The man says *passwords* must be *more than five characters*, and *j0Hn* is only four, so (**A**) is incorrect. The man also mentions *you can't use the @ sign*, so (**B**) is wrong. He then says *you should have at least one symbol for the password to be accepted*. (**C**) has no *symbol* so it's incorrect. (**D**) is the only option which is *more than five characters*, a *combination of letters and numbers*, *capitals*, no @ or *underscore*, and a *symbol*, so it's correct.

78. (A)

The question asks what you do NOT need to do to achieve 'Confirmed' status. The man says you must add *copies of your degrees and certificates, as well as your passport*, i.e. *ID* evidence, so (B) and (C) are wrong. The man also says *you'll need to add details on what kind of work you are looking for*, i.e. your *preferences*, so (D) is wrong. (A) is the correct answer because what you *need to upload* is *a short bio*, i.e. a paragraph about you, not *a short video*.

79. (C)

The question asks what the man says at the end. While the man says you need to *wait for the person offering the project to pick someone*, he never says how long they *take*, so (A) is wrong. The man also says *you can't bid on projects you're not qualified to work on*, which means you are not *allowed to bid on all projects*, so (B) is wrong. (D) is incorrect because the man never says anything about *communicating* with *people offering projects* and whether it's allowed or not. (C) is the correct answer because the man says *projects you're not qualified to work on* will be *filtered out so you won't even be able to see them*, which means they will be *hidden*.

80. (D)

The question asks what can be inferred about the woman from the speech. The woman says *I was told by Marina that you used to do these Monday morning...well, I don't really want to call them meetings*. The *meetings* take place on *Monday morning* but the woman never comments on whether she *likes Monday mornings*, so (A) is incorrect. The woman then says about *meetings* that they *can often be dull and repetitive and I don't want you to think of this like that*, which means she wants them not to *think of this* as a *meeting*, not to *change* the length of the meeting, so (B) is incorrect. While the woman mentions *Marina*, she never says who she is and whether she has been *replaced* by her or not, so (C) is wrong. However, the fact the woman needed *Marina* to tell her they *used to* have *Monday morning meetings* means she hasn't been in *the company* very long, so (D) is correct.

81. (A)

The question asks which of the following the woman does NOT suggest as topics for the catch-up. The

woman mentions that in this *catch-up* they can mention a *recent success*, something (i.e. a *lesson*) *learned through trial and error* and *something* they *need help* (i.e. *assistance*) *with*, so (B), (C) and (D) are wrong. The woman says about *meetings* that people have them to *come up with a solution to something* and then says the *catch-up* is not a *meeting*, so she doesn't want this to be a *topic for the catch-up*, so (A) is correct.

82. (C)

The question asks what the woman says about the catch-up at the end. The woman says they can *try it out* for *a month*, not that it *will happen once a month*, so (A) is wrong. The point of the *trial* will be to decide if it is *beneficial* – the woman never says *she thinks it will be*, so (B) is wrong. The woman says the *catch-up* will be a *five-minute* one, but never says it *will start in five minutes*, so (D) is wrong. (C) is correct because the woman says that if the *catch-up* is not seen as *beneficial*, then *we can always discuss different ways of catching up* – which means *she will stop them*.

83. (A)

The question asks what is wrong with the cell phones being recalled. The man talks about a *fault that is making Spring Mini 6 phones shut down unexpectedly* – which means they *switch off out of the blue*, so (A) is correct. (B) is wrong because a *software update* is the solution, not the *fault*. (C) is wrong because the man talks about *tracing the origin of the fault*, not a 'trace' feature, and (D) is wrong because it's the *phone* that *shuts down randomly*, not *applications*.

84. (B)

The question asks what the speaker is referring to when he says, "This is commendable." The man says the *company* reps *encourage customers who have purchased a Spring Mini 6 to bring it in to a Spring Mobile store even if it hasn't exhibited the behavior reported*. He then says *I think this is commendable*, which means he is talking about the fact that the *company* is *inviting all customers* – so (B) is correct. The man *urges* people not to follow this advice to avoid *long queues*, so (A) is wrong. The man does not mention the fact the *company* is *recalling* its product or *admitting* the issue's *origin* when he says *this is commendable*.

85. (D)

The question asks which cell phone model from the graph below cannot be fixed. The man continuously mentions the *cell phone model* as *Spring Mini 6*, so (A) and (B) are incorrect. He then says the one being *recalled* is *from the November 2018 batch*, i.e. *11/2018*, so (D) is the right answer. (C) is wrong as it's from October (*10/2018*).

86. (D)

The question asks why the project with the woman's company is not going ahead. The woman says *at first I thought it was because they were going with a competitor or because they'd just run out of budget*, but then she says that's not it, so (A) and (B) are incorrect. The woman then says *Desmond told me the main reason is that they've decided to focus on what they already have rather than attacking new markets or launching in new regions and countries*. This means that (D) is correct, whereas (C) is incorrect because the client has clearly not *decided to attack a new market*.

87. (C)

The question asks what Desmond says about the project. The woman says *they anticipate to be looking into it in a year or two*; however, she then says *Desmond's not so sure we'll be in the running after our poor performance in Las Vegas*. Not being *in the running* means not being *considered* as a candidate – so (C) is correct. The woman says *they anticipate looking into it in a year or two*, so the clients are planning to expand, they are just delaying that decision, (D) is not the answer.

88. (D)

The question asks which month from the table the woman is referring to in her speech. The woman says: *Look at this: this month is one of the busiest in their Mississippi stores, and it was one of the worst-performing months in Las Vegas*. The *busiest* for *Mississippi* are *January* and *April*, at *$170,000-172,000*, so (B) and (C) are wrong. The *worst-performing months* for *Las Vegas* are *February* and *April*, at *$22,000-23,000* – however, as we've already rejected *February*, the correct answer is (D) *April*.

89. (B)

The question asks what the caller can do online. The recording says *to inquire about our services or make a new booking, please press 2 or visit our website at www.joesmoving.com*, which means you can *find out more about the company's services*, so (B) is correct. (A) is wrong because the recording says that to *modify* a *booking* you need to *press 4 or 5*. (C) is wrong because the recording asks to *have your booking reference ready* but doesn't say where to *find* it. (D) is incorrect because the recording mentions you may have *received a text message* but doesn't say how to *request it*.

90. (C)

The question asks which number the caller should press to cancel a paid-for booking. The recording says *to modify or cancel a booking for which you have been charged* (i.e. *paid-for*), *please press 4* – so (C) is correct. (A) is wrong because *1* is for *questions about a booking not taking place today*. (B) is wrong because *2* is for *bookings today* where the called has *not yet received a text message* or the *driver is not picking up their phone*. (D) is wrong because *5* is to *cancel a booking for which you have not been charged*, i.e. not already *paid for*.

91. (D)

The question asks which number the caller should press to make changes to an unpaid booking. The recording says *to modify* (i.e. *make changes*) *or cancel a booking for which you have not been charged yet, please press 5*, so (D) is correct. As in the previous question, (A) is wrong because *1* is for *questions about a booking not taking place today* and (B) is wrong because *2* is for *bookings today* where the called has *not yet received a text message* or the *driver is not picking up their phone*. Finally, (C) is wrong because *4* is to *modify* a *booking for which you have been charged*.

92. (C)

The question asks which government promise the speaker does NOT mention. The woman says the *government* said *they'd introduce new measures to tackle knife crime in the capital*, so (A) is incorrect. She also says *they would fix healthcare*, so (B) is incorrect. She then mentions *their promise to limit university fees*, so (**D**) is incorrect. (**C**) is the correct answer because the woman says *all I've heard is crickets* after mentioning the *promises* about *knife crime*, which is an expression that means *all* she has *heard* is silence – she never mentions a real *cricket population*.

93. (B)

The question asks which university from the graph the speaker attends. The woman says about her *university* that *they currently charge more than $5,000 per semester – that's more than $10,000 a year*. The table shows prices *per annum*, i.e. per *year*, not per *semester*, so (**A**) is incorrect. (**D**) is incorrect because the woman says *more than $10,000*, not exactly that – and (**C**) is incorrect because she says *with the new prices, they'll be able to charge $12,000 a year*, but the table says *current*, not future *fees*. The correct answer is (**B**), which at *$10,800 currently* exceeds *$10,000*.

94. (B)

The question asks how the speaker is likely to feel. The woman says *we will fight this* and *we will protest and take the fight to parliament*. All of this suggests she is the opposite of *unmotivated*, so (**A**) is incorrect. She's also not *glum* or *despondent*, which are synonyms and mean depressed and without hope. The correct answer is (**B**), as she is clearly *determined* to *fight*.

95. (A)

The question asks what the woman calls strange about the weather. The woman says *what's most surprising is not the ferocity with which these adverse weather phenomena have hit us – it is the way it happened, so abruptly*. This means that (**B**) is wrong, and (**A**) is correct – as *abruptly* is a synonym of *suddenly*. (**C**) is wrong because the woman never calls the *weather untypical*, and (**D**) is wrong because, while the woman says the *weather* turned *late this Wednesday*, she never calls this *strange*.

96. (C)

The question asks what is NOT forecasted for Sunday. The woman says *this drop is expected to continue well into the weekend*, so (**D**) *low temperatures* is wrong. She also says *strong gusts*, i.e. *wind*, will be around *until next Monday*, so (**A**) is wrong. She then says *snowfall, as you can imagine, is expected*

in the northernmost regions of the state throughout this time, so (**B**) is incorrect. What she does say is *the heavy downpour is not expected to ease until Saturday evening*, which means the *downpour* (i.e. *rain*) will stop before *Sunday*, so (**C**) is correct.

97. (B)

The question asks What CANNOT be inferred from the speech. The woman says *hospitals are braced for a busy weekend*, so (**A**) is incorrect. She then mentions *potential road accidents*, so (**C**) is incorrect. According to the woman, the *government* has *recommended that people keep an eye on older family members or neighbors*, which means they *might need assistance*, so (**D**) is incorrect. Near the end, though, the woman says *the last time we experienced such weather was ten years ago*, which means the *weather* is not *often this bad*, so (**B**) is correct.

98. (C)

The question asks what can be inferred about the woman from the speech. The woman says *I have a five-year-old daughter and every Sunday morning we go to a reading group for kids* and goes on to explain why this is so important for her *daughter*, so (**C**) is the correct answer. (**A**) is wrong because, while the woman mentions *Mr. Smith's plan to close 30 libraries*, she never says anything to suggest she *just found out*. (**B**) is wrong because the woman explicitly says *you might think libraries are a luxury, Mr. Smith, but they're not*. (**D**) is wrong because the woman says it's her *neighbors* who *can't afford to buy books*, not herself.

99. (B)

The question asks which of the following important library services is NOT mentioned. The woman mentions *unemployed adults*, i.e. people *looking for a job, can receive help with their resumes*, so (**A**) is incorrect. The woman also says *teenagers whose parents can't afford to buy them a laptop can use the computers to do research and write essays for school*, which means they have access to *technology*, so (**C**) is incorrect. However, the woman only says they can *write essays* on the *computers*, not that the *libraries* give *essay-writing help*, so (**B**) is the correct answer. Finally, (**D**) is wrong because the woman says *children learn to love books*.

100. (A)

The question asks what the woman recommends to save libraries. While the woman mentions *recruiting volunteers*, she never says they should *replace staff*, so (**B**) is wrong. She also never says anything about *closing* any of the *libraries*, so (**C**) is wrong. The woman does not suggest selling *books*, so (**D**) can be eliminated. (**A**) is the correct answer because the woman says *why not move some of the libraries?* And to *relocate* means to *move*.

Reading

Part V—Incomplete Sentences

101. (D)

The missing word is a verb, preceded by the adverb *still*. Since the sentence is talking about a *move* that's happening the future (*in April or May*), we can't use the past, so (**A**) *decided* and (**C**) *didn't decide*, both in the past simple, are wrong. The word *still* suggests something ongoing, but (**B**) *have decided* is in the present perfect simple, which suggests the decision would happen momentarily, so it's wrong. (**D**) *haven't decided* is the correct answer because the lack of a decision can be ongoing.

102. (B)

The missing word is part of the verb, the rest of which is in the sentence: *it is being*. Since we are using the verb 'be' twice (*is being*), this verb is in the passive voice, so we are missing the past participle, (**B**) *monitored*. This means that (**A**) is wrong because *monitor* is the infinitive or present simple, (**C**) is wrong because *monitoring* is the gerund, and (**D**) is wrong because *monitors* is the present simple.

103. (B)

The missing word is a phrasal verb that means to leave one's post. The correct phrasal verb for that is (**B**) *stand down*. (**A**) *stand out* means to be noticeable. (**C**) *stand away* means to literally move away from the something, and (**D**) *stand off* is not a verb; it's a noun that means a deadlock.

104. (C)

The missing word is a noun that means productive, as an *agreement* is *expected very soon*. The correct word for this is (**C**) *fruitful*, which means useful. (**A**) *frugal* means economical, (**B**) *frivolous* means silly, and (**D**) *fractious* means irritable (usually for children).

105. (B)

The missing word is a preposition that collocates with someone's (in this case *the victim's*) *name* to mean on behalf of them, or to honor them. The correct preposition for this is (**B**) *in*. This means that (**A**) *at*, (**C**) *for* and (**D**) *by* are all wrong.

106. (A)

The missing word is a verb which means to claim. (**A**) is correct because to *profess* something means to claim it. (**B**) is wrong because *propounded* means to put forward an idea for others' consideration. (**C**) is wrong because *proffered* means to give someone something by extending your arm, and (**D**) is wrong because *protracted* means to prolong.

107. (D)

The missing word is the verb of the sentence. The first sentence talks about *a terrible decision* in the past (*was*), and the second sentence talks about the better option, so the missing verb must also be in the past. This means (**A**) *must use* and (**C**) *should use* are both wrong because they're in the present. (**B**) *must have used* is wrong because we use *must* in the past to speculate, not to describe an option which was better but not used. To do that, we use *should* in the past, so (**D**) *should have used* is the correct answer.

108. (B)

The missing word is a verb which works as a synonym for 'taking into account'. (**A**) *provided* is wrong because we use *provided* as a synonym of 'assuming', not when we already know something and need to take it into account. (**C**) is wrong because *supposed* can't be used like this at all: we can only use 'supposing' as a synonym, again, of 'assuming'. (**D**) is wrong because, like *supposed*, it can't be used like this: 'considering' would've been a synonym of 'taking into account'. (**B**) is correct because *given* means 'taking into account'.

109. (D)

The missing word is a verb that means to follow rules. (D) is the correct answer because to *comply* means exactly that. (A) *compel* means to oblige, (B) *compete* means to have a competition, and (C) *compose* means to create or constitute.

110. (A)

The missing word is the verb – and since the *movie* has been called *disappointing*, the verb must mean to criticize. (A) *panned* means exactly that, so it's correct. (B) *penned* means to author, (C) *praised* means the exact opposite of criticize, and (D) *pounded* means to hit.

111. (C)

The missing word is a verb which means blocked, or busy, and collocates with *traffic*. (C) *congested* is the correct answer. (A) *constructed* is wrong because it means created, or made. (B) *contorted* is wrong because it means to twist, and (D) *confounded* is wrong because it means to surprise.

112. (C)

The missing word describes how *critics*, according to the *president, have attempted to mislead*. Since we already have the full verb (*have attempted*), the missing word can't be a verb, so (D) *deliberated* is wrong. (A) *deliberate* can be a verb, but it can also be an adjective; however, adjectives are followed by nouns, not verbs, so it's also wrong. (B) *deliberation* is wrong because it's a noun, and nouns can't go in the middle of a verb. The only type of word that can go in the middle of a verb is an adverb, to describe how the action was done – so (C) *deliberately*, which is an adverb and means 'on purpose', is correct.

113. (B)

The missing word is a verb which follows the verb *stopped*. The verb *stop* can be followed by either the infinitive with 'to' or gerund. This means that (A) *collect*, which is an infinitive without 'to', and (D) *to collecting*, which is the preposition 'to' with the gerund, are both wrong. The decision to use infinitive with 'to' or gerund depends on the meaning: to show that an action was interrupted, we use the gerund. To show that an action started after another was interrupted, we use infinitive with 'to'. Here, the speaker *stopped* with their car and then *collected Amy from her house*, so it's the latter and we need to use infinitive with 'to'. This means that (B) *to collect* is the correct answer, and (C) *collecting* is wrong.

114. (B)

The missing word is part of a conditional sentence. The condition is for the *unions' demands* to be met. Without that condition, they will *go ahead with their planned action*. (C) *if* and (D) *provided* are both used to show that a condition is met – but it's illogical here for the *unions* to strike if their *demands are met*, so both are wrong. (A) *whether* is used to give two binary options of a condition, which is not the case here, so it's also wrong. (B) *unless* is correct because it's used to show a condition has not been met.

115. (C)

The missing word follows the preposition *with*. After prepositions, we should always use the gerund – so (C) *arriving* is correct. This means that (A) *arrive* is wrong because it's the infinitive or present tense and (D) *arrived* is wrong because it's the past tense. We can also use nouns after prepositions, and (B) *arrival* is a noun. However, we already have a noun after *with* (*the first exit polls*) and we can't have two consecutive nouns without them being linked, so it's wrong. The correct structure would be *with the arrival of the first exit polls…*

116. (D)

The missing word describes how *the app* has been *crashing*. Only adverbs can describe how something happens, so (D) *unexpectedly* is correct. (A) *expect* is wrong because it's a verb. (B) *expected* is wrong because it's either a verb or an adjective, and (C) *unexpected* is wrong because it's an adjective.

117. (B)

The missing word is a verb that means to ask people to return something they have purchased. The correct verb for this is (B) *recall*. (A) *rehash* means to reuse (usually an idea), (C) *retrain* means to train again, and (D) *remit* means to cancel a payment or to send money as a present.

118. (B)

The missing word is the correct preposition that completes the phrasal verb *crack down* to mean to take measures against something or someone. The correct preposition for this is (**B**) *on*, so (**A**) *in*, (**C**) *at* and (**D**) *with* are all wrong.

119. (B)

The missing word is a verb that means to strengthen, and collocates with *rumors*. The correct verb for this is (**B**) *fueled*, as it means to give power to *rumors* like giving *fuel* to a fire or a vehicle. (**A**) *fortified* means to create a fort as protection, (**C**) *fabricated* means to invent lies, and (**D**) *fulminated* means to protest.

120. (B)

The missing word is a noun that describes a *period* during which a change takes place, or is *implemented* – so the correct answer is (**B**) *implementation*. (**A**) *aberration* means deviation, (**C**) *capitulation* means surrender, and (**D**) *delimitation* means creating limits.

121. (A)

The missing word is a verb that collocates with *to pressure* to means that you listen to *pressure*. The correct collocation for this is *bow*, so (**A**) is the correct answer. That means that (**B**) *fall*, (**C**) *give* and (**D**) *obey* are all wrong, because none of them collocates with *pressure*. There is a synonymous collocation with the verb *give* (*give in to pressure*), but only as a phrasal verb, as *give in* means to surrender.

122. (C)

The missing word is a verb that means to destroy. *Decimated* is a synonym of destroy, so (**C**) is the correct answer. (**A**) *dedicated* means to devote, so it's wrong. (**B**) *deprecated* means to disapprove, so it's also wrong. Finally, (**C**) *desecrated* means to disrespect something sacred, so it's wrong.

123. (C)

The missing word follows the verb *have a hard time*. This verb is always followed by the gerund, so (**C**) *passing* is correct. This means that (**A**) is wrong because *pass* is the infinitive or present tense, (**B**) because *to pass* is the infinitive with 'to, and (**D**) because *to be passed* is the infinitive with 'to' in the passive voice.

124. (B)

The missing word is a verb that collocates with *confidence* to mean to cause it. The correct verb for this collocation is *inspire*, so (**B**) is correct. (**A**) *import* means to bring from elsewhere, and does not collocate with *confidence*. (**C**) *increase* could potentially collocate with *confidence*, but not with *much confidence* because *much confidence* is a defined amount and you cannot *increase* an amount while defining it at the same time. (**D**) *intone* is a way of speaking and does not collocate with *confidence*.

125. (A)

The missing word is a noun that might mean something like unfair, or biased, as he has hired someone he is close to that is not qualified for the job. The correct word for this is (**A**) *favoritism*, he favored his nephew because of their relationship. (**B**) *clientelism* is the practice of gaining financial or political support through forms of bribery. (**D**) *bruxism* is the habit of grinding teeth, and (**C**) *protectionism* is the method of protecting local produce by imposing high tax on imports.

126. (D)

The missing word is an expression that means so far. (**A**) *hence* means therefore, so it's wrong. (**B**) *henceforth* means from now on, so it's also wrong. (**C**) *this far* is wrong because it shows distance; the correct expression would be thus *far*, so (**D**) is correct.

127. (B)

The missing word is an adjective that describes the *activities* of the *mayor* – and since they caused *his immediate resignation*, they must be bad. This rules out (**A**) *decorous*, which means polite, as well as (**C**) *scrupulous* and (**D**) *assiduous* which both mean careful. (**B**) *sordid* is the only option, as it means immoral.

128. (A)

The missing word is an adjective that describes a feeling that causes one to need *fresh air*. (**A**) is correct because *perturbed* means upset. (**B**) *unruffled* means the complete opposite, so it's wrong. (**C**) *biased* means prejudiced, whereas (**D**) *percipient* means perceptive.

129. (C)

The missing word is the preposition that follows the verb *to invest*. The correct preposition for this is *in*, so (**C**) is the correct answer. This means that (**A**) *on*, (**B**) *at* and (**D**) *to* are all wrong.

130. (D)

The missing word is verb that begins the subordinate clause in the beginning of the sentence. Since there is no conjunction such as 'and' or 'although', we cannot have a verb: we can only have the infinitive with 'to' (if we want to show purpose) or gerund (if we want to show an action that happened before or simultaneously). This means that (**A**) *discuss* and (**C**) *have discussed*, which are neither, are wrong. Since *Claire has agreed* on something, the *discussion* with her must be finished. Ergo, we can't use (**B**) *discussing*, as it would suggest the *discussion* is happening simultaneously. The only option is (**D**) *having discussed*, as it means the *discussion* is finished.

Part VI—Text Completion

131. (D)

The missing word the verb that follows the expression *thank you*. To give the reason for giving *thanks* to someone, we always use the preposition *for*. Therefore, (**A**) *to contact* and (**B**) *to contacting* are both wrong. Since *for* is a preposition, it must be followed by the gerund, not the infinitive, so (**C**) *for contact* is wrong and (**D**) *for contacting* is the correct answer.

132. (C)

The missing word follows *you are* and comes before *to our monthly HDTV service*. Since we already have a verb (*are*), we don't need another – so (**A**) *subscribe* is wrong. Since the word *you* refers to the recipient of the email, *Will*, we need a word that describes him. This means that (**D**) is wrong because *Will* is a person, so he can't be a *subscription*, which is a *service*. (**B**) is also wrong because, while *Will* can be a *subscriber*, this is a countable noun so it would need an article before it: a *subscriber*. (**C**) is the correct answer because *you are*

subscribed is the passive voice, and it means somebody *subscribed* him to the *service*.

133. (B)

The missing word is a phrasal verb which means to log in. The correct phrasal verb for this is (**B**) *sign in*. To (**A**) *sign up* means to join, and you wouldn't normally be asked to *upgrade* as soon as you joined. To (**C**) *sign off* means to use your signature to approve something, and to (**D**) *sign over* means to give up ownership of something (e.g. a property) by *signing* an official document.

134. (A)

The missing word is a verb which means to stop something. A synonym for stopping something, particularly a service, is (**A**) *discontinue*. (**B**) *disallow* means to forbid. (**C**) *dismember* means to remove someone's limbs, and (**D**) *dislodge* means to knock out of position.

135. (B)

The missing sentence follows the author's offering of *congratulations*, and precedes another sentence which explains why the team deserve the *congratulations*, as their *talent* and *commitment* led to winning the *award*. The missing sentence should therefore focus on the *congratulations* as well. It's illogical to switch to when the *results were announced* or how *close* the *race* was – and the *hope* to *continue to win* would fit as a conclusion, not a comment in between. The only logical sentence, therefore, is (**B**), which focuses on complimenting the team.

136. (C)

In this sentence, we are missing the verb. The text talks about an *award* that the company has received – and it was because of the employees' *commitment* that they won. Since they already won the award, we need to use the past tense, so (**A**) *will never come*, which is the future, (**B**) *would never come*, which is the present or future, and (**D**) *never come*, which is the present, are all wrong. The only option in the past is (**C**) *never would've come*, so it's correct.

137. (B)

In this sentence, we are missing the correct word to introduce a subordinate clause. Before the gap we have *Laura*, so the missing word must refer to her. Since Laura is a person, we can't use (**D**) *which*. After the gap, we have *New Talent graduate scheme*, which belongs to *Laura*, so the missing word must show possession. The word that shows possession is (**B**) *whose*, so it's correct. (**A**) *who* describes a person, not a possession, so it's wrong. Finally, (**C**) is wrong because it's a contraction of *who is* – although *whose* is often misspelled that way.

138. (A)

In this sentence, we are missing the verb that collocates with *thanks* to show that one gives *thanks* to someone. The correct collocation for this is to *extend thanks*, so (**A**) is correct. (**B**) *expand* means to enlarge, (**C**) *expose* means to reveal and (**D**) *extoll* means to praise, and none of these collocate with *thanks*.

139. (C)

In this sentence, we are missing the structure that follows the verb *regret*. The verb *regret* can be followed by the gerund or the infinitive with *to*, so (**A**) and (**D**) are incorrect. *Regret* followed by the gerund is used when we *regret* something we have already done, whereas *regret* with infinitive with *to* is used when we are sorry for something we are about to do. Since the *regret* here is about *informing* the email recipient of something, the author is sorry for what they are doing, so the correct answer is (**C**).

140. (B)

In this sentence, we are missing the adjective that collocates with the noun *competition* to mean strong. The correct collocation for this is *fierce*, so (**B**) is correct. None of the other adjectives collocate with *competition*, nor would it make sense for them to be used with it as (**A**) *foul* means bad, (**C**) *facetious* means whimsical and (**D**) *forthcoming* means honest or yet to arrive.

141. (A)

The missing sentence is in a paragraph that explains the author of the email liked the recipient and their *interview* was good, which means they have a chance to work in the company *in the future*. Since the author is actively *encouraging* the recipient to *apply* for other *opportunities* in *the future*, (**A**) is correct. (**B**) is wrong because the recipient did not get the *role*, so they

cannot *accept* it, whereas (**C**) and (**D**) are standard phrases used in rejection emails and letters, which do not fit with the author's *encouragement* and suggestion that the recipient can *work* in the company *in the future*.

142. (D)

In this sentence, we are missing the word before the noun *feedback*. Since *feedback* is a noun and the gap is preceded by *more*, which is an adverb, the missing word must be an adjective. (**A**) and (**C**) are either nouns or verbs, whereas (**B**) is a verb or gerund, so they're wrong. (**D**) *detailed* is the only adjective, so it's correct.

143. (A)

In this sentence, we are missing a verb that means to consider something *appropriate*. (**A**) *deem* is a synonym of consider, so it is correct. To (**B**) *adjourn* means to interrupt or postpone. To (**C**) *submit* means offer or present, and to (**D**) *confer* means to discuss. None of these options can be followed by an adjective like *appropriate*, so they're all incorrect.

144. (B)

We know from the word *an* that the missing word must begin with a vowel; eliminate (**C**) and (**D**). *Adjacent* does not describe a type of vote, so (**B**), anonymous must be the correct answer.

145. (C)

In this sentence, we are missing the word that collocates with *vote* to describe *voting* via *post* instead of in person. The correct collocation for this is *postal vote*, so (**C**) is correct. This means that (**A**) *post* (**B**) *posted* and (**D**) *postage* are all incorrect, as none of them collocates with *vote*.

146. (A)

Before the missing sentence, the paragraph describes what the *voters* need to carry to the *club* in order to *vote*. It therefore makes sense for the next sentence to clarify that these (*I.D.* and *proxy form*) are necessary and you can't *vote without these*. (**A**) is therefore correct. Mentioning when *non-members* can *vote* or when the *results* will be *posted* is not consistent with the rest of the paragraph, which focuses on the *voting* procedure itself – while the need to *book a room* is completely irrelevant to this paragraph.

Part VII—Reading Comprehension

147. (C)

The question asks what the purpose of this email is. The email starts with *we are happy to hear that you are considering becoming an adoptive parent*. It then goes on to answer the *questions* the sender might *have* and to explain about the *FAQ* and *guides* available. All of this suggests this is the first time the sender is contacting the agency, which means this is an *initial query*, so (C) is correct. While the email does *explain how to book an appointment*, this is in the context of general information – and while *guides to adoption* are mentioned, they are not attached. Finally, since the sender is *considering becoming an adoptive parent*, they can't have sent an *application* yet, so (B) is incorrect.

148. (B)

The question asks what the email says about the first meeting with the agency. The email says the *meeting is not considered part of the application process*, so (A) is wrong. It also says *no notes are taken*, so (C) is wrong. While the email does mention the *meeting* will be with a *social worker*, it never says that this will be the *social worker* who will be assigned to the *applicant's case*. (B) is the correct answer as the *meeting* is described as a *casual chat*, which means it *will not be formal*.

149. (D)

The question asks which of the positions [1], [2], [3] or [4] the following sentence best belong in: "If you have any further questions, please do not hesitate to get in touch." This is a typical closing sentence, inviting the recipient to *get in touch* if the present email has not given them all the answers they needed. This, combined with *I look forward to hearing from you*, is a very appropriate ending to the email, so [4] is the correct position. While there are things the recipient might have *questions* about in the other three positions, e.g. the *guides* or the *meeting* with the *social worker*, this sentence does not fit anywhere but at the end of the email, as in any other position it would only invite *questions* arising from that particular paragraph, rather than the entire email.

150. (C)

The question asks what can be inferred about Orpheus Cruises from the ad. The ad mentions *Promo Code Summer*, but this does not mean that the company only operates during the summer. *Rome* and *America* are not mentioned in the text. The text mentions *14-day cruises* which is equivalent to two weeks, so (C) is the answer.

151. (C)

The question asks which statement is NOT TRUE about Orpheus Cruises. The ad says *breakfast and dinner included*, so (A) is true. It also mentions *excellent discounts at local bars and restaurants*, which must mean they have *an agreement with certain bars. Open bar from noon till midnight* means that This means that *customers can drink for free on the ship from 12 at noon to 12 at night*, so (D) is true. (C) is NOT TRUE because, while the text does say *Spend a week touring the Greek islands from as little as $1,399*, a week is *7 days* and there are also *4-day cruises* available, which must be *cheaper* than the *week*-long ones.

152. (B)

The question asks at how many islands the 7-day cruise spends the night. The text says *1 overnight stay* (i.e. *spending the night*) *for 4-day cruises, 2 overnight stays for all other cruises*. This means that (B) is the correct answer. (A) applies to *4-day cruises*, not *7-day*, (C) is not mentioned as an option anywhere, and (D) is the total number of *islands* where *overnight stays* can take place, but none of the *cruises* offers *4 overnight stays*.

153. (B)

The question asks you to find the item that cost the least in total, so check the final column in the table for the smallest number, as this will be the answer. The lemon and poppy seed muffin is only $1.14, so (B) is the correct answer.

154. (D)

The question asks which type of milk is cheapest per unit. *Per unit* means we shouldn't care about whether the *milk* in the *unit* is *1.5L* or *1L*: we should be looking only at the *price per unit*. Based on that, (D) is the correct answer as the *soya milk* is charged at *0.71 per* unit – even though in reality it's not the cheapest type of *milk*, as with just 0.08 more you get *1.5L* of *full-fat milk* rather than the *1L* included in the *unit* of *soya*.

155. (B)

The question asks which of the products the largest number of units will be sent. This means that the question is asking which *product* has the largest *quantity* of *units* in the *purchase order*. (A) *croissant* has *10*; (B) *white sandwich bread loaf* has *20*; (D) *white baguette* has *15*. This means that (B) is correct. While (C) *coffee beans (1kg)* is the most expensive *product* at *8.45 per unit*, the *quantity* ordered is only *3*, so it's incorrect.

156. (D)

The question asks why bigger platforms are more popular according to the author. While the author mentions you will need a *high rating* on those websites, they never say this is why they are *popular*, so (A) is incorrect. (B) is incorrect because the *fee* they *charge* is called *unattractive*, which is the opposite of *small*, and is actually given as a *downside*. (C) is wrong because the author never comments on the quality of their *customer service*, just the size of the *pool of potential customers*. (D) is the correct answer because the author says their *insurance makes them less stressful to use*, which means they *offer peace of mind*.

157. (C)

The question asks what the author does NOT say about meeting a buyer. The author says *meet during daylight*, which means you shouldn't *meet at night*, so (A) is wrong. The author also says to meet *at a public place*, i.e. *somewhere with other people around*, so (B) is also wrong. The author also says anywhere meeting *monitored by CCTV*, i.e. *with cameras around, is good*, so (D) is wrong. The author mentions you should *keep in mind your safety, especially if the value of the product you're selling is high*, but never suggests you shouldn't *meet a buyer* if that's the case, so (C) is the correct answer.

158. (B)

The question asks which of the following is usually fine to give out to buyers. The author explicitly says *do not*

give out your home address or cell phone number, so (C) and (D) are wrong. The author also says to *have a separate email address for selling online*, which means your *personal email address* should remain private – making (B) also wrong. Finally, the author says *don't give out your full name, either – keep your last name private*. Presumably, then, your *first name* is *fine to give out*, so (A) is correct.

159. (B)

The question asks what can be inferred from the text. The author says *it's up to you to decide the way in which you are comfortable with conducting business online* and never advocates using *bigger platforms* over *free platforms*, so (A) is incorrect. They also describe the *rules* as *common sense*, which means no *expertise* is needed to *sell online*, so (C) is incorrect. While the author does say *many first-time sellers naively forget to take precautions when selling their stuff online*, that doesn't automatically mean *you will most probably have issues* – just that you're more likely to *have issues*, so (D) is incorrect. What the author says is that a *prepared seller is a happy seller*, which means that *selling online* can be fun, but only *if you take precautions* – so (B) is the correct answer.

160. (B)

The question asks why Yussef has contacted Bill. Yussef starts by asking Bill if he is *in the office*. Then, when Bill confirms, Yussef adds: *My computer's frozen, I can't access any of the files*. However, the purpose is not to *inform* him about the *IT issue*: the very next thing he says is *can you ping IT and ask them to take a look?* This means that Yussef needs Bill's *assistance*, so (B) is correct. While the two men do *make plans for Friday*, this is not why Yussef has got in touch – and it's Bill who *asks* Yussef *how he is*, not the other way around.

161. (A)

The question asks, in line 3, what the word "ping" is closest in meaning to. To *ping* someone means to *message* them, so (A) is correct. While to *call*, *query* or *walk over to IT* would have also made sense in the gap, none of these are synonyms of *ping*, so (B), (C) and (D) are all wrong.

162. (C)

The question asks why Yussef is working from home. In the conversation, Bill asks *Yussef* how *the leg* is, and Yussef says the *cast should be coming off soon*. If he's wearing a *cast*, it must mean he has *broken his leg*. Bill then says *so y will be coming back to the office soon*, suggesting that the *broken leg* is the reason Yussef is *working from home*. (C) is, therefore, correct. While Yussef mentions a *doctor's appointment*, that was *2 days ago* and he never links it to *working from home*. He also never says he's *ill*, and *remote work* is never mentioned – just *remote access* for *IT*, which means *accessing* someone's computer *remotely*.

163. (B)

The question asks what the purpose of Will's email is. The opening sentence of the email is *it is with great sadness I must announce my departure from the company at the end of this month*. This means that the *purpose* of the *email* is to *announce* the *departure* of *Will*. As he is the person resigning, he cannot be accepting another person's resignation. Moreover, the rest of the email goes on to *thank* everyone and list the things he enjoyed, and how to keep in touch. This must mean he is *bidding his colleagues farewell*, so (B) is correct. While *Will* does mention his *new role*, he is not *applying* for it through this *email* nor is the *purpose* solely to talk about the *new role*, which cannot be a promotion as he is moving to a different company.

164. (A)

The question asks what can be inferred from the email. Will writes: *We've had our highs and our lows (particularly during the move to the swanky new offices earlier this year!)* If they *moved* to *new offices earlier this year*, this means the *company relocated recently*, so (A) is correct. While Will explains his new role is a *Manager*, he never mentions what his current role is, so it's impossible to know if it's *higher-level* or not. Similarly, while Will mentions making *friends*, he never mentions his *best friend*. Finally, there's nothing to suggest a *high turnover rate*: Will is leaving after *five years*, and even if he were leaving sooner, we don't know how soon his colleagues are leaving so we can't determine what the *turnover* is.

165. (D)

The question asks who this article is aimed at. The article talks about a *company's point of view* in the third paragraph, and then focuses on *employees* and what they can do *when you find yourself romantically interested in one of your colleagues* in the fourth paragraph. This means the text is not solely *aimed at companies* or *employees* but both, i.e. (D) *all of the above*.

166. (B)

The question asks which of the following employees need to decide before starting an office romance. While the text does ask *employees* to check what the *dating policy* is at their *company*, *employees* don't get to *decide* the *policy*, so (A) is incorrect. What the text does ask them to *decide* is, *is it worth it?* This means: are the *advantages* more than the *disadvantages*? So, (B) is correct. While the text does say *sexual harassment claims are unpleasant*, it never asks the reader to *decide* how to *avoid* them – and the text is very clear that *employees* must *follow* their *company's dating rules*.

167. (A)

The question asks what the phrase "keep your relationships on the down low" in paragraph 4, line 7 is closest in meaning to. To *keep* something *on the down low* means to *hide* it, so (A) is correct.

168. (B)

The question asks which of the positions [1], [2], [3] or [4] the following sentence best belongs in: "It is, of course, natural for relationships to blossom in the workplace." The sentence might have worked in position [1] if the question following it marked the contrast in the arguments by adding the word 'but' in the beginning: "But *should it be allowed?*" The same applies to position [4]: the surrounding sentences take a negative view and the missing sentence takes a positive view, so the contrast should be marked with a linking word: "*Regardless of how your employer feels about it*, however…" The sentence doesn't work in position [3] because the paragraph talks about the implications of *office romance* for a *company*, not whether it's *natural* or not. The only logical position for the missing sentence is [2], as it serves as an introduction to a paragraph that explains why *office romance* occurs.

169. (C)

The question asks which of the following is NOT an issue with the current reporting system. The *process* is described as *manual*, i.e. *not automated*, so (A) is clearly an issue. It's also described as *not billable*, which means the *company* has to pay, i.e. *swallow the cost*. Finally, it *takes up a lot of time*, which means it's *time-consuming*. (C) is not an issue because what the email says is that Massimo and Lucas *manipulate it to translate it into a presentable PDF*, which means the *PDF* is *presentable* in the end.

170. (A)

The question asks why Massimo can't change the status quo with his client. What Massimo says is *At this point, the client has certain expectations, so we can't go back and ask him to pay or tell him we won't be providing this service anymore*. To *build an expectation* means to *set a precedent*, so (A) is correct. (B) is incorrect because Massimo says they *can't ask him to pay*, which means they haven't yet. (C) is incorrect because Massimo says *the current process is not sustainable*, not a potential new *process*. Finally, (D) is incorrect because Massimo says they can't *tell* the *client* that they *won't be providing this service anymore* – which means it hasn't been *discontinued*.

171. (B)

The question asks how the author of this email is likely to feel. The topic of this email is a request for a solution, and Massimo closes the email with *I look forward to your thoughts* and *I'm sure you'll come up with something brilliant*. If he's *sure* a solution will be found, that must mean he feels hopeful, i.e. (B) *sanguine*. This means he can't be (A) *forlorn*, i.e. sad, (C) *apprehensive*, i.e. fearful, or (D) *overwrought*, i.e. anxious.

172. (C)

The question asks which of the following is true about local resident discount card applications. The text says *you might be able to apply in person* and adds *please check your local council's website for further information*. This means it's only possible *in some councils*, so (C) is correct. While the text offers the option to *apply online*, it also says this can be done *in person* or *via post*, so (A) and (B) are incorrect. Finally,

(D) is incorrect because the text says you *must email your personal documents* after you *apply online*, but doesn't say this also applies if you *apply in person* or *via post*.

173. (C)

The question asks which of the following is not a valid supporting document. The text says that *to support your Local Resident Discount Card, you will need*, first of all, a *national ID card*, i.e. *identity card*. A *proof of address* is also needed, which can be an *official letter* from a *medical practice*, i.e. *your doctor*, and *photographs*, i.e. *pictures*, *of you*. What is explicitly described as not acceptable is *cellular phone bills*, i.e. *bills from a cell phone carrier*, so (C) is correct.

174. (A)

The question asks what CANNOT be inferred from the conversation. Ross says *boss says jump* at the end to explain why he has no choice but to miss the *meeting*. "When someone *says jump* you say *how high?*" is an expression that means you have no choice but to do what told, and since *Pete* is the one who told Ross to do something, he must be his *boss*, so (A) is incorrect. (B) is incorrect because Rahul says *2nd time rescheduling* and (D) is incorrect because, if they are *rescheduling for* Ross, it must mean he needs to be *present*. (C) is the correct answer because there's nothing to suggest it was *Rahul* who *scheduled* the *meeting* – Ross may have chosen to text him for a number of reasons.

175. (A)

The question asks why Ross says "Boss says jump…" As mentioned in question 174, "When someone *says jump* you jump" is an expression that means you have no choice but to do what told. This means that (A) is the correct answer. Ross says nothing about *not wanting* to join the *meeting*, and the fact that he says *not my fault* means he expects *Miranda* to get *upset*. He also never comments on the fact that the *meeting* will need to be *rescheduled*.

176. (D)

The question asks which of the following is NOT listed as available at 365 HOLIDAY apartments. (A) is incorrect because the *apartment* has a *kitchen or kitchenette*, where one can *cook*. (**B**) is incorrect because the *apartment* also has a *safe*, which is where you put *personal belongings* to *protect* them. (**C**) is incorrect because the ad mentions a *range of activities, both for adults and for children*. (**D**) is the right answer because the ad mentions *boat moorings*, i.e. space for *boats* to park, not *boat tours*.

177. (C)

The question asks what can be inferred from the first text. The text mentions that *you also receive a regular cleaning service every two days, which is included in the price* – but never says you can request it *more often for a small fee*, so (**A**) is incorrect. (**B**) is wrong because the ad says *we even throw in a free massage at the local massage salon if you book before 31st January* – which means this is an offer, not something *included in the price* normally. (**D**) is wrong because no *early-bird discount* is mentioned – what you get if you *book early* is the *massage*. (**C**) is the correct answer because the ad mentions *private beaches*, so some of the apartments must be located by the beach.

178. (B)

The question asks what the first issue Jonathan Wells encountered was. The review says: *while, according to the package my wife and I had purchased, we were entitled to a suitcase of 23kg each, the booking made by 365 HOLIDAY only included hand luggage.* This means that *Jonathan paid for* something but the *company didn't book* it, so (**B**) is correct. (**A**) is wrong because the review never says anything about the *flight* being *delayed*. (**C**) is wrong because the *company* forgot to add the *luggage* to the *tickets*, but the *tickets* themselves were not *wrong*. (**D**) is wrong because *Jonathan* had to pay *$50* for the *suitcases* to the airline – he wasn't *overcharged* by the *company*.

179. (B)

The question asks how Jonathan and his wife were likely to feel after they arrived at the apartment. *Jonathan* says *nothing could've prepared* us, which means they were surprised, i.e. *flabbergasted*, so (**B**) is correct. (**A**) is incorrect because *relieved* is a positive feeling, and the *apartment* having *mold*, *rust* and noisy *renovations* probably wouldn't make them feel happy. (**C**) is incorrect for the same reason: *euphoric* means

extremely happy. (**D**) is incorrect because *assertive* means confident and forceful, and *Jonathan* says nothing about *feeling* that way when *they arrived*.

180. (B)

The question asks what Jonathan says about compensation. (**A**) is incorrect because he says nothing about *suing the company*. (**C**) is incorrect because he *has requested a refund* already. (**B**) is correct because he says he is *not holding* his *breath*, which is an expression that means he *doesn't expect* a result. This means that (**D**) is incorrect because he wouldn't be saying he *doesn't expect* a result if he had *been offered a refund* already.

181. (A)

The question asks with whom Lachlan McDowell is likely to cohabit based on the bank statement. (**A**) is the correct answer because *Peter Andrews* put *$750.00* into *Lachlan's* account with the reference *Rent & Bills*, and *Lachlan* then paid out *$1213.00* with the reference *Rent*, which must mean *Peter* contributes his half to *Lachlan* and then *Lachlan* pays the landlord. (**B**) is wrong because *Lilith Jones* is the one *Lachlan* paid *$1213.00* to, meaning she must be the landlord. (**C**) is wrong because *Oscar Thompson* received *$250.00* from *Lachlan* with the reference *personal trainer*, which must mean he is *Lachlan's personal* gym *trainer*. (**D**) is wrong, finally, because *Amparo Perez* received *$180.00* from *Lachlan* with the reference *Spanish class*, which must mean she is his *Spanish* teacher.

182. (D)

The question asks for which of the following activities there is no charge in Lachlan's bank statement. (**A**) is incorrect because there is a charge of *$250.00* from *Oscar Thompson* with the reference *personal trainer*, and a *personal trainer* helps you to exercise. (**B**) is incorrect because there's a charge of *$180.00* from *Amparo Perez* for *Spanish* lessons. (**C**) is incorrect because there's a charge of *$38.40* from *FOREVER TV*, and *TV* is a form of *home entertainment*. (**D**) is the correct answer because there is something called *The Slender Box Concert* in the statement, it's a *refund* of *$89.00*, which means it's money going *in*, not *out*.

183. (B)

The question asks what can be inferred about Lachlan from the email. (A) is incorrect because the email says *please note that, in urgent cases such as this, it is preferable to contact us through our web chat feature*, which must mean he didn't *use* it this time. (C) is incorrect because, while the email mentions what to do in *urgent cases*, there's nothing to suggest *Lachlan didn't think* this was one – perhaps he just didn't know what to do. (D) is incorrect because the email mentions the *suspicious charge* came from a *shop called "Spices and Places"*, there's nothing to suggest that *Lachlan frequents* it. The opposite, in fact, as if he did *frequent* it he would recognize the charge. (B) is the correct answer because the email says the *web chat feature* is *available at all times to customers with hearing loss*, which they wouldn't mention unless they knew *Lachlan* had *hearing loss*, such as being *deaf*.

184. (C)

The question asks what Lachlan does NOT need to do, based on the email. (A) is wrong because the email says *please note that, in urgent cases such as this, it is preferable to contact us through our web chat feature*. (B) is wrong because the email also says *if this purchase sounds familiar, please let us know*. (D), finally, is wrong because the email says *I have also attached a short form for you to complete and return to us*. (C) is correct because, while the email says the *refund* will *reach* the *account by close of business today at the latest*, it never says *Lachlan* should *let the bank know* when it does.

185. (A)

The question asks what Riley says about the refund. (A) is the correct answer because *contingent* means dependent, and from the fact that *Riley* says *your refund will be processed regardless of when you submit this form*, it's clear the *refund is not contingent upon completion of the short form*. (B) is incorrect because the email says the *refund* will arrive *by close of business today*, which is before *tomorrow*. (C) is incorrect because the email says that *Riley* has *authorized* the *refund* already and it will *reach* the *account by close of business*, and *Riley* never asks *Lachlan* to *confirm he doesn't recognize the charge* –

only to let them know if he does *recognize* it. Finally, (D) is incorrect because the email says *your refund will be processed regardless of when you submit this form*, so the two are clearly not depending upon each other.

186. (A)

The question asks in which month the ad was most likely published. The ad refers to a *New Year's resolution* and a *Christmas turkey meal*. Both of these suggest it was *published* right after *Christmas* and *New Year*, i.e. *January*. (A) is therefore correct.

187. (C)

The question asks what can be inferred from Gaby's message. Gaby does mention she has two *pools* near her: *I live near your 31st Street branch, and I also work near the 77th Street branch*. However, she then says about the latter that she would *prefer* it as *I'd like to also have access to a swimming pool*. This must mean that the former *doesn't have a pool*, so (C) is correct. Gabby never says anything about *wanting access to two pools* or *preferring* the one *near work* because she like to *go to the gym after work*. She also explicitly asks to be contacted via *email* rather than *social media*, which she *uses* infrequently.

188. (B)

The question asks what can be inferred from Jared's response. Jared's email says *we are currently running a new promotional offer which is quite similar and, unlike our previous offer, also includes access to our swimming pools*. If the *new offer* is *unlike* the last one through its *access* to *swimming pools*, this means the *New Year, New Rules deal didn't give access to swimming pools*, so (B) is correct. Jared mentions *12 months* for the *new deal*, and mentions the previous *offer expired on 31st January*, not the *new* one. Also, while he might mention higher *prices* for the *deal* in his email, that *deal* is described as *gym + swim*, whereas we know the previous *deal* didn't include *swim*, so the *prices* are different because of this, not because they went up.

189. (C)

The question asks, in Jared's email, in paragraph 3, what the phrase "I will be happy to throw in a free month" is closest in meaning to. To *throw in* something to an *offer* means to add it for *free*, so (C) is the correct answer. (A) and (B) are wrong because Jared says *you do have to pay the registration fee*, so it's clearly not *free* - and (D) is wrong because he never mentions a *trial* – just a *free month*.

190. (C)

The question asks, in Jared's email, in paragraph 4, what "Please let me know if this sounds good to you" refers to. *This* must refer to the most recently mentioned thing, and the last thing Jared mentioned is *I will be happy to throw in a free month for a 12-month membership*, so (C) is correct. (A) is incorrect because the *New Year, New Rules plan* is no longer available. (B) is wrong because the *registration fee* has to be paid, and (D) is wrong because *being contacted over the phone to arrange everything* would be the result of confirming *this sounds good to you*, not the *this* itself.

191. (C)

The question asks which of the following is NOT TRUE about the advertised role based on Sarah's post. Sarah describes the *company* as *San Francisco-based*, so (A) is true. She also describes the *role as home-based*, so (B) is true. She says the *salary* is *$22-25k depending on experience*, which means it's *negotiable*, so (D) is true. The only thing she doesn't call the *position* is *freelance*: Diego mentions his *freelance work*, but she never uses that word, so (C) is the correct answer.

192. (B)

The question asks, in Sarah's post, in line 4, what the phrase "notable academic performance" is closest in meaning to. *Notable* means something *remarkable*, and *academic* refers to *education*, so (B) is correct. (A) is wrong because *academic* is about school, not *work*, whereas (C) and (D) are wrong because *many years in education* and *a university degree* do not tell us anything about *performance*.

193. (D)

The question asks which of the following Diego is worried about. (A) is wrong because Diego mentions

his *experience* in an *advertising company* but doesn't ask if it's *relevant*. (C) is wrong because Diego mentions a previous job in *Chicago* but doesn't even say if he still lives there. (B) is wrong because Diego mentions that he has a *1-month notice*, which means he knows already *his current job will ask for* it. (D) is correct because Diego mentions his *holiday*, i.e. *vacation*, in *July* and asks if it's *all right*, which means he is *worried about* it.

194. (B)

The question asks what "I wouldn't worry about it" in Sarah's DM, in line 7 refer to. The full sentence in the DM is *they'd also prefer an immediate start, but most candidates have a 1-month notice so I wouldn't worry about it*. This must mean she is referring to the *1-month notice*, so (B) is the correct answer. Sarah refers to *Diego's location* earlier in the DM when she asks him if he is *willing to move*, so it clearly would be something to *worry about* if he can't. She addresses the *holidays* right after the quoted sentence by saying *not sure about the holidays but I can't imagine them posing an issue, either*. Finally, while Diego mentions *references*, she never addresses them herself.

195. (A)

The question asks what Diego does NOT need to do for his application to be considered. Sarah says *I'll send you a task the company would like you to complete – it's nothing complicated, just designing a logo*, so Diego needs to *design something*. Sarah also says *can you send me your resume*, so he needs to *forward* it. Before that, she says: *Are you based in Chicago? If so, are you willing to move? The role is home-based but the company would prefer candidates based in SF*. This means (D) is incorrect, too. The correct answer is (A) because Diego says *have a look at my portfolio* in his message, and Sarah says *I've looked at your portfolio* - which means he has already *shared* it and does not need to do it anymore.

196. (A)

The question asks what can be inferred from the entrance pass. The pass says *you and your guest must remain together throughout your visit to the fair*. This means it is impossible to *attend different shows*, so (**A**) is the correct answer. (**B**) is wrong because the pass says it is for *throughout the duration of the fair*. (**C**) is wrong because the pass mentions *random ticket inspections are carried out*. (**D**) is wrong for the same reason as (**C**).

197. (B)

The question asks on which day the ticket holder visited *Absolutely Vegan*. While the pass says *12th – 15th March* at the top, the receipt says *03/13/18*, which means *13th March*, so (**B**) is correct and all the other options are wrong.

198. (C)

The question asks Which of the following Silvia does NOT mention as proof that the entrance pass is valid for two. Silvia says the *pass is valid for two according to your website and the confirmation email I received after I purchased this ticket*, so (**A**) and (**B**) are incorrect. She also says *this is also clearly marked on the pass itself*, so (**D**) is incorrect. She never mentions *ticket inspectors*, however, so (**C**) is the correct answer.

199. (B)

The question asks how Silvia is likely to feel based on her email. Silvia mentions *unacceptable behavior* and that she wants a *refund* plus *compensation for the*

way she was *treated*. All of this suggests she is not happy, and in fact that she feels quite frustrated, or *exasperated* with her experience. (**B**) is, therefore, the correct answer. She is unlikely to feel *exhilarated*, i.e. very happy, or *exuberant*, i.e. excited and energetic. Finally, *exfoliated* is not a feeling: it is an action, more specifically the action of removing dead skin cells from your body.

200. (B)

The question asks which of the positions [1], [2], [3] or [4] the following sentence best belong in: "Despite our protestations, they did not relent." To *relent* means to change your mind, and *protestations* are a form of complaint, so the sentence is clearly talking about the fact that Silvia and her *partner* were not allowed to *attend* a *show* at *Absolutely Vegan* with their *pass*. Position [1] is therefore wrong, as that issue has not been mentioned yet. Position [3] is wrong because of the word *however* in the next sentence: the word *however* introduces contrast, and there is no contrast between the fact that *Absolutely Vegan did not relent* and that they *expect a full refund*. Position [4] is wrong because the fact that they *did not relent* is no longer relevant once the request for a *refund* has been made, as everything has been explained already. The only logical position is [2], as it explains a logical sequence of events: Silvia and her *partner* were told their *pass was not valid*. They *protested*, but this did not achieve anything and *in fact*, it only made *Absolutely Vegan* react *rudely*.

PRACTICE TEST 5 ANSWER KEY

Part I	Part II	Part III	Part IV	Part V	Part VI	Part VII
1. C	7. C	32. B	71. B	101. D	131. B	147. A
2. C	8. A	33. A	72. A	102. A	132. D	148. C
3. B	9. B	34. A	73. A	103. A	133. A	149. C
4. D	10. A	35. C	74. B	104. D	134. A	150. D
5. C	11. A	36. A	75. A	105. B	135. C	151. D
6. B	12. C	37. D	76. D	106. B	136. D	152. B
	13. C	38. B	77. D	107. A	137. A	153. C
	14. A	39. B	78. A	108. A	138. B	154. B
	15. A	40. A	79. C	109. B	139. C	155. B
	16. A	41. D	80. D	110. C	140. C	156. C
	17. B	42. B	81. C	111. C	141. B	157. A
	18. C	43. A	82. B	112. A	142. D	158. D
	19. A	44. C	83. D	113. A	143. A	159. B
	20. B	45. A	84. A	114. B	144. A	160. B
	21. C	46. A	85. A	115. B	145. C	161. B
	22. A	47. C	86. B	116. B	146. D	162. C
	23. B	48. C	87. A	117. C		163. A
	24. A	49. B	88. C	118. A		164. A
	25. C	50. D	89. D	119. D		165. B
	26. A	51. A	90. A	120. D		166. B
	27. B	52. B	91. B	121. A		167. A
	28. B	53. B	92. A	122. C		168. D
	29. A	54. A	93. B	123. D		169. A
	30. A	55. C	94. C	124. D		170. A
	31. B	56. B	95. B	125. D		171. D
		57. C	96. A	126. B		172. C
		58. A	97. A	127. C		173. C
		59. D	98. A	128. C		174. B
		60. A	99. A	129. A		175. B
		61. C	100. A	130. D		176. A
		62. C				177. B
		63. D				178. B
		64. C				179. B
		65. D				180. B
		66. B				181. D
		67. A				182. A
		68. A				183. C
		69. C				184. A
		70. B				185. A
						186. B
						187. C
						188. D
						189. B
						190. D
						191. D
						192. A
						193. B
						194. A
						195. C
						196. D
						197. A
						198. D
						199. C
						200. A

PRACTICE TEST 5

Part I—Photographs

1. (C)

The photograph shows a woman talking to someone and taking notes. (C) best describes the photograph. They are *talking*, not having a *walk*. They could be having a meeting, but they're not in a *conference room*. She's taking notes, not *noticing the time*.

2. (C)

The photograph shows three shelves with plates, bowls and a teapot on them. The teapot is on the bottom shelf. The plates are stacked, they have not *fallen down*. There is a cup and saucer on the middle shelf, but no *sauce*. The dishes are on the shelves, not being *cleared*.

3. (B)

The photograph shows a group of cyclists on the road. (B) best describes the photograph. They're pedalling their bikes, but the pedals aren't *being pulled up*. They're cycling, but the *gears* are not *on the move*. They are cycling on the road, not *renewing* their *cycles*.

4. (D)

The photograph shows a man showing a group of people a tablet. (D) best describes the photograph. They're looking at a tablet, not a *table, cell phone,* or *laptop*.

5. (C)

The photograph shows two groups of people on a conference call. (C) best describes the photograph; they're taking part in a meeting. They're having a meeting, not *discussing the weather*. They're all seated, so there is *enough seating*. They're talking on a video link, not *looking at the photograph*.

6. (B)

The photograph shows a ballerina dancer putting on her shoes. (B) best describes the photograph. She is sitting down, she has not *fallen down*. She's *getting ready*, not *taking a break*. She is a dancer, not *learning to dance*.

Part II—Question-Response

7. (C)

The question is in the *past simple* and asks *when*. This means (C) is the correct answer. (A) is wrong because it's in the *present*. (B) is not possible because it answers *where*, not *when*.

8. (A)

The question is in the *present perfect* and it checks information about a *recent past*. (B) and (C) are incorrect because they're in the *future*. This means (A) is the only possible answer.

9. (B)

(A) is wrong because it answers *when,* not *where*. (C) is not possible because you wouldn't name a city if someone asked you where to find a password. This means (B) is the right answer.

10. (A)

The question wants to know *in which department* Mr. Nazario works. The only alternative to talk about company departments is (A), so this is the correct answer. (B) is incorrect because it doesn't say *which department*. (C) talks about *tea,* so it's not possible either.

11. (A)

The question asks *where* and (A) is the only alternative that provides a location. (B) is wrong because it answers *when*. (C) is also incorrect because it answers *how*.

12. (C)

The question asks *what time* and (C) is the only alternative that answers that. (A) is wrong because it answers *where*. (B) is not possible because it answers *how many times*.

13. (C)

The question refers to *BWC Bank*, which is a company. (A) is wrong because we don't know who *he* is. (B) is not possible because it refers to *her,* and not a bank. This means (C) is the only possible answer.

14. (A)

The question asks if the person could send a fax. (**B**) is incorrect because it says *when something arrived*. (**C**) is also wrong because you don't refuse a request by saying *No, I don't.* This means (**A**) is the correct alternative.

15. (A)

The question asks *when,* so (**A**) is the only possible answer. (**B**) is wrong because it doesn't answer *when.* (**C**) is incorrect because it answers *how.*

16. (A)

In this question, *how soon* means *when something will happen.* (**B**) is wrong because it doesn't say *when.* (**C**) is not possible because it's in the *past.* This means (**A**) is the right answer.

17. (B)

Restroom means *toilet,* so (**A**) is not possible. (**C**) is also wrong because it doesn't say whether the door is locked or not. This means (**B**) is the only possible answer.

18. (C)

The question asks *who.* (**C**) is the only alternative to answer that, so it's correct. (**A**) is wrong because it doesn't answer *who.* (**B**) is incorrect because it answers *where.*

19. (A)

(**B**) is wrong because it talks about measurements, not time length. (**C**) is incorrect because it doesn't answer *how long.* This means (**A**) is the correct alternative.

20. (B)

The question asks *whose* and (**B**) answers *Nora's,* so this is the correct alternative. (**A**) is wrong because it gives a phone number. (**C**) talks about text messages, so it's also incorrect.

21. (C)

The question asks *where* and (**C**) is the only alternative to provide this information. (**A**) is wrong because it answers *when.* (**B**) is not possible because it talks about a pen, not signing up for the basketball team.

22. (A)

The question *May I borrow* is a request, so (**A**) is the correct answer. You can't refuse a request by saying *No, you won't,* so (**B**) is not possible. (**C**) is incorrect because it answers *how often.*

23. (B)

(**A**) is wrong because the question asks *how old,* not *how long ago,* so we need an age, not a time period. (**B**) answers the question. (**C**) gives a number of children, but we need to know *how old* they are, not *how many* there are.

24. (A)

When the question asks *how much* it refers to money, so (**A**) is the correct answer. (**B**) doesn't answer *how much,* so it's not possible. (**C**) is wrong because it talks about *years,* not money.

25. (C)

The question asks *where* and (**A**) answers *when,* so it's wrong. (**B**) is also incorrect because it answers *how.* This means (**C**) is the correct alternative.

26. (A)

The question asks *when* and (**B**) answers *how,* so it's incorrect. (**C**) is wrong because it talks about an *appointment* and the question asks about an *invoice.* This means (**A**) is the right answer.

27. (B)

The question asks for a *ZIP CODE* and (**B**) is the only answer to provide that. People aren't usually proud of ZIP codes, so (**A**) is incorrect. (**C**) is also wrong because it talks about an object, not a ZIP code.

28. (B)

The question asks *how many people* and (**B**) answers *50, 60,* so this is the correct answer. (**A**) talks about food and a DJ but doesn't say *how many people,* so it's incorrect. (**C**) is wrong because it talks about a swimming pool.

29. (A)

The speaker is about to fire the other person and asks for a reason not to. (B) is wrong because it talks about the weather. (C) is also incorrect because it talks about firemen, and not *fire* as a verb. This means (A) is the correct answer.

30. (A)

(B) is wrong because we shouldn't use *doesn't* to answer a question asked with *is* as an auxiliary verb. The question asks about a *photocopier* and (C) talks about coffee, so it's not possible either. This means (A) is the only possible answer.

31. (B)

The question wants to know if something is good. (A) talks about *being tired,* so it's not related to the topic. (C) is wrong because it says *no* but then says *it's excellent,* which means one part of the answer contradicts the other. Therefore, (B) is the only possible answer.

Part III—Short Conversations

32. (B)

The man says *I can't find my jacket,* so (B) is the correct answer. (A) is wrong because he thinks his jacket might be in the car, but doesn't say anything about *car keys.* (C) is wrong because the woman says *They can scan it straight from the phone screen* when talking about the tickets that were in his jacket. (D) is not possible because they're going to the theater.

33. (A)

The woman says *We don't need to print those things anymore. They can scan it straight from the phone screen,* so (A) is the correct answer. (B) is incorrect because she says *We don't need to print those things anymore.* (C) is also wrong because he thinks his jacket might be in the car, not a taxi. (D) is not possible because they don't talk about the price.

34. (A)

The woman says *But don't take too long. Mark and Vera are waiting for us,* so (A) is the right answer. She

doesn't say she doesn't like being late, so (B) is wrong. Even though she says the taxi is downstairs waiting, she doesn't say anything about the taxi leaving without them. This means (C) is also incorrect. (D) is not possible because she says *Mark and Vera are waiting for us,* but doesn't say where.

35. (C)

(C) is the best answer because the woman says *You said you were coming on Monday and then you had a problem with your van. Then on Tuesday it was the snow. And now you're telling us you can't give us a quote until Friday?,* which indicates that she doesn't trust Mr. Wells. (A) is not possible because she doesn't talk about the size of the problem. (B) is not possible because they need a quote. (D) is incorrect because they need the job done before the Chinese arrive, but don't say when that is.

36. (A)

The woman says *You said you were coming on Monday and then you had a problem with your van,* so (A) is the right answer. (B) is wrong because she says *Then on Tuesday it was the snow.* Then she says *And now you're telling us you can't give us a quote until Friday?,* so we can safely assume they're having this conversation on a Wednesday. This means (C) and (D) are not possible.

37. (D)

She says *We have a leak in the office,* so (D) is the correct alternative. She says *The door is on your left. Take care and good luck* when asking Mr. Wells to leave, so (A) is wrong. (B) is also incorrect because Mr. Wells is a plumber. Mr. Wells says *I'd have to check with my men what their availability is,* but that doesn't mean he knows they're not available. Therefore, (C) is not possible either.

38. (B)

(B) is the correct answer because she says *We've recently managed to take two major clients from one of our main competitors.* She also says *everything's fine* in Buenos Aires but that doesn't mean she loves the atmosphere there, so (A) is incorrect. She says *We've recently managed to take two major clients from one of our main competitors* but we don't know if they're powerful or not. This means **(C)** is also wrong. **(D)** is not possible because she doesn't say anything about Denver.

39. (B)

Buzz means a *feeling of excitement or euphoria,* so **(B)** is the best answer. He misses setting up new businesses, but that does not necessarily mean he misses working or travelling to new places. Therefore, alternatives **(A)** and **(D)** are not possible. **(C)** is wrong because he doesn't say anything about decorating offices.

40. (A)

He says *I left you alone with a roomful of new new clients and rushed to the hospital* when talking about the birth of his first child, so **(A)** is the correct answer. He left Gabriela alone, so **(B)** is wrong. **(C)** is also incorrect because he doesn't say anything about the presentation being successful. We don't know if he regrets having left in the middle of the presentation, so **(D)** is not possible either.

41. (D)

One of the women says *Shall we go that new place on 52nd? Jackie said their risotto is to die for,* so **(D)** is the correct alternative. The restaurant is new but they don't say who the owner is, so **(A)** is wrong. **(B)** is also incorrect because one of them wants to invite Manuel, not Jackie. They don't say anything about an argument between Jackie and Manuel. It's one of them who doesn't want to see Manuel, so **(C)** is not possible either.

42. (B)

One of them says *One o' clock it is then,* so **(B)** is the correct answer. The other woman says *we could meet downstairs in half an hour* but that doesn't mean she's talking about 30 minutes after the hour, so **(A)** and **(C)** are wrong. **(D)** is not possible because they don't say anything about *two o' clock.*

43. (A)

The woman starts the conversation by saying *What do you want for lunch? I feel like Italian today* and the other replies *Italian is fine,* so **(A)** is the correct answer. Only one of them needs to see Manuel, so **(B)** is

incorrect. **(C)** is wrong because one of them doesn't want to see Fiona. **(D)** is not possible because even though they talk about a project in Helsinki, they don't say anything about going there.

44. (C)

(C) is the correct answer because the man says *He's giving two of my best clients to Clara.* **(A)** is wrong because it is the manager who is giving them to Clara. **(B)** is also wrong because he says *I'll be getting the usual 20%.* **(D)** is not possible because we don't know if Boris and Clara were in a relationship.

45. (A)

The woman says *You have to take it to the board,* so **(A)** is the right answer. She doesn't say anything about Clara, so **(B)** is not possible. The manager is the one causing the problems, so **(C)** is also wrong. **(D)** is incorrect because even though she says *If Mr. Fernandez finds out, he'll put an end to this,* she doesn't say anything about an email.

46. (A)

(A) is the correct alternative because the woman says *Since the merger he's been giving all the good clients to his people.* Boris will be getting his commission until July, so **(B)** is not possible. **(C)** is wrong because they don't say anything about a promotion. They don't mention *last week,* so **(D)** is also incorrect.

47. (C)

The woman says *our budget is quite low,* so **(C)** is the best answer. She doesn't mention any financial problems, so **(A)** is wrong. **(B)** is also incorrect because even though she says *We're a new company,* that doesn't necessarily mean the company is very small. She doesn't mention any *markets,* so **(D)** is not possible.

48. (C)

(C) is the right answer because she says *They're staying at the Shelton.* The taxi company is called Maryland Taxis but that doesn't necessarily mean they are in Maryland, so **(A)** is incorrect. They'll be having dinner at the Royal Bath, so **(B)** is also wrong. **(D)** is not possible because they don't mention an airport.

49. (B)

They'll be using 3 cars for 12 passengers for $225.00, and each is 75 bucks, or $75. This means **(B)** is the only possible answer. **(A)** is not possible because they would need 4 cars. **(C)** is wrong because the total would be $300. **(D)** is also incorrect because she says *It's not a bad idea but I think I'll pass this time* when talking about the option of hiring a premium vehicle.

50. (D)

(D) is the right answer because Chuck says *Mrs. Walcott is waiting for us.* **(A)** and **(B)** are not possible because Chuck says *Murilo! Claire! I see you two have already met*, which means they have already met. **(C)** is incorrect for the same reason – Chuck is talking to Murilo and Claire and the only person not taking part in the conversation is Mrs. Walcott.

51. (A)

(A) is the most likely answer because Chuck says *Mrs. Walcott is waiting for us* and then he says *Mrs. Walcott called a meeting to introduce her to everyone in Finances. And that includes you, my friend.* Claire wants to go to reception, but that doesn't mean the men work there. Therefore, **(B)** is not possible. They'll take a shortcut through the warehouse, so **(C)** is also incorrect. **(D)** is wrong because they don't say anything about *IT.*

52. (B)

Claire initially wants to go to the *main reception*, but one of the men tells her they need to go to meet Mrs Walcott instead. **(C)** is incorrect. The will go through the warehouse but they are not going *to* the warehouse, eliminate **(D)**. **(A)** is incorrect as Claire's office is not mentioned. **(B)** is the correct answer, one of the men says *Mrs Walcott called a meeting.*

53. (B)

(B) is the right answer because the man says *Do you think it's a good idea? I'm not so sure.* He says *I'm not so sure,* but doesn't say he disagrees. This means **(A)** is wrong. **(C)** is incorrect because Mr. Honda is frustrated, not the man. **(D)** is not possible because the man says *I'm not so sure.*

54. (A)

The woman says *if we don't have the resources for manufacturing the goods here in the US, why not send it elsewhere* and the then the man says *I'm just worried what our customers might think when the word gets out.* This means **(A)** is the right answer. **(B)** is wrong because he doesn't say anything about losing customers. He's not worried about the designs, so **(C)** is not possible. **(D)** is also incorrect because they don't talk about prices.

55. (C)

The woman says it's a *calculated risk,* so it means Mr. Honda has thought about what might go wrong. Therefore, **(C)** is the right answer. **(A)** is not possible because even though she says *he's got a point there,* that doesn't mean she thinks it's a great idea. She says *calculated risk,* not *risky.* This means **(B)** is incorrect. **(D)** is also wrong because she says *he's got a point.*

56. (B)

(B) is the correct alternative because the woman says *They're trying to get the projector to work now since the screen is not working.* The man says *When's the presentation going to start,* so **(A)** is not possible. **(C)** is wrong because it is the man who says he's been working long hours. **(D)** is also incorrect because it's the man who works in compliances.

57. (C)

The man says *We're really short-staffed,* so **(A)** is not possible. **(B)** is wrong because the woman says *Our software is outdated.* **(D)** is wrong because the woman says *We still have fax machines.* This means **(C)** is the correct alternative.

58. (A)

(A) is the right answer because the woman says *She tells us that she has been in this business for 50 years and all that traditional non-sense.* The woman doesn't say anything about the woman not wanting to spend money, so **(B)** is not possible. **(C)** is incorrect because she doesn't say anything about Mrs. Pollain's skills as a saleswoman. **(D)** is also wrong because the woman says *She tells us that she has been in this business for 50 years and all that traditional non-sense.*

59. (D)

The woman says *I'm afraid Mrs. Kournikova is not in the office today,* so (D) is the right answer. If she's not in the office, (A) is not possible. (B) is incorrect because the woman says *She never returns anyone's emails.* (C) is also wrong because she says *She's attending a conference in Santiago and won't be back until Tuesday next week.*

60. (A)

The man says *We are happy with the dinner menu and wine selection,* so (A) is the best answer. (B) is not possible because the man doesn't mention an email from the guests. (C) is wrong because there's nothing that indicates the man wants to change the time of the event. The man says *we have increased the number of guests from 280 to 300,* but that doesn't mean he thinks there are too many of them. Therefore, (D) is not possible either.

61. (C)

(A) and (D) are not possible because he says *we have increased the number of guests from 280 to 300.* (B) is not possible because the man says *We are happy with the dinner menu.* This means (C) is the only possible answer.

62. (C)

The man says *I put the boxes next door.* (C) is the correct answer. The man also says *there wasn't room here in your office,* which makes (A) and (B) and (D) not possible.

63. (D)

The woman says *I really need to get this sorted. It's such a mess.* (D) is the right answer. The woman doesn't say anything about the size of her office so (A) and (B) are not possible. (C) is also incorrect because although the woman uses the word *mess,* she doesn't give a specific date for it to be cleaned.

64. (C)

The woman says *cocktails will be served at 6. The presentation itself should start an hour later.* An hour later is 7 o'clock; (C) is the correct answer. (A) gives the time at which cocktails will be served. (B)

discusses a time in the past tense, and the question refers to a future time (will). (D) is not mentioned in the conversation.

65. (D)

Mr. Cooper says *my manager asked me not to do any of the rooms upstairs* and then Mrs. Zhang replies *I see. In this case, I'm going to have a word with Mr. Beech this afternoon.* This means (D) is the right answer. (A) is not possible because Mrs. Zhang is the one who is annoyed by the fact that the rooms aren't clean. Mr. Cooper says *my manager asked me not to do any of the rooms upstairs,* so (B) is also incorrect. (C) is wrong because when Mrs. Zhang asks *Who's in charge of maintenance here?,* Lucas replies *That would be Mr. Silva.*

66. (B)

Mrs. Zhang says *I was just wondering why these rooms aren't being cleaned,* so (B) is the right answer. Mrs. Zhang says the rooms aren't being cleaned, but does not say that the furniture is *broken.* Therefore, (A) is not possible. (C) is wrong because Mrs. Zhang says *I'll make sure he sorts this mess himself.* (D) is also incorrect because her only complaint is that the rooms aren't being cleaned.

67. (A)

Mrs. Zhang says *I'm going to have a word with Mr. Beech,* so (A) is the correct alternative. She is talking to Lucas at the beginning of the conversation, so (B) is not possible. She mentions using one of the rooms for a talk, but doesn't say anything about postponing a talk. Therefore, (C) is incorrect. (D) is also wrong because she says *What if we had a problem with the auditorium downstairs and had to move one of the talks up here,* which means this is hypothetical situation.

68. (A)

The man says *the supervisor just sent me an email to see if he can visit the plant.* (A) is the correct answer. The woman says *I have a meeting in Denver at 3* when reacting to the man's announcement that the supervisor wants to see the plant, so the meeting is not the main topic of the discussion and (B) is wrong. There's no mention of a *presentation,* so (C) is not possible. (D) is not mentioned in the conversation.

69. (C)

The man says *if he can visit the plant tomorrow at lunchtime.* (C) is correct. (A) and (B) are morning hours, before lunchtime, so both options are wrong. (D) is afternoon, after lunchtime, so it's also incorrect.

70. (B)

The woman says *I have a meeting in Denver at 3. It'll take me at least an hour to get there.* The woman will have to travel to attend a meeting after seeing the visitor. (B) is the correct answer; she has a busy schedule. The woman talks about a meeting in Denver but doesn't say she lives there, so (A) is not possible. (C) repeats *plant* but uses it to mean plants as in trees and flowers, not factories, as it is used in the sentence. The man says *I think all he wants is to make sure the new machines are up and running*, but doesn't say anything about machines that *aren't working*, so (D) is incorrect.

Part IV—Short Talks

71. (B)

The woman says *She'll join us to learn more about our projects here in Minnesota*, so (B) is the right answer. (A) is incorrect because she doesn't say mention who's leading the new marketing campaign. (C) is also wrong because the woman talks about a new marketing campaign, not line of products. (D) is not possible because we don't know who's leading the brainstorming session.

72. (A)

The woman says *Customers have a lot of confidence in the quality of our baked goods*, so (A) is the right answer. (B) is incorrect because she says *but the same cannot be said about our range of kitchen appliances.* She doesn't talk about business strategies or models, so (C) and (D) are incorrect.

73. (A)

(A) is the correct alternative because the woman says *We believe that our previous marketing campaign gave too much importance to the looks and design of our range of appliances but did not emphasize their quality.* Since she says *gave too much importance to the looks*

and design, (B) is not possible. She doesn't talk about costs, so (C) is incorrect. (D) is also wrong because when she says *gave too much importance to the looks and design,* we can assume the campaign wasn't very successful.

74. (B)

The woman says *The luxurious shopping mall is located in a prime location,* so (B) is the right option. She doesn't mention movies, restaurants or cafés, so alternatives (A), (C) and (D) are not possible.

75. (A)

(A) is the right answer because the woman says Giggi Giglio is *one of the most revered brands in Europe.* Even though it is an international brand, she doesn't use the word luxurious to describe it. This means (B) is incorrect. The woman only mentions *Giggi Giglio* amongst the new shops, but that doesn't necessarily mean they were the highlight of the opening. Therefore, (C) is not possible. (D) is also wrong because she doesn't talk about prices.

76. (D)

The woman says *the newest development by Aaron Brothers,* so (A) is not possible. She also says *Giggi spoke of his love for the country,* which means (B) is also wrong. (C) is incorrect because she says *he was waiting for the correct opportunity to take his posh rags, as they're called by fashionistas.* This means (D) is the only possible answer.

77. (D)

(D) is the correct alternative because the woman says *Susie Crab, 44, has been charged with selling counterfeit Npads tablet computers.* The woman doesn't say anything about stealing, so alternatives (A) and (B) are not possible. (C) is incorrect because even though she was arrested in a parking lot, the woman doesn't say Susie attacked the man.

78. (A)

The woman says *She would place ads on different auction websites and then agree to meet the person to deliver the Npad computers,* so (A) is the right answer. We don't know how long she sold counterfeit items for, so (**B**) is incorrect. The woman says she was arrested in a parking lot but doesn't say she used to meet all her victims there, so (**C**) is also wrong. (**D**) is not possible because the woman says *Mrs. Crab could serve 10-15 years in a federal prison.*

79. (C)

(**C**) is the right answer because the woman class Susie a *trickster,* which means a person who cheats and deceives people. There's no mention of violence in the story, so (**A**) is not possible. We don't know if Susie was dangerous, so (**B**) is also wrong. (**D**) is incorrect because she sold counterfeit items, but the woman doesn't say if she smuggled them from another country.

80. (D)

The man says *British pop star Bob Jones,* so (**D**) is the correct alternative. Maurizio is the news reader, so (**A**) is wrong. Amy is the correspondent, so (**B**) is also wrong. (**C**) is incorrect because Ananada is a photographer and art collector.

81. (C)

(**C**) is the right answer because the man says *critics and art lovers are not sure what to expect.* The man says the exhibition is a mystery, so (**A**) is not possible. Even though Bob Jones is going to play there, the event is an exhibition, so (**B**) is wrong. (**D**) is also incorrect because even though drinks and food might be served during the opening of an art gallery, that doesn't mean it's a private party.

82. (B)

The man says they were childhood friends, so (**B**) is the correct answer. Ananada is a photographer, not a musician. This means (**A**) is not possible. The man doesn't say anything about the two of them being cousins, so (**C**) is incorrect. (**D**) is wrong because the man doesn't mention a school.

83. (D)

The recording says *Press 4 for traveler's checks and foreign currency,* so (**D**) is the right answer. The recording says *Press 1* (**A**) *for your current balance.*

Press 2 (**B**) *for PIN services and online banking ID. Press 3* (**C**) *for credit cards,* so these alternatives are all incorrect.

84. (A)

The recording says *one in five Americans have been victims of bank fraud,* so (**A**) is the correct alternative. She doesn't mention whether it has happened with their customers or not, so (**B**) is not possible. The recording doesn't mention an increase, so (**C**) is also wrong. (**D**) is not possible because she doesn't link the crime to vacations.

85. (A)

The recording says *Easysave is the ideal savings account for those who,* so (**A**) is the right answer. The woman doesn't mention any loans, so (**B**) is wrong. The same applies to (**C**) since mortgages aren't mentioned either. (**D**) is wrong because EasySave is one of their products.

86. (B)

The woman says *We have received your claim but would like to ask you a few questions before processing it,* so (**B**) is the correct answer. (**A**) is wrong because she doesn't mention a new policy. The man made the claim, so (**C**) is not possible. (**D**) is incorrect because she says *we have received your claim,* which means they're not renewing a policy.

87. (A)

The woman says *My name is Antonina Skrtel,* so (**B**) is incorrect. She also says *We have received your claim but would like to ask you a few questions before processing it,* which means (**C**) is not possible either. (**D**) is also wrong because she leavers a phone number and email. The answer must be (**A**), as the client's full name is not given.

88. (C)

The woman says *If you don't hear back from you by April 4th, we will not be able to process your claim,* so (**B**) and (**D**) are not possible. (**A**) is wrong because she says *It seems to me that you have not been living at the same address provided when you took out our policy.*

89. (D)

(D) is the correct alternative because the man says Mr. Hudson *transformed a small family company into a global force in Digital Marketing.* (A) is wrong because the mans says *Mr. Hudson is due to retire at the end of the year.* Mr. Hudson is the former chairman, so (B) is also incorrect. (C) is not possible because Ms. Flores developed the app.

90. (A)

To fill one's shoes means *to take the place of some other person and do their work satisfactorily.* This means (A) is the best answer. (B) and (D) are wrong because they're talking about the new chairman and no directors are mentioned. (C) is also incorrect because Ms. Flores is appointed as the new chairman.

91. (B)

(B) is the right answer because the man says *Ms. Flores, she is mastermind behind our DigiWorld app, which has allowed us to offer our products and services to small entrepreneurs all over the world.* (A) and (D) are wrong because Ms. Flores is the new chairman. We don't know who updates the app, so (C) is not possible.

92. (A)

The woman says *Your plane has been delayed,* so (A) is the correct answer. There's no mention of a cancellation, so (B) is not possible. The message says *we will inform you as soon as we have an approximate boarding time,* so (C) and (D) are both incorrect.

93. (B)

The man says *here in Dublin,* so (B) is the correct answer. (A) is wrong because London is the flight destination. Moscow is not mentioned, so (C) is not possible. (D) is wrong because even though the name of the airline is Saudi Airlines, that doesn't mean they're in Saudi Arabia.

94. (C)

The announcement mentions London as the destination, so (A) is wrong. He also mentions the *thick fog* in London Heathrow, so (B) is also incorrect. (D) is not possible because he says *we'll update you once the*

aircraft has left London Heathrow. This means (C) is the only possible answer.

95. (B)

Alan says *This is a beautiful, vibrant city,* so (B) is the right answer. He doesn't say the city is expensive, so (A) is not possible. Alan says *take a moonlit walk along the water if you prefer some peace and quiet,* but he is not describing the city as a whole. This means (C) is incorrect. The man doesn't use the word noisy to describe Ibiza, so (D) is also wrong.

96. (A)

The idiom *as certain as death and taxes* means that *something is inevitable.* Therefore, (A) is the correct alternative. He doesn't say how *most people* feel when they go to Ibiza, so (B) is incorrect. (C) is also wrong because he doesn't say Ibiza is tax free. (D) is not possible because even though this is true, that's not the reason why he uses the idiom.

97. (A)

The hotel is called Marina Hotel, so (B) is not possible. The man talks about clubs, moonlit walks, and other things people can do in Ibiza. This means (C) is also wrong. (D) is incorrect because he says *Please make sure your bag has a tag and has been taken off the bus.* (A) must be the answer.

98. (A)

The woman says *An immediate evacuation of warehouses A1, A2 and A3 is required due to fire,* so (A) is the best answer. There's no mention of any machinery or armed intruders, so (B) and (C) are not possible. There's nothing implying this is a drill, so (D) is not the correct anwer.

99. (A)

The woman says *go to the parking lot opposite the main building,* so (A) is the right answer. She says *opposite,* not *behind.* This means (B) is incorrect. (C) is not possible because she says *An immediate evacuation of warehouses A1, A2 and A3 is required due to fire.* (D) is also wrong because she says *Personnel in warehouses B1 and B2, or areas of the company not listed for evacuation should remain in place.*

100. (A)

The woman says *An immediate evacuation of warehouses A1, A2 and A3 is required due to fire,* so **(A)** is the correct alternative. The other alternatives are all wrong because she says *Personnel in warehouses B1 and B2, or areas of the company not listed for evacuation should remain in place.*

Reading

Part V—Incomplete Sentences

101. (D)

The phrases *It's about time* is usually followed by *subject + past simple,* so **(D)** is the correct answer. **(A)** and **(B)** are wrong because they're infinitive. **(C)** is wrong because it's gerund.

102. (A)

An is an article and should be followed by a *singular noun,* which means **(A)** is the only possible answer. **(B)** is an adjective, so it's incorrect. **(C)** is not possible because it's in the plural form. **(D)** is wrong because it's an adverb.

103. (A)

The noun *profit* collocates with the verb *make,* so **(A)** is the only possible answer. The verbs *buy, have,* and *do* do not go with the noun *profit.* This means alternatives **(B), (C)** and **(D)** are not possible.

104. (D)

Recruitment agency is an organization which finds new people to join a company. This means **(D)** is the right answer. *Recruitment* is a noun which is used as an adjective to form the word *recruitment agency.* Alternatives **(A), (B)** and **(C)** are not possible because they're verbs.

105. (B)

The gap needs a verb in the *future* in the *active* voice. **(A)** is wrong because it's in the present perfect. **(C)** is incorrect because it's passive. **(D)** is not possible because it's in the past perfect. This means **(B)** is the only possible answer.

106. (B)

On the verge of is a fixed phrase, so **(B)** is the only possible answer. Because it's a fixed phrase, other prepositions cannot be used. This means alternatives **(A), (C)** and **(D)** are not possible.

107. (A)

The sentence requires a passive form, which usually needs the verb *be* to be formed. This means **(A)** is the best answer. **(B)** and **(C)** are modal verbs and should not be followed by a verb in the past participle, so they're both incorrect. **(D)** is an auxiliary verb and should be followed by a verb in the infinitive, so this alternative isn't possible either.

108. (A)

The gap requires a verb which has the figurative meaning of *arrived in overwhelming amounts.* This is the meaning of *flooded,* so **(A)** is the correct answer. **(B)** can be used with a similar meaning but not followed by the preposition *in,* so it's incorrect. *Snowed in* means people can't leave a place because they're confined by a large quantity of snow, so **(C)** is also wrong. **(D)** is not possible because *storm in* means to *move angrily or forcefully into a place.*

109. (B)

The gap requires a verb in the *past participle* form to form the *passive voice.* This means **(B)** is the correct alternative. **(A)** is incorrect because it's in the *infinitive.* **(C)** is in the *gerund,* so it's also wrong. **(D)** is not possible because the verb is conjugated in the *present simple.*

110. (C)

The noun *floor* usually follows the preposition of place *on,* so **(C)** is the correct answer. *In, at,* and *by* cannot be used with the noun *floor,* so alternatives **(A), (B)** and **(D)** are incorrect.

111. (C)

(C) is the only possible answer because the gap needs an adjective in the *superlative.* **(A)** is an adjective in its original form, so it's wrong. **(B)** is incorrect because it's in the *comparative* form. **(D)** is another *comparative* form, so it's not possible either.

112. (A)

the gap needs a conjunction which means *in spite of the fact that,* so (**A**) is the right option. (**B**) is wrong because it means *immediately after.* (**C**) is incorrect because it means *except if.* (**D**) is not possible because it means *but.*

113. (A)

(**B**) is wrong because it should be followed by an *uncountable noun.* (**C**) is incorrect because it should either go *at the end of a sentence* or be followed by *of.* (**D**) is not possible because it should be followed by *an adjective.* This means (**A**) is the only possible answer.

114. (B)

To be seen as means *to be considered,* so (**B**) is the correct answer. *Like* when used as a preposition means *in the same way that* and is commonly used to draw a comparison between two things. This means (**A**) is incorrect. *For* is commonly used to express a *reason* or *result,* so (**C**) isn't possible either. *How* is usually used to express a *method,* so (**D**) is also wrong.

115. (B)

Post office means *the public department responsible for postal services,* so (**B**) is the correct alternative. A *postbox* is a *public box where post is placed for collection by the post office,* so (**A**) is incorrect. The correct collocation for services offered by the post office would be *postal* services, so (**C**) is not possible. *Post* and *mail* can sometimes be used as synonyms and don't usually go well together, so (**D**) is also wrong.

116. (B)

The gap requires an *adverb,* so (**B**) is the correct answer. (**A**) is wrong because it's an *adjective.* (**C**) is also incorrect because it's a *comparative adjective.* (**D**) is not possible because it's a *noun.*

117. (C)

(**A**) is wrong because it should be followed by a verb in the *infinitive.* (**B**) and (**D**) are incorrect because they would make a *passive* sentence, but the sentence should be active because the subject is the agent. This means (**C**) is the only possible answer.

118. (A)

Since is used in *present perfect* sentences to indicate the *point in time when the action started.* This means (**A**) is the correct answer. (**B**) is wrong because it should be followed by a *period of time. When* is not commonly used with the present perfect, so (**C**) is not possible. (**D**) is wrong because *from* is not commonly used with present perfect either.

119. (D)

The fixed phrase *only a matter of time* means *there will not be long to wait,* so (**D**) is the correct answer. Because it's a fixed phrase, the nouns *problem, issue,* and *concern* cannot be used. Therefore, alternatives (**A**), (**B**) and (**C**) are incorrect.

120. (D)

The sentence says *when she divorced last year,* so the other verb should be in the *past perfect.* This means (**D**) is the right answer. (**A**) is wrong because it's in the *future simple.* (**B**) is *present simple,* so it's also wrong. (**C**) is not possible because it's *present perfect.*

121. (A)

Lead to means *be a reason for,* so (**A**) is the correct answer. (**B**) and (**C**) should be followed by the preposition *in,* so they're both incorrect. (**D**) is also wrong because *make* isn't usually followed by *to.*

122. (C)

The gap needs a conjunction which means *because of,* so (**C**) is the correct alternative. (**A**) and (**B**) are wrong because it should be followed by a *clause.* (**D**) is also incorrect because it expresses a *result,* not a reason.

123. (D)

This is a third conditional sentence. *Had the firemen not arrived* is the same as *If the firemen had not arrived. If clauses* in the third conditional can have the conjunction *if* omitted by moving the auxiliary *had* to the beginning of the clause. This means (**D**) is the correct answer. (**A**) is wrong because the *if clause* in a third conditional should go in the *past perfect. Imagine* is commonly used in the second conditional, so (**B**) is also incorrect. *Should* can be used as a more formal alternative to *if* in the first conditional, so **(C)** is not possible either.

124. (D)

Should, must, and *might* cannot be followed by *to.* This makes **(D)** the only possible answer because **(A)**, **(B)** and **(C)** are all incorrect.

125. (D)

The gap requires an *adverb,* so **(D)** is the correct alternative. **(A)** is either a *noun* or a *verb,* so it's incorrect. **(B)** and **(C)** are wrong because they're adjectives.

126. (B)

(A) is wrong because it can't go after a preposition. **(C)** is also incorrect because it should not be used in *non-defining clauses* (in between commas). **(D)** is not possible because it refers to *something,* not *someone.* This means **(B)** is the only possible answer.

127. (C)

(C) is the only option that shouldn't be followed by *to,* so this is the correct answer. **(A)**, **(B)** and **(D)** should all be followed by the preposition *to,* so they're all incorrect.

128. (C)

The gap requires a conjunction which means *in order to,* so **(C)** is the right answer. *Due to* means *because of,* so **(A)** is wrong. **(B)** requires the preposition *to,* so it's also wrong. **(D)** is not possible because it should be followed by a *gerund.*

129. (A)

This is an indirect question, so the auxiliary verb should not be inverted. This means **(A)** is the correct alternative. *Contractions* should not be used at the end of indirect questions, so **(B)** is incorrect. The auxiliary verb *is not inverted* in indirect questions, so **(C)** is also wrong. **(D)** is not possible because it doesn't have the verb *be.*

130. (D)

The phrases *give someone a hand,* means to *help someone.* This means **(D)** is the right answer. Because

this is a fixed phrase, the verbs *take, do,* and *borrow* cannot be used. This means alternatives **(A)**, **(B)** and **(C)** are all incorrect.

Part VI—Text Completion

131. (B)

Means of transport means any vehicle that you can travel in, so **(B)** is the correct way. *Transport* and *ways* do not collocate, so **(A)** is incorrect. Even though *means* as plural noun means *method,* the nouns *transport* and *method* do not collocate. This means **(C)** is also wrong. **(D)** is not possible because we need a phrase which means *vehicles that you can travel in.*

132. (D)

The gap needs an adverb which means *it is unfortunate that,* so **(D)** is the correct alternative. **(A)** and **(B)** are wrong because they have the opposite meaning. **(C)** is not possible because it's an adjective.

133. (A)

The verb *improve* is commonly followed by an object and the preposition *by.* This means **(A)** is the only possible answer. The prepositions *for, at,* and *on* are not commonly used with the verb *improve.* This means alternatives **(B)**, **(C)** and **(D)** are incorrect.

134. (A)

The gap needs a noun which means *a rise in the amount. Increase* is both a verb and a noun, so **(A)** is the correct answer. Alternatives **(B)**, **(C)** and **(D)** are wrong because they're verbs.

135. (C)

(C) is the correct alternative because the gap requires an adverb which means *at the present time.* **(A)** is wrong because it means *in fact.* **(B)** is also incorrect because it means *in a decisive way.* **(D)** is not possible because it means *with a feeling of deep pleasure and satisfaction.*

136. (D)

(D) is the correct alternative because the gap needs a conjunction which means *except if.* **(A)** is wrong because it means *in spite of the fact that.* **(B)** is also incorrect because it means *without being affected by*. (**C**) is not possible because it means *as an extra thing*.

137. (A)

(**A**) is the correct answer because the gap needs a verb which means *have a similarity to*. (**B**) and (**C**) are not possible because it cannot be followed by *to*. (**D**) is wrong because it means *measure the similarity or dissimilarity between*.

138. (B)

(**A**) is wrong because the email doesn't say anything about the reader contacting the company. (**C**) is incorrect because the reader did not do or perform any activities with the company. The language in (**D**) is too casual, so it's not possible either. This means (**B**) is the only possible answer.

139. (C)

(**A**) is wrong because it should be followed by *to*. (**B**) is also incorrect as it should be followed by *at*. (**D**) should be followed by *in*, so it's not possible either. This means (**C**) is the only possible answer.

140. (C)

The gap requires an *adjective*, so alternatives (**A**) and (**D**) are not possible. (**B**) is wrong because *too confident* means *more confident than necessary*. This means (**C**) is the correct answer.

141. (B)

The gap needs a noun which means *a thing that is needed or wanted*. This means (**B**) is the correct answer. (**A**) is wrong because it means *the state of being required*. (**C**) is incorrect because it means *a thing that is or may be chosen*. (**D**) is not possible because it means *a duty or commitment*.

142. (D)

(**A**) is wrong because it should be followed by *to*. (**B**) and (**C**) are not possible because they should be followed by *in*. This means (**D**) is the only possible answer.

143. (A)

The beginning of the setnence talks about a grant application, and thanks the receipient, the most likely

answer is (**A**), the grant has been submitted. (**B**) and (**C**) are negative sentence endings, but these cannot be correct as the message goes on to give further instructions for the application process. (**D**) cannot be be correct, as *thank you* suggests that part of the application has already been submitted.

144. (A)

The sentence follows another sentence (*Your unique reference number is provided below.*). (**A**) has an object pronoun *it* which refers back to the object of the previous sentence (*your unique application number*), so this is the correct option. (**B**) is wrong because the number has already been provided. (**C**) is also incorrect because the person has already applied for the grant. (**D**) is not possible because it probably refers to a *medical prescription*.

145. (C)

(**C**) is the correct answer because *have access to* means *the opportunity to use something*. (**A**) is incorrect because it means *the opportunity to benefit from something*. (**B**) means *acquire*, so it is incorrect. The same applies to (**D**), which gives the idea of paying for something.

146. (D)

The gap needs a phrase which refers back to something previously mentioned and adds more information. This means (**D**) is the correct answer. (**A**) is wrong because it expresses *reason*. (**B**) is not possible as it expresses *contrast*. (**C**) is also incorrect because it is used to link ideas.

Part VII—Reading Comprehension

147. (A)

The email mentions three room types: *premier suite*, *family room*, and *family premium chalet*. This means (**A**) is the correct answer. The text says *all rooms are wheelchair accessible*, so (**B**) is wrong. There are two types of family rooms, so (**C**) is also wrong. The text doesn't say anything about room service, so (**D**)is not possible.

148. (C)

Room rates can be found after each room type, so (**A**) is incorrect. The email says *Please find attached* *file regarding the services and facilities at San Marco,* so **(B)** is also wrong. The text also says rooms are available from March 26, so **(D)** is not possible. This means **(C)** is the only possible answer.

149. (C)

The sentence says *please click on the link below,* so **(C)** is the right answer. **(A)** is not possible because the sentence is not an introduction. **(B)** is incorrect because room information should be presented before the sentence. **(D)** is also wrong because the sentence says *link below.*

150. (D)

The memo says *all employees are asked to attend,* so **(D)** is the correct answer. **(A)** is wrong because we know the date and location for this year's meeting, but that doesn't mean it always happens in the same month and place. **(B)** is wrong because staff should contact their department heads if they had any questions about the meeting. **(C)** is also incorrect because the text says *drinks and snacks,* not dinner.

151. (D)

The memo says *bring a copy of their appraisal forms,* so **(D)** is the correct alternative. *Drinks and snacks will be offered at the bar,* so **(A)** is wrong. The text doesn't say anything about *friends* or *family,* so **(B)** is not possible. **(C)** is not possible because the text doesn't say anything about *résumés* either.

152. (B)

The email says *your claim refers to the main water pipe,* so **(B)** is the right answer. **(A)** is wrong because the text doesn't say anything about a car. Mr. Noguira made an insurance claim. The text doesn't say anything about his position, so **(C)** is also incorrect. **(D)** is not possible because the email says *your claim refers to the main water pipe.*

153. (C)

The email says *I suggest you contact your water supplier,* so **(C)** is the right answer. **(A)** is wrong because the insurance company sent the email. **(B)** is also incorrect because the text says *under the terms of your policy, outdoor water and gas pipes are not covered,* but it doesn't say anything about *revising*

his policy. **(D)** is not possible because the text doesn't mention a *new claim.*

154. (B)

It is common practice to politely start an email that brings bad news. This means **(B)** is the correct answer. **(A)** is wrong because information is not usually given before the greeting. **(C)** and **(D)** are also incorrect because the phrase *we regret to inform* usually comes in an opening sentence.

155. (B)

The definition of *extravagant* is to spend money with little or not restraint. This means **(B)** is the correct alternative. We don't k now if the man spent all his money or not, so **(A)** is not possible. The text doesn't say anything about *borrowing money,* so **(C)** is incorrect. **(D)** is also wrong because *neighbors* aren't mentioned in the article.

156. (C)

(C) is the correct answer because the article says *seized the vehicle from the personal trainer's father.* **(A)** is wrong because the text says *a Ferrari F40 had been obtained from a car dealer in Beverly Hills.* The text says *obtained by deception,* which means the man didn't pay for the car and **(B)** is incorrect. **(D)** is wrong because the text says *federal agents located and seized the vehicle.*

157. (A)

The article says the man *has been jailed for drug dealing* **(D)**, *money laundering* **(C)** *and fraud* **(B)**, so these alternatives are wrong. This means **(A)** is the only possible answer.

158. (D)

This is a closing sentence and it says *all of the above offences.* This means **(D)** is the right answer. **(A)** is wrong because there's not enough information yet. **(B)** is wrong because it's followed by details of one of the offences. **(C)** is not possible because the man's arrest hasn't been mentioned yet.

159. (B)

The schedule says *the past, present and future of graphics design, developing autonomous designers* and *the impact of graphics design in advertising.* Since *graphic designers* are mentioned in three of the sessions, we can safely say that **(B)** is the best possible answer. *Students* aren't mentioned anywhere in the schedule, so **(A)** and **(D)** are not possible. **(C)** is wrong because the schedule doesn't say anything about *IT.*

160. (B)

The definition of monotony is *lack of interest, tedious repetition and routine.* This means *session 2* might be able to help and **(B)** is the correct answer. **(A)** is wrong because it focuses on the history of graphics design and has nothing to do with motivation. **(C)** is not possible because session 3 addresses *autonomy,* which means *working independently.* **(D)** is also incorrect because it talks about advertising.

161. (B)

The text says *08.00 – 08.30 – registration desk open,* so **(A)** is wrong. **(C)** is also incorrect because all the session numbers are followed by their topics. **(D)** is not possible because *coffee break* and *lunch times* can be found in the schedule. This means **(B)** is the only possible answer.

162. (C)

(A) is wrong because Deborah says *I recently applied for a job opening.* **(B)** is also incorrect because she doesn't ask for any other information about the job. **(D)** is not possible because *Ms. Maynard* is the one recruiting a professional, not Deborah. This means **(C)** is the only possible answer.

163. (A)

Deborah says *I recently applied for a job opening at Creative Minds,* so **(A)** is the correct answer. *BusinessLink* is either a forum or a social media website, so **(B)** is not possible. **(C)** is wrong because Deborah writes *on your online career site,* so there's nothing indicating the job is being advertised somewhere else. **(D)** is also incorrect because Deborah is the one who applied for a position.

164. (A)

Deborah says *truly appreciated your article on digital marketing,* so **(A)** is the correct answer. Deborah says she follows Ms. Maynard on BusinessLink. She doesn't

say that Ms. Maynard doesn't like being followed, so **(B)** is incorrect. They are very unlikely to be friends or Deborah wouldn't say *you can learn more about me,* so **(C)** is not possible. **(D)** is wrong because the email doesn't say anything about Ms. Maynard's schedule.

165. (B)

(A) is incorrect because the position hasn't been mentioned yet. **(C)** is incorrect because even though it comes after the position and her experience is mentioned, Deborah would not repeat exactly the same words *position* and *experience* in the following sentences. **(D)** is also wrong because it's in between sentences that talk about scheduling a meeting. This means **(B)** is the only possible answer.

166. (B)

The text says *There has been an increase of nearly 10% in the number of vegetarians,* so **(B)** is the correct answer. If the number increased by 10%, the total number of vegetarians is unlikely to be less than 10%. This means **(A)** is not possible. **(C)** is wrong because the text says *social media activists protesting against meat consumption and animal cruelty.* There's no mention of a protest being organized now, so **(D)** is incorrect.

167. (A)

The text mentions *social media activists* and *teen celebrities, youtubers* and *bloggers.* These people are all likely to have the same age, so **(A)** is the correct answer. The text doesn't say anything about *health,* so **(B)** is wrong. The article doesn't say anything about the *economy,* so **(C)** is also incorrect. **(D)** is not possible because *parents* aren't mentioned either.

168. (D)

The text says *The Animal Farming Association is planning to develop materials in an attempt to reestablish the image of a sector,* so **(D)** is the correct answer. The text says more teenagers are becoming vegetarians, but doesn't say anything about their image. This means **(A)** is wrong. **(B)** is also incorrect because it says they protest against meat consumption, but nothing about their image. **(C)** is wrong because the text doesn't anything about their image either.

169. (A)

The text says *Save up to $32 a year by setting up online billing,* so (A) is the right answer. (B) is wrong because the 15% discount refers to *setting up a calling circle.* Numbers (C) and (D) aren't mentioned in the text, so these alternatives are not possible.

170. (A)

The idiom *won't cost you a dime* means that something is *free,* so (A) is the correct answer. If it's free, options (B) and (C) are both incorrect. (D) is not possible because the text says it's free to set up a calling circle. It doesn't say that the calls are free.

171. (D)

(A) is wrong because this is not an introductory sentence. (B) is also incorrect because the features the sentence refer to haven't been mentioned yet. (C) is not possible because this paragraph doesn't talk about any features, it talks about setting up a calling circle. This means (D) is the only possible answer.

172. (C)

(C) is the correct alternative because the email says *The course in International Law (by distance learning) is designed for lawyers with over 2 years of experience in a corporate environment.* This is a Master's Degree course, so (A) is not possible. (B) contains some true information but is incomplete since it doesn't mention the 2 year's experience required. (D) is wrong because *International Law* is the Master's Degree course being offered by the university.

173. (C)

The email says *please note the fees for 2018/19 have not been confirmed yet,* so (C) is the correct answer. The text says *please find attached: reference forms* and then *PG Prospectus.* This means (A) and (D) are not possible. (B) is wrong because the text says *For any academic-related queries please contact Dr. Fiona Copper, our Program Director, at: f.m.copper@ lawuniversityarizona.com.*

174. (B)

(A) is wrong because the job only requires 2 years' experience and needs someone *with the ability to work in a team environment.* (C) is not possible because the job ad says they want someone with *a vast working knowledge of the building and planning regulations.* (D) is also incorrect because the text says they need an architect that likes to *innovate* and *work on a range of modern building projects.* This means (B) is the only possible answer.

175. (B)

(B) is the correct answer because job requirements are listed under this position. (A) is wrong because this is not an introductory sentence. (C) and (D) are also incorrect because they come after the job requirements.

176. (A)

Javier's first message says *got my email Sal?,* so (A) is the correct answer. (B) is wrong because he doesn't say anything about needing *help.* (C) is not possible because he asks if Sal read hos email. He invites Sal for dinner and not lunch, so (D) is also incorrect.

177. (B)

Javier writers *I owe you big time* in an email to Sal and Mari, so he must be saying something to them, not Mr Schmidt or Pete, eliminate (A) and (D). (B) is most likely to be correct, because the forwarded email is about a job, not about money. The correct answer is (B).

178. (B)

The email says *Our manager, Mr. Schmidt, was very impressed,* so (B) is the correct answer. Sal is Javier's friend, so (A) is wrong. (C) is incorrect because the texts don't say anything about Mari. (D) is wrong because even though Pete Sanders is the one who wrote the email, he uses the adjective *impressed* when talking about the manager.

179. (B)

(A) is wrong because he invites Sal for dinner. (B) is not mentioned so it must be the correct answer. (C) is given in the subject of the email (Bid Writer).

180. (B)

This is an introductory sentence, so (B) is the best answer. (A) is not possible because it's part of the message Javier wrote when he forwarded the email to

Sal and Mari. **(C)** is wrong because the results of trial have already been given. **(D)** is also incorrect because it requires a closing sentence.

181. (D)

The review says *I considered many other printers and this one seemed to be the best option available within this price-range,* so **(D)** is the correct alternative. **(A)** is wrong because the text says *This is the perfect kit for a first time printer builder.* **(B)** is also incorrect because the text says *The frame is cut to the right length, making it perfectly square.* **(C)** is not possible because the text says *making it perfectly square and easier for manual levelling.*

182. (A)

The review says *The install time depends on the builders' knowledge,* so **(A)** is the right answer. The text says the frame makes manual levelling easier but doesn't say anything about different users, so **(B)** is not possible. The text only says parts are well packaged, so **(C)** is wrong. **(D)** is also incorrect because *performance* is not mentioned in either text.

183. (C)

The idiom *will not break the bank* means something is not too expensive, so **(C)** is the correct answer. Even though we can assume the discount is a great opportunity, neither text say anything about *opportunities,* so **(A)** is not the best answer. He bought the printer, so **(B)** is not possible. He doesn't say anything about *borrowing money,* so **(D)** is also wrong.

184. (A)

(B) is wrong because the review mentions many of the features. **(C)** is wrong because Lawrence's last text message says the name of the shop, *TechPak.* The printer model is mentioned in one of the texts (*TriD 3500S*), so **(D)** is also incorrect. This means **(A)** is the only possible answer.

185. (A)

(A) must be the answer because the sentence says *before I go into detail,* so it must come at the earliest opportunity.

186. (B)

The notice says *Customer catalogues will not be available for this collection,* so **(B)** is the right answer. **(A)** is not

possible because the new line of products will arrive later, but the customer catalogues have been discontinued. **(C)** and **(D)** are wrong because the notice says *Please check staff catalogue for full collection and product information.*

187. (C)

Humdrum means *boring.* This means **(C)** is the correct alternative. **(A)** is wrong because the meaning is the opposite. **(B)** is also incorrect because it refers to something specific and not things in general. **(D)** is not possible because the phrase is talking about fashion, not advertisements.

188. (D)

The article says *giving old styles a reenergized exotic, look that conveys both nature and the wild,* so **(D)** is the correct answer. **(A)** is wrong because the ad says *designers endured a long journey in the depths of the Brazilian rainforest,* but doesn't the clothes are actually made there. **(B)** is not possible because the designers are men (*Kevin Alonso and Osvaldo da Silva*). The ad says *designed for the modern woman,* but doesn't say the designers themselves are modern. This means **(C)** is also incorrect.

189. (B)

Marisa Stones wrote the article in which she says *such designs never had the opportunity to leave the catwalk and be embraced by the public. Well, I'm glad this is about to end.* This means **(B)** is the right answer. **(A)** is wrong because the notice doesn't say anything about that. **(C)** and **(D)** are wrong because the article doesn't say anything about the designers being happy.

190. (D)

This is a closing sentence, so **(D)** is the only possible answer. **(A)**, **(B)** and **(C)** are all wrong for the same reason. The collection hasn't been mentioned before so the sentence wouldn't make any sense if it came before the second paragraph.

191. (D)

(D) is the correct answer because the job ad says *McQueen offers the opportunity to develop and progress, whilst gaining formal qualifications.* **(A)** is wrong because the ad doesn't say how many years of experience is required. **(B)** is also incorrect because even though the ad says *This role involves working as one member of a two-person aggregation team,* we don't know if both positions are available. **(C)** is not possible because the ad doesn't say anything about travelling.

192. (A)

Bo says *go to careers* and *once in a lifetime opportunity.* Later in the email Samuel says *thanks for the referral,* so we can safely assume that Bo thought the job suited him and **(A)** is the correct answer. **(B)** is not possible because Bo doesn't say anything about *revising* a text. **(C)** is incorrect because Bo doesn't mention an interest in the position. **(D)** is also wrong because Bo doesn't ask for help.

193. (B)

The idiom *to tick all the (right) boxes* means *to fulfill all the necessary requirements.* This means **(B)** is the only possible answer. **(A)** is wrong because even though we know Samuel has applied for the job, this is not the reason why he says he *ticks all the boxes.* We know Samuel is interested ion the job because he has applied for it. However, this is not why he uses the idiom, which makes **(C)** incorrect. **(D)** is not possible because nothing suggests Bo is interested in the job.

194. (A)

(A) is the right answer because Samuel writes *I have always dreamed about living in New York.* Even though everybody knows New York is a big city, Samuel doesn't say anything about that. This means **(B)** is wrong. **(C)** is also incorrect because New York is known as the *city that never sleeps* due to the fact that there is always something happening there with restaurants and clubs being open until late. This doesn't mean it's difficult to sleep there. **(D)** is wrong because Samuel mentions the Italian restaurants as a good thing, not because there are too many of them.

195. (C)

(A) is wrong because people don't usually *send regards* in an opening sentence. This is something which is usually done in a closing sentence. **(B)** is not possible because the next paragraph still asks for information about Bo and Sue. **(D)** is also incorrect because it is not common to write a sentence in that position between

the closing phrase and the signature. This means **(C)** is the only possible answer.

196. (D)

The ad says *You can choose from a range of 6 different colors,* so **(D)** is the correct alternative. **(A)** is wrong because the ad says *easy to move* and *you're free to take it with you anywhere.* **(B)** is also incorrect because the ad says *connect up to 6 wireless speakers,* which means *five other speakers.* **(C)** is not possible because the ad says *water-resistant surface.*

197. (A)

The email written by Theo says *Bought those speakers we talked about last week* and then *Since Christmas's at yours this years, I asked them to deliver them to you.* This means **(A)** is the correct answer. If Theo is the one who bought the speakers, alternatives **(C)** and **(D)** are incorrect. None of the texts mention a *birthday,* so **(C)** is not possible either.

198. (D)

The invoice shows that the yellow speakers were 10% cheaper than the others, so **(D)** is the right answer. Alternatives **(A)**, **(B)** and **(C)** are wrong because they have the same price in the invoice.

199. (C)

The colloquial phrase *and stuff* is *said in reference to additional things of a similar nature.* This means **(C)** is the best possible answer. **(A)** is wrong because *and stuff* refers to similar things, not different types of the same thing. **(B)** is also wrong because the phrase implies additional things, not alternatives. The same applies to **(D)** because drinks can't be considered *of the similar nature* as desserts.

200. (A)

The email says *how's Livy doing? Did she like the ring? Bella was over the moon when I told her about the engagement,* so **(A)** is the correct alternative. The email doesn't say anything about Bella loving spending Christmas at Noah's, so **(B)** is wrong. **(C)** is not possible because the email doesn't link Bella to the speakers. **(D)** is also wrong because even though the email says *mom said she's going to make the turkey,* it doesn't say that Bella likes it.

PRACTICE TEST 6 ANSWER KEY

Part I	Part II	Part III	Part IV	Part V	Part VI	Part VII
1. A	7. B	32. B	71. B	101. D	131. C	147. D
2. D	8. C	33. C	72. C	102. C	132. B	148. C
3. C	9. A	34. D	73. A	103. B	133. B	149. D
4. D	10. C	35. B	74. D	104. C	134. B	150. B
5. A	11. A	36. C	75. A	105. A	135. D	151. C
6. B	12. C	37. B	76. B	106. B	136. B	152. A
	13. A	38. C	77. D	107. C	137. C	153. D
	14. C	39. A	78. D	108. B	138. A	154. C
	15. A	40. D	79. B	109. B	139. A	155. B
	16. C	41. B	80. B	110. A	140. C	156. C
	17. A	42. A	81. B	111. C	141. B	157. B
	18. B	43. C	82. A	112. A	142. D	158. C
	19. C	44. D	83. B	113. D	143. A	159. A
	20. A	45. C	84. B	114. B	144. B	160. B
	21. A	46. A	85. A	115. B	145. B	161. A
	22. B	47. B	86. B	116. A	146. C	162. D
	23. C	48. B	87. C	117. D		163. D
	24. B	49. D	88. B	118. A		164. C
	25. B	50. B	89. D	119. B		165. C
	26. B	51. C	90. B	120. D		166. C
	27. C	52. D	91. C	121. A		167. B
	28. A	53. C	92. B	122. C		168. B
	29. B	54. D	93. A	123. D		169. A
	30. C	55. A	94. A	124. B		170. A
	31. B	56. C	95. B	125. B		171. D
		57. A	96. D	126. C		172. C
		58. B	97. C	127. B		173. C
		59. D	98. A	128. A		174. C
		60. C	99. D	129. D		175. A
		61. C	100. C	130. B		176. B
		62. D				177. A
		63. B				178. B
		64. B				179. D
		65. B				180. C
		66. C				181. C
		67. A				182. D
		68. A				183. C
		69. C				184. A
		70. B				185. B
						186. D
						187. A
						188. C
						189. C
						190. A
						191. C
						192. A
						193. D
						194. C
						195. A
						196. B
						197. C
						198. A
						199. B
						200. C

PRACTICE TEST 6

Part I—Photographs

1. (A)

The photograph shows a city with skyscrapers. The tallest building is on the right, (A) best describes the photograph. The buildings are complete, not being *constructed*. There are no *gherkins being eaten* in the photograph. The city has lots of *buildings*, not *fillings*.

2. (D)

The photograph shows three students using their laptops to work outside. (D) best describes the photograph. The pupils are working, not taking a *vacation*. They're on their laptops, but they're not in a *lecture*. They're working, but he is not *offended by her comments*.

3. (C)

The photograph shows a group of colleagues in an office. The women are laughing together. Only one man is on the phone, not all of them. The colleagues are working individually, not presenting together. The people are colleagues, not family members.

4. (D)

The photograph shows two people reading the label on a bottle of wine. (D) best describes the photograph. He's reading the label, not the *headlines*. The bottle is sealed, the wine has not *spilled*. The bottle of wine is new, not *old and dusty*.

5. (A)

The photograph shows a group of people looking at pictures. (A) best describes the photograph. They're looking at pictures, not having their work graded. They're looking at pictures informally, they're not at an art gallery. They're looking at pictures, not stories.

6. (B)

The photograph shows a florist on the phone, taking down notes while he talks. He is most likely taking an order for a customer. He's on the phone, not *closing his shop*. The shop has flowers, not *the garden*. He is a florist, he is not *ordering flowers*.

Part II—Question-Response

7. (B)

The question is *have you decided on a name yet?* This means they're talking about a baby. (A) talks about how the speaker was *named*, not the baby. (C) talks about someone being *named Salesperson of the year*, which is an award, not a baby name. (B) explains they can't choose a *name* because they *don't even know the gender*.

8. (C)

The sentence is *I hate speaking on the phone.* (C) agrees with the speaker and explains they *prefer texting*. (A) talks about *ringing* someone, but not about whether they like *speaking on the phone*, and (B) talks about a *payphone* location, not preferences in terms of calling people.

9. (A)

The question is *Did you apply for the job?* (A) explains they didn't because they *missed the deadline* for it. (B) talks about whether they *got* the job, not whether they *applied for* it, and (C) agrees about *wishing* to have the first speaker's *job*, but that's not what the first speaker said.

10. (C)

The question is *what did you want to be when you were a kid?* This means what job they wanted to have as kids, not what food they liked, so (A) is wrong because it talks about food (*cheese* and *vegetables*). (B) is wrong because it talks about whether they *have kids* or not, not about when they *were a kid*. (C) is correct because it gives job options: *astronaut* and *football player*.

11. (A)

The question is *did you renew your membership after all?* (A) explains they *negotiated a discount first* before they *renewed*. (B) talks about *options* for the first speaker, but the first speaker is asking about the second speaker's *membership*. (C) talks about *helping out*, not *renewing* anything.

12. (C)

The sentence is *I'm feeling a bit under the weather this morning.* This means they're a bit ill, or *sick*, which means (C) is correct as it says the speaker *must've caught something* from *the office* – and the correct collocation for an illness is to *catch* it. (A) talks about the *forecast*, i.e. the actual *weather* – not the expression of being *under the weather*. The same applies to (B), which talks about a *beautiful morning*.

13. (A)

The question is *what's gotten into him?* If something *has gotten into* somebody, it means they're *upset*, so (A) is correct. (B) is wrong because to be *into* someone means to like them, and (C) is wrong because it talks about getting a new car, but not why someone might be upset.

14. (C)

The question is *did she tell you what she's bringing to the party?* (C) explains they are *bringing* a *casserole*. (A) talks about the date of the *party (Saturday)*, not what someone is *bringing*, and (B) talks about what the speaker is *bringing (nothing)*, not what a third person (*she*) is bringing.

15. (A)

The question is *Whose song is this?* (A) answers that it's from *an indie band*, i.e. an independent music *band*. (B) is wrong because it talks about whether the speaker *listens to music*, not about a specific *song*. (C) is wrong because it talks about *singing in the shower* rather than a specific *song*.

16. (C)

The question is *did you go for the first or the second candidate?* (A) talks about a measurement of time (*second* – of which there are sixty in a minute), not the number (*second candidate*). (B) talks about an *interview* they *tanked*, i.e. failed, which means they were the *candidate* themselves, not the one choosing. (C) explains they are *still deciding*, so it's the correct answer.

17. (A)

The question is *what were you guys talking about?* (A) explains the conversation started because *he just*

wanted to know what time we're meeting tomorrow. (B) talks about *offending* the other speaker, but the other speaker said nothing about being *offended*. (C) says they'll *go and talk to her right now*, but the *talk* has already happened in the question, as it's in the past.

18. (B)

The question is *did I do something to upset you?* (B) says *I just wish you'd listen to me sometimes*, which is a legitimate reason to get *upset*. (A) talks about someone else being *upset*, not the speaker, and (C) talks about not *having done it yet*, which is not a reason to get *upset* with someone else.

19. (C)

The question is *are you going to the coffee shop?* (A) gives the location to the *coffee shop*, but doesn't answer if they are *going* or not. (B) talks about whether someone else *drinks coffee*, but doesn't say if they're going to the coffee shop or not. (C) answers *yes* and asks if they *want anything*, so it's correct.

20. (A)

The question asks *why didn't you just bring him with you?* (A) explains *this is not his kind of thing*, which means he wouldn't like it, and that's why they *didn't just bring him*. (B) talks about *looking* for an *assistant*, which is irrelevant. (C) talks about *forgetting to bring glasses*, not a person.

21. (A)

The sentence says *I wouldn't take it personally if I were you.* (A) says *I know, everyone says this is just how he is*, which is a reason not to *take it personally*. (B) talks about *the right kind of person for the job*, not someone who treated someone in a way they might *take personally*. (C) talks about being *allowed* to *take* something *with* them, not *taking* something *personally*.

22. (B)

The question is *do you prefer pancakes or scones for breakfast?* (B) asks for *croissants instead*, which are a different kind of *breakfast food*. (A) talks about when *breakfast is served*, but not what it will be, and (C) talks about the fact they *haven't eaten*, but not what they *prefer* to eat.

23. (C)

The question asks *do you want to give it a go?* To *give* something *a go* means to try it. (C) says *I'm good*, which means they don't want to try. (A) talks about *giving* something physically, not trying something. (B) talks about having a *long way to go*, so not trying something either.

24. (B)

The question is *what is wrong with the printer?* (B) explains *it's jammed*, which means there is paper stuck in it. (A) talks about *printing*, but doesn't explain what is *wrong with the printer*, and (C) talks about where the *printer* is (*in the printer room*), but not what's *wrong* either.

25. (B)

The question asks *did you understand what he said?* (B) answers *yeah* and explains *he said to meet him there*. (A) talks about whether they *know* him, not *what he said*. (C) says *he hasn't told me yet*, which doesn't make sense as the person they're talking about already *said* something.

26. (B)

The sentence is *this is all I could find*. (B) says *it'll have to do*, which means they will *have* to use it since there is nothing else available. (A) talks about *finding* something *hard*, not physically *finding* something. (C) talks about *finding out*, i.e. discovering something, not *finding* it physically.

27. (C)

The question is *you didn't need to pay much, did you?* (A) talks about forms of payment accepted (*credit* and *cash*) but doesn't say how *much*. (B) talks about being *paid enough for* something, which is an expression usually used by employees to explain why they refuse to do something asked of them. (C) explains that the item was *half price*, so they *didn't need to pay much*.

28. (A)

The question is *can you tell me where the bathroom is?* (A) gives directions: *down the corridor, on your left*. (B) talks about being *all right*, but doesn't say *where the bathroom is*. (C) talks about how many *rooms* a *house* has, not *where the bathroom is*.

29. (B)

The question is *what happened between them?* (B) explains *they had a massive fight*. (A) talks about something *happening this weekend*, not something *happening between* two people. (C) talks about something *between 3 and 5 p.m.*, which are timings – not a situation *between* two people.

30. (C)

The question is *do you like the blue or the red tie more?* (A) talks about *wearing* a *blue suit*, but doesn't answer which *tie* is better. (B) talks about wanting *to be there*, but also doesn't address the question of the *tie*. (C) suggests the speaker *wear a bow tie* instead of a *tie*, so it's correct.

31. (B)

The sentence is *I brought you some sweets from Europe*. (A) talks about someone being *sweet*, which for a person means being kind and has nothing to do with actual *sweets*, i.e. candy. (C) talks about how many times they've *been to Europe*, which is irrelevant to the offer of *sweets from Europe*. (B) says *you shouldn't have*, which is what people say as a form of thanking someone for a gift.

Part III—Short Conversations

32. (B)

The man says *My wife bought it for my 40th*, which means his *wife picked* it for his *40th birthday present*, so (A) and (C) are incorrect. (D) is wrong because the man describes the *sweater* as *striped blue*, and *stripes* are a *pattern*. The correct answer is (B) is wrong because the man says *it was on the back of my chair before I went to my 10 a.m. meeting*, which means he wasn't wearing it then.

33. (C)

The man says *I hope no one took it* and one woman replies *they wouldn't...* which is why the other woman says *oh, I don't know about that*. This is an expression of doubt when you disagree with someone, so this means the second woman *thinks someone might've stolen the sweater*, making (**C**) the correct answer. The woman is suggesting that someone would steal the sweater, not that she doesn't know the answer, so (**A**) is wrong. (**B**) is wrong because the woman is not asked *where the sweater is* before she says *I don't know about that*, and (**D**) is incorrect because, while the woman does say *things are going missing in the office*, this is to support her argument that *someone might've stolen the sweater* and she never focuses on *why*.

34. (D)

The man has lost his *favorite sweater*, which is a *birthday present* from his *wife*. As such, he must be *feeling* quite upset and *distressed*, so (**D**) is correct. The man could've felt (**A**) *moody*, i.e. irritable, but the way he reacts (*damn it…*) suggests distress rather than irritability. There's also nothing to suggest he's (**C**) *tenacious*, i.e. determined, and it's unlikely he would *feel* (**B**) *grateful* for losing his *sweater*.

35. (B)

The man says *I was looking for the 7th of April but it's all extremely expensive, and then I'm on holiday between the 15th and the 22nd and the show finishes on the 23rd so I went for the 13th.* Since the *7th* is *expensive*, (**A**) is wrong. So are (**C**) and (**D**), as the man is *on holiday* between those dates. The man says *I went for the 13th*, which means he selected it, so (**B**) is the correct answer.

36. (C)

The woman says *I'm working late every Friday this month* and the man says *that sucks*, so (**C**) is correct. The woman says she doesn't want to *pay more than $100*, not that she *can't*. She does say *Friday* is no good, but the man selected a *Tuesday* so that's not a problem. Finally, it's the man who mentions *the show finishes on the 23rd* but he says *that sucks* much further down the conversation.

37. (B)

The woman says *I'm not paying for than $100 for theater tickets*, so (**A**) is wrong. She also says *I might get vertigo if we're high up* and *I'd rather pick orchestra seats*, so (**D**) is wrong as it's the *balcony*, not the *orchestra*. Finally, the woman says *I think it's*

worth paying a bit extra so we're in the middle. If they're paying a bit extra, they've *selected* the more expensive tickets from the ones remaining. In addition, *middle* is the same as *center*, so (**B**) is correct and (**C**) is wrong.

38. (C)

One of the men mentions they are at an *exhibition* and another says *it's a shame* the *photograph* he *really liked* has been *sold*. Though they could be *exhibited* there, it's unlikely *photographs* would be sold at a *college*, a *museum* or a *photography class*. The only place that might *sell photographs* is an *art gallery*, so (**C**) is correct.

39. (A)

The woman says *my photographs are doing quite well and I haven't even finished school yet*, which mean *she sells photographs* and *she's a student*, so (**B**) and (**C**) are wrong. She also says she's *surprised* at the *exhibition's* success because *it's good* but *not that good*, which means it's *overrated*. While the woman mentions *her photographs* and that they're *doing quite well*, she never says they're *better*, so (**A**) is correct.

40. (D)

One of the men says *they're all about everyday life and how common it can be* and the other man says *I agree with Tom*. That's when the woman says *yeah, I get that* – and explains she *also gets why people like it*, but she doesn't *get why they like it so much*. Since she *doesn't get why they like it so much*, (**C**) is incorrect. While the *men* do *agree with each other* and *disagree with her*, the woman doesn't focus on this: she focuses on the reasoning they give for the *photographs* being *common*, i.e. the *theme* of the *photographs*, and the woman says she *gets* that. Therefore, (**D**) is correct.

41. (B)

The man says to the woman *can you come over to my desk and help me to install Yellow Studio? I tried looking for it on the shared drive, but I couldn't find it.* This means he *knows how to install* the *program he needs*, but *he can't locate* it, so (**B**) is correct. While he did *spill tea on his laptop* and *need a replacement*, that happened a while ago and he's just explaining this is why he *needs* the *program* again.

42. (A)

The woman asks *how in the world did you manage that*, and the man, thinking she means how he *spilled tea*, starts to explain *the mug kind of flew out of* his hand before the woman interrupts him and says *no, I mean, how did you manage to get a replacement*. That's when the man says *oh, right*, and answers her question. He has therefore now *realized* what she was actually asking, so (**A**) is correct. While we can say *oh, right* when we *remember something* or when we are *being sarcastic*, this is not the case here – and normally we would just say *right*, not *oh, right* when we *agree with something*.

43. (C)

The woman says *Andrew's notoriously susceptible to bribery in the form of any kind of chocolate.* This means *Andrew* must *really like chocolate*, so (**C**) is correct. It does not mean *he needs bribery* for everything, so (**B**) is wrong. (**A**) is wrong because *Andrew* plans to *give remote worker privileges* to the man, not the woman – and (**D**) is incorrect because the woman says *that'll do the trick* when the man explains how he convinced *Andrew* to replace his *laptop*. Thus, *that'll do the trick* means 'this is how you do it', not that *Andrew* is *a tricky person to deal with.*

44. (D)

The question asks for the Gist of the conversation. The speaker says 'have you two met the new COO yet?', and the rest of the conversation is mainly about the new COO: when they will meet her, what she is like, and what she will do. The speakers are mainly talking about a new member of staff. (**D**) is correct. *Mr. Renton, lunch* and *staff dinner* are all mentioned in the conversation, but they do not give the man topic of the conversation.

45. (C)

The question asks what the COO is going to do, so you should listen actively to the conversation for the COO being mentioned in the future tense. The man says 'isn't she planning to shorten lunch breaks and crack-down on late arrivals?' Shortening lunch breaks will create longer working hours, so (**C**) is correct. The COO wants to *shorten* lunch breaks, not remove them

altogether. It is Mr. Renton, not the new COO who has organized a dinner for the team to introduce the new member of staff to the rest of the team.

46. (A)

The question asks what the man disagrees with the two women about. The man says that the COO is going to 'shorten lunch breaks and crack-down on late arrivals,' which one of the women says is 'exactly what we need' and the other woman says 'her changes could make us so much more efficient,' but the man disagrees, saying 'No! I like the way things are now. Working in a relaxed environment is so much more enjoyable.' (**A**) is correct; the man doesn't think the changes are a good thing. (**B**), (**C**) and (**D**) are all mentioned in the conversation, but the speakers do not disagree about these points.

47. (B)

The woman says her website is called *www. beatricetraveldeals.com*, so her company is most likely to be a travel agency. (**B**) is correct.

48. (B)

The man says *with the Gold Plan you get more GBs of RAM and you have access to our tech support 24/7 365 days a year*, so (**A**) and (**C**) are *perks*. The man also says *you also get help in setting up your control panel in a way that works for you*, i.e *assistance with customizing*, so (**D**) is a *perk* too. (**B**) is the right answer because it's *with the Silver plan you only get tech support during business hours*, not the *Gold plan*.

49. (D)

The woman says *I think 30 bucks is a reasonable price so let's go for that.* According to the table, the *Gold Plan* costs *$29.99 per month*, which is almost $30. This means (**D**) is correct. (**A**) and (**B**) are wrong because the woman currently has the *Bronze Plan*, and wants to *upgrade*, i.e. get a better one. (**C**) is wrong because the woman chooses *$29.99* rather than *$12.99* after the man compares the two *options*.

50. (B)

The man says *you speak Spanish, right?* And the woman says *yeah* and *why? What's up?* Since the question about *Spanish* has prompted her answer, she can't be asking *how the man is*, or *why* he is *sad* or *what* his *plans are*. The only logical meaning for her question is *what's going on* that makes him want to know if she *speaks Spanish*. (**B**) is, therefore, the correct answer.

51. (C)

The woman says *your contact in New York must've misinformed him*, to which the man responds *this is so typical of Chris*. *Chris* must therefore be the *contact in New York*, so (**C**) is correct. *Carol* is the name of the woman and *Alex* is the name of the man, whereas *Agustin* is the guy who sent the *email*, i.e. the guy from *Chile*.

52. (D)

The woman asks *do you want me to write a reply to him?* But the man replies *no, I don't want to set a precedent*. To *set a precedent* means to create an *expectation*, and the woman meant to *write a reply* in *Spanish*, so (**D**) is correct. (**A**) is wrong because the man plans to *call* himself, not to *wait* for it. (**B**) and (**C**) are wrong because the man never says *he wants to write his own email* or that *he doesn't know what* to put in it.

53. (C)

This is an Inference question, asking who the speakers are talking about. The man says *I wonder who is going to take over his current job here*, so they must be talking about a *co-worker*; (**C**) is correct. (**A**) and (**B**) are not mentioned in the conversation. Bobby Edmonds will work for a newspaper publication (*The Herald*), but he is not a *newspaper salesman*.

54. (D)

The woman says *have you heard the news about Bobby Edmonds? He's moving over to the Herald*. (**D**) is correct. (**A**) and (**C**) are not mentioned in the conversation. (**B**) repeats *column* but does not answer the question

55. (A)

This is a Gist question, asking where the speakers work. The man says *he's a great writer and copyeditor*

and the woman says *he asked... for his own column and online blog*. The speakers most likely work at an online publication; (**A**) is correct. (**B**), (**C**) and (**D**) are not mentioned in the conversation.

56. (C)

The woman says *I've been out of the office for a while this summer doing database programming training at the regional training center in Colorado*. (**D**) is correct. (**A**) repeats *Suzuki Building*, but this is where the woman *usually works*, not where she has been working *during the summer*. (**B**) and (**D**) are not mentioned in the conversation.

57. (A)

The man says *are you still working in the finance and accounting department*, to which the woman answers in the affirmative. (**A**) is correct. (**B**) and (**D**) are not mentioned in the text. (**C**) repeats *database*, but does not give the *department* the woman works in.

58. (B)

The woman says *sounds great. Let's do lunch*. (**B**) is correct. (**A**) repeats *database* but does not answer the question. (**D**) repeats *eighteenth floor*, but the speakers do not make plans to go there. (**C**) is not mentioned in the conversation.

59. (D)

The man says *Professor Whitworth* has *Crime and Media Representation*. However, the woman says *it's not Professor Whitworth anymore*, so (**A**) is incorrect. The man mentions that, like *Professor Whitworth*, *Professor Stone* has *retired*, so (**B**) is wrong. The woman then says *I thought it was Professor Dominguez but if you look at the schedule, it's actually Professor Fuller*, which means (**D**) is correct.

60. (C)

The woman says *I know you're not going to be able to wake up in time for a class at 9, so these two are out*. (**A**) *History of Crime and Punishment* and (**B**) *Penology* are at *9 a.m.* so they must be the *two* she is referring to. The man then says he *normally* would rather have a class in the *evening*, but he then says *the late morning one sounds much more interesting* and

the woman says *let's go for that, then.* This means that
(D) *Sociology of Violence*, which is *evening*, is out
and they have selected **(C)** *Youth and Crime*, which is
late morning.

61. (C)

The woman says *I can't believe it will all be over in six
months* and the man says *I know, right?* This suggests
they will be graduating soon, which means they are
seniors, so **(C)** is correct. **(A)** is wrong because the man
says he's *trying not to think about it*, which means he
can't be excited about it. **(B)** is wrong because it's the
man who *doesn't like early mornings*, not the woman,
and **(D)** is wrong because the only thing we know is
the man *prefers evenings*, but we don't know if that's
because he *has a job* or for some other reason.

62. (D)

The man says *I miss my old commute*, and the woman
says *you were lucky before* and *a 25-minute commute
is the dream*, suggesting that's how long his *commute*
was. Therefore, **(A)** is correct. *40 to 50 minutes* is how
long it *takes* the woman *to get to work*, and *45 minutes*
is the man's current *commute*.

63. (B)

The man explicitly says he's *taking the bus*, so **(A)** is
incorrect. He also says his *new colleagues* are *all right*,
but *not like* his previous ones, whom he *misses*, so
(C) is incorrect. He also describes the *new colleagues*
as *uptight*, which is the opposite of *chatty*. **(B)** is the
correct answer because, when the woman asks him how
his *new colleagues* are, the man says *not like you guys*
– suggesting she was a *colleague* of his in the past.

64. (B)

After the woman says *finding nice colleagues is so
hard*, the man says *tell me about it* and describes his
new colleagues as *robots*. The expression *tell me about
it* can be used to show agreement, and since the man
goes on to give an example of how *hard* it is to *find nice
colleagues*, it seems to suggest he is *agreeing* with the
woman's point, so **(B)** is correct. **(C)** is therefore wrong,
and so is **(D)**, as you can't *agree* with something you
don't understand. The man never asks the woman to
elaborate or *share something*, so **(A)** is wrong, too.

65. (B)

The man says *my wallet has just been stolen on the
subway.* **(B)** is correct. The man's *wallet* was *stolen*. He
did not lose his *credit card*, or *misplace* his *ATM card*.
(D) is not mentioned in the conversation.

66. (C)

The man says *I need to cancel my ATM card and
credit card and would like to request new ones.* **(C)**
is correct. **(B)** repeats *cancel*, but the man wants to
cancel his *cards*, not his *bank accounts*. **(A)** and **(D)**
are not mentioned in the conversation. **64. (A)** The man
says *I'll need to go and find a bank statement for my
account number.* **(A)** is correct. **(B)**, **(C)** and **(D)** are not
mentioned in the conversation.

67. (A)

The man says *I'll need to go and find a bank statement
for my account number.* **(A)** is correct. **(B)**, **(C)** and **(D)**
are not mentioned in the conversation.

68. (A)

The woman tells the man *I told you it was good*, which
suggests she *recommended* it, so **(A)** is correct. The
woman never says she *didn't expect* him to *like* it – it's
the man who says he is *surprised* with how much he
liked it, so **(B)** is wrong. So is **(C)**, as to find something
a *slog* means to find it difficult to get through, and the
man calls the *book beautiful*. **(D)** is wrong, finally,
because the man says he's an *impatient reader* in
general but never links this to the book in question.

69. (C)

The man says the reason he's *not into romance novels*
is *not because I don't think it has its merits*, so **(A)** is
incorrect. He also clearly says *I don't like literary
fiction*, so **(B)** is incorrect. He never comments on how
commercial it is; the woman is the one who calls it
commercial. What he does say is he thinks the *prose*
is *too elaborate* – and since the *prose* is the *style of
writing*, **(C)** is correct.

70. (B)

The man calls the prose in romance novels too
elaborate and says this is why he dislikes it – and says

it's the same with literary fiction. The woman then says literary fiction tends to be flowery and bombastic. Bombastic is a synonym for pompous, so (**B**) is correct. The man says he prefers science fiction, but the woman does not agree with that, so (**A**) is wrong. Neither of them calls science fiction commercial, and the man clearly says he doesn't think the language in romance novels isn't simple, so (**C**) and (**D**) are wrong.

Part IV—Short Talks

71. (B)

The speaker says *Hello everyone, thanks for giving me such a warm welcome. Well, I think we all know why we're here tonight, but let me just take a few moments to remind you all. We're here to support Janet Richardson and her school for disadvantaged young children.* The speaker is giving a formal speech at a private, non-business event. The answer is (**B**).

72. (C)

The speaker says *Next, we'll hear from the students themselves, who will tell us a bit about their lives before they found the school, and how things have changed for them since joining.* The answer must be (**C**).

73. (A)

The speaker says *I'd like to thank you all for coming tonight,* so the correct answer must be (**A**).

74. (D)

The question asks what the topic of this speech is. The woman says *a lot of people ask this question: how do I know what the right career is for me?* She then proceeds to explain how to find the *answer* and *identify the best career option,* so (**D**) is correct. (**A**) is incorrect because the woman never says *most people are not in the right career* – just that *a lot of people ask* the *question.* (**B**) is incorrect because, while the woman does suggest *we shouldn't listen to our parents,* this is in the context of answering the previous question. Finally, (**C**) is incorrect because, while the woman talks about *happiness,* it is again in the context of *the right career,* which will *make people happy.*

75. (A)

The question asks which of the following is NOT a reason parents sometimes give the wrong advice. The woman says *they want to see you in a field that makes money,* i.e. a *lucrative career,* so (**B**) is incorrect. The woman also says they *want* you *a field that they themselves built a career in* (i.e. the *family legacy) or always wanted to go into but never had the chance* (i.e. *their own past aspirations*), so (**C**) and (**D**) are incorrect. (**A**) is correct because the woman says the exact opposite: *parents tend to think more pragmatically.*

76. (B)

The question asks what the woman says about jealousy at the end. The woman says *the person you envy the most probably has the thing you want the most, and that's what you need to get to make yourself happy.* This means the *thing you want* will be the *source of happiness,* not *jealousy* itself, so (**A**) is incorrect. *Jealousy,* however, will *reveal* this to you, what *you want the most,* i.e. *your true desire,* so (**B**) is correct. (**C**) is incorrect because the woman says *we're constantly bombarded with ideas about the source of happiness,* not *ideas about what jealousy means.* Finally, (**D**) is wrong because the woman mentions a *colleague's promotion* and a *neighbor's successful career* as examples of what can make us *jealous,* but never says that *jealousy* is *often the result* of such things.

77. (D)

The question asks which country first introduced alcohol-free January. The man questions whether the *USA* could adopt the *custom,* which means it didn't originate there, so (**A**) is wrong. The man also says *Dry January* can be attributed to a *British charity.* However, he then mentions that *Dry January* has been *going on since 1942 when the Finnish government attempted to persuade its citizens to observe what they called 'Sober January'.* This means it was *Finland* that started the *custom,* not *Great Britain,* so (**B**) is wrong and (**D**) is correct. Finally, (**C**) is incorrect because the *Soviet Union* is mentioned to have been at *war* with *Finland,* not to observe *Dry January* or have come up with it.

78. (D)

The question asks why Dry January critics dislike the choice of January. The man says *January is a popular choice because it's the start of a new year*, not *disliked*, so (A) is incorrect. While the man mentions that *January comes after Christmas, when most of us have spent weeks binge drinking and eating*, he never says it's *harder to stop drinking* because of this, so (B) is wrong. The man never mentions the *weather in January*, so (C) is wrong. He does say *January* is *the worst* choice because of *post-Christmas blues*, i.e. *depression* after *Christmas*, so (D) is the right answer.

79. (B)

The question asks what the speech says about doctors and psychologists. The man says that *while some participants and doctors claim abstaining from alcohol can have a positive effect on mood, sleep and energy, psychologists warn that it can actually induce feelings of sadness. Sadness* is a negative *mood*, which means *doctors* and *psychologists disagree on how Dry January affects mood*, so (B) is correct. This also means (A) is incorrect as they clearly don't *agree on the effects*. (C) is wrong because the man doesn't say what *psychologists* think about *sleeping patterns*, and (D) is wrong because the man says nothing about the *priorities* of *doctors* and *psychologists*.

80. (B)

The question asks how many surveys received a response from every person surveyed, i.e. a *100% response rate*. According to the man, *only 18 surveys had a 100% response rate*, so (B) is correct. (A) is incorrect the man mentions *10% of the surveys receiving a response from more than 70% of the participants*, and (C) and (D) are incorrect because *55-60%* is the *average response rate*, not the number of *surveys* with a *100% response rate*.

81. (B)

The question asks what was the thing most visitors disliked about the vineyard visit. The man says *the least popular part of everyone's visit was overwhelmingly the film*, i.e. *the video*, so (B) is correct. The man also says *the most popular response was "the tasting session", followed by the "tour"*, so (A) and (C) are

wrong. (D) is wrong because *the timings offered* are never mentioned in that context.

82. (A)

The question asks what solution the man offers at the end. The man says *perhaps we should consider changing the time of the second tour* because *afternoon visitors are more likely to be hungry by the time the tour takes place* – so an *earlier tour* would solve the problem – thus, (A) is correct. (B) is wrong because, while *survey respondents* say the *tour "could be shorter"*, the man never *offers* it as a *solution*. (C) is wrong because the man says *afternoon visitors are more likely to be hungry by the time the tour takes place, so they're more eager to have some snacks and taste our wines*, which suggests that *snacks are already offered*, and (D) is wrong because the man never mentions *removing the second tour*.

83. (B)

The question asks on which floor the room in which the guests will be having their breaks is. The man says *we did decide to use the small conference room on the first floor as the break room*, so (B) is correct. The *basement floor* is where the *event* will take place, not the *breaks* – and the *rooms* on the *second* and *third floor* were considered but rejected for the *event*.

84. (B)

The question asks whose duty it is to prepare the identification for the guests. The man says *Mario will have lanyards ready for everyone*, and *lanyards* are what you use to wear a *name tag*, i.e. *identification*, so (B) is correct. *Tanya* is responsible for asking about *dietary requirements*, while *Joao* and *the speaker* will be responsible for *setting up* the *room* in preparation for the *event*.

85. (A)

The question asks at what time the Paris group presentation starts based on the graph. According to the graph, the *London group presentation starts* at *9:30 a.m.* and the *Paris group presentation starts at 1 p.m.* However, the man says *there's a mistake in the program* and that *the Paris group will be presenting first, not the London group*. This means the two have been swapped, so the *Paris group will be presenting* at *9:30 a.m.* (**A**) is, therefore, the correct answer.

86. (B)

The question asks which number the caller should press if they can't make their appointment. If you *can't make* an *appointment*, you need to either *reschedule* it or *cancel* it, and the voice says *if you would like to reschedule or cancel your appointment, please press 2*, so (**B**) is correct. (**A**) *1* is what you need to *press* to *book* an *appointment*, whereas *3* is for *setting up online accounts* and *4* is for *test results*.

87. (C)

The question asks what the caller needs to do to activate their online account. The voice message says *you will need to come in with your passport to activate your online account*. This means you will have to *visit the medical practice*, so (**C**) is correct. *Pressing 3* will only *set up* the *account*, not *activate* it, and the voice message doesn't say you can *send a picture of* your *passport*: you need to bring it in. The *website* is where you would *book* an *appointment*, but the voice message does not say you can *activate* an *online account* there.

88. (B)

The question asks how many people are on the line before the caller. The voice message says *you are the... fifth person in line*. This means there are *4 people on the line before the caller*, so (**B**) is correct. *3* is a menu option, not a number of *people*, and *8* is never mentioned in the voice message. *10* is the *average waiting time* in *minutes*, not a number of *people*.

89. (D)

The question asks what can be inferred from the speech. The man *says we've merged two roles into one*, which is what the guy you met on Friday, *Mateusz*, will *be doing at the head office*. If the *merge* happened now, *Mateusz* must be a *new recruit*, and if the team *met* him on Friday, he must've *visited* them, so (**D**) is correct. (**A**) is wrong because, while *three people* did leave, *two roles* were *merged into one*, which means only two *people* are needed. The man says nothing to suggest he himself has *resigned* or is *moving to the head office*: this is all other people, not him.

90. (B)

The question asks where the man works based on the graph. The man says *we have the second lowest percentage of shoe sales in the region*. The *lowest* is *Store 199* with *10%*, and the *second lowest* is *541* with *12%*, so (**B**) is correct. *Store 235* has the highest *percentage*, and *Store 675* the *second* highest.

91. (C)

The question asks what will be changing at the store where the man works. The man says *men and women's clothing won't be affected* by the *changes*, so (**A**) is incorrect. He also says *we won't be stocking as many shoes anymore*, which means they will *be stocking* some, so (**B**) is wrong. (**D**) is wrong because it's the other way around: the *shoe corner will be turning into a children's corner*. The correct answer, therefore, is (**C**), as without a *shoe corner* the *dedicated shoe section* will disappear.

92. (B)

The question asks what can be inferred about the woman from the speech. The woman says *this research illustrates the point I've made since the moment I took office*, which means she *holds a public office position*, so (**B**) is correct. If she *took office*, she can't be a *member of the public*, so (**A**) is incorrect. (**C**) is incorrect because the woman specifically refers to the *Transport Minister*, so she can't be them, and the woman never says anything to suggest she is the one who *carried out the research* she's talking about.

93. (A)

The question asks, when the speaker says "Isn't that appalling", what she is referring to. The woman mentions *the fact that some motorcyclists don't wear a helmet* and talks about *the results of the research in general*. However, she then concludes with: *and the government is doing nothing to address this. Isn't that appalling?* Which means that what she finds *appalling* is the fact that the *government is doing nothing*, i.e. *the government's inaction*, so (**A**) is correct. The woman doesn't even refer to the *lives lost* until much later, so it's unlikely she's calling that *appalling*.

94. (A)

The question asks how many accidents that kill people happen each week. The woman says *for the past four years, we've had 3 deadly vehicle accidents per week, and 8 to 9 non-deadly accidents*. Therefore, *4* is the number of *years* this trend has been present for, and *8 to 9* is the number of *non-deadly accidents*. *3*, on the other hand, is the number of *deadly accidents*, i.e. *accidents that kill people*, so (A) is correct.

95. (B)

The question asks what can be inferred from the speech. The woman says *I'm a bit surprised at the backlash that this is receiving, especially from teachers*. If *backlash* is coming from *teachers*, then they are against, not *for the idea*, so (A) is wrong. (C) is wrong because the woman never refers to herself as a *teacher*. (D) is wrong because the woman mentions her *children* but never mentions their opinions on *uniforms*. The correct answer is (B) because the woman mentions a *backlash* which *surprises* her, meaning that most people are against the decision.

96. (D)

The question asks why the woman says "Please". The woman says: *Do you think kids can't tell if a uniform is brand new or if it's a hand-me-down from an older sibling or second-hand bought from a charity shop? Please. Trust me, it's quite easy to spot the difference.* So, the woman mentions an opinion (that it's hard to *tell if a uniform is brand new*), then says *please* and then disagrees with the opinion (*it's quite easy*). This means she's clearly not *asking for something*, *confirming* it, or *begging*. What she is doing is *expressing* her *incredulity*, as she clearly disagrees with this opinion. (D) is, therefore, the correct answer.

97. (C)

The question asks which of the following arguments the woman does NOT mention. The woman talks about the *message* that *uniforms* give and says: *we should be encouraging them to thrive on their individuality, not suppressing it*. (A) is, therefore, mentioned as an *argument*. The woman also says *I don't think that uniforms make all kids look the same, rich or poor*, so (B) is wrong. The woman then says *kids know how to*

dress appropriately, so (D) is wrong. While the woman mentions that *dress codes* must be *logical*, however, she never says *uniforms* are not *logical*, so (C) is correct.

98. (A)

The question asks what the finalist in second place will get. The woman says the *runner-up will be going home with a $1,000 cash prize*, so (A) is the correct answer. The $5,000 and the *opportunity to exhibit their art* will go to the *winner*, not the *runner-up* – and since the *runner-up* is getting a *cash prize*, they are not getting *nothing*.

99. (D)

The question asks which finalist from the graph has removed themselves from the competition. The woman says *one of the contestants has decided to remove herself from the competition as she was offered an opportunity elsewhere – which is not surprising, considering she had the second highest score given by the judges*. The *highest score given by the judges* is *9.1* to *Maria Santxez*, followed by *9* to *Rose O'Brien*. Since *Rose O'Brien* has the *second highest score*, (D) is correct. The other two *finalists*, *John Krakow* and *Donald Wreck*, have the third and fourth *highest score* respectively.

100. (C)

The question asks how the woman is likely to feel as she announces the results. The woman says *is … Oh, wow … Incredibly, the winner is our youngest contestant, with no formal art training*, the woman is surprised that the finalist with the least experience has won, so the answer is (C).

Reading

Part V—Incomplete Sentences

101. (D)

The missing word is preceded by the adjective *open*. To be *open to* something means to be susceptible, rather than closed off, and it is followed by the preposition 'to' and either a noun or a gerund. This means that (D) *to discussing* is the correct answer, as it is the preposition *to* and a gerund. (A) is wrong because *discuss* is an infinitive or verb, and (**B**) is wrong because it's the infinitive with *to*. (**C**) is wrong, finally, because it's the gerund without the preposition *to*.

102. (C)

The missing word introduces a condition. The result of the condition is *dire consequences for the country's economy*. Since *dire* means terrible and the condition is to *find a solution*, we need a word or expression that excludes this condition for the sentence to make sense. The only word that can do that is (**C**) *unless*, so it is the right answer. (**A**) *if*, (**B**) *when* and (**D**) *as soon as* are positive, so the sentence wouldn't make sense with them: with a *solution*, the *consequences* would be avoided, not *dire*.

103. (B)

The missing word is a verb. The *survey* has revealed that *public opinion* has changed since *six months ago*, so we need a synonym for change. That synonym is (**B**) *shifted*. (**A**) *swaggered* means to walk with confidence. (**C**) *shunted* means to push or shove something, and (**D**) *swirled* means to move in a twisting pattern, so none of these are correct.

104. (C)

The missing word is a phrasal verb that means that someone has abandoned or left their *role*. To (**C**) *step down* means exactly that, so it's the correct answer. To (**A**) *step off* is a physical movement, such as *stepping off* a train. So is to (**B**) *step out*, e.g. *stepping out* of the house. To (**D**) *step over* means to move over something or someone.

105. (A)

The missing word is an adjective that describes how people view the decision to *donate to charity*. Since it's something *even* the *most outspoken critics* will *agree* on, it must be something positive. (**A**) *commendable* means something that people would congratulate you on, so it is the correct answer. (**B**) is incorrect because *ceremonial* means related to public events and ceremonies. (**C**) is also wrong because *cantankerous* means bad-tempered, and (**D**) is wrong because *convalescent* describes someone recovering from an illness.

106. (B)

The missing word is part of a collocation starting with *in the* that means something was in progress of being made. The correct collocation is *in the making*, so (**B**) is the right answer. This means that (**A**) *make*, (**C**) *makes* and (**D**) *makings* are all incorrect.

107. (C)

The missing word is the preposition that follows the noun *concerns*. *Concern* is usually followed by either *about* or *over*. The only option present from these two is (**C**) *over*, so it is the correct answer. This means that (**A**) *at*, (**B**) *for* and (**D**) *in* are all wrong.

108. (B)

The missing word is a verb that means the *cost of installing ramps* should be picked up by the council and the *school*, not the *parents*. (**B**) is correct because to *subsidize* means to pay part of something. (**A**) is wrong because to *conflate* means to combine. (**C**) is wrong because, while *allocate* means to distribute and the cost could be distributed to the council, *allocate* is followed by the preposition 'to', not *by*. (**D**) is wrong because *destabilized* means to cause unrest.

109. (B)

The missing word is an adjective that describes *accusations* against a *media mogul* as described by the *mogul* themselves. The *mogul* would probably defend themselves, so they would describe the *accusations* as wrong, or baseless, i.e. (**B**) *unfounded*. (**A**) is wrong because *unctuous* means excessively flattering. (**C**) is wrong because *unruly* means rowdy, or disorderly, and (**D**) is wrong because *unabashed* means unashamed.

110. (A)

The missing word is the preposition that follows the verb *provide* to mean providing food, shelter and other necessities to someone. The correct preposition is (**A**) *for*. (**B**) is incorrect because it would be missing the noun – you can *provide* food *to* your *children*, for example, but '*provide to your children*' is an incomplete sentence. (**C**) *with* is incorrect because you can *provide* someone *with* something, e.g. *provide* your *children with* food, but you can't *provide with* someone.

(**D**) *over* is wrong because the preposition *over* does not collocate with the verb *provide*.

111. (C)

The missing word is the verb. Since the speaker says they *cannot book* anything before they *hear back*, this must mean they don't have *confirmation*. This is further evidenced by the word *yet*, which can only be used in questions or negative forms. Since this is not a question, we need a negative – so (**A**) *received*, a positive, is wrong. (**B**) is wrong because the word order is wrong: it should be *we have not yet received*, not *we have yet not received*. (**D**) is wrong because it's impossible to say *we have yet not to receive*, as it would mean that so far they have been *receiving confirmation* continuously. (**C**) is the correct answer because *we have yet to receive* something means we have not *received* it *yet*.

112. (A)

The missing word is an adjective that describes someone's *need to micromanage* – and since it *has left him with few friends*, this *need* is a bad thing. This automatically excludes (**B**) *inalienable*, which describes something that can't be taken away (e.g. human rights) and (**C**) *infallible*, which describes something that is never wrong. (**D**) *inadmissible* describes something invalid (such as evidence in court). The only logical option is (**A**) *inexorable*, as it describes something impossible to prevent.

113. (D)

The missing word is a noun that describes a *company's* mistake. The word *blunder* is a synonym for mistake, so (**D**) is correct. (**A**) is wrong because a *blister* is a bubble on the skin, (**B**) is wrong because *blather* is long-winded talk, and (**C**) is wrong because a *blinker* is a vehicle indicator.

114. (B)

The missing word is a preposition that completes the expression *take _ storm* to mean to make an impression. The correct preposition for this is *by*, so (**B**) is the correct answer. This means that (**A**) *on*, (**C**) *at* and (**D**) *with* are wrong.

115. (B)

The missing word is the verb that completes the subordinate clause. The clause talks about the speaker's *father*, who *died* before *visiting Europe*. Since the *father* is dead, it is impossible for them to *visit Europe* in the present, so the verb has to be in the past. Therefore, (**A**) *never visits* and (**C**) *has never visited* are both incorrect, as they are present tenses. (**D**) is also wrong because *had never visited* is in the past perfect, which is used to show something happened before something else – but here we don't have anything else that happens after. (A correct version would've been *my father, who had never visited Europe before he died...*) (**B**) *never visited* is in the past simple tense, so it's correct.

116. (A)

The missing word is part of a collocation starting with the verb *run* to mean something *runs wild*. The correct collocation for this is *run rampant*, so (**A**) is the right answer. This means that (**B**) *raucous* (i.e. noisy), (**C**) *restless* (i.e. uneasy) and (**D**) *ruthless* (i.e. cruel) are all incorrect, as none of them collocates with *run*.

117. (D)

The missing word is the verb of the sentence. The sentence begins with *not once*, which is always followed by inversion to show emphasis – so the auxiliary verb needs to come before the main verb. (**A**) *we offered* and (**B**) *offered we* have no auxiliary verb, so they are wrong. (Inversion cannot happen with the subject and verb, as in *offered we*. The correct inversion would be *did we offer*.) (**C**) *we were offered* and (**D**) *were we offered* are both in the passive voice, but only (**D**) is inverted, so it's the correct answer.

118. (A)

The missing word is the verb that means to focus on something. (**A**) *zero in on* means exactly that, so it's correct. (**B**) *zero out on*, (**C**) *zero off of* and (**D**) *zero on in* are all wrong because they are not common phrases.

119. (B)

The missing word is an expression that explains why the *client* wants to *move* the *meeting back by half an hour*. The reason is she wants to *make it on time*. (**A**) *as long as* is wrong because it expresses a condition, not a purpose or hope. (**C**) *in order to* expresses purpose, but is followed by an infinitive, not a clause (*she can make it on time*), so it's wrong. (**D**) is wrong for a similar reason: *in hopes of* expresses *hope*, but is followed by a gerund. (**B**) is the correct answer because *so that* shows purpose and is followed by a clause.

120. (D)

The missing word is between *which is* and *the reason*. (**A**) *presumed* is wrong because we can't say something is *presumed the reason*: we can only say *presumed to be* the *reason*. (**B**) is incorrect because *the reason* is a noun and *presumption* is also a noun, and the verb 'to be' cannot have two objects. (**C**) is wrong because *presumptive* is an adjective and adjectives generally come before a noun and after the article, so *presumptive the reason* is impossible – we can only say *the presumptive reason*. (**D**) is the correct answer because *presumably* is an adverb, so it can go between the verb and noun to mean it is *presumed* to be *the reason*.

121. (A)

The missing word is a verb that means to impose and collocates with *accusations*. *Levied* is a synonym of impose, so (**A**) is the correct answer. (**B**) *levitated* means to hover, so it's wrong. (**C**) *levered* means to use a *lever* to lift something. Its spelling is very close to the word 'leveled', which would've worked on this occasion. Finally, (**D**) *leveraged* means to use something to your advantage.

122. (C)

The missing word is the verb of the sentence. The subject of the sentence is *people* and the verb is followed by *to avoid travelling*. Since the verb is *warn*, if the *people* were the ones doing the *warning*, we would need an object: whom are they *warning*? The only other option is that the *people* are receiving the *warning*, which means we need the passive voice.

The only option in the passive voice is (**C**) *are being warned*, so it's the correct answer. (**A**) and (**B**) are wrong because they're in the active voice, and (**D**) is wrong because it's not a verb – it's the gerund, and the sentence does not have a verb so it needs one.

123. (D)

The missing word is the preposition that follows the verb *struggle*. The verb *struggle* can be followed by either *to* or *with*, so (**B**) *at* and (**C**) *on* are wrong. The difference between *to and with* is that *to* is followed by the infinitive and *with* is followed by the gerund. Since after the gap we have *paying off*, which is a gerund, (**D**) is the correct answer.

124. (B)

The missing word is an adjective that can describe *performance*. Since the person in question didn't have their *contract renewed*, and the *performance played a role*, the missing adjective must be a negative word. (**A**) is wrong because *performance* can't be *unreasonable*; only behavior can. (**C**) is wrong for the same reason: a person can be *unrelenting*, but their *performance* can't. (**D**) is wrong because *unrequited* describes love which is not reciprocated, so nothing to do with *performance*. The correct answer is (**B**), as *unremarkable* means not special, and not special *performance* can be a bad thing.

125. (B)

The missing word is an expression that collocates with *best interests* to mean you want the best for someone. The correct collocation for this is (**B**) *at heart*. (**A**) *at hand* means to keep something close, whereas (**C**) *at mind* and (**D**) *at arms* are not common expressions. (To keep someone's *best interests* in *mind* might've worked.)

126. (C)

The missing word is the verb that completes a conditional sentence. Since the person *does not want to think about* what could've happened, it's impossible for it to happen, which means the sentence is talking about the past. The clause with the missing verb starts with *if*, which means it's a conditional sentence, and conditional sentences in the past use the past perfect, i.e. (**C**) *hadn't raised*. (**A**) *didn't raise* and (**B**) *haven't raised* can only be used in conditional sentences referring to the future. (**D**) *wouldn't have raised* is used in the results clause of a conditional sentence, not the condition clause.

127. (B)

The missing word is a verb that means to succumb to. To resort to is the closest match, so thise answer must be (**B**).

128. (A)

The missing word is the noun that describes how someone feels about someone, and collocates with *have nothing but*. Since the person they are speaking about is the reason a *proposal* was *unsuccessful*, the feelings must be negative. (**B**) *respect* and (**D**) *avidity*, i.e. enthusiasm, are wrong. (**A**) *contempt* and (**C**) *hostility* are both negative, but only *contempt* collocates with *have nothing but*, so (**A**) is correct.

129. (D)

The missing word is the preposition that follows the verb *wade* to mean participating in a conflict to help out. The correct preposition for this is *in to*, so (**D**) is the correct answer. This means that (**A**) *on*, (**B**) *in* and (**D**) *to* are all wrong.

130. (B)

The missing word is the verb that begins the expression *as it may*. This is a set expression and the only way it can be said is *be that as it may*, so (**B**) is correct. This means that (**A**) *is*, (**C**) *being* and (**D**) *was* are all wrong.

Part VI—Text Completion

131. (C)

In this sentence, we are missing the verb structure that completes the subordinate clause. Since there is no linking word such as 'which', this is a participle clause describing the noun of the main clause: *maintenance work*. There are two types of participle clauses: active with the gerund, and passive with the past participle. Since the *work commences* and is not *commenced*, this participle clause

is active, so it needs the gerund: (**C**) *commencing*. This means that (**B**), which is the past participle used in passive clauses, is wrong. (**A**) and (**D**) are wrong because they can't introduce participle clauses.

132. (B)

In this sentence, we are missing the linking word that connects the main and subordinate clause. The *cold water supply will not be affected* by the *works*, but the *hot water supply will*, according to the text – so we need a linking word that shows contrast. The only options that introduce contrast are (**B**) *while* and (**D**) *however*: (**A**) *when* expresses simultaneity, and (**C**) *as* expresses simultaneity and reason. *However*, though, cannot introduce subordinate clauses: it can only be used in main clauses. *While*, therefore, is the only option.

133. (B)

The missing clause is part of a sentence that finishes with *and will be during working hours*. Since the second part of the sentence does not have a subject (what *will be during working hours*?), the subject must be in the missing part of the sentence. In (**A**) and (**D**) the subject is *you*, which doesn't make sense. Neither does (**C**) *we*. The only logical subject is *this* from (**B**), which refers to *switching off* the *cold water supply*. The correct answer is, therefore, (**B**).

134. (B)

The missing sentence follows a request to inform *tenants* about *the works* and the *potential disruption*. A *request* requires *cooperation* to be fulfilled, so (**B**) is correct.

135. (D)

In this sentence, we are missing the verb. The sentence is talking about a *course* that the recipient will be attending. Since the email is to *confirm* the *course*, the recipient must have *booked* it already. We do not know, however, when she *booked* it, so we need the present perfect. This means that (**A**) and (**B**) are wrong. Since the recipient did the *booking*, and the *course* is the subject of the sentence, we need the passive voice – so (**D**) *has been booked* is correct.

136. (B)

The missing sentence comes after an explanation that the particular *school* has a *partnership* with various *schools* to use their buildings, so the *locations* might vary. After the missing sentence comes a promise that *directions* will be sent *before* the *course* starts. **(A)** is wrong because the *directions* have not arrived yet, so it's impossible to *confirm receipt*. **(C)** is wrong because no reference is made to a need for *enough bookings* in the text, and **(D)** is wrong because what the *partner schools offer* is irrelevant. **(B)** explains where *all* the *locations* are, so it's correct.

137. (C)

In this sentence, we are missing the word that introduces a condition, and the condition is that *this is the first time* they are *booking*. The word *only* cannot introduce a condition, so **(A)** is incorrect. (*Only if* would've been correct.) *Whether* can only introduce a condition when we only have two options, which is not the case here, so **(B)** is incorrect, too. *While* is used to introduce contrast, not a condition, so **(D)** is wrong. The correct answer is **(C)** *if*, which introduces a condition.

138. (A)

In this sentence, we are missing the verb that means to receive or be given, i.e. to **(A)** *obtain*. To **(B)** *contrive* means to create or manufacture. To **(C)** *ordain* means to anoint or make someone a minister, and to **(D)** *undertake* means to take on or guarantee.

139. (A)

In this sentence, we are missing the verb that describes transferring what you imagine *in your mind* to *paper*. *Transfer* is correct. You can only *transcribe* words, not drawings, and to *transpire* means to happen, and is an intransitive verb, i.e. does not take an object (*what you see in your mind* is the object here). *Transport* also means to move something, but it is used for physical objects, not mental images.

140. (C)

In this sentence, we are missing the verb. Since the gap is followed by the preposition *by*, the missing verb must be in the passive voice, which means

(A) and **(B)** are incorrect. However, since this clause is at the beginning and describes the *course*, it is an adjectival clause – and adjectival clauses can only begin with the gerund (in active voice) or the past participle (in passive voice). **(C)** *taught* is the past participle, so it's correct. Another way to know **(D)** is wrong is that the verb *were* is in the plural, but the *course* is singular.

141. (B)

The missing word is the preposition that follows the verb *aimed*. The verb *aimed* can only be followed by the preposition *at*, so **(B)** is correct. This means that **(A)** *to*, **(C)** *on* and **(D)** *for* are all wrong.

142. (D)

The missing sentence is part of the advert's closing statement, followed by the recommendation to *book now*. **(A)** cannot be the answer, as the writer will not be in touch, the reader must get in touch. **(B)** is an incomplete sentence, as it's missing the verb. It would've been correct if the gap were followed by a comma that connected it to *book now*. **(C)** is an irrelevant statement at this stage with no context whatsoever. **(D)** is the only logical answer, as it has the same tone as the *book now* suggestion.

143. (A)

The missing sentence is the beginning of the email. **(B)** is wrong because it's the woman writing this email who has *chosen* this restaurant, not the other way around. **(C)** is wrong because *we look forward to your reply* is how you would close, not open an email. **(D)** is wrong because the woman needs to first explain what she needs before she explains how she can be *contacted*. The only logical option is **(A)**, which is a standard phrase for starting an email.

144. (B)

In this sentence, we are missing the adjective that collocates with *requirements* to describe anything someone cannot or does not want to eat. The correct collocation for this is *dietary requirements*, so **(B)** is correct. **(A)** *diet* and **(C)** *dieting* do not collocate with requirements, whereas **(D)** *dietician* is a job, not a *requirement*.

145. (B)

In this sentence, we are missing the adjective that describes the *vegetarian options* in the *menu*. Since the woman says she does not anticipate any *problems*, the adjective must be positive. This means (A) is incorrect, as *edible* means it can be eaten, but does not describe the quality of the food. (C) *edifying* describes something that provides moral instructions, whereas (D) *duplicitous* means deceitful, neither of which fit here. The correct answer is (B) *delectable*, which is a synonym for delicious.

146. (C)

In this sentence, we are missing the verb that gives the time of *arrival*. Since we are talking about a booking in the future, the *arrival* will be in the future, too – so (A) *arrived* and (B) *have arrived* are wrong, as they are in the past and present respectively. (C) and (D) are in the future, but (D) *will have arrived* is normally used to show that something will happen before a set deadline, and the deadline is expressed through the preposition 'by', not *at* (which is what we have in the text). Therefore, only (C) can be used here.

Part VII—Reading Comprehension

147. (D)

The question asks how much money Dana offered for the job Will posted. Will says *one person - Dana Johnson - submitted a bid of double the maximum amount of $500*. Double of $500 is $1,000, so (D) is correct. $500 is the *budget*, or *maximum amount*, whereas $300 to $450 is the *range* of *offers* received from *most of the people who use* the *website*.

148. (C)

The question asks how Will is likely to feel based on the email. Will talks about how *Dana* has targeted him with *a barrage of abusive remarks* and *tracked* him down *on social media*, sending him *a steady stream of abuse* and even contacting his *employer*. All of this is unlikely to please Will, so (A) *overjoyed*, which means extremely happy, is wrong. From the fact that Will is sending an email to complain and that he is threatening to *press charges against* the woman, it is clear he is

not *nonchalant* or *lackadaisical*, both of which mean indifferent. The correct answer Is (C), as *vexed* means irritated and concerned.

149. (D)

The question asks which of the positions the following sentence best belong in: "I'm at the end of my rope here." This sentence describes someone who is fed up, and Will is clearly fed up with the woman's behavior. [1] and [2] are therefore wrong, as he has not yet described what the woman's behavior is. [3] is also wrong because both before (*I was subjected*) and after the gap we have the past tense (*I reported the message*), which means that Will is describing something that happened, and the sentence is in the present tense, so it doesn't fit into his narration. The only logical position is [4], as it is preceded by the current actions of the woman (*I have been on the receiving end... she has even emailed my employer...*) and followed by the actions Will plans to take (*I'm also very close to pressing charges...*) in the near future.

150. (B)

The question asks what the purpose of Ian's text is. Ian asks Kris if she *has a minute* because he *got a call from Alice* about the *hotel* they *booked* and the fact that *there's no booking*. Kris's reaction is to ask for *the hotel name & booking ref* so she can *call* them. Since Kris immediately explains what she will do to help, it's safe to assume the *purpose of Ian's text* is to *ask for* her *assistance*, not to *complain* or to *inform Kris about a mistake* which we cannot even tell if *she made* or not. Finally, even though *Kris* says *she's off*, he does not ask about it. Therefore, (B) is correct.

151. (C)

The question asks why Kris says "What's up?" Ian asks Kris if she *has a minute* and that *it's urgent*, which is when she asks *what's up*. If *it's urgent*, it must mean *Ian needs her*, so (C) is correct. You can't say *what's up* to ask *where* someone is, and Ian doesn't say *how* he *feels* after Kris asks *what's up*. Finally, it's safe to assume Kris already knows that *Ian is at work*, as he has asked for *urgent* help and she replies she is *off today*.

152. (A)

The question asks, based on the conversation, how Kris thinks Ian feels. Kris tells Ian *don't freak out*, so clearly she thinks he is stressed, so **(A)** is the correct answer. To be *grief-stricken* would be a bit extreme, as Ian hasn't lost someone or something special to him. *Frustrated* means annoyed, but Ian is worried, and *nonplussed* means surprised, but Ian does not comment on whether what has happened with the *hotel* is surprising or not.

153. (D)

The question asks which of the following customers CANNOT do based on the ad. The ad says *customers* are able to *buy two pairs of prescription glasses, two pairs of sunglasses, or one of each*, so **(A)** and **(B)** are wrong. The ad also says it's possible to *buy two pairs from our own range*. However, the ad also says *only 2 pairs per person*, so **(D)** is not possible, as It's a total of 4 *pairs*.

154. (C)

The question asks which of the following is NOT free in the 2-for-1 deal. The ad says they offer a *free appointment with our optometrist*, so **(D)** is free. They also say *cheapest pair free*; however, they say *deal only includes frames*, not *lenses*, so **(C)** is not free.

155. (B)

The question asks which of the following is NOT TRUE based on the ad. **(A)** is true because the ad mentions a *stylish range of frames for all ages*, i.e. *both young and old*. **(C)** is true because the ad says *orders must be placed on or before 31st July 2018*, and *on* means that it *can still be used on* that date. **(D)** is true because the ad says the *deal cannot be combined with any other voucher or deal*. **(B)** is the correct answer because the ad says the *optician appointment normal price of $20 will be discounted from 2-for-1 purchase*, which means not *everyone* gets *free optometrist appointments*: only those who use the *2-for-1 deal*.

156. (C)

The question asks who this article is aimed at. The article author addresses the reader a few times and

mentions, at least twice, *your business* – which means that they expect the reader to be a **(C)** *business owner*. **(A)** is incorrect because, while *customers* are mentioned in the article, it's always in the third person. The same applies to **(B)** *employees* and **(D)** *shop assistants*, so all of these are wrong.

157. (B)

The question asks which of the following benefits of name badges is NOT mentioned in the article. The text says *name badges allow customers to start a conversation with your employees*, i.e. *chat* to them, so **(A)** is incorrect. It also says they *will make it easier for them to complain*, so **(C)** is incorrect. The article mentions that *employees will be more motivated to do their best when helping a customer*, so their *service* will be *better*, so **(D)** is incorrect. **(B)** is correct because the article says *customers* can *name the employee who made them happy with their visit in feedback forms*, but it never says the *feedback* overall will be *more positive*.

158. (C)

The question asks what the word "seasoned" in paragraph 3 means in this occasion. The text is talking about *entrepreneurs* giving advice, so *seasoned* is likely to mean experienced, or *accomplished*, so **(C)** is correct. **(A)** is incorrect because *rudimentary* means basic or simple. **(B)** is incorrect because *callow* means the opposite of *seasoned*: young and inexperienced. **(D)** is incorrect because *cumbersome* means inefficient and unwieldy.

159. (A)

The question asks what can be inferred about millennials from the article. The article says *millennials hate name badges*, not *working in customer service*, so **(B)** is incorrect. **(C)** is incorrect because the text says *unhappy employees make unhappy customers*, not *millennials*. **(D)** is incorrect because the text says *employees, particularly millennials, tend to hate name badges* – so their *opinions* don't *differ*, they are similar. **(A)** is the correct answer because the text says that nowadays *privacy is valued* and that's why *employees, particularly millennials, hate badges* – which must mean *millennials value privacy more*.

160. (B)

The question asks why Elliott missed Wolfgang's call. Elliott says *I was dragged into a meeting out of the blue and it lasted until late in the evening*. If Elliott *was dragged into* the *meeting out of the blue*, it means it was not *scheduled* and he was *asked to join*. (B) is, therefore, correct. (C) is wrong because there is nothing to suggest the call was *in the evening* - the *evening* is just when the *meeting* finished. (D) is wrong because *out of the blue* means suddenly and has nothing to do with *feeling blue*, which means to feel sad or melancholy.

161. (A)

The question asks, in paragraph 2, line 5, what the phrase "take a peek" is closest in meaning to. To *take a peek* means to *have a* quick *look*, so (A) is correct. It does not mean to *examine closely*, *make a decision* or *share your thoughts*, though all of these would have also made sense in the gap, so (B), (C) and (D) are all wrong.

162. (D)

The question asks which of the positions [1], [2], [3] or [4] the following sentence best belongs in: "Shall we have a call tomorrow?" The sentence cannot go in [1] because of the sentence after, which explains why Elliott *missed* the original *call* (he was in a *meeting*). The sentence might have fit after the explanation, at the end of the paragraph. There is no reason for Elliott to suggest a *call* while he is explaining the outcome of the *B2C role* interviews so far, so [2] is wrong. [3] is wrong because the next paragraph focuses on another *advertised role*, the *B2B role*. It would make sense for Elliott to explain everything that needs to be discussed on the *call* before suggesting the *call*. In fact, the suggestion for a *call* makes a perfect closing statement, so [4] is correct.

163. (D)

The question asks what CANNOT be inferred about the author from the post. The author calls the reader a *fellow American*, which means he is *American* himself. He also says he has *lived in London for 10 years* and on the left column his *age* is stated as *41*, so he was *31* when he *moved*. On the left column we can also see

he *joined* back in *2011*, but the post is made in 2018, so (C) can be inferred. (D) is correct because the only thing we know is that the author has *lived in London for 10 years* but we do not know if he was a *tourist* when he first came.

164. (C)

The question asks what the author means by "layers are your friend" in the last bullet point. While *wearing a coat* and *waterproof clothing* and a *t-shirt in case the sun comes out* are all valid advice based on the fact that, according to the author, *you can have four seasons in a day*, to dress in *layers* means to *wear many garments on top of each other* so that you can take them off or put them back on depending on how the weather changes during a day. Therefore, (C) is correct.

165. (C)

The question asks what the phrase "WiseWay is finally starting to feel the heat" in paragraph 1, line 2 is closest in meaning to. To *feel the heat* is an idiom, which means to be in an uncomfortable situation (as uncomfortable as a *heated* room). It has negative connotations and can also suggest that those who *feel the heat* are under pressure to take action to prevent something bad from becoming worse. Therefore, here it must mean the bad *consequences of the strike are becoming apparent*, so (C) is correct. The text is not talking about literal *heat*, and *WiseWay* is clearly not *coming up with solutions* yet, nor does the text say anything to suggest they are *getting angry*.

166. (C)

The question asks Which of the following CANNOT be inferred from the text. The text says *for the last three years, salaries have remained pretty much stagnant, growing at a much slower rate than inflation* while *top-level salaries and bonuses, in the meantime, have skyrocketed*, suggesting this *disparity* is a reason for the *strike*. It also says there were *failed talks between the union and the management* before the *strike* was *announced*. Finally, it says *customers* are *overwhelmingly on the employees' side*. What it doesn't say, however, is that *WiseWay has announced they want to reach an agreement soon*. While the author does think this will happen, their prediction is based on *history*, not any announcement made by *WiseWay*, so (**C**) is correct.

167. (B)

The question asks, based on the article, how does the author feel towards the cause of the employees. The author says *WiseWay's employees have every right to be upset* – and later on describes their *demands* as *reasonable*. The author never says anything to suggest he thinks they are *petulant* or *exaggerating*, and he is clearly taking a *view*, so all the other options are wrong.

168. (B)

The question asks which of the positions [1], [2], [3] or [4] the following sentence best belongs in: "This isn't the first time WiseWay has been in trouble." In the first paragraph, the text mentions the company's *400 stores* and then says *11 are open*. After position [1], it continues to say *the rest are barricaded*. These sentences naturally connect as they all talk about the *stores*, not *WiseWay*, so the missing sentence does not belong there. It also doesn't belong in position [3], as paragraph 2 ends with a suggestion that *WiseWay* must be *regretting* allowing *unions* to form, and paragraph 3 starts with a contrast: *however, the employees have every right to be upset*. The missing sentence would interrupt the contrast. As for position [4], the paragraph is talking about *salaries* and how they *grow slowly* for *employees* but *have skyrocketed* for the *management*. There's no mention of *trouble* in the past, so the missing sentence doesn't fit. The correct position is [2], as the missing sentence comes after a paragraph that explains the current *trouble* (the *strikes*) and the sentence after position [2] focuses on the past *trouble* (the lawsuit in *2015*). (**B**) is the correct answer.

169. (A)

The question asks why it took Andrea so long to complete the manual. Andrea says *with all the last-minute meetings and stuff, I've only just managed to get round to it*. The *last-minute meetings and stuff* must've kept her busy, meaning *she didn't have the time* to do it, so (**A**) is correct. Andrea never says *she forgot*, and

there's nothing to suggest *she didn't have everything she needed*. Finally, the *meeting with the Marketing Team* was when the *manual* and the *changes* needed were discussed; Andrea doesn't say anything to suggest she *needed* another *meeting*.

170. (A)

The question asks which of the following Andrea does not ask the team to check the manual for. Andrea says *let me know if there's anything I've missed*, so she wants them to *check* for *incomplete sections*. She also draws attention to parts where she's *not sure about the wording*, i.e. worried about *sentence structure*. Finally, she *asks* them to *check* any parts where *the procedures described are different now*, i.e. where the *information* is *outdated*. The only thing she doesn't *ask* for is help with *grammatical mistakes or typos*, so (**A**) is correct.

171. (D)

The question asks which of the positions [1], [2], [3] or [4] the following sentence best belongs in: "I look forward to your thoughts." This missing sentence clearly refers to the recipients' *thoughts* on the *manual* that Andrea has *attached* to her email. [1] is therefore wrong, as she has not yet mentioned the *manual*. [2] is wrong because it's right in the middle of a paragraph explaining what she has *changed* in the *manual*, so it would make sense to ask for *thoughts* after she has explained. [3], however, which comes after, is also wrong because in the very next sentence she asks them to *check* for her, so if the sentence went here it would be repetitive. The only possible option is [4], which comes after a paragraph explaining what the team's *thoughts* should focus on.

172. (C)

The question asks on which of the following occasions you do NOT get a free coffee. The ad says *get your 10th cup of coffee for free after nine beverage purchases*, so (**A**) is incorrect. It also says *get 2 coffees + 2 desserts for free on your birthday*, so (**B**) is incorrect. Finally, it also says *collect points which can be used on anything in store*, so (**D**) is incorrect. However, when you *buy a special occasion cake* you only get a *10% discount*, not a *free coffee*, so (**C**) is correct.

173. (C)

The question asks how many points per dollar you get if you buy a travel mug. The text mentions *merchandise such as travel mugs*, so *travel mugs* count as *merchandise*. It then says you get *10 points per dollar spent on food and merchandise*, so (B) is correct. (A) is wrong because *5 points* are for *drinks*, and (C) and (D) are wrong because the text says *100 points are equivalent to 50 cents*, but doesn't say you get either with a *travel mug*.

174. (C)

The question asks which building Rhian is looking for. Rhian says in his texts that he's *looking 4 the blue front door but all are brown*. This means the *building* needs to have a *blue door*, so (A) and (B) are incorrect. Tim then says *28th, not 38th! corner of 28th and 9th!* This means the *building* must be on the *corner of 9th and 28th*, so (C) is correct.

175. (A)

The question asks how Rhian is likely to feel at the end of this conversation. When Tim tells Rhian *28th, not 38th! corner of 28th and 9th* and asks him if *Maria* told him *about the mistake in the form*, Rhian replies *WHAT? NO. Great, now gotta run 10 streets in 5 mins! YAY*. To *run 10 streets in 5 mins* must be very stressful, so Rhian probably feels *stressed*. There's no reason for him to be scared, or *terrified*, and he can't be *fortunate* if he went to the wrong address. Since he doesn't question what Rhian told him, he can't be *skeptical*, either.

176. (B)

The question asks, from the people who signed out, who stayed in the premises for the shortest time. (D) is incorrect because *Anna Vandi* didn't *sign out*. From the people that did *sign out*, *Lachlan Summers* stayed for 45 minutes, *Jessica Thorne* for 15 minutes, and *Kana Sato* for 30 minutes. (B) is, therefore, correct.

177. (A)

The question asks which person had the most visitors. This information can be found in the *here to visit* column. While *Wren Tyler*'s name appears 3 times in the *signed out by* column, he doesn't appear at all in the

here to visit column, so (C) is incorrect. (D) is incorrect because *Cordelia Fuller* was only visited by one person. *Amy Jones* was visited by two people (not to be confused with *Amy James*, who was visited by one), and *Rian Dodeigne* by three people. (A) is therefore the correct answer.

178. (B)

The email says that guests are not allowed to leave the building without being escorted, and highlights the fact that some visitors were not signed out or escorted, so (C) is the best answer.

179. (D)

The question asks what the phrase "if push comes to shove, contact someone from reception or HR" in paragraph 3, line 4, is closest in meaning to. *When push comes to shove* is an expression that describes a situation where there's a lot of pressure and someone has to make a decision. Before this sentence, the email gives options in terms of what to do when someone has a *visitor*: *you should always allow extra time between meetings to escort guests out and if for any reason you are unable to do so, you should either ask one of your colleagues to do so for you*. That's when it adds the final option, which is to *contact* either *reception or HR*. This means that they *should be* the *last choice* – not the *first* one, or how often they *should* be *informed* (*always* or *never*). (D) is, therefore, correct.

180. (C)

The question asks what is NOT mentioned as a consequence of not following the rules. The text says *repeated failure to comply with this very important rule may lead beyond verbal warnings to disciplinary action or even dismissal*. *Dismissal* is synonymous with *being fired*, so (A) is incorrect. A *verbal warning* is a *spoken warning*, so (B) is also incorrect. *Disciplinary action* is the same as *disciplinary measures*, so (D) is incorrect. The only thing not mentioned is *performance reviews*, so (C) is correct.

181. (C)

The question asks on which day Giulio has the most interviews. Having a look at Giulio's calendar, and ignoring everything that is not an *interview* (such as *meetings*), we can see that on *June 4th* and *June 5th* he has 3 *interviews*, on *June 6th* he has 4 *interviews* and on *June 7th* he has 2 *interviews*. *June 6th* is therefore the day with the *most interviews*, and (C) is the correct answer.

182. (D)

The question asks which time is always free of meetings and interviews on Giulio's calendar. Looking at his calendar, we can see there's no empty line and there is always something. Giulio has a *meeting* on *June 6th* at the *09:00-10:00* slot. He has three different *meetings* at the *10:00-11:00* slot, and three different *interviews* at the *12:00-13:00* slot. The only thing he has at the *13:00-14:00* slot, however, is a *team lunch* on *June 5th*. *Team lunch* is neither a *meeting* nor an *interview*, so (D) is correct.

183. (C)

The question asks which of the following is NOT a reason Giulio wants Bozena to help with the interviews. In his email, Giulio says *since you will be working closely with the new recruit it will be better for you to play a role in the decision-making process to ensure you get along with them*. To *get along with* someone you must *like* them, so (A) is incorrect. He also says *I think it would be great experience for you*, which means it would *increase her familiarity with the process*, so (B) is incorrect. Finally, he says *you were right when you said we should hire Raymond, so I trust your insights*, which means he *believes she will be good at selecting the right candidate*, so (D) is incorrect. (C) is the correct answer because, while Giulio mentions *Phoebe from HR*, all he says about her is that she's *on holiday*, not that she *recommended* Bozena.

184. (A)

The question asks which interview Giulio is referring to in his email when he says "I've booked one of the interviews in the wrong room". Giulio says *we're supposed to be having all interviews in either the boardroom or the meeting room, but they were both busy*. This means that the *interview in the wrong room* must be in a different room. (B) is wrong because Giulio has a *meeting with Allie*, not an *interview*. (C) is wrong because the *interview with Sami* is in the *meeting room*, and (D) is wrong because the *interview with Willa* is in the *boardroom*. (A) is correct because the *interview with George* is in the *blue room*.

185. (B)

The question asks what the phrase "Phoebe will bite my head off" in paragraph 3, line 4, is closest in meaning to. To *bite* someone's *head off* means to yell at them because they did something wrong. If you yell at someone, you are usually not *indifferent towards* them, so (D) is wrong. (C) is incorrect because yelling at someone is not the same as *not wanting to speak to* them. (A) is incorrect because the feeling of *disappointment* is not as strong as yelling would suggest – but someone who is *furious* might yell, so (B) is the correct answer.

186. (D)

The question asks which of the following is NOT mentioned as a perk in the advertisement. The ad mentions *mini fridge and coolers*, which are both *places to store cold drinks*, so (A) is wrong. It also calls the *back spacious*, which means there's *abundance of room*, so (B) is wrong. It also mentions *A/C*, i.e. *air conditioning*, so (C) is wrong. While it mentions *fiber optic lighting*, however, it says it's in the *back*, not *exterior*, so (D) is correct.

187. (A)

The question asks how much the deposit for Rainbow Party Limos is. In the first post, Jess says *on their website they say they only need a $100 deposit*, so (A) is correct. According to the same post, the other options apply to *other companies*, not *Rainbow Party Limos*: *every other company I've contacted either want the full amount upfront or they ask for $300-$400 deposit*.

188. (C)

The question asks what the phrase "what's the verdict?" in the first post, in line 8, is closest in meaning to. A *verdict* is usually the result of a trial, where the judge declares someone guilty or not guilty, but the expression *what's the verdict* can be used in other situations where there's an either/or choice of *good* or *bad*, and as the author says *I don't wanna use them if anyone else has had any bad experience with them* before asking for the *verdict*, (C) is correct. While all the other questions are valid and some, such as (A) and (B), are either implied in the post or linked to the question, they are not the same as *what's the verdict*, so they're wrong.

189. (C)

The question asks which of the following is TRUE about the friend of the second post's author. (**A**) is wrong because the post says *she contested the charge and got her money back from the bank*. (**B**) is incorrect because she was *celebrating her sister's bachelorette party*, not *21st birthday*. (**D**) is wrong because it's the *author* of the *second post* who *recommends Lime Limo or Treasure Bus*, not the *friend*. (**C**) is the correct answer because the post says *my friend was lured in by the same promotion that caught your eye* and the *promotion* is the *10% discount* referenced in the first post.

190. (A)

The question asks, based on the second post, what is the author's opinion on Rainbow Party Limos. The author starts with *STAY AS FAR AWAY AS POSSIBLE FROM RAINBOW PARTY LIMOS* and goes on to say *you should not give any of your hard-earned cash to these scammers*. A *scammer* is someone who tries to trick you out of your money; based on this, it's clear the author thinks the company is definitely not *magnificent*, or even *mediocre* or *average*: they must think the *company* is *horrendous*, i.e. awful, so (**A**) is the correct answer.

191. (C)

The question asks how much a 70-year-old man needs to pay for a 1-hour tour. A *70-year-old man* is *over 65*, so he would count as a *senior*. The price for a *senior ticket* for the *1-hour*, i.e. *60-minute tour* is *$12*, so (**C**) is correct. *$7* is a *child ticket*, *$10* is a *student ticket* and *$15* is an *adult ticket*, so they're all wrong.

192. (A)

The question asks what combination of tickets has been charged in the receipt. In the *receipt* we can see *two $18 tickets*, and *$18* is the price for a *90-minute adult ticket*, which means these *two tickets* are for *adults*, making (**C**) and (**D**) wrong. The remaining *ticket* is *$15*, which is the price for a *90-minute tour senior ticket*, so (**A**) is correct and (**B**) is wrong.

193. (D)

The question asks how the author of the email is NOT likely to feel. The author of the email talks about how they were *overcharged* and then not allowed to *request a refund*, and how the *mistake* was *not identified* by anyone. Based on this, it's quite *likely* the man feels *cheated*, *galled* (i.e. annoyed) and *exasperated*, but it's extremely unlikely he feels *ebullient*, i.e. full of enthusiasm and energy. (**D**) is, therefore, the correct answer.

194. (C)

The question asks why the man was refused a refund at the ticket office. The email says *we were told that it's company policy not to offer refunds once a ticket has been stamped as "used"*. This means the *ticket had been used already*, so (**C**) is the correct answer. While the man indeed *didn't notice the mistake*, that's not offered as a reason for no *refund* – and the company has a *no-refund policy* under certain conditions (a *stamped ticket*), not in general. Finally, the *tour guide* did *examine the ticket* – they just didn't notice the mistake.

195. (A)

The question asks what the phrase "I take issue with this policy" in the email, in paragraph 4, line 3, is closest in meaning to. To *take issue with* something means to have a problem with it, i.e. not to be *happy about* it, so (**A**) is correct. It doesn't mean you *don't understand how* it *works*, or that you were *not aware of* it or that you *think* it *doesn't apply to* your *situation*, so all the other options are wrong.

196. (B)

The question asks, according to the card, why the driver did not deliver the parcel. The *card* offers four options: *the shipment was too big* (i.e. *too large*), *a signature was required* (i.e. it *needs* to be *signed*), *it was not safe* (i.e. *unsafe*) to do so and *other*. The only one ticked, however, is *a signature was required*, so (**B**) is the correct answer. A *neighbor* is not even mentioned in that section: they are mentioned above, in the empty *we left your shipment* section.

197. (C)

The question asks what can be inferred from Silas's email. (**A**) is incorrect because Silas says it was a *birthday present* for his *son*, not his *wife*. (**D**) is incorrect because he was *on hold for half an hour* with the *offices*: the *driver never* even *picked up*. Silas says *if this is how you treat loyal, long-term customers, I dread to imagine how you treat newcomers*, suggesting he is a *loyal customer*. (**C**) is, therefore, the correct answer.

198. (A)

The question asks, based on his email, how is Silas likely to feel. Silas clearly says he is *furious*, i.e. incredibly *cross*, in his email because of the terrible service he has received. (**A**) is, therefore, correct. It's unlikely he would feel *content*, i.e. happy, or *complacent*, i.e. smug, or even *callous*, i.e. uncaring.

199. (B)

The question asks what the phrase "we do not have delivery quota for our drivers" in the second email, in paragraph 1, line 3, is closest in meaning to. A *quota* is a *minimum* number, so to *not have quota* means to not have a *minimum of deliveries*, so (**B**) is correct. *Quotas* have nothing to do with a *specific time* or *trying* your *hardest*, and just because the company has no *quota* does not mean they *do not ask our drivers how many deliveries they made at the end of the day*, so all other options are wrong.

200. (C)

The question asks which of the following FLP does NOT offer to Silas Till. (**A**) is wrong because the email says *please let me know if you would like to be informed of the outcome of our investigation*. (**B**) is incorrect because the email says *we have arranged for special evening delivery for you today at no cost to you*, i.e. for *free*. (**D**) is incorrect because the email says *we would also like to offer you a $20 voucher for any future services you purchase with us*. (**C**) is the correct answer because the email mentions a *free special delivery* for this occasion, not a *future purchase*.